Medizinisches Wörterbuch der deutschen und englischen Sprache

Medical Dictionary of the English and German Languages

Medizinisches Wörterbuch

der deutschen und englischen Sprache

Von Dr. med. Dieter Werner Unseld

Chefarzt der inneren Abteilung
des Kreiskrankenhauses Hechingen (Hohenzollern)

7., neubearbeitete und erweiterte Auflage

Zwei Teile in einem Band:

Erster Teil: Englisch–Deutsch
Zweiter Teil: Deutsch–Englisch

Wissenschaftliche Verlagsgesellschaft mbH Stuttgart
1978

Medical Dictionary

of the English and German Languages

By Dr. med. Dieter Werner Unseld

Chefarzt der inneren Abteilung
des Kreiskrankenhauses Hechingen (Hohenzollern)

Seventh Edition, revised and enlarged

Two Parts in one Volume:

First Part: English–German
Second Part: German–English

Wissenschaftliche Verlagsgesellschaft mbH Stuttgart
1978

CIP-Kurztitelaufnahme der Deutschen Bibliothek

Unseld, Dieter Werner
Medical Dictionary of the English and German
Languages: 2. parts in 1 vol./by Dieter Werner Unseld. –
7. ed., rev. and enl. –
Stuttgart: Wissenschaftliche Verlagsgesellschaft,
1978.
Enth.: P. 1. English–German. – P. 2. German–English.

ISBN 3-8047-0567-7

Alle Rechte, auch die des auszugsweisen Nachdrucks, der photomechanischen Wiedergabe (durch Photokopie, Mikrofilm oder irgendein anderes Verfahren) und der Übersetzung, vorbehalten.

© 1978 Wissenschaftliche Verlagsgesellschaft mbH, Stuttgart

Printed in Germany

Satz: W. Hädicke, Stuttgart. Druck: Zechnersche Buchdruckerei, Speyer

Inhaltsverzeichnis — Index

Vorwort	6
Preface	7
Vorbemerkungen	9
Introductory Notes	11
Erster Teil (Englisch–Deutsch)	13
First Part (English–German)	13
Zweiter Teil (Deutsch–Englisch)	268
Second Part (German–English)	268
Anhang (Maße, Gewichte, Temperaturen)	518
Appendix (Measures, weights, temperatures)	518

Vorwort zur dritten Auflage

Seit dem Erscheinen der zweiten Auflage des Wörterbuchs haben zahlreiche neue Begriffe in der Medizin und ihren Grenzgebieten Eingang gefunden und sind zu festen Bestandteilen des ärztlichen Sprachschatzes geworden. Dieser Tatsache, der sich jeder Autor eines Wörterbuches, und zumal eines medizinischen, von Auflage zu Auflage erneut gegenübergestellt sieht, habe ich dadurch Rechnung getragen, daß ich – unter weitgehender Beibehaltung der ursprünglichen, bewährten, zusammen mit *M. Goertz* bei der Erstauflage ausgeführten Anordnung des Buches – den Text vollkommen neu bearbeitet und die Zahl der Stichwörter erheblich vermehrt habe. Dabei war ich bestrebt, meine Bemühungen ganz auf die Handlichkeit und Zuverlässigkeit des Buches, auf die praktischen Bedürfnisse seines Benutzers und auf das Beiseitelassen unnötigen Ballastes zugunsten der Erschwinglichkeit und Preiswürdigkeit des Werkes zu richten. Bei dieser Zielsetzung konnte unter Berücksichtigung des Umstandes, daß beim Benutzer des Buches grundsätzliche Kenntnisse der fremden Sprache vorausgesetzt werden dürfen, auf terminologische Erläuterungen weitgehend, auf phonetische Bezeichnungen im Text vollkommen verzichtet werden. Wer außer der Hilfe beim Übersetzen medizinischer Texte auch sprachwissenschaftliche Belehrung sucht, sei auf die entsprechenden größeren, damit natürlich auch kostspieligeren Spezialwerke verwiesen.

Möglichst großzügig verfahren bin ich hingegen mit der Heranziehung des Sprachgutes der Wissensgebiete, die mit der Humanmedizin in mehr oder weniger enger Beziehung stehen. Ich hoffe, daß das Buch dadurch wie bisher nicht nur praktisch und wissenschaftlich tätigen Ärzten, sondern auch Zahnärzten, Psychologen, Pharmazeuten, Chemikern, Physikern, Dolmetschern, ärztlichen Hilfspersonen und auf dem Medizinalmarkt tätigen Kaufleuten und Technikern nützliche Dienste zu leisten imstande sein wird.

Bei der Ergänzung des Wortschatzes hat mir Herr *Rurik Dames*, Berlin, mehrfach in freundlicher und uneigennütziger Weise Rat und Unterstützung zuteil werden lassen. Die Bearbeitung von Übersetzungen aus dem Bereiche der Zahnmedizin wurde durch das Entgegenkommen von Herrn Dr. med. dent. *Kurt Krau*, Ulm, wesentlich gefördert. Beiden Herren sei an dieser Stelle für ihre Hilfe herzlich gedankt. In gleicher Weise gebührt Dank Frau *Elfriede Unseld* für die mühevolle Hilfe bei der alphabetischen Ordnung der Stichwörter. Dankend sei schließlich der verständnisvollen Unterstützung gedacht, welche der Unterzeichnete vom Verleger, Herrn Prof. Dr. *Schmiedel*, in stets gleichbleibender Weise erfahren durfte.

Ulm/Donau, den 25. April 1960　　　　　　　　　　　　　　　　*D.W. Unseld*

Preface to the third edition

Since the second edition of the dictionary was published, many new terms in medicine and its related sciences have emerged and have become an indispensable part of the medical vocabulary. This has led to a considerable increase in the number of words included in the present edition, and the opportunity has been taken to revise the text completely. Nevertheless the original arrangement of the first edition, for which Mr. *M. Goertz* was partly responsible, has been retained. I have tried to keep the book reliable and convenient to use, and have omitted all unnecessary details in order to keep the price reasonably low. Since a basic knowledge of the foreign language may be assumed on the part of the user, it has been possible to limit terminological explanations and to completely omit phonetic instructions in the text. If anyone wants further philological information than that required for the translation of medical texts, he may refer to the more comprehensive and therefore more expensive special reference books.

As to the vocabulary of subjects more or less closely related to medicine, I have been as liberal as possible. I hope therefore the book will be of good service not only to practising and research physicians, but also to dentists, psychologists, pharmacists, chemists, physicists, interpreters, medical assistants and those concerned with the supply and servicing of medical requisites.

In supplementing the vocabulary I was most kindly and frequently aided and advised by Mr. *Rurik Dames*, Berlin. Dr. med. dent. *Kurt Krau*, Ulm, was good enough to read through the translation referring to dental medicine. Many thanks are offered here to both gentlemen for their help. The same thanks are given to Mrs. *Elfriede Unseld* for her great help in arranging the catchwords alphabetically. Finally the undersigned would like to mention with gratitude the ever sympathetic assistance of the publisher, Professor Dr. *Schmiedel*, Stuttgart.

Ulm, April 25, 1960

D.W. Unseld

Vorwort zur siebten Auflage

Erneut ist unter Berücksichtigung der jüngsten Entwicklungen der Medizin der Wortschatz des Buches vergrößert worden. Seit der 4. Auflage wurden auch zahlreiche Begriffe aus dem Bereich der Tierheilkunde neu aufgenommen, sodaß das Buch auch dem Tierarzt ebenso wie dem Arzt und dem Zahnarzt bei Übersetzungen eine Hilfe bieten kann. Grundsätzliche Änderungen gegenüber der dritten bis sechsten Auflage haben sich nicht als erforderlich erwiesen.

Hechingen (Hohenzollern), 31. Januar 1978 *D.W. Unseld*

Preface to the seventh edition

The number of words contained in the dictionary has again had to be increased, as a result of the latest developments in the field of medicine. The fourth, the fifth, the sixth and present edition contain also numerous veterinary terms; it is hoped that the dictionary will be useful to translators in the field of veterinary medicine as well as in the fields of human medicine and of dentistry. – Otherwise only few changes have been made since the third edition.

Hechingen (Hohenzollern), January 31, 1978 *D.W. Unseld*

Vorbemerkungen

1. Die lateinischen „nomina anatomica" sind international und deswegen in der Regel nicht angeführt. Lediglich Körperteile, welche in einer der beiden oder in beiden Sprachen im klinischen Gebrauche vorzugsweise mit abweichenden oder besonderen Bezeichnungen benannt werden, sind angegeben. Bei der Aussprache der anatomischen Namen ist das unter 2. Erwähnte zu beachten.

2. Die Aussprache von Wörtern, welche dem Lateinischen oder Griechischen nachgebildet sind, ist im Englischen meist nicht dieselbe wie im Deutschen, erfolgt vielmehr nach den allgemeinen Regeln der englischen Phonetik.

   Beispiele: encephalitis sprich: ensephalaitis
   pneumonitis sprich: njumonaitis.

3. Für manche Diagnosen, Symptome u. a. sind im Deutschen wie im Englischen mehrere Bezeichnungen gebräuchlich. Findet man einen Ausdruck nicht angeführt, so suche man also nach gleichbedeutenden Bezeichnungen, evtl. auch nach dem entsprechenden lateinischen Namen. Sollte eine selten vorkommende oder wenig gebräuchliche Krankheitsbezeichnung auch, nachdem man wie angegeben vorgegangen ist, nicht zu finden sein, so benütze man den lateinischen Terminus. Bei Bezeichnungen, die an einen Eigennamen gebunden sind, setze man diesen in den sächsischen Genitiv und füge dann den allgemeinen Begriff, z. B. „disease" oder „symptom", an.

4. Manche Wörter sind unter dem Stichwort des Sammelbegriffs rubriziert, z. B. „Mandelsäure" unter: „Säure, Mandel-" bzw. im englisch-deutschen Teil „mandelic acid" unter: „acid, mandelic".

5. Wird ein Wort in beiden Sprachen gleich geschrieben, so steht meist statt der Wiederholung

    e.e. = englisch ebenso bzw. d.e. = deutsch ebenso.

Es ist jedoch dabei zu beachten, daß im Englischen außer Eigen- und Ländernamen und einigen anderen, in diesem Zusammenhang weniger interessierenden Besonderheiten alle Hauptwörter mit kleinen Anfangsbuchstaben geschrieben werden. Die Tatsache, daß in Zeitungsüberschriften oder an sonstigen Stellen, welche die Aufmerksamkeit des Lesers wachrufen sollen, manchmal die Substantive oder sogar auch die Zeit- und Eigenschaftswörter mit großen Anfangsbuchstaben geschrieben werden, muß als Ausnahme von obiger Regel aufgefaßt werden.

Vorbemerkungen　　　　　　　　　　　　　　　　　　　　　　　　　　　10

6. In manchen Fällen sind bei englischen Wörtern zwei verschiedene Möglichkeiten der Rechtschreibung gegeben. Häufig wird dann die eine Form vorzugsweise in Großbritannien, die andere vorzugsweise in den USA gebraucht. In diesem Buch ist im allgemeinen nur eine Schreibweise angegeben. Nur in Fällen, in denen der Unterschied zwischen englischer und amerikanischer Schreibweise obligatorisch ist, wurden beide Formen verzeichnet und die englische Schreibweise mit (e), die amerikanische mit (a) kenntlich gemacht. In anderen Fällen bedeutet (a) einen nur in Amerika, (e) einen nur in England üblichen Ausdruck.

   Verschiedene Schreibweise ist z. B. möglich in folgenden Fällen:

   Endung -isation oder -ization (hospitalisation, hospitalization)
   Endung -ic oder -ical (analytic, analytical)
   Endung -in oder -ine (thiamin, thiamine)
   Endung -pathy oder -pathia (myelopathy, myelopathia).

7. Im englisch-deutschen Teil ist das Geschlecht deutscher Substantive mit

   m. = männlich
   f. = weiblich
   n. = sächlich

   angegeben, sofern es nicht schon aus anderen Gründen (z. B. durch Adjektive) ersichtlich ist. Das Geschlecht lateinischer Hauptwörter ist nicht angegeben. – Weitere Abkürzungen, soweit sie sich nicht von selbst verstehen:

   pl. = Plural
   (veter.) = veterinärmedizinischer Ausdruck
   (dent.) = zahnärztlicher Ausdruck.

8. Im alphabetischen Register sind die Buchstaben ä, ö, ü unter ae, oe, ue eingeordnet.

9. Bei deutschen Wörtern wurde in einschlägigen Fällen die Schreibung mit Z bzw. mit K der Schreibung mit C vorgezogen. Man suche aber doch unter dem Buchstaben C, wenn unter Z bzw. K nichts zu finden ist.

10. Die Wiedergabe von Markenbezeichnungen, Gebrauchs- und Handelsnamen berechtigt auch dann, wenn keine nähere Kennzeichnung erfolgt ist, nicht zu der Annahme, daß diese im Sinne der Warenzeichen- und Markenschutzgesetzgebung als frei zu betrachten wären und deshalb von jedermann benutzt werden dürften.

Introductory Notes

1. The Latin "nomina anatomica" are international and therefore omitted, except those terms of the parts of the body which have a special name in clinical usage in one or both of the two languages. Regarding the pronunciation of the anatomical terms see 2.

2. Words derived from Latin or Greek are pronounced in the German language according to the rules of Latin or Greek phonetics.

3. For certain diagnoses, symptoms etc. several terms are used in German as well as in English. If you cannot find a term, look for an equivalent or take the suitable Latin expression. If the term is connected to a proper noun, use the suffix "sche" (resp. "scher", "sches") and add the general term, e.g. "Krankheit" or "Symptom".

   Examples: Beck's disease = Becksche Krankheit f.
             Umber's test = Umberscher Test m.
             Ott's sign = Ottsches Zeichen n.

4. Some words are listed under the catchword of the collective noun, e.g. "mandelic acid" under: "acid, mandelic", and in the German-English part, "Mandelsäure" under: "Säure, Mandel-".

5. Words of the same spelling in both languages: to avoid repetition the following abbreviations are used:

         e.e. = the same in Englisch
         d.e. = the same in German.

   However it must be remembered that capitals are used as the initial letters for all the German nouns including such as are derived from the Latin or Greek languages. If Latin nouns are necessary in the German text, capitals have in most cases been used for them too.

   Example: erysipeloid = d.e.n. (= Erysipeloid n.)

6. The sign (e) means English method of spelling or a term in general use in Great Britain. The sign (a) indicates American spelling or form in use in USA.

7. The gender of Germans nouns is listed in the English-German part of the dictionary as follows:

           m. = masculine
           f. = feminine
           n. = neuter

except when it ist obvious, e.g. through adjectives. The gender of Latin nouns is omitted. – Further abbreviations, which may not be comprehensible without explanation, are

              pl. = plural
      (veter.) = term of veterinary medicine
      (dent.) = term of dentistry.

8. The German letters ä, ö, ü are listed under ae, oe, ue.

9. As to German words the spelling of Z or K is preferred to C. But please refer to the letter C nevertheless, if you fail to find a word under Z or K.

10. The reproduction of trade-marks and trade-names in the dictionary does not imply (unless otherwise indicated) that their use is not restricted under the Trade Marks Registration Acts.

ERSTER TEIL

Englisch-Deutsch

FIRST PART

English-German

A

A.A. (= Alcoholics Anonymous) anonyme Alkoholiker m. pl.
aasmus Asthma n.
abacterial abakteriell
abaction künstliche Fehlgeburt f.
Abadie's sign Abadiesches Zeichen n.
abalienated geistesgestört
abalienation Geistesverwirrung f.
abasia Abasie f.
abasic abasisch
abatement Nachlassen n.
abattage Schlachten n.
abattoir Schlachthaus n.
abaxial d. e.
abbreviation Abkürzung f.
A.B.C. (= axiobuccocervical) axiobukkozervikal
Abderhalden's reaction Abderhaldensche Reaktion f.
abdomen Abdomen n., Bauch m.
abdomen, pendulous Hängebauch m.
abdomen, scaphoid Kahnbauch m.
abdominal d. e.
abdominalgia Abdominalgie f., Bauchschmerz m.
abdominal pregnancy Bauchhöhlenschwangerschaft f.
abdominal surgery Bauchchirurgie f.
abdominal wall Bauchwand f.
abdominoanterior d. e.
abdominocentesis Abdominozentese f.
abdominocystic abdominozystisch
abdominogenital d. e.
abdominohysterectomy abdominale Hysterektomie f.
abdominohysterotomy abdominale Hysterotomie f.
abdominoperineal d. e.
abdominoposterior d. e.
abdominothoracic abdominothorakal
abdominous dickleibig
abdominovaginal d. e.
abdominovesical abdominovesikal
abducens nerve Nervus abducens
abduct, to abduzieren
abduction Abduktion f.
abduction splint Abduktionsschiene f.
aberrant aberrierend
aberrant ventricular conduction ventrikuläre Erregungsausbreitungsstörung f.
aberration Aberration f., Abweichung f.
A.B.G. (= axiobuccogingival) axiobukkogingival
ability Fähigkeit f.
abiotrophical abiotrophisch
abiotrophy Abiotrophie f.
abiogenesis Abiogenese f.
abiogenetic abiogenetisch
abiotic abiotisch
A.B.L. (= axiobuccolingual) axiobukkolingual
ablactation Ablaktation f.
ablate, to ablösen, loslösen, abtragen
ablation Loslösung f., Abtragung f.
able fähig, tauglich
ablution Abwaschung f.
abnormal abnorm, anomal, regelwidrig
abnormality Abnormität f.
aboral d. e.

abort, to abortieren
abortion Abort m., Fehlgeburt f.
abortion, artificial künstliche Fehlgeburt f.
– **cervical** Zervikalabort m.
– **complete** kompletter Abort m.
– **complicated** komplizierter Abort m.
– **criminal** krimineller Abort m.
– **febrile** fieberhafter Abort m.
– **imminent** Abortus imminens
– **incomplete** inkompletter Abort m.
– **induced** artefizieller Abort m.
– **septic** septischer Abort m.
– **uncomplicated** unkomplizierter Abort m.
abortionist Abtreiber m., Abtreiberin f.
abortive abortiv; Abortivum n.
abortus fever Bangsche Krankheit f.
abrade, to abschaben, ausschaben
abrasion Ausschabung f.; Abschürfung f.
abreaction Abreagieren n.; Katharsis f.
abrupt d. e.
abscess Abszeß m.
abscess, Brodie's Brodiescher Abszeß m.
abscess, cold kalter Abszeß m.
abscess, hot heißer Abszeß m.
abscess lancet Abszeßmesser n.
abscess, pericemental Wurzelhautabszeß m.
abscess, sudoriparous Schweißdrüsenabszeß m.
abscissa Abszisse f.
absence Abwesenheit f.
absent abwesend
absent-minded geistesabwesend, zerstreut
absent-mindedness Zerstreutheit f.
absolute absolut
absorb, to absorbieren, resorbieren
absorbability Absorptionsfähigkeit f.

absorbent Absorbens n.
absorption d. e. f., Resorption f.
absorptive absorbierend
abstain, to sich enthalten
abstinence Abstinenz f., Enthaltsamkeit f.
abstinent d. e., enthaltsam
abstract abstrakt
abstraction Abstraktion f.
abulia Abulie f.
abulic abulisch
abuse Mißbrauch m.
abuse, to mißbrauchen
abutment (dent.) Pfeiler m.
A.C. (= **anodal closure**) Anodenschließung f.
acacia Gummi arabicum
academic akademisch; Akademiker m.
academy Akademie f.
acanthoma Akanthom n.
acanthosis Akanthose f.
acanthosis nigricans d. e.
acapnia Akapnie f.
acaryote kernlos
accelerate, to beschleunigen
acceleration Beschleunigung f.
accent Akzent m.
accentuate, to akzentuieren
accentuation Akzentuation f.
access Zugang m., Zutritt m.
accessible zugänglich
accessory akzessorisch, nebensächlich
accident Zufall m., Unfall m., Zwischenfall m.
accident neurosis Unfallneurose f.
accidental zufällig; unfallbedingt
acclimation Akklimatisation f.
acclimatization Akklimatisation f.
acclimatize, to akklimatisieren
accommodate, to akkommodieren
accommodation Akkommodation f.
accouchement Entbindung f.
accretion Akkretion f., Anwachsen n.

accumulation Anhäufung f., Ansammlung f.
accumulator Akkumulator m.
accuracy Genauigkeit f.
accuracy check Genauigkeitsprüfung f.
accustom, to angewöhnen
acebutolol Azebutolol n.
acescent säuerlich
acetabuloplasty Azetabuloplastik f.
acetaldehyde Azetaldehyd m.
acetanilid Azetanilid n.
acetate Azetat n.
acetazoleamide Azetazolamid n.
acetonaemia; acetonaemic (e) Azetonämie f.; azetonämisch
acetone Azeton n.
acetone body Azetonkörper m.
acetonemia; acetonemic (a) Azetonämie f.; azetonämisch
acetonide Azetonid n.
acetonitrate Azetonitrat n.
acetonitrile Azetonitril n.
acetonuria Azetonurie f.
acetophenetidin Phenazetin n.
acetophenone Azetophenon n.
acetylacetone Azetylazeton n.
acetylate, to azetylieren
acetylation Azetylierung f.
acetylcholine Azetycholin n.
acetylcholinesterase Azetylcholinesterase f.
acetylene Azetylen n.
acetylglucosamine Azetylglukosamin n.
acetylsalicylic acid (ASA) Azetylsalizylsäure f. (ASS)
achalasia Achalasie f.
ache Schmerz m., Pein f.
ache, to schmerzen
Achilles reflex Achillessehnenreflex m.
Achilles tendon Achillessehne f.
achillodynia Achillodynie f.
achillorrhaphy Achillorrhaphie f.
achillotomy Achillotomie f.

achlorhydria Achlorhydrie f.
achlorhydric achlorhydrisch
acholia Acholie f.
acholic acholisch
acholuria Acholurie f.
acholuric acholurisch
achondroplasia Achondroplasie f.
achoresis Achorese f.
achrestic achrestisch
achromat d. e. m.
achromate Farbenblinder m., Farbenblinde f.
achromatic achromatisch
achromatopsia Achromatopsie f.
achromia Achromie f.
achromic achromisch
achylia Achylie f.
achylic achylisch
acid Säure f.; sauer
acid, abietinic Abietinsäure f.
– absinthic Absinthsäure f.
– acetic Essigsäure f.
– acetylenic Azetylensäure f.
– acetylsalicylic Azetylsalizylsäure f.
– acetyltannic Azetylgerbsäure f.
– aconitic Akonitsäure f.
– acrylic Akrylsäure f.
– adenosine phosphoric Adenosinphosphorsäure f.
– adenylic Adenylsäure f.
– aetianic Aetiansäure f.
– agaricic Agarizinsäure f.
– aldonic Aldonsäure f.
– aliphatic aliphatische Säure f.
– alloxanic Alloxansäure f.
– amido Amidosäure f.
– amino Aminosäure f.
– aminoacetic Aminoessigsäure f., Glykokoll n.
– aminobutyric Aminobuttersäure f.
– aminocaproic Aminokapronsäure f.
– aminoisobutyric Aminoisobuttersäure f.
– anthranilic Anthranilsäure f.

acid, arachidic Arachidonsäure f.
- arachidonic Arachidonsäure f.
- aromatic aromatische Säure f.
- arsenic Arsensäure f.
- arsenous arsenige Säure f.
- arsinic Arsinsäure f.
- arsonic Arsonsäure f.
- aryloxyacetic Aryloxyessigsäure f.
- ascorbic Askorbinsäure f.
- asparaginic Asparaginsäure f.
- aspartic Asparaginsäure f.
- auric Goldsäure f.
- barbituric Barbitursäure f.
- behenic Behensäure f.
- benzoic Benzoesäure f.
- betaoxybutyric Betaoxybuttersäure f.
- bile Gallensäure f.
- boric Borsäure f.
- butylethylbarbituric Butyläthylbarbitursäure f.
- butyric Buttersäure f.
- cacodylic Kakodylsäure f.
- camphoglycuronic Kamphoglukuronsäure f.
- camphoric Kampfersäure f.
- cantharidic Kantharidinsäure f.
- capric Kaprinsäure f.
- caproic Kapronsäure f.
- caprylic Kaprylsäure f.
- carbamic Karbamidsäure f.
- carbolic Karbolsäure f.
- carbonic Kohlensäure f.
- cephalinic Cephalinsäure f.
- cerebronic Cerebronsäure f.
- cerotinic Cerotinsäure f.
- chaulmoogric Chaulmoograsäure f.
- chelidonic Chelidonsäure f.
- chenodeoxycholic Chenodesoxycholsäure f.
- chloracetic Chloressigsäure f.
- chloric Chlorsäure f.
- chlorous chlorige Säure f.
- cholesterinic Cholesterinsäure f.
- cholic Cholsäure f.
- chondroitic Chondroitinsäure f.

acid, chondroitin-sulfuric (a) Chondroitinschwefelsäure f.
- chondroitin-sulphuric (e) Chondroitinschwefelsäure f.
- chromic Chromsäure f.
- chrysophanic Chrysophansäure f.
- cinnamic Zimtsäure f.
- citric Zitronensäure f.
- cresylic Kresylsäure f.
- crotonic Krotonsäure f.
- cytidylic Cytidylsäure f.
- decenoic Decensäure f.
- dehydrocholic Dehydrocholsäure f.
- deltaaminolaevulinic (e) Deltaaminolävulinsäure f.
- deltaaminolevulinic (a) Deltaaminolävulinsäure f.
- deoxyribonucleic Desoxyribonukleinsäure f.
- desoxycholic Desoxycholsäure f.
- diacetic Azetessigsäure f.
- diaminoacetic Diaminoessigsäure f.
- dibasic zweibasige Säure f.
- dichloracetic Dichloressigsäure f.
- diethylbarbituric Diäthylbarbitursäure f.
- diethylene triamine pentaacetic Diäthylentriaminpentaessigsäure f.
- dihydrofolic Dihydrofolsäure f.
- epsilon-aminocaproic Epsilon-Aminokapronsäure f.
- ergotinic Ergotinsäure f.
- ethacrynic Etacrynsäure f.
- ethylenediamine tetraacetic Äthylendiamintetraessigsäure f.
- etianic Aetiansäure f.
- fatty Fettsäure f.
- folic Folsäure f.
- folinic Folinsäure f.
- formiminoglutamic Formiminoglutaminsäure f.
- formic Ameisensäure f.

acid, fumaric Fumarsäure f.
- fuming nitric rauchende Salpetersäure f.
- galacturonic Galakturonsäure f.
- gallic Gallussäure f.
- gastric Magensäure f.
- glacial acetic Eisessig f.
- gluconic Glukonsäure f.
- glucuronic Glukuronsäure f.
- glutamic Glutaminsäure f.
- glutaminic Glutaminsäure f.
- glutaric Glutarsäure f.
- glyceric Glyzerinsäure f.
- glycerophosphoric Glycerophosphorsäure f.
- glycocholic Glykocholsäure f.
- guanylic Guanylsäure f.
- helvellic Helvellasäure f.
- heptacosanic Heptacosansäure f.
- hexose-diphosphoric Hexosediphosphorsäure f.
- hexuronic Askorbinsäure f.
- hippuric Hippursäure f.
- homogentisic Homogentisinsäure f.
- homopiperidinic Homopiperidinsäure f.
- hyaluronic Hyaluronsäure f.
- hydracrylic Hydrakrylsäure f.
- hydrobromic Bromwasserstoffsäure f.
- hydrochloric Salzsäure f.
- hydrocyanic Blausäure f.
- hydrofluoric Fluorwasserstoffsäure f.
- hydroxy Hydroxysäure f.
- hypophosphorous unterphosphorige Säure f.
- indolacetic Indolessigsäure f.
- inosinic Inosinsäure f.
- iodic Jodsäure f.
- iodogorgoric Jodgorgosäure f., Dijodtyrosin n.
- isovalerianic Isovaleriansäure f.
- keto Ketosäure f.
- ketoisocaproic Ketoisokapronsäure f.

acid, lactic Milchsäure f.
- laevulinic (e) Lävulinsäure f.
- lauric Laurinsäure f.
- levulinic (a) Lävulinsäure f.
- lignoceric Lignocerinsäure f.
- linoleic Linolsäure f.
- linolenic Linolensäure f.
- lithocholic Lithocholsäure f.
- lysergic Lysergsäure f.
- malic Apfelsäure f.
- mandelic Mandelsäure f.
- manganic Mangansäure f.
- margaric Margarinsäure f.
- melissic Melissinsäure f.
- mercapturic Merkaptursäure f.
- metaphosphoric Metaphosphorsäure f.
- monobasic einbasige Säure f.
- monochloracetic Monochloressigsäure f.
- mucic Schleimsäure f.
- mucoitin-sulfuric (a) Mukoitinschwefelsäure f.
- mucoitin-sulphuric (e) Mukoitinschwefelsäure f.
- muriatic Salzsäure f.
- myristic Myristinsäure f.
- nalidixic Nalidixinsäure f.
- neuraminic Neuraminsäure f.
- nicotinic Nikotinsäure f.
- nitric Salpetersäure f.
- nitrohydrochloric Königswasser n.
- nitromuriatic Königswasser n.
- nitrosonitric rauchende Salpetersäure f.
- nitrous salpetrige Säure f.
- nonacosanic Nonacosansäure f.
- nucleic Nukleinsäure f.
- nucleinic Nukleinsäure f.
- octacosanic Montansäure f.
- octanoic Oktansäure f.
- oleic Ölsäure f.
- orotic Orotsäure f.
- orthoaminosalicylic Orthoaminosalizylsäure f.

acid, orthophosphoric Orthophosphorsäure f.
- osmic Osmiumsäure f.
- oxalic Kleesäure f.
- palmitic Palmitinsäure f.
- pantothenic Pantothensäure f.
- paraaminobenzoic Paraaminobenzoesäure
- paraaminohippuric Paraaminohippursäure
- paraaminosalicylic Paraaminosalizylsäure f.
- paraffinic Paraffinsäure f.
- pelargonic Pelargonsäure f.
- penicillanic Penicillansäure f.
- pentacosanic Pentacosansäure f.
- peracetic Peressigsäure f.
- perboric Perborsäure f.
- permanganic Permangansäure f.
- phenylacetic Phenylessigsäure f.
- phenylethylbarbituric Phenyläthylbarbitursäure f.
- phenylcinchoninic Phenylchinolinkarbonsäure f.
- phosphatidic Phosphatidsäure f.
- phosphoribosylimidazole-acetic Phosphoribosylimidazolessigsäure f.
- phosphoric Phosphorsäure f.
- phosphorous phosphorige Säure f.
- phosphotungstic Phosphorwolframsäure f.
- phthalic Phthalsäure f.
- picric Pikrinsäure f.
- piperidinic Piperidinsäure f.
- propionic Propionsäure f.
- prostanic Prostansäure f.
- prussic Blausäure f.
- Pteroylglutamic Pteroylglutaminsäure f.
- pyrogallic Pyrogallussäure f.
- pyrophosphoric Pyrophosphorsäure f.
- pyrosulfuric (a) rauchende Schwefelsäure f.

acid, pyrosulphuric (e) rauchende Schwefelsäure f.
- pyruvic Brenztraubensäure f.
- quinic Chinasäure f.
- rhodanic Rhodansäure f.
- ribonucleic Ribonukleinsäure f.
- ricinolic Rizinolsäure f.
- rosolic Rosolsäure f.
- salicylic Salizylsäure f.
- salicylous salizylige Säure f.
- santalinic Santalinsäure f.
- santoninic Santoninsäure f.
- selenic Selensäure f.
- silicic Kieselsäure f.
- sorbic Sorbinsäure f.
- sozoiodolic Sozojodolsäure f.
- stearic Stearinsäure f.
- succinic Bernsteinsäure f.
- sulfanilic (a) Sulfanilsäure f.
- sulfosalicylic (a) Sulfosalizylsäure f.
- sulfuric (a) Schwefelsäure f.
- sulfurous (a) schweflige Säure f.
- sulphanilic (e) Sulfanilsäure f.
- sulphosalicylic (e) Sulfosalizylsäure f.
- sulphuric (e) Schwefelsäure f.
- sulphurous (e) schweflige Säure f.
- tannic Gerbsäure f.
- tartaric Weinsäure f.
- taurocholic Taurocholsäure f.
- tetrabasic vierbasige Säure f.
- tetracosanic Tetracosansäure f.
- tetrahydrofolic Tetrahydrofolsäure f.
- thioacetic Thioessigsäure f.
- thioaminopropionic Thioaminopropionsäure f., Thioalanin n.
- thymidylic Thymidylsäure f.
- tranexamic Tranexamsäure f.
- tribasic dreibasige Säure f.
- trichloroacetic Trichloressigsäure f.
- tricosanic Tricosansäure f.

acid, triiodothyroacetic Trijodthyroessigsäure f.
— triphosphoric Triphosphorsäure f.
— tropic Tropasäure f.
— uric Harnsäure f.
— ursodeoxycholic Ursodesoxycholsäure f.
— valerianic Baldriansäure f.
— vanadic Vanadinsäure f.
— vanillic Vanillesäure f.
— vanillin-mandelic Vanillinmandelsäure f.
— weak schwache Säure f.
acidaemia; acidaemic (e) Azidämie f.; azidämisch
acidalbumin Azidalbumin n.
acidaminuria Azidaminurie f.
acid-base balance Säure-Basen-Gleichgewicht n.
acid-base equilibrium Säure-Basen-Gleichgewicht n.
acidemia; acidemic (a) Azidämie f.; azidämisch
acid-fast säurefest
acid-forming säurebildend
acidify, to säuern, sauer machen
acidimeter Azidimeter n.
acidity Azidität f.
acidity, total Gesamtazidität f.
acidophilic azidophil
acidoresistance Säureresistenz f.
acidoresistant säureresistent
acidosis Azidose f.
acidosis, lactic Laktatazidose f.
acidotic azidotisch
acidulous schwach sauer, säuerlich
acinotubular azinotubulär
acinous azinös
acne Akne f.
acne conglobata d. e.
acne keratosa d. e.
acne rosacea d. e.
acne varioliformis d. e.
acne vulgaris d. e.
aconite Akonit n.
aconitine Akonitin n.

acoustic akustisch
acoustic neurinoma Akustikusneurinom n.
acoustics Akustik f.
acquire, to erwerben, sich zuziehen
acridine Acridin n.
acriflavine hydrochloride Trypaflavin n.
acrocephaly Turmschädel m.
acrocyanosis Akrozyanose f.
acrocyanotic akrozyanotisch
acrodynia Akrodynie f.
acrognosis Akrognosis f.
acrohyperhidrosis Akrohyperhidrose f.
acromegalic akromegal
acromegaly Akromegalie f.
acromioclavicular akromioklavikular
acromioscapular akromioskapular
acromiothoracic akromiothorakal
acronyx eingewachsener Nagel m.
acropachy Akropachie f.
acroparaesthesia (e) Akroparästhesie f.
acroparaesthetic (e) akroparästhetisch
acroparesthesia (a) Akroparästhesie f.
acroparesthetic (a) akroparästhetisch
acrylamide Acrylamid n.
acrylate Acrylat n.
acting out d. e. n., Ausagieren n.
actinide Aktinid n.
actinium Aktinium n.
actinobacillosis Aktinobazillose f.
Actinobacillus mallei Rotzbazillus m.
actinological strahlenkundlich
actinology Strahlenkunde f.
actinomycin d. e. n.
actinomycosis Aktinomykose f.
actinomycotic aktinomykotisch
actinotherapy Strahlenbehandlung f.

action 22

action Aktion f., Handlung f., Tätigkeit f.
action, mode of Wirkungsweise f.
activate, to aktivieren
activation Aktivierung f.
activator Aktivator m.
active aktiv
activity Aktivität f.
actomyosin Aktomyosin n.
acuity Akuität f.
acuity, visual Sehschärfe f.
acupuncture Akupunktur f.
acute akut
acute yellow atrophy akute gelbe Atrophie f.
acyclic azyklisch
acyl Radikal n. einer organischen Säure
acylguanidine Acylguanidin n.
acylureidomethylpenicillin d. e. n.
A.D. (= axiodistal) axiodistal
adamantine Adamantin n.
adamantinoma Adamantinom n.
adamantoblast d. e. m.
Adam's apple Adamsapfel m.
adamsite Adamsit n.
Adams-Stokes disease Adams-Stokessches Syndrom n.
adaptation d. e. f.
adapter d. e. m.
A.D.C. (= axiodistocervical axiodistozervikal
addict süchtig
addiction Sucht f.
addiction, alcohol Alkoholsucht f.
addiction, drug Arzneimittelsucht f.
addisonism Addisonismus m.
Addison's anaemia (e) perniziöse Anämie f.
Addison's anemia (a) perniziöse Anämie f.
Addison's disease Addisonsche Krankheit f.
addition d. e. f.
additional zusätzlich

additional food Beikost f., Zusatzkost f.
adduct, to adduzieren
adduction Adduktion f.
adductor Adduktor m.
adelomorphous adelomorph
adelomorphous cell Hauptzelle f.
adenine Adenin n.
adenitic adenitisch
adenitis d. e. f.
adeno-acanthoma Adenoakanthom n.
adeno-angiosarcoma Adenoangiosarkom n.
adenoblast d. e. m.
adenocarcinoma Adenokarzinom n.
adenocele d. e. f., Adenozele f.
adenochondroma Adenochondrom n.
adenochondrosarcoma Adenochondrosarkom n.
adenofibroma Adenofibrom n.
adenohypophysis Adenohypophyse f.
adenoid d. e.
adenoidectomy Adenoidektomie f.
adenoids adenoide Vegetationen f. pl.
adenolipomatosis Adenolipomatose f.
adenoma Adenom n.
adenoma, islet Insulom n.
adenoma sebaceum d. e.
adenoma sudoriparum Adenoma sudoriferum
adenomatosis Adenomatose f.
adenomatous adenomatös
adenomyoma Adenomyom n.
adenosclerosis Adenosklerose f., Drüsensklerose f.
adenosine Adenosin n.
adenosine triphosphate Adenosintriphosphat n.
adenotome Adenotom n.
adenotomy Adenotomie f.
adenoviral infection Adenovirus-Infektion f.

adenovirus d. e. n.
adenylate Adenylat n.
adequate adäquat
adermin d. e. n.
A.D.G. (= axiodistogingival) axiodistogingival
adhere, to anhaften, anhängen, festkleben
adhesion Adhäsion f.
adhesion, denture Zahnprothesenhaftung f.
adhesive adhäsiv
adhibit, to anwenden
A.D.I. (= axiodistoincisal) axiodistoinzisal
adiabatic adiabatisch
adiadokokinesis Adiadochokinese f.
adiaphoresis Adiaphorese f.
adiaphoretic adiaphoretisch
Adie's syndrome Adiesches Syndrom n.
adipocere Leichenwachs n.
adipose fettsüchtig, adipös
adipose cell Fettzelle f.
adiposis Fettsucht f.
adiposis dolorosa Dercumsche Krankheit f.
adiposity Fettsucht f.
adiposogenital d. e.
adiposogenital syndrome Dystrophia adiposogenitalis
adipsia Adipsie f.
adjust, to anpassen
adjustable verstellbar
adjustment Anpassung f.
adjuvant Adjuvans n.
administration Verwaltung f.; Verabfolgung f., Anwendung f.
admission Zulassung f., Annahme f., Aufnahme f.
admission to a hospital Krankenhausaufnahme f.
admixture Beimischung f.
adnexitic adnexitisch
adnexitis d. e. f.
adnexopexy Adnexopexie f., Adnexanheftung f.
A.D.O. (= axiodistoocclusal) axiodistookklusal
adolescence Adoleszenz f.
adolescent Adoleszent m.
adonidin d. e. n.
adonitol Adonit n.
adopt, to adoptieren
adoption d. e. f.
adrenal d. e.
adrenal cortex Nebennierenrinde f.
adrenal cortical hypofunction Nebennierenrindenunterfunktion f.
adrenalectomize, to adrenalektomieren
adrenalectomy Adrenalektomie f., Nebennierenentfernung f.
adrenal gland Nebenniere f.
adrenalin d. e. n.
adrenal insufficiency Nebenniereninsuffizienz f.
adrenal marrow Nebennierenmark n.
adrenal medulla Nebennierenmark n.
adrenergic adrenergisch
adrenoceptor Adrenorezeptor m.
adrenocorticotropic adrenokortikotrop
adrenocorticotropic hormone adrenokortikotropes Hormon n.
adrenolytic adrenolytisch
adrenoreceptor Adrenorezeptor m.
adrenotropic adrenotrop
adriamycin d. e. n.
adsorb, to adsorbieren
adsorption d. e. f.
adult erwachsen; Erwachsener m., Erwachsene f.
advanced fortgeschritten
advancement Verlagerungsoperation f.
advantageous vorteilhaft
adventitia d. e. f.
advice Rat m.

advise, to raten, beraten
advisory center Beratungsstelle f.
adynamia Adynamie f.
aegophony (e) Ägophonie f.
aerate, to belüften
aeration Belüftung f.
Aerobacter aerogenes Bacillus lactis aerogenes
aerobe Aerobier m.
aerobic aerob
aerocystoscopic aerozystoskopisch
aerocystoscopy Aerozystoskopie f.
aerogram Aerogramm n.
aerographic aerographisch
aerography Aerographie f.
aeromedical luftfahrtmedizinisch
aeroneurosis Aeroneurose f.
aerophagy Aerophagie f.
aerosol d. e. n.
aesculin (e) Äsculin n.
aesthetical (e) ästhetisch
aestival (e) sommerlich
aestivoautumnal malaria (e) Malaria tropica
aetiological (e) ätiologisch
aetiology (e) Ätiologie
aetioporphyrin Ätioporphyrin n.
afebrile afebril
affect Affekt m.
affect, to befallen, affizieren, angreifen
affected, to be befallen sein
affect epilepsy Affektepilepsie f.
affection Affektion f., Befall m.
affective affektiv
affective instability Affektlabilität f., Affektschwäche f.
afference Afferenz f.
afferent d. e.
affinity Affinität f.
affix, to anheften
afflux d. e. m.
affusion according to Kneipp Kneippscher Guß m.
afibrinogenaemia (e) Afibrinogenämie f.

afibrinogenemia (e) Afibrinogenämie f.
aflatoxin d. e. n.
after-birth Nachgeburt f.
afterbleeding Nachblutung f.
after-care Nachbehandlung
after-condensation Nachkondensation f.
after-discharge Nacherregung f., Nachentladung f.
after-effect Nachwirkung f.
after-examination Nachuntersuchung f., Nachprüfung f.
after-image Nachbild n.
afterload Nachbelastung f.
after-pains Nachwehen f. pl.
after-result Spätergebnis n., Spätresultat n.
after-treatment Nachbehandlung f.
A.G. (= axiogingival) axiogingival
agalactia Agalaktie f.
agammaglobulinaemia (e) Agammaglobulinämie f.
agammaglobulinemia (a) Agammaglobulinämie f.
aganglionosis Aganglionose f.
agar d. e. m.
agar, ascitic fluid Aszitesagar m.
— **bile salt** Gallensalzagar m.
— **blood** Blutagar m.
— **brilliant green** Brillantgrünagar m.
— **dextrose** Dextroseagar m.
— **Dieudonné's** Dieudonné-Agar m.
— **Drigalski's** Drigalski-Agar m.
— **fuchsin** Fuchsinagar m.
— **gelatin** Gelatineagar m.
— **glucose** Glukoseagar m.
— **Löffler's** Löffler-Agar m.
— **potato-blood** Kartoffel-Blut-Agar m.
— **Serum** Serumagar m.
— **tellurite** Telluritagar m.
agar-agar d. e. m.
agaric Blätterpilz m.
agaric, fly Fliegenpilz m.
agaric, larch Lärchenschwamm m.

agaricin Agarizin n.
agastric agastrisch
agate Achat m.
age Alter n., Lebensalter n.
age, advanced höheres Alter n.
age changes Altersveränderungen f. pl.
age-dependent altersabhängig
ageing Altern n.
age-limit Altersgrenze f.
agenitalism Agenitalismus m.
agent Agens n.
agent, polishing Poliermittel n.
ageusia Ageusie f.
age worn altersschwach
agglomerate Agglomerat n.
agglutinable agglutinabel
agglutination d. e. f.
agglutinin d. e. n.
agglutinogen d. e. n.
aggravate, to aggravieren
aggravation d. e. f.
aggregate Aggregat n.
aggregation d. e. f.
aggression d. e. f.
aggressive aggressiv
aging Altern n.
agitation d. e. f.
aglucon Aglykon n.
aglucone Aglykon n.
aglycone Aglykon n.
agnosia Agnosie f.
agonal d. e.
agonist d. e. m.
agony Agonie f.
agoraphobia Agoraphobie f.
agrammatism Agrammatismus m.
agranulocytic agranulozytisch
agranulocytic angina Angina agranulocytica
agranulocytosis Agranulozytose f.
agraphia Agraphie f.
agrypnia Agrypnie f.
agree, to übereinstimmen
agreeable angenehm
agreement Übereinkommen n., Übereinstimmung f.

ague Malariafieber n.; hitziges Fieber n.
Ahlfeld's sign Ahlfeldsches Zeichen n.
A.I. (= axioincisal) axioinzisal
ail, to unpäßlich sein, schmerzen
ailing unpäßlich, leidend
ailment Unpäßlichkeit f.
ainhum Dactylolysis spontanea
air Luft f.
air bath Luftbad n..
air, complemental Komplementärluft f.
air-cooled luftgekühlt
air-cushion Luftkissen n.
air embolism Luftembolie f.
air hunger Kußmaulsche Atmung f.
air inflation Lufteinblasung f.
airing worthy fliegertauglich
air pressure Luftdruck m.
air, reserve Reserveluft f.
air, residual Residualluft f.
air sickness Luftkrankheit f.
air tight luftdicht
air, trapped Blähluft f.
airway Luftweg m.
ajmaline Ajmalin n.
akinaesthesia (e) Akinästhesie f.
akinesia Akinesie f.
akinesthesia (a) Akinästhesie f.
akinetic akinetisch
alabamine Alabamin n.
alanine Alanin n.
alarm d. e. m.
alastrim d. e. f.
Albers-Schönberg marble bones disease Albers-Schönbergsche Marmorknochenkrankheit f.
albinism Albinismus m.
albino d. e. m.
albinotic albinotisch
Albright's disease Albrightsches Syndrom n.
albuginea d. e. f.
albugineotomy Albugineotomie f.
albumen Eiweiß n.

albumin d. e. n.
albuminimeter d. e. n.
albuminuric albuminurisch
albuminuria Albuminurie f.
albumose d. e. f.
Alcaligenes faecalis Bacillus faecalis alcaligenes
alcapton Alkapton n.
alcaptonuria Alkaptonurie f.
alcian blue Alcianblau n.
alcohol Alkohol m.
alcohol, absolute absoluter Alkohol m.
– allyl Allylalkohol m.
– amyl Amylalkohol m.
– amylic Amylalkohol m.
– aromatic aromatischer Alkohol m.
– butyl Butylalkohol m.
– cetyl Cetylalkohol m.
– dehydrated dehydrierter Alkohol m.
– diluted verdünnter Alkohol m.
– embittered vergällter Alkohol m.
– ethyl Äthylalkohol m.
– methyl Methylalkohol m.
– primary primärer Alkohol m.
– propyl Propylalkohol m.
– secondary sekundärer Alkohol m.
– tertiary tertiärer Alkohol m.
– unsaturated ungesättigter Alkohol m.
alcohol addiction Alkoholsucht f.
alcohol block Alkoholblockade f.
alcoholic alkoholisch; Alkoholiker m., Alkoholikerin f.
alcoholic liquors alkoholische Getränke n. pl.
alcoholics anonymous anonyme Alkoholiker m. pl.
alcoholism Alkoholismus m.
aldehyde Aldehyd m.
aldocorticosterone Aldokortikosteron n.
aldohexose d. e. f.
aldol d. e. n.

aldolase d. e. f.
aldose d. e. f.
aldosterone Aldosteron n.
aldosteronism Aldosteronismus m.
aldrin d. e. n.
alerting system retikuläres Aktivierungssystem n.
aleukaemia (e) Aleukämie f.
aleukaemic (e) aleukämisch
aleukemia (a) Aleukämie f.
aleukemic (a) aleukämisch
aleukia Aleukie f.
Alexander-Adams operation Alexander-Adams-Operation f.
alexia Alexie f.
alexin d. e. n.
algebra d. e. f.
alginate Alginat n.
Alice in wonderland syndrome Depersonalisationssyndrom n.
alicyclic alizyklisch
alienation Geistesstörung f.
alienist Irrenarzt m.
alien substance Fremdstoff m.
alimentary alimentär
alimentary tract Verdauungstrakt m.
alimentation Ernährung f.
aliphatic aliphatisch
alizarin d. e. f.
alizarin yellow Alizaringelb n.
alkali d. e. n.
alkalify, to alkalisieren
alkaline alkalisch
alkalinity Alkalinität f., Alkaligehalt m.
alkalinization Alkalisierung f.
alkalinize, to alkalisieren
alkalization Alkalisierung f.
alkalize, to alkalisieren
alkaloid d. e. n.
alkalosis Alkalose f.
alkalotic alkalotisch
alkapton d. e. n.
alkaptonuria Alkaptonurie f.
alkyl d. e. n.
alkylamine Alkylamin n.

alkylate, to alkylieren
allantoin d. e. n.
allantois d. e. f.
allelomorphic allelomorph
allelomorphism Allelomorphie f.
Allen-Doisy test Allen-Doisy-Test m.
allergen d. e. n.
allergic allergisch
allergization Allergisierung f.
allergize, to allergisieren
allergosis Allergose f.
allergy Allergie f.
alleviate, to erleichtern, lindern
alleviation Erleichterung f., Linderung f.
alligator d. e. m.
allobiosis Allobiose f.
allobiotic allobiotisch
allopathical allopathisch
allopathist Allopath m.
allopathy Allopathie f.
allopregnandiol d. e. n.
allopregnane Allopregnan n.
allopregnanolone Allopregnanolon n.
allopsychosis Allopsychose f.
allopsychotic allopsychotisch
allopurinol d. e. n.
allorhythmia Allorhythmie f.
allorhythmic allorhythmisch
all or none law Alles-oder-Nichts-Gesetz n.
allotypic allotypisch
alloxan d. e. n.
alloxazine Alloxazin n.
alloxin d. e. n.
alloy Legierung f., Mischung f.
allyl d. e. n.
allyl isothiocyanate Senföl n., Allylisothiozyanat n.
almond Mandel f.
almoner Fürsorger m.
aloe d. e. f.
aloin d. e. n.
alopecia Alopezie f.
alphabetic alphabetisch

alpha cell Alphazelle f.
alpha emitter Alphastrahler m.
alpha globulin Alpha-Globulin n.
alpha-methyl-dopa Alpha-Methyldopa n.
alpha-ray Alpha-Strahl m.
alpha receptor Alpha-Rezeptor m.
alpha wave Alphawelle f.
alprenolol d. e. n.
alteration d. e. f.
alternating alternierend
alternating current Wechselstrom m.
altitude Höhe f.
altitude sickness Höhenkrankheit f.
alum Alaun m.
alumina Aluminiumoxyd n.
aluminate Aluminat n.
aluminated alaunhaltig
aluminium d. e. n.
aluminium acetate (e) essigsaure Tonerde f.
aluminosis Aluminose f.
aluminum (a) Aluminium n
aluminum acetate (a) essigsaure Tonerde f.
alveobronchiolitis d. e. f.
alveolar alveolär
alveolar air Alveolarluft f.
alveolectomy Alveolektomie f.
alveolitis d. e. f.
alveoloarterial alveoloarteriell
alveolocapillary alveolokapillär
alveoloclasia Alveoloklasie f.
alveolodental d. e.
alveoloplasty Alveoloplastik
alveolotomy Alveolotomie f.
alveolovenous alveolovenös
alveolus Alveole f.
alveolysis Alveolyse f.
alymphia Alymphie f.
Alzheimer's disease Alzheimersche Krankheit f.
A.M. (= axiomesial) axiomesial
amalgam d. e. n.
amalgamate, to amalgamieren

amalgamator Amalgammischer m.
amalgam carrier Amalgamträger m.
amalgam plugger Amalgamstopfer m.
amalgam spoon Amalgamlöffel m.
amanita, deadly Knollenblätterpilz m.
amastia Amastie f.
amaurosis Amaurose f.
amaurotic amaurotisch
amber Bernstein m.
ambient air Raumluft f.
ambivalence Ambivalenz f.
ambivalent d. e.
amblyopia Amblyopie f.
amboceptor d. e. m.
ambosexual bisexuell
ambulance Krankenwagen m.; Feldlazarett n.
ambulance station Unfallstation f.
ambulance train Lazarettzug m.
ambulant d. e.
ambulatorium Ambulanz f.
ambulatory ambulant
A.M.C. (= axiomesiocervical) axiomesiozervikal
A.M.D. (= axiomesiodistal) axiomesiodistal
ameba (a) Amöbe f.
ameboid (a) amöboid
amelia Amelie f.
ameliorate, to verbessern
amelioration Verbesserung f., Besserung f.
ameloblast d. e. m., Adamantoblast m.
ameloblastoma Ameloblastom n.
amelo-dentinal d. e.
amenorrhea (a) Amenorrhöe f.
amenorrheal (a) amenorrhoisch
amenorrhoea (e) Amenorrhöe f.
amenorrhoic (e) amenorrhoisch
amentia d. e. f.
ametropia Ametropie f.
amidase d. e. f.
amide Amid n.

amiloride Amilorid n.
amimia Amimie f.
aminase d. e. f.
amine Amin n.
amine oxidase Monaminoxydase f.
amino acid Aminosäure f.
aminopeptidase d. e. f.
aminophenazole Aminophenazol n.
aminophylline Aminophyllin n.
aminoprotease d. e. f.
aminopyrine Dimethylaminophenazon n.
aminoquinoline Aminochinolin n.
aminothiazole Aminothiazol n.
aminotransferase d. e. f.
amitotic amitotisch
amitriptyline Amitriptylin n.
ammonia Ammoniak m.
ammonia water Salmiakgeist m.
ammonium d. e. n.
ammonium acetate Ammoniumazetat n.
ammonium carbonate Ammoniumkarbonat n.
ammonium chloride Ammoniumchlorid n.
ammonium salicylate Ammoniumsalizylat n.
Ammon's horn Ammonshorn n.
amnesia Amnesie f.
amnestic amnestisch
amniographical amniographisch
amniography Amniographie f.
amnion d. e. n.
amoeba (e) Amöbe f.
amoeboid (e) amöboid
amorphous amorph
amoxicillin d. e. n.
ampere Ampere n.
amphetamine Amphetamin n.
amphiarthrosis Amphiarthrose f.
amphibium Amphibie f.
amphibolic amphibol
amphoric amphorisch
amphoteric amphoter
amphotericin d. e. n.
ampicillin d. e. n.

amplitude d. e. f.
ampoulate, to ampullieren
ampoule Ampulle f., Glasampulle f.
ampule Ampulle f., Glasampulle f.
ampulla Ampulle f.
ampullar ampullär
amputate, to amputieren
amputation d. e. f.
amputation stump Amputationsstumpf m.
amputee Amputierter m.
amusia Amusie f.
amusic amusisch
amygdalin d. e. n.
amyl d. e. n.
amylase d. e. f.
amylene Amylen n.
amylene hydrate Amylenhydrat n.
amyl nitrite Amylnitrit n.
amyloid Amyloid n.; amyloid
amyloidosis Amyloidose f.
amylomaltase d. e. f.
amylopectin Amylopektin n.
amylopsin Diastase f. (enzymol.)
amylose d. e. f.
amyostatic amyostatisch
amyotrophic amyotrophisch
amyotrophy Amyotrophie f.
anabiosis Anabiose f.
anabiotic anabiotisch
anabolic anabolisch; Anabolikum n.
anachoresis Anachorese f.
anachoric anachoretisch
anacid anazid
anacidity Anazidität f.
anaclitic anaklitisch
anaemia (e) Anämie f.
anaemia, aplastic (e) aplastische Anämie f.
– due to infection (e) Infektanämie f.
– haemolytic (e) hämolytische Anämie f.
– hyperchromic (e) hyperchrome Anämie f.

anaemia, hypochromic (e) hypochrome Anämie f.
– megaloblastic Megaloblastenanämie f.
– pernicious (e) perniziöse Anämie f.
– secondary (e) sekundäre Anämie f.
anaemic (e) anämisch
anaerobe Anaerobier m.
anaerobic anaerob
anaesthesia (e) Anästhesie f.; Narkose f.
–, basal (e) Basisnarkose f.
–, conduction (e) Leitungsanästhesie f.
–, endotracheal (e) Intubationsnarkose f.
–, infiltration (e) Infiltrationsanästhesie f.
–, inhalation (e) Inhalationsnarkose f.
–, local (e) Lokalanästhesie f.
–, refrigeration (e) Kälteanästhesie f.
–, surface (e) Oberflächenanästhesie f.
– tube (e) Narkosetubus m.
anaesthesiologic (e) anästhesiologisch
anaesthesiology (e) Anästhesiologie f.
anaesthetic (e) anästhetisch; Anaestheticum n.
– apparatus (e) Narkoseapparat m.
– inhaler (e) Narkosemaske f.
anaesthetist (e) Anästhesist m., Anästhesistin f.; Narkotiseur m.
anaesthetize, to (e) anästhesieren, narkotisieren
anal d. e.
analbuminaemia (e) Analbuminämie f.
analbuminemia (a) Analbuminämie f.
analeptic analeptisch; Analeptikum n.

analgesia Analgesie f.
analgesic analgetisch;
 Analgetikum n.
analog (a) d. e.
analogous analog
analogue (e) analog
analogy Analogie f.
analysis Analyse f.
analytic analytisch
analyze, to analysieren
anamnesis Anamnese f.
anamnestic anamnestisch
anaphase d. e. f.
anaphoresis Anaphorese f.
anaphylactic anaphylaktisch
anaphylaxis Anaphylaxie f.
anaplasia Anaplasie f.
anaplasmosis Anaplasmose f.
anaplastic anaplastisch
anastigmat d. e. n.
anastigmatic anastigmatisch
anastomose, to anastomosieren
anastomosis Anastomose f.
anastomotic anastomotisch
anatomic anatomisch
anatomist Anatom m.
anatomy Anatomie f.
anatoxin d. e. n.
anchor Anker m.
anchorage Verankerung f.
ancrod d. e. n.
Ancylostoma duodenale
 Ankylostoma duodenale
ancylostomiasis Ankylostomiasis f.
andradiol d. e. n.
androgen d. e. n.
androgenic androgen
androgynism Androgynie f.
andrology Andrologie f.
androstandiol d. e. n.
androstandion d. e. n.
androstane Androstan n.
androstendion d. e. n.
androstenolone Androstenolon n.
androsterone Androsteron n.
anemia (a) Anämie f.
—, aplastic (a) aplastische Anämie f.

anemia due to infection (a)
 Infektanämie f.
—, hemolytic (a) hämolytische
 Anämie f.
— hyperchromic (a) hyperchrome
 Anämie f.
— hypochromic (a) hypochrome
 Anämie f.
— megaloblastic (a) Megaloblastenanämie f.
— pernicious (a) perniziöse
 Anämie f.
— secondary (a) sekundäre
 Anämie f.
anemic (a) anämisch
anencephaly Anenzephalie f.
anergic anergisch
anergy Anergie f.
anesthesia (a) Anästhesie f.;
 Narkose f.
—, basal (a) Basisnarkose f.
—, conduction (a) Leitungsanästhesie f.
—, endotracheal (a) Intubationsnarkose f.
—, infiltration (a) Infiltrationsanästhesie f.
—, inhalation (a) Inhalationsnarkose f.
—, local (a) Lokalanästhesie f.
—, refrigeration (a) Kälteanästhesie f.
—, surface (a) Oberflächenanästhesie f.
— tube (a) Narkosetubus m.
anesthesiologic (a) anästhesiologisch
anesthesiology (a) Anästhesiologie f.
anesthetic (a) anästhetisch;
 Anaestheticum n.
— apparatus (a) Narkoseapparat m.
— inhaler (a) Narkosemaske f.
anesthetist (a) Anästhesist m.,
 Anästhesistin f.; Narkotiseur m.
anesthetize, to (a) anästhesieren,
 narkotisieren

aneurin d. e. n.
aneurysm Aneurysma n.
aneurysmal aneurysmatisch
aneurysmatic aneurysmatisch
angiectasis Angiektasie f.
angiectatic angiektatisch
angiectomy Angiektomie f.
angiitis d. e. f.
angina d. e. f.
—, lacunar Angina lacunaris
—, follicular Angina follicularis
— pectoris d. e.
—, Vincent's Angina Plaut-Vincent
anginous anginös
angioblastoma Angioblastom n.
angiocardiogram Angiokardiogramm n.
angiocardiographic angiokardiographisch
angiocardiography Angiokardiographie f.
angioendothelioma Angioendotheliom n.
angiofibroma Angiofibrom n.
angiogliomatosis Angiogliomatose f.
angiographic angiographisch
angiography Angiographie f.
angiokeratosis Angiokeratose f.
angiologic angiologisch
angiology Angiologie f.
angiolymphoma Angiolymphom n.
angiolysis Angiolyse f.
angioma Angiom n.
angiomatosis Angiomatose f.
angiomatosis, encephalotrigeminal Sturge-Webersches Syndrom n.
angiomyoma Angiomyom n.
angiomyoneuroma Angiomyoneurom n.
angiomyosarcoma Angiomyosarkom n.
angioneurosis Angioneurose f.
angioneurotic angioneurotisch
angioplasty Angioplastik f., Gefäßplastik f.
angiorrhaphy Gefäßnaht f.
angiorrhexis Gefäßriß m.
angiosarcoma Angiosarkom n.
angiospasm Gefäßspasmus m.
angiospastic angiospastisch
angiostomy Angiostomie f.
angiotensin d. e. n.
angiotensinase d. e. f.
angiotomy Angiotomie f.
angiotonin d. e. n., Hypertensin n.
angle Winkel m., Ecke f.
angle, cerebellopontine Kleinhirnbrückenwinkel m.
angle of view Blickwinkel m.
anglepiece Winkelstück n.
Ångström unit Ångström-Einheit f.
angular winkelig, eckig
angulation Abwinkelung f., Knickung f.
anhepatic anhepatisch
anhydraemia (e) Anhydrämie f.
anhydraemic (e) anhydrämisch
anhydrase d. e. f.
anhydremia (a) Anhydrämie f.
anhydremic (a) anhydrämisch
anhydride Anhydrid n.
anhydrous anhydrisch
anicteric anikterisch
anilid d. e. n.
anilide Anilid n.
aniline Anilin n.
animal Tier n.; animalisch
animal cage Tierstall m.
animal experiment Tierversuch m.
animal, experimental Versuchstier n.
animal kingdom Tierreich n.
animal pathology Tierpathologie f.
animate, to beleben
anion d. e. n.
aniridia Aniridie f.
anise Anis m.
anisine Anisin n.
anisochromasia Anisochromasie f.
anisochromatic anisochromatisch
anisocoria Anisokorie f.
anisocytosis Anisozytose f.
anisometropia Anisometropie f.

anisotonic anisotonisch
ankle Sprunggelenk n.
ankle clonus Fußklonus m.
ankyloblepharon d. e. n.
ankylopoietic ankylopoetisch
ankylosing ankylosierend
– spondylarthritis Spondylarthritis ankylopoetica
ankylosis Ankylose f.
ankylotic ankylotisch
anlage d. e. f.
anneal, to ausglühen
annihilate, to vernichten
annihilation Vernichtung f.
annular ringförmig
annuloplasty Annuloplastik f.
anode d. e. f.
anodinia schmerzlose Geburt f.
anodontia Anodontie f.
anodyne schmerzlindernd; schmerzlinderndes Mittel n.
anodynia Schmerzlosigkeit f.
anoint, to salben, schmieren
anointment Salbe f.
anomalous anomal
anomaly Anomalie f.
anomeric anomer
anonymous anonym
anoperineal d. e.
Anopheles d. e. f.
anophthalmia Anophthalmie f.
anopsia Anopsie f.
anorchism Anorchismus m.
anorectal anorektal
anorexia Anorexie f.
anorganic anorganisch
anosmia Anosmie f.
anovesical anovesikal
anovulatory anovulatorisch
anoxaemia (e) Anoxämie f.
anoxaemic (e) anoxämisch
anoxemia (a) Anoxämie f.
anoxemic (a) anoxämisch
anoxia Anoxie f.
antacid antazid; Antazidum n.
antagonism Antagonismus m.
antagonist d. e. m.

antagonistic antagonistisch
antasthmatic antiasthmatisch; Antiasthmaticum n.
antefixation d. e. f.
anteflexion d. e. f.
antegrade antegrad
antelope Antilope f.
antenatal d. e.
antenna Antenne f.
anteposition d. e. f.
anteriocclusion Vorbißstellung f.
anterior chamber Vorderkammer f.
anterior lobe of the pituitary gland Hypophysenvorderlappen m.
anterior pituitary hypofunction Hypophysenvorderlappenunterfunktion f.
anterior wall Vorderwand f.
anterodorsal d. e.
anteroinferior d. e.
anterolateral d. e.
anteroposterior d. e.
anterosuperior d. e.
anteversion d. e. f.
anteverted antevertiert
anthelminthic Anthelminthicum n., Wurmmittel n.
anthelmintic Anthelminthicum n., Wurmmittel n.
anthracene Anthrazen n.
anthracosis Anthrakose f.
anthramine Anthramin n.
anthraquinone Anthrachinon n.
anthrarobin d. e. n.
anthrax Milzbrand m.
–, symptomatic Rauschbrand m.
anthropologic anthropologisch
anthropologist Anthropologe m., Anthropologin f.
anthropology Anthropologie f.
antiaditis Tonsillitis f.
antiallergic antiallergisch; Antiallergicum n.
antianaemic (e) antianämisch
antianemic (a) antianämisch
antiarrhythmic antiarhythmisch
antiarthritic antiarthritisch

antiasthmatic antiasthmatisch; Antiasthmaticum n.
antibacterial antibakteriell
antibechic hustenstillend; hustenstillendes Mittel n.
antibilious antibiliös
antibiotic antibiotisch; Antibioticum n.
antiblennorrhagic antigonorrhoisch
antibody Antikörper m.
antibody deficiency Antikörpermangel m.
anticarcinogenic antikarzinogen
anticariogenic antikariös
anticatarrhal antikatarrhalisch
anticathode Antikathode f.
anticellular antizellulär
anticholinergic anticholinergisch; Anticholinergicum n.
anticholinesterase d. e. f.
anticoagulant Antikoagulans n.
anticoagulative antikoagulierend
anticomplement Antikomplement n.
anticomplementary antikomplementär
anticoncipient empfängsniverhütend
anticonvulsive antikonvulsiv
anticytolysin Antizytolysin n.
antidepressant antidepressiv; Antidepressivum n.
antidiabetic antidiabetisch; Antidiabeticum n.
antidiabetogenic antidiabetogen
antidiphtheritic antidiphtherisch
antidiuretic antidiuretisch; Antidiureticum n.
antidote Antidot n.
antidromic antidrom
antiemetic antiemetisch; Antiemeticum n.
antienzyme Antienzym n.
antiepileptic antiepileptisch; Antiepilepticum n.
antiestrogen (a) Antiöstrogen n.
antifebrile antifebril

antiferment d. e. n.
antigen d. e. n.
antigenic antigen
antigenicity Antigenität f.
antiglobulin d. e. n.
antihaemolytic (e) antihämolytisch
anithaemophilic (e) antihämophil
antihaemorrhagic (e) antihämorrhagisch
antihemolytic (a) antihämolytisch
antihemophilic (a) antihämophil
antihemorrhagic (a) anithämorrhagisch
antihistaminic antihistaminisch; Antihistaminicum n.
antihypertensive antihypertonisch
antiinflammatory entzündungswidrig, entzündungshemmend
antiketogenic antiketogen
antilipolytic antilipolytisch
antiluetic antiluetisch; Antilueticum n.
antilymphocyte serum Antilymphozytenserum n.
antilymphocytic antilymphozytär
antimetabolite Antimetabolit m.
antimicrobial antimikrobiell
antimony Antimon n.
– **and potassium tartrate** Tartarus stibiatus
antimycotic antimykotisch; Antimycoticum n.
antineoplastic antineoplastisch
antineuralgic antineuralgisch; Antineuralgicum n.
antineuritic antineuritisch
antioestrogen (e) Antiöstrogen n.
antiparasitic antiparasitär
antipathy Antipathie f.
antiperistalsis Antiperistaltik f.
antiperistaltic antiperistaltisch
antiphlogistic antiphlogistisch; Antiphlogisticum n.
antiplasmin d. e. n.
antipruriginous antipruriginös
antipruritic antipruritisch, juckreizlindernd

antipyretic antipyretisch; Antipyreticum n.
antipyrine Antipyrin n.
antirachitic antirachitisch
antireticuloendothelial serum Bogomoletzserum n.
antirheumatic antirheumatisch; Antirheumaticum n.
anti-Rh-serum Anti-Rh-Serum n.
antisepsis d. e. f.
antiseptic antiseptisch; Antisepticum n.
antiserotonin d. e. n.
antiserum d. e. n.
antisialogogue speichelhemmend
antispasmodic antispastisch; Antispasticum n.
antistaphylolysin d. e. n.
antistreptolysin d. e. n.
antisyphilitic antisyphilitisch; Antisyphiliticum n.
antitetanic antitetanisch
antithrombin d. e. n.
antithromboplastic antithromboplastisch
antithrombotic antithrombotisch; Antithromboticum n.
antitoxic antitoxisch
antitoxin d. e. n.
antitrypsin d. e. n.
antituberculotic antituberkulös
antitussive hustenlindernd
antivaccinationist Impfgegner m., Impfgegnerin f.
antivenin antitoxisches Serum n., antitoxisches Schlangenserum n.
antiviral agent Antivirusmittel n.
antivitamin d. e. n.
antixerophthalmic antixerophthalmisch
antrectomy Antrektomie f.
antronasal d. e.
antroscope Antroskop n.
antroscopic antroskopisch
antroscopy Antroskopie f.
antrostomy Antrostomie f.
antrotomy Antrotomie f.

antrotympanic antrotympanisch
anuresis Anurie f.
anuria Anurie f.
anuric anurisch
anus, praeternatural (e) Anus praeternaturalis
−, preternatural (a) Anus praeternaturalis
anvil Amboß m.
anxiety Angst f., Beklemmung f.
anxiety, basic Grundangst f.
anxiety neurosis Angstneurose f.
anxiolytic angstlösend; angstlösendes Mittel n.
A.O. (= anodal opening) Anodenöffnung f.
aorta d. e. f.
aortic aortal
 − arch Aortenbogen m.
 − insufficiency Aorteninsuffizienz f.
 − stenosis Aortenstenose f.
 − valve Aortenklappe f.
aortitis d. e. f.
aortography Aortographie f.
aortoiliac aortoiliakal
A.P. (= axiopulpal) axiopulpal
aparalytic aparalytisch
apareunia Apareunie f.
apathetic unpathetisch
apathic apathisch
apathy Apathie f.
apatite Apatit m.
ape Affe m.
 − fissure Affenspalte f.
apertognathia offener Biß m.
aperture Apertur f.
apex Spitze f.
apex beat Spitzenstoß m.
apex beat, heaving hebender Spitzenstoß m.
aphakia Aphakie f.
aphasia Aphasie f.
aphasic aphasisch
aphonia Aphonie f.
aphonic aphonisch
aphrodisiac Aphrodisiacum n.

aphtha Aphthe f.
aphthous aphthös
apical apikal
apicitis Apizitis f.
apicoectomy Wurzelspitzenresektion f.
apicogram Apexkardiogramm n., Apikogramm n.
apicolysis Apikolyse f.
apicostomy Apikostomie f.
apiol d. e. n.
aplanat d. e. m.
aplanatic aplanatisch
aplasia Aplasie f.
aplastic aplastisch
apnea (a) Apnoe f.
apneic (a) apnoisch
apnoea (e) Apnoe f.
apnoic (e) apnoisch
apocrine apokrin
apo-enzyme Apoenzym n.
apoferritin d. e. n.
apomorphine Apomorphin n.
aponeurosis Aponeurose f.
apophysary apophysär
apophysis Apophyse f.
apophysitis d. e. f.
apoplectic apoplektisch
apoplectiform apoplektiform
apoplexy Apoplexie f.
apoprotein d. e. n.
apothecary Apotheker m., Apothekerin f.
apotoxin d. e. n.
apparatus Apparat m.
apparatus, attachment Halteapparat m.
apparatus, masticatory Kauapparat m.
apparent death Scheintod m.
appease, to Hunger stillen; beruhigen
appendage Anhängsel n., Anhangsgebilde n.
appendage, atrial, of the heart Herzohr n.
appendectomy Appendektomie f.

appendicitic appendizitisch
appendicitis Appendizitis f.
apperception Apperzeption f., Wahrnehmung f.
apperceptive apperzeptiv
appetite Appetit m.
appetite depressant Appetitzügler m.
appliance Gerät n., Vorrichtung f.
applicant Bewerber m., Bewerberin f.
application Applikation f., Anwendung f., Anlegung f.; Bewerbung f.
application, manner of − Anwendungsart f.
applied biology angewandte Biologie f.
apply, to applizieren, anwenden, anlegen
apposition d. e. f.
appraisal Bewertung f.
apprentice Lehrling m.
approach Annäherung f.; Betrachtungsweise f.
approximal d. e.
apractic apraktisch
apraxia Apraxie f.
apron Schurz m., Schürze f.
aquaeduct (e) Aquädukt m.
aqueduct (a) Aquädukt m.
aqueous wässerig
aquocobalamine Aquokobalamin n.
arabinose d. e. f.
arabinoside Arabinosid n.
arabinosuria Arabinosurie f.
arachnida d. e. n. pl.
arachnitis d. e. f.
arachnodactylia Arachnodaktylie f.
arachnoid Arachnoidea f.
arachnoidal d. e.
arbitration expertise Gutachten n.
arborization Arborisation f.
arbutin d. e. n.
arc Bogen m.
arcade Arkade f.

arch Bogen m.; Gewölbe n.
arch, dental Zahnbogen m.
arch, zygomatic Jochbogen m.
archaic archaisch
archetype Archetyp m.
architectonic architektonisch; Architektonik f.
archive Archiv n.
arch support Senkfußeinlage f.
area Gebiet n., Bezirk m., Fläche f.
arecaline Arecolin n.
areflexia Areflexie f.
aregenerative aregenerativ
areolar areolär
argentaffine argentaffin
argentaffinoma Argentaffinom n.
argentophil d. e.
argillaceous earth Tonerde f.
arginase d. e. f.
arginine Arginin n.
argininosuccinase Argininosukzinase f.
argon d. e. n.
argyria Argyrie f.
argyrophil d. e.
ariboflavinosis Ariboflavinose f.
arithmomania Arithmomanie f.
Arkansas oil stone Arkansasabziehstein m.
arm d. e. f.
arm bath Armband n.
armour heart Panzerherz n.
armpit Achselhöhle f.
arm-sling Armtragschlinge f.
army surgeon Feldchirurg m.
Arndt-Schulz law Arndt-Schulzsches Gesetz n.
Arning's tincture Arningsche Tinktur f.
aroma d. e. n.
aromatic aromatisch
arousal reaction Weckreaktion f.
arrested aufgehalten, zum Stillstand gekommen
arrhenoblastoma Arrhenoblastom n.

arrhythmia Arhythmie f.
arrhythmic arhythmisch
arrosion d. e. f.
arrow poison Pfeilgift n.
arsenic arsenhaltig (fünfwertig); Arsen n.
− trioxide Arsenik n.
arsenious arsenhaltig (dreiwertig)
arsenite Arsenit n.
arsenotherapy Arsenbehandlung f.
arsenous arsenhaltig (dreiwertig)
arsine Arsin n.
arsonate Arsonat n.
artefact Artefakt m.
arterial arteriell
arterialization Arterialisierung f.
arterialize, to arterialisieren
arteriocapillary arteriokapillar
arteriogram Arteriogramm n.
arteriographical arteriographisch
arteriography Arteriographie f.
arteriolar arteriolär
arteriole d. e. f.
arteriolosclerosis Arteriolosklerose f.
arteriolosclerotic arteriolosklerotisch
arteriorrhaphy Arteriennaht f.
arteriosclerosis Arteriosklerose f.
arteriosclerotic arteriosklerotisch
arteriovenous arteriovenös
arteritis Arteriitis f.
artery Arterie f., Schlagader f.
−, basilar Arteria basilaris
−, brachial Arteria brachialis
−, cerebellar Arteria cerebellaris
−, cerebral Arteria cerebralis
−, clamp Gefäßklemme f.
−, common carotid Arteria carotis communis
−, copper-wire Kupferdrahtarterie f.
−, corkscrew Korkzieherarterie f.
−, coronary Koronararterie f., Kranzschlagader f.
−, deep femoral Arteria profunda femoris

artery, epigastric Arteria epigastrica
—, **femoral** Arteria femoralis
—, **frontal** Arteria frontalis
—, **gastroduodenal** Arteria gastroduodenalis
—, **gastroepiploic** Arteria gastroepiploica
—, **haemorrhoidal** (e) Arteria haemorrhoidalis
—, **hemorrhoidal** (a) Arteria haemorrhoidalis
—, **hepatic** Arteria hepatica
—, **iliac** Arteria ilica
—, **inferior epigastric** Arteria epigastrica caudalis
—, **innominate** Truncus brachiocephalicus
—, **internal auditory** Arteria labyrinthi
—, **lingual** Arteria lingualis
—, **maxillary** Arteria maxillaris
—, **meningeal** Arteria meningica
—, **mesenteric** Arteria mesenterica
—, **obturator** Arteria obturatoria
—, **occipital** Arteria occipitalis
— **of retina, central** Arteria centralis retinae
— **of tibia, nutrient** Arteria nutricia tibiae
— **of Zinn** Arteria centralis retinae
—, **ophthalmic** Arteria ophthalmica
—, **palatine** Arteria palatina
— **pancreaticoduodenal** Arteria pancreaticoduodenalis
—, **perineal** Arteria perinealis
—, **peroneal** Arteria fibularis
—, **pharyngeal** Arteria pharyngica
—, **popliteal** Arteria poplitea
—, **pudendal** Arteria pudendalis
—, **pulmonary** Arteria pulmonalis
—, **radial** Arteria radialis
—, **renal** Arteria renalis
—, **spermatic** Arteria spermatica
—, **splenic** Arteria lienalis
—, **subclavian** Arteria subclavia
—, **subscapular** Arteria subscapularis

artery, **superior thyroid** Arteria thyreoidea cranialis
—, **temporal** Arteria temporalis
—, **thoracic** Arteria thoracalis
—, **thyroid** Arteria thyreoidea
—, **tibial** Arteria tibialis
—, **umbilical** Arteria umbilicalis
—, **uterine** Arteria uterina
—, **vertebral** Arteria vertebralis
arthralgia Arthralgie f.
arthritic arthritisch
arthritis d. e. f.
—, **atrophic** primär chronischer Gelenkrheumatismus m.
—, **climactic** klimakterische Arthropathie f.
—, **degenerative** Arthrosis deformans
—, **hypertrophic** Arthrosis deformans
—, **infectional** Infektarthritis f.
—, **menopausal** klimakterische Arthropathie f.
—, **rheumatoid** primär chronischer Gelenkrheumatismus m.
arthritism Arthritismus m.
arthrodesis Arthrodese f.
arthrolysis Arthrolyse f.
arthropathic arthropathisch
arthropathy Arthropathie f.
arthropoda d. e. n. pl.
arthrotomy Arthrotomie f.
Arthus's phenomenon Arthus-Phänomen n.
article, original Originalartikel m.
articular artikulär
articulate, to artikulieren
articulated gegliedert, artikuliert
articulation Artikulation f.
articulator Artikulator m.
artifact Artefakt m.
artificial artefiziell, künstlich
artless kunstlos, ungeschickt
aryepiglottic aryepiglottisch
aryl d. e. n.
arylamidase d. e. f.
arylation Arylierung f.

arytaenoid cartilage (e) Ary-Knorpel m.
arytenoid cartilage (a) Ary-Knorpel m.
ASA (= acetylsalicylic acid) ASS (= Azetylsalizylsäure) f.
asbestos Asbest m.
asbestosis Asbestose f.
ascariasis Askaridiasis
ascaris Askaris m.
ascending aszendierend
Aschheim-Zondek test Aschheim-Zondek-Test m.
Aschoff's nodule Aschoffsches Knötchen n.
Aschoff-Tawara node Aschoff-Tawara-Knoten m.
ascites Aszites m.
ascorbate Askorbat n.
asemia Asemie f.
asepsis d. e. f.
aseptic aseptisch
ash Asche f.
ash, to veraschen
asher Veraschungsgerät n.
ashing Veraschung f.
asialia Asialie f., Aptyalismus m.
Asian influenza Asiatische Grippe f.
asiderosis Asiderose f.
asleep, to fall einschlafen
asocial asozial
asparaginase d. e. f.
asparaginate Asparaginat n.
asparagine Asparagin n.
aspartate Asparaginat n.
aspect Aspekt m.
aspergillosis Aspergillose f.
aspermia Aspermie f.
asphyctic asphyktisch
asphyxia Asphyxie f.
asphyxiation Erstickung f.
aspidinol d. e. n.
aspidium, rhizome of – Rhizoma filicis
aspirate, to aspirieren
aspiration d. e. f.

aspirator d. e. m.
ass Esel m.
assay Erprobung f., Test m., Prüfung f.
assignment, stationary stationäre Einweisung f.
assimilate, to assimilieren
assimilation d. e. f.
assist, to assistieren; helfen, beistehen
assistance Assistenz f.; Beistand m.
assistant Assistent m.; Gehilfe m.
– **chemist** Laborant m., Laborantin f.
– **dental** zahnärztliche Helferin f.
association Assoziation f.
assortment Sortiment n.
astasia Astasie f.
asteatosis Asteatose f.
astereognosis Astereognosie f.
astereognostic astereognostisch
asthenia Asthenie f.
asthenic asthenisch
asthenopia Asthenopie f.
asthma d. e. n.
–, **bronchial** Bronchialasthma n.
–, **cardiac** Herzasthma n.
asthmatic asthmatisch
astigmatic astigmatisch
astigmatism Astigmatismus m.
astringent adstringierend; Adstringens n.
astrocyte Astrozyt m.
astrocytoma Astrozytom n.
astronautics Astronautik f.
asylum Asyl n.
asymmetric asymmetrisch
asymmetrogammagram Asymmetrogammagramm n.
asymmetry Asymmetrie f.
asymptomatic asymptomatisch
asymptotical asymptotisch
asynchronous asynchron
asynclitic asynklitisch
asynclitism Asynklitismus m.
asynergic asynergisch

asynergy Asynergie f.
asystolia Asystolie f.
atactic ataktisch
ataractic ataraktisch;
  Ataracticum n.
ataraxy Ataraxie f.
atavism Atavismus m.
atavistic atavistisch
ataxia Ataxie f.
ataxic ataktisch
atelectasis Atelektase f.
atelectatic atelektatisch
atenolol d. e. n.
atherogenic atherogen
atherogenous atherogen
atheroma Atherom n.
atheromatosis Atheromatose f.
atheromatous atheromatös
atherosclerosis Atherosklerose f.
atherosclerotic atherosklerotisch
athetosic athetotisch
athetosis Athetose f.
athlete's foot Athletenfuß m.
athlete's heart Sportherz n.
athletic athletisch
athyreosis Athyreose f.
atloido-occipital atlantookzipital
atmocausis Atmokausis f.
atmosphere Atmosphäre f.
atmospheric atmosphärisch
atom d. e. n.
atomic atomar
atomic weight Atomgewicht n.
atomization Atomisierung f.;
  Versprühung f.
atomizer Atomiseur m.
atonic atonisch
atony Atonie f.
atopy spezifische Überempfindlichkeit f.
atoxyl d. e. n.
atransferrinaemia (e) Atransferrinämie f.
atransferrinemia (a) Atransferrinämie f.
atresia Atresie f.
atresic atresisch

atrial ectopic beat Vorhofextrasystole f.
atrial pressure Vorhofdruck m.
atrichia Atrichie f.
atrioventricular atrioventrikulär
– **valves, left** Mitralklappen f. pl.
– **valves, right** Trikuspidalklappen f. pl.
atrium of the heart Herzvorhof m.
atrophic atrophisch
atrophy Atrophie f.
–, **cortical** Rindenatrophie f.
atropine Atropin n.
atropinization Atropinisierung f.
attachment Befestigung f.;
  Geschiebe n.
attendant Wärter m., Wärterin f.
attention Aufmerksamkeit f.
attenuate, to verdünnen
attenuation Verdünnung f.
attest d. e. n.
–, **to** attestieren
attraction Anziehungskraft f.,
  Attraktion f.
attrition Abkauung f.
atypia Atypie f.
atypical atypisch
audiometer d. e. n.
audiometric audiometrisch
audiometry Audiometrie f.
audiovisual audiovisuell
audition Hören n., Hörvermögen n.,
  Gehör n.
auditory auditorisch, akustisch
– **passage** Gehörgang
– **vertigo** otogener Schwindel m.
Auerbach's plexus Auerbachscher
  Plexus m.
aura d. e. f.
aural toilet Ohrtoilette f.
auricle Aurikel f., Ohrmuschel f.;
  Herzvorhof m.
auricular aurikulär
– **fibrillation** Vorhofflimmern n.
– **flutter** Vorhofflattern n.
auriculoventricular aurikuloventrikulär

auriculoventricular valves, left
  Mitralklappen f. pl.
- valves, right Trikuspidalklappen f. pl.
auriscope Otoskop n.
aurothiomalate Aurothiomalat n.
auscultate, to auskultieren
auscultation Auskultation f.
auscultatory auskultatorisch
author Autor m., Autorin f.
autism Autismus m.
autistic autistisch
- thinking autistisches Denken n.
autoagglutination d. e. f.
auto-antibody Auto-Antikörper m.
autoblood Eigenblut n.
autocannibalism Autokannibalismus m.
autochthonous autochthon
autoclave Autoklav m.
autodigestion Selbstverdauung f.
autogenous autogen
autohaemolysin (e) Autohämolysin n.
autohaemolysis (e) Autohämolyse f.
autohaemotherapy (e) Eigenblutbehandlung f.
autohemolysin (a) Autohämolysin n.
autohemolysis (a) Autohämolyse f.
autohemotherapy (a) Eigenblutbehandlung f.
autohypnosis Autohypnose f.
autoimmune autoimmun
autoimmunization Selbstimmunisierung f.
autoinfection Autoinfektion f.
autointoxication Autointoxikation f.
autoisolysin d. e. n.
autologous autolog
autolysate Autolysat n.
autolysin d. e. n.
autolysis Autolyse f.
autolytic autolytisch
autolyze, to autolysieren
automatic automatisch

automatization Automatisierung f.
automatism Automatismus m.
autonomic autonom
autonomic nervous disorder
  vegetative Dystonie f.
- nervous system vegetatives
  Nervensystem n.
autonomy Autonomie f.
autophagy Autophagie f.
autophobia Autophobie f.
autoplastic autoplastisch
autoplasty Autoplastik f.
autopraecipitin (e) Autopräzipitin n.
autoprecipitin (a) Autopräzipitin n.
autoprotection Selbstschutz m.
autopsy Autopsie f.
autoradiography Autoradiographie f.
autoregulation Selbstregulierung f.
autosome Autosom n.
autosomal d. e.
autosuggestion d. e. f.
autotoxin d. e. n.
autotransfusion d. e. f.
autotransplantation d. e. f.
autovaccination Autovakzination f.
autovaccine Autovakzine f.
auxiliary auxiliär
auxin d. e. n.
A.V. (= atrioventricular)
  atrioventrikulär
availability Verfügbarkeit f.
available verfügbar
average Durchschnitt m.,
  Mittelwert m.
aversion Widerwille m., Aversion f.
avert, to abwenden
aviation medicine Luftfahrtmedizin f.
aviator's disease Fliegerkrankheit f.
avirulent d. e.
avitaminosis Avitaminose f.

Avogadro's constant Loschmidtsche Konstante f.
Avogadro's law Avogadrosches Gesetz n.
avulsion Abriß n.
axanthopsia Axanthopsie f., Gelbblindheit f.
axial d. e.
axial shift Achsenverschiebung f.
axilla Achselhöhle f.
axillary line, anterior vordere Axillarlinie f.
axiobuccocervical axiobukkozervikal
axiobuccogingival axiobukkogingival
axiobuccolingual axiobukkolingual
axiodistal d. e.
axiodistocervical axiodistozervikal
axiodistogingival d. e.
axiodistoincisal axiodistoinzisal
axiodistoocclusal axiodistookklusal
axiogingival d. e.
axioincisal axioinzisal
axiomesial d. e.
axiomesiocervical axiomesiozervikal
axiomesiodistal d.e.

axiopulpal d. e.
axis Achse f.
− cylinder Achsenzylinder m.
− -traction forceps Achsenzugzange f.
axolotl d. e. m.
axon reflex Axonreflex m.
axoplasm Axoplasma n.
Ayerza's disease Ayerzasche Krankheit f.
azaadenine Azaadenin n.
azahypoxanthine Azahypoxanthin n.
azathioprin d. e. n.
azauracil d. e. n.
azauridine Azauridin n.
azo compound Azo-Verbindung f.
azolitmin d. e. n.
azoospermia Azoospermie f.
azorubin test Azorubintest m.
azotaemia (e) Azotämie f.
azotaemic (e) azotämisch
azote Stickstoff m.
azotemia (a) Azotämie f.
azotemic (a) azotämisch
azole Azol n.
azure Azur m.
azurophilia Azurophilie f.
azurophilic azurophil
azygos vein Vena azygos

B

B.A. (= buccoaxial) bukkoaxial
babesiasis Babesiose f.
babesiosis Babesiose f.
Babinski's reflex Babinski-Reflex m.
Babinski's sign Babinskisches Zeichen n.
baboon Pavian m.
baby napkin (e) Windel f.

baby nursery Säuglingsheim n.
B.A.C. (= buccoaxiocervical) bukkoaxiozervikal
bacillaemia (e) Bazillämie f.
bacillary bazillär
bacillemia (a) Bazillämie f.
bacilliform bazilliform
bacillogenic bazillogen
bacillophobia Bazillophobie f.

bacillosis Bazillose f.
bacilluria Bazillurie f.
bacillus Bazillus m.
—, **acid-fast** säurefestes Stäbchen n.
bacillus anthracis d. e.
bacitracin d. e. n.
back Rücken m.
backache Rückenschmerz m.
backbone Rückgrat n.
backflow, pyelovenous pyelovenöser Reflux m.
back titration Rücktitration f.
bacteriaemia (e) Bakteriämie f.
bacteriaemic (e) bakteriämisch
bacterial bakteriell
bactericholia Baktericholie f.
bactericidal bakterizid
bactericide bakterizid; bakterizides Mittel n.
bacteriemia (a) Bakteriämie f.
bacteriemic (a) bakteriämisch
bacteriocholia Bakteriocholie f.
bacteriological bakteriologisch
bacteriologist Bakteriologe m., Bakteriologin f.
bacteriology Bakteriologie f.
bacteriolysis Bakteriolyse f.
bacteriolytic bakteriolytisch
bacteriophage Bakteriophage m.
bacteriophagia Bakteriophagie f.
bacteriophobia Bakteriophobie f.
bacteriostatic bakteriostatisch
bacteriotropic bakteriotrop
bacterium Bakterium n.
bacteriuria Bakteriurie f.
Bacteroides d. e. m.
bag, hot water Wärmflasche f.
—, **ice** Eisbeutel m.
—, **laundry** Wäschesack m.
—, **physician's** Ärztetasche f., Arzttasche f.
—, **sand** Sandsack m.
bake, to backen
bakelite Bakelit n.
balance Gleichgewicht n.; Waage f.

balanitis d. e. f.
balanoposthitis d. e. f.
balantidiasis d. e. f.
Balantidium coli d. e.
bald kahl
baldhead Kahlkopf m.
baldheaded kahlköpfig
ball Ball m., Kugel f.
ball- and socket joint Nußgelenk n.
ballism Ballismus m.
ballistocardiogram Ballistokardiogramm n.
ballistocardiographic ballistokardiographisch
ballistocardiography Ballistokardiographie f.
ball of the thumb Daumenballen m.
balloon Ballon m.
ballottement d. e. n.
balm Balsam m.
balneary Bäderabteilung f., Bäderinstitut n.
balneation Balneotherapie f.
balneological balneologisch
balneologist Balneologe m.
balneology Balneologie f.
balneotherapy Balneotherapie f.
balsam d. e. m.
—, **Canada** Canadabalsam m.
—, **Peruvian** Perubalsam m.
— **of Tolu** Tolubalsam m.
band d. e. n.
bandage Binde f., Verband m.
—, **abdominal** Leibbinde f.
—, **Barton's** Capistrum n.
—, **circular** zirkulärer Verband m.
—, **Desault's** Desaultverband m.
—, **flannel** Flannellbinde f.
—, **pressure** Druckverband m.
—, **Priessnitz's** Priessnitzwickel m.
—, **protective** Schutzverband m.
—, **roller** Bindenwickler m.
— **scissors** Verbandschere f.
—, **spica** Spica f.
—, **starch** Stärkebinde f., Stärkeverband m.

bandage, suspensory Suspensorium n.
bandage, to verbinden, bandagieren
bandager Bandagist m., Bandagistin f.
bandaging material Verbandmaterial n.
Bandl's ring Bandlsche Furche f.
bandy leg X-Bein n.
banisterine Banisterin n.
banthine Banthin n.
Banti's disease Bantisyndrom n.
bar Barriere f., Bügel m.
Bárány's test Bárányscher Versuch m.
barbed wire disease Stacheldrahtkrankheit f.
barbital Diäthylbarbitursäure f.
barbitone Diäthylbarbitursäure f.
barbiturate Barbiturat n.
barium d. e. n.
barium enema Kontrasteinlauf m.
– **meal** Bariummahl n.
– **sulfate** (a) Bariumsulfat n.
– **sulphate** (e) Bariumsulfat n.
bark Borke f., Rinde f.
baroreceptor Barorezeptor m.
barrel chest faßförmiger Thorax m.
barren unfruchtbar
barrenness Unfruchtbarkeit f.
barrier Schranke f.
Bartholin's gland Bartholinsche Drüse f.
Bartonella d. e.
bartonelliasis d. e. f.
basal d. e.
basal cell Basalzelle f.
– **metabolic rate** Grundumsatz m.
basaloma Basalzellenkarzinom n.
base Basis f.; Base f. (chem.)
base (of an artificial denture) Gaumenplatte f. (eines künstlichen Gebisses)
base, cranial Schädelbasis f.
base hospital Hauptverbandplatz m.

baseline Grundlinie f.
base plate Basisplatte f.
Basedow's disease Basedowsche Krankheit f.
basic basisch
basin Becken n.
basis d. e. f.
basophil, basophile basophil; basophile Zelle f.
basophilia Basophilie f.
basophilic basophil
Bassini's operation Bassini-Operation f.
basswood Schusterspan m.
bastard d. e. m.
bat Fledermaus f.
batch Schub m.; Menge f., Portion f.
bath Bad n.
–, **full** Vollbad n.
–, **half** Halbbad n.
–, **medicated** Medizinalbad n.
–, **moor** Moorbad n.
–, **partial** Teilbad n.
–, **permanent** Dauerbad n.
–, **pine** Fichtennadelbad n.
–, **sweat** Schwitzbad n.
–, **vapor** (a) Dampfbad n.
–, **vapour** (e) Dampfbad n.
bathmotropic bathmotrop
bathyaesthesia (e) Tiefensensibilität f.
bathyesthesia (a) Tiefensensibilität f.
battered child syndrome Folgeerscheinungen f. pl. von Mißhandlung und Vernachlässigung von Kindern
battery Batterie f.
Bauhin's valve Bauhinsche Klappe f.
bay horse Braune m. (veter.)
bayonet Bayonett n.
B.D. (= **buccocervical**) bukkozervikal
BCG vaccination BCG-Impfung f.
BCG vaccine BCG-Vakzine f.

B.D. (= buccodistal) bukkodistal
bdella Blutegel m.
beads, rachitic rechitischer Rosenkranz m.
beak Schnabel m.
beaker Becherglas n.
beam Strahl m.
beam, to strahlen
bear Bär m.
bear, to tragen, ertragen, leiden; gebären
beard Bart m.
bearing Tragen n., Ertragen n.
beat Schlag m., Schlagen n., Pulsieren n.
beat, to schlagen, pulsieren
beatin d. e. n.
beaver Biber m.
Bechterew's disease Bechterewsche Krankheit f.
Bechterew's reflex Bechterewscher Reflex m.
becquerel d. e. n.
bed Bett n.
bedbug Bettwanze f.
bedlam Irrenanstalt f.
bedpan Bettschüssel f., Schieber m.
bed rest Bettruhe f.
bedridden bettlägerig
bedside teaching Unterricht m. am Krankenbett
beef tapeworm Rinderbandwurm m.
bee's sting Bienenstich m.
behaviour Verhalten n., Benehmen n.
Behcet's syndrome Behcet Syndrom n.
belching Rülpsen n.
Bell's palsy Fazialisparese f.
Bell's phenomenon Bellsches Phänomen n.
belladonna d. e. f.
Bellocq's cannula Bellocqsche Röhre f.
belly Bauch m.
belt Gürtel m., Binde f., Leibbinde f.
benazine Benazin n.
Bence-Jones protein Bence-Jonesscher Eiweißkörper m.
Benedict's test Benedictsche Probe f.
benfotiamine Benfotiamin n.
benign, benignant benigne, gutartig
benignness Gutartigkeit f.
benorylate Benorylat n.
bentyl d. e. n.
benzaldehyde Benzaldehyd m.
benzanilide Benzanilid n.
benzanthrene Benzanthren n.
benzene Benzol n.
benzidine Benzidin n.
benzine Benzin n.
benzoate Benzoat n.
benzochinone Benzochinon n.
benzodiazepine Benzodiazepin n.
benzodioxane Benzodioxan n.
benzothiadizine Benzothiadizin n.
benzoyl d. e. n.
benzpyrene Benzpyren n.
benzyl d. e. n.
benzyl orange Benzylorange n.
Berger wave Alpha-Welle f.
beriberi d. e. m.
Berkefeld filter Berkefeldfilter n.
Berlin blue Berliner Blau n.
beryllium d. e. n.
beta-adrenergic beta-adrenergisch
beta blocker Betarezeptorenblocker m.
beta cell Beta-Zelle f.
beta emitter Betastrahler m.
– globulin Betaglobulin n.
betaine Betain n.
betalactamase d. e. f.
betamethasone Betamethason n.
betaoxybutyric acid Betaoxybuttersäure f.
beta ray Betastrahl m.
beta receptor Beta-Rezeptor m.
betatron d. e. n.

betatron therapy Betatron-
Therapie f.
beta wave Betawelle f.
betel nut Betelnuß f.
betweenbrain Zwischenhirn n.
between-meal Zwischenmahlzeit f.
bevel, to abflachen, abschrägen
beverage Getränk n.
Bezold's mastoiditis Bezoldsche
Mastoiditis f.
B.G. (= buccogingival) bukkogingival
bias schräg, schief
bibliographical review Literaturübersicht f.
bicarbonate Bikarbonat n.
bichloride Bichlorid n.
bicuspid zweizipflig, zweihöckerig
bicuspid tooth Prämolar m.
bicycle ergometry Fahrrad-
Ergometrie f.
BID (bis in die) zweimal täglich
bier Totenbahre f.
Biermer's anaemia (e) Biermersche
Anämie f.
Biermer's anemia (a) Biermersche
Anämie f.
Bier's hyperaemia (e) Stauungshyperämie f.
Bier's hyperemia (a) Stauungshyperämie f.
bifascicular bifascicular
bifocal bifokal
bifurcation Bifurkation f.
bigeminal pulse Pulsus bigeminus
bigeminy Bigeminie f.
big liver disease (veter.)
Leukämie f.
biguanide Biguanid n.
bilateral d. e.
bile Galle f.
– **acid** Gallensäure f.
bilharziasis Bilharziose f.
biliary biliär
biliary ducts Gallenwege m. pl.
biliary tract Gallentrakt m.

biliflavin d. e. n.
bilifuscin d. e. n.
bilious biliös
bilirubin d. e. n.
–,**direct reacting** direktes Bilirubin n.
–,**indirect reacting** indirektes
Bilirubin n.
bilirubinaemia (e) Bilirubinämie f.
bilirubinemia (a) Bilirubinämie f.
bilirubinuria Bilirubinurie f.
biliverdin d. e. n.
Billroth I/II operation
Billroth I/II-Operation f.
bilophodont d. e.
bimanual bimanuell
bimaxillary bimaxillär
binary binär, dual
binaural d. e.
bind, to binden, verbinden
binding Bindung f.
bindweb Bindegewebe n.
Binet-Simon test Binet-Simon-
Test m.
binocular binokulär
binovular zweieiig
bioassay Tierexperiment n.
bioavailability biologische Verfügbarkeit f.
biochemical biochemisch
biochemist Biochemiker m.;
Biochemikerin f.
biochemistry Biochemie f.
bioclimatology Bioklimatologie f.
bioelectric bioelektrisch
biogenesis Biogenese f.
biogenetic biogenetisch
biogenous biogen
biologic biologisch
biologist Biologe m., Biologin f.
biology Biologie f.
biomedicine Biomedizin f.
biometeorological biometeorologisch
biometeorology Biometeorologie f.
bionics Bionik f.
biopharmaceutics Biopharmazie f.

biophysics Biophysik f.
biopsy Biopsie f.
bioscopy Bioskopie f.
biosphere Biosphäre f.
biosynthesis Biosynthese f.
biotelemetry Biotelemetrie f.
Biot's respiration Biotsche Atmung f.
biotin d. e. n.
biotransformation d. e. f.
biotropic biotrop
biotropism Biotropie f.
bipara Zweitgebärende f.
biparietal d. e.
biparous zweitgebärend
bipartite zweigeteilt
biphasic biphasisch
bipolar d. e.
bird Vogel m.
birdlike vogelartig
bird mite Vogelmilbe f.
birefractive doppeltbrechend
birefrigent doppeltbrechend
birth Geburt f.
— **palsy** Geburtslähmung f.
—,**postterm** Spätgeburt f.
—,**premature** Frühgeburt f.
— **room** Kreißsaal
— **trauma** Geburtstrauma n.
—, **to give** — gebären
birthmark Muttermal n.
bisection Zweiteilung f.
bisexual bisexuell
Bismarck brown Bismarckbraun n.
bismuth Wismut n.
bison d. e. m.
bistable bistabil
bistoury Bistouri m.
bisulfate (a) Bisulfat n.
bisulfide (a) Bisulfid n.
bisulfite (a) Bisulfit n.
bisulphate (e) Bisulfat n.
bisulphide (e) Bisulfid n.
bisulphite (e) Bisulfit n.
bitartrate Bitartrat n.
bitch Hündin f.

bite Biß m.
bite analysis (dent.) Bißanalyse f.
bite, close Tiefbiß m.
bite, edge-to-edge Kopfbiß m.
bite, locked Zwangsbiß m.
bite, open offener Biß m.
bite, to beißen
— **block** Beißblock m.
bitemporal d. e.
bite-taking Bißnahme f.
bitewing Flügelbißfilm m.
bitter d. e.
biuret d. e. n.
— **test** Biuretprobe f.
bivalence Bivalenz f., Zweiwertigkeit f.
bivalent d. e., zweiwertig
B.L. (= buccolingual) bukkolingual
black disease Schwarzkrankheit f.
black fever Rocky Mountain-Fieber n.
blackhead (med.) Mitesser m.
blackhead (veter.) Enterohepatitis f.
blackleg Rauschbrand m.
black quarter Rauschbrand m.
black spaul Rauschbrand m.
blackwater fever Schwarzwasserfieber n.
bladder Blase f.
blade Klinge f.
blain Geschwür n.
blanch, to weißen, bleichen
blank test Leerversuch m.
blastoderm d. e. n.
blastoma Blastom n.
blastomatous blastomatös
blastomycosis Blastomykose f.
blastulation d. e. f.
Blaud's pill Blaudsche Pille f.
bleaching agent Bleichmittel n.
blear-eye Triefauge n.
— **-eyed** triefäugig
bleed, to bluten
bleeder Bluter m.
bleeding Blutung f.; Aderlaß m.

bleeding time Blutungszeit f.
–, **withdrawal** Abbruchblutung f.
blennorhagia Blennorrhagie f.
blennorrhagic blennorhagisch
blennorrhea (a) Blennorrhöe f.
blennorrheal (a) blennorrhoisch
blennorhoea (e) Blennorrhöe f.
blennorrhoeal (e) blennorrhoisch
blepharitis d. e. f.
blepharoplasty Blepharoplastik f.
blepharoptosis Blepharoptose f.
blepharospasm Blepharospasmus m.
blind d. e.
blind, to grow – erblinden
blindgut Blinddarm m.
blind man Blinder m.
blindness Blindheit f.
blindspot blinder Fleck m.
blind staggers Coenurose f., Drehkrankheit f.
blind study, simple/double einfacher/doppelter Blindversuch m.
blister Blase f., Hautblase f.; blasenziehendes Mittel n.
bloat Tympanie f. des Pansens
block d. e. m.
block, bilateral bundle branch trifaszikulärer Block m.
–, **hisian** His-Bündel-Block m.
block, to blockieren
blockade d. e. f.
blocker blockierendes Mittel n.
blocking Blockade f., Blockieren n.
blond d. e.
blood Blut n.
– **-alcohol testing** Blutalkoholbestimmung f.
– **bank** Blutbank f.
– **-cerebrospinal fluid barrier** Blut-Liquor-Schranke f.
– **circulation** Blutkreislauf m.
– **collecting needle** Blutentnahmekanüle f.
– **count** Blutbild n.
– **culture** Blutkultur f.

blood donor Blutspender m.
– **examination** Blutuntersuchung f.
– **-fed (well/poorly)** (gut/schlecht) durchblutet
– **-flow** Blutstrom m.
– **forming organ** blutbildendes Organ n.
–, **fresh** Frischblut n.
– **group (0, A, B, AB)** Blutgruppe (0, A, B, AB)
– **grouping** Blutgruppenbestimmung f.
– **lancet** Blutentnahmelanzette f.
bloodless blutlos, blutleer, blutarm
bloodletting Aderlaß m.
blood picture Blutbild n.
– **poisoning** Blutvergiftung f.
– **pressure** Blutdruck m.
– **pressure drop** Blutdruckabfall m.
– **pressure rise** Blutdruckanstieg m.
– **preserve** Blutkonserve f.
– **-relation** Blutsverwandtschaft f.
– **-serum** Blutserum n.
– **sludge** intrakapilläre Blutzellaggregation f.
– **smear** Blutausstrich m.
– **-stanching** blutstillend
– **substitute** Blutersatz m.
– **sugar** Blutzucker m.
– **supply** Blutversorgung f., Durchblutung f.
– **test** Blutprobe f.
– **transfusion** Bluttransfusion f.
– **-urea** Blutharnstoff m.
– **vessel** Blutgefäß n.
bloody blutig, blutbefleckt
bloody murrain Rauschbrand m.
blottingpaper Fließpapier n.
blower Gebläse n.; Bläser m.
blow in, to einblasen
blow one's nose, to schneuzen
blowfly Schmeißfliege f.
blown (veter.) Tympanie f. des Pansens
blue blindness Blaublindheit f.
blues Gemütsverstimmung f.

blue-yellow blindness Blau-Gelb-Blindheit f.
Blumberg's sign Blumbergsches Zeichen n.
blunt stumpf
blur Fleckschatten m., Trübung f.
blurring, movement Bewegungsunschärfe f.
B.O. (= buccoocclusal) bukkookklusal
board Brett n.
board-like rigidity of the abdominal wall brettharte Bauchdeckenspannung
bodily körperlich
– **weakness** Körperschwäche f.
body Körper m., Leib m.
– **culture agent** Körperpflegemittel n.
– **fluid** Körperflüssigkeit f.
– **heat** Körperwärme f.
– **linen** Leibwäsche f.
– **weight** Körpergewicht n.
Boeck's sarcoid Boecksches Sarkoid n.
Böhler splint Böhler-Schiene f.
boil Beule f.; Furunkel m.
boil, to sieden
boiling pan Kochkessel m.
boiling point Siedepunkt m.
bolete, satanic Satanspilz m.
bolometer d. e. n.
bolster Polster n.
bolster, to polstern
Bolton point Boltonscher Punkt m.
bolus d. e. m.
bombard, to bombardieren
bombardment Bombardierung f.
bombesine Bombesin n.
bone Knochen m.
bone bank Knochenbank f.
bone conduction Knochenleitung f.
– **-conduction hearing aid** Knochenhörer m.
– **-conduction of sound waves** Knochenleitung f. des Schalls

bone curette scharfer Löffel m.
– **formation** Knochenbildung f., Verknöcherung f.
– **fragment** Knochensplitter m.
– **marrow** Knochenmark n.
– **marrow insufficiency** Knochenmarkinsuffizienz f.
boneplasty Knochenplastik f.
bone plate Knochenplatte f.
– **screw** Knochenschraube f.
bony knöchern
booster Förderer m.; Zusatzdynamo m.
booster-shot Wiederholungsimpfung f.
borate Borat n.
borax d. e. m.
border cell Belegzelle f.
borderland Grenzgebiet n.
borderline Grenzlinie f.
borderline ray Grenzstrahl m.
Bordetella pertussis Bordet-Gengou-Bazillus m.
bore, to bohren
Borna disease Bornasche Krankheit f.
Borna sickness Bornasche Krankheit f.
borneol d. e. n.
Bornholm disease Bornholmkrankheit f.
bornyval d. e. n.
boron Bor n.
borosilicate Borsilikat n.
Borrelia duttoni Spironema Duttoni
– **kochi** Spironema Kochi
– **novyi** Spironema Novyi
– **recurrentis** Spironema recurrentis (Obermeyer)
– **vincenti** Spirillum Vincenti
bosom Busen m., Brust f.
botanical botanisch
botany Botanik f.
botch, to verpfuschen
botfly Dasselfliege f.
bothriocephalus d. e. m.

botryomycosis Botryomykose f.
bottle Flasche f.
−, dropping Tropfflasche f.
− -fed infant Flaschenkind n.
bottom Boden m., Grund m.
Bottom disease Schweinsberger-
 krankheit f.
botulism Botulismus m.
bougie d. e. m.
bouginage Bougierung f.
bouillon d. e. f.
bound gebunden, begrenzt
bout Attacke f., Anfall m.
bovine bovin
bovine serum Rinderserum n.
bowel Darm m.
bowel sound Darmgeräusch n.
bowl, emetic Brechschale f.
Bowman's capsule Bowmansche
 Kapsel f.
box lock Durchsteckverschluß m.
Bozeman's catheter Bozeman-
 Katheter m.
b.p. (boiling point) Siedepunkt m.
BP (= blood pressure) Blutdruck
 m.
B.P. (= buccopulpal) bukkopulpal
brachial d. e.
brachialgia Brachialgie f.
brachial plexus Plexus brachialis
brachiocephalic brachiozephal
brachydactyly Brachydaktylie f.
brachymetropia Brachymetropie f.,
 Myopie f.
bradsot Magenpararauschbrand m.
bradycardia Bradykardie f.
bradycardic bradykard
bradykinesia Bradykinesie f.
bradykinetic bradykinetisch
bradykinin d. e. n.
bradylalia Bradylalie f.
bradyphrasia Bradyphrasie f.
bradyphrenia Bradyphrenie f.
bradyteleokinesis Bradyteleokinese f.
bradytrophia Bradytrophie f.

bradytrophic bradytroph
bradyuria Bradyurie f.
braille Blindenschrift f.
brain Gehirn n., Hirn n.
− injured hirnverletzt
− mantle Hirnmantel m.
− research Hirnforschung f.
− stem Hirnstamm m.
− work geistige Arbeit f.
brake Bremse f.
branched verzweigt
branchiogenous branchiogen
brandy Branntwein m.
brassard Rote-Kreuz-Armbinde f.
Braun's anastomosis Braunsche
 Anastomose f.
braxy Magenpararauschbrand m.
breach Lücke f., Bruch m., Riß m.
break, to brechen
breakbone fever Denguefieber n.
breakpoint Fixpunkt m.
breakthrough Durchbruch m.
breast Brust f.
− -fed baby Brustkind n.
− pump Milchpumpe f.
− support Brusthalter m.
breastings Vormilch f.
breath Atemluft f., Atem m.
breath sounds Atemgeräusch n.
breath sounds, bronchial
 Bronchialatmen n.
breath sounds, diminished abgeschwächtes Atmungsgeräusch n.
− sounds, vesicular Bläschenatmen n.
breathe, to atmen
breathing Atmen n., Atmung f.
breathing capacity, maximal
 Atemgrenzwert m.
breathing exercise Atemübung f.
breathless atemlos
breathlessness Atemlosigkeit f.
breech Steiß m.
− presentation Steißlage f.
breeding Zucht f., Aufzucht f.
Brenner tumor (a) Brenner-
 tumor m.

Brenner tumour (e) Brenner-
  tumor m.
brenzcatechin Brenzkatechin n.
bretylium tosylate Bretyliumtosylat n.
bridge Brücke f.; Zahnbrücke f.
bridgework Zahnbrücke f.
brightening screen Aufhellschirm m.
brightness contrast Helligkeitsumfang m.
brillant green brillantgrün;
  Brillantgrün n.
Brill's disease Brillsche Krankheit f.
Brill-Symmers disease Brill-
  Symmerssche Krankheit f.
brittle bones Osteogenesis
  imperfecta
brittle diabetes Brittle-Diabetes m.
broach Wurzelkanalinstrument n.
Broadbent's sign Broadbentsches
  Zeichen n.
broad spectrum Breitspektrum n.
Broca's center Brocasches
  Zentrum n.
brochure Broschüre f.
Brocq's disease Brocqsche
  Krankheit f.
Brodie's abscess Brodie-
  Abszeß m.
broken home gestörter familiärer
  Bereich m.
bromacetone Bromazeton n.
bromate Bromat n.
bromcresol green Bromkresolgrün n.
bromcresol purple Bromkresolpurpur m.
bromelin d. e. n.
bromic bromhaltig
bromide Bromid n.
bromine Brom n.
brominism Bromismus m.
bromism Bromismus m.
bromobenzene Brombenzol n.
bromocriptin d. e. n.
bromoform d. e. n.

bromphenol blue Bromphenolblau n.
bromphenol red Bromphenolrot n.
bromsulfalein test (a) Bromsulfaleintest m.
bromsulphalein test (e) Bromsulfaleintest m.
bromthymol blue Bromthymolblau n.
bronchadenitis d. e. f.
bronchial d. e.
bronchial breath sounds
  Bronchialatmen n.
bronchiectasis Bronchiektasie f.
bronchiectatic bronchiektatisch
bronchiloquy Bronchiloquie f.
bronchiolar bronchiolär
bronchiole d. e. f.
bronchiolitis d. e. f.
bronchiospasm Bronchospasmus m.
bronchiostenosis Bronchialstenose f.
bronchitic bronchitisch
bronchitis d. e. f.
bronchoadenitis d. e. f.
bronchoalveolitis Bronchopneumonie f.
bronchoblennorrhea (a) Broncho-
  blennorrhöe f.
bronchoblennorrhoea (e) Broncho-
  blennorrhöe f.
bronchoconstriction Bronchokonstriktion f.
bronchogenic bronchogen
bronchogenic carcinoma
  Bronchialkarzinom n.
bronchogram Bronchogramm n.
bronchographical bronchographisch
bronchography Bronchographie f.
broncholithiasis d. e. f.
bronchology Bronchologie f.
bronchoplasty Bronchoplastik f.
bronchopleuropneumonia
  Bronchopleuropneumonie f.
bronchopneumonia Bronchopneumonie f.

bronchopneumonic bronchopneumonisch
bronchoscope Bronchoskop n.
bronchoscopic bronchoskopisch
bronchoscopy Bronchoskopie f.
bronchospasm Bronchialspasmus m.
bronchospirometry Bronchospirometrie f.
bronchostomy Bronchostomie f.
bronchotomy Bronchotomie f.
bronchovesicular bronchovesikulär
bronzed diabetes Bronzediabetes m.
brood, foul Faulbrut f. (veter.)
broth Brühe f., Fleischbrühe f.
brow Braue f.
brown braun
Brown-Séquard's disease Brown-Séquardsche Halbseitenlähmung f.
Brucella abortus d. e.
− **melitensis** d. e.
brucellosis Brucellose f.
Brudzinski's sign Brudzinskisches Zeichen n.
bruise, to quetschen
bruit Geräusch n.
Brunner's gland Brunnersche Drüse f.
brush Bürste f.
brush, to bürsten
Bruton's disease Antikörpermangelsyndrom n.
Bryant's triangle Bryantsches Dreieck n.
B.S. (= breath sounds) Atemgeräusch n.
buba Frambösie f.
bubble Blase f.
bubo d. e. m.
bubonic plague Beulenpest f.
buccal bukkal
buccoaxial bukkoaxial
buccoaxiocervical bukkoaxiozervikal
buccocervical bukkozervikal
buccodistal bukkodistal
buccogingival bukkogingival
buccolabial bukkolabial
buccolingual bukkolingual
buccomesial bukkomesial
bucco-occlusal bukko-okklusal
buccopharyngeal bukkopharyngeal
buccopulpal bukkopulpal
buck Bock m.
bucket Eimer m., Kübel m.
Bucky diaphragm Buckyblende f.
bud Knospe f.
Budd's jaundice akute gelbe Leberatrophie f.
budgerigar Wellensittich m.
Budin's rule Budinsche Regel f.
Bülau's method Bülausche Drainage f.
Buerger's disease Buergersche Krankheit f., Winiwarter-Buergersche Krankheit f.
bufallo Büffel m.
buffer Puffer m.
buffer, to puffern
buffering Pufferung f.
buffer value Pufferungsvermögen n.
buffy coat Speckhaut f.
bug Wanze f.
bug-bite Wanzenstich m.
bulb Bulbus m.
bulbar bulbär
bulbitis d. e. f.
bulbocapnine Bulbocapnin n.
bulbogastrone Bulbogastron n.
bulboscope Bulboskop n.
bulboscopic bulboskopisch
bulboscopy Bulboskopie f.
bulbourethral d. e.
− **gland** Cowpersche Drüse f.
bulimia Bulimie f.
bulk Masse f.
bull Stier m.
bulletin Krankheitsbericht m.
bullock junger Stier m.
bullosis Bullose f.
bullous bullös
bundle Bündel n.

bundle branch block, left/right
linksseitiger/rechtsseitiger
Schenkelblock m.
bungle, to verpfuschen
bunitrolol d. e. n.
bunodont d. e.
bunolophodont d. e.
bunoselenodont d. e.
buphthalmus d. e. m.
bupranolol d. e. n.
bur Bohrer m.
burden Last f.
burden, to belasten
burdening Belastung f.
bur-drill Zahnbohrer m.
burette Bürette f.
burial Begräbnis n.
burimamide Burimamid n.
buring dust Bohrstaub m.
Burkitt's lymphoma Burkitt-Tumor m.
burn (of first/second/third degree) Verbrennung f. (ersten/zweiten/dritten Grades)
burn, to verbrennen
burner Brenner m.
Burnett syndrom Milch-Alkali-Syndrom n.
burning brennend; brennendes Gefühl n.
burning feet burning feet-Syndrom n.
burnisher Zahnpolierinstrument n.
Burri's stain Burritusche f.
bursectomize, to bursektomieren
bursectomy Bursektomie f.
bursitis d. e. f.
burst, to bersten, platzen
Burton's line Bleisaum m. am Zahnfleisch
bust Büste f.
butadiene Butadien n.
butalamine Butalamin n.
butandiol d. e. n.
butane Butan n.
butanol Butylalkohol m.
butterfly vertebra Schmetterlingswirbel m.
buttermilk Buttermilch f.
buttock Hinterteil n., Gesäß n.
butyl d. e. n.
butyl biguanide Butylbiguanid n.
butylene Butylen n.
butyramide Butyramid n.
butyrate Butyrat n.
butyrophenone Butyrophenon n.
bypass Umgehung f.
bypass, to umgehen, umfahren
byssinosis Byssinose f.
bythus

C

cabin Kabine f.
cable Kabel n.
Cabot's ring Cabotscher Ring m.
cacaine Theobromin n.
cacao Kakao m.
cachectic kachektisch
cachexia Kachexie f.
cacodyl Kakodyl n.
cacodylate Kakodylat n.
cadaver Leiche f., Kadaver m.
cadaver blood Leichenblut n.
cadaveric rigidity Leichenstarre f., Totenstarre f.
cadaverine Kadaverin n.
cadaverous smell Leichengeruch m.
caddis fly Köcherfliege f.
cadmium d. e. n.
caduca Dezidua f.
caecal (e) zökal
caecum (e) Coecum n., Zökum n.

caesarean section (e) Kaiserschnitt m.
caesium (e) Zäsium n.
cafard Gemütsverstimmung f.
caffeine Coffein n., Koffein n.
caffeine, citrated Coffeinzitrat n.
– with sodium benzoate Coffeinum-Natrium benzoicum
caisson disease Caissonkrankheit f.
Calabar bean Calabarbohne f.
calamine Galmei m.
calcaneoplantar d. e.
calcarea Kalziumoxyd n.
calciferol d. e. n.
calcification Verkalkung f.
– of cartilage Knorpelverkalkung f.
calcify, to verkalken
calcinosis Kalzinose f.
calcipriv kalzipriv
calcitonin d. e. n.
calcium Kalzium n.
– carbonate Kalziumkarbonat n.
– chloride Kalziumchlorid n.
– gluconate Kalziumglukonat n.
– hydroxide Kalziumhydroxyd n.
calciuria Kalziurie f.
calculation Berechnung f.
calculus Konkrement n., Steinbildung f.
–, alvine Kotstein m.
–, biliary Gallenstein m.
–, dental Zahnstein m.
–, oxalate Oxalatstein m.
–, pancreatic Pankreasstein m.
–, renal Nierenstein m.
–, urate Uratstein m.
–, vesical Blasenstein m.
Caldwell-Luc operation Caldwell-Luc-Operation f.
calf Wade f.
calf (veter.) Kalb n.
caliber Kaliber n.
caligo Augentrübung f.
caliper Tasterzirkel m.
calix Kelch m.
calling program Abrufprogramm n.

callosity Verhornung f., Schwiele f.
callous kallös
callus Kallus m.
– formation Kallusbildung f.
calm, to beruhigen, ruhigstellen
calomel Kalomel n.
caloric kalorisch
calorie (small/large) (kleine/ große) Kalorie f.
calorigenic kalorigen
calorimeter Kalorimeter n.
calorimetric kalorimetrisch
calorimetry Kalorimetrie f.
calorose d. e. f.
calory Kalorie f.
calve, to kalben
camazepam d. e. n.
camel Kamel n.
camisole Zwangsjacke f.
camomile Kamille f.
camphor Kampfer m.
– and soap liniment Opodeldok m.
camphorated oil Kampferöl n.
canal Kanal m.
canalicular kanalikulär
canalization Kanalisierung f.
canal, semicircular Bogengang m.
canal, vidian Canalis pterygoideus
canary Kanarienvogel m.
cancellation Löschung f.
cancer Krebs m. (med.), Karzinom n.
cancerogenic kanzerogen
cancerotoxic kanzerotoxisch
cancerous kanzerös, krebsig, krebsartig
cancroid kankroid; Kankroid n.
candela d. e. f.
canine madness Tollwut f.
– tooth Eckzahn m.
canities Grauhaarigkeit f.
canker Mundulzeration f.
cannabine Cannabin n.
cannibalism Kannibalismus m.
cannula Kanüle f.

cantering rhythm Galopprhythmus m.
cantharides Kanthariden f. pl.
canula Kanüle f.
caoutchouc Kautschuk m.
cap, operating Operationsmütze f.
capable fähig
– **of begetting** zeugungsfähig
– **of living** lebensfähig
capacity Kapazität f.
capillaroscopical kapillarmikroskopisch
capillaroscopy Kapillarmikroskopie f.
capillary kapillär; Kapillare f.
capping Überkappung f.
capreomycin d. e. n.
caproate Caproat n.
caprylate Caprylat n.
caprylic acid Caprylsäure f.
capsular kapsulär
capsule Kapsel f.
– **staining** Kapselfärbung f.
captodiamine Captodiamin n.
carbamate Karbamat n.
carbamazepine Karbamazepin n.
carbamazine Karbamazin n.
carbamic acid Karbamidsäure f.
carbamide Harnstoff m.
carbamoyltransferase Karbamoyltransferase f.
carbamyl Karbamyl n.
carbamylase Karbamylase f.
carbazone Karbazon n.
carbenicillin d. e. n.
carbenoxolone Carbenoxolon n.
carbide Karbid n.
carbimazole Carbimazol n.
carbohydrase Karbohydrase f.
carbohydrate Kohlehydrat n.
carbolfuchsin Karbolfuchsin n.
carbolic acid Karbolsäure f.
carbomycin d. e. n.
carbon Kohlenstoff m.
– **arc lamp** Kohlenbogenlampe f.
carbonate Karbonat n.

carbon dioxide Kohlendioxyd n.
– **dioxide bath** Kohlendioxydbad n.
carbonic acid Kohlensäure f.
– **anhydrase** Karboanhydrase f.
– **anhydrase inhibitor** Karboanhydrasehemmer m.
carbonize, to verkohlen
carbon monoxide Kohlenmonoxyd n.
–, **tetrachloride** Tetrachlorkohlenstoff m.
carbonyl Karbonyl n.
carborundum Karborund n.
carboxamide Karboxamid n.
carbonyl Karbonyl n.
carboxamide Karboxamid n.
carboxyl Karboxyl n.
carboxylase Karboxylase f.
carboxylation Karboxylierung f.
carbuncle Karbunkel m.
carbutamide Karbutamid n.
carcinoembryogenic antigen karzinoembryogenes Antigen n.
carcinogen Karzinogen n.
carcinogenic karzinogen, krebserzeugend
carcinogenous karzinogen
carcinoid Karzinoid n.
carcinoma Karzinom n., Krebs m. (med.)
– **bronchogenic** Bronchialkarzinom n.
carcinomatosis Karzinomatose f.
carcinomatous karzinomatös
carcinophobia Karzinophobie f.
carcinosarcoma Karzinosarkom n.
carcinosis Karzinose f.
cardboard splint Pappschiene f.
card file Kartothek f.
cardia d. e. f.
cardiac kardial; Herzpatient m., Herzpatientin f.
– **arrest** Herzstillstand m.
– **asthma** Herzasthma n.
– **catheterization** Herzkatheterisierung f.

cardiac massage Herzmassage f.
- massage, closed chest äußere Herzmassage f.
- massage, open chest direkte Herzmassage f.
- minute output Herzminutenvolumen n.
- murmur Herzgeräusch n.
- neurosis Herzneurose f.
- palpitation Herzklopfen n.
cardinal kardinal
card index Kartei f.
cardiogram Kardiogramm n.
cardiographic kardiographisch
cardiography Kardiographie f.
cardiolipin d. e. n.
cardiologic kardiologisch
cardiologist Kardiologe m., Herzspezialist m.
cardiology Kardiologie f.
cardiolysis Kardiolyse f.
cardiomalacia Herzerweichung f.
cardiomyopathy Kardiomyopathie f.
cardioneurosis Herzneurose f.
cardiopathy Herzkrankheit f., Kardiopathie f.
cardioportal kardioportal
cardiospasm Kardiospasmus m.
cardiosurgery Herzchirurgie f.
cardiotherapy Herzbehandlung f.
cardiotocography Kardiotokographie f.
cardiovascular kardiovaskulär
- disease Herz- und Kreislaufkrankheit f.
cardioversion Kardioversion f.
carditis Karditis f.
care Fürsorge f., Pflege f.
- of the mouth Mundpflege f.
caries Karies f.
carinamide Karinamid n.
carindacillin d. e. n.
carious kariös
carisoprodol d. e. n.
Carlsbad salt Karlsbader Salz n.

carminative blähungswidrig; Carminativum n.
carmine Karmin n.
carneous fleischig
carnification Karnifikation f.
carnify, to karnifizieren
carotene Karotin n.
carotid artery Arteria carotis
carpal karpal
carpal tunnel syndrome Karpaltunnelsyndrom n.
carpopedal karpopedal
carrageen Irländisches Moos n.
carragheen Irländisches Moos n.
carrier Träger m.
carrier, chronic Dauerausscheider m.
Carrión's disease Oroyafieber n.
carry, to tragen; verschleppen
car sickness Eisenbahnkrankheit f.; Autokrankheit f.
cartilage Knorpel m.
cartilage knife Knorpelmesser n.
cartilaginification Verknorpelung f.
cartilaginous knorpelig
carver Modellierinstrument n.
caryotin Chromatin n.
cascade stomach Kaskadenmagen m.
cascara sagrada, extract of – Cascara-Sagrada-Extrakt m.
case Fall m., Kasus m.; Behälter m.
- mailing culture – Versandgefäß n.
- history Krankengeschichte f.
- of death Todesfall m.
-, operating Operationsbesteckkasten m.
-, postmortem Sektionsbesteckkasten m.
caseation Verkäsung f.
casein Kasein n.
caseinogen d. e. n.
caseinogenate Caseinogenat n.
caseous käsig
cassette Kassette f.

cast Ausgußkörper m.;
 Zylinder m.; Strabismus m.
– crown Gußkrone f.
–, hyaline hyaliner Zylinder m.
–, Külz's Komazylinder m.
casting Gießen n.; Guß m.
casting machine Gußmaschine f.
Castle's factor Castle-Faktor m.
castor oil Rizinusöl n.
castrate Kastrat m.
castrate, to kastrieren
castration Kastration f.
casualty department Unfallstation f.
casuistic kasuistisch
casuistics Kasuistik f.
cat Katze f.
catabiosis Katabiose f.
catabiotic katabiotisch
catabolic katabolisch; Katabolikum n.
catabolism Katabolismus m.
catabolize, to katabolisieren
catalase Katalase f.
catalepsy Katalepsie f.
cataleptic kataleptisch
catalog Katalog
catalysis Katalyse f.
catalytic katalytisch
catalyze, to katalysieren
catalyzer Katalysator m.
catamnesis Katamnese f.
catamnestic katamnestisch
cataphoresis Kataphorese f.
cataphoretic kataphoretisch
cataplasia Kataplasie f.
cataplasm Kataplasma n.
cataplastic kataplastisch
cataplexy Kataplexie f.
cataract Katarakt f., Star m. (med.)
cataract knife Starmesser n.
catarrh Katarrh m.
catarrhal katarrhalisch
catatonic katatoni
catatony Katatonie f.
catch a cold, to sich erkälten

catechin Katechin n.
catechol Brenzkatechin n.
catecholamine Brenzkatechinamin n.
catechu Katechu n.
category Kategorie f.
catering Verpflegung f., Versorgung f.
catgut Katgut n.
catharsis Katharsis f.
cathartic kathartisch
cathepsin Kathepsin n.
catheter Katheter m.
–, balloon Ballonkatheter m.
–, de Pezzer Pezzerkatheter m.
–, indwelling Verweilkatheter m.
–, irrigation Spülkatheter m.
–, Mercier's Mercierkatheter m.
–, Nélaton's Nélatonkatheter m.
–, ureteral Harnleiterkatheter m.
catheterism Katheterisierung f.
catheterization Katheterisierung f.
catheterize, to katheterisieren
cathode Kathode f.
cathode ray Kathodenstrahl m.
cation Kation n.
cation exchange Kationenaustausch m.
cattle Vieh n., Rindvieh n.
cattle plague Rinderpest f.
caudad kaudalwärts
caudal kaudal
caul Epiploon n.
causal kausal
causalgia Kausalgie f.
causalgic kausalgisch
causation Verursachung f.
causative verursachend, ursächlich
cause Ursache f.
cause, to bewirken, verursachen, veranlassen
caustic kaustisch; Kaustikum n.
cauter Kauter m.
cauterization Kauterisation f.
cauterize, to kauterisieren
cautery Kaustik f.
caution Vorsicht f.

cave Höhle f.
cavern Kaverne
cavernoma Kavernom n.
cavernosography Kavernosographie f.
cavernous kavernös
cavitation Höhlenbildung f., Kavernisierung f.
cavity Höhle f., Kavität f.
cavity liner (dent.) Unterfüllung f.
cavography Kavographie f.
CBC (complete blood count) ganzes Blutbild n.
C.C. (cathodal closure) Kathodenschließung f.
cecal (a) zökal
cecum (a) Zökum n., Coecum n.
cedarwood oil Zedernholzöl n.
cefamandol d. e. n.
cefazolin d. e. n.
cefoxitin d. e. n.
cefuroxime Cefuroxim n.
celandine Chelidonium n.
celiac disease (a) Zöliakie f.
celiotomy (a) Laparotomie f.
cell Zelle f.
cell division Zellteilung f.
cell-free zellfrei
celliform zellenförmig
cellobiase Zellobiase f.
cellobiose Zellobiose f.
cellophane Zellophan n.
cellular zellulär
− tissue Zellgewebe n.
cellulase Zellulase f.
cellulitis Zellgewebeentzündung f.
cellulose Zellulose f.
celom (a) Zölom n.
cement Zement m.
cementification Zementbildung f.
cementoblast Zementoblast m.
cementoclasia Zementoklasie f.
cementoclast Zementklast m.
cementocyte Zementozyt m.
cementom Zementom n.
cementosis Zementose f.

center Zentrum n.
center, motor motorisches Zentrum n.
centrad zentralwärts
central zentral
− cell Hauptzelle f.
− gray zentrales Grau n.
− nervous system Zentralnervensystem n.
centre Zentrum n.
centre dialysis Zentrumsdialyse f.
centrifugal zentrifugal
centrifugation Zentrifugierung f.
centrifuge Zentrifuge f.
centrifuge, to zentrifugieren
centrilobular zentrilobulär
centriole Zentriole f.
centripetal zentripetal
centrosome Zentrosom n.
cephalalgia Kopfschmerz m.
cephalexin d. e. n.
cephalhaematoma (e) Kephalhämatom n.
cephalhematoma (a) Kephalhämatom n.
cephalic vein Vena cephalica
cephalin Kephalin n.
cephalometer Kephalometer n.
cephalometry Schädelmessung f.
cephaloridine Cephaloridin n.
cephalosporin d. e. n.
cephalosporinase d. e. f.
cephalothin d. e. n.
cephalotripsy Kephalotripsie f.
cephalozin d. e. n.
cephradine Cephradin n.
ceramic keramisch
ceramics Keramik
cercaria Zerkarie f.
cerebellar zerebellar
cerebellopontile zerebellopontin
cerebellopontine zerebellopontin
cerebellopontine angle Kleinhirnbrückenwinkel m.
cerebellorubrospinal zerebellorubrospinal
cerebellum Kleinhirn n.

cerebral **zerebral**
cerebration **Hirntätigkeit f.**
cerebromeningeal **zerebromeningeal**
cerebrosclerosis **Zerebralsklerose f.**
cerebroside **Zerebrosid n.**
cerebrospinal **zerebrospinal**
cerebrum **Gehirn n.**
cerium **Zer n., Cer n.**
certifiable **meldepflichtig**
certificate **Bescheinigung f., Zeugnis n.**
certificate of death **Totenschein m.**
ceruloplasmin (a) **Coeruloplasmin n.**
cerumen **Ohrschmalz n.**
ceruminal **zeruminal**
cervical **zervikal**
– plexus **Plexus cervicalis**
– rib **Halsrippe f.**
– spinal column **Halswirbelsäule f.**
– spinal cord **Halsmark n.**
– vertebra **Halswirbel m.**
cervicoaxial **zervikoaxial**
cervicobuccal **zervikobukkal**
cervicolingual **zervikolingual**
cervix **Zervix f., Cervix f.**
cesarean section (a) **Kaiserschnitt m.**
cesium (a) **Zäsium n.**
cessation **Aufhören n.**
cestode **d. e. f.**
chafe, to **reiben, wundreiben**
Chagas's disease **Chagaskrankheit f.**
chain **Kette f.**
– hook **Kettenhaken m.**
– saw **Kettensäge f.**
chair, dental **zahnärztlicher Stuhl m.**
chalazion **d. e. n.**
chalicosis **Chalikose f.**
chalk **Kalk m.; Kreide f.**
chamber **Kammer f.**
chamomile **Kamille f.**
champagne **Champagner m.**

chancre **Schanker m.**
chancroid **weicher Schanker m.**
change **Veränderung f.**
channel **Kanal m.**
Chaoul therapy **Chaoulsche Nahbestrahlung f.**
character **Charakter m.**
characteristical **charakteristisch**
characterize, to **charakterisieren**
characterology **Charakterkunde f.**
charbon **Milzbrand m.**
charcoal, activated **Medizinalkohle f.**
–, animal **Tierkohle f.**
–, wood **Holzkohle f.**
Charcot-Leyden crystal **Charcot-Leydenscher Kristall m.**
Charrière scale **Charrièresche Skala f.**
charting **Eintragung f., Registrierung f.**
chaulmoogra oil **Chaulmoograöl n.**
check, to **steuern**
check, final **Abschlußkontrolle f., Endkontrolle f.**
check up, to, a patient **einen Patienten gründlich untersuchen**
checkbite **Bißnahme f.**
checking **Steuerung f.**
check up (a) **Kontrolle f.**
Chediak's test **Chediaksche Reaktion f.**
cheek **Wange f., Backe f.**
cheek pouch **Backentasche f.**
cheek retractor **Wangenhalter m.**
cheesy **käsig**
cheilitis **d. e. f.**
cheiloplasty **Lippenplastik f.**
chelate **Chelat n.**
chelating agent **Chelatbildner m.**
chelen **Äthylchlorid n.**
chelometry **Chelometrie f.**
chemical **chemisch**
chemicals **Chemikalien f. pl.**
chemicophysiologic **physiologisch-chemisch**
chemism **Chemismus m.**

chemist Chemiker m., Chemikerin f.
chemist's shop (e) Apotheke f.
chemistry Chemie f.
−, **physiologic** physiologische Chemie f.
chemodectoma Chemodektom n.
chemophysiology physiologische Chemie f.
chemoprophylaxis Chemoprophylaxe f.
chemoresistance Chemoresistenz f.
chemoresistant chemoresistent
chemosis d. e. f.
chemotactic chemotaktisch
chemotaxis d. e. f.
chemotherapeutical chemotherapeutisch
chemotherapy Chemotherapie f.
chenotherapy Chenotherapie f.
chest Brustkasten m., Thorax m.
chestnut Kastanie f.
chest Brustkasten m., Thorax m.
chestnut Kastanie f.
chest wall Brustwand f.
chew, to kauen
Cheyne-Stokes respiration Cheyne-Stokessche Atmung f.
Chiari disease Budd-Chiari-Syndrom n.
chiasm Chiasma n.
chick Küken n.
chicken Küken n.
chicken cholera Geflügelcholera f.
chickenpest Hühnerpest f.
chickenpox Windpocken f. pl.
chief cell Hauptzelle f.
chief resident Oberarzt m., Oberärztin f.
chilblain Frostbeule f.
childbed Kindbett n.
− **fever** Kindbettfieber n.
childbirth Geburt f., Gebären n.
childhood Kindheit f.
childish kindisch
chill Frösteln n.; Erkältung f.
−, **shaking** Schüttelfrost m.

chilly fröstelnd; mutlos
−, **to feel** − frösteln
chimpanzee Chimpanse m.
chin Kinn n.
− **holder** Kinnstütze f.
chinone Chinon n.
chiropody Hand- und Fußpflege f.
chiropractic Chiropraxis f.; chiropraktisch
chiropractor Chiropraktiker m.
chisel Flachmeißel m.
−, **bone** Knochenmeißel m.
−, **enamel** Schmelzmeißel m.
chitin d. e. n.
Chlamydia d. e.
chloasma d. e. n.
chloracne Chlorakne f.
chloral d. e. n.
− **hydrate** Chloralhydrat n.
chloralose d. e. f.
chlorambucil d. e. n.
chloramine Chloramin n.
chloramphenicol d. e. n.
chlorate Chlorat n.
chlordiazepoxide Chlordiazepoxid n.
chloride Chlorid n.
chlorinate, to chlorieren
chlorine Chlor n.
chlorite Chlorit n.
chlormadinone Chlormadinon n.
chlorobutanol Trichlorisobutylalkohol m.
chloroform d. e. n.
chloroform, to chloroformieren
chloroformization Chloroformierung f.
chlorolymphosarcoma Chlorolymphosarkom n.
chloroma Chlorom n.
chlorophyll d. e. n.
chloropurine Chloropurin n.
chloroquine Chlorochin n.
− **diphosphate** Chlorochindiphosphat n.
chlorosis Chlorose f.
chlorothiazide Chlorothiazid n.

chlorotic chlorotisch
chlorphenol d. e. n.
chlorphenol red Chlorphenolrot n.
chlorpromazine Chlorpromazin n.
chlorpropamide Chlorpropamid n.
chlorprothixene Chlorprothixen n.
chlortetracycline Chlortetracyclin n.
chlorthalidone Chlorthalidon n.
Chlumsky's solution Chlumskysche Lösung f.
choana Choane f.
chocolate cyst Schokoladenzyste f.
choke Erstickungsanfall m.; Drossel f. (techn.)
choke, to ersticken, drosseln, erdrosseln, verstopfen
choking Erstickung f., Erdrosselung f.; Drosselung f., Verstopfung f.
cholaemia (e) Cholämie f.
cholaemic (e) cholämisch
cholagogue Cholagogum n.; cholagog
cholangiogram Cholangiogramm n.
cholangiographic cholangiographisch
cholangiography Cholangiographie f.
cholangiolitis d. e. f.
cholangioma Cholangiom n.
cholangiopancreaticography Cholangiopankreatikographie f.
cholangioscopy Cholangioskopie f.
cholangiostomy Cholangiostomie f.
cholangiotomy Cholangiotomie f.
cholangitic cholangitisch
cholangitis d. e. f.
cholanthrene Cholanthren n.
cholate Cholat n.
cholecystectomy Cholezystektomie f.
cholecystitic cholezystitisch
cholecystitis Cholezystitis f.

cholecystoduodenostomy Cholezystoduodenostomie f.
cholecystogastrostomy Cholezystogastrostomie f.
cholecystogram Cholezystogramm n.
cholecystographic cholezystographisch
cholecystography Cholezystographie f.
cholecystoileostomy Cholezystoileostomie f.
cholecystojejunostomy Cholezystojejunostomie f.
cholecystokinin d. e. n.
cholecystopathy Cholezystopathie f.
cholecystopexy Cholezystopexie f.
cholecystostomy Cholezystostomie f.
cholecystotomy Cholezystotomie f.
choledochectomy Choledochektomie f.
choledochoduodenostomy Choledochoduodenostomie f.
choledochoenterostomy Choledochoenterostomie f.
choledocholithiasis d. e. f.
choledochoplasty Choledochusplastik f.
choledochorrhaphy Choledochorrhaphie f.
choledochostomy Choledochostomie f.
choledochotomy Choledochotomie f.
cholelithiasis d. e. f.
cholemia (a) Cholämie f.
cholemic (a) cholämisch
choleperitonitis gallige Peritonitis f.
cholera d. e. f.
cholera, pancreatic Verner-Morrison-Syndrom n.
choleresis Cholerese f.
choleretic Cholereticum n.; choleretisch

choleric cholerisch
cholestasis Cholostase f.
cholestatic cholostatisch
cholesteatoma Cholesteatom n.
cholesterol Cholesterin n.
cholestyramine Cholestyramin n.
choline Cholin n.
cholinergic cholinergisch
cholinesterase d. e. f.
—, inhibiting cholinesterase-hemmend
cholopoiesis Gallenbildung f.
cholostasis Cholostase f.
cholostatic cholostatisch
choluria Cholurie f.
chondrification Verknorpelung f., Knorpelbildung f.
chondrin d. e. n.
chondritis d. e. f.
chondroadenoma Chondroadenom n.
chondroangioma Chondroangiom n.
chondroblast d. e. m.
chondroblastoma Chondroblastom n.
chondrocalcinosis Chondrokalzinose f.
chondroclast Chondroklast m.
chondrocyte Chondrozyt m.
chondrodysplasia Chondrodysplasie f.
chondrodystrophy Chondrodystrophie f.
chondrogenesis Chondrogenese f., Knorpelbildung f.
chondroitin d. e. n.
chondrolysis Chondrolyse f.
chondroma Chondrom n.
chondromalacia Condromalazie f.
chondromatosis Chondromatose f.
chondromyxoma Chondromyxom n.
chondroosteodystrophy Chondroosteodystrophie f.

chondroplastic chondroplastisch
chondroplasty Knorpelplastik f.
chondrosarcoma Chondrosarkom n.
chondrotomy Chondrotomie f.
Chopart's amputation Chopartsche Amputation f.
chordata d. e. n. pl.
chorditis d. e. f.
chordoblastoma Chordoblastom n.
chordotomy Chordotomie f.
chorea d. e. f.
—, chronic Chorea Huntington f.
—, Huntington's Chorea Huntington f.
—, Sydenham's Chorea minor Sydenham f.
choreatic choreatisch
choreiform d. e.
choreo-athetoid d. e.
— -athetosis Choreoathetose f.
choreomania Choreomanie f.
chorial d. e.
chorioangioma Chorioangiom n.
chorioepithelioma Chorionepitheliom n.
choriocarcinoma Chorionkarzinom n.
chorioma Choriom n.
choriomeningitis d. e. f.
chorion d. e. n.
corioptic itch Chorioptesräude f.
chorioretinitis d. e. f.
choroid Chorioidea f.
choroidal chorioidal
choroidectomy Chorioidektomie f.
choroiditis Chorioiditis f.
Christmas factor Christmasfaktor m.
chromaffin d. e.
chromaffinoma Chromaffinom n.
chromargentaffin d. e.
chromate Chromat n.
chromatic chromatisch
chromatin d. e. n.
chromatogenous chromatogen

chromatographic chromatographisch
chromatography Chromatographie f.
chromatophilia Chromatophilie f.
chromatophilic chromatophil
chromatopsia Chromatopsie f.
chromatoskiameter d. e. n.
chrome plated verchromt
chromidrosis Chromhidrose f.
chromium Chrom n.
– trioxide Chromsäure f.
chromocystoscopical chromozystoskopisch
chromocystoscopy Chromozystoskopie f.
chromogen d. e. n.
chromogenic chromogen
chromogranin d. e. n.
chromophobic chromophob
chromoscope Chromoskop n.
chromoscopic chromoskopisch
chromoscopy Chromoskopie f.
chromosome Chromosom n.
chromotropic chromotrop
chronaxia Chronaxie f.
chronaximeter d. e. n.
chronaximetric chronaximetrisch
chronaximetry Chronaximetrie f.
chronic chronisch
chronicity Chronizität f.
chronotropic chronotrop
chrysarobin d. e. n.
chrysoidin d. e. n.
chrysotherapy Chrysotherapie f.
chrysotoxin d. e. n.
chuck (dent.) Futter n.
Chvostek's sign Chvosteksches Zeichen n.
chyle Chylus m.
chylomicron d. e. n.
chylopericardium Chyloperikard n.
chyloperitoneum d. e. n.
chylothorax d. e. m.
chylous chylös
chyluria Chylurie f.
chymase d. e. f.

chyme Chymus m.
chymotrypsin d. e. n.
chymous chymös
CI (colo(u)r index) Färbeindex m.
cibisotome Starmesser n.
cicatricial narbig
cicatrization Vernarbung f.
cicatrize, to vernarben
cilia Zilie f.
ciliary body Ziliarkörper m.
ciliata d. e. n. pl.
cimetidine Cimetidin n.
Cimex lectularius d. e.
Cinchona Chinarinde f.
cinchophen Phenylchinolinkarbonsäure f.
cinder Schlacke f.
cinematography Kinematographie f.
cineradiography Kineradiographie f.
cineroentgenography Kineröntgenographie f.
cinnamon Zimt m.
cinnarizin d. e. n.
circadian zirkadisch, einen 24-Stunden-Rhythmus betreffend
circinate kreisförmig, zirzinär
circle Zirkel m., Kreis m.
circle of Willis Circulus arteriosus
circuit Stromkreis m., Kreislauf m., Umlauf m.; Ableitung f. (EKG)
– short Kurzschluß m.
circular zirkulär
circulate, to zirkulieren
circulation Zirkulation f., Kreislauf m.
–, collateral Kollateralkreislauf m.
–, portal Pfortaderkreislauf m.
–, pulmonary kleiner Kreislauf m., Lungenkreislauf m.
–, systemic großer Kreislauf m.
circulatory zirkulatorisch

circumanal zirkumanal
circumarticular zirkumartikulär
circumcision Zirkumzision f., Umschneidung f., Beschneidung f.
circumduction Zirkumduktion f.
circumference Umfang m.
circumoral zirkumoral
circumorbital zirkumorbital
circumpulpal zirkumpulpal
circumscribe, to umschreiben
circumvascular zirkumvaskulär
circumventricular zirkumventrikulär
cirrhosis Zirrhose f.
cirrhotic zirrhotisch
cirsenchysis Krampfaderverödung f.
cistern Zisterne f.
cisternal zisternal
– puncture Subokzipitalpunktion f.
cite, to zitieren
citochol reaction Citocholreaktion f.
citrate Zitrat n.
citrin Zitrin n.
citrovorum factor Citrovorum-Faktor m.
citrulline Zitrullin n.
citrullinuria Citrullinurie f.
cladosporiosis Cladosporiose f.
clamp Klammer f., Klemme f.
–, adjustable verstellbare Klemme f.
clamp, intestinal Darmklemme f.
clamp, to klemmen, abklemmen
clap Tripper m.
clarification Klärung f., Reinigung f.
clarify, to klären, reinigen
Clarke's column Clarkesche Säule f.
clasp Haken m., Klammer f., Spange f.
class Klasse f.
classical klassisch
classification Klassifizierung f.
classify, to klassifizieren

clastic klastisch
Clauberg's culture medium Claubergscher Nährboden m.
claudication Hinken n.
–, intermittent intermittierendes Hinken n.
claustrophilia Klaustrophilie f.
claustrophobia Klaustrophobie f.
clavicepsin d. e. n.
clavicle Schlüsselbein n.
clavicular klavikular
clavus Leichdorn m., Hühnerauge n.
claw Klaue f., Kralle f., Pfote f.
claw elevator Krallenheber m.
clawfoot Klauenfuß m.
clawhand Klauenhand f.
clean rein, sauber
clean, to reinigen
cleanse, to säubern; ausspülen
cleanser Reiniger m.
clear klar, hell, sauber
clear, to klären, reinigen, aufhellen
clear cell Klarzelle f.
clearance Klärung f.; Räumung f.; Clearance f.
–, urea Harnstoffclearance f.
clearing Klärung f., Aufhellung f.
cleavage Segmentierung f., Spaltung f., Spaltbarkeit f.
cleft Spalte f.
–, palate Gaumenspalte f.
cleidotomy Kleidotomie f.
client Klient m., Klientin f.
climacteric Klimakterium n.
climacterium Klimakterium n.
climate Klima n.
climatic klimatisch
climatological klimatologisch
climatology Klimatologie f.
climatotherapy Klimabehandlung f.
climax Höhepunkt m., Gipfel m.
clindamycin d.e.n.
clinic Klinik f.
clinical klinisch

clinical course klinischer Verlauf m., Krankheitsverlauf m.
clinical history Krankheitsgeschichte f.
clinician Kliniker m.
clippers, hair Haarschneidemaschine f.
cloaca Kloake f.
cloacogenic kloakogen
clofenapate Clofenapat n.
clofibrate Clofibrat n.
clonic klonisch
clonicotonic klonisch-tonisch
clonidine Clonidin n.
clonorchiosis Clonorchiose f., Leberegelbefall m.
Clonorchis sinensis d. e.
clonus Klonus m.
close, to schließen
Clostridium botulinum Bacillus botulinus
− oedematis maligni Bacillus oedematis maligni
− putrificum Bacillus putrificus
− tetani Bacillus tetani
− welchii Bacillus perfringens
closure Verschließen n., Verschluß m.
clot Gerinnsel n.
clotrimazole Clotrimazol n.
clot, to gerinnen
clotting Gerinnung f.
clotting time Gerinnungszeit f.
clotting timer Gerinnungsmeßgerät n.
clouding Trübung f.
cloudy trüb
cloxacillin d. e. n.
clubbed fingers Trommelschlägelfinger m. pl.
clubfoot Klumpfuß m.
clyster Klystier n.
CNS (central nervous system) ZNS (Zentralnervensystem)
C.O. (cathodal opening) Kathodenöffnung f.
coagglutinin Koagglutinin n.

coagulability Koagulabilität f.
coagulant koagulierend; Koagulans n.
coagulase Koagulase f.
coagulate, to koagulieren
coagulation Koagulation f.
− test Kochprobe f.
coagulative koagulativ
coagulopathy Koagulopathie f.
coalescence Vereinigung f., Zusammenwachsen n.
coal tar Steinkohlenteer m.
coarctation Einschnürung f., Einengung f.
− of aorta Aortenisthmusstenose f.
coasting Kontaktstörung f. bei Gefangenen
coat Belag m., Bedeckung f., Überzug m.
coated belegt, bedeckt, überzogen
cobalamine Kobalamin n.
cobalt Kobalt m.
cobalt irradiation Kobaltbestrahlung f.
cobamide Cobamid n.
cobbler's chest Schusterbrust f.
cobra Kobra f.
− venom Kobragift n.
cocaine Kokain n.
cocainism Kokainismus m.
cocainist Kokainist m., Kokainistin f.
cocainization Kokainisierung f.
cocainize, to kokainisieren
cocarboxylase Kokarboxylase f.
coccidioidomycosis Coccidioidomykose f.
coccidiosis Coccidiose f.
coccygodynia Coccygodynie f.
coccyx Steiß m.
cochlear kochlear
cochlear joint Schraubengelenk n.
cochleography Cochleographie f.
cock Hahn m.
cockerel Hähnchen n.
cocoa Kakao m.

cocoa butter Kakaobutter f.
coconut Kokosnuß f.
cocoon Kokon m.
code d. e. m.
code of medical ethics ärztliche Berufsordnung f.
codehydrase d. e. f., Kodehydrase f.
codehydrogenase d. e. f.
codeine Kodein n.
coding Codierung f.
cod liver oil Lebertran m.
coecal (e) zökal
coefficient Koeffizient m.
coelenterata d. e. n. pl.
coeliac disease (e) Zöliakie f.
coeliotomy (e) Laparotomie f.
coelom (e) Zölom n.
coenurosis Coenurose f., Drehkrankheit f.
coenzyme Koenzym n.
coeruloplasmin (e) d. e. n.
co-factor Ko-Faktor m.
coferment Koferment n.
coffee Kaffee m.
coffin Sarg m.
coffin bone Hufbein n.
cognition Erkenntnis f.
cohabitation Kohabitation f.
coherent kohärent
cohesion Kohäsion f.
cohobation Redestillation f.
cohydrogenase d. e. f.
coil Spule f., Rolle f.
−, induction Induktionsspule f.
− kidney Spulenniere f.
coincidence Koinzidenz f.
coin lesion of the lung münzenförmige Lungenverschattung f.
coition Koitus m.
coitus Koitus m.
colation Kolation f.
colchicine Colchicin n.
cold kalt; Kälte f.; Erkältung f.
− agglutination Kälteagglutination f.

cold agglutinin Kälteagglutinin n.
−, to catch a − sich erkälten
coldsore Herpes labialis
cold water treatment Kaltwasserkur f.
coleitis Vaginitis f.
coleoptosis Scheidenvorfall m.
coles Penis m.
colic Kolik f.
−, ureteral Harnleiterkolik f.
colica mucosa d. e.
colipyelitis Coli-Pyelitis f.
colitis d. e. f.
−, ulcerative Colitis ulcerosa
collagen Kollagen n.
− disease Kollagenkrankheit f.
collagenic kollagen
collagenosis Kollagenose f.
collagenous kollagen
collapse Kollaps m.
collapsotherapy Kollapstherapie f.
collateral kollateral
collecting tubule Sammelröhrchen n.
collegue Kollege m.
colliculitis d. e. f.
Collin's lock Lappenverschluß m.
− lock, double Doppellappenverschluß m.
Collip unit Collip-Einheit f.
colliquation Kolliquation f., Einschmelzung f., Verflüssigung f.
colliquative kolliquativ
collochemistry Kolloidchemie f.
collodion Collodium n.
colloid Kolloid n.
collodial kollodial
colloid goiter Kolloidkropf m.
− osmotic kolloidosmotisch
collutory Spülflüssigkeit f.
collyrium Augenspülflüssigkeit f.
coloboma Kolobom n.
colocynth Colocynthe f.
colon Colon n., Kolon n.
−, subphrenic displacement of Chilaiditi-Syndrom n.
colonic wall Dickdarmwand f.

colony Kolonie f.
colopexy Colopexie f., Kolopexie f.
colophony Kolophonium n.
coloptosis Coloptose f., Koloptose f.
color (a) Farbe f.
— blindness (a) Farbenblindheit f.
— index (a) Färbeindex m.
Colorado tick fever Coloradozeckenfieber n.
colorimeter Kolorimeter n.
colorimetric kolorimetrisch
colorimetry Kolorimetrie f.
coloscope Koloskop n.
coloscopic koloskopisch
coloscopy Koloskopie f.
colostomy Colostomie f., Kolostomie f.
colostrum Vormilch f.
colotomy Colotomie f., Kolotomie f.
colour (e) Farbe f.
— blindness (e) Farbenblindheit f.
— index (e) Färbeindex m.
colpeurynter Kolpeurynter m.
colpitic kolpitisch
colpitis Kolpitis f.
colpocystocele Kolpozystozele f.
colpocystoplasty Blasenscheidenplastik f.
colpoperineoplasty Scheidendammplastik f.
colpoplasty Scheidenplastik f.
colporrhaphy Kolporrhaphie f.
colposcope Kolposkop n.
colposcopical kolposkopisch
colposcopy Kolposkopie f.
colt Fohlen n.
column Säule f.
— chromatography Säulenchromatographie f.
colytic hemmend
coma Coma n., Koma n.
comatose komatös
combined spectacles and hearing aid Hörbrille f.
combustion Verbrennung f.

combustor Verbrennungsofen m.
comedo Komedo m.
commissure Kommissur f.
commissurotomy Kommissurotomie f.
commit suicide, to sich entleiben, Selbstmord verüben
committee Komitee n.
common bile duct Ductus choledochus
— cold Erkältung f., Schnpfen m.
communicable übertragbar
communicate, to kommunizieren
communication Kommunikation f.
—,personal persönliche Mitteilung f.
communition Zerbröckelung f.
compact kompakt
comparison Vergleich m.
compatibility Kompatibilität f., Verträglichkeit f.
compatible verträglich
compensate, to kompensieren
compensation Kompensation f.
compensation neurosis Begehrungsneurose f., Entschädigungsneurose f.
compensatory kompensatorisch
competition Wettbewerb m.
competitive kompetitiv, wettbewerbsfähig, wettbewerbsmäßig
complain of, to leiden an, klagen über
complaint Leiden m., Klage f., Beschwerde f.
complement Komplement n.
— fixation Komplementbindung f.
complementary komplementär
complete vollständig, komplett
completion Vervollständigung f.
— of a cure Nachkur f.
complex Komplex m.; komplex
— of symptoms Symptomenkomplex m.
complexing agent Komplexbildner m.
complexion Gesichtsfarbe f.

complexometric komplexometrisch
complexometry Komplexometrie f.
compliance Dehnbarkeit f.
complicate, to komplizieren
complicated kompliziert
complication Komplikation f.
component Komponente f.
composition Zusammensetzung f.
compound Verbindung f., Zusammensetzung f.
compress Kompresse f.
—, long Longuette f.
compress, to komprimieren, zusammendrücken
compression Kompression f.
— fracture Kompressionsfraktur f.
compressor Kompressor m.
compressorium Kompressorium n.
compulsion Zwang m.
compulsion neurosis Zwangsneurose f.
compulsive zwangsmäßig
computed tomography Computer-Tomographie f.
computer Rechenmaschine f., Computer m.
concave konkav, hohl
— mirror Hohlspiegel m.
concavity Konkavität f.
concentrate Konzentrat n.
—, to konzentrieren
concentrating ability Konzentrationsvermögen n.
concentration Konzentration f.
— test Konzentrationsversuch m.
concentric konzentrisch
concept Vorstellungsbild n., Konzept n.
conception Befruchtung f., Empfängnis f.
conceptive empfängnisfähig
conchotome Conchotom n.
conchotomy Conchotomie f.
concoction Abkochung f.
concomitant begleitend
concrement Konkrement n.
concrescence Verwachsung f.

concrete konkret
concretion Konkretion f., Verdichtung f., Verwachsung f.; Konkrement n.
concussion Erschütterung f.
— of the brain Gehirnerschütterung f.
condensate Kondensat n.
condensation Kondensation f.
condenser Kondensor m.; Stopfer m.
condiment Gewürz n.
condition Kondition f., Bedingung f., Verfassung f.
condom Kondom m.
conductance Leitfähigkeit f.
conduction Konduktion f., Leitung f., Überleitung f.
— of sound waves Schalleitung f.
conduction system of the heart Erregungsleitungssystem n., Reizleitungssystem n.
conduction velocity Leitgeschwindigkeit f.
conductivity Leitfähigkeit f.
conductor Leiter m., Leitmaterial n.; Träger m., Konduktor m.
condurango d. e. f.
condyloma Kondylom n.
condylomatosis Kondylomatose f.
condylomatous kondylomatös
condylotomy Kondylotomie f.
cone Konus m., Keil m.
cones and rods, retinal Zapfen m. pl. und Stäbchen n. pl. der Retina
confabulate, to konfabulieren
confabulation Konfabulation f.
confection Zubereitung f.
conference Konferenz f.
confidential vertraulich
— medical officer Vertrauensarzt m.
configurate, to konfigurieren
configuration Konfiguration f.
conflict Konflikt m.

confluent konfluierend
confusion Konfusion f., Verwirrung f.
congelation Frostbeule f., Erfrierung f.
congenital kongenital
congestion Blutandrang m., Blutüberfüllung f., Stauung f.
congestive kongestiv
– **cirrhosis** Stauungscirrhose f.
– **heart failure** Stauungsinsuffizienz f. des Herzens, deskompensierte Herzinsuffizienz f.
conglobation Zusammenballung f.
conglomerate Konglomerat n.
Congo red Kongorot n.
– **trypanosomiasis** afrikanische Schlafkrankheit f.
conical konisch
coniine Koniin n.
coniotomy Koniotomie f.
conjugal ehelich
conjugase Konjugase f.
conjugate gepaart, konjugiert; Konjugat n.; Konjugata f.
conjunction Verbindung f.
conjunctiva Augenbindehaut f.
conjunctival konjunktival
– **sac** Konjunktivalsack m.
conjunctivitis Konjunktivitis f.
conjunctivoplasty Bindehautplastik f.
connatal konnatal
connection Verbindung f.
connective tissue Bindegewebe n.
Conn's syndrome Conn-Syndrom n.
conquer, to überwinden
consanguinity Blutsverwandtschaft f.
conscious bewußt
consciousness Bewußtsein n.
consensual konsensuell
conservative konservativ
consolidate, to konsolidieren
consolidation Konsolidierung f.

consonant Konsonant m.
constant konstant; Konstante f.
constipated obstipiert
constipation Obstipation f., Verstopfung
constitution Konstitution f.
constitutional konstitutionell
constrict, to zusammenziehen
constriction Zusammenziehung f.
constrictive konstriktorisch, konstriktiv
constrictor Konstriktor m.
constructive konstruktiv
consult, to konsultieren
consultant beratender Arzt m.
consultation Konsultation
consumption Verbrauch m., Aufbrauch m., Auszehrung f.
consumptive zehrend
contact Kontakt m.
contact area Kontaktfläche f.
contact lense Kontaktlinse, Haftschale f.
contagion Ansteckung f.
contagiosity Ansteckungsfähigkeit f.
contagious ansteckend, kontagiös
contain, to enthalten
container Behälter m.
contamination Verunreinigung f.
content Inhalt m., Gehalt m.
content of the stomach Mageninhalt m.
contiguity Kontiguität f.
continuity Kontinuität f.
continuous kontinuierlich, beständig, ununterbrochen
contour Kontur f.
contoured konturiert
contra-aperture Gegeninzision f.
contraception Empfängnisverhütung f.
contraceptive empfängnisverhütend; empfängnisverhütendes Mittel n.
contraceptive, oral Antibaby-Pille f., orales Antikonzipiens n.

contract, to kontrahieren
contractile kontraktil
contractility Kontraktilität f.
contraction Kontraktion.;
 Kontraktur f.
contraction, anodal closure
 Anodenschließungszuckung f.
contraction, anodal opening
 Anodenöffnungszuckung f.
contraction, cathodal closure
 Kathodenschließungszuckung f.
contraction, cathodal opening
 Kathodenöffnungszuckung f.
contractor Schließer m.,
 Schließmuskel m.
contracture Kontraktur f.
contra-incision Gegeninzision f.
contraindicant kontraindiziert
contraindication Kontra-
 indikation f., Gegenanzeige f.
contrainsular kontrainsulär
contralateral kontralateral
contrary gegensätzlich, konträr
− to rule regelwidrig
− to taste geschmackswidrig
contrast Kontrast m.
− foot bath Wechselfußbad n.
− medium Kontrastmittel n.
contrecoup d. e. m.
contribution Beitrag m.
control Kontrolle f.
control, to kontrollieren, steuern
− desk Schalttisch m.
− lever Schalthebel m.
− subject Kontrollperson f.
controversial kontrovers
contusion Kontusion f.,
 Quetschung f.
convalescence Rekonvaleszenz f.
convalescent Rekonvaleszent m.,
 Rekonvaleszentin f.
convallamarin d. e. n.
convallarin d. e. n.
convallatoxin d. e. n.
convergence Konvergenz f.
convergent konvergent
conversion Konversion f.

convex konvex
convexity Konvexität f.
convoluted tubules Tubuli contorti
convolution Windung f.;
 Gehirnwindung f.
convulsant krampfauslösend;
 Krampfmittel n.
convulsion Konvulsion f.,
 Zuckung f., Krampf m.
convulsive zuckend, krampfend
convulsive disorder Krampf-
 leiden n.
cook Koch m.
cook, to kochen
cool kühl; Kühle f.
cool, to kühlen, erkalten
cooling Kühlung f.
Cooley's anaemia (e) Cooleysche
 Anämie f.
− anemia (a) Cooleysche Anämie f.
cooperate, to zusammenarbeiten
cooperation Zusammenarbeit f.
coordinate, to koordinieren
coordination Koordination f.
copious kopiös
copper Kupfer n.
copraemia (e) Koprämie f.
copremia (a) Koprämie f.
coprolith Kotstein m.
coprophilia Koprophilie f.
coprophilous koprophil
coproporphyrin Koproporphyrin n.
coprostanol Koprosterin n.
copulation Geschlechtsverkehr m.
coracoacromial korakoakromial
coracoclavicular korakoklavikular
coracoid process Processus
 coracoideus
cord Strang m., Kabel n.
− blood Nabelschnurblut n.
− handle Kabelgriff m.
−, vocal Stimmband n.
cordate herzförmig
cordial herzstärkend
cordiform herzförmig
cordotomy Cordotomie f.
core Kern m.

corepressor Korepressor m.
corium Lederhaut f.
cork Kork m.
corkscrew Korkenzieher m.
corn (med.) Hühnerauge n.
cornea d. e. f.
—, opacity of — Hornhauttrübung f.
cornification Verhornung f.
cornify, to verhornen
cornutine Cornutin n.
coronaritis Koronariitis f.
coronary koronar
coronary care unit Herzinfarkt-Intensivstation f.
coroner Leichenschauer m.
coronet (veter.) Hufkrone f.
corporal körperlich
corporeal körperlich
corpse Leiche f.
corpulency Korpulenz f.
corpulent korpulent
corpuscle Korpuskel n., Körperchen n.
corpuscular korpuskulär
corpus luteum hormone Corpus luteum-Hormon n.
correlation Korrelation f.
correlative korrelativ
corresponding to nature naturgemäß
corrigent Korrigens n.; korrigierend
corrode, to ätzen, zerfressen
corrosion Korrosion f.
corrosive korrosiv, Ätzmittel n.
corset Korsett n.
cortex Rinde f.
cortexolone Cortexolon n.
cortexone Cortexon n., Desoxycorticosteron n.
cortical kortikal
— blindness Rindenblindheit f.
— epilepsy Rindenepilepsie f.
corticomedullary kortikomedullär
corticospinal kortikospinal
corticosteroid d. e. n.
corticosterone Corticosteron n.

corticotropic kortikotrop
corticotropin Corticotropin n.
— releasing factor corticotropinfreisetzender Faktor m.
cortin d. e. n.
cortisol Cortisol n., Hydrocortison n.
cortisone Cortison n.
Corti's organ Cortisches Organ n.
Corynebacterium diphtheriae Diphtheriebazillus m.
Corynebacterium pseudodiphtheriae Pseudodiphtheriebazillus m.
— xerosis Xerosebazillus m.
coryza Schnupfen m.
cosmesis Kosmetik f.
cosmetic kosmetisch; kosmetisches Mittel n.
cosmetics Kosmetik f.
cosmic kosmisch
costive obstipiert
costiveness Obstipation f.
costophrenic angle Zwerchfellrippenwinkel m.
costovertebral kostovertebral
cotarnine Cotarnin n.
co-trimoxazol d. e. n.
cotton Baumwolle f.; Watte f.; baumwollen
— bandage Baumwollbinde f.
— carrier Watteträger m.
— holder Watteträger m.
— roll Watterolle f.
cough Husten m.
cough, to husten
— slightly, to hüsteln
coulomb d. e. n.
coumarin Cumarin n.
counter Zähler m.
countercurrent Gegenstrom m.
counterextension Gegenextension f., Gegenzug m.
counterlight Gegenlicht n.
counteropening Gegenöffnung f.
counterpoison Gegengift n.
counterregulation Gegenregulation f.

countertraction Gegenzug m.
counting cell Zählkammer f.
– chamber Zählkammer f.
couple Paar n.
couple, to paaren
course Kurs m., Lauf m.
courses Monatsblutung f.
court-physician Hofarzt m.
Courvoisier's sign Courvoisiersches Zeichen n.
cover Decke f.
cover, to bedecken, zudecken
coverglass Deckglas n.
covering Auskleidung f., Überzug m.
cow Kuh f.
cow horn beak Kuhhornschnabel m.
coworker Mitarbeiter m., Mitarbeiterin f.
Cowper's gland Cowpersche Drüse f.
cowperitis d. e. f.
coxa valga d. e.
– vara d. e.
coxitis d. e. f.
Coxsackie virus Coxsackievirus n.
cozymase Kozymase f.
crab louse Filzlaus f.
Cramer's splint Cramerschiene f.
cramp Krampf m.
crampus neurosis Krampusneurose f.
cranial kranial
craniectomy Kraniektomie f.
craniocaudal kraniokaudal
craniocerebral kraniozerebral
cranioclast Kranioklast m.
craniometry Schädelmessung f.
craniopharyngeal kraniopharyngeal
craniopharyngioma Kraniopharyngiom n.
cranioplasty Schädelplastik f.
craniotabes Kraniotabes f.
craniotomy Kraniotomie f.
crank, revolving Drehkurbel f.

crataegin d. e. n.
Crataegus oxyacantha d. e.
crater Krater m.
crazy verrückt; gebrechlich
crazy disease Bornasche Krankheit f.
cream Rahm m., Sahne f.
creatine Kreatin m.
creatinine Kreatinin n.
creative kreativ
creativity Kreativität f.
creature Kreatur f.
Credé's method Credéscher Handgriff m.
cremation Einäscherung f.
crematory Krematorium n.
creosol Kreosol n.
creosote Kreosot n.
crepitant krepitierend
crepitation Krepitation f.
crescendo d. e.
cresol Kresol n.
cresol phthalein Kresolphthalein n.
cresol purple Kresolpurpur m.
cresol red Kresolrot n.
–, saponated solution of – Kresolseifenlösung f.
crest Leiste f.
cresyl Kresyl n.
cretin Kretin m.
cretinism Kretinismus m.
crevice, gingival Subgingivalspalt m.
CRF (corticotropin releasing factor) corticotropin-freisetzender Faktor m.
cricoidectomy Krikoidektomie f.
cricopharyngeal krikopharyngeal
cricotomy Krikotomie f.
crime Verbrechen n.
criminal kriminell; Verbrecher m., Verbrecherin f.
cripple Krüppel m.
cripple, to verkrüppeln
crisis Krise f.

cristothermographical cristothermographisch
cristothermography Cristothermographie f.
criterion Kriterium n.
critical kritisch
critique Kritik f.
crocodile Krokodil n.
Crohn's disease Morbus Crohn
cross, to kreuzen
− reaction Kreuzreaktion f.
− resistance gekreuzte Resistenz f.
− -section Querschnitt m.
− typing Kreuzprobe f.
crossing Kreuzung f.
croton oil Krotonöl n.
croup Croup m., Krupp m.
croupous croupös, kruppös
crown Krone f.; Zahnkrone f.
crown, cast Gußkrone f.
crowning Einschneiden n. (obstetr.)
crown pusher Kronensetzer m.
crownwork Überkronung f.
crucible Tiegel m.
crude roh
cruor clot Cruorgerinnsel n.
crural ulcer Unterschenkelgeschwür n.
crush, to quetschen, zermalmen
crushing Quetschung f.
crush syndrome Crush-Syndrom n.
crust Kruste f., Borke f.
Crustacea d. e. n. pl.
crutch Krücke f.
crymotherapy Kälteanwendung f.
cryogenic kryogen
cryoglobulin d. e. n.
cryotherapy Kälteanwendung f.
crypt Krypte f.
cryptic kryptisch
cryptococcosis Kryptokokkose f.
cryptogenetic kryptogenetisch
cryptorchidism Kryptorchismus m.
crystal Kristall n.
crystalline kristallisch
crystalluria Kristallurie f.

c.s.f. (= cerebrospinal fluid) Liquor cerebrospinalis
cube root Kubikwurzel f.
cubic meter Kubikmeter m.
cubital kubital
cuff Manschette f.
culdoscopy Culdoskopie f.
culicide Mückenvertilgungsmittel n.
cultivation Kultivierung f.
cultural kulturell
culture Kultur f.
− medium Nährboden m.
cumulate, to kumulieren
cumulative kumulativ
cumulation Kumulation f.
cuneiform keilförmig
cunnilingus d. e.
cup (med.) Schröpfkopf m.; Exkavation f.
cup, to schröpfen
cupping glass Schröpfkopf m.
cupreine Cuprein n.
cupric sulfate (a) Kupfervitriol m.
− sulphate (e) Kupfervitriol m.
curable heilbar
curableness Heilbarkeit f.
curare Curare n., Kurare n.
curarine Curarin n., Kurarin n.
curarization Kurarisierung f.
curdled mild Sauermilch f.
cure Kur f.; Heilung f.
cure, to kurieren, heilen
curet Kürette f.
curettage Kürettage f.
curette Kürette f.
curie d. e. n.
current Strom m.; elektrischer Strom m.
−, alternating Wechselstrom m.
−, constant Gleichstrom m.
−, continuous Gleichstrom m.
−, faradic faradischer Strom m.
−, galvanic galvanischer Strom m.
−, heating Heizstrom m.
−, swelling Schwellstrom m.
−, three phase Drehstrom m.

current curve of the brain Hirnstromkurve f.
Curschmann's spiral Curschmannsche Spirale f.
curvature Kurvatur f.
curve Kurve f.
curved gebogen
Cushing's disease Cushingsche Krankheit f.
cushion Kissen n.
cusp Zipfel m.; Höcker m.
cuspid Eckzahn m.
cut Schnitt m., Einschnitt m.
cut, to schneiden
– in, to einschneiden
– open, to aufschneiden
– to pieces, to zerschneiden, zerstückeln
cutaneous kutan
– test Hauttest m.
– tolerance Hautverträglichkeit f.
cuticle Häutchen n.; Epidermis f.
cuticularization Überhäutung f.
cutireaction Hautreaktion f.
cutter Schneidegerät n.
cyanamide Zyanamid n.
cyanate Zyanat n.
cyanidanol Zyanidanol n.
cyanide Zyanid n.
cyanoacrylate Zyanoakrylat n., Cyanoacrylat n.
cyanocobalamine Zyanokobalamin n., Vitamin B_{12} n.
cyanosed zyanotisch
cyanosis Zyanose f.
cyanotic zyanotisch
cybernetic kybernetisch
cyclamate Cyclamat n.
cyclase d. e. f.
cyclazocine Cyclazocin n.
cycle Zyklus m.
cycle per second Hertz n.
cyclic zyklisch
cyclitis Zyklitis f.
cyclohexane Hexamethylen n.

cyclopenthiazide Zyklopenthiazid n.
cyclophrenia Zyklothymie f.
cyclopropane Zyklopropan n.
cycloserine Zykloserin n.
cyclothymia Zyklothymie f.
cyclothymiac Zyklothymer m., Zyklothyme f.
cyclothymic zyklothym
cyclotron Zyklotron n.
cylinder Zylinder m.
cylindrical zylindrisch
cylindroma Zylindrom n.
cylindruria Zylindrurie f.
cymarin Zymarin n.
cymarose Zymarose f.
cymogen Zymogen n.
cyproheptadine Cyproheptadin n.
cyst Zyste f.
cystadenoma Zystadenom n.
cysteamine Zysteamin n.
cysteine Zystein n.
cystic zystisch
cysticercosis Zystizerkose f.
cystine Zystin n.
cystinosis Zystinose f.
cystinuria Zystinurie f.
cystitic zystitisch
cystitis Zystitis f.
cystocele Zystozele f.
cystography Zystographie f.
cystoma Zystom n.
cystopexy Blasenfixation f.
cystoplasty Blasenplastik f.
cystopyelitis Zystopyelitis f.
cystorrhaphy Blasennaht f.
cystoscope Zystoskop n.
cystoscopic zystoskopisch
cystoscopy Zystoskopie f.
cystotomy Zystotomie f., Blasenschnitt m.
cysto-urethroscope Zystourethroskop n.
cytidin Zytidin n.
cytidylate Cytidylat n.
cytoarchitectonic zytoarchitektonisch

cytoarchitecture Zytoarchitektonik f.
cytochalasin d.e.n.
cytochemical zytochemisch
cytochemistry Zellularchemie f.,
   Zytochemie f.
cytochrome Zytochrom n.
cytogenesis Zytogenese f.
cytogenetic zytogenetisch
cytogenetics Zytogenetik f.
cytoglobin Zytoglobin n.
cytohormone Zellhormon n.
cytologic zytologisch
cytology Zytologie f.
cytolysis Zytolyse f.
cytolytic zytolytisch
cytomegalic inclusion zytomegaler
   Einschluß m.
cytomegaly Zytomegalie f.
cytomembrane Zellmembran f.
cytometaplasia Zellmetaplasie f.
cytomorphology Zellmorphologie f.
cytopathology Zellularpathologie f.
cytophysiology Zellphysiologie f.
cytoplasm Zytoplasma n.
cytoplasmic zytoplasmatisch
cytosine Zytosin n.
cytosome Zytosom n.
cytostasis Zytostase f.
cytostatic zytostatisch;
   Zytostatikum n.
cytotherapy Zellulartherapie f.
cytotoxic zytotoxisch

D

dacryadenitis Dakryoadenitis f.
dacryocanaliculitis Dakryokanalikulitis f.
dacryocystectomy Dakryo-
   zystektomie f.
dacryocystitis Dakryozystitis f.
dacryolithiasis Dakryolithiasis f.
dactylogram Fingerabdruck m.
Dakin's solution Dakinsche
   Lösung f.
daltonism Farbenblindheit f.
damage Schaden m.
dandruff Haarschuppen-
   krankheit f.
danger Gefahr f.
− to life Lebensgefahr f.
dangerous gefahrvoll, gefährlich
dangerously ill todkrank
dap, to tupfen
Darier's disease Dariersche
   Krankheit f.
dark adaptation Dunkel-
   anpassung f.
darkfield Dunkelfeld n.
darkground Dunkelfeld n.
darkroom Dunkelkammer f.
dartre Herpes m.
data file Datei f.
data processing Daten-
   verarbeitung f.
daunorubicin d. e. n.,
   Rubidomycin n.
day blindness Tagesblindheit f.
dazzle, to blenden
deacidification Entsäuerung f.
deacidify, to entsäuern
deacon Diakon m.
deaconess Diakonisse f.
deacylase Desazylase f.
dead tot, abgestorben
− body Leiche f.
deaden, to abtöten, töten
deadly todbringend, tödlich
deadspace Totraum m.
deaf taub
− and dumb taubstumm

deaf-mutism Taubstummheit f.
deafness Taubheit f.
deamidase Desamidase f.
deamidization Desamidierung f.
deaminase Desaminase f.
deamination Desaminierung f.
death Tod m.
− **-cup** Knollenblätterpilz m.
− **rate** Sterblichkeitsquote f.
− **struggle** Todeskampf m.
debile debil
debility Debilität f.
deblock, to entblocken
débridement Wundausschneidung f.
debris Detritus m.
debugging Entstörung f.
decalcification Entkalkung f.
decalcify, to entkalken
decannulation Kanülenentfernung f.
decanoate Decanoat n.
decantation Dekantierung f.
decapeptide Dekapeptid n.
decapitate, to enthaupten, dekapitieren
decapitation Enthauptung f.
decapsulate, to dekapsulieren
decapsulation Dekapsulation f.
decarboxylase Dekarboxylase f.
decarboxylation Dekarboxylierung f.
decay Fäulnis f.
decay, to faulen, zerfallen
decease, to ableben, sterben
decerebrate, to enthirnen
decerebration Enthirnung f.
dechloridation Entchlorung f.
decholesterolize, to entcholesterinisieren
decibel Dezibel n.
decidua d. e. f.
decidual d. e.
deciduous teeth Milchgebiß n.
decimeter wave Dezimeterwelle f.
declination Deklination f.
decoction Abkochung f.
decollation Enthauptung f.
decolorize, to entfärben

decompensate, to dekompensieren
decompensation Dekompensation f.
decomposition Dekomposition f., Verwesung f.
decompression Dekompression f.
decongestant abschwellend; abschwellendes Mittel n.
decortication Dekortikation f., Entrindung f.
decrease Verminderung f., Abnahme f.
decrease, to vermindern, abnehmen
decrescendo d. e. n.
decrudescence Dekrudeszenz f.
decrustation Krustenentfernung f.
decubitus Dekubitus m.
decussation Dekussation f., Kreuzung f.
dedifferentiate, to entdifferenzieren
dedifferentiation Entdifferenzierung f.
deep tief
− **action** Tiefenwirkung f.
− **roentgen therapy** Röntgentiefenbestrahlung f.
− **-seated** tiefsitzend
deer Rotwild n.
defaecate, to (e) defäkieren
defaecation (e) Defäkation f.
defatigation Ermüdung f., Ermattung f.
defatted entfettet
defecate, to (a) defäkieren
defecation (a) Defäkation f.
defect Defekt m., Fehler m., Mangel m.
− **of the interventricular septum** Ventrikelseptumdefekt m.
defective defekt, mangelhaft, fehlerhaft
defemination Entweiblichung f.
defence (e) Abwehr f.
defence mechanism (e) Abwehrmechanismus m.

defense (a) Abwehr f.
defense mechanism (a) Abwehrmechanismus m.
defensive defensiv
deferentitis d. e. f.
defervescence Deferveszenz f.
defibrillate, to defibrillieren
defibrillation d. e. f.
defibrillator d. e. m.
defibrinate, to defibrinieren
defibrination Defibrinierung f.
deficiency Defizit n., Mangel m., Fehlen n.
− disease Mangelkrankheit f.
deficient fehlend, mangelhaft, mangelnd
deficit, pulse − Pulsdefizit n.
definition d. e. f.
deflection Deflexion f., Ablenkung f., Abbiegung f., Abweichung f.
defloration d. e. f., Entjungferung f.
deform, to deformieren, entstellen
deformation d. e. f., Entstellung f.
deformity Deformität f.
defurfurate, to abschilfern
degassing Entgasung f.
degeneracy Entartungszustand m.
degenerate, to degenerieren
degeneration d. e. f.
degenerative degenerativ
deglutition Schlucken n.
degradation Degradierung f., Abbau m.
degrade, to degradieren, abbauen, abwerten
degranulation d. e. f., Entgranulierung f.
degree Grad m.
− of cold Kältegrad m.
− of heat Wärmegrad m.
degustation Schmecken n., Geschmack m.
dehiscence Dehiszenz f.
dehydrate, to dehydrieren, entwässern

dehydration Dehydrierung f., Entwässerung f.
dehydrocorticosterone Dehydrokortikosteron n.
dehydroemetine Dehydroemetin n.
dehydrogenase d. e. f.
dehydropeptidase d. e. f.
dehydroxylation Dehydroxylation f.
déjà vu d. e.
Dejerine's sign Dejerinesches Zeichen n.
Deiters' nucleus Deitersscher Kern m.
dekapeptide Dekapeptid n.
delactation Abstillen m.
delay Verzögerung f., Aufschub m.
delay, to verzögern, verschleppen
delead, to entbleien
deleterious deletär
delicate delikat, empfindlich, zart
deligation Abbindung f.
delimitation Abgrenzung f.
delirious delirant
delirium d. e. n.
− tremens d. e.
deliver, to entbinden
delivery Entbindung f.
−, forceps Zangenentbindung f.
delomorphous cell Belegzelle f.
Délorme's operation Délormesche Operation f.
delousing Entlausung f.
delusion Wahn m.
delusion of grandeur Größenwahn m.
delusion of persecution Verfolgungswahn m.
delusion of reference Beziehungswahn m.
delusional wahnhaft
demand ventilation Abrufbeatmung f.
demarcation Demarkation f.
dement dement; Dementer m., Demente f.
dementia Demenz f.

dementia praecox (hebephrenic/ catatonic/paranoid type) Schizophrenie f. (hebephrener/ katatoner/paranoider Typ)
demethylate, to demethylieren
demethylchlor-tetracycline Demethylchlortetrazyklin n.
demineralization Demineralisation f.
demodicosis d. e. f., Demodexausschlag m.
demodulate, to demodulieren
demonstrate, to demonstrieren
demonstration d. e. f.
demyelinization Entmyelinisierung f., Entmarkung f.
demyelinize, to entmyelinisieren
denaturation Denaturierung f.
denature, to denaturieren
dendrite Dendrit m.
denervate, to entnerven
denervation Entnervung f.
dengue Denguefieber n.
denicotinize, to entnikotinisieren
dense dicht
densiometry Densiometrie f.
density Dichte f.
density-gradient electrophoresis Dichtegradient-Elektrophorese f.
densography Densiographie f.
dental d. e.
− **depot** Dentaldepot n.
dental technician Zahntechniker m.
dentifrice Zahnpulver n., Zahnpflegemittel n.
dentin d. e. n.
dentinoblast d. e. m.
dentino-cemental dentinozemental
dentino-enamel amelodentinal
dentinoma Dentinom n.
dentist Zahnarzt m., Zahnärztin f.
dentist's forceps Zahnzange f.
dentistry Zahnheilkunde f.
dentistry, operative konservierende Zahnheilkunde f.
dentition d. e. f.
− **primary** erste Dentition f.

dentition secondary zweite Dentition f.
dentoalveolar d. e.
denture Gebiß n., künstliches Gebiß n.
− **adaption** Zahnprothesenanpassung f.
−,**complete** Vollprothese f.
−,**lower** Unterkieferprothese f.
−,**partial** Teilprothese f.
− **supporting** (dent.) prothesenstützend
−,**temporary** provisorische Prothese f.
−,**upper** Oberkieferprothese f.
denudation Freilegung f., Entblößung f.
deodorant desodorierend; desodorierendes Mittel n.
deodorization Desodorierung f.
deodorize, to desodorieren
deontology Standeskunde f.
deoxidation Desoxydation f.
deoxidize, to desoxydieren
deoxygenation Sauerstoffentladung f.
deoxyribonuclease Desoxyribonuklease f.
depancreatize, to pankreatektomieren
dependence Abhängigkeit f.
dependent abhängig
depersonalization Entpersönlichung, Depersalisierung f.
dephosphorylate, to dephosphorylieren
depilate, to enthaaren
depilation Enthaarung f.
depilatory Enthaarungsmittel n.
deplete, to entleeren
depletion Entleerung f.
depolarization Depolarisation f.
depolarize, to depolarisieren
depolymerase d. e. f.
depolymerize, to depolymerisieren
deposit Ablagerung f., Sediment n.

deposit, brick dust Ziegelmehlsediment n.
depot d. e. n.
− insulin Depotinsulin n.
− penicillin Depotpenicillin n.
depravation Verschlechterung f.,
 Verderbnis f.
depraved verschlechtert, verdorben
depressant depressorisch
depressed eingedrückt
− fracture of skull Schädelimpressionsfraktur f.
depression d. e. f.
−,reactive reaktive Depression f.
depressive depressiv
deprival Verlust m., Fehlen n.
deprivation Beraubung f.,
 Entzug m., Verlust m.
−,maternal Verlust m.
 der mütterlichen Fürsorge
depurated gereinigt
derangement Störung f.
− of mind Geistesverwirrung f.
Dercum's disease Dercumsche
 Krankheit f.
derivation Ableitung f.
derivative ableitend; ableitendes
 Mittel n.; Derivat n.
dermatitis d. e. f.
dermatitis, atopic allergisches
 Ekzem n.
dermatological dermatologisch
dermatologist Dermatologe m.,
 Dermatologin f.
dermatology Dermatologie f.
dermatome Dermatom n.
dermatomycosis Dermato-
 mykose f.
dermatomyositis d. e. f.
dermatophytide Dermatophytid n.
dermatophytosis Dermatophytose f.
dermatosis Dermatose f.
dermographia Dermographie f.
dermographism Dermo-
 graphismus m.
dermoid dermoid; Dermoid n.
− cyst Dermoidzyste f.

desalination Entsalzung f.
Desault's bandage Desaultscher
 Verband m.
Descemet's membrane Des-
 cemetsche Membran f.
descemetitis d. e. f.
descend, to abstammen, absteigen,
 abfallen
descendant Nachkomme m.
descent Abstieg m., Abfall m.,
 Abstammung.f.
Deschamps' needle Deschamps-
 Nadel f.
description Beschreibung f.
descriptive deskriptiv
desensitization Desensibilisierung f.
desensitize, to desensibilisieren
deserpidine Deserpidin n.
desferrioxamine Desferrioxamin n.
desiccate, to austrocknen
desiccation Austrocknung f.
desmethylimipramine Demethylimipramin n.
desmodontal d. e.
desmolase d. e. f.
desmology Desmologie f.
desobliteration d. e. f.
desoxycorticosterone Desoxykortikosteron n.
desoxyribonuclease Desoxyribonuklease f.
desoxyribose d. e. f.
despeciate, to entarten
despeciation Entartung f.
d'Espine's sign d'Espinesches
 Zeichen n.
desquamate, to schuppen,
 abschuppen
desquamation d. e. f.
 Abschuppung f.
desquamative desquamativ
destruct, to zerstören
destruction Destruktion f.,
 Zerstörung f.
destructive destruktiv

detachment Loslösung f., Ablösung f.
deterioration Verschlechterung f.; Verstimmung f.
determination Bestimmung f.
determination, rapid Schnellbestimmung f.
detoxicate, to entgiften
detoxication Entgiftung f.
detoxification Entgiftung f.
detoxify, to entgiften
detritus d. e. m.
detumescence Abschwellung f.
deuteranopia Deuteranopie f., Grünblindheit f.
deuterium d. e. n.
deuteron d. e. n.
devascularize, to devaskularisieren
develop, to entwickeln
developer Entwickler m.
development Entwicklung f.
developmental entwicklungsmäßig
deviation d. e. f.
– **of the left** Linksverschiebung f.
device Gerät n.
device, intrauterine Intrauterinspirale f.
devil's grip Pleurodynie f.
devitalize, to devitalisieren, abtöten
devour, to verschlingen
dew-claw Afterklaue f.
deworming Wurmkur f.
dexamethasone Dexamethason n.
dexiocardia Dextrokardie f.
dextran d. e. n.
dextrin d. e. n.
dextroamphetamine Dextroamphetamin n.
dextromanual rechtshändig
dextroposed dextroponiert
dextroposition d. e. f.
dextrorotation Rechtsdrehung f.
dextrorotatory rechtsdrehend
dextrose d. e. f.
dextroversion d. e. f.
dextroverted dextrovertiert
dezymotize, to entfermentieren

diabetes d. e. m.
– **insipidus** d. e.
–, **insulin-deficient** Insulinmangeldiabetes m.
– **mellitus** d. e.
– **renalis** d. e.
–, **to regulate a** – einen Diabetes einstellen
diabetic diabetisch; Diabetiker m., Diabetikerin f.
diabetogenic diabetogen
diacetate Diazetat n.
diacetic acid Azetessigsäure f.
diacetyl Diazetyl n.
diacetylmorphine Diazetylmorphin n., Heroin n.
diad zweiwertig
diadokokinesia Diadochokinese f.
diagnose, to diagnostizieren
diagnosis Diagnose f.
diagnostic diagnostisch
– **set** Untersuchungsbesteck n.
diagnostician Diagnostiker m., Diagnostikerin f.
diagram Diagramm n.
diallyl d. e. n.
dialysate Dialysat n.
dialysis Dialyse f.
dialysis fluid Dialysierflüssigkeit f.
dialyze, to dialysieren
dialyzer Dialysator m.
diameter Durchmesser m.
diamide Diamid n.
diamido-monoester Diamidomonoester m.
diamine Diamin n.
diaminodiphosphatide Diaminodiphosphatid n.
diaminomonophosphatide Diaminomonophosphatid n.
diamniotic diamniotisch
dianisidine Dianisidin n.
diapedesis Diapedese f.
diaper (a) Windel f.
diaphanoscopy Diaphanoskopie f.
diaphorase d. e. f.
diaphoresis Diaphorese f.

diaphoretic diaphoretisch,
schweißtreibend; Diaphoreticum n., schweißtreibendes Mittel n.
diaphragm Zwerchfell n.; Scheidewand f.; Blende f.
diaphragmatic diaphragmatisch
diaphysary diaphysär
diaphyseal diaphysär
diaphysis Diaphyse f.
diaplacental diaplazental
diarginyl d. e. n.
diarrhea (a) Diarrhöe f.
diarrhea, white bacillary (a) Kückenruhr f.
diarrheal (a) diarrhoisch
diarrhoea (e) Diarrhöe f.
diarrhoea, white bacillary (e) Kückenruhr f.
diarrhoeal (e) diarrhoisch
diarthrosis Diarthrose f., Kugelgelenk n.
diascopy Diaskopie f.
diastase d. e. f.
diastasis Diastase f. (anatom.)
– **recti abdominis** Rektusdiastase f.
diastole d. e. f.
diastolic diastolisch
diathermy Diathermie f.
diathesis Diathese f.
diathetic diathetisch
diazepam d. e. n.
diazepine Diazepin n.
diazepoxide Diazepoxid n.
diazine Diazin n.
diazo compound Diazoverbindung f.
– **reaction** Diazoreaktion f.
diazoxide Diazoxyd n., Diazoxid n.
dibasic zweibasig
dibenamine Dibenamin n.
dibenzanthracene Dibenzanthracen n.
dibenzazepine Dibenzazepin n.
dibromide Dibromid n.
dibutyl d. e. n.
dibutyryladenosinemonophosphate Dibutyryladenosinmonophosphat n.
dichloramine Dichloramin n.
dichloride Dichlorid n.
dichotomy Dichotomie f.
dichromatopsia Dichromatopsie f.
Dick test Dick-Test m.
diclofenac d. e. n.
dicloxacillin d. e. n.
dicoumarin Dikumarin n.
dicrotic dikrot
dicrotism Dikrotie f.
dictating machine Diktiergerät n.
dicumarol d. e. n.
dicyandiamide Dicyandiamid n.
didactic didaktisch
die (dent.) Gußform f.
die, to sterben
dieldrin d. e. n.
dielectric dielektrisch
diencephalic dienzephal
diene Dien n.
diester d. e. m.
diet Diät f.
–, **low gluten** glutenarme Diät f.
dietary Diätschema n.
dietetic diätetisch
dietetics Diätetik f.
diethylamide Diäthylamid n.
diethylcarbamazine Diäthylkarbamazin n.
diethylpropion Diäthylpropion m.
dietitian Diätetiker m., Diätetikerin f.
dietotherapy Diätbehandlung f.
difference Differenz f.
differential d. e.
differential diagnosis Differentialdiagnose f.
differentiate, to differenzieren
differentiation Differenzierung f.
diffuse diffus
diffuse, to diffundieren
diffusion d. e. f.
– **capacity** Diffusionskapazität f.
digest, to verdauen

digestible verdaulich
digestion Verdauung f.
digestive digestiv; Verdauungsmittel n.
− **tract** Verdauungstrakt m.
digital d. e.
digital display Digitalanzeige f.
digitalin d. e. n.
digitalis d. e. f.
digitalization Digitalisierung f.
digitalize, to digitalisieren
digitaloid d. e. n.
digitalose d. e. f.
digitogenin d. e. n.
digitonin d. e. n.
digitoxin d. e. n.
digitoxose d. e. f.
diguanidine Diguanidin n.
dihydrate Dihydrat n.
dihydrocodeinone Dihydrocodeinon n.
dihydroergotamine Dihydroergotamin n.
dihydrofolate Dihydrofolat n.
dihydrophenylalanine Dihydrophenylalanin n.
dihydrostreptomycin d. e. n.
dihydrotachysterol Dihydrotachysterin n.
dihydrotheelin Östradiol n.
diiodide Dijodid n.
diiodotyronin Dijodtyronin n.
diiodotyrosine Dijodtyrosin n.
dilatable erweiterungsfähig
dilatation d. e. f., Erweiterung f.
dilate, to dilatieren, erweitern
dilator Dilatator m., Dehner m., Erweiterer m.
diluent Verdünnungsmittel n.
dilute, to verdünnen
dilution Verdünnung f.
− **curve** Verdünnungskurve f.
− **test** Verdünnungsversuch m.
dimethylamine Dimethylamin n.
dimethylaminoazobenzene Dimethylaminoazobenzol n.

dimethylbiguanide Dimethylbiguanid n.
dimethylguanidine Dimethylguanidin n.
dimethyl sulfoxide (a) Dimethylsulfoxyd n.
− **sulphoxide** (e) Dimethylsulfoxyd n.
diminished breath sounds abgeschwächtes Atmungsgeräusch n.
diminution Verminderung f., Verkleinerung f.
dinitrate Dinitrat n.
dinitrophenol d. e. n.
dinucleotide Dinukleotid n.
diode d. e. f.
diopter Dioptrie f.
dioptry Dioptrie f.
dioxane Dioxan n.
dioxide Dioxyd n.
dipeptidase d. e. f.
dipeptide Dipeptid n.
diphasic diphasisch
diphenicillin d. e. n.
diphenyl d. e. n.
diphenylamine Diphenylamin n.
diphenylhydantoin d. e. n.
diphenylmethane Diphenylmethan n.
diphosphatase d. e. f.
diphosphate Diphosphat n.
diphosphonucleoside Diphosphonukleosid n.
diphtheria Diphtherie f.
diphtheric diphtherisch
diphtheroid d. e.
Diphyllobothrium latum Fischbandwurm m., Bothriocephalus latus
dipicrylamine Dipikrylamin n.
diplegia Diplegie f.
diplegic diplegisch
diplobacillus Diplobazillus m.
diplococcus Diplokokkus m.
diploid d. e.
diplopia Diplopie f.

dipper Löffel m.
dipsomania Dipsomanie f.
dipyridamol d. e. n.
direct direkt
dirt Kot m.
disabled person versehrte Person f.
disaccharidase d. e. f.
disaccharide Disaccharid n.
disacidify, to entsäuern
disaccustom, to entwöhnen
disappear, to verschwinden
disappearing bone disease kryptogenetische progressive Osteolyse f.
disappearance rate Abklingquote f.
disc look for:/siehe bei: disk
discharge Entlassung f., Freisetzung f.; Ausfluß m.
discharge, to entlassen, freisetzen
discission Diszission f.
discoloration (a) Verfärbung f.
discolouration (e) Verfärbung f.
discontinuation of a therapy Absetzen n. einer Therapie
discontinue a treatment, to eine Behandlung absetzen
discovery Entdeckung f.
discrepancy Diskrepanz f.
discrete diskret
discussion Diskussion f.
disdain, to verschmähen
disease Krankheit f.
disequilibrium Gleichgewichtsstörung f.
disfigure, to entstellen
disgust, to ekeln, verekeln
disgusting widerlich
dish Schüssel f., Schale f.
—, evaporating Abdampfschale f.
—, kidney Nierenschale f.
—, Petri Petrischale f.
disinfect, to desinfizieren
disinfectant desinfizierend; Desinfektionsmittel n.
disinfection Desinfektion f.

disinfestation Entwesung f.; Entlausung f.
disinhibition Enthemmung f.
disinsectization Insektenvernichtung f.
disintegration Desintegration f.
disk Scheibe f.
disk, choked Stauungspapille f.
dislocate, to dislozieren, ausrenken
dislocation Dislokation f.
— of (lateral/mesial) articular cartilage of the knee Dislokation des (lateralen/medialen) Meniskus am Knie
dismiss, to entlassen
dismissal Entlassung f.
dismissal slip Entlassungsschein m.
dismutase d. e. f.
disodium salt Dinatriumsalz n.
disopyramide Disopyramid n.
disorder Unordnung f.
disorganization Desorganisation f., Zerrüttung f.
disorientation Desorientierung f., Desorientiertheit f.
disoriented desorientiert
dispareunia Dispareunie f.
dispensary Dispensarium n., Krankenhausapotheke f.
dispense, to dispensieren
dispensing Rezeptur f.
disperse dispers
dispersion d. e. f.
dispersonalization Entpersönlichung f.
displacement Verlagerung f., Verdrängung f.
disposition d. e. f.
disproportion Mißverhältnis n.
disproportional d. e.
Disse, space of Dissescher Raum m.
dissect, to sezieren, präparieren (anatom.)
dissecting set Präparierbesteck n.

dissection Leichensektion f.
disseminated disseminiert
dissemination d. e. f.
dissertation d. e. f.
dissimilate, to dissimilieren, abbauen
dissimilation d. e. f., Abbau m.
dissociate, to dissoziieren
dissociation Dissoziation f.
dissolution Auflösung f., Lösung f.
dissolve, to auflösen, lösen
distad distalwärts
distal d. e.
distance Distanz f.
distemper Hundestaupe f.
distention Ausdehnung f.
distil, to destillieren
distillate Destillat n.
distillation Destillation f.
distilling apparatus Destillierapparat m.
distoangular distoangulär
distobuccal distobukkal
distobuccoocclusal distobukkookklusal
distobuccopulpal distobukkopulpal
distocclusion Distokklusion f.
distolabial d. e.
distolingual d. e.
distomiasis d. e. f.
distomolar d. e.
distortion Distorsion f.
distoversion d. e. f.
distract, to zerstreuen
distraction Zerstreuung f.
distress Elend n., Not f., Bedrängnis f.
distribution Verteilung f.
distributor Verteiler m.
disturb, to stören
disturbance Störung f.
disulfate (a) Disulfat n.
disulfide (a) Disulfid n
disulphate (e) Disulfat n.
disulphide (e) Disulfid n.

dithiocarbamoylhydrazine Dithiokarbamoylhydrazin n.
dithiol d. e. n.
dithizone Dithizon n.
Dittrich's plugs Dittrichsche Pfröpfe m. pl.
diuresis Diurese f.
diuretic diuretisch; Diureticum n.
divalent bivalent, zweiwertig
diver Taucher m.
divergence Divergenz f.
divergent d. e.
diversion Umleitung f.
diverticulitis d. e. f.
diverticulosis Divertikulose f.
diverticulum Divertikel n.
division Teilung f.
dizziness leichter Schwindel m.
DNA Desoxyribonukleinsäure f.
doctor Doktor m., Arzt m.; Doktorin f., Ärztin f.
doctor in attendance diensttuender Arzt m., diensttuende Ärztin f.
doctor's office Arztpraxis f., Praxisräume m. pl. des Arztes
doctor's report Arztbericht m.
doe Ricke f.
Döderlein's bacillus Döderleinscher Bazillus m.
Döhle's inclusion body Döhlesches Einschlußkörperchen n.
dog Hund m.
dog-bite Hundebiß m.
dogmatic dogmatisch
Dold's test Doldscher Test m.
dolichocephalic dolichozephal
dolphin Delphin m.
dome of diaphragm Zwerchfellkuppel f.
domiciliary häuslich
dominance Dominanz f.
dominant d. e.
Donath-Landsteiner test Donath-Landsteinerscher Test m.
donator Spender m.

donee Empfänger m., Empfängerin f.
donkey Esel m.
donor Spender m., Spenderin f.
dopa d. e. n.
dopamine Dopamin n.
dopaoxidase Dopaoxydase f.
dope Aufputschmittel n.
doping Aufputschen n.
dormancy Ruhestadium n.
dormouse Haselmaus f.
dorsad dorsalwärts
dorsal d. e.
dorsoanterior d. e.
dorsoposterior d. e.
dorsoradial d. e.
dosage Dosierung f.
–, high hohe Dosierung f.
–, increased erhöhte Dosierung f.
–, low niedrige Dosierung f.
–, reduced erniedrigte Dosierung f.
dose Dosis f.
– -dependent dosisabhängig
–, effective Wirkungsdosis f.
–, incident Einfallsdosis f.
–, protective Schutzdosis f.
– -related dosisbezogen, dosisabhängig
dosimeter d. e. n.
dosimetric dosimetrisch
dosimetry Dosimetrie f.
dot Fleck m., Tupfen m.
dotage Vergreisung f., senile Geistesschwäche f.
dotard geistesschwacher Greis m.
double blind study Doppelblindversuch m.
double blind trial Doppelblindversuch m.
douche Dusche f.
Douglas' cul-de-sac Douglasscher Raum m.
dourine Beschälseuche f.
Dover's powder Doversches Pulver v.
dowel crown Stiftzahn m.
doxepin d. e. n.

doxycycline Doxycyclin n.
draft (a) Trank m.; Zugluft f.
dragée d. e. n.
drain d. e. m.
drainage d. e. f.
– clip Drainageklammer f.
dramatic dramatisch
drastic drastisch; drastisches Abführmittel n.
draught (e) Trank m.; Zugluft f.
draw off, to entziehen, ableiten
dream Traum m.
dream, to träumen
drench (veter.) Trank m.
drepanocyte Drepanozyt m.
dress, to anziehen; verbinden
dressing Verband m.
– drum Verbandstofftrommel f.
– forceps Kornzange f.
–, occlusive Okklusivverband m.
Dreuw's paste Dreuwsche Paste f.
Drigalski medium Drigalski-Nährboden m.
drill Bohrer m.
drink Getränk n.
drink, to trinken
drip, to tröpfeln
– intravenous intravenöse Dauertropfinfusion f.
driving ability Fahrtauglichkeit f.
dromedary Dromedar n.
dromotropic dromotrop
drop Tropfen m.
drop, to tropfen, tröpfeln
– in, to einträufeln
droplet Tröpfchen n.
dropper Tropfer m.
dropping bottle Tropfflasche f.
drop seizure Sturzanfall m.
drop tube Tropfrohr n.
dropsical wassersüchtig
dropsy Wassersucht f.
drostanolone Drostanolon n.
drown, to ertränken
drowned, to be – ertrinken
drug Droge f., Arzneiware f.

drug, delayed action – Depot-Arzneimittel n., Retard-Arzneimittel n.
drug, slow release Depot-Arzneimittel n., Retard-Arzneimittel n.
drug addiction Arzneimittelsucht f.
drug dependence Arzneimittelabhängigkeit f.
druggist Drogist m., Apotheker m.; Drogistin f., Apothekerin f.
drug induced arzneimittelinduziert, arzneimittelbedingt
drug reaction Arzneimittelreaktion f.
– **resistance** Arzneimittelresistenz f.
– **store** (a) Apotheke f.
– **therapy** Arzneimitteltherapie f., Pharmakotherapie f.
drum Trommel f.; Mittelohr n.
drunkard Säufer m., Trinker m.; Trinkerin f.
drunken betrunken
drunkenness Trunkenheit f., Rausch m.
druse d. e. f.
dry trocken
– **cough** Reizhusten m.
drying oven Trockenschrank m.
dual d. e.
dualism Dualismus m.
dualistic dualistisch
Dubin-Johnson syndrome Dubin-Johnson-Syndrom n.
duck Ente f.
duct Gang m., Durchgang m.
ductless gland endokrine Drüse f.
dull dumm; dumpf, gedämpft
dulness Dämpfung f.
dumb stumm
dumdum fever tropische Splenomegalie f.
dump, to auswerfen, ausstoßen
dumping syndrome Dumpingsyndrom n.
duodenal d. e.

duodenal papilla Vatersche Papille f.
– **ulcer** Zwölffingerdarmgeschwür n.
duodenitis d. e. f.
duodenobiliary duodenobiliär
duodenocholecystostomy Duodenocholezystostomie f.
duodenocholedochotomy Duodenocholedochotomie f.
duodenojejunal d. e.
duodenoscopic duodenoskopisch
duodenoscopy Duodenoskopie f.
duodenostomy Duodenostomie f.
duodenum d. e. n., Zwölffingerdarm m.
duplication Verdoppelung f.
Dupuytren's contraction Dupuytrensche Kontraktur f.
durable dauerhaft
dural d. e.
duraplasty Duraplastik f.
duration Dauer f.
duration of survival Überlebensdauer f.
Duroziez's sign Duroziezsches Doppelgeräusch n.
dust Staub m.
dwarf Zwerg m.
dwarfishness Zwergwuchs m.
dwarfism Zwergwuchs m.
dye Farbe f., Farbstoff m.
dye-dilution curve Farbstoffverdünnungskurve f.
dye, to färben
dynamic dynamisch
dynamics Dynamik f.
dynamo d. e. m.
dynamometer d. e. n.
dysacousia Dysakusis f.
dysarthria Dysarthrie f.
dysbasia Dysbasie f.
dyschezia Dyschezie f.
dyscrasia Dyskrasie f.
dyscrasic dyskrasisch
dysdiadokokinesia Dysdiadochokinesie f.

dysenteric dysenterisch
dysentery Dysenterie f., Ruhr f.
–, bacillary Bazillenruhr f.
–, amoebic (e) Amöbenruhr f.
–, amebic (a) Amöbenruhr f.
dysergia Dysergie f.
dysergic dysergisch
dysergy Dysergie f.
dysergy, neurovegetative vegetative Neurodysergie f., vegetative Dystonie f.
dysfunction Dysfunktion f.
dysgenesia Dysgenesie f.
dysgerminoma Dysgerminom n.
dyshidrosis Dyshidrose f.
dyshidrotic dyshidrotisch
dyshormonal dyshormonell
dyskeratosis Dyskeratose f.
dyskinesia Dyskinesie f.
dyskinetic dyskinetisch
dyslexia Dyslexie f.
dysmenorrhea (a) Dysmenorrhöe f.
dysmenorrhoea (e) Dysmenorrhöe f.
dysostosis Dysostose f.
dysovarism Dysovarismus m.
dyspareunia Dyspareunie f.
dyspepsia Dyspepsie f.
dyspeptic dyspeptisch
dysphagia Dysphagie f.
dysphasia Dysphasie f., Sprachstörung f.

dyspituitarism Hypophysenstörung f.
dysplasia Dysplasie f.
dysplastic dysplastisch
dyspnea (a) Dyspnöe f.
– on exertion (a) Belastungsdyspnoe f.
dyspneic (a) dyspnoisch
dyspnoea (e) Dyspnöe f.
– on exertion (e) Belastungsdyspnoe f.
dyspnoic (e) dyspnoisch
dyspraxia Dyspraxie f.
dysprosium d. e. n.
dysproteinaemia (e) Dysproteinämie f.
dysproteinemia (a) Dysproteinämie f.
dysrhaphic dysrhaphisch
dysrhythmia Dysrhythmie f.
dysrhythmic dysrhythmisch
dyssynergia Dyssynergie f.
dysthymia Dysthymie f.; Melancholie f.
dysthyreosis Dysthyreose f.
dystonia Dystonie f.
dystonic dystonisch
dystopy Dystopie f.
dystopic dystopisch
dystrophy Dystrophie f.
dystrophic dystrophisch
dysuria Dysurie f.
dysuric dysurisch

E

eager gierig
eagerness Gier f.
ear Ohr n.
–, prominent abstehendes Ohr n.
earache Ohrschmerz m.
ear-cap Ohrenklappe f.
ear-drum Mittelohr n.; Trommelfell n.

earlap Ohrläppchen n.
early detection Früherkennung f., Frühentdeckung f.
earth connection Erdung f.
ear-trumpet Hörrohr n.
ear-wax Ohrenschmalz n.
eat, to essen
eatable eßbar, genießbar

Eberthella typhosa Typhusbazillus m.
Ebstein's anomaly Ebsteinsche Anomalie f.
eccentric exzentrisch
ecchondroma Ekchondrom n.
ecchymosis Ekchymose f.
eccrine exkretorisch
e.c.g. (= electrocardiogram) EKG (Elektrokardiogramm)
ecgonine Ekgonin n.
echinococcosis Echinokokkose f.
echinococcus Echinokokkus m.
echinuriosis Echinuriose f.
echo d. e. n.
echocardiographical echokardiographisch
echocardiography Echokardiographie f.
echoencephalography Echoenzephalographie f.
echographic echographisch
echography Echographie f.
echoscopic echoskopisch
echoscopy Echoskopie f.
echosonic echosonisch
echotomography Echo-Tomographie f.
ECHO-virus ECHO-Virus n.
Eck's fistula Ecksche Fistel f.
eclampsia Eklampsie f.
eclamptic eklamptisch
ecology (a) Ökologie f.
economy Ökonomie f.
ectasy Ektasie f.
ecthyma Ekthym n.
ectoderm Ektoderm n.
ectodermal ektodermal
ectoglia Ektoglia f.
ectomy Ektomie f., Ausschneidung f.
ectoparasite Ektoparasit m.
ectopic ektopisch
– **beat** Extrasystole f.
ectoplasm Ektoplasma n.
ectopy Ektopie f.
ectropion Ektropion n.

ectropionize, to ektropionieren
eczema Ekzem n.
eczematization Ekzematisierung f.
eczematous ekzematös
edema (a) Ödem n.
–, **malignant** (a) malignes Ödem n.
–, **pulmonary** (a) Lungenödem n.
edematous (a) ödematös
edentulous zahnlos
edetate Edetat n.
edible eßbar
Edinger's nucleus Edingerscher Kern m.
edulcorate, to süßen
e.e.g. (= electroencephalogram) EEG (= Elektroenzephalogramm)
eelworm Spulwurm m.
efface, to auswischen
effect Effekt m., Wirkung f.
–, **protective** Schutzwirkung f.
effect, to bewirken
effective effektiv
effectiveness Wirksamkeit f.
effectiveness, loss of Wirkungsverlust m.
effemination Verweiblichung f.
efferent d. e.
effervescent powder Brausepulver n.
efficiency Leistungsfähigkeit f.
–, **masticatory** Kautüchtigkeit f.
efficient leistungsfähig
efflorescence Effloreszenz f.
effort Anstrengung f.
effusion Erguß m.
– **of blood** Bluterguß m.
egg Ei n.
egg cell Eizelle f.
egocentric egozentrisch
egophony (a) Ägophonie f.
Ehrlich's reaction Ehrlichsche Reaktion f.
eidetical eidetisch
Eisenmenger complex Eisenmengerkomplex m.
ejaculate Ejakulat n.
ejaculation Ejakulation f.

ejection time Austreibungszeit f.
ejector, apical fragment Wurzelspitzenheber m.
ektebin d. e. n.
elaidin d. e. n.
elaidinize, to elaidinisieren
elastase d. e. f.
elastic elastisch
– tissue elastisches Gewebe n.
elasticity Elastizität f.
elastin d. e. n.
elastinase d. e. f.
elastogenesis Elastogenese f.
elastolysate Elastolysat n.
elastomer d. e. n.
elastometer d. e. n.
elastoproteinase d. e. f.
elastosis Elastose f.
elbow Ellenbogen m.
elbow, capped (veter.) Ellenbogenhygrom n.
elective elektiv
electric elektrisch
– shock Elektroschock m.
– torch Taschenlampe f.
electricity Elektrizität f.
electrify, to elektrifizieren
electrization Elektrisierung f.
electroanalysis Elektroanalyse f.
electroanalytic elektroanalytisch
electrobiological elektrobiologisch
electrobiology Elektrobiologie f.
electrocardiogram Elektrokardiogramm n.
electrocardiograph Elektrokardiograph m.
electrocardiographic elektrokardiographisch
electrocardiography Elektrokardiographie f.
 (lead I–II–III) (Ableitung I–II–III)
 (P-wave) (P-Zacke f.)
 (QRS-complex) (QRS-Komplex m.)
 (T-wave) (T-Zacke f.)

electrocardiophonography Elektrokardiophonographie f. elektrische Herzschallschreibung f.
electrocautery Elektrokauter m.
electrocoagulation Elektrokoagulation f.
electrode Elektrode f.
electrode, coagulation – Koagulationselektrode f.
electroencephalogram Elektroenzephalogramm n.
electroencephalograph Elektroenzephalograph m.
electroencephalographic elektroenzephalographisch
electroencephalography Elektroenzephalographie f.
electroenterography Elektroenterographie f.
electrolysis Elektrolyse f.
electrolyte Elektrolyt m.
electrolytic elektrolytisch
electromagnet Elektromagnet m.
electromagnetic elektromagnetisch
electromassage Elektromassage f.
electrometer Elektrometer n.
electromicroscope Elektronenmikroskop n.
electromyographical elektromyographisch
electromyography Elektromyographie f.
electron Elektron n.
–, fast schnelles Elektron n.
– microscope Elektronenmikroskop n.
electronarcosis Elektronarkose f.
electronegative elektronegativ
electroneurolysis Elektroneurolyse f.
electronic elektronisch
electro-nystagmography Elektronystagmographie f.
electrophoresis Elektrophorese f.

electrophoresis, continuous flow Durchflußelektrophorese f.
—, filter paper Papierelektrophorese f.
—, high voltage Hochspannungselektrohprese f.
electrophoretic elektrophoretisch
electrophotometer Elektrophotometer n.
electrophotometry Elektrophotometrie f.
electrophysiological elektrophysiologisch
electrophysiology Elektrophysiologie f.
electroplating bath Galvanisierbad n.
electropositive elektropositiv
electroretinography Elektroretinographie f.
electrospectrography Elektrospektrographie f.
electrostatic elektrostatisch
electrosurgery Elektrochirurgie f.
electrosurgical elektrochirurgisch
electrotherapeutical elektrotherapeutisch
electrotherapeutist Elektrotherapeut m.
electrotherapy Elektrotherapie f.
electrothermometer Elektrothermometer n.
electrotonic elektrotonisch
electrotonus Elektrotonus m.
electuary Elektuarium n.
element d. e. n.
elementary elementar
elephant Elefant m.
elephantiasic elephantiastisch
elephantiasis d. e. f.
elevate, to elevieren
elevation d. e. f., Anhebung f., Hochlagerung f.
elevator d. e. m.
eliminase d. e. f.
eliminate, to eliminieren
elimination d. e. f.

elixir Elixier n.
ellipsoid joint Ellipsoidgelenk n.
elliptical elliptisch
elliptocyte Elliptozyt m.
elliptocytosis Elliptozytose f.
elute, to eluieren, auswaschen
elution d. e. f.
emaciated abgemagert
emaciation Abmagerung f.
emanation d. e. f.
enarthrosis Enarthrose f., Nußgelenk n.
enbalming Einbalsamierung f.
embed, to einbetten
embedding Einbettung f.
embitter, to vergällen
embolectomy Embolektomie f.
embolic embolisch
embolism Embolie
embolus d. e. m.
embrasure Interdentalraum m.
embrocate, to einreiben
embrocation Einreibung f.
embryocardia Embryokardie f.
embryogeny Embryogenese f.
embryological embryologisch
embryologist Embryologe m., Embryologin f.
embryology Embryologie f.
embryoma Embryom n.
embryonal d. e.
embryonary embryonal
embryotomy Embryotomie f.
emedullate, to entmarken
emergency Notlage f., Dringlichkeit f.
emergency dressing Notverband m.
emergency endoscopy Notfallendoskopie f.
emergency measure Sofortmaßnahme f.
emergent dringlich, notfallmäßig
emery Schmirgel m.
emetic emetisch; Brechmittel n.
emetine Emetin n.
eminence Vorwölbung f.
emission d. e. f.

emission computed tomography
Emissionscomputertomographie f.
emmetropia Emmetropie f.
emmetropic emmetrop
emodin d. e. n.
emollient weichmachend; weichmachendes Mittel n.
emotion d. e. f., Gemütsbewegung f.
emotional emotionell
– **stability** ausgeglichene Gemütsverfassung f.
emphysema Emphysem n.
–,**pulmonary** Lungenemphysem n.
emphysematous emphysematös
empiric empirisch; Empiriker m. Empirikerin f.
empiricism Empirie f.; Quacksalberei f.
empty leer
empyema Empyem n.
emulsify, to emulgieren
emulsion d. e. f.
enamel (med.) Zahnschmelz m.
– **cleaver** Schmelzspalter m.
– **hatchet** Schmelzmesser n.
–,**mottled** gesprenkelter Zahnschmelz m.
enanthema Enanthem n.
enanthematous enanthematös
enantiomorphic enantiomorph
enarthrosis Enarthrose f.
en bloc d. e.
encapsulate, to einkapseln, verkapseln
encapsulation Einkapselung f., Verkapselung f.
enceinte schwanger
encephalitic enzephalitisch
encephalitis Enzephalitis f.
encephaloarteriography Enzephaloarteriographie f.
encephalocele Enzephalocele f.
encephalogram Enzephalogramm n.
encephalograph Enzephalograph m.
encephalographic enzephalographisch
encephalography Enzephalographie f.
encephalomalacia Enzephalomalazie f.
encephalomeningitis Enzephalomeningitis f.
encephalomyelitis Enzephalomyelitis f.
–,**equine** Bornasche Krankheit f.
encephalopathy Enzephalopathie f.
encephalosis Enzephalose f.
encephalotrigeminal enzephalotrigeminal
enchondroma Enchondrom n.
enchondromatosis Enchondromatose f.
encopresis Stuhlinkontinenz f.
end Ende n.
end, to beendigen
Endamoeba histolytica Entamoeba histolytica
endangiitis d. e. f.
endarterectomy Endarterektomie f.
endarteritis Endarteriitis f.
end-artery Endarterie f.
end diastolic enddiastolisch
endemic endemisch; Endemie f.
endexpiratory endexspiratorisch
ending Endigung f.
endoantitoxin d. e. n.
endocardial endokardial
endocarditic endokarditisch
endocarditis Endokarditis f.
–,**subacute bacterial** Endokarditis lenta
endocardium Endokard n.
endocellular intrazellulär
endocervical endozervikal
endocochlear endokochleär
endocranial endokranial
endocrine endokrin
endocrinological endokrinologisch

endocrinologist Endokrinologe m., Endokrinologin f.
endocrinology Endokrinologie f.
endocrinous endokrin
endocytosis Endozytose f.
endodontia Endodontie f.
endoenzyme Endoenzym n.
endogenous endogen
endognathion d. e. n.
endolabyrinthitis d. e. f.
endolaryngeal d. e.
endolumbar endolumbal
endolymph Endolymphe f.
endometrial d. e.
endometriosis Endometriose f.
endometritis Endometritis f.
endometrium d. e. n.
endomyocarditis Endomyokarditis f.
endonasal d. e.
endoneural d. e.
endoperitoneal d. e.
endoperoxide Endoperoxid n.
endophlebitis d. e. f.
endophthalmitis d. e. f.
endophyte Endophyt m.
endoplasm Endoplasma n.
endoplasmic endoplasmatisch
end-organ Endorgan n.
endosalpingitis d. e. f.
endoscope Endoskop n.
endoscopic endoskopisch
endoscopy Endoskopie f.
endosecretory innersekretorisch
Endo's medium Endo-Nährboden m.
endosmosis Endosmose f.
endosteitis Endostitis f.
endosteoma Endosteom n.
endothelial d. e.
endotheliitis d. e. f.
endothelioblastoma Endothelioblastom n.
endothelioma Endotheliom n.
endotheliosis Endotheliose f.
endotoxic endotoxisch
endotoxin d. e. n.

endotracheal d. e.
– anaesthesia (e) Endotrachealnarkose f.
– anesthesia (a) Endotrachealnarkose f.
endourethral d. e.
endouterine endouterin
endovenous intravenös
endovesical endovesikal
end-plate Endplatte f.
end to end anastomosis End-zu-End-Anastomose f.
– to side anastomosis End-zu-Seit-Anastomose f.
endure, to erdulden, aushalten, ertragen
enema Klistier n.
energetic energetisch
energetics Energielehre f.
energy Energie f.
enervate, to entnerven
engagement (obst.) Geburtsbeginn m.
engine, dental zahnärztliche Bohrmaschine f.
engram Engramm n.
enhance, to erhöhen
enjoyment Genuß m.
enlargement Verbreitung f.
enol d. e. n.
enolase d. e. f.
enophthalmos Enophthalmus m.
enostosis Enostose f.
enrich, to anreichern
enrichment Anreicherung f.
enrol, to immatrikulieren
ensanguino-transfusion Eigenblutübertragung f.
ENT (= ear, nose, throat) HNO (= Hals, Nase, Ohren)
entelechy Entelechie f.
enteral d. e.
enteritis d. e. f.
enteroanastomosis Enteroanastomose f.
enterobiliary enterobiliär

Enterobius vermicularis Oxyuris vermicularis
enterocele d. e. f.
enterocholecystostomy Enterocholezystostomie f.
enterocholecystotomy Enterocholezystotomie f.
enterococcus Enterokokkus m.
enterocolitis d. e. f.
enterocolostomy Enterocolostomie f.
enteroglucagon Enteroglukagon n.
enterohepatic enterohepatisch
enterohepatitis d. e. f.
enterohormone Enterohormon n.
enterokinase d. e. f.
enterolithiasis d. e. f.
enterology Enterologie f.
enteropathy Enteropathie f.
–, protein-losing eiweißverlierende Enteropathie f.
enteropexy Enteropexie f.
enteroptosis Enteroptose f.
enterorrhaphy Darmnaht f., Enterorrhaphie f.
enterostomy Enterostomie f.
enterotomy Enterotomie f.
enterotoxin d. e. n.
enterovirus d. e. n.
entity Sein n., Dasein n., Entität f.
entocone Entokon m.
entoconid Entokonid m.
entoderm d. e. n.
entomology Entomologie f.
entrails Eingeweide n. pl.
entropion d. e. n.
enucleate, to enukleieren
enucleation Enukleation f.
enumeration Auszählung f.
enuresis d. e. f.
environment Umwelt f.
encironment protection Umweltschutz m.
environmental conditions Umweltbedingungen f. pl.
enzootic enzootisch

enzymatic enzymatisch
enzyme Enzym n.
enzymic regulation Enzymregulation f.
enzymology Enzymologie f.
enzymolysis Enzymolyse f.
eosin d. e. n.
eosinopenia Eosinopenie f.
eosinophil eosinophiler Leukozyt m.
eosinophile eosinophil
eosinophilia Eosinophilie f.
eosinophilic eosinophil
eosinophilous eosinophil
ependyma Ependym n.
ependymal d. e.
ependymitis d. e. f.
ependymoma Ependymom n.
ephedrine Ephedrin n.
ephemeral ephemer
ephetonine Ephetonin n.
epicanthus d. e. m.
epicardia Epikardia f.
epicardial epikardial
epicardiectomy Epikardiektomie f.
epicardium Epikard n.
epicarin d. e. n.
epicillin d. e. n.
epicondylitis d. e. f.
epicrisis Epikrise f.
epicritic epikritisch
epidemic epidemisch; Epidemie f.
epidemiological epidemiologisch
epidemiology Epidemiologie f.
epidermal d. e.
epidermis d. e. f.
epidermolysis Epidermolyse f.
epidermophytid d. e. n.
epidermophytosis Epidermophytose f.
epidiascope Epidiaskop n.
epididymis Nebenhoden m.
epididymitis d. e. f.
epididymoorchitis d. e. f.
epidural d. e.
epigastric epigastrisch
epiglottic epiglottisch

epiglottis d. e. f.
epignathus d. e. m.
epilation d. e. f.
epilatory epilatorisch, haarentfernend; Haarentfernungsmittel n.
epilepsy Epilepsie f.
—, jacksonian Jackson-Epilepsie f.
epileptic epileptisch
epileptiform d. e.
epileptogenic epileptogen
epileptoid d. e.
epinephrine Suprarenin n.
epineural d. e.
epipharyngitis d. e. f.
epiphora d. e. f.
epiphyseal epiphysär
— separation Epiphysenlösung f.
epiphysiolysis Epiphysiolyse f.
epiphysis Epiphyse f.
epiphysitis d. e. f.
epiplocele d. e. f.
epiplopexy Epiplopexie f., Netzanheftung f.
episcleral episkleral
episcleritis Episkleritis f.
episcope Episkop n.
episioplasty Dammplastik f.
episiorrhaphy Dammnaht f.
episiotomy Episiotomie f., Dammschnitt m.
episode, schizophrenic schizophrener Schub m.
epispadias Epispadie f.
epistaxis d. e. f., Nasenbluten n.
epistemology Erkenntnistheorie f.
episternal d. e.
epitestosterone Epitestosteron n.
epithalamic epithalamisch
epithelial d. e.
epithelioma Epitheliom n.
—, basal Basalzellenepitheliom n.
—, squamous Deckzellenepitheliom n.
epitheliosis Epitheliose f.
epithelium Epithel n.

epithelium, ciliated Flimmerepithel n.
—, columnar Zylinderepithel n.
—, cubical kubisches Epithel n.
—, germinal Keimepithel n.
—, glandular Drüsenepithel n.
—, pavement Plasterepithel n.
—, squamous Plattenepithel n.
—, stratified mehrschichtiges Epithel n.
epithelization Epithelisierung f.
epituberculosis Epituberkulose f.
epizootic epizootisch
epulis d. e. f.
equation Gleichung f.
equilibration Äquilibrierung f.
equilibriometry Äquilibriometrie f.
equilibrium Gleichgewicht n.
equimolecular äquimolekular
equine equin
equinia Malleus m.
equipment Ausrüstung f.
equivalence Äquivalenz f.
equivalent äquivalent; Äquivalent n.
eradicate, to ausrotten
eradication Ausrottung f.
erbium d. e. n.
Erb's paralysis Erbsche Lähmung f.
— point Erbscher Punkt m.
— sign Erbsches Zeichen n.
ERCP (= endoscopic retrograde cholangiopancreaticography) endoskopische retrograde Cholangiopankreatikographie f. (ERCP)
erect, to aufrichten
erection Erektion f.
erepsin d. e. n.
erethism Erethismus m.
erethistic erethisch
erg d. e. n.
ergochrysin d. e. n.
ergoclavine Ergoclavin n.
ergocornine Ergocornin n.

ergocristine Ergocristin n.
ergograph d. e. m.
ergographic ergographisch
ergography Ergographie f.
ergokryptine Ergokryptin n.
ergometer d. e. n.
ergometric ergometrisch
ergometrine Ergometrin n.
ergometrinine Ergometrinin n.
ergometry Ergometrie f.
ergomonamine Ergomonamin n.
ergonomics Ergonomie f.
ergonovine Ergometrin n.
ergosine Ergosin n.
ergosinine Ergosinin n.
ergospirometric ergospirometrisch
ergospirometry Ergospirometrie f.
ergosterol Ergosterin n.
ergot Mutterkorn n.
ergotamine Ergotamin n.
ergotaminine Ergotaminin n.
ergothioneine Ergothionein n.
ergotine Ergotin n.
ergotinine Ergotinin n.
ergotism Ergotismus m.
ergotoxine Ergotoxin n.
ergotropic ergotrop
Erlenmeyer flask Erlenmeyerkolben m.
erogenous erogen
erosion d. e. f.
erotic erotisch
erotomania Erotomanie f.
error range Fehlerbereich m.
eructation Rülpsen n.
eruption d. e. f., Ausbruch m.
– of a tooth Zahndurchbruch m.
eruptive eruptiv
erysipelas Erysipel n.
erysipeloid d. e. n., Schweinerotlauf m.
Erysipelothrix insidiosa d. e.
erythema Erythem n.
erythematous erythematös
erythraemia (e) Erythrämie f.
erythraemic (e) erythrämisch
erythrasma d. e. n.

erythremia (a) Erythrämie f.
erythremic (a) erythrämisch
erythroblast d. e. m.
erythroblastic erythroblastisch
– anaemia (e) Erythroblastenanämie f.
– anemia (a) Erythroblastenanämie f.
erythroblastosis Erythroblastose f.
erythrocyanosis Erythrozyanose f.
erythrocyte Erythrozyt m.
erythrocytic erythrozytär
erythrocytosis Erythrozytose f.
erythroderma Erythrodermie f.
erythrokinetic erythrokinetisch
erythroleukaemia (e) Erythroleukämie f.
erythroleukemia (a) Erythroleukämie f.
erythrol tetranitrate Erythroltetranitrat n.
erythromelalgia Erythromelalgie f.
erythromelia Erythromelie f.
erythromycin d. e. n.
erythrophagocytosis Erythrophagozytose f.
erythropia Rotsehen n.
erythropoiesis Erythropoese f.
erythropoietic erythropoetisch
erythrose d. e. f. (chem.)
erythrosis Erythrose f. (dermatol.)
erythrulose d. e. f.
erythruria Erythrurie f.
Esbach's reagent Esbachsches Reagens n.
escape beat Ersatzschlag m.
eschar Schorf m.
escharotic ätzend; ätzendes Mittel n.
Escherichia coli Colibazillus m., Bacillus coli communis
esculent eßbar
esculin (a) Äsculin n.
eserine Eserin n.
Esmarch's bandage Esmarchsche Binde f.
esodic zentripetal

esophagectasia (a) Speiseröhrenektasie f.
esophagitis (a) Ösophagitis f., Speiseröhrenentzündung f.
esophagoduodenostomy (a) Ösophagoduodenostomie f.
esophagogastrostomy (a) Ösophagogastrostomie f.
esophagojejunogastrostomy (a) Ösophagojejunogastrostomie f.
esophagoplasty (a) Speiseröhrenplastik f.
esophagoscope (a) Ösophagoskop n.
esophagoscopical (a) ösophagoskopisch
esophagoscopy (a) Ösophagoskopie f.
esophagostomy (a) Ösophagostomie f.
esophagus (a) Ösophagus m., Speiseröhre f.
esotric esoterisch
ESR (= erythrocyte sedimentation rate) BSG (= Blutsenkungsgeschwindigkeit)
essence Essenz f.
essential essentiell; wesentlich
establishment Anstalt f., Einrichtung f.
ester d. e. m.
esterase d. e. f.
esterification Veresterung f.
esterify, to verestern
esterize, to verestern
esterolysis Esterolyse f.
esterolytic esterolytisch
esthetical (a) ästhetisch
estimation Bestimmung f.
estivoautumnal malaria (a) Malaria tropica
estradiol (a) Östradiol n.
estrane (a) Östran n.
estrangement Entfremdung f.
estriol (a) Östriol n.
estrogen (a) Östrogen n.
estrogenic (a) östrogen

estrone (a) Östron n.
ethambutol Äthambutol n.
ethane Äthan n.
ethanol Äthylalkohol m.
ether Äther m.
 – for anaesthesia (e) Narkoseäther m.
 – for anesthesia (a) Narkoseäther m.
ethical ethisch
ethinyl Äthinyl n.
ethionamide Äthionamid n.
ethmoid bone Siebbein n.
ethmoidal d. e.
ethmoiditis d. e. f.
ethnographic ethnographisch
ethnography Ethnographie f.
ethnological ethnologisch
ethnology Ethnologie f.
ethyl Äthyl n.
 – alcohol Äthylalkohol m.
 – chloride Chloräthyl n.
ethylation Äthylierung f.
ethylene Äthylen n.
ethylenediamine Äthylendiamin n.
ethyleneimino group Äthylenimino-Gruppe f.
ethylism Äthylismus m.
ethylmorphine hydrochloride Äthylmorphinhydrochlorid n.
etiandiolone Ätiandiolon n.
etianolone Ätianolon n.
etiologic (a) ätiologisch
etiology (a) Ätiologie f.
etioporphyrin Ätioporphyrin n.
eucalyptol Eukalyptol n.
eucalyptus Eukalyptus m.
eucapnia Eukapnie f.
euchinine Euchinin n.
eugenic eugenisch
eugenics Eugenik f.
eugenol d. e. n.
eugenolate Eugenolat n.
euglobulin d. e. n.
eumetabolic eumetabolisch, stoffwechselgesund
eumydrine Eumydrin n.

eunuch d. e. m.
eunuchoid d. e.
eunuchoidism Eunuchoidismus m.
eupeptic eupeptisch
euphoria Euphorie f.
euphoric euphorisch
euphoristic euphorisierend
eurhythmia Eurhythmie f.
eurhythmic eurhythmisch
europium d. e. n.
eustachian tube Eustachische Röhre f.
eutectic eutektisch; Eutektikum m.
euthanasia Euthanasie f.
evacuation Entleerung f.
evagination Ausstülpung f.
evaluate, to auswerten
evaluation Auswertung f.
Evan's blue Evan-Blau n.
evaporate, to verdampfen, evaporieren
evaporation Verdampfung f.
even gerade, gleichmäßig, eben
eventration d. e. f.
eversion Umstülpung f., Auswärtsdrehung f.
evert, to umstülpen, auswärtsdrehen
every hour stündlich
evidence Evidenz f., Klarheit f.
evidence, medical ärztliches Gutachten n.
evident d. e.
eviration Entmannung f.
evisceration Eviszeration f.
evolution d. e. f., Entwicklung f.
evolutive evolutiv
Ewald's test meal Ewaldsches Probefrühstück n.
Ewing's tumor (a) Ewing-Tumor m.
– tumour (e) Ewing-Tumor m.
exacerbation Exazerbation f.
exacrinous exokrin
exact exakt, genau
exaggerate, to übertreiben

exaltation d. e. f.
examination Prüfung f., Untersuchung f.
examine, to prüfen, untersuchen
– by the microscope, to mikroskopisch untersuchen
examinee Prüfling m.
examiner Prüfer m., Prüferin f., Untersuchender m., Untersuchende f.
exanthem d. e. n.
exanthema Exanthem n.
exanthema, vesicular Exanthema vesculosum, Bläschenausschlag m.
exanthematous exanthematisch
exarticulation Exartikulation f.
excavation Exkavation f.
excavator Exkavator m.
exceed, to überschreiten, übertreffen
excentric exzentrisch
excerebration Enthirnung f., Exzerebration f.
excess Exzeß m., Übermaß n., Überschuß m.
exchangeable auswechselbar
exchangeable lenses Auswechseloptik f.
exchanger Austauscher m.
exchange transfusion Austauschtransfusion f.
excise, to exzidieren, ausschneiden
excision Exzision f., Ausschneidung f.
–, exploratory Probeexzision f.
excitability Erregbarkeit f.
excitable erregbar
excitant Erregungsmittel n.
excitation Erregung f.
excite, to erregen
excited, to be – aufgeregt sein
excitement Aufregung f.
excitatory erregend
exclusion Ausschaltung f., Ausschluß m.
– principle Ausschlußprinzip n.

excochleation Exkochleation f.
excoriation Exkoriation f., Schürfwunde f.
excrement Exkrement n.
excrescence Wucherung f., Auswuchs m.
excrete Exkret n.
excrete, to ausscheiden
excretion Ausscheidung f., Exkretion f.
excretion urography Ausscheidungsurographie f.
excretory exkretorisch
excursion Exkursion f.
exenteration d. e. f.
exercise Übung f.
exercise, physical körperliche Übung f.; körperliche Belastung f.
exercise, to üben
– bone Exerzierknochen m.
exeresis Exhairese f.
exfoliate, to abblättern
exfoliation d. e. f.
– of teeth Zahnausfall m.
exfoliative exfoliativ
exhalation d. e. f.
exhaust, to erschöpfen, ausschöpfen
exhaustible erschöpflich
exhaustion Erschöpfung f.
exhibitionism Exhibitionismus m.
exhibitionist Exhibitionist m., Exhibitionistin f.
exhumation Exhumierung f.
exhume, to exhumieren
existence Existenz f.
existential existentiell
exit dose Austrittsdosis f.
exocrine exokrin
exocytosis Exozytose f.
exodic zentrifugal
exodontology Zahnextrationslehre f.
exogenic exogen
exogenous exogen
exonerate, to entlasten

exoneration Entlastung f.
exophthalmic exophthalmisch
– goiter Glotzaugenkrankheit f.
exophthalmos Exophthalmus m.
exostosis Exostose f.
exotic exotisch
exotoxin d. e. n.
expander d. e. m.
expansion d. e. f.
expansive expansiv
expect, to abwarten, erwarten
expectant abwartend
– mother werdende Mutter f.
expectation neurosis Erwartungsneurose f.
expectation of life Lebenserwartung f.
expectorant Expektorans n.
expectorate, to expektorieren
expectoration Expektoration f.
expel, to austreiben
expenditure Aufwand m.
experience Erfahrung f.
experiment d. e. n.
experiment, to experimentieren
experimental experimentell
expert sachverständig, erfahren; Sachverständiger m., Sachverständige f.; Gutachter m., Gutachterin f.
expertise Gutachtertätigkeit f.; Sachkenntnis f.; Gutachten n.
expiration Exspiration f., Ausatmung f.
expiratory exspiratorisch
expiratory flow rate exspiratorische Atemstromstärke f.
– volume Exspirationsvolumen n.
expire, to exspirieren, ausatmen
explain, to erklären
explanation Erklärung f.
explant Explantat n.
explant, to explantieren
explantation d. e. f.
explode, to explodieren
exploration d. e. f., Erforschung f.

exploratory exploratorisch
- **excision** Probeexzision f.
- **laparotomy** Probelaparotomie f.

explore, to explorieren, erforschen, ausforschen
explorer Sonde f.
explosive explosiv
exponent d. e. m.
expose, to exponieren, aussetzen; belichten
exposure Aussetzung f.; Belichtung f., Bestrahlung f.
- **dose** Bestrahlungsdosis f.
- **latitude** Belichtungsspielraum m.

express, to ausdrücken
expression Ausdrücken n.; Ausdruck m.
exsanguinate, to blutleer machen, ausbluten
exsanguination Entblutung f., Verblutung f.
exsanguinotransfusion Austauschtransfusion f.
exsiccate, to austrocknen
exsiccation Austrocknung f.
exsiccosis Exsikkose f.
extend, to dehnen; sich erstrecken
extension d. e. f.
- **stirrup** Extensionsbügel m.

extensor Strecker m., Streckmuskel m.
external extern, äußerlich
extinguish, to auslöschen
extirpation Exstirpation f.
extraarticular extraartikulär
extrabulbar extrabulbär
extracapsular extrakapsulär
extracardial extrakardial
extracellular extrazellulär
extracorporeal extrakorporal
extracranial extrakranial
extract Extrakt m.
extract, to extrahieren
extractable extrahierbar
extracting forceps Zahnzange f.
extraction Extraktion f.
extractor Extraktor m.

extradural d. e.
extrafascial extrafaszial
extragastric extragastral
extragenital d. e.
extrahepatic extrahepatisch
extramarital außerehelich
extramaxillary extramaxillär
extramedullary extramedullär
extramural d. e.
extraoral d. e.
extraosseous extraossär
extraovarian extraovariell
extrapancreatic extrapankreatisch
extraperitoneal d. e.
extrapleural d. e.
extrapulmonary extrapulmonal
extrapyramidal d. e.
extrarenal d. e.
extrasensory außersinnlich
extrasystole d. e. f.
extratracheal d. e.
extrauterine extrauterin
extravaginal d. e.
extravasation Blutaustritt m. ins Gewebe, Flüssigkeitsaustritt m. ins Gewebe
extravascular extravaskulär
extraventricular extraventrikulär
extreme extrem
extremity Extremität f.
extrinsic factor Extrinsic-Faktor m.
extroversion d. e. f.
extubate, to extubieren
extubation d. e. f.
exuberant überschießend
exudate Exsudat n.
exudation Exsudation f.
exudative exsudativ
exungulation Ausschuhen n.
eye Auge n.; Öhr n.
eyeball Augapfel m.
eyebrow Augenbraue f.
eyeground Augenhintergrund m.
eyelash Augenwimper f.
eyelid Augenlid n.
eye-lotion Augenwasser n.

eyepiece Okular n.
eye shield Augenklappe f.
– specialist Augenspezialist m., Augenspezialistin f.

eye speculum Augenlidhalter m.
eyestrain Asthenopie f.
eyewater Augenwasser n.

F

face Gesicht n.
facet Facette f.
faceted facettiert
facial muscle Gesichtsmuskel m.
– nerve Nervus facialis
facial paralysis Fazialislähmung f.
facilitation Bahnung f., Erleichterung f.
facing Facette f.
facioplasty Gesichtsplastik f.
factitious künstlich
factor Faktor m.
facultative fakultativ
faculty Fakultät f.; Fähigkeit f.
– of smelling Geruchsvermögen n.
fading Abblassen n.
faecal (e) fäkal
– fistula (e) Kotfistel f.
faeces (e) Kot m.
fagopyrism Buchweizenvergiftung f.
fail, to fehlen; schwächer werden; versagen; versäumen
failure Versagen n., Ausbleiben n.
failure rate Ausfallquote f.
faint matt, schwach, ohnmächtig; Ohnmacht f.
faint, to ohnmächtig werden
fainting fit Ohnmachtsanfall m.
fair blond; unparteiisch
falling sickness Fallsucht f.
fallopian tube Eileiter m.
false conclusion Trugschluß m.
familial familiär
family doctor Hausarzt m.
– medicine-chest Hausapotheke f.

family planning Familienplanung f.
– tree Stammbaum m.
famine fever Rückfallfieber n.
fancy, to sich einbilden, Gefallen finden
fango d. e. m.
farad d. e. n.
faradic faradisch
faradization Faradisation f.
faradize, to faradisieren
far advanced in pregnancy hochschwanger
farina Mehl n.
farinaceous mehlig
farmer's lung Farmerlunge f.
farsighted weitsichtig
farsightedness Weitsichtigkeit f.
farcy chronischer Rotz m.
fascia Faszie f.
fasciaplasty Faszienplastik f.
fascicular faszikulär
Fasciola hepatica d. e.
fasciotomy Fasziotomie f.
fast fest, resistent
fast, to fasten
fasting blood glucose Nüchternblutzucker m.
fat fett; Fett n.
– cell Fettzelle f.
– embolism Fettembolie f.
– -soluble fettlöslich
– splitting fettspaltend
fatal verhängisvoll; tödlich
fatherhood Vaterschaft f.
fatigability Ermüdbarkeit f.
fatigable ermüdbar

fatigue Ermüdung f.
fatty fettig
– **degeneration** fettige Degeneration f.
– **meal** Fettmahlzeit f.
– **tissue** Fettgewebe n.
fault Gebrechen n.
faulty diet Diätfehler m.
fauna d. e. f.
favism Favismus m.
favorable (a) günstig
favourable (e) günstig
favus Erbgrind m., Favus m.
fawn Rehkalb n., Hirschkalb n.
FBS (= **fasting blood sugar**) Nüchternblutzucker m.
fear of death Todesangst f.
feature (med.) Gesichtszug m.
febrifacient fiebererzeugend
febrifugal fiebersenkend
febrifuge fiebersenkendes Mittel n.
febrile febril, fieberhaft
fecal (a) fäkal
– **fistula** (a) Kotfistel f.
feces (a) Kot m.
fecundation Befruchtung f.
fecundity Fruchtbarkeit f.
fee Gebühr f., Honorar n.
feeble schwächlich, matt
feebleminded schwachsinnig
feeblemindedness Schwachsinn m.
feed, to füttern, ernähren
feedback Rückkopplung f.
feeding Fütterung f., Ernährung f.
feel, to fühlen, verspüren
feeling Gefühl n.
– **of repletion** Völlegefühl n.
Feer's disease Feersche Krankheit f.
fees, to pay – honorieren, Honorar bezahlen
Fehling's solution Fehlingsche Lösung f.
– **test** Fehlingsche Probe f.
feign, to fingieren, täuschen
felon Panaritium n.
felt Filz m.

Felty's syndrome Felty-Syndrom n.
female weiblich; weibliches Wesen n.
feminization Verweiblichung f.
feminize, to verweiblichen
femoral d. e.
fenestrate, to fenstern
fenestration Fensterung f.
fennel Fenchel m.
ferment d. e. n.
fermental fermentativ
fermentation d. e. f., Gärung f.
– **test** Gärungsprobe f.
fern Farn m.
Ferrata's cell Ferratazelle f.
ferret Frettchen n.
ferric ammonium sulfate (a) Eisenammoniumsulfat n.
– **ammonium sulphate** (e) Eisenammoniumsulfat n.
– **compound** dreiwertige Eisenverbindung f.
ferricyanide Ferrizyanid n.
ferrioxamine Ferrioxamin n.
ferrite Ferrit n.
ferritin d. e. n.
ferrotherapy Eisentherapie f.
ferrous compound zweiwertige Eisenverbindung f.
fertile fruchtbar
fertility Fruchtbarkeit f.
fertilize, to fruchtbar machen
fester, to eitern
festoon, gum Zahnfleischrandwulst m.
fetal (a) fötal
fetid (a) fötid
fetishism Fetischismus m.
fetishist Fetischist m., Fetischistin f.
fetlock Fesselhaar n.; Fesselgelenk n.
fetlock joint Fesselgelenk n.
fetlow Hufgeschwür n., Klauengeschwür n.
fetoprotein Fetoprotein n., Fötoprotein n.

fetor (a) Fötor m.
fetus (a) Fötus m.
fever Fieber n.
– -heat Fieberhitze f.
feverish fiebernd, fiebrig
fever therapy Fiebertherapie f.
fiber Faser f.
fiberscope Fiberskop n.
fibre Faser f.
fibril Fibrille f.
fibrillary fibrillär
fibrillate, to fibrillieren
fibrillation Flimmern n., Muskelflimmern n.
fibrin d. e. n.
fibrinogen d. e. n.
fibrinogenic fibrinogen
fibrinogenopenia Fibrinogenopenie f.
fibrinoid d. e. n.
fibrinokinase d. e. f.
fibrinolysin d. e. n.
fibrinolysis Fibrinolyse f.
fibrinolysokinase d. e. f.
fibrinolytic fibrinolytisch
fibrinopenia Fibrinopenie f.
fibrinous fibrinös
fibroadenia Fibroadenie f.
fibroadenoma Fibroadenom n.
fibroblast d. e. m.
fibrocarcinoma Fibrokarzinom n.
fibrocartilage Faserknorpel m.
fibrocyte Fibrozyt m.
fibroelastosis Fibroelastose f.
fibroglioma Fibrogliom n.
fibroid d. e.
fibrolipoma Fibrolipom n.
fibrolysin d. e. n.
fibroma Fibrom n.
fibromatosis Fibromatose f.
fibromatous fibromatös
fibromyoma Fibromyom n.
fibromyxoma Fibromyxom n.
fibromyxosarcoma Fibromyxosarkom n.
fibroplasia Fibroplasie f.
fibroplastic fibroplastisch

fibroplastin d. e. n.
fibrosarcoma Fibrosarkom n.
fibrosis Fibrose f.
fibrositis d. e. f.
fibrous fibrös
fibular d. e.
field hospital Feldlazarett n.
– of operation Operationsgebiet n.
– of vision Gesichtsfeld n.
figure Figur f., Gestalt f.; Ziffer f.
fig wart Feigwarze f.
filament Faden m.
Filaria bancrofti d. e.
filariasis d. e. f.
file Feile f.
–, finishing Finierfeile f.
filiform d. e., fadenförmig
fill, to füllen
fillet Schleife f.
filling Füllung f.
– defect Füllungsdefekt m.
– pressure Füllungsdruck m.
–, temporary Einlage f. (dent.)
film Film m.; Häutchen n., Belag m.; Abstrich m.
–, X-ray Röntgenfilm m.
filmaron d. e. n.
filter d. e. m.
filter, to filtrieren
filth Schmutz m.
fitrable filtrabel, filtrierbar
filtrate Filtrat n.
Filtration d. e. f.
fimbria Fimbrie f.
final d. e.
finding Befund m.
findings on admission Aufnahmebefund m.
fine structure Feinstruktur f.
finger d. e. m.
– -joint Fingergelenk n.
– -nose test Finger-Nasenversuch m.
fingerprint Fingerabdruck m.
finger protector Fingerschützer m.
– -tip Fingerspitze f.

finishing instrument Finierinstrument n.
Finkelstein's albumin milk Finkelsteinsche Eiweißmilch f.
Finsen light Finsenlampe f.
fireproof feuerfest
first aid Erste Hilfe f.
– aid man Sanitäter m.
fish Fisch m.
fishhook stomach Angelhakenmagen m.
fish-oil Lebertran m.
fish tapeworm Fischbandwurm m.
fissile spaltbar
fission Spaltung f.
– product Spaltprodukt n.
fissionable spaltbar
fissure Fissur f.
– of anus Analfissur f.
fist Faust f.
fistula Fistel f.
–, biliary Gallenfistel f.
–, rectovesical Blasenmastdarmfistel f.
fistulization Fistelbildung f.
fistulous fistulös
fit Anfall m.
fix, to fixieren; ruhigstellen
fixation Fixierung f., Bindung f.
fixative Fixiermittel n.
fixing agent Fixiermittel n.
fixing bath Fixierbad n.
flabby welk
flaccid schlaff
flagellata d. e. n. pl.
flake Flocke f.
flaky flockig
flamelike flammig
flame photometry Flammenphotometrie f.
flamingo d. e. m.
flap Lappen m., Gewebelappen m.
flare up Aufflackern n.
flare up, to aufflackern
flash Blitz m., Strahl m.
flask, Erlenmeyer Erlenmeyerkolben m.

flatfoot Plattfuß m.
flatfooted plattfüßig
flatulence Flatulenz f.
flatulent blähend
flavin d. e. n.
flavone Flavon n.
flavonoid d. e. n.
flavoprotein d. e. n.
flea Floh m.
flesh Fleisch n.
flexibility Biegbarkeit f., Gelenkigkeit f.
flexible biegbar, biegsam
flexile biegbar, biegsam
Flexner's bacillus Flexner-Bazillus m.
flexure Flexur f.
flightiness Zerfahrenheit
flight of ideas Gedankenflucht f.
Flint's murmur Flintsches Geräusch n.
floating flottierend
flocculation Flockung f., Ausflockung f.
flocculoreaction Flockungsreaktion f.
flora d. e. f.
flotation d. e. f.
flour Mehl n.
flow Fluß m., Strom m.
flow, to fließen, rinnen
flowing off Abfluß m.
flowmeter Flußmesser m.
flow property Fließeigenschaft f.
flu grippaler Infekt m.
flucloxapenicillin d. e. n.
fluctuant fluktuierend
fluctuation Fluktuation f.
fluid flüssig; Flüssigkeit f.
fluidextract Fluidextrakt m.
fluid substitution Flüssigkeitsersatz m.
fluke Trematode f.
flumethiazide Flumethiazid n.
flunitrazepam d. e. n.
fluocinolone Fluocinolon n.
fluocortolone Fluocortolon n.

fluorenylacetamide Fluorenylazetamid n.
fluorescein Fluoreszin n.
fluorescence Fluoreszenz f.
fluorescent fluoreszierend
fluorescent screen Röntgenschirm m.
fluorinate, to fluorieren
fluorine Fluor n.
fluorohydrocortisone Fluorohydrocortison n.
fluoroprednisolone Fluoroprednisolon n.
fluoropyrimidine Fluoropyrimidin n.
fluoroscopy Durchleuchtung f.
fluorosis Fluorose f., Fluorvergiftung f.
flurazepam d. e. n.
flush Gesichtsrötung f.
flutamide Flutamid n.
flutter Flattern n.
flux Fluß m., Fließen n.; Flußmittel n.
fluxion Fluß m.
fly Fliege f.
fly, bluebottle Schmeißfliege f.
foal Fohlen n.
foal, to fohlen
foam Schaum m.
− bath Schaumbad n.
− cell Schaumzelle f.
− -forming schaumbildend
− rubber Schaumgummi m.
focal fokal
− infection Herdinfektion f.,
  Fokalinfektion f.
focal toxicosis Fokaltoxikose f.
focus Fokus m.
Förster's operation Förstersche
  Operation f.
foetal (e) fötal
foetid (e) fötid
foetoprotein (e) Fötoprotein n.,
  Fetoprotein n.
foetor (e) Fötor m.
foetus (e) Fötus m., Leibesfrucht f.
fog dichter Nebel m.

foil Folie f.
folate Folat n.
fold Falte f.
folie Geisteskrankheit f.
folinerin d. e. n.
follicle Follikel m.
− -stimulating hormone Follikelreifungshormon n.
follicular follikulär
− hormone Follikelhormon n.
folliculitis d. e. f.
follow-up Katamnese f.
fominoben d. e. n.
fontanel Fontanelle f.
fontanelle Fontanelle f.
food Nahrung f., Kost f.
− allergy Nahrungsmittelallergie f.
− poisoning Lebensmittel-
  vergiftung f.
foot Fuß m.
− -and mouth-disease Maul- und
  Klauenseuche f.
− -bath Fußbad n.
− easer Plattfußeinlage f.
− powder Fußpuder m.
force Kraft f.
forced forciert
forceps Zange f., Klemme f.,
  Pinzette f.
−, angiotribe Druckklemme f.
−, approximation Wundrandpinzette f.
−, artery Arterienklemme f.
−, biopsy Biopsiezange f.
−, bone rongeur Hohlmeißelzange f.
−, chalazion Chalazionpinzette f.
−, clip applying Wundklammer-
  zange f.
−, cover glass Deckglaspinzette f.
−, crushing Quetschklemme f.
−, dissecting anatomische
  Pinzette f.
−, entropium Entropionpinzette f.
−, fixation Fixierpinzette f.
−, foreign body removing Fremdkörperzange f.

forceps, grasping Greifzange f., Faßzange f.
—, gum guillotine Zahnfleischkappenstanze f.
—, haemostatic (e) Gefäßklemme f.
—, hemostatic (a) Gefäßklemme f.
—, intestinal Darmfaßzange f., Darmklemme f.
—, iris Irispinzette f.
—, midwifery Geburtszange f.
—, mosquito Moskitoklemme f.
—, nasal dressing Nasentamponpinzette f.
—, obstetrical Geburtszange f.
—, ovum Abortuszange f.
—, polypus Polypenzange f.
—, rectal biopsy Mastdarmbiopsiezange f.
—, scoop Löffelzange f.
—, skull Schädelzange f.
—, slide holding Objektträgerpinzette f.
—, specimen Probeexzisionszange f.
—, splinter Splitterpinzette f.
—, sterilizing Sterilisierpinzette f.
—, strabismus Schielpinzette f.
—, tenaculum Hakenzange f.
—, tissue Hakenpinzette f., chirurgische Pinzette f.
—, tongue Zungenzange f.
—, towel Tuchklemme f.
—, uterine dressing Uterustamponzange f.
—, wire twisting Drahtspannzange f.
—, wound clip Wundklammerpinzette f.
forcible feeding Zwangsernährung f.
forearm Unterarm m.
forehead Vorderhaupt n.
— position Vorderhauptshaltung f.
foreign body Fremdkörper m.
forensic forensisch
foreskin Vorhaut f.
foreword Vorwort n.
forget, to vergessen
forgetful vergeßlich

forgetfulness Vergeßlichkeit f.
fork Gabel f.
form Form f., Gestalt f.
formaldehyde Formaldehyd m.
format d. e. n.
formation Bildung f.; Gebilde n.
formication Ameisenlaufen n.
formolgel test Formolgeltest m.
formula Formel f.
formula, dental Zahnformel f.
formula, structural Strukturformel f.
formulary Formelsammlung f.
form wrongly, to verbilden, verbauen
fornix Gewölbe n.
foul brood Faulbrut f. (veter.)
founder Rehe f., Hufrehe f. (veter.)
four-legged vierbeinig
fourth disease Rubeola scarlatinosa
fovea d. e. f.
foveate grubenförmig
foveola Grübchen n.
fowl Geflügel n.
fowl plague Hühnerpest f.
Fowler's solution Fowlersche Lösung f.
fox Fuchs m.
Fox-Fordyce disease Fox-Fordycesche Krankheit f.
foxglove Digitalis f.
Foxia mansoni d. e.
f.p. (= freezing point) Gefrierpunkt m.
fraction Fraktion f.
fractional fraktioniert
— removal of the gastric juice fraktionierte Magenaushebung f.
fractionate, to fraktionieren
fractionation Fraktionierung f.
fracture fraktur f.
—, comminuted Splitterfraktur f.
—, compound komplizierte Fraktur f.

fracture, compound comminuted komplizierte Splitterfraktur f.
–, fatigue Ermüdungsfraktur f.
–, greenstick Grünholzfraktur f.
–, march Marschfraktur f.
–, simple einfache Fraktur f.
fracture, to frakturieren, brechen
Fränkel's bacillus Fränkelscher Bezillus m.
fragility Brüchigkeit f.
fragment d. e. n.
fragmentation d. e. f.
frambesia (a) Frambösie f.
framboesia (e) Frambösie f.
frame Gefüge n., Bau m., Gerüst n., Rahmen m.
framework Bau m., Einfassung f.
Frankenhäuser's ganglion Frankenhäusersches Ganglion n.
Fraunhofer's line Fraunhofersche Linie f.
freckle Sommersprosse f.
free frei
– from complaints beschwerdefrei
– HCl freie Salzsäure f.
– sale drug Handverkaufsmedikament n.
freeze-drying Gefriertrocknung f.
freeze, to gefrieren, erstarren; zum Gefrieren bringen
– to death, to erfrieren
freezing apparatus Gefrierapparat m.
– point Gefrierpunkt m.
Frei test Freische Probe f.
fremitus d. e. m.
frenzy Tobsucht f., Raserei f.
frequency Frequenz f., Häufigkeit f.
frequent d. e.
friction Reibung f., Abreibung f.
Friedländer's bacillus Friedländerscher Bazillus m.
Friedreich's ataxia Friedreichsche Ataxie f.
fright Schrecken m.
frigid d. e.

frigidity Frigidität f.
frivolity Frivolität f.
frivolous frivol
Fröhlich's syndrome Fröhlichsches Syndrom n.
frog Frosch m.
frog (veter.) Strahl m.
– belly Froschbauch m.
front Stirn f.
frontal d. e.
frontobasal d. e.
frontomalar frontozygomatisch
frontonasal d. e.
frontooccipital frontookzipital
frontoparietal d. e.
frontotemporal d. e.
frost-bite Erfrierung f. (eines Körperteils)
frostbitten erfroren
fructokinase Fruktokinase f.
fructose Fruktose f.
fructosuria Fruktosurie f.
fruit Frucht f.
fruitful fruchtbar
frustrane frustran
fry, to schmoren
fuadin d. e. n.
fuchsin d. e. n.
fuchsinophilous fuchsinophil
fucosamine Fucosamin n.
fucose d. e. f.
fuel Brennstoff m., Kraftstoff m.
fulgurant blitzartig
full bath Vollbad n.
fullbreasted vollbrüstig
fulminant d. e.
fumarate Fumarat n.
fumigate, to räuchern, ausräuchern
fumigation Ausräucherung f.
function Funktion f.
– test Funktionsprüfung f.
functional funktionell
fundament d. e. n.
fundamental d. e.
fundus d. e. m.

fundus of the eye Augenhintergrund m.
fungal fungös
fungicidal fungizid
fungous fungös
fungus Pilz m.
funicular funikulär
funicular myelosis funikuläre Spinalerkrankung f.
funiculitis Funikulitis f.
funnel Trichter m.
− chest Trichterbrust f.
−, separating Scheidetrichter m.
− -shaped trichterförmig
fur Belag m.
furan d. e. n.
furane Furan n.
furanose d. e. f.
furazone Furazon n.
furfuran Furan n.
furred belegt, bedeckt
furrow Furche f.
furuncle Furunkel m.
furuncular furunkulös
furunculosis Furunkulose f.
furylalanine Furylalanin n.
fuscin d. e. n.
fusiform d. e.
Fusiformis dentium Fusobacterium fusiforme
fusing Schmelzen n.
fusion Verschmelzung f.
− defect Hemmungsmißbildung f.
Fusobacterium fusiforme d. e., Bacillus fusiformis
fusospirillary fusospirillär
future expectation Zukunftserwartung
futurology Futurologie f.

G

gadfly Viehbremse f., Bremse f.
gadolinium d. e. n.
Gärtner's bacillus Gärtnerscher Bazillus m.
Gaffkya tetragena Mikrokokkus tetragenus
gag Mundsperrer m.
gait Gangart f., Gang m., Gehen n.
galactagogue milchtreibend; Laktagogum n.
galactokinase Galaktokinase f.
galactophoritis Milchgangentzündung f.
galactorrhea (a) Galaktorrhöe f.
galactorrhoea (e) Galaktorrhöe f.
galactosamine Galaktosamin n.
galactose Galaktose f.
− tolerance Galaktosetoleranz f.
galactose tolerance test Galaktosebelastungsprobe f.
galactosidase Galaktosidase f.
galactoside Galaktosid n.
galactostasis Milchstauung f.
galactosuria Galaktosurie f.
galenic galenisch
galenics Galenik f.
gall Galle f.
gallate Gallat n.
gallbladder Gallenblase f.
gallium d. e. n.
gallop rhythm Galopprhythmus m.
gallsickness Anaplasmose f.
gallstone Gallenstein m.
Galton's whistle Galtonsche Pfeife f.
galvanic galvanisch
galvanization Galvanisierung f.
galvanize, to galvanisieren

galvanocautery Galvanokaustik f.
galvanometer d. e. n.
galvanotactic galvanotaktisch
galziekte Anaplasmose f.
Gambian horse sickness Gambiafieber n.
gamete Gamet m.
gametocyte Gametozyt m.
gametogony Gametogonie f.
gamma emitter Gammastrahler m.
− globulin Gammaglobulin n.
− ray Gamma-Strahl m.
gammatron d. e. n.
gangliectomy Gangliektomie f.
ganglioglioma Gangliogliom n.
ganglioma Gangliom n.
ganglion Ganglion n., Überbein n.
ganglion cell Ganglienzelle f.
ganglionectomy Ganglionektomie f.
ganglioneuroma Ganglioneurom n.
ganglionic blocking agent Ganglienblocker m.
ganglionitis d. e. f.
ganglioplegic ganglioplegisch; Ganglioplegikum n.
ganglioside Gangliosid n.
gangrene Gangrän f.
gangrenous gangränös
gap Lücke f.
gargarism Gurgelwasser n.
garget (veter.) Euterentzündung f., Brustdrüsenentzündung f.
gargle Gurgelwasser n., Mundspülwasser n.
gargle, to gurgeln
gargoylism Pfaundler-Hurlersche Krankheit f.
Garland's triangle Garlandsches Dreieck n.
garlic Knoblauch m.
gas d. e. n.
− analysis Gasanalyse f.
− chromatography Gaschromatographie f.
− gangrene Gasbrand m.

gas gangrene antitoxin Gasbrandantitoxin n.
gaseous gasförmig, gasartig
gas-filled gasgefüllt
gasoline Benzin n.
gasp, to keuchen, schwer atmen
gasserian ganglion Gassersches Ganglion n.
gastralgia Gastralgie f.
gastralgic gastralgisch
gastrectasis Gastrektasie f.
gastrectomy Gastrektomie f.
gastric gastrisch
− acid Magensäure f.
− function test Magenfunktionsprüfung f.
− juice Magensaft m.
− lavage Magenspülung f.
− tolerance Magenverträglichkeit f.
− ulcer Magengeschwür n.
gastrin d. e. n.
gastritic gastritisch
gastritis d. e. f.
gastrocardiac gastrokardial
gastrocolostomy Gastrokolostomie f.
gastroduodenal d. e.
gastroduodenitis d. e. f.
gastroduodenostomy Gastroduodenostomie f.
gastroenteritic gastroenteritisch
gastroenteritis d. e. f.
gastroenterocolitis Gastroenterokolitis f.
gastroenterological gastroenterologisch
gastroenterologist Gastroenterologe m.
gastroenterology Gastroenterologie f.
gastroenteroptosis Gastroenteroptose f.
gastroenterostomy Gastroenterostomie f.
gastrogavage Magenfistelernährung f.
gastrogenic gastrogen

gastrointestinal d. e.
gastrojejunostomy Gastrojejunostomie f.
gastrolienal d. e.
gastropathic gastropathisch
gastropathy Gastropathie f.
gastrophiliasis d. e. f.
gastroplegia Gastroplegie f.
gastroptosis Gastroptose f.
gastroscope Gastroskop n.
gastroscopic gastroskopisch
gastroscopy Gastroskopie f.
gastrostomy Gastrostomie f.
gastrosuccorrhea (a) Gastrosukkorrhöe f.
gastrosuccorrhoea (e) Gastrosukkorrhöe f.
gastrotomy Gastrotomie f.
gastrula d. e. f.
gastrulation d. e. f.
gathering Abszeß m.; Schwellung f.
gatism Inkontinenz f.
Gaucher's disease Gauchersche Speicherkrankheit f.
gauge Maß n.; Kaliber n.
—, **to** eichen
gauze Gaze f.
— **bandage** Mullbinde f.
— **packer** Tamponstopfer m.
gavage Sondenernährung f.
Gay-Lussac's law Gay-Lussacsches Gesetz n.
gazelle d. e. f.
Gee's disease Zöliakie f.
Geiger counter Geiger-Zählrohr n.
gel d. e. n.
gelatin Gelatine f.
gelatinize, to gelatinieren
gelatinous gelatinös
geld, to kastrieren
gelding Wallach m.
gelosis Gelose f.
gelotripsy Gelotripsie f.
gelsemine Gelsemin n.
gene Gen n.
genealogy Genealogie f.
general generell, allgemein

general paralysis of the insane Dementia paralytica
— **paresis** Dementia paralytica
— **state of health** Allgemeinbefinden
generalize, to generalisieren
general-purpose machine Allzweckmaschine f.
generation d. e. f.
—, **spontaneous** Urzeugung f.
generative generativ
generator d. e. m.
generic name Trivialbezeichnung f.
genesis Genese f.
genetic genetisch
geneticist Genetiker m., Genetikerin f.
genetics Genetik f.
genital d. e.
— **organ** Geschlechtsorgan n.
genitourinary urogenital
genito-urinary organ Harn- und Geschlechtsorgan n.
genoblast d. e. m.
genome Genom n.
genotype Genotyp m.
genotypic genotypisch
gentamycin d. e. n.
gentian Enzian m.
— **violet** Gentianaviolett n.
geomedicine Geomedizin f.
geometrical geometrisch
geometry Geometrie f.
Gerhardt's reaction Gerhardtsche Probe f.
geriatric geriatrisch
geriatrics Geriatrie f.
germ Keim m.
germanium d. e. n.
German measles Röteln f. pl.
German silver Neusilber n.
germ-cell Keimzelle f.
germ content Keimgehalt m.
germfree keimfrei
germicidal keimtötend
germicide keimtötendes Mittel n.
germinate, to keimen

germinative germinativ
germ-plasm Keimplasma n.
gerontological gerontologisch
gerontologist Gerontologe m., Gerontologin f.
gerontology Gerontologie f.
Gerson-Hermannsdorfer diet Gerson-Hermannsdorfersche Diät f.
gestagen d. e. n.
gestation d. e. f., Schwangerschaft f.
gestosis Gestose f.
gesture Gebärde f.
Ghon tubercle Ghonscher Tuberkel m.
giant Riese m.
– cell Riesenzelle f.
Giardia lamblia Lamblia intestinalis
gibbus d. e. m.
gid Drehkrankheit f., Coenurose f.
giddiness Schwindel m., Schwindelgefühl n.
Giemsa's staining method Giemsafärbung f.
gigantism Riesenwuchs m., Gigantismus m.
– hypophysial hypophysärer Gigantismus m.
gigantoblast d. e. m.
gigantocyte Gigantozyt m.
Gigli's saw Giglische Säge f.
Gimbernat's ligament Ligamentum Gimbernati
ginger Ingwer m.
gingival d. e.
gingivectomy Gingivektomie f.
gingivitis d. e. f.
ginglymus Scharniergelenk n.
girdle Gürtel m.
gitalin d. e. n.
gitogenin d. e. n.
gitoxigenin d. e. n.
gitoxin d. e. n.
give in, to eingeben
glaciated vereist

glaciation Vereisung f.
gland Drüse f.
–, lacrimal Tränendrüse f.
–, sudoriparous Schweißdrüse f.
glanders Rotz m., Malleus m.
glandular glandulär
– fever Pfeiffersches Drüsenfieber n.
glare Blendung f.
glare, to blenden, strahlen
glass Glas n.
glasses Brille f.
glassy glasig
Glauber's salt Glaubersalz n.
glaucoma Glaukom n.
glaucomatous glaukomatös
glaze Glasur f.
gleet chronischer Harnröhrentripper m.
gleet, nasal (veter.) Nasenkatarrh m., nasaler Rotz m.
glibenclamide Glibenclamid n.
glibornuride Glibornurid n.
glioblastoma Glioblastom n.
glioma Gliom n.
gliomatosis Gliomatose f.
gliosarcoma Gliosarkom n.
gliosis Gliose f.
glipizide Glipizid n.
glisoxepide Glisoxepid n.
Glisson's capsule Glissonsche Kapsel f.
– sling Glissonsche Schlinge f.
global d. e.
globin d. e. n.
globule Kügelchen n.
globulin d. e. n.
glomangiosis Glomangiose f.
glomerular glomerulär
glomerulitis d. e. f.
glomerulonephritis d. e. f.
glomerulosclerosis Glomerulosklerose f.
glossectomy Glossektomie f.
Glossina morsitans d. e.
– palpalis d. e.
glossitis d. e. f.

glossodynia Glossodynie f.
glossolalia Glossolalie f.
glossoplasty Zungenplastik f.
glossoplegia Glossoplegie f.
glossopyrosis Zungenbrennen n.
glossotrichia Haarzunge f.
glossy glänzend
glottic glottisch
glove Handschuh m.
glucagon Glukagon n.
glucocorticoid Glukokortikoid n.
glucokinase Glukokinase f.
gluconate Glukonat n.
glucosamine Glukosamin n.
glucose Glukose f., Glykose f.
glucose load Glukosebelastung f.
glucosidase Glykosidase f.
glucoside Glykosid n.
glucuronate Glukuronat n.
glucuronidase Glukuronidase f.
glukagon d. e. n.
gluside Saccharin n.
glutamate Glutamat n.
glutamic acid Glutaminsäure f.
 – **oxalacetic transaminase** Glutaminsäure-Oxalessigsäure-Transaminase f.
 – **pyruvic transaminase** Glutaminsäure-Brenztraubensäure-Transaminase f.
glutaminase d. e. f.
glutamine Glutamin n.
glutarate Glutarat n.
glutathione Glutathion n.
gluten d. e. n.
 – **-free diet** glutenfreie Diät f.
glutethimide Glutethimid n.
glycaemia (e) Glykämie f.
glycaemic (e) glykämisch
glycemia (a) Glykämie f.
glycemic (a) glykämisch
glycerate Glyzerat n.
glyceric aldehyde Glyzerinaldehyd m.
glyceride Glyzerid n.
glycerin Glyzerin n.
glycerite Glyzerit n.

glycerokinase Glyzerokinase f.
glycerol Glyzerin n.
glycerophosphatase Glyzerophosphatase f.
glycerophosphate Glyzerophosphat n.
glycerophosphatide Glyzerophosphatid n.
glyceryl Glyzeryl n.
 – **trinitrate** Nitroglyzerin n.
glycinamide Glycinamid n.
glycine Glykokoll n.
glycocoll Glykokoll n.
glycocyamine Glykozyamin n.
glycodiazine Glycodiazin n., Glykodiazin n.
glycogen Glykogen n.
glycogenase Glykogenase f.
glycogenesis Glykogenese f.
glycogenolysis Glykogenolyse f.
glycogenolytic glykogenolytisch
glycogenosis Glykogenspeicherkrankheit f.
glycogeny Glykogenie f.
glycolipid Glykolipid n.
glycolysis Glykolyse f.
glycolytic glykolytisch
glyconeogenesis Glykoneogenese f.
glycoprivous glykopriv
glycoprotein Glykoprotein n.
glycosidase Glykosidase f.
glycoside Glykosid n.
glycosuria Glykosurie f.
glycuronate Glykuronat n.
glycyl Glyzyl n.
glycyrrhizin Glyzyrrhizin n.
glyoxalase d. e. f.
glyoxalate Glyoxalat n.
glyoxalyl urea Glyoxalylharnstoff m.
Gmelin's test Gmelinsche Probe f.
gnat (a) Steckmückchen n.
gnat (e) Moskito m.
gnathoplasty Kieferplastik f.
gnathoschisis Kieferspalte f.
gnotobiotic gnotobiotisch
goat Ziege f.
goat's milk Ziegenmilch f.

goblet cell Becherzelle f.
goggles, X-ray Röntgenbrille f.
goiter Kropf m., Struma f.
goitre Kropf m., Struma f.
goitrigenous kropferzeugend
goitrogenic kropferzeugend
goitrogenous kropferzeugend, strumigen
goitrous kropfig
gold d. e. n.
– **sol test** Goldsolreaktion f.
Golgi's apparatus Golgi-Apparat m.
– **corpuscle** Golgi-Körperchen n.
gonad Keimdrüse f., Geschlechtsdrüse f.
gonadal dysgenesis Gonadendysgenesie f.
gonadectomy Keimdrüsenentfernung f.
gonadorelin d. e. n.
gonadotropic gonadotrop
gonadotropin d. e. n.
–, **chorionic** Choriongonadotropin n.
gonarthritis d. e. f., Kniegelenksentzündung f.
goniometer d. e. n.
gonioscope Gonioskop n.
gonioscopical gonioskopisch
gonioscopy Gonioskopie f.
gonitis d. e. f.
gonoblennorrhea (a) Gonoblennorrhöe f.
gonoblennorhoea (e) Gonoblennorrhöe f.
gonococcal infection Gonokokkeninfektion f.
gonococcus Gonokokkus m.
gonorrhea (a) Gonorrhöe f.
genorrheal (a) gonorrhoisch
gonorrhoea (e) Gonorrhöe f.
gonorrhoeal (e) gonorrhoisch
Goodpasture's syndrome Goodpasture-Syndrom n.
goose Gans f.
Gordon's sign Gordonsches Zeichen n.

Gordon's test Gordontest m.
gorge Gurgel f.
gorilla d. e. m.
gouge Hohlmeißel m.
gout Gicht f.
gouty gichtisch
GP (= general practitioner) Allgemeinpraktiker m.
graafian follicle Graafscher Follikel m.
gracile grazil
gradation Gradierung f.
grade Neugrad m.
Gradenigo's syndrome Gradenigo-Syndrom n.
gradient d. e. m.
gradual graduell
graduate graduiert; promovierte Person f.
graduate, to graduieren
graduation Graduierung f.; Promotion f.
Graefe's sign Graefesches Zeichen n.
graft Transplantat n., Implantat n.
graft, to verschieben, verpflanzen, transplantieren, implantieren
gram Gramm n.
gramicidin d. e. n.
graminol d. e. n.
gramme Gramm n.
gram-negative gramnegativ
gram-positive grampositiv
Gram's staining method Gramfärbung f.
grand mal d. e. n.
granular granulär
– **cast** granulierter Zylinder m.
granulation d. e. f.
– **tissue** Granulationsgewebe n.
granule Körnchen n.
granulocyte Granulozyt m.
granulocytopenia Granulozytopenie f.
granulocytopenic granulozytopenisch

granulocytopoiesis Granulozytopoese f.
granulocytopoietic granulozytopoetisch
granuloma Granulom n.
− **inguinale** Granuloma venereum pudendi
granulomatosis Granulomatose f.
granulomatous granulomatös
granulosis Granulose f.
grape sugar Traubenzucker m.
graph graphische Darstellung f.
graphic graphisch
graphological graphologisch
graphologist Graphologe m., Graphologin f.
graphology Graphologie f.
grasp Griff m.
grass disease Graskrankheit f.
Gratiolet's optic radiation Gratioletsche Sehstrahlung f.
gravel Nierengrieß m., Harngrieß m.
Graves' disease Basedowsche Krankheit f.
gravid schwanger
gravidity Schwangerschaft f.
gravimeter d. e. n.
gravimetric gravimetrisch
gravimetry Gravimetrie f.
gravitation d. e. f.
gravity Gewicht n., Schwere f.
−, **specific** spezifisches Gewicht n.
gravewax Leichenwachs n.
Grawitz's tumor (a) Grawitztumor m.
− **tumour** (e) Grawitztumor m.
gray, nervous graue Substanz f. des Nervensystems
grazing shot Streifschuß m.
grease Schmalz n.
grease, to einfetten
grease-heel Fußekzem n. (veter.)
greater curve große Kurvatur f.
great tubercle Tuberculum majus
greediness Gier f.
grenz ray Grenzstrahl m.

grey-haired grauhaarig
grid Gitter n.; Raster m.
grief Gram m., Kummer m.
Griesinger's sign Griesingersches Zeichen n.
grind, to schleifen; knirschen
grinder Molar m.
grinding Knirschen n., Schleifen n.
grinding surface Kaufläche f.
grip Griff m.; Grippe f.
gripe Darmgrimmen n.
grippal d. e.
grippe d. e. f.
griseofulvin d. e. n.
gristle Knorpel m.
grit Grieß m.
Gritti's amputation Grittische Amputation f.
groan, to ächzen, stöhnen
Grocco's triangle Rauchfuß-Groccosches Dreieck n.
groin Leistengegend f.
groove Furche f., Rinne f.
ground substance Grundsubstanz f.
group Gruppe f.
− **psychotherapy** Gruppenpsychotherapie f.
growing, rapidly schnellwachsend
−, **slowly** langsamwachsend
growth Wuchs m., Wachstum n.
− **hormone** Wachstumshormon n.
growth-regulating wachstumsregulierend
Gruber-Widal reaction Gruber-Widalsche Reaktion f.
gruel Haferschleim m.
guaiacol Guaiakol n.
guanase d. e. f.
guanethidine Guanethidin n.
guanidase d. e. f.
guanidine Guanidin n.
guanine Guanin n.
guanosine Guanosin n.
guanoxane Guanoxan n.
Guarnieri's corpuscle Guarnierisches Körperchen n.

Günzburg's test Günzburgsche Probe f.
Guillain-Barré syndrome Guillain-Barré-Syndrom n.
guinea-pig Meerschweinchen n.
gullet Speiseröhre f., Schlund m.
Gullstrand's lamp Gullstrandsche Spaltlampe f.
gum Gummi m.; Zahnfleisch n.
– lancet Zahnfleischmesser n.
– scissors Zahnfleischschere f.
gumma d. e. n.
gummatous gummös
gummose d. e. f.
Gumprecht's shadow Gumprechtsche Scholle f.
Gunn's syndrome Gunnsches Zeichen n.
gunshot wound Schußwunde f.
gush, to quellen
gustation Geschmackssinn m., Geschmack m.
gustatory geschmacklich
gustatory organ Geschmacksorgan n.
gustometer d. e. n.
gustometry Gustometrie f.
gut Darm m.
gutta-percha Guttapercha f.
guttural d. e.
gymnastic gymnastisch
gymnastics Gymnastik f.
–, medical Heilgymnastik f.
gynaecological (e) gynäkologisch
gynaecologist (e) Gynäkologe m., Gynäkologin f.
gynaecology (e) Gynäkologie f.
gynaecomastia (e) Gynäkomastie f.
gynandroblastoma Gynandroblastom n.
gynatresia Gynatresie f.
gynecological (a) gynäkologisch
gynecologist (a) Gynäkologe m., Gynäkologin f.
gynecology (a) Gynäkologie f.
gynecomastia (a) Gynäkomastie f.
gypsum Gips m.

H

habit Gewohnheit f.; Prädisposition f.; Körperverfassung f.
habitual habituell
habituation Gewöhnung f., Angleichung f.
haema... (e) look for:/siehe bei: hema... (a)
haeme (e) Häm n.
haemin (e) Hämin n.
haemo... (e) look for:/siehe bei: hemo... (a)
Haff disease Haffkrankheit f.
hafnium d. e. n.
Hageman factor Hageman-Faktor m.
hair Haar
hair follicle Haarbalg m.
hairless haarlos
hairy cell Haarzelle f.
half bath Halbbad n.
half-life period Halbwertzeit f.
half wave Halbwelle f.
halide kochsalzähnlich; Halid n.
halisteresis Halisterese f.
halitosis Foetor ex ore
Hallervorden-Spatz disease Hallervorden-Spatzsche Krankheit f.
hallucination Halluzination f.
hallucinogenic halluzinogen
hallucinosis Halluzinose f.
hallux valgus d. e.
– varus d. e.
halogen d. e. n.

halogenate, to halogenieren
halometer d. e. n.
halometric halometrisch
halometry Halometrie f.
haloperidol d. e. n.
halothane Halothan n.
Halsted's operation Halstedsche Operation f.
hamamelin d. e. n.
harmartoma Hamartom n.
Hamman-Rich syndrome Hamman-Rich-Syndrom n.
Hammarsten's test Hammarstensche Probe f.
hammer, percussion Perkussionshammer m.
hammer toe Hammerzehe f.
hamster d. e. m.
hamycin d. e. n.
hand Hand f.
handbarrow Trage f.
handbook Handbuch n.
handicapped behindert
handle Handgriff m., Griff m.
handpiece Handstück n.
Hand-Schueller-Christian disease Hand-Schüller-Christiansche Krankheit f.
hang, to hängen
Hanganutziu-Deicher test Hanganutziu-Deicher-Test m.
hanging drop hängender Tropfen m.
hangover Kater m. (= schlechtes Befinden)
Hanot's cirrhosis Hanotsche Cirrhose f.
haplodont d. e.
haploid d. e.
hapten d. e. n.
haptene Hapten n.
haptoglobin d. e. n.
haptophore Haptophor m.
harden, to härten, abhärten
hardening Verhärtung f.; Härten n.
hardness Härte f.

hard of hearing schwerhörig
– **ray method** Hartstrahltechnik f.
hare Hase m.
harelip Hasenscharte f.
harmine Harmin n.
harpoon Harpune f.
hashish Haschisch n.
hatch Brut f.
–, **to** brüten, ausbrüten
hatchet Beil n.
–, **claw** Klauenbeil n.
hatching Inkubationszeit f.
haunch Hüfte f.
haustration Haustrierung f.
Havers' canal Haverssches Kanälchen n.
hawk's bill Habichtschnabel m.
Hayem's solution Hayemsche Lösung f.
hay fever Heufieber n., Heuschnupfen m.
haze Dunst m.
head Kopf m., Haupt n.
headache Kopfschmerz m.
headband mirror Stirnreflektor m.
head lamp Stirnlampe f.
headlight Kopflicht n.
head louse Kopflaus f.
– **of femur** Oberschenkelkopf m.
– **of humerus** Oberarmkopf m.
– **of pancreas** Pankreaskopf m.
– **physician** Oberarzt m., Oberärztin f.
Head's zone Headsche Zone f.
heal, to heilen
healing Heilung f.
– **by first intention** Heilung f. per primam intentionem
– – **second intention** Heilung f. per secundam intentionem
– **power** Heilkraft f.
health Gesundheit f.
– **resort** Kurort m.
healthy gesund
heal up, to zuheilen
hear, to hören

hearing Gehör n., Hören n.
- **aid** Hörapparat m.
- **precipitation** Hörsturz m.

heart Herz n.
- **,armored** (a) Panzerherz n.
- **,armour** (e) Panzerherz n.
- **beat** Herzschlagen n., Herztätigkeit f.
- **block** Herzblock m.
- **block, auriculo-ventricular** atrioventrikulärer Herzblock m.
- **block, bundle branch** Schenkelblock m.
- **block, sino-auricular** sinoaurikulärer Herzblock m.

heartburn Sodbrennen n.

heart catheterization Herzkatheterisierung f.
- **cell** Herzfehlerzelle f.
- **disease** Herzleiden n., Herzkrankheit f.
- – –,**arteriosclerotic** arteriosklerotisches Herzleiden n.
- – – **cell** Herzfehlerzelle f.
- – –,**hypertensive** Herzleiden n. bei Hypertonie
- – –,**hyperthyroid** hyperthyreotisches Herzleiden n.
- – –,**syphilitic** syphilitisches Herzleiden n.
- – –,**rheumatic** rheumatisches Herzleiden n.
- – –,**valvular** Herzklappenerkrankung f.
- –,**drop** Tropfenherz n.
- **failure** Herzversagen n.
- – – **cell** Herzfehlerzelle f.
- – –,**congestive** dekompensierte muskuläre Herzinsuffizienz f., Stauungsinsuffizienz f. des (rechten) Herzens
- **function test** Herzfunktionsprüfung f.
- **lesion cell** Herzfehlerzelle f.
- **-lung machine** Herz-Lungenmaschine f.
- **rate** Herzfrequenz f.

heart shadow Herzschatten m.
- **-shaped** herzförmig
- **sound** Herzton m.
- – –,**split** gespaltener Herzton m.

heat Hitze f.;
(veter.) Brunst f.
- –,**to** erhitzen
- **conductor** Wärmeleiter m.
- **prostration** Hitzschlag m.
- **-resisting** hitzebeständig
- **-stable** hitzebeständig
- **stroke** Hitzschlag m.

heaves (veter.) paroxysmale Dyspnoe f.

heavy metal Schwermetall n.
hebephrenia Hebephrenie f.
hebephrenic hebephren
Heberden's node Heberdenscher Knoten m.
hebosteotomy Hebosteotomie f., Pubiotomie f.
Hebra's ointment Hebrasche Salbe f.
hectic hektisch
heel Ferse f.
- **-knee test** Knie-Hacken-Versuch m.

Heerfordt's disease Heerfordtsche Krankheit f.
Hegar's dilator Hegarstift m.
Heinz body Heinzsches Innenkörperchen n.
heliation Besonnung f.
heliophobia Heliophobie f., Lichtscheu f.
heliotherapy Heliotherapie f.
helium d. e. n.
hellebore Helleborus m.
helminth Eingeweidewurm m.
helminthiasis d. e. f., Wurmbefall m.
helminthological helminthologisch
helminthology Helminthologie f.
hema... (a), **haema...** (e) häma...
hemacytometer Hämazytometer n.
hemagglutination Hämagglutination f.

hemagglutinin Hämagglutinin n.
hemangioendothelioma Hämangioendotheliom n.
hemangioma Hämangiom n.
hemapoiesis Blutbildung f.
hemarthrosis Hämarthros m., blutiger Gelenkerguß m.
hematemesis Hämatemesis f., Bluterbrechen n.
hematin Hämatin n.
hematinuria Hämatinurie f.
hematoblast Hämatoblast m.
hematocele Hämatocele f.
hematocolpos Hämatokolpos m.
hematocrit Hämatokrit n.
hematocyturia Hämatozyturie f.
hemato-encephalic barrier Blut-Liquorschranke f.
hematogenesis Blutbildung f.
hematogenic hämatogen
hematogenous hämatogen
hematogone Hämatogonie f.
hematoidin Hämatoidin n.
hematological hämatologisch
hematologist Hämatologe m., Hämatologin f.
hematology Hämatologie f.
hematoma Hämatom m.
hematomyelia Hämatomyelie f.
hematoporphyrin Hämatoporphyrin n.
hematothorax Hämatothorax m.
hematotoxic hämatotoxisch
hematoxylin Hämatoxylin n.
hematuria Hämaturie f.
heme (a) Häm n.
hemeralopia Hemeralopie f.
hemiachromatopsia Hemiachromatopsie f.
hemialbumose d. e. f.
hemialgia Hemialgie f.
hemiamblyopia Hemiamblyopie f.
hemianaesthesia (e) Hemianästhesie f.
hemianesthesia (a) Hemianästhesie f.
hemianopsia Hemianopsie f.

hemianopsia, binasal binasale Hemianopsie f.
 —, **bitemporal** bitemporale Hemianopsie f.
 —, **heteronymous** heteronyme Hemianopsie f.
 —, **homonymous** homonyme Hemianopsie f.
 —, **quadrantic** Quadrantenhemianopsie f.
hemianoptic hemianoptisch
hemiapraxia Hemiapraxie f.
hemiataxia Hemiataxie f.
hemiathetosis Hemiathetose f.
hemiatrophy Hemiatrophie f.
hemiballism Hemiballismus m.
hemiblock d. e. m.
hemicellulase Hemizellulase f.
hemicellulose Hemizellulose f.
hemichorea d. e. f., Halbseitenchorea f.
hemicorporectomy Hemikorporektomie f.
hemicrania Hemikranie f.
hemiepilepsy Hemiepilepsie f., Halbseitenepilepsie f.
hemigastrectomy Hemigastrektomie f.
hemihydrate Hemihydrat n.
hemihyperidrosis Hemihyperhidrose f.
hemilaminectomy Hemilaminektomie f.
hemin (a) Hämin n.
hemiparaesthesia (e) Hemiparästhesie f.
hemiparesis Hemiparese f.
hemiparesthesia (a) Hemiparästhesie f.
hemipelvectomy Hemipelvektomie f.
hemiplegia Hemiplegie f.
hemiplegic hemiplegisch
hemisphere Hemisphäre f.
hemispherectomy Hemisphärektomie f.
hemisuccinate Hemisukzinat n.

hemo... (a), haemo... (e) hämo...
hemoblast Hämoblast m.
hemoblastosis Hämoblastose f.
hemochromatosis Hämochromatose f.
hemochromometer Hämochromometer n.
hemoculture Blutkultur f.
hemodialysis Hämodialyse f.
hemodynamic hämodynamisch
hemodynamics Hämodynamik f.
hemoglobin Hämoglobin n.
hemoglobinolysis Hämoglobinolyse f.
hemoglobinometer Hämoglobinometer n.
hemoglobinuria Hämoglobinurie f.
hemoglobinuric fever Schwarzwasserfieber n.
hemogram Hämogramm n., Blutbild n.
hemolysin Hämolysin n.
hemolysis Hämolyse f.
hemolytic hämolytisch
hemolyzate Hämolysat n.
hemolyzation Hämolysierung f.
hemolyze, to hämolysieren
hemometer Hämometer n.
hemoperfusion Hämoperfusion f.
hemopericardium Hämoperikard n.
hemophilia Hämophilie f.
hemophiliac Bluter m.
hemophilic hämophil
Hemophilus influenzae Influenzabazillus m.
– of Ducrey Streptobacterium ulceris mollis
– of Koch-Weeks Koch-Weeks-Bakterium n.
– of Morax-Axenfeld Morax-Axenfeld-Bazillus m.
– pertussis Bordet-Gengou-Bazillus m.

hemophthalmos Hämophthalmus m.
hemopoiesis Hämopoese f.
hemopoietic hämopoetisch
hemoptysis Hämoptyse f., Hämoptoe.f.
hemopyrrol Hämopyrrol n.
hemorrhage Hämorrhagie f., Blutung f., Blutsturz m.
–, cerebral Gehirnblutung f.
–, intestinal Darmblutung f.
– into the adrenal gland Nebennierenblutung f.
– of pregnancy Schwangerschaftsblutung f.
–, pulmonary Lungenblutung f.
–, subarachnoid Subarachnoidalblutung f.
–, subdural Subduralblutung f.
hemorrhagic hämorrhagisch
hemorrhoid Hämorrhoide f.
hemorrhoidal hämorrhoidal
hemosiderin Hämosiderin n.
hemosiderosis Hämosiderose f.
hemostasis Hämostase f., Blutstillung f.
hemostatic hämostatisch, hämostyptisch; Hämostypticum n.
– forceps Gefäßklemme f.
hemostyptic hämostyptisch; Hämostypticum n.
hemothorax Hämothorax m., Hämatothorax m.
hemotoxin Hämotoxin n., Blutgift n.
hen Huhn n., Henne f.
Henle's loop Henlesche Schleife f.
henry d. e. n.
heparin d. e. n.
heparinization Heparinisierung f.
heparinize, to heparinisieren
hepatargy Hepatargie f.
hepatic hepatisch
– and biliary ducts Leber- und Gallenwege m. pl.
hepaticoduodenostomy Hepatikoduodenostomie f.

hepaticostomy Hepatikostomie f.
hepaticotomy Hepatikotomie f.
hepatitis d. e. f.
–, **infectious** (a) Hepatitis epidemica
–, **infective** (e) Hepatitis epidemica
hepatization Hepatisation f.
hepatized hepatisiert
hepatocholangioduodenostomy Hepatocholangioduodenostomy f.
hepatocholangitis d. e. f.
hepatocyte Hepatozyt m.
hepatogastric hepatogastrisch
hepatogenous hepatogen
hepatography Hepatographie f.
hepatolenticular hepatolentikulär
hepatolienal d. e.
hepatomegaly Hepatomegalie f.
hepatopathy Hepatopathie f.
hepatorenal d. e.
hepatosis Hepatose f.
hepatosplenomegaly Hepatosplenomegalie f.
hepatotherapy Lebertherapie f.
hepatotoxic hepatotoxisch
hepatotropic hepatotrop
heptane Heptan n.
heptose d. e. f.
heptulose d. e. f.
herb Kraut n.
herbal Kräuterbuch n.
hereditable vererbbar
hereditary erblich
heredity Erblichkeit f., Vererbung f.
heritable vererbbar
hermaphrodite Zwitter m.
hermaphroditism Hermaphroditismus m.
hermetical hermetisch
hernia Hernie f.
–, **cicatrical** Narbenhernie f.
–, **crural** Schenkelhernie f.
–, **diaphragmatic** Zwerchfellhernie f.
–, **hiatal** Hiatushernie f.
–, **inguinal** Leistenhernie f.

hernia, irreducible irreponible Hernie f.
–, **reducible** reponible Hernie f.
–, **scrotal** Skrotalhernie f.
–, **strangulated** eingeklemmte Hernie f.
–, **Treitz's** Treitzsche Hernie f.
–, **umbilical** Nabelhernie f.
–, **vesical** Blasenbruch m.
hernial sac Bruchsack m.
herniation Hernienbildung f.
– **of intervertebral disk** Bandscheibenvorfall m.
herniotomy Herniotomie f., Bruchoperation f.
heroin d. e. n.
herpangina d. e. f.
herpes d. e. m.
– **zoster** d. e. m., Zoster m., Gürtelrose f.
herpetic herpetisch
herpetiform d. e.
herpetism Herpetismus m.
Herter's disease Zöliakie f.
Herxheimer's reaction Herxheimersche Reaktion f.
hesperidin d. e. n.
hetacillin d. e. n.
heteroautoplasty Heteroautoplastik f.
heterocentric heterozentrisch
heterochromia Heterochromie f.
heterochromosome Heterochromosom n.
heterochromous heterochrom
heterocomplement Heterokomplement n.
heterocyclic heterozyklisch
heterodont d. e.
heteroinfection Heteroinfektion f.
heteroinoculation Heteroinokulation f.
heterointoxication Heterointoxikation f.
heterokinesis Heterokinese f.
heterologous heterolog
heterology Heterologie f.

heteronomous heteronom
heteronymous heteronym
heterophagy Heterophagie f.
heterophilic heterophil
heterophonic heterophon
heterophoria Heterophorie f.
heteroplasia Heteroplasie f.
heteroplastic heteroplastisch
heteroploid d. e.
heteroscopy Heteroskopie f.
heterosexual heterosexuell
heterosuggestion d. e. f.
heterotopic heterotop
heterotopy Heterotopie f.
heterotoxin d. e. n.
heterotransplantation d. e. f.
heterozygous heterozygot
Heubner's disease Heubnersche Krankheit f.
hexagonal sechseckig
hexahydrate Hexahydrat n.
hexamethonium d. e. n.
hexamethonium bromide Hexamethoniumbromid n.
hexamethylenamine Hexamethylentetramin n.
hexamethylendiamine Hexamethylendiamin n.
hexamethylenetetramine Hexamethylentetramin n.
hexamine (e) Hexamethylentetramin n.
hexane Hexan n.
hexanicotinate Hexanikotinat n.
hexanoate Hexanoat n.
hexapeptide Hexapeptid n.
hexavalent sechswertig
hexazonium d. e. n.
hexetidine Hexetidin n.
heximide Heximid n.
hexokinase d. e. f.
hexopeptidase d. e. f.
hexosamine Hexosamin n.
Hexose d. e. f.
– diphosphate Hexosediphosphat n.

Hexose monophosphate Hexosemonophosphat n.
hexosephosphatase d. e. f.
hexuronate Hexuronat n.
hexyl d. e. n.
hexylamine Hexylamin n.
hexylresorcinol Hexylresorzin n.
hiatal hernia Hiatushernie f.
hibernation Winterschlaf m.
–, artificial künstlicher Winterschlaf m.
hiccough Schluckauf m.
hiccup Schluckauf m.
hide Haut f., Fell n.
hide, to verbergen
hidradenitis d. e. f.
hidradenoma Hidradenom n.
hidrosis Hidrose f.
hidrotic hidrotisch
high-altitude health resort Höhenkurort m.
high calcium diet kalziumreiche Diät f.
– energy phosphate energiereiches Phosphat n.
– frequency Hochfrequenz f.
– grade hochgradig
– molecular hochmolekular
– protein diet eiweißreiche Diät f.
– vitamin diet vitaminreiche Diät f.
– voltage Hochspannung f.
highly inflammable feuergefährlich
hilar hilär
hilitis d. e. f.
hillock Vorwölbung f.
hind Hirschkuh f.
hinge Scharnier n.
hinge joint Scharniergelenk n.
hip Hüfte f.
– joint Hüftgelenk n.
hippocampus major Ammonshorn n.
hippocratic oath hippokratischer Eid m.
hippurate Hippurat n.

hippuric acid Hippursäure f.
Hirschsprung's disease Hirschsprungsche Krankheit f.
hirsutism Hirsutismus m.
hirudin d. e. n.
hirudinea d. e. n. pl.
His' bundle Hissches Bündel n.
histaminase d. e. f.
histamine Histamin n.
histidase d. e. f.
histidinase d. e. f.
histidine Histidin n.
histidyl d. e. n.
histioblast d. e. m.
histiocyte Histiozyt m.
histiocytic histiozytär
histiocytosis Histiozytose f.
histoadhesive Gewebe-Klebstoff m.
histochemical histochemisch
histochemistry Histochemie f.
histogenesis Histogenese f.
histological histologisch
histologist Histologe m., Histologin f.
histology Histologie f.
histolysis Histolyse f.
histolytic histolytisch
histomorphological histomorphologisch
histomorphology Histomorphologie f.
histone Histon n.
histopathological histopathologisch
histopathology Histopathologie f.
histoplasmosis Histoplasmose f.
history of medicine Medizingeschichte f.
histotropic histiotrop
hives Nesselsucht f.
hoarse heiser
hoarseness Heiserheit f.
hobble, to hinken, humpeln
Hochsinger's phenomenon Hochsingersches Zeichen n.
Hodge's pessary Hodge-Pessar n.

Hodgkin's disease Lymphogranulomatose f.
hoe Hacke f.
hog Schwein n.
holder Halter m.
hole Loch n.
hollow of the knee Kniekehle f.
holmium d. e. n.
holocrine holokrin
holography Holographie f.
Holzknecht space Holzknechtscher Raum m.
homalography Homalographie f.
homatropine Homatropin n.
– **hydrobromide** Homatropinhydrobromid n.
home dialysis Heimdialyse f.
homeopathical (a) homöopathisch
homeopathist (a) Homöopath m., Homöopathin f.
homeopathy (a) Homöopathie f.
homeostasis (a) Homöostase f.
homoeopathical (e) homöopathisch
homeotherapy (a) Homöotherapie f.
homeotransplantation (a) Homöotransplantation f.
homesickness Heimweh n.
Home's lobe Homescher Lappen m.
homicide Totschlag m.
homocentric homozentrisch
homocyclic homozyklisch
homocystine Homozystin n.
homoeopathical (e) homöopathisch
homoeopathist (e) Homöopath m., Homöopathin f.
homoeopathy (e) Homöopathie f.
homoeostasis (e) Homöostase f.
homoeotherapy (e) Homöotherapie f.
homoeotransplantation (e) Homöotransplantation f.
homoerotic homoerotisch
homogenate Homogenat n.
homogeneity Homogenität f.

homogeneous homogen
homogenization Homogenisierung f.
homogenize, to homogenisieren
homolateral d. e.
homologen Homolog n.
homologous homolog
− **serum hepatitis** homologe Serumhepatitis f.
homologue Homolog n.
homology Homologie f.
homonomous homonom
homonymous homonym
homoplastic homoplastisch
homoplasty Homoplastik f.
homoserine Homoserin n.
homosexual homosexuell
homosexuality Homosexualität f.
homotransplantation d. e. f.
homozygosis Homozygotie f.
homozygous homozygot
honey Honig m.
honey-bee Honigbiene f.
hoof Huf m.
hoof-beat Hufschlag m.
hoof-bound zwanghufig
hoofed animal Huftier n.
hook Haken m.
− **retractor** Muskelhaken m.
−, **sharp** scharfer Haken m.
hookworm Hakenwurm m.
hoove Tympanie f. des Pansens
hooven Tympanie f. des Pansens
hop Hopfen m.
hopogan Magnesiumperoxyd n.
horary stündlich
horizon Horizont m.
horizontal d. e.
hormonal hormonell
hormone Hormon n.
hormonotherapy Hormontherapie f.
horn d. e. n.
Horner's syndrome Hornersches Syndrom n.
horny hornig
horse Pferd n.

horse, bay Braune m., braunes Pferd n.
horse, black Rappe m.
horse chestnut Roßkastanie f.
horse-knacker Abdecker m.
horse leech Pferdeegel m.
− **serum** Pferdeserum n.
− **sickness** Pferdepest f., Paardenziekte f.
−, **sorrel** Fuchs m. (Pferd)
−, **white** Schimmel m. (Pferd)
horseradish Meerrettich m.
horseshoe Hufeisen n.
hospital Krankenhaus n.
− **for incurables** Pflegeanstalt f.
− **regional** Kreiskrankenhaus n.
hospitalism Hospitalismus m.
hospitalization Hospitalisierung f., Krankenhauseinlieferung f., Krankenhausaufnahme f.
hospitalize, to hospitalisieren, in ein Krankenhaus einliefern, in einem Krankenhaus aufnehmen
host Wirt m.
hot air Heißluft f.
− **pack** heiße Packung f.
Hottentot apron Hottentottenschürze f.
hot-water bottle Wärmflasche f.
hourglass contraction of stomach Sanduhrmagen m.
hour of death Todesstunde f.
hoven Tympanie f. des Pansens
Howell's body Jolly-Körper m.
hubble, to humpeln
hum, venous Nonnensausen n.
human menschlich, human
human growth hormone menschliches Wachstumshormon n.
humanity Menschlichkeit f., Humanität f.
humeroscapular humeroskapular
humidity Feuchtigkeit f., Feuchtigkeitsgrad m.
humor (a) Flüssigkeit f.; Hautleiden n.

humour (e) Flüssigkeit f.; Hautleiden n.
humoral d. e.
hunger Hunger m.
hungry hungrig
Hunt's test Hunt-Test m.
Hunter's canal Adduktorenkanal m.
Hunter's glossitis Huntersche Glossitis f.
Huntington's chorea Huntingtonsche Chorea f.
Hurler's syndrome Hurler-Syndrome n.
hurt, to beschädigen, verletzen
hurtfull schädlich
Hutchinson's triad Hutchinsonsche Trias f.
hyalin d. e. n.
hyaline hyalin
− cast hyaliner Zylinder m.
hyalitis d. e. f.
hyaloplasm Hyaloplasma n.
hyaluronate Hyaluronat n.
hyaluronidase d. e. f.
hybrid Hybride f.
hybridization Hybridation f.
hydantoin d. e. n.
hydatid Hydatide f.
− disease Echinokokkose f.
− fremitus Hydatidenschwirren n.
hydraemia (a) Hydrämie f.
hydraemic (e) hydrämisch
hydralazine Hydralazin n.
hydramine Hydramin n.
hydramnion d. e. n.
hydrastine Hydrastin n.
hydrastinine Hydrastinin n.
hydrate Hydrat n.
hydrate, to hydrieren
hydration d. e. f.
hydraulic hydraulisch
hydrazide Hydrazid n.
hydrazine Hydrazin n.
hydrazinophthalazine Hydrazinophthalazin n.

hydrazone Hydrazone n.
hydremia (a) Hydrämie f.
hydremic (a) hydrämisch
hydroa vacciniforme d. e.
hydrobilirubin d. e. n.
hydrobromate Hydrobromat n.
hydrobromide Hydrobromid n.
hydrocarbon Kohlenwasserstoff m.
hydrocele d. e. f.
hydrocephalus d. e. m.
−, acute tuberkulöse Meningitis f.
hydrochloric acid Salzsäure f.
hydrochloride Hydrochlorid n.
hydrochlorothiazide Hydrochlorothiazid n.
hydrocholesterol Hydrocholesterin n.
hydrocortisone Hydrocortison n.
hydrocupreine Hydrocuprein n.
hydrodynamic hydrodynamisch
hydrodynamics Hydrodynamik f.
hydroflumethiazide Hydroflumethiazid n.
hydrogen Wasserstoff m.
−, heavy schwerer Wasserstoff m.
− ion concentration Wasserstoffionenkonzentration f.
− peroxide Wasserstoffsuperoxyd n.
− sulfide (a) Schwefelwasserstoff m.
− sulphide (e) Schwefelwasserstoff m.
hydrogenase d. e. f.
hydrolase d. e. f.
hydrolysate Hydrolysat n.
hydrolysis Hydrolyse f.
hydrolytic hydrolytisch
hydrolyze, to hydrolysieren
hydronephrosis Hydronephrose f.
hydropathic hydropathisch
hydrophilia Hydrophilie f.
hydrophilous hydrophil
hydrophobia Hydrophobie f.
hydrophthalmos Hydrophthalmus m.
hydropic hydropisch

hydrops d. e. m.
hydroquinone Hydrochinon n.
hydrorrhea (a) Hydrorrhöe f.
hydrorrhoea (e) Hydrorrhöe f.
hydrosalpinx d. e. f.
hydrotherapeutical hydrotherapeutisch
hydrotherapeutics Hydrotherapie f.
hydrotherapy Hydrotherapie f.
hydrothorax d. e. m.
hydrous wasserhaltig
hydroxide Hydroxyd n.
hydroxybutyrate Hydroxybutyrat n.
hydroxychloroquine Hydroxychlorochin n.
hydroxycobalamine Hydroxykobalamin n.
hydroxycodeine Hydroxykodein n.
hydroxycorticosteroid Hydroxykortikosteroid n.
hydroxyethyl starch Hydroxyäthylstärke f.
hydroxyl d. e. n.
hydroxylamine Hydroxylamin n.
hydroxylase d. e. f.
hydroxylate, to hydroxylieren
hydroxyproline Hydroxyprolin n.
hydroxysteroid d. e. n.
hydroxytryptamine Hydroxytryptamin n.
hydroxytryptophan d. e. n.
hyena Hyäne f.
hygiene d. e. f.
hygienic hygienisch
hygienics Hygiene f.
hygienist Hygieniker m., Hygienikerin f.
hygroma Hygrom n.
hygrometer d. e. n.
hygrometric hygrometrisch
hygrometry Hygrometrie f.
hygroscopic hygroskopisch
hymen d. e. n.
hymenectomy Hymenektomie f.
hymenitis d. e. f.
hymenolepiasis d. e. f.
hyoscyamine Hyoszyamin n.
hypacid subazid
hypacidity Hypazidität f., Subazidität f.
hypaesthesia (e) Hypästhesie f.
hypaesthetic (e) hypästhetisch
hypalbuminosis Hypalbuminämie f.
hypalgesia Hypalgesie f.
hypalgesic hypalgetisch
hyperacid superazid, hyperazid
hyperacidity Superazidität f. Hyperazidität f.
hyperacousia (e) Hyperakusis f.
hyperactivity Hyperaktivität f.
hyperacusis (a) Hyperakusis f.
hyperadrenalism Hyperadrenalismus m.
hyperaemia (e) Hyperämie f.
hyperaemic (e) hyperämisch
hyperaesthesia (e) Hyperästhesie f.
hyperaesthetic (e) hyperästhetisch
hyperalbuminosis Hyperalbuminose f., Hyperalbuminämie f.
hyperaldosteronism Hyperaldosteronismus m.
hyperalgesia Hyperalgesie f.
hyperalgesic hyperalgetisch
hyperalgia Hyperalgie f.
hyperalimentation Überernährung f.
hyperbaric hyperbar
hyperbilirubinaemia (e) Hyperbilirubinämie f.
hyberbilirubinaemic (e) hyperbilirubinämisch
hyperbilirubinemia (a) Hyperbilirubinämie f.
hyperbilirubinemic (a) hyperbilirubinämisch
hyperbola Hyperbel f.
hypercalcaemia (e) Hyperkalzämie f.
hypercalcemia (a) Hyperkalzämie f.

hypercapnia Hyperkapnie f.
hypercementosis Hyperzementose f.
hyperchloraemia (e) Hyperchlorämie f.
hyperchloraemic (e) hyperchlorämisch
hyperchloremia (a) Hyperchlorämie f.
hyperchloremic (a) hyperchlorämisch
hyperchlorhydria Hyperchlorhydrie f.
hyperchlorhydric hyperchlorhydrisch
hypercholesteraemia (e) Hypercholesterinämie f.
hypercholesteremia (a) Hypercholesterinämie f.
hyperchromatic hyperchromatisch
hyperchromatism Hyperchromasie f.
hyperchromatosis Hyperchromasie f.
hyperchromic hyperchrom
hypercupraemia (e) Hypercuprämie f.
hypercupremia (a) Hypercuprämie f.
hyperdense hyperdens
hyperdicrotism Hyperdikrotie f.
hyperemesis d. e. f.
hyperemia (a) Hyperämie f.
hyperemic (a) hyperämisch
hypereosinophilia Hypereosinophilie f.
hyperergic hyperergisch
hyperergy Hyperergie f.
hyperesthesia (a) Hyperästhesie f.
hyperesthetic (a) hyperästhetisch
hyperextension d. e. f.
hyperfibrinolysis Hyperfibrinolyse f.
hyperfibrinolytic hyperfibrinolytisch
hyperflexion d. e. f.

hyperfunction Überfunktion f., Hyperfunktion f.
hypergalactia Hypergalaktie f.
hypergenitalism Hypergenitalismus m.
hyperglobulia Hyperglobulie f.
hyperglobulinaemia (e) Hyperglobulinämie f.
hyperglobulinemia (a) Hyperglobulinämie f.
hyperglycaemia (e) Hyperglykämie f.
hyperglycaemic (e) hyperglykämisch
hyperglycemia (a) Hyperglykämie f.
hyperglycemic (a) hyperglykämisch
hypergonadism Keimdrüsenüberfunktion f.
hyperhidrosis Hyperhidrose f.
hyperinsulinism Hyperinsulinismus m.
hyperirritability Übererregbarkeit f.
hyperirritable übererregbar
hyperkalaemia (e) Hyperkaliämie f.
hyperkalemia (e) Hyperkaliämie f.
hyperkeratosis Hyperkeratose f.
hyperkinesia Hyperkinese f.
hyperkinetic hyperkinetisch
hyperleukocytosis Hyperleukozytose f.
hyperlipaemia (e) Hyperlipämie f.
hyperlipemia (a) Hyperlipämie f.
hyperlipoproteidaemia (e) Hyperlipoproteidämie f.
hyperlipoproteidemia (a) Hyperlipoproteidämie f.
hyperluteinization Hyperluteinisierung f.
hypermagnesaemia (e) Hypermagnesiämie f.
hypermagnesemia (a) Hypermagnesiämie f.
hypermature überreif

hypermenorrhea (a) Hypermenorrhöe f.
hypermenorrhoea (e) Hypermenorrhöe f.
hypermetropia Hypermetropie f.
hypermetropic hypermetrop
hypermotility Hypermotilität f.
hypernephroma Hypernephrom n.
hypernormal d. e., übernormal
hypernutrition Überernährung f.
hyperopia Hyperopie f., Weitsichtigkeit f.
hyperopic hyperopisch
hyperostosis Hyperostose f.
hyperoxaluria Hyperoxalurie f.
hyperoxaluric hyperoxalurisch
hyperoxia Hyperoxie f.
hyperparathyroidism Epithelkörperchenüberfunktion f.
hyperpathia Hyperpathie f.
hyperperistalsis Hyperperistaltik f.
hyperphagia Hyperphagie f.
hyperpiesia essentielle Hypertonie f.
hyperpigmentation d. e. f., Überpigmentierung f.
hyperpituitarism Hypophysenüberfunktion f.
hyperplasia Hyperplasie f.
hyperplastic hyperplastisch
hyperpnea (a) Hyperpnoe f.
hyperpnoea (e) Hyperpnoe f.
hyperpotassaemia (e) Hyperkaliämie f.
hyperpotassemia (a) Hyperkaliämie f.
hyperproinsulinaemia (e) Hyperproinsulinämie f.
hyperproinsulinemia (a) Hyperproinsulinämie f.
hyperproteinaemia (e) Hyperproteinämie f.
hyperproteinemia (a) Hyperproteinämie f.
hyperpyretic hyperpyretisch
hyperpyrexia Hyperpyrexie f.
hyperreflexia Hyperreflexie f.

hypersecretion Hypersekretion f.
hypersecretory hypersekretorisch
hypersegmented übersegmentiert, hypersegmentiert
hypersensibility Überempfindlichkeit f.
hypersensible überempfindlich
hypersensitive hypersensitiv, überempfindlich
hypersensitiveness Hypersensitivität f., Überempfindlichkeit f.
hypersomnia Schlafsucht f.
hypersplenia Hypersplenie f.
hypersplenism Hypersplenie f.
hypersthenuria Hypersthenurie f.
hypersystole d. e. f.
hypertensin d. e. n.
hypertension d. e. f., Hochdruck m.
–, essential essentielle Hypertonie f.
–, Goldblat Goldblat-Hypertonie f.
–, neurogenic essentielle Hypertonie f.
–, pale blasser Hochdruck m.
–, red roter Hochdruck m.
hypertensive hypertensiv
hyperthermia Hyperthermie f.
hyperthymia Hyperthymie f.
hyperthymic hyperthym
hyperthymism Thymusdrüsenüberfunktion f.
hyperthymization Thymusdrüsenüberfunktion f.
hyperthyreosis Hyperthyreose f.
hyperthyroid hyperthyreotisch
hyperthyroidism Hyperthyreose f.
hypertonia Hypertonie f.
hypertonic hypertonisch
hypertrichosis Hypertrichose f.
hypertrophic hypertrophisch
hypertrophy Hypertrophie f.
hyperuricaemia (e) Hyperurikämie f.
hyperuricemia (a) Hyperurikämie f.
hyperventilation d. e. f.
hypervitaminosis Hypervitaminose f.

hypervolaemia (e) Hypervolämie f.
hypervolemia (a) Hypervolämie f.
hypesthesia (a) Hypästhesie f.
hypesthetic (a) hypästhetisch
hyphaemia (e) Hyphäma n.
hyphemia (a) Hyphäma n.
hypinosis Hypinose f.
hypnoanalysis Hypnoanalyse f.
hypnosis Hypnose f.
hypnotic hypnotisch
hypnotism Hypnotismus m.
hypnotist Hypnotiseur m.
hypnotization Hypnotisierung f.
hypnotize, to hypnotisieren
hypoalimentation Unterernährung f.
hypobaropathy Höhenkrankheit f.
hypocalcaemia (e) Hypokalzämie f.
hypocalcaemic (e) hypokalzämisch
hypocalcemia (a) Hypokalzämie f.
hypocalcemic (a) hypokalzämisch
hypocapnia Hypokapnie f.
hypochloraemia (e) Hypochlorämie f.
hypochloraemic (e) hypochlorämisch
hypochloremia (a) Hypochlorämie f.
hypochloremic (a) hypochlorämisch
hypochlorhydria Hypochlorhydrie f.
hypochlorhydric hypochlorhydrisch
hypochlorite Hypochlorit n.
hypocholesteraemia (e) Hypocholesterinämie f.
hypocholesteremia (a) Hypocholesterinämie f.
hypochondriac Hypochonder m.
hypochondriacal hypochondrisch
hypochondriasis Hypochondrie f.
hypochromasia Hypochromasie f.
hypochromatic hypochromatisch
hypochromia Hypochromie f.
hypochromic hypochrom

hypoconid Hypokonid m.
hypoconulid Hypokonulid m.
hypocorticalism Nebennierenrindenunterfunktion f.
hypodense hypodens
hypodermic subkutan
hypodermoclysis subkutane Infusion f.
hypodynamic hypodynamisch, hypodynam
hypofibrinogenaemia (e) Hypofibrinogenämie f.
hypofibrinogenemia (a) Hypofibrinogenämie f.
hypofunction Unterfunktion f.
hypogalactia Hypogalaktie f.
hypogammaglobulinaemia (e) Hypogammaglobulinämie f.
hypogammaglobulinemia (a) Hypogammaglobulinämie f.
hypogastric hypogastrisch
hypogenitalism Hypogenitalismus m.
hypoglycaemia (e) Hypoglykämie f.
hypoglycaemic (e) hypoglykämisch
hypoglycemia (a) Hypoglykämie f.
hypoglycemic (a) hypoglykämisch
hypogonadism Keimdrüsenunterfunktion f.
hypokalaemia (e) Hypokaliämie f.
hypokalemia (a) Hypokaliämie f.
hypokinesis Hypokinese f.
hypokinetic hypokinetisch
hypomagnesaemia (e) Hypomagnesiämie f.
hypomagnesemia (a) Hypomagnesiämie f.
hypomania Hypomanie f.
hypomanic hypomanisch
hypomenorrhea (a) Hypomenorrhöe f.
hypomenorrhoea (e) Hypomenorrhöe f.
hyponatraemia (e) Hyponatriämie f.

hyponatremia (a) Hyponatriämie f.
hypoparathyroidism Epithelkörperchenunterfunktion f.
hypophamine Hypophysenhinterlappenhormon n.
hypopharyngeal d. e.
hypophosphate Hypophosphat n.
hypophosphite Hypophosphit n.
hypophysectomize, to hypophysektomieren
hypophysectomy Hypophysektomie f.
hypophysial hypophysär
hypophysin d. e. n.
hypophysis Hypophyse f.
—,anterior lobe Hypophysenvorderlappen m.
—,posterior lobe Hypophysenhinterlappen m.
hypophysitis d. e. f.
hypopiesia arterielle Hypotonie f.
hypopituitarism Hypophysenunterfunktion f.
hypoplasia Hypoplasie f.
hypoplastic hypoplastisch
hypopotassaemia (e) Hypokaliämie f.
hypopotassemia (a) Hypokaliämie f.
hypoproteinaemia (e) Hypoproteinämie f.
hypoproteinemia (a) Hypoproteinämie f.
hypoprothrombinaemia (e) Hypoprothrombinämie f.
hypoprothrombinemia (a) Hypoprothrombinämie f.
hypopyon d. e. n.
hyporeflexia Hyporeflexie f.
hypospadias Hypospadie f.
hypostasis Hypostase f.
hypostatic hypostatisch
hyposthenuria Hyposthenurie f.
hypotension Hypotonie f., Hypotension f.

hypotensive hypotensiv
hypothalamic hypothalamisch
hypothermia Hypothermie f.
—,accidental Spontanhypothermie f.
hypothesis Hypothese f.
hypothetical hypothetisch
hypothyreosis Hypothyreose f.
hypothyroid hypothyreotisch
hypotonia Hypotonie f.
hypotonic hypotonisch
hypotrichosis Hypotrichose f.
hypoventilation d. e. f.
hypovitaminosis Hypovitaminose f.
hypovolaemia (e) Hypovolämie f.
hypovolemia (a) Hypovolämie f.
hypoxaemia (e) Hypoxämie f.
hypoxaemic (e) hypoxämisch
hypoxanthine Hypoxanthin n.
hypoxemia (a) Hypoxämie f.
hypoxemic (a) hypoxämisch
hypoxia Hypoxie f.
hypsarrhythmia Hypsarrhythmie f.
hypsodont d. e.
hysterectomy Hysterektomie f.
hysteresis Hysterese f.
hysteria Hysterie f.
hysteriac Hysteriker m., Hysterikerin f.
hysterical hysterisch
hysterics Hysterieanfall m.
hysterocervicotomy Hysterozervikotomie f.
hysteroepilepsy Hysteroepilepsie f.
hysterographical hysterographisch
hysterography Hysterographie f.
hysteronarcolepsy Hysteronarkolepsie f.
hysteroptosis Hysteroptose f.
hysterosalpingography Hysterolapingographie f.
hysterosalpingostomy Hysterosalpingostomie f.
hysterotomy Hysterotomie f.
hysterotonin d. e. n.

I

IA (= intraarterial) i.a. (= intraarteriell)
iatrogenic iatrogen
ibuprofen d. e. n.
ice bag Eisbeutel m.
ichthyosis Ichthyose f.
ichthyotic ichthyotisch
icteric ikterisch
icterus Ikterus m.
idea Gedanke m., Idee f.
ideal ideal; Ideal n.
ideation d. e. f.
identical identisch
identification Identifizierung f.
identify, to identifizieren
identity Identität f.
ideomotor ideomotorisch
idiocratic idiokratisch
idiocy Idiotie f.
idioisoagglutinin d. e. n.
idioisolysin d. e. n.
idiolysin d. e. n.
idiopathic idiopathisch
− **steatorrhea** (a) Zöliakie f.
− **steatorrhoea** (e) Zöliakie f.
idiosyncrasy Idiosynkrasie f.
idiosyncratic idiosynkratisch
idiot d. e. m., Idiotin f.
idiotic idiotisch
idiotype Idiotyp m.
idiotypic idiotypisch
ignipuncture Ignipunktur f.
iguana Leguan m.
ileitis d. e. f.
−, **terminal** Ileitis terminalis
ileocaecal (e) ileozökal
ileocecal (a) ileozökal
ileocolic ileokolisch
ileocolitis Ileokolitis f.
ileocolostomy Ileokolostomie f.
ileocolotomy Ileokolotomie f.
ileo-ileostomy Ileo-Ileostomie f.
ileoproctostomy Ileoproktostomie f.

ileosigmoidostomy Ileosigmoidostomie f.
ileostomy Ileostomie f.
ileotomy Ileotomie f.
ileotransversostomy Ileotransversostomie f.
ileum d. e. n.
ileus d. e. m.
iliac crest Darmbeinkamm m.
iliopubic iliopubisch
ill krank, übel; Krankheit f.
−, **to fall** − krank werden, erkranken
−, **mentally** geisteskrank; Geisteskranker m., Geisteskranke f.
illness Krankheit f., Erkrankung f.
illegitimate ungesetzlich, illegitim
illumination Beleuchtung f.
illusion d. e. f.
illusional illusionär
image Bild n.
− **intensifier** Bildverstärker m.
imaginary imaginär
imagination Einbildungskraft f., Vorstellung f.
imagine, to sich einbilden, sich vorstellen
imaging, medical medizinisches bildgebendes System n.
imbalance Gleichgewichtsstörung f.
− **of the autonomic nervous system** vegetative Dystonie f.
imbecile imbezill, schwachsinnig
imbecility Imbezillität f.
imbibition d. e. f.
imide Imid n.
iminazole Iminazol n.
iminodibenzyl d. e. n.
iminostilbene Iminostilben n.
imipramine Imipramin n.
immature unreif
immaturity Unreife f.
immediate unmittelbar

immerse, to eintauchen
immersion d. e. f.
imminent drohend, bevorstehend
immiscible unmischbar
immitigable unstillbar
immobile unbeweglich, immobil
immobility Unbeweglichkeit f.
immobilize, to immobilisieren
immoral unmoralisch
immune from immun gegen
immunity from Immunität f. gegen
immunizate, to immunisieren
immunization Immunisierung f.
− register Impfliste f.
immunoblastic immunoblastisch
immunochemical immunochemisch
immunochemistry Immunchemie f.
immunochromatography Immunochromatographie f.
immunodiffusion d. e. f.
immunoelectrophoresis Immunelektrophorese f.
immunofluorescence Immunofluoreszenz f.
immunoglobulin Immunglobulin n.
immunological immunologisch
immunology Immunologie f.
immunoreaction Immunoreaktion f.
immunoreactive immunoreaktiv
immunoreactivity Immunreaktionsfähigkeit f.
immunosuppression d. e. f.
immunosuppressive immunsuppressiv
immunotherapy Immunotherapie f.
impacted eingeklemmt, eingekeilt
impaction Einklemmung f., Einkeilung f.
impairment Störung f., Schwächung f.
impalement Pfählung f.
impassibility Teilnahmslosigkeit f.
impedance Impedanz f.

impede, to erschweren, behindern
impenetrable undurchdringlich
impenetrability Undurchdringlichkeit f.
imperceptible unmerklich, nicht wahrnehmbar
impermeable undurchgängig
impervious undurchgängig
impetiginization Impetiginisierung f.
impetiginous impetiginös
impetigo d. e. f.
implant Implantat n.
implant, to implantieren, einpflanzen
implantation d. e. f.
implantology Implantologie f.
implication Übergreifen n., Einbeziehung f.; Folgerung f.
impotence Impotenz f.
impotent d. e.
impregnate, to imprägnieren; schwängern
impregnation Imprägnation f.; Schwängerung f.
impression Impression f., Eindruck m., Abdruck m.
− tray Abdrucklöffel m.
improper unpassend, unrichtig, ungenau
improve, to bessern, verbessern
improvement Besserung f.
impulse Impuls m.
impure unrein, unsauber
inactivate, to inaktivieren
inactivation Inaktivierung f.
inactive inaktiv
inadequacy Inadäquanz f.
inadequate inadäquat
inanition d. e. f.
inappetence Inappetenz f.
inborn angeboren
inbreeding Inzucht f.
incalculable unberechenbar
incarcerate, to inkarzerieren
incarceration Inkarzeration f.
incest Inzest m., Blutschande f.

incidence Häufigkeitsquote f., Vorkommen n.
incident Zwischenfall m.
incineration Veraschung f.
incision Einschnitt m., Inzision f.
incisor Schneidezahn m.
incisure Inzisur f.
incitement Anregung f.
inclination Inklination f., Neigung f.
inclusion Einschluß m.
inclusion body Einschlußkörperchen n.
incoherent inkohärent
incompatibility Inkompatibilität f., Unverträglichkeit f.
incompatible unverträglich
incompetence Insuffizienz f.; Inkompetenz f.
incompetency Insuffizienz f.; Inkompetenz f.
incomplete unvollständig
inconscious unbewußt
inconstancy Unbeständigkeit f., Inkonstanz f.
inconstant unbeständig, inkonstant
incontinence Inkontinenz f.
incontinence of urine Harninkontinenz f.
incontinent inkontinent
incorporate, to einverleiben
incorporation Einverleibung f.
increase Steigerung f., Zunahme f.
increase, to steigern, vermehren
– in weight Gewichtszunahme f.
incretory inkretorisch
incrustation Krustenbildung f.
incubate, to inkubieren
incubation Inkubation f.
incubator Inkubator m.; Brutofen m.
incubus Alpdrücken n.
incurable unheilbar
indenture Zähnelung f.
independent unabhängig
indestructible unzerstörbar

index Index m.; Zeigefinger m.
indican Indikan n.
indicanuria Indikanurie f.
indicate, to anzeigen, indizieren
indication Indikation f.
indicator Indikator m.; Zeigefinger m.
indifferent d. e.
indigestible unverdaulich
indigestion Verdauungsstörung f., d. e. f.
indigo d. e. m.
indigo blue Indigoblau n.
indigo carmine Indigokarmin n.
indirect indirekt, mittelbar
indisposed indisponiert, unpäßlich
indisposition d. e. f., Unpäßlichkeit f.
indissoluble unauflösbar, unauflöslich
indistinct undeutlich
indium d. e. n.
individual individuell
individualize, to individualisieren
indocyanine green Indozyaningrün n.
indolamine Indolamin n.
indole Indol n.
indolence Indolenz f.
indolent d. e.
indomethacin d. e. n.
indophenol d. e. n.
indoxyl d. e. n.
induce, to induzieren
inductance Selbstinduktion f.
induction Induktion f.
inductor Induktor m.
indurate, to indurieren
induration d. e. f.
indurative indurativ
industrial medicine Gewerbemedizin f.
ineducable unerziehbar
inefficient wirkungslos, unwirksam, unergiebig
infancy Säuglingsalter n.
infant Kleinkind n., Säugling m.

infant welfare Säuglingsfürsorge f.
infantile infantil
infantilism Infantilismus m.
−,intestinal Herter-Heubnersche Krankheit f.
infarct Infarct m.
infarction Infarzierung f.
−,silent stumme Infarzierung f.
infect, to infizieren, verseuchen
infection Infektion f.
infectiosity Infektiosität f.
infectious infektiös
− disease Infektionskrankheit f.
− erythema Erythema infectiosum
infecundity Unfruchtbarkeit f.
infertibility Unfruchtbarkeit f.
infertility Unfruchtbarkeit f.
infestation Befall m.
infestment Befall m.
infiltrate Infiltrat n.
−,to infiltrieren
infiltration d. e. f.
infinitesimal d. e.
infirmary Sanitätseinrichtung f., Verbandplatz m., Krankenhaus n., Behandlungsstation f.
inflame, to entzünden
inflammation Entzündung f.
inflammatory entzündlich
inflation Aufblasung f., Einblasung f.
influenza d. e. f., Grippe f.
information d. e. f.
infraaxillary infraaxillär
infraclavicular infraklavikulär
infraction Infraktion f.
infradiaphragmatic infradiaphragmatisch
infraglottic infraglottisch
infrahisian unterhalb des His-Bündels
inframammary inframammär
inframandibular inframandibulär
inframaxillary inframaxillär
infraocclusion Infraokklusion f.
infraorbital d. e.

infrapatellar d. e.
infra-red Infrarot n.; infrarot
infra-red thermography Infrarotthermographie f.
infrascapular infraskapulär
infrasellar infrasellär
infraspinal d. e.
infraspinous infraspinal
infravalvular infravalvulär
infriction Einreibung f.
infundibular infundibulär
infusion d. e. f.
infusion pump Infusionspumpe f.
infusoria Infusorien n. pl.
ingestion Nahrungsaufnahme f.
ingredient Ingredienz f.
inguinal d. e.
− ring Inguinalring m.
ingrown eingewachsen
inhabit, to bewohnen, innewohnen
inhalation d. e. f.
inhale, to inhalieren
inhaler Inhalationsapparat m.
inhaler, pocket Tascheninhalator m.
inherit, to erben, vererben
inheritance Vererbung f., Erbgang m.
inherited vererbt
inhibin d. e. n.
inhibit, to hemmen
inhibition Hemmung f.
inhibitor d. e. m.
inhibitory hemmend
inhomogenous inhomogen
inhuman unmenschlich
inhumanity Unmenschlichkeit f.
initial d. e.
− sclerosis Initialsklerose f.
− stage Initialstadium n., Anfangsstadium n.
inject, to injizieren, einspritzen
injection Injektion f., Einspritzung f.
−,ready for − spritzfertig, spritzbereit
injure, to verletzen
injurious schädlich

injury Verletzung f., Schaden m.
ink Tinte f.
inlay (dent.) Gußfüllung f.
INN (= international nonproprietary name) generische Bezeichnung f.
innate angeboren
inner ear Innenohr n.
innervate, to innervieren
innervation d. e. f.
innocent unschädlich
innocuous unschädlich
innoxious unschädlich
inoculate, to inokulieren
inoculation Inokulation f.
inoperable inoperabel
inorganic anorganisch
inosine Inosin n.
inositol Inosit n.
inotropic inotrop
in-patient stationärer Patient m., stationäre Patientin f.
input Eingabe f.
inructation Luftschlucken n.
inquest, to hold an – obduzieren
insalivation Speicheldurchmischung f.
insane geisteskrank, geistesgestört
insanitary unhygienisch
insanity Geisteskrankheit f., geistige Störung f.
inscription Inskription f.
insect Insekt n.
– powder Insektenpulver n.
insecticide insektizid; Insektenvertilgungsmittel n.
insecure unsicher
insecurity Unsicherheit f.
insemination d. e. f., Besamung f.
insenescence Altern n.
insensible gefühllos, unempfindlich
insensibility Gefühllosigkeit f., Unempfindlichkeit f.
insensitive (to) unempfindlich (gegen)
insertion d. e. f.
insight Einblick m.

insolation Sonnenbestrahlung f.
insoluble unlöslich, unlösbar
insomnia Schlaflosigkeit f.
inspection Inspektion f.
inspector of butcher's meat Fleischbeschauer m.
inspiration d. e. f.
inspiratory inspiratorisch
inspiratory flow rate inspiratorische Atemstromstärke f.
inspire, to inspirieren
inspissate, to verdicken
instabile instabil
instability Instabilität f., Unbeständigkeit f., Haltlosigkeit f.
– of a joint Wackelgelenk n.
instantaneous augenblicklich, momentan
instep Rist m.
– -raiser Senkfußeinlage f.
instill, to instillieren
instillation d. e. f.
instinct Instinkt m.
instinctive instinktiv
institute Institut n.
instruction Instruktion f., Unterricht m.
–, programmed programmierter Unterricht m.
instrument d. e. n.
–, double-ended Doppelinstrument n.
instrumental instrumentell
instrumentation Instrumentierung f.
instrument holder Instrumentenhalter m.
insufficiency Insuffizienz f.
insufficient insuffizient
insufflation d. e. f., Einblasung f.
insular insulär
insular tissue Inselgewebe n.
insulin d. e. n.
insulin, bovine Rinderinsulin n.
insulin, monospecies Monospeciesinsulin n.
insulin, porcine Schweineinsulin n.

insulinase d. e. f.
insulin deficiency Insulinmangel m.
insulin-dependent insulinbedürftig
insulin resistance Insulinresistenz f.
insulinizate, to insulinisieren
insulinization Insulinisierung f., Insulinbehandlung f.
insulinotropic insulinotrop
insulin-zinc suspension Insulinzinksuspension f.
insuloma Insulom n.
insurance Versicherung f.
−, **social health** Sozialversicherung f.
intake Einnahme f.
intact intakt
integral d. e.
integrate, to integrieren
integration d. e. f.
integrity Integrität f.
integument Haut f.
intellect Intellekt m.
intellectual intellektuell
intelligence Intelligenz f.
− **test** Intelligenztest m.
intelligent d. e.
intemperance Maßlosigkeit f.
intensification Intensivierung f.
intensify, to intensivieren
intensity Intensität f.
intensive intensiv
intensive care Intensivpflege f.
intensive care unit Intensivpflegestation f.
intensive nursing Intensivpflege f.
intensive therapy Intensivbehandlung f.
intention Absicht f.; Naturvorgang m.; Zweck m.
intentional absichtlich, beabsichtigt; zweckbestimmt
interaction Wechselwirkung f.
interaural d. e.
interbulbar interbulbär
intercellular interzellulär
interchange Austausch m.
interchangeable auswechselbar

intercondylar interkondylär
intercourse Verkehr m.; geschlechtlicher Verkehr m.
intercurrent interkurrent
intercuspidation Interkuspidation f.
interdental d. e.
interdigital d. e.
interfere, to interferieren, überlagern, störend einwirken
interference Interferenz f.
interferometer d. e. n.
interferometry Interferometrie f.
interferon d. e. n.
intergrade Zwischenstufe f., Zwischenstadium n.
interindividual interindividuell
interior inneres; Inneres n.
interlobar interlobär
interlobular interlobulär
interlock, to ineinandergreifen
intermaxillary intermaxillär
intermediary intermediär
intermediate result Zwischenergebnis n.
intermedin d. e. n.
intermenstruum d. e. n.
intermission d. e. f.
intermit, to intermittieren, zeitweilig aussetzen
intermittent intermittierend
− **fever** Wechselfieber n.
intermuscular intermuskulär
intern Krankenhaushilfsarzt m., Krankenhaushilfsärztin f.
internal intern, innerlich
− **medicine** Innere Medizin f.
internist d. e. m., Internistin f.
internodal d. e.
interocclusal interokklusal
interphase Zwischenphase f.
interpolated interpoliert
interposition d. e. f.
interproximal d. e.
interradicular interradikulär
interrelationship Beziehung f.
interrenalism Interrenalismus m.

interrenin Nebennierenrinden-
    hormon n.
interrupt, to unterbrechen
interruption d. e. f., Unter-
    brechung f.
intersex d. e. m.
intersexual intersexuell
intersexuality Intersexualität f.
interstice Interstitium n.
interstitial interstitiell
intertrabecular intertrabekulär
intertriginous intertriginös
intertrigo d. e.
intertrochanteric intertrochan-
    terisch
interval Intervall n.
intervention d. e. f.
intervention, surgical chirurgischer
    Eingriff m.
interventricular interventrikulär
intervertebral d. e.
– disk Zwischenwirbelscheibe f.
intervillous intervillös
intestinal d. e.
– infantilism Herter-Heubnersche
    Krankheit f.
intestine Darm m.
intimal d. e.
intimitis d. e. f.
intoe Hallux valgus
intolerance Intoleranz f., Unver-
    träglichkeit f.
intolerant d. e.
intoxicate, to vergiften
intoxication Intoxikation f.,
    Vergiftung f.
intraabdominal d. e.
intraacinous intraazinös
intraarterial intraarteriell
intraarticular intraartikulär
intrabronchial d. e.
intracanalicular intrakanalikulär
intracapsular intrakapsulär
intracardiac intrakardial
intracellular intrazellulär
intracerebral intrazerebral
intracervical intrazervikal

intracisternal intrazisternal
intracranial intrakraniell
intradermal d. e.
intraduodenal d. e.
intradural d. e.
intragastric intragastral
intraglandular intraglandulär
intrahepatic intrahepatisch
intraindividual intraindividuell
intralaryngeal d. e.
intralingual d. e.
intralobar intralobär
intralobular intralobulär
intralumbar intralumbal
intramammary intramammär
intramaxillary intramaxillär
intramedullary intramedullär
intrameningeal d. e.
intramural d. e.
intramuscular intramuskulär
intranasal d. e.
intraneural d. e.
intranuclear intranukleär
intraocular intraokulär
intraocular pressure Augeninnen-
    druck m.
intraoral d. e.
intraossal d. e.
intraosseous intraossär
intrapancreatic intrapankreatisch
intraperitoneal d. e.
intraplacental intraplazental
intrapleural d. e.
intrapulmonary intrapulmonal
intrarectal intrarektal
intrarenal d. e.
intrascrotal intraskrotal
intraspinal d. e.
intrasplenic intralienal
intrasternal d. e.
intrasynovial d. e.
intrathecal intrathekal
intrathoracic intrathorakal
intrathyroid intrathyreoidal
intratracheal d. e.
intraurethral d. e.
intrauterine intrauterin

intrauterine device Intrauterinspirale f.
intravaginal d. e.
intravascular intravaskulär
intravenous intravenös
intraventricular intraventrikulär
intraventricular pressure Ventrikeldruck m.
intravesical intravesikal
intravital d. e.
intrinsic factor Intrinsic-Faktor m.
introduction Introduktion f., Einführung f.
introversion d. e. f.
introvert, to introvertieren
intrusion d. e. f.
intubate, to intubieren
intubation d. e. f.
intumescence Intumeszenz f., Anschwellung f.
intussusception Intusseszeption f.
inulase d. e. f.
inulin d. e. n.
inunction Inunktion f.
invade, to eindringen
invagination d. e. f.
invalid Invalide m.; invalid
– **wheel chair** Krankenfahrstuhl m.
invalidity Invalidität f.
invasion d. e. f.
invasive invasiv
invasiveness Eindringungsvermögen n.
inversion d. e. f.
invert sugar Invertzucker m.
invertose Invertzucker m.
invest, to (dent.) einbetten, einhüllen
investigate, to forschen, erforschen
investigation Forschung f., Erforschung f.
investigator Forscher m.
invisible unsichtbar
in vitro d. e.
in vivo d. e.

involuntary unfreiwillig
involution d. e. f.
involutional involutionell
involve, to befallen
involvement Befall m.
iodate Jodat n.
iodide Jodid n.
iodine Jod n.
iodize, to jodieren
iodized oil Jodöl n.
iodoform Jodoform n.
iodometric jodometrisch
iodometry Jodometrie f.
ion d. e. n.
ionization Ionisierung f.
ionize, to ionisieren
ionogram Ionogramm n.
ionometer d. e. n.
ionometric ionometrisch
ionometry Ionometrie f.
iontophoresis Iontophorese f.
iontophoretical iontophoretisch
IP (= **intraperitoneal**) intraperitoneal
ipecac Brechwurzel f.
– **and opium powder** Pulvis ipecacuanhae opiatus
ipratropiumbromide Ipratropiumbromid n.
iproniazid d. e. n.
ipsilateral d. e., gleichseitig
iridectomize, to iridektomieren
iridectomy Iridektomie f.
iridium d. e. n.
iridocele d. e. f.
iridochoroiditis Iridochoroiditis f.
iridocyclitis Iridozyklitis f.
iridodiagnosis Irisdiagnose f., Augendiagnose f.
iridodialysis Iridodialyse f.
iridodonesis Irisschlottern n.
iridoplegia Iridoplegie f.
iridosclerotomy Iridosklerotomie f.
iridoscope Iridoskop n.
iridoscopical iridoskopisch
iridoscopy Iridoskopie f.
iridotomy Iridotomie f.

iris d. e. f.
iritis d. e. f.
iron Eisen n.
- **binding capacity** Eisenbindungskapazität f.
- **deficiency** Eisenmangel m.
iron, reduced Ferrum reductum
irradiate, to bestrahlen; ausstrahlen
irradiation Bestrahlung f.; Ausstrahlung f.
-, **moving field** Bewegungsbestrahlung f.
-, **short distance** Nahbestrahlung f.
irregular irregulär, regelwidrig, unregelmäßig
irregularity Irregularität f.
irreversibility Irreversibilität f.
irreversible irreversibel
irrevocable unwiderruflich
irrigate, to ausspülen
irrigation d. e. f., Spülung f., Ausspülung f.
- **instrument** Spülinstrument n.
irrigator d. e. m.
irrigoscopy Irrigoskopie f.
irritability Reizbarkeit f.
irritable reizbar
irritable heart Effort-Syndrom n.
irritant irritierend; Reizmittel n.
irritate, to reizen, irritieren
irritation d. e. f., Reizung f.
ischaemia (e) Ischämie f.
ischaemic (e) ischämisch
ischemia (a) Ischämie f.
ischemic (a) ischämisch
ischiopubic ischiopubisch
ischiorectal ischiorektal
ischuria paradoxa d. e.
island of Langerhans Langerhanssche Insel f.
Isle of Wight disease Milbenseuche f. der Honigbiene
isoagglutination d. e. f.
isoagglutinin d. e. n.
isoalloxazine Isoalloxazin n.
isoantibody Isoantikörper m.

isocarboxazide Isocarboxazid n.
isochromatic isochromatisch
isochronia Isochronie f.
isochronous isochron
isocomplement Isokomplement n.
isocoria Isokorie f.
isocytosis Isozytose f.
isodense isodens
isodont d. e.
isodynamic isodynamisch
isoelectric isoelektrisch
isoenergetic isoenergetisch
isogamous isogam
isohaemolysin (e) Isohämolysin n.
isohemolysin (a) Isohämolysin n.
isohydria Isohydrie f.
isoimmunization Isoimmunisation f.
isolate, to isolieren
isolation Isolierung f.
- **ward** Isolierstation f.
isoleucine Isoleucin n.
isolysin d. e. n.
isomaltase d. e. f.
isomaltose d. e. f.
isomer d. e. n.
isomerase d. e. f.
isomeric isomer
isomerism Isomerie f.
isometric isometrisch
isometropia Isometropie f.
isomorphous isomorph
isoniazid d. e. n.
isoprenaline Isoprenalin n.
isoprene Isopren n.
isopropamide Isopropamid n.
isopropyl d. e. n.
isopropylarterenol d. e. n.
isopropylhydrazine Isopropylhydrazin n.
isoproterenol Isopropylnoradrenalin n.
isosexual isosexuell
isosorbide dinitrate Isosorbiddinitrat n.
Isospora belli/hominis d. e.
isosthenuria Isosthenurie f.
isosthenuric isosthenurisch

isothiazole Isothiazol n.
isothiocyanate Isothiozyanat n.
isotonia Isotonie f.
isotonic isotonisch
isotope Isotop n.
isotransplantation d. e. f.
isotropic isotrop
isovolumetric isovolumetrisch
isoxazole Isoxazol n.
isoxazolidone Isoxazolidon n.
isoxazolyl d. e. n.
isozyme Isozym n.
isthmian isthmisch
isthmic isthmisch
isthmus d. e. m.

itch Jucken n.; Krätze f.
itch, mad Pseudowut f., Aujeszkysche Krankheit f.
itch, to jucken
IU (= **international unit**) internationale Einheit f.
IUD (= **intrauterine device**) Intrauterinspirale f.
IV (= **intravenous**) i.v. (= intravenös)
ivory Elfenbein n.; Dentin n.
− **bones** Marmorknochenkrankheit f.
Ixodes d. e. m.
ixodiasis d. e. f., Zeckenbefall m.

J

jaborine Jaborin n.
jackal Schakal m.
jacket crown Jacketkrone f.
jackscrew Dehnungsschraube f.
jacksonian epilepsy Jackson-Epilepsie f.
Jacobson's anastomosis Jacobsonsche Anastomose f.
jaguar d. e. m.
jalapin d. e. n.
Janus green Janusgrün n.
jar Krug m.
Jarisch-Herxheimer phenomenon Jarisch-Herxheimersche Reaktion f.
jaundice Gelbsucht f.
−,**acute infectious** Weilsche Krankheit f.
−,**Budd's** akute gelbe Leberatrophie f.
−,**homologous serum** − Inokulationshepatitis f., homologe Serumhepatitis f.
−,**leptospiral** Weilsche Krankheit f.

jaundice, obstructive Verschlußikterus m.
−,**virus** Virushepatitis f.
jaundiced gelbsüchtig
Javal's ophthalmometer Javal-Ophthalmometer n.
jaw Kiefer m.
− **bone, lower** Unterkiefer m.
− −,**upper** Oberkiefer m.
−,**lumpy** Aktinomykose f.
− **angle** Kieferwinkel m.
−,**underhung** Progenie f.
jejunal d. e.
jejunitis d. e. f.
jejunocolostomy Jejunokolostomie f.
jejunoileostomy Jejunoileostomie f.
jejunojejunostomy Jejunojejunostomie f.
jejunostomy Jejunostomie f.
jelly Gallerte f.
Jendrassik's maneuver Jendrassikscher Handgriff m.
jerk Reflexbewegung f., Zuckung f.

jerk, ankle Achillessehnenreflex m.
johimbine Johimbin n.
Johne's disease (veter.) Paratuberkulose f.
joint Gelenk n.
joint, to gliedern
jointless gelenklos
Jolly's body Jollykörper m.
joule d. e. n.
jugular jugulär
juice Saft m.

junction Verbindungsstelle f., Verbindung f.
Jüngling's disease Jünglingsche Krankheit f.
justomajor bulb Megabulbus m.
justominor bulb Mikrobulbus m.
juvenile juvenil, jugendlich
juxtaarticular juxtaartikulär
juxtaglomerular juxtaglomerulär
juxtaposition d. e. f.
juxtapyloric juxtapylorisch

K

Kafka's reaction Kafka-Reaktion f.
Kahler's disease Kahlersche Krankheit f.
Kahn's test Kahnsche Reaktion f.
kalaazar d. e. f.
kaliuresis Kaliurese f.
kallidin d. e. n.
kallikrein d. e. n.
kanamycin d. e. n.
kangaroo Känguruh n.
kaolin d. e. n.
Kaposi's varicelliform eruption Ekzema vaccinatum
Karell's treatment Karellkur f.
Kartagener's syndrome Kartagenersches Syndrom n.
karyolysis Karyolyse f.
karyolytic karyolytisch
karyoplasm Karyoplasma n.
katabolic katabolisch
katalase d. e. f.
katamnesis Katamnese f.
Kaufmann's test Kaufmannscher Versuch m.
kefir d. e. m.
Keith-Flack node Keith-Flackscher Knoten m.
keloid d. e. n.
kelotomy Kelotomie f.

kelvin d. e. n.
Kent's bundle Kentsches Bündel n.
kerasin d. e. n.
keratin d. e. n.
keratinization Verhornung f., Keratinisierung f.
keratinize, to verhornen
keratitis d. e.
keratocentesis Keratozentese f.
keratoconjunctivitis Keratokonjunktivitis f.
keratoconus Keratokonus m.
keratoderma d. e. n.
keratodermia Keratodermie f.
keratohyaline keratohyalin
keratolysis Keratolyse f.
keratolytic keratolytisch
keratoiritis d. e. f.
keratoma Keratom n.
keratomalacia Keratomalazie f.
keratoscopy Keratoskopie f.
keratosis Keratose f.
kerion of Celsus Kerion Celsi
Kerkring's fold Kerkringsche Falte f.
kernicterus Kernikterus m.
Kernig's sign Kernigsches Zeichen n.

ketobutyrate Ketobutyrat n.
keto compound Ketoverbindung f.
ketogenic ketogen
ketoglutarate Ketoglutarat n.
ketohexose d. e. f.
ketolytic ketolytisch
ketonaemia (e) Ketonämie f.
ketone Keton n.
− **body** Ketonkörper m.
ketonemia (a) Ketonämie f.
ketonuria Ketonurie f.
ketose d. e. f.
ketosis Ketosis f., Ketose f.
ketosteroid d. e. n.
khellidine Khellidin n.
khelline Khellin n.
khellinine Khellinin n.
kidney Niere f.
−, **artificial** künstliche Niere f.
− **biopsy** Nierenbiopsie f.
− **function test** Nierenfunktionsprüfung f.
Kienböck's disease Kienböcksche Krankheit f.
kieselguhr Kieselgur f.
Kiesselbach's area Kiesselbachscher Ort m.
Killians' operation Killiansche Operation f.
kilogram Kilogramm n.
kilohertz d. e. n.
kiloliter d. e. n.
kilometer d. e. n.
kilovolt d. e. n.
kilowatt d. e. n.
kinaesthesia (e) Kinästhesie f.
kinaesthetic (e) kinästhetisch
kinase d. e. f.
kind Art f., Gattung f.
kineradiography Kineradiographie f.
kineroentgenography Kineröntgenographie f.
kinesitherapy Bewegungstherapie f.
kinesthesia (a) Kinästhesie f.
kinesthetic (a) kinästhetisch
kinetic kinetisch

kinetics Kinetik f.
kinetism Kinetik f.
kinetosis Kinetose f.
kinin d. e. n.
kininase d. e. f.
kininogen d. e. n.
kininogenase d. e. f.
kink Knoten m., Knick m.
kissing spine Osteoarthrosis interspinalis
kitten Kätzchen n.
Kjeldahl's method Kjeldahlverfahren n.
Kjelland's forceps Kjellandzange f.
Klapp's creeping treatment Klappsche Kriechbehandlung f.
Klebsiella ozaenae d. e., Bacterium ozaenae
Klebsiella pneumoniae Pneumobazillus Friedländer
Klebsiella rhinoscleromatis d. e., Rhinosklerombazillus m.
Kleine-Levin syndrome Klein-Levinsches Syndrom n.
kleptomania Kleptomanie f.
kleptomaniac Kleptomane m., Kleptomanin f.
Klinefelter's syndrome Klinefelter-Syndrom n.
Klippel-Feil disease Klippel-Feilsche Krankheit f.
Klumpke's paralysis Klumpkesche Lähmung f.
knead, to kneten
knee Knie n.
knee-crooking Kniebeuge f.
kneepan Kniescheibe f.
kneel, to knien
kneippism Kneippbehandlung f.
knife Messer n.
−, **amputating** Amputationsmesser n.
−, **cartilage** Knorpelmesser n.
−, **cataract** Starmesser n.
−, **folding** Bistouri m.
−, **operating** Operationsskalpell n.
−, **plaster** Gipsmesser n.

knife, tonsil Tonsillenmesser n.
knob Knopf m.
knock-kneed X-beinig
knot Knoten m.
Koch's bacillus Kochscher Bazillus m., Tuberkelbazillus m.
Koch-Weeks bacillus Koch-Weeks-Bazillus m.
Kocher's operation Kochersche Operation f.
Köhler's disease Köhlersche Krankheit f.
Kohlrausch's fold Kohlrauschsche Falte f.
kola d. e. f.
Kollmann's dilator Kollmann-dilatator m.
Koplik's spot Koplikscher Flecken m.
Korsakoff's psychosis Korsakoffsche Psychose f.
koumiss Kumyss m.
kraurosis Kraurose f.
Kristeller's technic Kristellerscher Handgriff m.
Krönlein's operation Krönleinsche Operation f.

Kromayer's lamp Kromayerlampe f.
Krukenberg's arm Krukenbergarm m.
krypton d. e. n.
kryptorchism Kryptorchismus m.
Külz's cast Komazylinder m.
Küster's operation Küstersche Operation f.
Küstners' sign Küstnersches Zeichen n.
Kuhn's mask Kuhnsche Maske f.
kumyss d. e. m.
Kupffer's cell Kupffersche Sternzelle f.
Kussmaul-Kien respiration Kussmaulsche Atmung f.
kwashiorkor d. e. m.
kymogram Kymogramm n.
kymograph d. e. m.
kymographic kymographisch
kymography Kymographie f.
kyphoscoliosis Kyphoskoliose f.
kyphosis Kyphose f.
kyphotic kyphotisch

L

label, to markieren
lab ferment Labferment n.
labial d. e.
labial angle Mundwinkel m.
labile labil
lability Labilität f.
labiodental d. e.
labionasal d. e.
labioplasty Lippenplastik f.
labor (a) Arbeit f.; Geburt f., Gebären n.
laboratorian Laborant m., Laborantin f.

laboratory Laboratorium n., Labor n.
laboratory report Laborbericht m., Laborbefund m.
labour (e) Arbeit f.; Geburt f., Gebären n.
labyrinth d. e. n.
labyrinthectomy Labyrinthektomie f.
labyrinthine labyrinthär
labyrinthine disturbance Labyrinthstörung f.
labyrinthitis d. e. f.

lacerate, to zerreißen
laceration Zerreißung f.; Rißwunde f.
laceration, Mallory-Weiss
 Mallory-Weiss-Syndrom n.
lachrymation Tränen n.
lack of blood Blutarmut f.
lacmoid Lakmoid n.
lacrimal lakrimal
− duct Tränengang m.
− gland Tränendrüse f.
− obstruction Tränengang-
 verstopfung f.
− sac Tränensack m.
lacrimation Tränen n.
lactacidogen Laktazidogen n.
lactalbumin Laktalbumin n.
lactam d. e. n.
lactamase d. e. f.
lactate Laktat n.
lactation Laktation f.
lactigenous milchbildend
lactim d. e. n.
Lactobacillus acidophilus d. e.
− bifidus d. e.
− bulgaricus d. e.
lactobionate Laktobionat n.
lactoflavin Laktoflavin n.
lactogen, human placenta
 menschliches Plazenta-Laktationshormon n.
lactogenic laktogen; milchtreibend
lactone Lakton n.
lactose Laktose f., Milchzucker m.
lactotropic laktotrop
lactulose Laktulose f.
lacuna Lakune f.
lacunar lakunär
ladle Löffel m., Schöpflöffel m.
lady doctor Ärztin f.
Laennec's cirrhosis Laennecsche
 Cirrhose f.
laevallorphan (e) Lävallorphan n.
laevorotation (e) Linksdrehung f.
laevorotatory (e) linksdrehend
laevulose (e) Lävulose f.

laevulosuria (e) Lävulosurie f.
lag Latenzzeit f.
lagging Nachhinken n.
lagophthalmos Lagophthalmus m.
laical laienhaft
lalling Lallen n.
lalophobia Lalophobie f.
laloplegia Laloplegie f.
lamb Lamm n.
lamb, to lammen
lambdoid suture Lambdanaht f.
lambliasis d. e. f.
lame lahm
lame, to go − hinken
lamella Lamelle f.
lamellar lamellär
lamina aggregation test Plättchenaggregationstest m.
laminar d. e.
laminar air flow Lamellenluftstrom m.
lamination Schichtung f.
laminectomy Laminektomie f.
laminotomy Laminotomie f.
lamp Lampe f.
lampas (veter.) Gaumen-
 geschwulst f.
lamziekte d. e. f.
lance, to aufschneiden, spalten
lancet Lanzette f.
lancinating lanzinierend
Landry's paralysis Landrysche
 Paralyse f.
Langenbeck's operation Langenbecksche Operation f.
Langerhans' island Langerhanssche Insel f.
Langhans' cell Langhanssche
 Zelle f.
language disturbance Sprachstörung f.
languish, to erschlaffen, ver-
 schmachten, dahinsiechen
lanthanide Lanthanid n.
lanthanum Lanthan n.
laparoscope Laparoskop n.
laparoscopical laparoskopisch

laparoscopy Laparoskopie f.
laparotomize, to laparotomieren
laparotomy Laparotomie f.
lard Schweinefett n.
large intestine Dickdarm m.
larva Larve f., Finne f.
larva migrans d. e.
larvate, to larvieren
larvicide Larvenvertilgungsmittel n.
laryngeal d. e.
laryngectomy Laryngektomie f.
laryngitic laryngitisch
laryngitis d. e. f.
laryngographical laryngographisch
laryngography Laryngographie f.
laryngological laryngologisch
laryngologist Laryngologe m., Laryngologin f.
laryngology Laryngologie f.
laryngopharyngeal d. e.
laryngoplasty Kehlkopfplastik f.
laryngoplegia Laryngoplegie f.
laryngoscope Laryngoskop n., Kehlkopfspiegel m.
laryngoscopical laryngoskopisch
laryngoscopy Laryngoskopie f.
laryngospasm Laryngospasmus m.
laryngostenosis Kehlkopfstenose f.
laryngostomy Laryngostomie f.
laryngotomy Laryngotomie f.
laryngotracheoscopy Laryngotracheoskopie f.
Laséque's sign Laséquesches Zeichen n.
LASER ray LASER-Strahl m.
Lassar's paste Lassarsche Paste f.
late spät
— **damage** Spätschaden n.
— **result** Spätresultat n.
latency Latenz f.
latent d. e.
lateral d. e.
— **sclerosis, primary** spastische Spinalparalyse f.
lateroposition d. e. f.
lateroventral d. e.

latex drop test Latex-Tropfentest m.
lathyrism Lathyrismus m.
latitude Ausdehnung f., Breite f.
latrine d. e. f.
latrodectism Latrodectismus m., Giftspinnenbiß m.
lattice Gitter n.
laudanum Opiumtinktur f.
laugh Lachen n.
laughing gas Lachgas n.
laughter Lachen n., Gelächter n.
laureate Preisträger m., Preisträgerin f.
Laurence-Biedl syndrome Laurence-Biedlsches Syndrom n.
lauryl d. e. n.
lavage Waschung f., Spülung f.
lavage solution Spüllösung f.
lavation Waschung f., Spülung f.
lavatory Waschraum m., Toilette f.
lavement Waschung f., Spülung f.
lavender Lavendel m.
law, all or none — Alles-oder-Nichts-Gesetz n.
law of mass action Massenwirkungsgesetz n.
laxative laxierend; Laxativum n., Abführmittel n.
laxity Schlaffheit f.
layer (med.) Schicht f., Lage f.
layer, germinal Keimschicht f.
layman Laie m.
LD (= lethal dose) Dosis letalis
lead Blei n.; EKG-Ableitung f.
— **acetate** Bleiazetat n.
— **apron** Bleischürze f.
— **glove** Bleihandschuh m.
leakage Lecksein n., Undichtigkeit f.
lean hager, mager
L.E. cell L.E.-Zelle f.
lecithin Lezithin n.
lecithinase Lezithinase f.
lecture Vorlesung f.

Lederer's anaemia (e) Lederer-
 Anämie f.
− anemia (a) Lederer-Anämie f.
leech Blutegel m.
left anterior oblique projection
 zweiter Schrägdurchmesser m.
left-handed linkshändig
left-handedness Linkshändigkeit f.
left-to-right shunt Links-Rechts-
 Shunt m.
leg Schenkel m., Bein n.
Legal's test Legalsche Probe f.
leg-holder Beinhalter m.
leguminous leguminös
leiomyoma Leiomyom n.
leiomyosarcoma Leiomyo-
 sarkom n.
Leishmania donovani d. e.
leishmaniasis Leishmaniose f.
Lembert's suture Lembertnaht f.
lemon Zitrone f.
lemur Lemure m., Halbaffe m.
lengthen, to verlängern
lengthening Verlängerung f.
− of life Lebensverlängerung f.
lenitive lindernd; Linderungsmittel n.
lens Linse f.
lenticulothalamic lentikulothalamisch
lentigo Sommersprosse f.
leopard d. e. m.
lepidosis Schuppenausschlag m.
leproma Leprom n.
leprosary Leprosorium n.
leprosy Lepra f.
leprous leprös
leptomeningitis d. e. f.
leptosomatic leptosom
Leptospira autumnalis d. e.
− canicola d. e.
− grippotyphosa d. e.
− icterohaemorrhagiae Leptospira icterogenes
− morsus muris Spirillum
 morsus muris
leptospirosis Leptospirose f.

Leptothrix d. e. f.
Leriche's operation periarterielle
 Sympathektomie f. nach Leriche
lesbian lesbisch
lesbianism lesbische Liebe f.
lesion Läsion f., Verletzung f.
lesser curve kleine Kurvatur f.
− tubercle Tuberculum minus
lethal letal
lethality Letalität f.
lethargy Lethargie f.
lethe Gedächtnisverlust m.
Letterer Siwe disease Letterer-
 Siwesche Krankheit f.
leucine Leucin n.
leucine aminopeptidase Leucin-
 Aminopeptidase f.
leukaemia (e) Leukämie f.
−, lymphoblastic (e) lymphatische
 Leukämie f.
−, myeloid (e) myeloische
 Leukämie f.
leukaemic (e) leukämisch
leukaemoid (e) leukämoid
leukanaemia (e) Leukanämie f.
leukanemia (a) Leukanämie f.
leukemia (a) Leukämie f.
−, lymphoblastic (a) lymphatische
 Leukämie f.
−, myeloid (a) myeloische
 Leukämie f.
leukemic (a) leukämisch
leukemoid (a) leukämoid
leukocyte Leukozyt m.
leukocytic leukozytär
leukocytopenia Leukozytopenie f.
leukocytosis Leukozytose f.
leukoderma Leukodermie f.
leukoencephalitis Leuko-
 enzephalitis f.
leukoma Leukom n.
leukopenia Leukopenie f.
leukopenic leukopenisch
leukoplakia Leukoplakie f.
leukopoiesis Leukopoese f.
leukopoietic leukopoetisch
leukorrhea (a) Leukorrhöe f.

leukorrhoea (e) Leukorrhöe f.
leukosis Leukose f.
leukotomy Leukotomie f.
leukotoxic leukotoxisch
leukotrichia Leukotrichie f.
levallorphan (a) Lävallorphan n.
level Ausgangspunkt m., Niveau n.; Schaltstelle f., Stufe f.
lever Hebel m.
levorotation (a) Linksdrehung f.
levorotatory (a) linksdrehend
levulose (a) Lävulose f.
levulosuria (a) Lävulosurie f.
Leydig's cell Leydigsche Zwischenzelle f.
liberate, to befreien, freisetzen
liberation Befreiung f., Freisetzung f.
libidinous libidinös
libido d. e. f.
Libman-Sacks syndrome Libmann-Sacks-Syndrom n.
library Bücherei f.; Bibliothek f.
lice Laus f.
licence Lizenz f.
lichen d. e. m.
lichenification Lichenifizierung f.
lichenoid d. e.
licorice (a) Lakritze f.
licorice root (a) Süßholzwurzel f.
lid Lid n.; Deckel m.
–, sliding Schiebedeckel m.
lidoflazine Lidoflazin n.
Lieben's test Liebensche Probe f.
Lieberkühn's crypt Lieberkühnsche Krypte f.
lienal d. e.
life Leben n.
– expectancy Lebenserwartung f.
lifeless leblos
lifelessness Leblosigkeit f.
life span Lebensdauer f.
–, -threatening lebensbedrohlich
lifter Heber m.
ligament Ligament n., Band n.
ligase d. e. f.
ligate, to ligieren, unterbinden

ligation Unterbindung f.
ligature Ligatur f.
– cutter Fadenabschneider m.
– knife Ligaturmesser n.
light Licht n.
– bath Lichtbad n.
– bulb Glühlampe f.
lightning shock Schock m. durch Blitzschlag
light threshold Lichtschwelle f.
limb Glied n., Extremität f.
–, artificial Kunstglied n.
limbal limbisch
limbic limbisch
limbs Gliedmaßen f. pl.
lime Kalk m., Kalziumoxyd n.
lime water Kalkwasser n.
limit Grenze f.
limitation Begrenzung f.
limp, to hinken
lincomycin d. e. n.
lincture Latwerge f.
linctus Latwerge f.
line Linie f.
line, blue Bleisaum m. am Zahnfleisch
line, Burton's Bleisaum m. am Zahnfleisch
line, Ellis-Garland Ellis-Garlandsche Linie f.
line, Fraunhofer's Fraunhofersche Linie f.
line, midclavicular Medioklavikularlinie f.
–, Monro-Richter Monro-Richtersche Linie f.
– of demarcation Demarkationslinie f.
linear d. e.
liner, cavity Kavitätenschutzlack m.
lingual d. e.
Linguatula serrata d. e.
liniment d. e. n.
lining Auskleidung f.
linitis d. e. f.
linkage Bindung f.
linking Bindung f.

linoleate Linoleat n.
linolein d. e. n.
linseed Leinsamen m.
– **oil** Leinöl n.
lint Verbandsstoff m.
lion Löwe m.
lioness Löwin f.
liothyronine Liothyronin n.
lip Lippe f.
– **retractor** Lippenhalter m.
lipaemia (e) Lipämie f.
lipaemic (e) lipämisch
lipase d. e. f.
lipemia (a) Lipämie f.
lipemic (a) lipämisch
lipid d. e. n.
lipin Lipid n.
lipocaic factor Lipocaic-Faktor m.
lipochrome Lipochrom n.
lipodystrophy Lipodystrophie f.
lipofuscin d. e. n.
lipogenic lipogen
lipogranulomatosis Lipogranulomatose f.
lipoid lipoid; Lipoid n.
lipoidosis Lipoidose f.
lipoiduria Lipoidurie f.
lipolysis Lipolyse f.
lipolytic lipolytisch
lipoma Lipom n.
lipomatosis Lipomatose f.
lipomyoma Lipomyom n.
lipomyxoma Lipomyxom n.
lipopexia Lipopexie f.
lipophagocytosis Lipophagozytose f.
lipophil d. e.
lipoprotein d. e. n.
liposarcoma Liposarkom n.
lipping Randwulstbildung f.
lipuria Lipurie f.
lipuric lipurisch
liquefaction Verflüssigung f.
liquefy, to verflüssigen
liquid flüssig; Flüssigkeit f.
– **extract** (c) Fluidextrakt m.
liquor d. e. m., Flüssigkeit f.

liquorice (e) Lakritze f.
liquorice root (e) Süßholzwurzel f.
liquorrhea (a) Liquorrhöe f.
liquorrhoea (e) Liquorrhöe f.
listen, to horchen, hören, abhorchen
Listerella monocytogenes Listeria monocytogenes
Listerellosis Listeriose f.
Listeria monocytogenes d. e.
listeriosis Listeriose f.
Lisfranc's joint Lisfrancsches Gelenk n.
literature Literatur f.
literature source Literaturquelle f.
lithium d. e. n.
– **oxalate** Lithiumoxalat n.
lithocholate Lithocholat n.
lithotomy Lithotomie f., Steinschnitt m.
– **position** Steinschnittlage f.
lithotripsy Lithotripsie f.
lithotriptor Lithotripter m.
litmus Lackmus n.
litter Tragbahre f.
Little's disease Littlesche Krankheit f.
Littre's hernia Littresche Hernie f.
Litzmann's obliquity Litzmannsche Obliquität f.
live, to leben
liver Leber f.
– **abscess** Leberabszeß m.
– **biopsy** Leberbiopsie f.
– **fluke** Leberegel m.
– **function test** Leberfunktionsprüfung f.
– **injection** Leberextraktinjektion f.
livid livide
living lebend; Lebensweise f.
Loa loa Filaria loa f.
load Ladung f.
load, to laden, beladen
loading Laden n., Ladung f., Belastung f.
lobar lobär
– **pneumonia** Lobärpneumonie f.

lobe Lappen m.
- **knife** Lappenmesser n.
lobectomy Lobektomie f.
lobeline Lobelin n.
lobotomy Lobotomie f.
Lobstein's disease Osteogenesis imperfecta
lobular lobulär
lobulation Lappung f.
lobule Läppchen n.
- **of the ear** Ohrläppchen n.
local lokal, örtlich
localization Lokalisierung f., Lokalisation f.
localize, to lokalisieren
location Ortung f.
lochia Lochien f. pl.
lochiometra d. e. f.
lock Verschluß m.
locking Arretierung f.
lockjaw Trismus m.
locomotion Bewegung f.
locomotor lokomotorisch
- **ataxia** Tabes dorsalis f.
- **system** Bewegungsapparat m.
locomotorium Bewegungsapparat m.
Löffler's stain Löfflerfärbung f.
logarithm Logarithmus m.
logic logisch
logical logisch
logorrhea (a) Logorrhöe f.
logorrhoea (e) Logorrhöe f.
loin Lende f.
long-acting langwirkend
longevity Langlebigkeit f.
longitudinal d. e.
long-lasting langdauernd
longsighted weitsichtig
longsightedness Weitsichtigkeit f.
long-term memory Langzeitgedächtnis n.
long-term therapy Langzeitbehandlung f.
long wave Langwelle f.
loop Schleife f., Öse f.
- **of Henle** Henlesche Schleife f.

loosening, tooth - Zahnlockerung f.
lorazepam d. e. n.
lordosis Lordose f.
lordotic lordotisch
lose weight, to abmagern
loss Verlust m.
- **in weight** Gewichtsverlust m.
lotion Waschflüssigkeit f.
louchettes Schielbrille f.
loupe Lupe f.
louping ill Springkrankheit f. (der Schafe)
louse Laus f.
-, **body** Kleiderlaus f.
-, **crab** Filzlaus f.
-, **head** Kopflaus f.
lousiness Verlausung f.
low back pain Kreuzschmerz m.
- **calcium diet** kalkarme Kost f.
- **frequency** Niederfrequenz f.
- **gluten diet** glutenarme Diät f.
- **grade** geringgradig
- **molecular** niedermolekular
- **protein diet** eiweißarme Kost f.
- **salt syndrome** Salzmangelsyndrom n.
- **vitamin diet** vitaminarme Kost f.
lower abdomen Unterbauch m.
- **leg** Unterschenkel m.
- **lip** Unterlippe f.
- **jaw** Unterkiefer m.
loxia Schiefhals m.
lozenge Tablette f.
lucid interval lichter Augenblick m.
Ludwig's angina Angina Ludovici
lues d. e. f.
luetic luetisch; Luetiker m., Luetikerin f.
Lugol's solution Lugolsche Lösung f.
lumbago d. e.
lumbar lumbal
- **region** Lendengegend f.
- **spinal column** Lendenwirbelsäule f.
- **vertebra** Lendenwirbel m.

lumbodorsal d. e.
lumbosacral lumbosakral
lumen d. e. n.
luminescence Lumineszenz f.
lunacy Wahnsinn m.
lunatic wahnsinnig, irr, geistesgestört
– **asylum** Irrenanstalt f.
lung Lunge f.
– **field** Lungenfeld n.
lung volume Lungenvolumen n.
lupinosis Lathyrismus m.
lupoid d. e.
lupus erythematosus Erythematodes m.
– **erythematosus, systemic** generalisierter Erythematodes m.
– **vulgaris** d. e.
lutecium Lutetium n.
lutein d. e. n.
luteinization Luteinisierung f.
luteinize, to luteinisieren
luteinizing hormone Luteinisierungshormon n.
Lutembacher's syndrome Lutembacher-Syndrom n.
lux d. e. n.
luxate, to verrenken, luxieren
luxation d. e. f.
lycopodium d. e. n.
lye Lauge f.
lying-in hospital Entbindungsanstalt f.
lying-in woman Wöchnerin f.
lymph Lymphe f.
– **node** Lymphknoten m.
– **vessel** Lymphgefäß n.
lymphadenitis d. e. f.
lymphadenoma Lymphadenom n.
lymphadenopathy Lymphadenopathie f., Lymphknotenerkrankung f.
lymphadenosis Lymphadenose f.
–, **acute** akute Lymphadenose f.
–, **aleukaemic** (e) aleukämische Lymphadenose f.

lymphadenosis, aleukemic (a) aleukämische Lymphadenose f.
–, **chronic** chronische Lymphadenose f.
–, **leukaemic** (a) leukämische Lymphadenose f.
–, **leukemic** (a) leukämische Lymphadenose f.
lymphangiectasis Lymphangiektasie f.
lymphangioendothelioma Lymphangioendotheliom n.
lymphangioma Lymphangiom n.
lymphangitic lymphangitisch
lymphangitis d. e. f.
lymphatic lymphatisch
– **duct** Lymphgang m.
– **scissure** Lymphspalte f.
– **vessel** Lymphgefäß n.
lymphatism lymphatische Diathese f.
lymphoadenoma Lymphoadenom n.
lymphoangiosarcoma Lymphangiosarkom n.
lymphoblast d. e. m.
lymphoblastic lymphoblastisch
lymphoblastoma Lymphoblastom n.
lymphocyte Lymphozyt m.
lymphocytic lymphozytär
lymphocytopenia Lymphozytopenie f.
lymphocytopoiesis Lymphozytopoese f.
lymphocytosis Lymphozytose f.
lymphogenous lymphogen
lymphogranuloma Lymphogranulom n.
–, **venereal** Lymphogranuloma inguinale
lymphogranulomatosis Lymphogranulomatose f.
lymphoid d. e.
lymphoidocyte Lymphoidozyt m.
lymphology Lymphologie f.
lymphoma Lymphom n.
lymphomatosis Lymphomatose f.
lymphomatous lymphomatös

lymphopenia Lymphopenie f.
lymphopenic lymphopenisch
lymphopoiesis Lymphopoese f.
lymphopoietic lymphopoetisch
lymphorrhea (a) Lymphorrhöe f.
lymphorrhoea (e) Lymphorrhöe f.
lymphosarcoma Lymphosarkom n.
lymphosarcomatosis Lymphosarkomatose f.
lynx Luchs m.
lyophile lyophil
lyophilic lyophil

lyophilization Lyophilisierung f.
lyophilize, to lyophilisieren
lyophobe lyophob
lyotropic lyotrop
lysin d. e. n.
lysine Diaminokapronsäure f.
lysis Lyse f.
lysoform d. e. n.
lysosome Lysosom n.
lysozyme Lysozym n.
lyssa Tollwut f.
lytic lytisch

M

macerate, to mazerieren
maceration Mazeration f.
macroblast Makroblast m.
macrocephalous makrozephal
macrocyte Makrozyt m.
macrocytic makrozytär
macrodontia Makrodontie f.
macroglobulin Makroglobulin n.
macroglobulinaemia (e) Makroglobulinämie f.
macroglobulinemia (a) Makroglobulinämie f.
macromelia Makromelie f.
macromolecular makromolekular
macromolecule Makromolekül n.
macroscopic makroskopisch
macrosomy Makrosomie f.
macula Fleck m.
macular makulär
maculation Tüpfelung f.
maculopapular makulopapulös
mad wahnsinnig
mad-doctor Irrenarzt m.
madefaction Befeuchtung f., Anfeuchtung f.
Madelung's neck Madelungscher Fetthals m.
mad-house Irrenanstalt f.

mad itch Pseudowut f.
madness Wahnsinn m., Verrücktheit f.
maduromycosis Madurafuß m.
maggot Made f.
maggotty madig
magistery Rezepturarznei f.
magistral d. e.
magma of magnesia Magnesiamilch f.
magnesia d. e. f.
magnesium d. e. n.
– sulfate (a) Magnesiumsulfat n.
– sulphate (e) Magnesiumsulfat n.
magnet d. e. m.
– probe Magnetsonde f.
magnetic magnetisch
magnetize, to magnetisieren
magnification Vergrößerung f.
magnify, to vergrößern
magnifying glass Vergrößerungsglas n.
– lens Vergrößerungsglas n., Lupe f.
Mahler's sign Mahlersches Zeichen n.
maid Jungfrau f.

maidenhood Jungfräulichkeit f.
maidism Pellagra f.
mailing case Versandgefäß n.
maim, to verstümmeln
maintenance Erhaltung f., Aufrechterhaltung f., Wartung f.
− **dose** Erhaltungsdosis f.
major surgery große Chirurgie f.
malabsorption intestinale Resorptionsstörung f.
malachite Malachit n.
malacia Malazie f., Erweichung f.
malacic malazisch
malady Krankheit f.
malaise Unwohlsein n., Unpäßlichkeit f.
malalignment, dental Zahnstellungsanomalie f.
malanders Mauke f.
malar zygomatisch
malaria d. e. f.
−, **benignant** Malaria tertiana
−, **falciparum** Malaria tropica
−, **malignant** Malaria tropica
−, **pernicious** Malaria tropica
−, **quartan** Malaria quartana
−, **subtertian** Malaria subtertiana
−, **tertian** Malaria tertiana
−, **tropical** Malaria tropica
malariotherapy Malariatherapie f.
malate Malat n.
mal de caderas Mal de Caderas m.
− − **coit** Beschälseuche f.
maldevelopment Fehlentwicklung f.
maldigestion Verdauungsstörung f.
male männlich; Mann m.; Männchen n.
maleate Maleat n.
maleimide Maleimid n.
malformation Verbildung f., Mißbildung f.
Malgaigne's fracture Malgaignesche Fraktur f.
− **hernia** Malgaignesche Hernie f.
malignancy Malignität f.

malignant bösartig, maligne
− **pustule** Pustula maligna
malignization bösartige Umwandlung f.
malignolipin d. e. n.
malignoma Malignom n.
malingerer Simulant m.
malingering Simulation f.
mallein d. e. n.
malleolar malleolär
malleolus Knöchel m.
mallet Hammer m.
−, **surgical metal** chirurgischer Metallhammer m.
Mallory-Weiss, syndrome of −
 Mallory-Weiss-Syndrom n.
malnutrition Unterernährung f.
malocclusion Malokklusion f.
malodorous übelriechend
malonyl d. e. n.
malpighian corpuscle Malpighisches Körperchen n.
malposed tooth Zahn m. in schlechter Stellung
malpractice Fehlbehandlung f.; unkorrekte Praxisführung f.
malt Malz n.
Malta fever Maltafieber n.
malthusianism Malthusianismus m.
maltase d. e. f.
maltose d. e. f.
maltreat, to mißhandeln, schlecht behandeln
maltreatment Mißhandlung f., schlechte Behandlung f.
mammal Säugetier n.
mammalian Säugetier ...
mammary mammär
− **gland** Brustdrüse f.
mammilary mamillär
mammilitis Brustwarzenentzündung f.
mammography Mammographie f.
mammotropin Laktationshormon n.
management Behandlung f.; Handhabung f., Leitung f.

mandelate Mandelat n.
mandible Unterkiefer m., Mandibel f.
mandibular mandibulär
Mandl's solution Mandlsche Lösung f.
mandrin d. e. m.
mane Mähne f. (veter.)
maneuver Handgriff m., Manöver n.
manganese Mangan n.
mange Räude f.
mangy räudig
manhood Männlichkeit f.
mania Manie f., Sucht f.
– for drinking Trunksucht f.
maniacal manisch
manic manisch
– depressive psychosis manisch-depressives Irresein n.
manifestation d. e. f.
manikin anatomisches Modell n.
manipulation d. e. f.
manner Art f., Gestalt f.
– of death Todesart f.
mannitol Mannit m.
mannokinase d. e. f.
mannose d. e. f.
manometer d. e. n.
manometric manometrisch
manslaughter Totschlag m.
mantle Mantel m.
Mantoux test Mantoux-Probe f.
manual manuell
maple Ahorn m.
marantic marantisch
marasmic marantisch
marasmus d. e. m.
marble bones disease Marmorknochenkrankheit f.
marbleization Marmorisierung f.
mare Stute f.
Marfan syndrome Marfan-Syndrom n.
margarine d. e. f.
margin Rand m.
marginal d. e.

marihuana d. e. n.
marital ehelich
mark Marke f., Merkmal n.
marmoration d. e. f., Marmorisierung f.
marriage counselling Eheberatung f.
– guidance Eheberatung f.
marrow Mark n.
– bone Markknochen m.
marsh fever Malaria f.
marshmallow root Radix Althaeae
marsupial Beuteltier n.
marsupialization Marsupialisation f.
masculine maskulin, männlich
masculinity Männlichkeit f.
masculinization Vermännlichung f.
masculinize, to vermännlichen
MASER ray MASER-Strahl m.
mash Maische f.
mask Maske f.
mask, to maskieren
masked maskiert
masochism Masochismus m.
masochist d. e. m., Masochistin f.
masochistic masochistisch
masquerade, to maskieren
mass Masse f.
– radiography Röntgenreihenuntersuchung f.
massage d. e. f.
–, to massieren
massagist Masseur m., Masseuse f.
masseur d. e. m.
masseuse d. e. f.
massive massiv
mast cell Mastzelle f.
mastectomy Mastektomie f., Ablatio mammae
mastic Mastix m.
– test Mastixreaktion f.
masticate, to kauen
mastication Kauen n.
masticatory mastikatorisch
mastitic mastitisch

mastitis d. e. f.
mastocyte Mastzelle f., Mastozyt m.
mastocytosis Mastozytose f.
mastodynia Mastodynie f.
mastoid Processus mastoides
mastoidal d. e.
mastoidectomy Mastoidektomie f.
mastoiditis d. e. f.
mastoidotomy Mastoidotomie f.
mastoidotympanectomy Mastoidotympanektomie f.
mastopathy Mastopathie f.
mastoptosis Mastoptose f.
mastosis Mastose f.
mastotomy Mastotomie f.
masturbate, to masturbieren
masturbation d. e. f.
match Zündholz n.
mate Genosse m., Genossin f., Gatte m., Gattin f.
material materiell; Material n.
maternal mütterlich
maternity Mutterschaft f.
− **hospital** Entbindungsanstalt f.
mathematical mathematisch
mathematician Mathematiker m., Mathematikerin f.
mating Paarung f.
matrix Matrize f.; Gebärmutter f.
matron Hausmutter f., Oberin f.
matter Substanz f.; Eiter m.
maturation Reifung f.
− **arrest** Reifungsstillstand m.
− **inhibition** Reifungshemmung f.
mature reif
maturity Reife f.
matutinal morgendlich
maxilla Kiefer m., Oberkiefer m.
−, **inferior** Unterkiefer m.
−, **superior** Oberkiefer m.
maxillary maxillär
maxillofacial maxillofazial
maxillomandibular maxillomandibulär
maximal d. e.

maximal allowable concentration maximal zulässige Konzentration f.
maza Mutterkuchen m.
McBurney's point McBurneyscher Punkt m.
meagre mager
meagreness Magerkeit f.
meal Mahlzeit f.
mean Mittelwert m.; Mittel n.
means of enjoyment Genußmittel n. pl.
measles Masern f. pl.
measly zystizerkös
measure Maß n.
−, **to** messen
measurement Messung f.
measuring point Meßstelle f.
meat Kochfleisch n.
− **diet** Fleischkost f.
mebanazine Mebanazin n.
mecamylamine Mekamylamin n.
mechanical mechanisch
mechanics Mechanik f.
mechanism Mechanismus m.
mechanotherapy Mechanotherapie f.
Meckel's diverticulum Meckelsches Divertikel n.
meclizine Meclizin n.
meconium Mekonium n.
mediad medialwärts
medial d. e.
median d. e.
− **nerve** Nervus medianus
mediastinal d. e.
mediastinitis d. e. f.
mediastinopericarditis Mediastinoperikarditis f.
mediastinoscopy Mediastinoskopie f.
mediastinum d. e. n.
medical ärztlich
− **establishment** Heilanstalt f.
− **opinion** ärztliches Gutachten n.
− **society** Ärzteverein m., ärztliche Gesellschaft f.

medical treatment ärztliche
 Behandlung f., Heilverfahren n.
medicament Medikament n.,
 Heilmittel n.
medication Medikation f.
medicinal medizinisch
− **spring** Heilquelle f.
medicine Medizin f.; Heilmittel n.
medicolegal medikolegal,
 gerichtsmedizinisch
medicomechanical medikomechanisch
medicotechnical medizinisch-
 technisch
mediolateral d. e.
Mediterranean fever
 Maltafieber n.
**Mediterranean fever, exanthema-
 tous** Olmersche Krankheit f.
Mediterranean fever, familial
 familiär gehäuft auftretendes
 Fieber der Mittelmeerländer
− **yellow fever** Morbus Weil
medium d. e. n.; Nährboden m.
−,**curative** Kurmittel n.
−,**separating** Separiermittel n.
medley Mischung f.
medroxyprogesterone
 Medroxyprogesteron n.
medulla d. e. f., Mark n.
medullary medullär
medulloblast d. e. m.
medulloblastoma Medulloblastom n.
medulloculture Markkultur f.,
 Knochenmarkkultur f.
megacolon Megakolon n.
megahertz d. e. n.
megakaryoblast d. e. m.
megakaryocyte Megakaryozyt
 m.
megaloblast d. e. m.
megaloblastosis Megaloblastose f.
megalocyte Megalozyt m.
megalocytic megalozytär
megalocytosis Megalozytose f.

meibomian gland Meibomsche
 Drüse f.
Meinicke reaction Meinickereaktion f.
Meissner's plexus Meissnerscher
 Plexus m.
melaena (e) d. e. f.
melancholia Melancholie f.
−,**involutional** Rückbildungsmelancholie f.
melancholiac melancholisch
melanin d. e. n.
melanoblast d. e. m.
melanoblastoma Melanoblastom n.
melanocarcinoma Melanokarzinom n.
melanocyte Melanozyt m.
melanoderma Melanodermie f.
melanogen d. e. n.
melanogenic melanogen
melanoma Melanom n.
melanosarcoma Melanosarkom n.
melanosis Melanose f.
melanotic melanotisch
melanuria Melanurie f.
melasma d. e. n.
melena (a) Melaena f.
melissa Melisse f.
melorheostosis Melorheostose f.
melt, to schmelzen
melting point Schmelzpunkt m.
melting range Schmelzbereich n.
 m.
member Glied n.
memberment Gliederung f.
membranaceous membranös
membrane Membran f.
−,**basement** Basalmembran f.
−,**periodontal** Wurzelhaut f.
membranous membranös
memory Gedächtnis n.
menadione Menadion n.
menarche d. e. f.
Mendel's law Mendelsches
 Gesetz n.
Mendel-Mantoux test Mendel-
 Mantoux-Probe f.

Mendel's reflex Mendel-
Bechterewscher Reflex m.
mendelize, to mendeln
Menge's pessary Menge-Pessar n.
Ménière's syndrome Ménièrescher
Symptomenkomplex m.
meninge Hirnhaut f.
meningeal d. e.
meningioma Meningeom n.
meningism Meningismus m.
meningitic meningitisch
meningitis d. e. f., Hirnhautentzündung f.
–, **acute aseptic** akute aseptische
Meningitis f.
–, **epidemic cerebrospinal**
Meningitis epidemica
–, **lymphocytic** lymphozytäre
Meningitis f.
–, **purulent** eitrige Meningitis f.
–, **serous** seröse Meningitis f.
–, **tuberculous** tuberkulöse
Meningitis f.
meningocele Meningozele f.
meningococcus Meningokokkus m.
meningoencephalitis Meningoenzephalitis f.
meningoencephalomyelitis
Meningoenzephalomyelitis f.
meningovascular meningovaskulär
meniscotomy Meniskotomie f.,
Meniskusoperation f.
– **knife** Meniskusmesser n.
meniscus Meniskus m.
menometrorrhagia Menometrorrhagie f.
menopause d. e. f.
menorrhagia Menorrhagie f.
menses Monatsblutung f.
Mensinga diaphragm Mensingapessar n.
menstrual menstruell
menstruate, to menstruieren
menstruation d. e. f.
–, **silent** uterine Schmierblutung f.
mensual monatlich
mensuration Messung f.

mental geistig; mental
– **deficiency** Schwachsinn m.
– **disease** Geisteskrankheit f.
– **disorder** Geistesstörung f.
– **disturbance** Geistesverwirrung f.
mentality Mentalität f.
menthol d. e. n.
mentoanterior d. e.
mentolabial d. e.
mentoposterior d. e.
mepazine Mepazin n.
meperidine Meperidin n.
mephenesin d. e. n.
meprobamate Meprobamat n.
mepyramine Mepyramin n.
meralgia Meralgie f.
– **paraesthetica** d. e.
mercaptan Merkaptan n.
mercaptopurine Merkaptopurin n.
mercurial quecksilberhaltig
– **ointment** graue Salbe f.
mercurialism Merkurialismus m.
mercurialization Quecksilberbehandlung f.
mercuric quecksilberhaltig
(zweiwertig)
– **chloride** Quecksilberchlorid n.,
Sublimat n.
mercurous quecksilberhaltig
(einwertig)
– **chloride** Quecksilberchlorür n.,
Kalomel n.
mercury Quecksilber n.
– **bichloride** Quecksilberchlorid n.
– **quartz lamp** Quecksilberdampfquarzlampe f.
meridian d. e. m.
meridional d. e.
merocrine merokrin
Merseburg triad Merseburger Trias f.
Merzbacher-Pelizaeus disease
Merzbacher-Pelizaeussche
Krankheit f.
mesad medianwärts
mesaortitis d. e. f.
mescaline Meskalin n.

mesencephalic mesenzephal
mesencephalitis Mesenzephalitis f.
mesencephalon Mittelhirn n.
mesenchyma Mesenchym n.
mesenchymal d. e.
mesenteric mesenterisch
mesentery Mesenterium n.
mesh Masche f.
mesial d. e.
mesioangular mesioangulär
mesiobuccal mesiobukkal
mesiodiencephalic mesiodienzephal
mesiodistal d. e.
mesiolingual d. e.
mesioocclusal mesiookklusal
mesoaortitis Mesaortitis f.
mesobilirubin d. e. n.
mesobilirubinogen d. e. n.
mesoblast d. e. m.
mesoderm d. e. n.
mesodermal d. e.
mesodiastolic mesodiastolisch
mesoinositol Mesoinosit n.
mesometritis d. e. f.
mesosystolic mesosystolisch
mesothelioma Mesotheliom n.
mesoxalyl urea Mesoxalylharnstoff m.
mesterolone Mesterolon n.
metabolic metabolisch, stoffwechselmäßig
metabolism Stoffwechsel m.
metabolite Stoffwechselprodukt n.
metacarpal metakarpal
metachromasia Metachromasie f.
metachromatic metachromatisch
metahexamide Metahexamid n.
metal Metall n.
–, noble Edelmetall n.
– rack Metallständer m.
metallic metallisch
metalloid d. e. n.
metallurgy Metallurgie f.
metamorphosis Metamorphose f.
metamyelocyte Metamyelozyt m.
metaniline yellow Metanilgelb n.

metaphysis Metaphyse f.
metaplasia Metaplasie f.
metaplastic metaplastisch
metapneumonic metapneumonisch
metastasis Metastase f.
metastasize, to metastasieren
metastatic metastatisch
metasyphilis d. e. f.
metasyphilitic metasyphilitisch
metatarsal d. e.
metatarsalgia Metatarsalgie f.
metazoa d. e. n. pl.
metencephalon Hinterhirn n.
meteorism Meteorismus m.
meteorological meteorologisch
meteorology Meteorologie f.
metformin d. e. n.
methadone Methadon n.
methaemoglobin (e) Methämoglobin n.
methaminodiazepoxide Methaminodiazepoxid n.
methamphetamine Methamphetamin n.
methandrostenolone Methandrostenolon n.
methane Methan n.
methanol Methylalkohol m.
methantheline Methanthelin n.
methaqualone Metaqualon n.
methemoglobin (a) Methämoglobin n.
methenamine Hexamethylentetramin n.
methicillin d. e. n.
methionine Methionin n.
method Methode f.
methodology Methodologie f.
methonium d. e. n.
methopterine Methopterin n.
methopyrapone Methopyrapon n.
methotrexate Methotrexat n.
methoxamine Methoxamin n.
methyl d. e. n.
methylase d. e. f.
methylate Methylat n.

methylate, to methylieren
methylation Methylierung f.
methylcholine Methylcholin n.
methyldimethoxyamphetamine Methyldimethoxyamphetamin n.
methyl dopa Methyldopa n.
methylene Methylen n.
− blue Methylenblau n.
methylhydrocortisone Methylhydrocortison n.
methyliodide Methyljodid n.
methyl orange Methylorange n.
methylphenidylate Methylphenidylat n.
methylphenylhydrazine Methylphenylhydrazin n.
methylprednisolone Methylprednisolon n.
methyl red Methylrot n.
methylrosanilin d. e. n.
methyltestosterone Methyltestosteron n.
methylthionine chloride Methylenblau n.
methyl thiouracil Methylthiouracil n.
methyltransferase d. e. f.
methyl violet Methylviolett n.
metiamide Metiamid n.
metoclopramide Metoclopramid n.
metoprolol d. e. n.
metrazol d. e. n.
metreurynter d. e. m.
metric metrisch
metritis d. e. f.
metropathia Metropathie f.
metropathic metropathisch
metrorrhagia Metrorrhagie f.
metrosalpingography Metrosalpingographie f.
metypranol d. e. n.
mezcaline Meskalin n.
mezlocillin d. e. n.
Michaelis' rhomboid Michaelissche Raute f.
microanalysis Mikroanalyse f.
microanalytic mikroanalytisch

microaneurysm Mikroaneurysma n.
microbe Mikrobe f.
microbial mikrobiell, mikrobisch
microbiological mikrobiologisch
microbiology Mikrobiologie f.
microbody Mikrokörper m.
microcephalia Mikrozephalie f.
microcephalic mikrozephal
microchemical mikrochemisch
microchemistry Mikrochemie f.
microcirculation Mikrozirkulation f.
micrococcus Mikrokokkus m.
microcurie Mikrocurie f.
microcyte Mikrozyt m.
microcytic mikrozytär
microcytosis Mikrozytose f.
microdetermination Mikrobestimmung f.
microdontia Mikrodontie f.
microelectrode Mikroelektrode f.
microelectrophoresis Mikroelektrophorese f.
microelement Mikroelement n.
microflocculation Mikroflockung f.
microglia Mikroglia f.
microgliomatosis Mikrogliomatose f.
microgram Mikrogramm n.
microhaemorrhage (e) Sickerblutung f.
microhemorrhage (a) Sickerblutung f.
microheating table apparatus Mikroheiztisch m.
microinjection Mikroinjektion f.
micro-leakage mikroskopische Undichtigkeit f.
microliter Mikroliter n.
micromelia Mikromelie f.
micrometer Mikrometer n.
micromethod Mikromethode f.
micromolecular mikromolekular
micromolecule Mikromolekül n.
micron Mikron n.
microorganism Mikroorganismus m.
microphone Mikrophon n.
microphthalmia Mikrophthalmie f.

microphysics Mikrophysik f.
micropinocytosis Mikropinozytose f.
micropsia Mikropsie f.
micropuncture Mikropunktion f.
microquantity Mikroquantität f.
microradiological mikroradiologisch
microradiology Mikroradiologie f.
microreaction Mikroreaktion f.
microscope (monocular/binocular) (monokuläres/binokuläres) Mikroskop n.
microscopic mikroskopisch
− **preparation** Ausstrich m., Abstrich m.
− **set** Mikroskopiebesteck n.
microscopy Mikroskopie f.
microsomal mikrosomal
microsome Mikrosom n.
Microsporon audouini Mikrosporon Audouini
− **furfur** Mikrosporon furfur
− **mentagrophytes** Mikrosporon mentagrophytes
− **minutissimum** Mikrosporon minutissimum
micro slide Objektträger m.
microtome Mikrotom n.
microtubule Mikrotubulus m.
miction Miktion f.
micturition Wasserlassen n.
micturition disorder Miktionsstörung f.
midbrain Mittelhirn n.
middle abdomen Mittelbauch m.
middle ear Mittelohr n.
middle finger Mittelfinger m.
middle point Mittelpunkt m.
middle position Mittellage f.
midpain Mittelschmerz m.
midriff Zwerchfell n.
midstream urine Mittelstrahlharn m.
midwife Hebamme f.
midwifery Geburtshilfe f.
migraine Migräne f.
migrate, to wandern

migration Wanderung f.
migratory wandernd
Mikulicz's cell Mikuliczsche Zelle f.
Mikulicz's disease Mikuliczsche Krankheit f.
mildew Mehltau m., Schimmel m. (botan.)
mile Meile f.
−, **nautical** Seemeile f.
miliaria crystallina Miliaria cristallina
miliary miliar
milk Milch f.
−, **diluted 50%** Halbmilch f.
− **teeth** Milchgebiß n.
Milkman's syndrome Milkman-Syndrom n.
milky milchig
Miller-Abbott tube Miller-Abbott-Sonde f.
milliampere d. e. n.
millibar d. e. n.
millicurie d. e. n.
milligram Milligramm n.
milliliter d. e. n.
millimicron Millimikron n.
millimol d. e. n.
mill in, to einschleifen
milling-in Einschleifen n.
millivolt d. e. n.
Millon's test Millonsche Probe f.
mimetic mimetisch
mind Geist m., Gemüt n., Seele f.
mindblindness Seelenblindheit f.
minddeafness Worttaubheit f.
mineral d. e. n.; mineralisch
− **bath** Mineralbad n.
− **oil** Mineralöl n.
− **waters** Mineralwasser n.
mineralization Mineralisation f.
mineralocorticoid Mineralokortikoid n.
minimal d. e.
ministry of health Gesundheitsministerium n.
mink Nerz n.
minocyclin d. e. n.

minor surgery kleine Chirurgie f.
minoxidil d. e. n.
minute volume Minutenvolumen n.
miosis d. e. f.
miotic miotisch; Miotikum n.
miraculin d. e. n.
mire Kot m.
mirror Spiegel m.
miry kotig
miscarriage Fehlgeburt f.
miscibility Mischbarkeit f.
miscible mischbar
misfortune Unglück n., Unglücksfall m.
missed abortion verhaltene Fehlgeburt f.
− **labor** (a) verhaltene Totgeburt f.
− **labour** (e) verhaltene Totgeburt f.
mist Nebel m.
mistakenly irrtümlich
mistletoe Mistel f.
misuse Mißbrauch m.
mite Milbe f.
mitella d. e. f.
mitigate, to mildern, lindern
mitigation Milderung f., Linderung f.
mitochondria Mitochondrien n. pl.
mitochondrial d. e.
mitosis Mitose f.
mitotic mitotisch
mitral insufficiency Mitralinsuffizienz f.
− **regurgitation** Mitralinsuffizienz f.
− **stenosis** Mitralstenose f.
− **valve** Mitralklappe f.
mix, to mischen, vermengen
mixed infection Mischinfektion f.
mixture Mixtur f., Mischung f.
Miyagawanella d. e.
mnemonics Mnemotechnik f.
mobile mobil, beweglich
mobility Mobilität f., Beweglichkeit f.
mobilization Mobilisierung f.

mobilize, to mobilisieren
modality Modalität f.
mode of action Wirkungsweise f.
mode of living Lebensweise f.
model Modell n.
modelling instrument Modellierinstrument n.
moderate mäßig
modification Modifikation f.
modify, to modifizieren
modulate, to modulieren
modulation d. e. f.
Möbius' sign Möbiussches Zeichen n.
Moeller-Barlow disease Moeller-Barlowsche Krankheit f.
Mönckeberg's sclerosis Mönckebergsche Sklerose f.
moist feucht
moisten, to befeuchten, anfeuchten
mol d. e. n.
molality Molalität f.
molar molar; Molar m., Mahlzahn m.
molarity Molarität f.
mold Schimmelpilz m., Schimmel m.; Gußform f.
molding fötale Konfiguration f. des Kopfes sub partu
mole d. e. f.; (zool.) Maulwurf m.
−, **blood** Blutmole f.
−, **carneous** Fleischmole f.
−, **fleshy** Fleischmole f.
−, **hydatid** Blasenmole f.
−, **hydatidiform** Blasenmole f.
−, **stone** Steinmole f.
−, **vesicular** Blasenmole f.
molecular molekular
molecular weight Molekulargewicht n.
molecule Molekül n.
Moll's gland Mollsche Drüse f.
mollusca d. e. n. pl.
molluscicidal molluskizid
molluscum contagiosum d. e.
molsidomine Molsidomin n.

molting Mauserung f.
molybdate Molybdat n.
molybdenum Molybdän n.
molybdic molybdänhaltig (sechswertig)
molybdous molybdänhaltig (dreiwertig)
Monakow's fasciculus Monakowsches Bündel n.
Monaldi's drainage Monaldidrainage f.
monamide Monamid n.
monamine Monamin n.
monamniotic monamniotisch
monarthritis d. e. f.
monarticular monartikulär
Mondor's disease Mondorsche Krankheit f.
mongolism Mongolismus m.
mongoloid d. e.
Monilia albicans Oidium albicans, Soorpilz m., d. e. f.
moniliasis d. e. f., Soor m.
monitor d. e. m.
monkey Affe m.
– paw Affenhand f.
monobasic monobasisch
monoblast d. e. m.
monochromatic monochromatisch
monochromatophil d. e.
monochromatophilic monochromatophil
monocular monokulär
monocyte Monozyt m.
monocytic monozytär
– leukaemia (e) Monozytenleukämie f.
monocytic leukemia (a) Monozytenleukämie f.
monocytosis Monozytose f.
monofascicular monofaszikulär
monoiodotyrosine Monojodtyrosin n.
monolayer culture Einschichtkultur f.
monomania Monomanie f.
mononuclear mononukleär

mononucleosis Mononukleose f.
mononucleotide Mononukleotid n.
monophasic monophasisch
monophosphate Monophosphat n.
monoplasmatic monoplasmatisch
monoplegia Monoplegie f.
monorchidism Monorchismus m.
monorchism Monorchismus m.
monosaccharide Monosaccharid n.
monosomal d. e.
monosymptomatic monosymptomatisch
monovalent d. e., einwertig
monoxide Monoxyd n.
monozygotic monozygot
Monro-Richter line Monro-Richtersche Linie f.
monstre Mißbildung f., Mißgeburt f.
monstrosity Mißbildung f.
Montgomery's gland Montgomerysche Drüse f.
monthlies Monatsblutung f.
mood Stimmung f., Laune f.
moon-shaped mondförmig
moor bath Moorbad n.
Morax-Axenfeld diplococcus Diplokokkus Morax-Axenfeld
Moraxella lacunata Diplokokkus Morax-Axenfeld
morbid d. e.
morbidity Morbidität f.
morbific krankmachend
morel Morchel f.
Morgagni's syndrome Morgagnisches Syndrom n.
moribund d. e.
Moro's test Moroprobe f.
moronity Debilität f.
morphea (a) umschriebene Sklerodermie f.
morphoea (e) umschriebene Sklerodermie f.
morphine Morphium n., Morphin n.
morphinism Morphinismus m.
morphinization Morphinbehandlung f.

morphinomania Morphinsucht f.
morphogenesis Morphogenese f.
morphogenetic morphogenetisch
morphologic morphologisch
morphology Morphologie f.
morphometric morphometrisch
mortal tödlich, sterblich
mortality Mortalität f.
mortar Mörser m.
mortify, to absterben
mortuary Leichenhalle f.
morula d. e. f.
morulation d. e. f.
mosquito Moskito m.
moss Moos n.
–, Iceland Isländisches Moos n.
–, Irish Irländisches Moos n.
mother complex Mutterkomplex m.
mother instinct Mutterinstinkt m.
mother's mark Muttermal n.
mother's milk Muttermilch f.
motile beweglich
motility Beweglichkeit f., Motilität f.
motion Bewegung f.
– sickness Reisekrankheit f., Kinetose f.
motionless regungslos
motor d. e. m.; motorisch
motorial motorisch
mottled enamel gefleckter Schmelz m.
mould Schimmelpilz m., Schimmel m.; Gußform f.
moulding fötale Konfiguration des Kopfes sub partu
mountain sickness Bergkrankheit f.
mouse Maus f.
mouth Mund m.
– breathing Mundatmung f.
– dryness Mundtrockenheit f.
– gag Mundsperrer m.
– lamp Mundlampe f.
– mirror Mundspiegel m.
– piece Mundstück n.
– protection cloth Mundschutztuch n.

mouth-to-mouth insufflation Mund-zu-Mund-Beatmung f.
mouth-to-nose insufflation Mund-zu-Nase-Beatmung f.
move, to bewegen
movement Bewegung f.
m.p. (= melting point) Schmelzpunkt m.
mucigenous schleimbildend
mucilage Schleim m. (pharm.)
mucin d. e. n., Muzin n.
mucinosis Muzinose f.
mucocele Mukozele f.
mucopeptide Mukopeptid n.
mucopolysaccharide Mukopolysaccharid n.
mucoprotein Mukoprotein n.
mucosa Schleimhaut f.
mucosaccharide Mukosaccharid n.
mucosal block Mucosa-Block m.
mucostatic mukostatisch
mucous mukös
– membrane Schleimhaut f.
mucoviscidosis Mukoviskidose f.
mucus Schleim m.
– thread Schleimfaden m.
mud Schmutz m., Schlamm m.
– bath Schlammbad n.
– fever Schlammfieber n.
muddy schlammig, schmutzig, trübe
mule Maultier n.
mull d. e. m.
multiarticular multiartikulär
multicapsular multikapsulär
multicellular multizellulär
multicenter study wissenschaftliche Gemeinschaftsarbeit f. mehrerer Kliniken, multizentrische Arbeit f.
multicentre study wissenschaftliche Gemeinschaftsarbeit f. mehrerer Kliniken
multicentric multizentrisch
multi-channel system Mehrkanalsystem n.
multicystic multizystisch

multidisciplinary multidisziplinär
multifocal multifokal
multiglandular multiglandulär
multilobular multilobulär
multilocular multilokulär
multinuclear multinukleär
multinucleate multinukleär
multipara d. e. f.
multiparous patient multipare Patientin f.
multiphasic multiphasisch, mehrphasig
multiple multipel
− **choice examination** Auswahlfragen − Examen n.
− **sclerosis** multiple Sklerose f.
multiply, to vervielfachen, multiplizieren
multipolar d. e.
multitude Menge f., Vielfalt f.
multivalent d. e.
multivitamin d. e. n.
mummification Mumifizierung f.
mumps d. e. m.
mural d. e.
muramidase d. e. f.
murder Mord m.
murexide Murexid n.
− **test** Murexidprobe f.
muriatic muriatisch
murmur Geräusch n.
muscarine Muskarin n.
muscle Muskel m.
muscular muskulär
− **dystrophy, progressive** Dystrophia musculorum progressiva (Erb)
− **rheumatism** Muskelrheumatismus m.
− **system** Muskulatur f.
− **tension** Muskelspannung f.
musculature Muskulatur f.
−, **smooth** glatte Muskulatur f.
−, **striated** quergestreifte Muskulatur f.
musculocutaneous muskulokutan

musculomembranous muskulomembranös
musculous muskulös
mushroom eßbarer Pilz m.; Ständerpilz m.; Egerling m.
musical musikalisch
mustard Senf m.
− **paper** Senfpapier n.
mutagenesis Mutagenese f.
mutase d. e. f.
mutation d. e. f.
mute stumm
mutilate, to verstümmeln
mutilation Verstümmelung f.
mutism Stummheit f.
mutual gegenseitig
myalgia Myalgie f.
myasthenia Myasthenie f.
myasthenia gravis Myasthenia gravis pseudoparalytica
myasthenic myasthenisch
myatonia Myatonie f.
myatrophic myatrophisch
myatrophy Myatrophie f.
mycelium Mycel n.
mycetoma Madurafuß m.
Mycobacterium leprae d. e., Leprabazillus m.
− **smegmatis** d. e., Smegmabazillus m.
− **tuberculosis** d. e., Tuberkelbazillus m.
− **tuberculosis avium** d. e.
− **tuberculosis bovis** d. e.
mycological mykologisch
mycologist Mykologe m., Mykologin f.
mycology Mykologie f.
mycoplasma d. e. n.
mycosis Mykose f.
− **fungoides** d. e.
mycotic mykotisch
mycotoxin Mykotoxin n.
mydriasis d. e. f.
mydriatic mydriatisch; Mydriatikum n.
myectomie Myektomie f.

myelencephalon Nachhirn n.
myelin d. e. n.
myelinization Myelinisierung f.
myelitic myelitisch
myelitis d. e. f.
myeloblast d. e. m.
myeloblastosis Myeloblastose f.
myelocele Myelozele f.
myelocyte Myelozyt m.
myelodysplasia Myelodysplasie f.
myelofibrosis Markfibrose f.
myelogenesis Myelogenese f.
myelogenic myelogen
myelogenous myelogen
myelogram Myelogramm n.
myelographical myelographisch
myelography Myelographie f.
myeloid d. e.
myeloma Myelom n.
myelomalacia Myelomalazie f.
myelomatosis Myelomatose f.
myelomeningocele Myelomeningozele f.
myelopathy Myelopathie f.
myelophthisis Myelophthise f.
myelosarcoma Myelosarkom n.
myelosclerosis Myelosklerose f.
myelosis Myelose f.
−,aleukaemic (e) aleukämische Myelose f.
−,aleukemic (a) aleukämische Myelose f.
−,funicular funikuläre Spinalerkrankung f.
−,leukaemic (e) leukämische Myelose f.
− leukemic (a) leukämische Myelose f.
myelotomy Myelotomie f.
myoarchitectonic myoarchitektonisch
myoblast d. e. m.
myocardial myokardial
− damage Herzmuskelschaden m.
− insufficiency muskuläre Herzinsuffizienz f.
myocarditic myokarditisch

myocarditis Myokarditis f.
myocardium Myokard n., Herzmuskel m.
myoclonia Myoklonie f.
myoclonic myoklonisch
myoclonus Myoklonus m.
− epilepsy Myoklonusepilepsie f.
myodegeneration d. e. f.
myodystrophy Muskeldystrophie f.
myoelectric myoelektrisch
myofibril Myofibrille f.
myofibroma Myofibrom n.
myofibrosis Myofibrose f.
myogelosis Myogelose f.
myogenous myogen
myoglobin d. e. n.
myoglobinuria Myoglobinurie f.
myoglobulin d. e. n.
myography Myographie f.
myohaemoglobin (e) Myohämoglobin n.
myohemoglobin (a) Myohämoglobin n.
myolipoma Myolipom n.
myology Myologie f.
myolysis Myolyse f.
myoma Myom n.
− screw Myomheber m.
myomalacia Myomalazie f.
myomatosis Myomatose f.
myomatous myomatös
myomectomy Myomektomie f.
myometritis d. e. f.
myoneural d. e.
myoneuroma Myoneurom n.
myopathic myopathisch
myopathy Myopathie f.
myopia Myopie f.
myopic myopisch
myoplasm Myoplasma n.
myoplasty Muskelplastik f.
myosarcoma Myosarkom n.
myosin d. e. n.
myositis d. e.
−,ossifying Myositis ossificans
myospasm Muskelspasmus m.
myotomy Myotomie f.

myotonia Myotonie f.
− **congenita** d. e., Thomsensche Krankheit f.
myotonic myotonisch
myringitis d. e. f.
myringotomy Myringotomie f.
myristicin d. e. n.
myrrh Myrrhe f.
myxadenoma Myxadenom n.
myxedema (a) Myxödem n.
myxedematous (a) myxödematös
myxoblastoma Myxoblastom n.
myxochondrofibrosarcoma Myxochondrofibrosarkom n.
myxochondroma Myxochondrom n.
myxochondrosarcoma Myxochondrosarkom n.
myxoedema (e) Myxödem n.
myxoedematous (e) myxödematös
myxoendothelioma Myxoendotheliom n.
myxofibroma Myxofibrom n.
myxofibrosarcoma Myxofibrosarkom n.
myxoglioma Myxogliom n.
myxolipoma Myxolipom n.
myxoma Myxom n.
myxomatosis Myxomatose f.
myxomatous myxomatös
myxomyoma Myxomyom n.
myxoneuroma Myxoneurom n.
myxoneurosis Myxoneurose f.
myxosarcoma Myxosarkom n.
myxovirus d. e. n.

N

Nägele's obliquity Nägelesche Obliquität f.
naevoid amentia (e) Sturge-Webersches Syndrom n.
naevus (e) d. e. m.
nagana d. e. f.
nail Nagel m.
−, **to** nageln
− **affection** Nagelerkrankung f.
− **bed** Nagelbett n.
− **biting** Fingernägelbeißen n.
− **cleaner** Nagelreiniger m.
− **clipper** Nagelzange f.
− **extractor** Nagelzieher m.
− **file** Nagelfeile f.
− **fold** Nagelfalz m.
−, **ingrowing** eingewachsener Nagel m.
−, **picked-up** (veter.) Nageltritt m.
− **root** Nagelwurzel f.
− **scissors** Nagelschere f.
− **wall** Nagelwall m.
naked nackt
naloxone Naloxon n.
nandrolone Nandrolon n.
nanism Zwergwuchs m.
nanogram Nanogramm n.
nanosomia Zwergwuchs m.
nanous zwergwüchsig
nape Nacken m.
naphthalene Naphthalin n.
naphthamine Hexamethylentetramin n.
naphthidine Naphthidin n.
naphthol d. e. n.
naphtholphthalein d. e. n.
naphthol violet Naphtholviolett n.
naphthoquinone Naphthochinon n.
naphthyl d. e. n.
naproxen d. e. n.
narcissism Narzismus n.
narcissistic narzistisch
narcoanalysis Narkoanalyse f.
narcolepsy Narkolepsie f.
narcoleptic narkoleptisch
narcosis Narkose f.

narcotic narkotisch; Narkotikum n.
narcotine Narcotin n.
narcotize, to narkotisieren
narcylen d. e. n.
nasal d. e.
nasoalveolar nasoalveolär
nasolabial d. e.
nasopalatine nasopalatinal
nasopharyngeal d. e.
nasopharyngitis d. e. f.
nasotracheal d. e.
natality Geburtenhäufigkeit f.
natamycin d. e. n.
natriuresis Natriurese f.
natron d. e. n.
natural natürlich
− law Naturgesetz n.
− science Naturwissenschaft f.
naturopath Naturheilkundiger m.
naturopathy Naturheilkunde f.
nausea Brechreiz m., Nausea f.
navel Nabel m.
navel string Nabelschnur f.
nead Naht f.
near-sighted kurzsichtig
neat Rind n.
nebulization Vernebelung f.
nebulize, to vernebeln
nebulizer Vernebler m.
Necator americanus d. e.
neck Hals m.
− of the femur Schenkelhals m.
− − − tooth Zahnhals m.
− − − womb Gebärmutterhals m.
− vein congestion Halsvenenstauung f.
−, vesical Blasenhals m.
necrobiosis Nekrobiose f.
necrobiotic nekrobiotisch
necrophilism Nekrophilie f.
necrophilous nekrophil
necropsy Nekropsie f., Autopsie f.; Leichenschau f.
necrosis Nekrose f.
necrosis, papillary Papillennekrose f.

necrospermia Nekrospermie f.
necrotic nekrotisch
necrotize, to nekrotisieren
necrotomy Nekrotomie f.
needle Nadel f.
− biopsy Nadelbiopsie f.
− holder Nadelhalter m.
−, intestinal Nadel f. für Darmnaht
−, ligature Unterbindungsnadel f.
−, post mortem Sektionsnadel f., Leichennadel f.
−, spinal puncture Lumbalpunktionsnadel
−, suture chirurgische Nadel f.
nefopam d. e. n.
negative negativ
negativism Negativismus m.
Negri's body Negrisches Körperchen n.
neighbouring benachbart
Neisseria gonorrhoeae Gonokokkus m.
− intracellularis Meningokokkus m.
− weichselbaumii Meningokokkus m.
Nélaton's catheter Nélatonkatheter m.
− line Nélatonsche Linie f.
nema Nematode f.
nematode d. e. f.
nematodiasis Nematodenbefall m.
neodymium Neodym n.
neoformation Neubildung f.
neon d. e. n.
neonatal period Neugeborenenperiode f.
neonate Neugeborenes n.
neoplasm Neoplasma n.
neoplastic neoplastisch
nephelometer d. e. n.
nephelometric nephelometrisch
nephelometry Nephelometrie f.
nephrectomy Nephrektomie f.
nephritic nephritisch

nephritis d. e. f., Nierenentzündung f.
—, **acute glomerular** akute Glomerulonephritis f.
—, **chronic** chronische Nephritis f.
—, **focal** Herdnephritis f.
—, **interstitial** interstitielle Nephritis f.
—, **war** Feldnephritis f.
nephrocapsectomy Nierendekapsulation f.
nephrogenous nephrogen
nephrolithiasis d. e. f.
nephrological nephrologisch
nephrologist Nephrologe m., Nephrologin f.
nephrology Nephrologie f.
nephropathy Nepropathie f.
nephroptosis Nephroptose f.
nephrosclerosis Nephrosklerose f.
nephrosclerosis, arteriolar Nierenarteriolosklerose f.
nephrosclerotic nephrosklerotisch
nephrosis Nephrose f.
—, **amyloid** Amyloidnephrose f.
—, **lipoid** Lipoidnephrose f.
nephrosonephritis Nephritis f. mit nephrotischem Einschlag
nephrostomy Nephrostomie f.
nephrotic nephrotisch
nephrotomy Nephrotomie f.
nephrotoxic nephrotoxisch
nerval d. e.
nerve Nerv m.
—, **abducent** Nervus abducens
—, **acoustic** Nervus acusticus
—, **cochlear** Nervus cochlearis
—, **facial** Nervus facialis
—, **femoral** Nervus femoralis
—, **genitofemoral** Nervus genitofemoralis
—, **glossopharyngeal** Nervus glossopharyngeus
— **growth factor** Nervenwachstumsfaktor m.
—, **hypoglossal** Nervus hypoglossus

nerve, iliohypogastric Nervus iliohypogastricus
—, **ilioinguinal** Nervus ilioinguinalis
—, **infraorbital** Nervus infraorbitalis
—, **intercostal** Nervus intercostalis
—, **intermediary** Nervus intermedius
—, **median** Nervus medianus
—, **obturator** Nervus obturatorius
—, **oculomotor** Nervus oculomotorius
—, **olfactory** Nervus olfactorius
—, **optic** Nervus opticus
—, **peroneal** Nervus peroneus
—, **phrenic** Nervus phrenicus
—, **pneumogastric** Nervus vagus
—, **radial** Nervus radialis
—, **recurrent** Nervus recurrens
—, **sciatic** Nervus ischiadicus
—, **splanchnic** Nervus splanchnicus
—, **sympathetic** Nervus sympathicus
—, **tibial** Nervus tibialis
—, **trifacial** Nervus trigeminus
—, **trochlear** Nervus trochlearis
—, **ulnar** Nervus ulnaris
—, **vagus** Nervus vagus
—, **vestibular** Nervus vestibularis
nervosity Nervosität f.
nervous nervös
— **attack** Nervenanfall m.
— **breakdown** Nervenzusammenbruch m.
— **complaint** Nervenleiden n.
— **debility** Nervenschwäche f.
— **pathway** Nervenbahn f.
— **system** Nervensystem n.
nervousness Nervosität f.
nettle rash Nesselsucht f.
network Netz n., Geflecht n., Fasernetz n., Faserwerk n.
neural d. e.
neuralgia Neuralgie f.
—, **intercostal** Interkostalneuralgie f.

neuralgia, trigeminal Trigeminusneuralgie f.
neuralgic neuralgisch
neuralgiform d. e.
neuraminidase d. e. f.
neurasthenia Neurasthenie f.
neurastheniac Neurastheniker m., Neurasthenikerin f.
neurasthenic neurasthenisch
neuraxon Achsenzylinderfortsatz m.
neurectomy Neurektomie f.
neurilemma Schwannsche Scheide f.
neurin d. e. n.
neurinoma Neurinom n.
neurite Neurit m.
neuritic neuritisch
neuritis d. e. f.
—, **diphtheric** diphtherische Neuritis f.
—, **multiple alcoholic** Polyneuritis alcoholica
—, **optic** Neuritis optica
—, **retrobulbar** Neuritis retrobulbaris
neuroblast d. e. m.
neuroblastoma Neuroblastom n.
neurocirculatory neurozirkulatorisch
neurodermatitis d. e. f.
neurodermatosis Neurodermatose f.
neurodermitis d. e. f.
neuroepithelial d. e.
neuroepithelioma Neuroepitheliom n.
neuroepithelium Neuroepithel n.
neurofibril Neurofibrille f.
neurofibrillar neurofibrillär
neurofibroma Neurofibrom n.
neurofibromatosis Neurofibromatose f.
neurogenic neurogen
neurogenous neurogen
neuroglia d. e. f.
neurogliocytoma Neurogliozytom n.
neuroglioma Neurogliom n.
neurogliosis Neurogliose f.
neurohormonal d. e.
neurohumoral d. e.
neurohypophyseal neurohypophysär
neurohypophysis Neurohypophyse f.
neurokinin d. e. n.
neuroleptanalgesia Neuroleptanalgesie f.
neuroleptic neuroleptisch; Neuroleptikum n.
neurological neurologisch
neurologist Neurologe m., Neurologin f.
neurology Neurologie f.
neurolues d. e. f.
neurolysis Neurolyse f.
neuroma Neurom n.
neuromuscular neuromuskulär
neuron d. e. n.
neuronal d. e.
neurone Neuron n.
neuronophagy Neuronophagie f.
neuroparalysis Neuroparalyse f.
neuroparalytic neuroparalytisch
neuropath Neuropath m., Neuropathin f.
neuropathic neuropathisch
neuropathologic neuropathologisch
neuropathology Neuropathologie f.
neuropathy Neuropathie f.
neurophysiological neurophysiologisch
neurophysiology Neurophysiologie f.
neuroplegic neuroplegisch; Neuroplegikum n.
neuropsychopharmacology Neuropsychopharmakologie f.
neuroretinitis d. e. f.
neurorrhaphy Nervennaht f.
neurosecretion Neurosekretion f.
neurosis Neurose f.
neurosis, cardiac Herzneurose f.
—, **vasomotor** Vasoneurose f.

neurosurgeon Neurochirurg m.
neurosurgery Neurochirurgie f.
neurosurgical neurochirurgisch
neurosyphilis d. e. f.
neurotic neurotisch
neurotomy Neurotomie f.
neurotoxic neurotoxisch
neurotropic neurotrop
neurotropism Neurotropie f.
neurovascular neurovaskulär
neurovegetative neurovegetativ
neurovegetative dysergy vegetative Neurodysergie f., vegetative Dystonie f.
neutral d. e.
– **fat** Neutralfett n.
– **red** Neutralrot n.
neutralization Neutralisierung f.
neutralize, to neutralisieren
neutron d. e. n.
neutropenia Neutropenie f.
neutropenic neutropenisch
neutrophil neutrophil; neutrophiler Leukozyt m.
neutrophilia Neutrophilie f.
neutrophilic neutrophil
nevoid amentia (a) Sturge-Webersches Syndrom n.
nevus (a) Naevus m.
new born Neugeborenes n.
newton d. e. n.
Newton's ring Newtonscher Ring m.
niacin Nikotinsäure f.
nialamide Nialamid n.
nibble, to nagen
niche Nische f.
nickel d. e. n.
– **-plated** vernickelt
Nicol prism Nicolsches Prisma n.
nicotinamide Nikotinamid n.
nicotinate Nikotinsäuresalz n.
nicotine Nikotin n.
– **poisoning** Nikotinvergiftung f.
nicotinic acid Nikotinsäure f.
– **acid amide** Nikotinsäureamid n.
nictitate, to blinzeln

nidation d. e. f.
Niemann-Pick disease Niemann-Picksche Krankheit f.
nifedipine Nifedipin n.
night blindness Nachtblindheit f.
night eating syndrome Nachtessersyndrom n.
nightmare Alpdrücken n.
nightshade Belladonna f.
nightsweats Nachtschweiß m.
night watch Nachtwache f.
night work Nachtarbeit f.
nihilism Nihilismus m.
ninhydrin d. e. n.
niobium Niob n.
nipple Brustwarze f.
nirvanol d. e. n.
Nissl's body Nisslsches Körperchen n.
nit Nisse f.
niter Kaliumnitrat n.
niton Radiumemanation f.
nitraemia (e) Niträmie f.
nitramine Nitramin n.
nitrate Nitrat n.
nitre Kaliumnitrat n.
nitremia (a) Niträmie f.
nitric stickstoffhaltig (fünfwertig)
nitric acid Salpetersäure f.
nitride Nitrid n.
nitrile Nitril n.
nitrite Nitrit n.
nitrobenzene Nitrobenzol n.
nitrofurantoin d. e. n.
nitrofurazone Nitrofurazon n.
nitrogen Stickstoff m.
nitrogen mustard Stickstofflost m.
nitrogenous stickstoffhaltig
nitroglycerin Nitroglyzerin n.
nitrophenol d. e. n.
nitroprusside Nitroprussid n.
nitrosamine Nitrosamin n.
nitrose stickstoffhaltig
nitrous stickstoffhaltig (dreiwertig)
Nobel prize Nobelpreis m.
noble gas Edelgas n.
– **metal** Edelmetall n.

Nocardia d. e.
nocardiosis Nocardiose f.
nociceptive nocizeptiv
nocturnal nächtlich
nodal d. e.
nodal rhythm Knotenrhythmus m.
node Knoten m.
nodular nodulär
nodule Knötchen n.
Noguchia granulosis Bacterium granulosis
noise apparatus Lärmapparat m.
noma Wasserkrebs m.
nomenclature Nomenklatur f.
nomogram Nomogramm n.
nomotopic nomotop
nonesterified unverestert, nicht verestert
non Hodgkin lymphoma nicht lymphogranulomatöses Lymphom n.
noninvasive nichtinvasiv
nonmetal Nichtmetall n.
Nonne-Apelt reaction Nonne-Apeltsche Reaktion f.
nonprotein nitrogen Reststickstoff m.
nonspecific nicht spezifisch, unspezifisch
nonsuppressible nicht unterdrückbar
noradrenaline Noradrenalin n.
norandrostenolone Norandrostenolon n.
norephedrine Norephedrin n.
norepinephrine Noradrenalin n.
norethandrolone Noräthandrolon n.
norethisterone Noräthisteron n.
norgestrel d. e. n.
norleucine Norleucin n.
norm Norm f.
normal d. e.
— **saline solution** physiologische Kochsalzlösung f.
normalization Normalisierung
normalize, to normalisieren

normergic normergisch
normoblast d. e. m.
normocyte Normozyt m.
normotensive normoton
normothermia Normothermie f.
normothermic normothermisch
norprogesterone Norprogesteron n.
nortestosterone Nortestosteron n.
nose Nase f.
nosebleed Nasenbluten n.
nosematosis Nosematose f.
nosological nosologisch
nosology Nosologie f.
nostalgia Heimweh n.
nostalgy Heimweh n.
nostril Nasenloch n.
notatin d. e. n.
notch Inzisur f.
note blindness Notenblindheit f.
nourish, to nähren, ernähren
nourishing nahrhaft
nourishment Speise f., Nahrung f., Ernährung f.
novobiocin d. e. n.
noxious schädlich
nozzle Düse f.
nuchal d. e.
nuclear nukleär
— **medical** nuklearmedizinisch
— **physics** Kernphysik f.
— **reactor** Kernreaktor m.
nuclease Nuklease f.
nucleated kernhaltig
nuclein Nuklein n.
nucleoalbumin Nukleoalbumin n.
nucleolar nukleolär
nucleoprotein Nukleoproteid n.
nucleosidase Nukleosidase f.
nucleoside Nukleosid n.
nucleotidase Nukleotidase f.
nucleotide Nukleotid n.
nuclide Nuklid n.
nude nackt
nudity Nacktheit f.
Nuhn's gland Nuhnsche Drüse f.
nullipara d. e. f.

nulliparous patient Nullipara f.
numb gefühllos
numerous zahlreich
nummiform münzenförmig
nurse Pflegeperson f., Krankenpfleger m., Krankenpflegerin f., Krankenschwester f.
–, **child's** Kinderpflegerin f., Kinderkrankenschwester f.
–, **community** Gemeindeschwester f.
–, **dry** Säuglingspflegerin f.
–, **head** Oberschwester f., Oberpfleger m.
–, **student** Schwesternschülerin f.; Pflegeschüler m.
–, **wet** Amme f.
nurse, to säugen; pflegen
nursing Pflege f., Krankenpflege f.; Stillen n., Säugen n.
– **education** Ausbildung f. in Krankenpflege
– **period** Stillperiode f.
– **personnel** Pflegepersonal n.
– –, **auxiliary** pflegerisches Hilfspersonal n.

nutmeg Muskatnuß f.
nutrient nährend; Kräftigungsmittel n.
nutriment Nahrung f., Nahrungsstoff m.
nutrition Ernährung f.
nutritional ernährungsmäßig, nutritionell
nutritionist Ernährungswissenschaftler m.
nutritious nahrhaft
nutritiousness Nahrhaftigkeit f.
nutritive nutritiv, nährend
– **quality** Nährwert m.
nux vomica d. e.
nyctalgia Nachtschmerz m.
nyctalopia Nachtblindheit f.
nycturia Nykturie f.
Nylander's test Nylandersche Probe f.
nymphomania Nymphomanie f.
nystagmogenic nystagmogen
nystagmograph d. e. m.
nystagmography Nystagmographie f.
nystagmus d. e. m.

O

oak, poison Rhus toxicodendron
oaric ovariell
oarium Eierstock m.
oatmeal Hafermehl n.
obdormition Eingeschlafensein n.
obduction Obduktion f.
Obermayer's test Obermayersche Probe f.
obese fettleibig
obesity Fettleibigkeit f., Fettsucht f.
– **with pituitary disturbance** hypophysäre Fettsucht f.
object Objekt n.

objective objektiv; Objektiv n.
obligate obligat
oblique schief, schräg
obliquity Obliquität f.
obliterate, to obliterieren
obliteration d. e. f.
oblongata d. e. f.
observation Beobachtung f.
obsession Zwangsvorstellung f.
obsolete obsolet
obstetrical geburtshilflich
obstetrician Geburtshelfer m.
obstetrics Geburtshilfe f.
obstruct, to verstopfen, verlegen

obstruction Verstopfung f., Verlegung f.
obtuse stumpf
obviate, to entgegentreten, vorbeugen
occasional gelegentlich
occipital okzipital
occipitoanterior okzipitoanterior
occipitocervical okzipitozervikal
occipitofrontal okzipitofrontal
occipitomental okzipitomental
occipitoparietal okzipitoparietal
occipitoposterior okzipitoposterior
occipitotemporal okzipitotemporal
occiput anterior position vordere Hinterhauptshaltung f.
– **posterior position** hintere Hinterhauptshaltung f.
occlude, to verschließen
occlusal okklusal
occlusion Okklusion f., Verschluß m.
occlusive okklusiv
occlusive disease, arterial arterielle Verschlußkrankheit f.
occlusive dressing Okklusivverband m.
occult okkult
occupation Beschäftigung f., Beruf m.
occupation neurosis Beschäftigungsneurose f.
occupational beruflich, berufsbedingt
– **disease** Berufskrankheit f.
– **therapy** Beschäftigungstherapie f.
ocelot Ozelot m.
ochronosis Ochronose f.
octagonal achteckig
octane Oktan n.
octavalent achtwertig
ocular okulär; Okular n.
oculist Augenarzt m., Augenärztin f.
oculomotor okulomotorisch
oculonasal okulonasal

odontalgia Zahnweh n., Zahnschmerz m.
odontiatria Zahnheilkunde f.
odontoblast d. e. m.
odontoblastoma Odontoblastom n.
odontoclast Odontoklast m.
odontograph d. e. m.
odontoma Odontom n.
odontotomy Zahntrepanation f.
odor (a) Geruch m., Duft m.
odorless (a) geruchlos
odour (e) Geruch m., Duft m.
odourless (e) geruchlos
oecology (e) Ökologie f.
oedema (e) Ödem n.
oedematous (e) ödematös
Oedipus complex Ödipuskomplex m.
oesophagectasia (e) Ösophagektasie f.
oesophagoscope (e) Ösophagoskop n.
oesophagoscopical (e) ösophagoskopisch
oesophagoscopy (e) Ösophagoskopie f.
oesophagus (e) Ösophagus m., Speiseröhre f.
oestradiol (e) Östradiol n.
oestrane (e) Östran n.
oestriol (e) Östriol n.
oestrogen (e) Östrogen n.
oestrogenic (e) östrogen
oestrone (e) Östron n.
offensive widerlich, ekelhaft
office Büro n., Amt n.
office, doctor's Arztpraxis f., Praxisräume m. pl. des Arztes
official offiziell; offizinell
offspring Nachkommenschaft f.
ohm d. e. n.
–, **reciprocal** Siemens n.
oidiomycosis Oidiomykose f.
oikology Oikologie f.
oil Öl n.
–, **to** ölen
– **bath** Ölbad n.

oil, castor Rizinusöl n.
–, cedarwood Zedernöl n.
–, cod liver Lebertran m.
– diffusion pump Öldiffusionspumpe f.
–, eucalyptus Eukalyptusöl n.
–, linseed Leinsamenöl n.
– of chaulmoogra Chalmoograöl n.
–, chenopodium Oleum Chenopodii anthelminthici
–, cinnamon Zimtöl n.
–, cloves Nelkenöl n.
–, coriander Korianderöl n.
–, gaultheria Gaultheriaöl n.
–, mustard Senföl n.
–, tar Teeröl n.
–, thuja Thujaöl n.
–, olive Olivenöl n.
– transformer Öltransformator m.
ointment Salbe f.
ointment base Salbengrundlage f.
ointment, emulsifying Emulsionssalbe f.
old people's home Altersheim n.
old tuberculin Alttuberkulin n.
oleaginous ölig
oleander d. e. m.
oleandomycin d. e. n.
oleandrin d. e. n.
oleate Oleat n.
olefin ungesättigter aliphatischer Kohlenwasserstoff m.
oleoresin d. e. n.
oleothorax d. e. m.
olfactometer Olfaktometer n.
olfactory olfaktorisch
oligaemia (e) Oligämie f.
oligaemic (e) oligämisch
oligemia (a) Oligämie f.
oligemic (a) oligämisch
oligodendroblastoma Oligodendroblastom n.
oligodendrocyte Oligodendrozyt m.
oligodendroglia d. e. f.
oligodynamic oligodynamisch

oligomenorrhea (a) Oligomenorrhöe f.
oligomenorrhoea (e) Oligomenorrhöe f.
oligomorphic oligomorph
oligophrenia Oligophrenie f.
oligozoospermatism Oligozoospermie f.
oliguresis Oligurie f.
oliguria Oligurie f.
olive d. e. f.
Oliver-Cardarelli sign Oliver-Cardarellisches Zeichen n.
olivomycin d. e. n.
omarthritis d. e. f.
Ombrédanne's mask Ombrédanne-Maske f.
omentopexy Omentopexie f.
omit, to unterlassen
omphalitis d. e. f.
omphalocele d. e. f.
onanism Onanie f.
onchocerciasis Onchozerkiasis f.
oncogenesis Geschwulstbildung f.
oncological onkologisch
oncology Onkologie f.
oncotic onkotisch
oncolysis Onkolyse f.
oncolytic onkolytisch
one-armed einarmig
one-dimensional eindimensional
one-eyed einäugig
onset Anfall m., Einsetzen n., Angriff m.
ontogenesis Ontogenese f.
ontogenetic ontogenetisch
onychogryposis Onychogrypose f.
onychomycosis Onychomykose f.
ooblast d. e. m.
oocyte Oozyt m.
oophorectomy Oophorektomie f.
oophoritis d. e. f.
oosporosis Oosporose f.
opacifying schattengebend, kontrastgebend
opacity Trübung f., Verschattung f.
opalescence Opaleszenz f.

opalescent opaleszierend
opaque lichtundurchlässig; trüb
OPC (= outpatient clinic) Poliklinik f.
OPD (= outpatient department) Ambulanz f.
open offen
open, to öffnen
— air Freiluft f.
opening Öffnung f.
— snap Öffnungston m.
operability Operabilität f.
operable operabel
operate, to operieren
operate upon, to operieren
operating surgeon Operateur m.
operation d. e. f.
operative operativ
operator Operateur m.
— gene Operator-Gen n.
operon d. e. n.
ophthalmia Opthalmie f.
ophthalmic ointment Augensalbe f.
ophthalmitis d. e. f.
ophthalmologic ophthalmologisch
— surgery Augenchirurgie f.
ophthalmologist Ophthalmologe m., Ophthalmologin f., Augenarzt m., Augenärztin f.
ophthalmology Augenheilkunde f.
ophthalmometer d. e. n.
ophthalmoplegia Ophthalmoplegie f.
ophthalmoplegic ophthalmoplegisch
ophthalmoscope Ophthalmoskop n., Augenspiegel m.
ophthalmoscopic ophthalmoskopisch
ophthalmoscopy Ophthalmoskopie f.
ophthalmotonometer d. e. n.
opiate Opiat n.
opinion, medical ärztliches Gutachten n.
opinion, medical, to call in a — —
  ein ärztliches Gutachten einholen
opinion, medical, to give a — —
  ein ärztliches Gutachten abgeben

opipramol d. e. n.
opisthotonos Opisthotonus m.
opium d. e. n.
opossum d. e. n.
Oppenheim's sign Oppenheimsches Zeichen n.
opportune günstig
opposite entgegengesetzt, gegenüberliegend
oppression Beklemmung f.
opsonin d. e. n.
opsonocytophagic opsonozytophagisch
opsonocytophagy Opsonozytophagie f.
optic optisch
— atrophy Sehnervatrophie f.
— disk Sehnervpapille f.
— fundus Augenhintergrund m.
— nerve Sehnerv m.
optician Optiker m.
optics Optik f.
optimal d. e.
optimistic optimistisch
optimize, to optimieren
optimum d. e. n.
oral d. e.
— cavity Mundhöhle f.
— hygiene Mundpflege f.
— wedge Mundkeil m.
orange d. e. f.
— flower Orangenblüte f.
orbit Orbita f.
orbital d. e.
orcein Orzein n.
orchectomy Orchiektomie f., Hodenentfernung f.
orchidectomy Hodenentfernung f.
orchiectomy Hodenentfernung f.
orchitis d. e. f.
orcin Orzin n.
orcinol Orzin n.
orciprenaline Orziprenalin n.
order Ordnung f., Anordnung f.
order, to ordnen; anordnen, verordnen
orderly Krankenwärter m.

ordinance Verordnung f.
ordinate d. e. f.
ordure Exkrement n.
organ d. e. n.
organ, adjacent Nachbarorgan n.
organella Organelle f.
organic organisch
organism Organismus m.
organization Organisation f.
organize, to organisieren
organophosphate Organophosphat n.
organotropic organotrop
orgasm Orgasmus m.
oriental boil Orientbeule f.
orientation Orientierung f.
orifice Öffnung f., Mündung f.
origin Ursprung m., Herkunft f.
ornipressin d. e. n.
ornithine Ornithin n.
Ornithodorus moubata d. e.
oro-facial orofazial
orotidyldecarboxylase Orotidyldekarboxylase f.
orotidylpyrosphosphorylase d. e. f.
orotracheal d. e.
Oroya fever Oroyafieber n.
orphenadrine Orphenadrin n.
orthochromatic orthochromatisch
orthodontia Orthodontie f.
orthodontic orthodontisch
orthodromic orthodrom
orthopaedic (e) orthopädisch
orthopaedics (e) Orthopädie f.
orthopaedist (e) Orthopäde m., Orthopädin f.
orthopedic (a) orthopädisch
orthopedics (a) Orthopädie f.
orthopedist (a) Orthopäde m., Orthopädin f.
orthophosphate Orthophosphat n.
orthopnea (a) Orthopnoe f.
orthopnoea (e) Orthopnoe f.
orthorhythmic orthorhythmisch
orthoscope Orthoskop n.
orthoscopic orthoskopisch
orthoscopy Orthoskopie f.

orthostatic orthostatisch
orthotonic orthotonisch
osazone Osazon n.
oscillation Oszillation f.
oscillogram Oszillogramm n.
oscillograph Oszillograph m.
oscillographic oszillographisch
oscillography Oszillographie f.
oscillometer Oszillometer n.
oscillometric oszillometrisch
oscillometry Oszillometrie f.
Osgood-Schlatter's disease Schlattersche Krankheit f.
Osler's disease Oslersche Krankheit f.
osmium d. e. n.
osmolality Osmolalität f.
osmolarity Osmolarität f.
osmometer d. e. n.
osmosis Osmose f.
osmotic osmotisch
ossein d. e. n.
osseofibrous osseofibrös
osseous knöchern
ossiferous knochenbildend
ossification Ossifikation f., Verknöcherung f.
ossify, to verknöchern
ostectomy Ostektomie f.
osteitis Ostitis f.
osteoarthritis Arthrosis deformans
osteoarthropathy Osteoarthropathie f.
osteoarthrosis Arthrosis deformans
osteoblast d. e. m.
osteoblastic osteoblastisch
osteoblastoma Osteoblastom n.
osteochondritis d. e. f.
– dissecans d. e.
osteochondrofibroma Osteochondrofibrom n.
osteochondroma Osteochondrom n.
osteochondromatosis Osteochondromatose f.
osteochondrosarcoma Osteochondrosarkom n.
osteochondrosis Osteochondrose f.

osteoclast Osteoklast m.
osteoclastic osteoklastisch
osteofibroma Osteofibrom n.
osteogenesis Osteogenese f., Knochenbildung f.
osteogenesis imperfecta d. e.
osteogeny Knochenbildung f.
osteologic osteologisch
osteology Osteologie f.
osteolysis Osteolyse f.
osteolytic osteolytisch
osteoma Osteom n.
osteomalacia Osteomalazie f.
osteomalacic osteomalazisch
osteomyelitic osteomyelitisch
osteomyelitis d. e. f.
osteoid d. e.
osteopathy Osteopathie f.
—, disseminated condensing Marmorknochenkrankheit f.
osteopetrosis Osteopetrose f.
osteophyte Osteophyt m.
osteoplastic osteoplastisch
osteoporosis Osteoporose f.
osteoporotic osteoporotisch
osteopsathyrosis Osteopsathyrose f.
osteosarcoma Osteosarkom n.
osteosclerosis Osteosklerose f.
osteosclerotic osteosklerotisch
osteosynthesis Osteosynthese f.
osteotome Osteotom n.
osteotomy Osteotomie f.
ostrich Strauß m. (Vogel)
otalgia Otalgie f.
othaematoma (e) Othämatom n.
othematoma (a) Othämatom n.
otiatric otiatrisch
otiatrics Otiatrie f.
otitis d. e. f.
— externa/interna/media d. e.
otogenous otogen
otological otologisch
otologist Otologe m., Otologin f.
otology Otologie f.
otomycosis Otomykose f.

otorhinolaryngologist Hals-Nasen-Ohrenarzt m., Hals-Nasen-Ohrenärztin f.
otorhinolaryngology Hals-Nasen-Ohrenheilkunde f.
otorrhea (a) Otorrhöe f.
otorrhoea (e) Otorrhöe f.
otosclerosis Otosklerose f.
otoscope Otoskop n.
otoscopic otoskopisch
otoscopy Otoskopie f.
ototoxic ototoxisch
ouabain g-Strophanthin n.
outbreak (of a disease) Ausbruch m. (einer Krankheit)
outburst Ausbruch m.
outfit Ausstattung f.
outflow Ausfluß m.
outlet of pelvis Beckenausgang m.
out-patient ambulanter Patient m., ambulante Patientin f.
outpatient clinic Ambulatorium n., Poliklinik f.
outpatient department Ambulanz f., Ambulatorium n.
output Ausstoßung f.
ovalocyte Ovalozyt m.
ovalocytosis Ovalozytose f.
ovarian ovariell
— hormone weibliches Keimdrüsenhormon n.
— insufficiency ovarielle Insuffizienz f.
ovariectomize, to ovarektomieren
ovariectomy Eierstockentfernung f., Ovarektomie f.
ovariotomy Ovariotomie f.
ovariosalpingectomy Ovariosalpingektomie f.
ovariprival ovaripriv
ovary Eierstock m., Ovar n.
overcome, to überkommen
overdosage Überdosierung f.
overeat, to überessen
overexert, to überanstrengen
overexertion Überanstrengung f.

overexposure Überbeanspruchung f.; Überbelichtung f.
overfeed, to überfüttern
overfeeding Überfütterung f.
overflow Überlauf m.
overhaul Überholung f., Reparatur f.; gründliche Untersuchung f.
overlapping Überlappung f.
overlapping toes übereinanderstehende Zehen f. pl.
overlay Überlagerung f.
overload, to überladen, überlasten
overloading Überlastung f., Überbelastung f.
overpressure Überdruck m.
oversaturate, to übersättigen
oversaturation Übersättigung f.
oversew, to übernähen
overshooting überschießend
overstain, to überfärben
overstrain, to überanstrengen
overtired übermüdet
overtrain, to übertrainieren
overweight Übergewicht n.
overwork Überarbeitung f.
overwork, to überarbeiten
oviduct Eileiter m.
ovulation d. e. f.
– inhibitor Ovulationshemmer m.
ovulatory ovulatorisch
ovule Ovulum m.
ovum Ei n.
oxacillin d. e. n.
oxalacetate Oxalazetat n.
oxalate Oxalat n.
oxalic acid Oxalsäure f.
oxalosis Oxalose f.
oxazol d. e. n.
oxazone Oxazon n.
oxbile Rindergalle f.
oxgall Rindergalle f.

oxi... look also for:/siehe auch bei: oxy...
oxidase Oxydase f.
– -negative oxydasenegativ
– -positive oxydasepositiv
oxidation Oxydation f.
oxidative oxydativ
oxide Oxyd n., Oxid n.
oxidize, to oxydieren
oxidoreductase Oxydoreduktase f.
oxprenolol d. e. n.
oxy... look also for:/siehe auch bei: oxi...
oxycephaly Turmschädel m.
oxyfedrine Oxyfedrin n.
oxygen Sauerstoff m.
– bath Sauerstoffbad n.
– breathing Sauerstoffatmung f.
– consumption Sauerstoffverbrauch m.
– cylinder Sauerstoffflasche f.
oxygenase d. e. f.
oxygenation Sauerstoffsättigung f., Sauerstoffbeladung f.
oxygenic sauerstoffhaltig
oxyhaemoglobin (e) Oxyhämoglobin n.
oxyhemoglobin (a) Oxyhämoglobin n.
oxymetrical oxymetrisch
oxymetry Oxymetrie f.
oxyntic cell Belegzelle f.
oxyphilous oxyphil
oxypurine Oxypurin n.
oxytetracycline Oxytetracyclin n.
oxytocin d. e. n.
oxyuriasis d. e. f.
Oxyuris vermicularis d. e.
ozaena (e) Ozaena f.
ozena (a) Ozaena f.
ozone Ozon m.

P

pacchionian depression Pacchionisches Grübchen m.
pacemaker Schrittmacher m.
pachydermia Pachydermie f.
pachymeningitis d. e. f.
pacing, cardiac Schrittmacherbehandlung f. des Herzens
pack Wickel m., Packung f.; Packet n., Pack m.
pad Polster n., Kissen n.
paederasty (e) Päderastie f.
paediatric (e) pädiatrisch
paediatrician (e) Pädiater m., Kinderarzt m.; Kinderärztin f.
paediatrics (e) Pädiatrie f.
paediatrist (e) Pädiater m., Kinderarzt m.; Kinderärztin f.
Paget's disease Pagetsche Krankheit f.
pain Schmerz m., Weh n.
pain, intermenstrual Mittelschmerz m.
painfulness Schmerzhaftigkeit f.
pain, labor (a) Wehe f.
pain, labour (e) Wehe f.
— **-deadening** schmerzstillend
painful schmerzhaft
painstaking gewissenhaft
palaeokinetic (e) paläokinetisch
palaeontology (e) Paläontologie f.
palaeopathology (e) Paläopathologie f.
palatal d. e.
palate Gaumen m.
palatine palatin
palatomaxillary palatomaxillär
palatonasal d. e.
palatopharyngeal d. e.
palatoplasty Gaumenplastik f.
pale blaß, bleich
paleness Blässe f.
paleokinetic (a) paläokinetisch
paleontology (a) Paläontologie f.

paleopathology (a) Paläopathologie f.
palindromic palindromisch
palisade d. e. f.
palladium d. e. n.
pallaesthesia (e) Pallästhesie f.
pallanaesthesia (e) Pallanästhesie f.
pallanesthesia (a) Pallanästhesie f.
pallescence Blässe f.
pallesthesia (a) Pallästhesie f.
palliative palliativ; Palliativum n.
pallid blaß
pallidectomy Pallidektomie f.
pallor Blässe f.
pallor, bitemporal bitemporale Abblassung f.
palm Handteller m.
palmar d. e.
palmitate Palmitat n.
palmitin d. e. n.
palpability Tastbarkeit f.
palpable palpabel, tastbar
palpate, to palpieren, tasten
palpation d. e. f.
palpebral d. e.
palpitation of the heart Herzklopfen m.
palsy Lähmung f.
—**, shaking** Paralysis agitans
paludism Malariakachexie f.
panacea Allerweltsmittel n.
panaesthesia (e) Panästhesie f.
panagglutination d. e. f.
panagglutinin d. e. n.
panaris Panaritium n.
panarteritis Panarteriitis f.
pancarditis Pankarditis f.
panchrest Allerweltsmittel n.
Pancoast's neoplasm Pancoasttumor m.
pancreas Bauchspeicheldrüse f.
pancreatectomize, to pankreatektomieren

pancreatectomy Pankreatektomie f.
pancreatic pankreatisch
pancreatic head Pankreaskopf m.
– **tail** Pankreasschwanz m.
pancreaticocholecystostomy Pankreatikocholezystostomie f.
pancreaticoduodenostomy Pankreatikoduodenostomie f.
pancreaticography Pankreatikographie f.
pancreatitis Pankreatitis f.
pancreatoenterostomy Pankreatoenterostomie f.
pancreatography Pankreatographie f.
pancreatotropic pankreatotrop
pancreozymin Pankreozymin n.
pancytopenia Panzytopenie f.
pandemic pandemisch; Pandemie f.
Pandy's test Pandysche Probe f.
panel doctor Kassenarzt m., Kassenärztin f.
panesthesia (a) Panästhesie f.
panic panisch; Panik f.
panmyelophthisis Panmyelophthise f.
panniculitis Fettgewebeentzündung f.
panophthalmitis d. e. f.
panoptic panoptisch
panotitis d. e. f.
pansinusitis d. e. f.
panther d. e. m.
pantoscopic pantoskopisch
pantothenate Pantothenat n.
pantothenic acid Pantothensäure f.
pap Brei m.
papain d. e. n.
papaverine Papaverin n.
papayotin d. e. n.
paper Papier n.
– **electrophoresis** Papierelektrophorese f.
–, **filter** Filtrierpapier f.

paper, impervious undurchlässiges Papier n.
papilla Papille f.
papillary papillär
papillectomy Papillektomie f.
papilledema (a) Papillenödem n.
papillitis d. e. f.
papilloedema (e) Papillenödem n.
papilloma Papillom n.
papillomacular papillomakulär
papillomatosis Papillomatose f.
papillomatous papillomatös
papillosphincterotomy Papillosphinkterotomie f.
pappataci fever Pappatacifieber n.
Pappenheim's staining Pappenheimfärbung f.
papular papulär, papulös
papule Papel f.
papuloerythematous papuloerythematös
papulopustular papulopustulär
papulosquamous papulosquamös
papulovesicular papulovesikulär
paraaminobenzoic acid Paraaminobenzoesäure f.
paraaminosalicylic acid Paraaminosalizylsäure f.
parabiosis Parabiose f.
parabiotic parabiotisch
parablastoma Parablastom n.
parabola Parabel f.
paracentesis Punktion f., Einstich m.
paracentesis abdominis Bauchpunktion f., Eröffnung f. des Abdomens
paracentesis tympani Trommelfellparazentese f.
paracentral parazentral
paracervical parazervikal
parachloromercuribenzoate Parachloromercuribenzoat n.
parachromatin d. e. n.
paracurarine Tubocurarin n.
paracusia Parakusis f.
paracusis Parakusis f.

paracystitis Parazystitis f.
paradental d. e.
paradentitis d. e. f.
paradentium d. e. n., Parodontium n., Zahnhalteapparat m.
paradentopathy Paradentopathie f.
paradentosis Paradentose f.
paradox Paradoxon n.
paradoxical paradox
paraduodenal d. e.
paraesthesia (e) Parästhesie f.
paraesthetic (e) parästhetisch
paraffin d. e. n.
paraffinoma Paraffinom n.
paraform d. e. n.
paraganglioma Paragangliom n.
paraganglion d. e. n.
parageusia Parageusie f.
paragglutination d. e. f.
paraglobulin d. e. n.
paragonimiasis d. e. f.
Paragonimus westermani Distomum pulmonale, Lungenegel m.
paragraphia Paragraphie f.
parahaemophilia (e) Parahämophilie f.
parahemophilia (a) Parahämophilie f.
parahepatic parahepatisch
parahypnosis Parahypnose f.
parainfection Parainfektion f.
parainfectious parainfektiös
parainfluenza d. e. f.
parakeet Sittich m.
parakeratosis Parakeratose f.
parakinesis Parakinese f.
parakinetic parakinetisch
paralalia Paralalie f.
paraldehyde Paraldehyd m.
paralexia Paralexie f.
parallax Parallaxe f.
parallel d. e.
parallergic parallergisch
parallergy Parallergie f.
paralogia Paralogie f.

paralysis Paralyse f., Lähmung f.
— agitans d. e.
—, bulbar Bulbärparalyse f.
—, general progressive Paralyse f.
— of ocular muscles Augenmuskellähmung f.
paralytic paralytisch; Gelähmter m., Gelähmte f.; Paralytiker m., Paralytikerin f.
paralyze, to lähmen, paralysieren
paramagnetic paramagnetisch
paramastitis d. e. f.
paramastoiditis d. e. f.
parameter d. e. m.
paramethasone Paramethason n.
parametritic parametritisch
parametritis d. e. f.
parametrium d. e. n.
paramnesia Paramnesie f.
paramolar d. e.
paramyelin d. e. n.
parmayeloblast d. e. m.
paramyeloblastic paramyeloblastisch
paramyoclonus multiplex Paramyoklonus multiplex
paramyotonia Paramyotonie f.
paranasal sinus Nasennebenhöhle f.
paraneoplastic paraneoplastisch
paranephritic paranephritisch
paranephritis d. e. f.
paraneural d. e.
paranoia d. e. f.
paranoiac Paranoiker m., Paranoikerin f.
paranoic paranoisch
paranoid d. e.
paranormal d. e.
parapancreatic parapankreatisch
paraparesis Paraparese f.
paraparetic paraparetisch
paraphasia Paraphasie f.
paraphasic paraphasisch
paraphimosis Paraphimose f.
paraphrenia Paraphrenie f.
paraphrenic paraphrenisch
paraplegia Paraplegie f.

paraplegic paraplegisch
paraprostatitis d. e. f.
paraprotein d. e. n.
paraproteinaemia (e) Paraproteinämie f.
paraproteinemia (a) Paraproteinämie f.
paraproteinuria Paraproteinurie f.
parapsoriasis d. e. f.
parapsychological parapsychologisch
parapsychology Parapsychologie f.
pararectal pararektal
parasagittal d. e.
parasalpingitis d. e. f.
parasite Parasit m.
parasitic parasitär
parasitological parasitologisch
parasitology Parasitologie f.
parasitotropic parasitotrop
paraspadia Paraspadie f.
paraspecific paraspezifisch
parasternal d. e.
parasympathetic Parasympathikus m.
parasympathetical parasympathisch
parasympatholytic parasympathikolytisch
parasympathomimetic parasympathikomimetisch
parasyphilis d. e. f.
parasyphilitic parasyphilitisch
parasystole d. e. f.
parathion d. e. n.
parathymia Parathymie f.
parathyroid Epithelkörperchen n.
– extract Epithelkörperchenextrakt m.
parathyroidal parathyreoidal
parathyroprival parathyreopriv
parathyrotropic parathyreotrop
paratuberculosis Paratuberkulose f.
paratuberculous paratuberkulös
paratyphlitis d. e. f.
paratyphoid A/B Paratyphus A/B m.

paraurethral d. e.
paravaginal d. e.
paravenous paravenös
paravertebral d. e.
paregoric schmerzstillend, hustenstillend; schmerzstillendes Mittel n., hustenstillendes Mittel n.
– elixir Tinctura opii camphorata
paregorism Opiumsucht f.
parenchyma Parenchym n.
parenchymatous parenchymatös
parental elterlich
parenteral d. e.
parents Eltern m. pl.
paresis Parese f.
–, general progressive Paralyse f.
paresthesia (a) Parästhesie f.
paresthetic (a) parästhetisch
paretic paretisch
pareunia Geschlechtsverkehr m.
parietal d. e.
parietal cell Belegzelle f.
parietooccipital parietookzipital
parietotemporal d. e.
parietovisceral parietoviszeral
Paris green Schweinfurter Grün n.
parkinsonian patient Parkinson-Patient m., Parkinson-Patientin f.
Parkinson's disease Parkinsonsche Krankheit f.
parkinsonism Parkinsonismus m.
parodontal d. e.
parodontitis d. e. f.
parodontosis Parodontose f.
paromomycin d. e.
paronychia Paronychie f.
paroophoritis d. e. f.
parophthalmia Parophthalmie f.
parotid gland Parotis f., Ohrspeicheldrüse f.
parotidectomy Parotidektomie f.
parotitis d. e. f.
paroxysm Paroxysmus m., Anfall m.
paroxysmal d. e., anfallsweise
paroxystic anfallsweise

parrot Papagei m.
parrot fever Psittakose f.
Parrot's sign Parrotsches Zeichen n.
part Teil m.
parthenogenesis Parthenogenese f.
partial pressure Partialdruck m.
participant Teilnehmer m., Teilnehmerin f.
participation Beteiligung f.
particle Teilchen n., Partikel f.
partner Partner m.; Partnerin f.
parturient gebärend; Gebärende f.
parturition Geburt f., Geburtsvorgang m.
parulis d. e. f.
parvule Pillchen n.
pascal d. e. n.
Paschen's body Paschensches Körperchen n.
pass, to passieren, vorbeigehen
– away, to weggehen, vergehen
– water, to harnen, Wasser lassen
passage d. e. f., Durchgang m.
Passavant's bar Passavantscher Wulst m.
passion Leiden n.; Sucht f.; Gemütsbewegung f.
passive passiv
passivity Passivität f.
paste d. e. f.
paste, to verkleben
Pasteurella pestis Pestbazillus m.
– tularensis Bacterium tularense
pasteurization Pasteurisierung f.
pasteurize, to pasteurisieren
patch Fleck m.
patch test Läppchenprobe f., Epikutantest m.
patella d. e. f.
– clonus Patellarklonus m.
patellar d. e.
– reflex Patellarsehnenreflex m.
patency Offenstehen n.
patent offen; Patent n.
patented patentiert
paternal väterlich

paternity Vaterschaft f.
path Nervenbahn f.
pathergic pathergisch
pathergy Pathergie f.
pathetic pathetisch
pathoanatomical pathoanatomisch
pathobiological pathobiologisch
pathobiology Pathobiologie f.
pathogenesis Pathogenese f.
pathogenetic pathogenetisch
pathogen-free room keimfreie Isoliereinheit f.
pathogenic pathogen
pathognomonic pathognomonisch
pathography Pathographie f.
pathological pathologisch
pathologist Pathologe m., Pathologin f.
pathology Pathologie f.
patience Geduld f.
patient Patient m., Patientin f.
pattern Form f., Modell n., Gruppierung f.
patulous ausgedehnt
Paul-Bunnell test Paul-Bunnell-Test m.
paunch Pansen m.
pause d. e. f.
–, compensatory kompensatorische Pause f.
pavement cell Pflasterzelle f.
Pavlov's reflex Pawlowscher Reflex m.
Payr's clamp Payrsches Darmkompressorium n.
PBI proteingebundenes Jod n.
peak Spitze f., Gipfel m.
Péan's forceps Péansche Klemme f.
pearl Perle f.
pearl disease Perlsucht f.
pea soup stool Erbsensuppenstuhl m.
pectin Pektin n.
pectinase Pektinase f.
pectoral pektoral
– powder Brustpulver n.

pectoriloquy Pektoriloquie f.
pedal d. e.
pederasty (a) Päderastie f.
pediatric (a) pädiatrisch
pediatrician (a) Pädiater m.,
  Kinderarzt m.; Kinderärztin f.
pediatrics (a) Pädiatrie f.
pediatrist (a) Pädiater m.,
  Kinderarzt m.; Kinderärztin f.
pediculicide Entlausungsmittel n.
pediculosis capitis/corporis/
  palpebrarum/pubis d. e.
pedigree Stammbaum m.
peduncle Stiel m.
peduncular pedunkulär
pedunculated gestielt
peel Schale f., Rinde f.
peel, to schälen
peg Pflock m., Stift m.
Pel-Ebstein disease Pel-Ebsteinsche Krankheit f.
pelada Alopecia areata
pelade Alopecia areata
pelagism Seekrankheit f.
Pelger's nuclear anomaly
  Pelgersche Kernanomalie f.
Pelizaeus-Merzbacher disease
  Pelizaeus-Merzbachersche
  Krankheit f.
pellagra d. e. f.
pellagral pellagrös
pellagrose pellagrös
pellagrous pellagrös
pellet Pillchen n.
pelletierine Pelletierin n.
pellicle Häutchen n.
peloid d. e.
pelveoperitonitis d. e. f.
pelvic floor Beckenboden m.
pelvigraphy Pelvigraphie f.
pelvimeter Beckenzirkel m.
pelvimetric pelvimetrisch
pelvimetry Pelvimetrie f.,
  Beckenmessung f.
pelviostomy Pelveostomie f.
pelviotomy Pelveotomie f.
pelvis Becken n.

pelvis, assimilation Assimilationsbecken n.
–, flat plattes Becken n.
–, floor of the – Beckenboden m.
–, generally contracted
  allgemein verengtes Becken n.
–, generally enlarged
  allgemein erweitertes Becken n.
–, inlet of the – Beckeneingang m.
–, justo major allgemein
  erweitertes Becken n.
–, justo minor allgemein
  verengtes Becken n.
–, Nägele's Nägelebecken n.
–, rachitic rachitisches Becken n.
–, renal Nierenbecken n.
pemphigus d. e. m.
pendulum therapy Pendeltherapie f.
penetrate, to penetrieren,
  eindringen
penetration d. e. f.
penguin Pinguin m.
penicillamine Penicillamin n.
penicillanate Penicillanat n.
penicillin d. e. n.
– sodium Penicillin-Natrium n.
penicillinase d. e. f.
penis d. e. m.
– clamp Harnröhrenklemme f.,
  Penisklemme f.
pensive tiefsinnig
pentaborate Pentaborat n.
pentabromide Pentabromid n.
pentachloride Pentachlorid n.
pentachlorophenol d. e. n.
pentagastrin d. e. n.
pentalogy of Fallot Fallotsche
  Pentalogie f.
pentane Pentan n.
pentapeptide Pentapeptid n.
pentavalent fünfwertig
pentazocine Pentazocin n.
pentdyopent d. e. n.
pentetate Pentetat n.
pentosan d. e. n.
pentosazon d. e. n.

pentose d. e. f.
pentoside Pentosid n.
pentosuria Pentosurie f.
pentoxide Pentoxyd n.
pentylene tetrazole Pentylentetrazol n.
pepper Pfeffer m.
peppermint Pfefferminze f.
pepsin d. e. n.
pepsinogen d. e. n.
peptase d. e. f.
peptic peptisch
peptic cell Hauptzelle f.
peptid d. e. n.
peptidase d. e. f.
peptide Peptid n.
peptidyl d. e. n.
peptone Pepton n.
peptonuria Peptonurie f.
peracetate Perazetat n.
peracute perakut
perazine Perazin n.
perceive, to wahrnehmen
percent Prozent n.
percentage Prozentsatz m.
perceptible wahrnehmbar
perception Wahrnehmung f.
perceptivity Wahrnehmungsvermögen n.
perchlorate Perchlorat n.
perchloride Perchlorid n.
percolate, to perkolieren
percolation Perkolation f.
percolator Perkolator m.
percuss, to perkutieren
percussion Perkussion f.
percutaneous perkutan
perfecting Vervollkommnung f.; Fortbildung f.
perforate, to perforieren
perforation d. e. f.
performance Leistung f., Durchführung f.
perfusion d. e. f.
perhexiline Perhexilin n.
periacinous periazinös
perianal d. e.

periapical periapikal
periappendicitis Periappendizitis f.
periarterial periarteriell
periarteritis Periarteriitis f.
periarthritis d. e. f.
periarticular periartikulär
peribronchial d. e.
peribronchiectatic peribronchiektatisch
peribronchiolar peribronchiolär
peribronchitis d. e. f.
pericanalicular perikanalikulär
pericapillary perikapillär
pericapsular perikapsulär
pericardial perikardial
pericardial friction rub Perikardreiben n.
pericardiectomy Perikardiektomie f.
pericardiolysis Perikardiolyse f.
pericarditic perikarditisch
pericarditis Perikarditis f.
pericardium Perikard n.
pericellular perizellulär
pericementitis Perizementitis f.
pericementoclasia Perizementoklasie f.
pericementum Wurzelhaut f.
pericentral perizentral
pericholangitis d. e. f.
pericholecystitic pericholezystitisch
pericholecystitis Pericholezystitis f.
perichondritis d. e. f.
pericolitis Perikolitis f.
pericolpitis Perikolpitis f.
pericorneal perikorneal
pericystitis Perizystitis f.
peridental d. e.
peridiverticulitis Peridivertikulitis f.
periduodenitis d. e. f.
peridural d. e.
perifocal perifokal
perifollicular perifollikulär
perifolliculitis Perifollikulitis f.

perigastric perigastrisch
perigastritis d. e. f.
periglandular periglandulär
perihepatic perihepatisch
perihepatitis d. e. f.
peril of life Lebensgefahr f.
perilabyrinthitis d. e. f.
perilaryngeal d. e.
perilaryngitis d. e. f.
perilobar perilobär
perilymph Perilymphe f.
perimetritic perimetritisch
perimetritis d. e. f.
perimuscular perimuskulär
perimysial d. e.
perimysium d. e. n.
perineal d. e.
perinephritic perinephritisch
perinephritis d. e. f.
perineum Damm m.
perineural d. e.
perineuritis d. e. f.
perinuclear perinukleär
periocular periokulär
period Periode f.
−,half-life Halbwertzeit f.
periodical periodisch; Zeitschrift f.
periodicity Periodizität f.
periodontal d. e.
periodontitis d. e. f.
periodontoclasia Periodontoklasie f., Alveolarpyorrhöe f.
perioral d. e.
periorbital d. e.
periorchitis d. e. f.
periosteal periostal
periosteum Periost n.
periostitis d. e. f.
periostosis Periostose f.
peripancreatic peripankreatisch
peripancreatitis Peripankreatitis f.
peripapillary peripapillär
peripharyngeal d. e.
peripharyngitis d. e. f.
peripheral peripher
periphery Peripherie f.

periphlebitis d. e. f.
peripleural d. e.
peripleuritis d. e. f.
periportal d. e.
periproctic periproktisch
periproctitic periproktitisch
periproctitis Periproktitis f.
periprostatitis d. e. f.
peripyloric peripylorisch
periradicular periradikulär
perirenal d. e.
− air insufflation perirenale Lufteinblasung f.
perisalpingitis d. e. f.
perish, to zugrundegehen, verenden, verderben
perishable verderblich
perish from cold, to erfrieren
perisigmoiditis d. e. f.
perisinusitis d. e. f.
perisplenitic perisplenitisch
perisplenitis d. e. f.
peristalsis Peristaltik f.
peristaltic peristaltisch
peristasis Peristase f., Umgebung f.
peristatic peristatisch
peristole d. e. f.
peristolic peristolisch
peritendinitis d. e. f.
− calcarea of shoulder joint Periarthritis humeroscapularis
peritoneal d. e.
peritoneal dialysis Peritonealdialyse f.
peritoneoscopy Peritoneoskopie f.
peritoneum d. e. n., Bauchfell n.
peritonism Peritonismus m.
peritonitic peritonitisch
peritonitis d. e. f.
peritonsillar peritonsillär
peritonsillitis d. e. f.
peritracheal d. e.
perityphlitic perityphlitisch
perityphlitis d. e. f.
periurethral d. e.
perivaginal d. e.

perivascular perivaskulär
perivenous perivenös
perleche Faulecke f.
perlingual d. e.
permanence Permanenz f.
permanent d. e.
– bath Dauerbad n.
– teeth bleibendes Gebiß n.
permanganate of potash übermangansaures Kali n.
permanganic übermangansauer
permeability Permeabilität f.
permeable permeabel
pernasal d. e.
pernicious perniziös
pernio Frostbeule f.
perniosis Kälteschaden m. der Haut
perone Wadenbein n.
peroral d. e.
peroxidase Peroxydase f.
peroxide Peroxyd n.
perphenazine Perphenazin n.
persecution mania Verfolgungswahn m.
perseveration d. e. f.
person d. e. f.
personality Persönlichkeit f.
– change Persönlichkeitsveränderung f.
perspiration Ausdünstung f.
perspire, to ausdünsten
persulfate (a) Persulfat f.
persulphate (e) Persulfat n.
peruvoside Peruvosid n.
Perthes' disease Perthessche Krankheit f.
pertrochanteric pertrochanter
pertubation d. e. f.
peruvian bark Chinarinde f.
peruvian balsam Perubalsam m.
pervasion Durchdringung f.
perverse pervers
perversion d. e. f.
perversity Perversität f.
pervious durchgängig, passierbar
pes cavus Hohlfuß

pes cavus planus Plattfuß m.
pessary Pessar n.
pessimism Pessimismus m.
pessimistic pessimistisch
pestilence Pestilenz f., Seuche f.
petechia Petechie f.
petechial d. e.
petit mal d. e. n.
Petri dish Petrischale f.
petrify, to versteinern
petrolatum gelbes Vaselin n.
–, liquid Paraffinum liquidum
–, white weißes Vaselin n.
petroleum d. e. n.
Petruschky's litmus whey Petruschkysche Lackmusmolke f.
Peyer's patch Peyerscher Lymphfollikelhaufen m.
Pfannenstiel's incision Pfannenstielscher Querschnitt m.
Pfeiffer's glandular fever Pfeiffersches Drüsenfieber n.
phacomalacia Linsenerweichung f.
phacoscopy Phakoskopie f.
phacoscotasmus Linsentrübung f.
phaenotype (e) Phänotyp
phaenotypic (e) phänotypisch
phaechromocytoma (e) Phäochromozytom n.
phagocyte Phagozyt m.
phagocytic phagozytär
phagocytize, to phagozytieren
phagocytolysis Phagozytolyse f.
phagocytosis Phagozytose f.
phagolysis Phagolyse f.
phakitis d. e. f.
phalangeal d. e.
phallic phallisch
phallitis d. e. f.
phantasy Phantasie f.
phantom d. e. n.
– limb Phantomglied n.
pharmacal pharmazeutisch
pharmaceutical pharmazeutisch
– chemist Pharmakochemiker m., Pharmakochemikerin f.

pharmaceutics Pharmazie f.
pharmacist Pharmazeut m.,
 Apotheker m.; Pharmazeutin f.,
 Apothekerin f.
pharmacochemical pharmakochemisch
pharmacochemistry Pharmakochemie f.
pharmacodynamic pharmako-
 dynamisch
pharmacodynamics Pharmakodynamik f.
pharmacognosy Pharmakognosie f.
pharmacokinetic pharmakokinetisch
pharmacokinetics Pharmakokinetik f.
pharmacological pharmakologisch
pharmacologist Pharmakologe m.,
 Pharmakologin f.
pharmacomania Arzneimittelsucht f.
pharmacopeia (a) Pharmakopöe f.
pharmacopoeia (e) Pharmakopöe f.
pharmacotherapeutic pharmakotherapeutisch
pharmacotherapy Pharmako-
 therapie f.
pharmacy Pharmazie f.;
 Apotheke f.
—, hospital Krankenhausapotheke f.
—, satellite Zweigapotheke f.
pharyngeal d. e.
pharyngitic pharyngitisch
pharyngitis d. e. f.
pharyngolaryngeal d. e.
pharyngoscope Pharyngoskop n.
pharyngoscopy Pharyngoskopie f.
pharyngospasm Pharyngo-
 spasmus m.
pharyngotomy Pharyngotomie f.
pharynx d. e. m., Rachen m.
phase d. e. f.
— contrast microscope Phasenkontrastmikroskop n.
— contrast microscopy Phasenkontrastmikroskopie f.
phenanthrene Phenanthren n.

phenanthroline Phenanthrolin n.
phenazine Phenazin n.
phenazone Phenazon n.
phenelzine Phenelzin n.
phenethicillin d. e. n.
phenethylbiguanide Phenyläthylbiguanid n.
phenetidin d. e. n.
phenformin d. e. n.
phenmetrazine Phenmetrazin n.
phenobarbital Phenyläthylbarbitursäure f.
phenobarbitone Phenyläthylbarbitursäure f.
phenol d. e. n.
phenolase d. e. f.
phenolate Phenolat n.
phenolate, to phenolieren
phenolphthalein d. e. n.
phenomenon Phänomen n.
phenothiazine Phenothiazin n.
phenotype (a) Phänotyp m.
phenotypic (a) phänotypisch
phenoxybenzamine Phenoxy-
 benzamin n.
phenprocoumon d. e. n.
phentolamine Phentolamin n.
phenyl d. e. n.
phenylalanine Phenylalanin n.
phenylbutazone Phenylbutazon n.
phenylchinoline Phenylchinolin n.
phenylcyclopropylamine Phenylzyklopropylamin n.
phenylene Phenylen n.
phenylenediamine Phenylendiamin n.
phenylethylamine Phenyl-
 äthylamin n.
phenylethylhydrazine Phenyläthylhydrazin n.
phenylhydrazine Phenylhydrazin n.
phenylketonuria Phenylketonurie f.
pheochromocytoma (a)
 Phäochromozytom n.
philosophical philosophisch
philosophy Philosophie f.

phimosis Phimose f.
phlebectasia Phlebektasie f.
phlebectomy Phlebektomie f.
phlebitic phlebitisch
phlebitis d. e. f.
phlebogram Phlebogramm n.
phlebographic phlebographisch
phlebography Phlebographie f.
phlebolith d. e. m.
Phlebotomus papatasii d. e.
phlebotomy Phlebotomie f.
phlegm Schleim m.
phlegmatic phlegmatisch
phlegmona diffusa Zellgewebeentzündung f.
phlegmonous phlegmonös
phlogistic phlogistisch,
 entzündlich
phlorhizin Phlorizin n.
phlorizin d. e. n.
phloroglucin Phloroglucin n.
phloxine Phloxin n.
phlyctaena (e) Phlyktäne f.
phlyctena (a) Phlyktäne f.
phobia Phobie f.
phobic phobisch
phocomelia Phokomelie f.
phon d. e. n.
phonangiography Phonangiographie f.
phonation d. e. f.
phonatory phonatorisch
phonendoscope Doppelmem-
 branstethoskop n.
phonetic phonetisch
phonetics Phonetik f.
phonocardiogram Phono-
 kardiogramm n.
phonocardiographical phonokardiographisch
phonocardiography Phono-
 kardiographie f., Herzschallschreibung f.
phosgene Phosgen n.
phosphagen d. e. n.
phosphagenic phosphatbildend
phosphamide Phosphamid n.

phosphatase d. e. f.
phosphate Phosphat n.
phosphatic phosphathaltig
phosphatide Phosphatid n.
phosphatidyl d. e. n.
phosphatine Phosphatin n.
phosphaturia Phosphaturie f.
phosphide Phosphid n.
phosphin d. e. n.
phosphite Phosphit n.
phosphoadenosine Phospho-
 adenosin n.
phosphodiesterase d. e. f.
phosphoglucose Phosphoglukose f.
phosphoglycerate Phospho-
 glyzerat n.
phospholinase d. e. f.
phospholipase d. e. f.
phospholipid d. e. n.
phospholipin Phospholipid n.
phosphomannoisomerase d. e. f.
phosphoprotein d. e. n.
phosphopyridine Phosphopyridin
 n.
phosphorated phosphoriert
phosphorescence Phosphoreszenz f.
phosphoribosylpyrophosphate
 Phosphoribosylpyrophosphat n.
phosphoric phosphorhaltig
 (fünfwertig)
phosphorous phosphorhaltig
 (dreiwertig)
phosphorus Phosphor m.
phosphoryl d. e. n.
phosphorylase d. e. f.
phosphorylate, to phosphorylieren
phosphorylation Phosphorylierung f.
phosphosulfate (a) Phosphosulfat n.
phosphosulphate (e) Phosphosulfat n.
phote Phot n.
photobiology Photobiologie f.
photocell Photozelle f.
photochemical photochemisch

photocoagulation Photokoagulation f., Lichtkoagulation f.
photocoagulation Photokoagulation f., Lichtkoagulation f.
photodermia Photodermie f.
photoelectric photoelektrisch
photographical photographisch
photography Photographie f.
photometer d. e. n.
photometric photometrisch
photometry Photometrie f.
photooxidation d. e. f.
photophosphorylation Photophosphorylierung f.
photophthalmia Photophthalmie f., Lichtblindheit f., Schneeblindheit f.
photoreceptor Photorezeptor m.
photosynthesis Photosynthese f.
phrenicoexairesis Phrenikusexairese f.
phrenocardia kardiovaskuläre Neurasthenie f.
phrenological phrenologisch
phrenology Phrenologie f.
Phrygian cap phrygische Mütze f.
phthalamidine Phthalamidin n.
phthalanilid d. e. n.
phthalanilide Phthalanilid n.
phthalate Phthalat n.
phthalein d. e. n.
phthalidolene Phthalidolon n.
phthalylsulfathiazole (a) Phthalylsulfathiazol n.
phthalylsulphathiazole (e) Phthalylsulfathiazol n.
phthiriasis inguinalis Filzlausbefall m.
phthisic phthisisch
phthisiogenesis Phthisiogenese f.
phthisis Phthise f.
phylogenesis Phylogenese f.
phylogenetic phylogenetisch
phylogenic phylogenetisch
physic Heilkunde f.; Heilmittel n.; Physik f.

physical physisch, körperlich; physikalisch
physically handicapped körperbehindert; Körperbehinderter m., Körperbehinderte f.
physician Arzt m., Ärztin f.
—, **referring** überweisender Arzt m.
physician sample Ärztemuster n.
physician's bag Arzttasche f.
physicist Physiker m.; Physikerin f.
physicochemical physikalischchemisch
physics Physik f.
physiochemical physiologischchemisch
physiochemistry physiologische Chemie f.
physiognomy Physiognomie f.
physiological physiologisch
physiologist Physiologe m., Physiologin f.
physiology Physiologie f.
physiopsychic physiopsychisch
physiotherapy Physiotherapie f.
physostigmine Physostigmin n.
phytate Phytin n.
phytoagglutinin d. e. n.
phytoglobulin d. e. n.
phytohaemagglutinin (e) Phytohämagglutinin n.
phytohemagglutinin (a) Phytohämagglutinin n.
phytotherapy Phytotherapie f.
phytotoxic phytotoxisch
phytotoxin d. e. n.
pian Frambösie f.
Pick's atrophy Picksche Atrophie f.
Pickwick syndrome Pickwick-Syndrom n.
picofarad d. e. n.
picrin Pikrin n.
picrotoxin Pikrotoxin n.
picture Bild n.
—, **clinical** klinisches Bild n.
—, **to take a** eine (Röntgen-)Aufnahme machen

piecemeal necrosis
Mottenfraßnekrose f.
pier Pfeiler m.
pierce, to durchbohren, erstechen
piesaesthesia (e) Drucksensibilität f.
piesthesia (e) Drucksensibilität f.
piezochemistry Piezochemie f.
piezoelectric piezoelektrisch
pig Schwein n.
pigeon Taube f.
pigment d. e. n.
– **cell** Pigmentzelle f.
pigment, to pigmentieren
pigmentation d. e. f., Pigmentierung f.
pigmented pigmentiert
pile Batterie f.; Hämorrhoide f.
pill Pille f.
pillar Säule f., Stütze f.
pillet Pillchen n.
pillow Kissen n.
pilocarpidine Pilokarpidin n.
pilocarpine Pilokarpin n.
pilojection Pilojektion f.
pilomotor pilomotorisch
pilose haarig
pilous haarig
pimelosis Verfettung f.; Fettsucht f.
pimple Papel f.; Pustel f.
pin Stift m.
pin and tube Stifthülse f.
pincers Zwickzange f.
pinch, to quetschen, klemmen
pinchcock clamp Quetschhahn m., Schlauchklemme f.
pindolol d. e. n.
pine away, to dahinsiechen
– **bath** Fichtennadelbad n.
– **tar** Pix liquida
pineal gland Zirbeldrüse f.
pinealectomy Pinealektomie f.
pinealoma Pinealom n.
pinguecula d. e.
pink disease Feersche Krankheit f.

pink-eye epidemische mukopurulente Augenbindehautentzündung f.
pinledge mit Stift verankertes Inlay n.
pinocytosis Pinozytose f.
pinworm Madenwurm m.
piperazine Piperazin n.
piperidine Piperidin n.
piperine Piperin n.
pipet Pipette f.
pipette d. e. f.
Pirogoff's amputation
Pirogoffsche Amputation f.
piroplasmosis Piroplasmose f.
Pirquet's reaction Pirquetsche Probe f.
Piskacek's sign Piskaceksche Ausladung f.
pit Grube f.
pitch Pech n.
pitchblende Pechblende f.
pitcher Krug m.
pith Mark n., Kraft f.
pituitary extract Hypophysenextrakt m.
– **fossa** Türkensattel m.
– **gland** Hypophyse f.
– –, **anterior lobe** Vorderlappen m.
– –, **posterior lobe** Hinterlappen m.
pituitary hyperfunction, anterior
Hypophysenvorderlappenüberfunktion f.
– **hypofunction, posterior** Hypophysenhinterlappenunterfunktion f.
pityriasis rosea/rubra/simplex/versicolor d. e.
pivampicillin d. e. n.
pivot (dent.) Zapfen m.
placebo d. e. n.
placenta Plazenta f., Mutterkuchen m.
– **praevia** (e) d. e.
– **previa** (a) Placenta praevia
placental plazental, plazentar
placental barrier Plazentaschranke f.

placentation Plazentation f.
placentitis Plazentitis f.
placentography Plazentographie f.
placentoma Plazentom n.
placentotoxin Plazentotoxin n.
place value Stellenwert m.
Placido's disk Placidosche Scheibe f.
plague Seuche f.; Pest f.
– **boil** Pestbeule f.
–, **bubonic** Beulenpest f.
–, **cattle** Rinderpest f.
–, **fowl** Hühnerpest f.
–, **pneumonic** Lungenpest f.
– **spot** Pestfleck m.
plain flach; Fläche f.
plane flach, eben; Fläche f., Ebene f.
plane, to glätten, ebnen, abhobeln
– **sickness** Fliegerkrankheit f.
planigraphy Planigraphie f.
plant Pflanze f.
plantar d. e.
plant protective Pflanzenschutzmittel n.
plasma d. e. n.
– **cell** Plasmazelle f.
–, **frozen** Gefrierplasma n.
– **protein** Plasmaeiweiß n.
plasmacytosis Plasmazellenvermehrung f.
plasmakinin d. e. n.
plasmal d. e. n.
plasmalogen d. e. n.
plasmapheresis Plasmapherese f.
plasmatic plasmatisch
plasmin d. e. n.
plasminogen d. e. n.
plasmocytoma Plasmozytom n.
plasmodiocidal plasmodientötend
Plasmodium falciparum d. e.
– **immaculatum** d. e.
– **malariae** d. e.
– **vivax** d. e.
plasmolysis Plasmolyse f.
plasmolytic plasmolytisch

plantigrade Sohlengänger m.
plaster Pflaster n.
plaster, to pflastern; gipsen
–, **adhesive** Heftpflaster n.
– **bandage** Gipsverband m.
– **bed** Gipsbett n.
– **cast** Gipsabdruck m., Gipsmodell n., Gipsabdruckform f.
– **dressing allowing the patient to walk** Gehgips m.
– **knife** Gipsmesser n.
– **of Paris** Gips m.
– **room** Gipsraum m.
– **saw** Gipssäge f.
– **shears** Gipsschere f.
– **spatula** Pflasterspatel m.
– **splint** Gipsschiene f.
– **spreader** Gipsspreizer m.
– **trephine** Gipsbohrer m.
plastic plastisch
plastic bag Plastikbeutel m.
plasticity Plastizität f.
plastics Plastik f.; plastisches Material n., Kunststoff m.
plastocyte Blutplättchen n.
plastogamy Plastogamie f.
plate Platte f., Teller m.
– **holder** Kassette f. (roentgenolog.)
plate shears Blechschere f.
platelet Plättchen n.
platinate Platinat n.
platinum Platin n.
– **loop** Platinöse f.
platyhelminth Plattwurm m., Plathelminth m.
pledget kleine Kompresse f.
pleiochromia Pleiochromie f.
pleocytosis Pleozytose f.
pleomorphic pleomorph
pleomorphous pleomorph
pleomorphism Pleomorphie f.
plethora d. e. f.
plethoric plethorisch
plethysmogram Plethysmogramm n.
plethysmograph d. e. m.

plethysmographical plethysmographisch
plethysmography Plethysmographie f.
pleura d. e. f., Brustfell n.
pleural d. e.
pleurectomy Pleurektomie f.
pleurisy Pleuritis f., Brustfellentzündung f.
pleuritic pleuritisch
pleurodynia Pleurodynie f.
pleuropericarditis Pleuroperikarditis f.
pleuroperitoneal d. e.
pleuroperitoneostomy Pleuroperitoneostomie f.
pleuropneumolysis Pleuropneumolyse f.
pleuropneumonia Pleuropneumonie f.
pleuroscopy Pleuroskopie f.
pleurotomy Pleurotomie f.
pleurovisceral pleuroviszeral
pleximeter Plessimeter n.; Glasspatel m.
plexus d. e. m.
pliable gelenkig
plicotomy Plikotomie f.
pliers Zange f.
plug Propf m., Stöpsel m.
plugger Stopfer m.
plugging Plombierung f., Ausstopfung f.
plumbic bleihaltig
plumbism Bleivergiftung f.
Plummer-Vinson syndrome Plummer-Vinson-Syndrom n.
pluriglandular pluriglandulär
pluripara d. e. f.
pluripolar d. e.
pluripotent d. e.
pneumatic pneumatisch
pneumatization Pneumatisierung f.
pneumatize, to pneumatisieren
pneumatosis Pneumatose f.
pneumaturia Pneumaturie f.
pneumectomy Pneumektomie f.

pneumocardial pneumokardial
pneumococcus Pneumokokkus m.
pneumocolon Pneumokolon n.
pneumoconiosis Pneumokoniose f.
pneumocystosis Pneumozystose f.
pneumocyte Pneumozyt m.
pneumoencephalography Pneumenzephalographie f.
pneumogastric nerve Nervus vagus
pneumography Pneumographie f.
pneumolysis Pneumolyse f.
pneumomediastinum d. e. n.
pneumonectomy Pneumonektomie f.
pneumonia Pneumonie f., Lungenentzündung f.
–, **aspiration** Aspirationspneumonie f.
–, **bilious** biliäre Pneumonie f.
–, **bronchial** Bronchopneumonie f.
–, **cheesy** käsige Pneumonie f.
– **due to pulmonary infarction** Infarktpneumonie f.
–, **hypostatic** hypostatische Pneumonie f.
–, **interstitial** chronische fibröse Pneumonie f.
–, **lobar** croupöse Pneumonie f.
–, **migratory** Wanderpneumonie f.
–, **primary atypical** primär atypische Pneumonie f.
–, **virus** Viruspneumonie f.
pneumonic pneumonisch
pneumonitis, acute interstitial akute interstitelle Pneumonie f.
pneumopaludism Lungenmalaria f.
pneumopericardium Pneumoperikard n.
pneumoperitoneography Pneumoperitoneographie f.
pneumoperitoneum d. e. n.
pneumopyelography Pneumopyelographie f.
pneumotachograph d. e. m.
pneumothorax d. e. m.
– **apparatus** Pneumothoraxapparat m.

pneumotropic pneumotrop
pock Pustel f., Blatter f.
pock-mark Blatternarbe f.
pocket Tasche f.
− set Taschenbesteck n.
− size Taschenformat n.
podagra d. e.
pododerm Huflederhaut f.
pododermatitis, verrucose Hufkrebs m.
podophyllin d. e. n.
podophyllotoxin d. e. n.
podotrochilitis Hufrollenentzündung f.
poikilocyte Poikilozyt m.
poikilocytosis Poikilozytose f.
poikiloderma d. e. n.
point Punkt m.
− of action Angriffspunkt m.
− of controversy Streitfrage f.
− of maximum Punctum maximum
Poiseuille's law Poiseuillesches Gesetz n.
poison Gift n.
poison, to vergiften
poisongas Giftgas n.
poisoning Vergiftung f.
−, murder by − Giftmord m.
poisonous giftig
poisonousness Giftigkeit f.
polar d. e.
polarimeter d. e. n.
polarimetric polarimetrisch
polarimetry Polarimetrie f.
polariscopy Polariskopie f.
polarity Polarität f.
polarization Polarisierung f.
polarize, to polarisieren
polarographic polarographisch
polarography Polarographie f.
pole Pol m.
police, sanitary Sanitätspolizei f., Gesundheitspolizei f.
policlinic Poliklinik f.
polioencephalitis Polioenzephalitis f.

poliomyelitic poliomyelitisch
poliomyelitis, acute anterior Poliomyelitis anterior acuta
polio vaccine Poliomyelitis-Impfstoff m.
polish, to polieren
politzerization Politzerverfahren n.
politzerize, to politzern
poll (veter.) Hinterhaupt n.
pollakiuria Pollakisurie f.
pollen d. e. n.
pollinosis Pollinose f., Pollenkrankheit f.
polliwog Kaulquappe f.
pollution d. e. f.
polonium d. e. n.
Polya's operation Polya-Operation f.
polyacrylamide Polyacrylamid n.
polyadenitis d. e. f.
polyaesthesia (e) Polyästhesie f.
polyalgesia Polyalgesie f.
polyarteritis Polyarteriitis f.
− nodosa Periarteriitis nodosa
polyarthritic polyarthritisch
polyarthritis d. e. f.
polyarticular polyartikulär
polyavitaminosis Polyavitaminose f.
polybasic polybasisch
polycentric polyzentrisch
polycholia Policholie f.
polychromasia Polychromasie f.
polychromatic polychromatisch
polychromatophilia Polychromatophilie f.
polychromatophilic polychromatophil
polycyclic polyzyklisch
polycystic polyzystisch
polycythaemia (e) Polyzythämie f.
polycythaemic polyzythämisch
polycythemia (a) Polyzythämie f.
polycythemic (a) polyzythämisch
polydactylism Polydaktylie f.

polydeoxyribonucleotide Polydesoxyribonukleotid n.
polydipsia Polydipsie f.
polyergic polyergisch
polyesthesia (a) Polyästhesie f.
polyethylene Polyäthylen n.
polygalactia Polygalaktie f.
polygalacturonase d. e. f.
polyglandular polyglandulär
polyglobulism Polyglobulie f.
polyhypermenorrhea (a) Polyhypermenorrhöe f.
polyhypermenorrhoea (e) Polyhypermenorrhöe f.
polyhypomenorrhea (a) Polyhypomenorrhöe f.
polyhypomenorrhoea (e) Polyhypomenorrhöe f.
polymenorrhea (a) Polymenorrhöe f.
polymenorrhoea (e) Polymenorrhöe f.
polymerase d. e. f.
polymeric polymer
polymerism Polymerie f.
polymerization Polymerisierung f.
polymerize, to polymerisieren
polymethylene Polymethylen n.
polymorph polymorphkerniger Leukozyt m.
polymorphic polymorph
polymorphism Polymorphie f.
polymorphonuclear polymorphkernig
polymorphous polymorph
polymyositis d. e. f.
polymyxin d. e. n.
polyneural d. e.
polyneuritic polyneuritisch
polyneuritis d. e. f.
polynuclear polynukleär
polynucleotide Polynukleotid n.
polyol d. e. n.
polyopsia Polyopsie f.
polyp d. e. m.
polypeptidase d. e. f.
polypeptide Polypeptid n.

polyphasic polyphasisch
polyphosphate Polyphosphat n.
polyploid d. e.
polyposis Polypose f.
polypous polypös
polypragmasy Polypragmasie f.
polypropylene Polypropylen n.
polypus Polyp m.
polyradiculitis Polyradikulitis f.
polyradiculoneuritis Polyradikoloneuritis f.
polyribosome Polyribosom n.
polysaccharide Polysaccharid n.
polyserositis d. e. f.
polysome Polysom n.
polystyrene Polystyrol n.
polythiazide Polythiazid n.
polytopical polytopisch
polytopy Polytopie f.
polyunsaturated mehrfach ungesättigt
polyuresis Polyurie f.
polyuria Polyurie f.
polyvalent d. e.
polyvinyl d. e. n.
pomatum Pomade f.
pompholyx bullöses Exanthem n.
Poncet's disease Poncetsches Rheumatoid n.
pontic Kunstzahn m.
pontile pontin
pontine pontin
pontocerebellar pontozerebellar
pony d. e. n.
pool Blutversackung f.; Vereinigung f.
pool, to vereinigen, zusammenlegen, sammeln
poor blooded ausgeblutet, blutarm
popliteal d. e.
poppy Schlafmohn m.
population d. e. f.
poradenitis d. e. f.
porcelain Porzellan n.
porcine das Schwein betreffend
porcupine Stachelschwein n.
porcupine disease Ichthyose f.

pore d. e. f.
porencephalia Porenzephalie f.
poriomania Poriomanie f.
pork tapeworm Schweinebandwurm m.
porous porös
porphin d. e. n.
porphobilinogen d. e. n.
porphyria Porphyrie f.
porphyrin d. e. n.
porphyrinuria Porphyrinurie f.
porridge Haferbrei m.
porrigo decalvans Alopecia areata
− favosa Favus m.
Porro's operation Porro-Operation f.
portable tragbar
portacaval portokaval
− shunt portokavale Anastomose f.
portal d. e.
− circulation Pfortaderkreislauf m.
− vein Pfortader f.
− vein thrombosis Pfortaderthrombose f.
portion d. e. f.
portography Portographie f.
position d. e. f.
−, lateral Seitenlage f.
positive positiv
positrocephalogram Positrozephalogramm n.
positrocephalographical positrozephalographisch
positrocephalography Positrozephalographie f.
positron d. e. n.
posology Posologie f.
postabortal d. e.
postapoplectic postapoplektisch
postclimacteric postklimakterisch
postcommisurotomy syndrome Postkommisurotomie-Syndrom n.
postconcussion syndrome Postkommotionssyndrom n.
postcontusion syndrome Postkontusionssyndrom n.
postdiphtheric postdiphtherisch
postencephalitic postenzephalitisch
postepileptic postepileptisch
posterior chamber of the eye hintere Augenkammer f.
posterior wall Hinterwand f.
posterolateral d. e.
posteroparietal d. e.
posterotemporal d. e.
post-examine, to nachuntersuchen
postfebrile postfebril
postganglionic postganglionär
postgraduate examinierte Person f.; examiniert
postgraduate training, medical ärztliche Weiterbildung f.
postgrippal d. e.
posthaemorrhage (e) Nachblutung f.
posthemorrhage (a) Nachblutung f.
postherpetic postherpetisch
posthitis d. e. f.
posthumous posthum
posthypnotic posthypnotisch
posthypophysis Hypophysenhinterlappen m.
postmastectomy syndrome Postmastektomiesyndrom n.
postmature überreif
postmenopausal postklimakterisch
postmenstrua Postmenstruum n.
postmortal d. e.
postmortem examination Leichenöffnung f., Obduktion f.
postmortem set Obduktionsbesteck n.
postnatal d. e.
postoperative postoperativ
postpartum postpartual
postpneumonic postpneumonisch
postpoliomyelitic postpoliomyelitisch

postpone, to verschieben, zurückstellen
postprandial d. e.
post puller Stiftzieher m.
poststenotic poststenotisch
posttraumatic posttraumatisch
postulate Postulat n.
postural haltungsmäßig, haltungsbedingt
posture Haltung f., Stellung f.
postuterine postuterin, retrouterin
postvaccinal postvakzinal
pot Kanne f.
potable trinkbar
potable water Trinkwasser n.
Potain's apparatus Potainscher Apparat m.
potash Pottasche f.
potassa Kaliumhydroxyd n.
potassa sulfurata (a) Schwefelleber f.
− sulphurata (e) Schwefelleber f.
potassic kaliumhaltig
potassium Kalium n.
− acetate Kaliumazetat n.
− and sodium tartrate Kaliumnatriumtartrat n.
− arsenite Kaliumarsenit n.
− bicarbonate Kaliumbikarbonat n.
− carbonate Kaliumkarbonat n.
− hydroxide Ätzkali n.
− permanganate Kaliumpermanganat n.
potato culture Kartoffelkultur f.
potency Potenz f., Leistungsfähigkeit f., Wirksamkeit f.
potent d. e.
potential potentiell; Potential n.
potentiate, to potenzieren
potentiation Potenzierung f.
potentiometer d. e. n.
potentiometric potentiometrisch
potentiometry Potentiometrie f.
potentize, to potenzieren
potion Trank m.
Pott's disease Wirbeltuberkulose f.
pouch Tasche f., Höhle f.

poultice Breiumschlag m.
poultry Geflügel n.
Poupart's ligament Poupartsches Band n.
pour out, to ausschütten
pouring out Ausschüttung f.
poverty Armut f., Fehlen n.
powder Puder n., Pulver n., Staub m.
powder, to pudern
− blower Pulverbläser m.
pox Hautausschlag m.; Syphilis f. (vulg.)
practice Praxis f., Ausübung f.
practice, general Allgemeinpraxis f.
practique Quarantänefreigabebescheid m.
practitioner Praktiker m.
practitioner, general praktischer Arzt m., praktische Ärztin f.
practolol d. e. n.
prae... look for/suche unter: pre...
pragmatic pragmatisch
pragmatism Pragmatismus m.
Prague maneuver Prager Handgriff m.
praseodymium Praseodym n.
Pravaz's syringe Pravazsche Spritze f.
prazosin d. e. n.
preagonal präagonal
prealbumin Präalbumin n.
precancerosis Präkanzerose f.
precancerous präkanzerös
precapillary Präkapillare f.; präkapillar
precarcinomatous präkarzinomatös
precarious präkariös
precaution Vorsicht f.
precautionary measure Vorsichtsmaßregel f.
precautions, to take − Vorkehrungen treffen
precentral präzentral
precipitate Präzipitat n.
−, white Hydrargyrum praecipitatum album

precipitate, yellow Hydrargyrum oxydatum flavum
precipitate, to präzipitieren, niederschlagen, fällen
precipitation Präzipitation f.
precipitin Präzipitin n.
precision Präzision f., Genauigkeit f.
preclimacteric präklimakterisch
preclinical vorklinisch
precocious frühreif, vorzeitig entwickelt
precociousness Frühreife f., vorzeitige Entwicklung f.
precocity Frühreife f., vorzeitige Entwicklung f.
precoma Präkoma n.
precomatose präkomatös
preconscious unterbewußt
precordial präkordial
precursor Vorläufer m., Vorstufe f.
predestination Vorherbestimmung f., Prädestination f.
prediabetes Prädiabetes m.
prediabetic prädiabetisch
prediastolic prädiastolisch
predictable vorhersehbar
predigestion Vorverdauung f.
predisposing prädisponierend
predisposition Prädisposition f.
prednisolone Prednisolon n.
prednisone Prednison n.
predominate, to vorherrschen
preeclampsia Präeklampsie f.
preface Vorwort n.
preform, to präformieren
preformation Präformation f.
prefrontal präfrontal
preganglionic präganglionär
Pregl's solution Preglsche Lösung f.
pregnancy Schwangerschaft f.
–, **abdominal** Bauchhöhlenschwangerschaft f.
–, **phantom** Phantomschwangerschaft f.

pregnancy, spurious Scheinschwangerschaft f.
– **test** Schwangerschaftstest m.
–, **tubal** Eileiterschwangerschaft f.
– **urine hormone** Choriongonadotropin n.
pregnandiol d. e. n.
pregnandion d. e. n.
pregnane Pregnan n.
pregnanol d. e. n.
pregnanolone Pregnanolon n.
pregnant schwanger
pregnene Pregnen n.
prehypophysis Hypophysenvorderlappen m.
preliminary einstweilig, vorläufig
premarital vorehelich
premature frühreif; vorzeitig
– **birth** Frühgeburt f.
prematurity Frühreife f.
premedication Prämedikation f.
premenopausal präklimakterisch
premenstrual prämenstruell
premitotic prämitotisch
premolar Prämolar m.
premonitory prämonitorisch
premorbid prämorbid
premyelocyte Promyelozyt m.
prenatal pränatal
preneoplastic präneoplastisch
prenylamine Prenylamin n.
preoperative präoperativ
preparalytic präparalytisch
preparate, to präparieren, vorbereiten, zubereiten
preparation Präparation f.; Präparat n.
–, **multicomponent** zusammengesetztes Präparat n.
prepatellar präpatellar
preperitoneal präperitoneal
prepotent vorherrschend
preprogrammed vorprogrammiert
prepuberty Präpubertät f.
prepuce Vorhaut f.
prepyloric präpylorisch
presacral präsakral

presbyophrenia Presbyophrenie f.
presbyopia Presbyopie f., Alterssichtigkeit f.
presbyopic alterssichtig
presclerosis Präsklerose f.
presclerotic präsklerotisch
preschool age Vorschulalter n.
prescribe, to vorschreiben, verschreiben, verordnen
prescription Vorschrift f., Verordnung f., Rezept n.
– **only medicine** verschreibungspflichtiges Arzneimittel n.
presenile präsenil
presentation vorangehender Eiteil m., Kindslage f.
–, **breech** Steißlage f.
–, **brow** Stirnlage f.
–, **cephalic** Schädellage f.
–, **face** Gesichtslage f.
–, **footling** Fußvorlagerung f.
–, **funis** Nabelschnurvorlagerung f.
–, **head** Kopflage f.
–, **pelvic** Beckenendlage f.
–, **shoulder** Schulterlage f.
–, **transverse** Querlage f.
–, **vertex** Hinterhauptlage f.
preservation Konservierung f., Erhaltung f.
preservative Konservierungsmittel n.; Präservativ n.
preserve Konserve f.
preserve, to konservieren, erhalten, bewahren
pressor substance Pressorsubstanz f.
pressosensitive pressosensitiv, pressorezeptiv
pressure Druck m.; Zwang m.
–, **distending** Blähdruck m.
–, **high** Hochdruck m.
–, **low** Tiefdruck m.
–, **intraocular** Augeninnendruck m.
–, **negative** Unterdruck m.
–, **positive** Überdruck m.
prestenotic prästenotisch

presystolic präsystolisch
pretibial prätibial
pretreatment Vorbehandlung f.
prevent, to vorbeugen, zuvorkommen
prevention Vorbeugung f.
preventive präventiv, vorbeugend; vorbeugendes Mittel n.
previous vorausgehend, vorangehend
– **treatment** Vorbehandlung f.
priapism Priapismus m.
Price-Jones curve Price-Jonessche Kurve f.
prick Stich m., Stachel m.
Priessnitz bandage Priessnitzwickel m.
primary primär
– **lateral sclerosis** primäre spastische Spinalparalyse f.
primate Primat m.
primipara d. e. f.
primiparous patient Primipara f.
primitive primitiv
primordial d. e.
principal cell Hauptzelle f.
principle Prinzip n.
prindolol d. e. n.
priority Priorität f.
prism Prisma n.
private privat
privy Scham f.; Toilette f.
– **parts** Geschlechtsteile m. pl.
proaccelerin d. e. n.
probe Sonde f.
–, **grooved, after Kocher** Kocherrinne f.
probe, to sondieren
proboscis Rüssel m.
procaine hydrochloride Prokainhydrochlorid n.
procedure Prozedur f., Verfahren n.
process Prozeß m.; Fortsatz m.
prochlorperazine Prochlorperazin n.
proconvertin Prokonvertin n.

procreate, to zeugen, erzeugen
procreation Zeugung f., Nachwuchserzeugung f.
procreative prokreativ
procteurysis Prokteuryse f.
proctitic proktitisch
proctitis Proktitis f.
proctocystotomy Proktozystotomie f.
proctogenic proktogen
proctological proktologisch
proctologist Proktologe m.
proctology Proktologie f.
proctoscopical proktoskopisch
proctoscopy Proktoskopie f.
proctosigmoidoscope Rektoromanoskop n.
proctosigmoidoscopy Rektoromanoskopie f.
proctostomy Proktostomie f.
proctotomy Proktotomie f.
prodromal d. e.
− **period** Prodromalstadium n.
prodrome Prodrom n.
product Produkt n.
production Produktion f.
productive produktiv
proerythroblast d. e. m.
proesterase Pro-Esterase f.
proferment d. e. n.
professional professionell, beruflich
professor d. e. m., Professorin f.
profile Profil n.
profuse profus
progestational phase Gelbkörperphase f.
progestin Gelbkörperhormon n.
progesterone Gelbkörperhormon n., Luteohormon n., Progesteron n.
progestogen d. e. n.
proglottis Bandwurmglied n.
prognathism Prognathie f.
prognosis Prognose f.
prognostic prognostisch
prognosticate, to prognostizieren, vorhersagen

prognostician Prognostiker m.
program controlled programmgesteuert
programmed programmiert
programming Programmierung f.
progress Fortschritt m., Verlauf m.
progression d. e. f.
progressive progressiv, fortschreitend
− **muscular dystrophy** Dystrophia musculorum progressiva (Erb)
proinsulin d. e. n.
projection Projektion f.
prolactin laktotropes Hypophysenvorderlappenhormon n., Prolaktin n.
prolamin d. e. n.
prolan d. e. n.
proliferate, to proliferieren
proliferation d. e. f.
proliferative proliferativ
prolinase d. e. f.
proline Prolin n.
prolong, to verlängern, prolongieren
prolongation Verlängerung f.
promazine Promazin n.
promethazine Promethazin n.
promethium d. e. n.
prominence Prominenz f.
promonocyte Promonozyt m.
promontory Promontorium n.
prompt d. e.
promyelocyte Promyelozyt m.
pronation d. e. f.
pronged gezackt, zackig
propaedeutic (e) propädeutisch
propaedeutics (e) Propädeutik f.
propagate, to fortpflanzen
propagation Fortpflanzung f.
propamide Propamid n.
propane Propan n.
propanol d. e. n.
propanolol d. e. n.
propedeutic (a) propädeutisch
propedeutics (a) Propädeutik f.

propensity Anfälligkeit f.
properdin d. e. n.
property Eigentum n., Eigentümlichkeit f.
prophylactic prophylaktisch
prophylaxis Prophylaxe f.
propicillin d. e. n.
propion d. e. n.
propionate Propionat n.
propionic acid Propionsäure f.
propionyl d. e. n.
proportion d. e. f.
proportional d. e.
propoxyphene Propoxyphen n.
propranolol d. e. n.
proprietary Arzneimittelspezialität f.
proprioceptive propriozeptiv
propulsion d. e. f.
propyl d. e. n.
propylamine Propylamin n.
propylene Propylen n.
propyl red Propylrot n.
propylthiouracil d. e. n.
prorsad vorwärts, nach vorne gerichtet
prosecretin Prosekretin n.
prosector Prosektor m.
prosopoplegia Prosopoplegie f., Gesichtslähmung f.
prostaglandin d. e. n.
prostate Vorsteherdrüse f.
prostatectomy Prostatektomie f.
prostatic prostatisch
prostaticovesical prostatikovesikal
prostatitic prostatitisch
prostatitis d. e. f.
prostatorrhea (a) Prostatorrhöe f.
prostatorrhoea (e) Prostatorrhöe f.
prostatotomy Prostatotomie f.
prosthesis Ersatz m.; Prothese f.
prosthetic prothetisch; prosthetisch
prosthodontia prothetische Zahnheilkunde f.
prostitution d. e. f.
prostration d. e. f.

protaminase d. e. f.
protamine Protamin n.
protease d. e. f.
protect, to schützen, beschützen
protection Schutz m.
protective schützend
– dose Schutzdosis f.
– effect Schutzwirkung f.
– film Schutzfilm m.
proteid d. e. n.
protein d. e. n., Eiweiß n.
– -bound eiweißgebunden
– fraction Eiweißfraktion f.
– -free eiweißfrei
– silver Argentum proteinicum
– splitting eiweißspaltend
proteinase d. e. f.
proteinosis Proteinose f.
proteinotherapy Proteinkörpertherapie f.
proteinuria Proteinurie f., Eiweißharnen n.
proteohormone Proteohormon n.
proteolysis Proteolyse f.
proteolytic proteolytisch
proteometabolism Eiweißstoffwechsel m.
proteose d. e. f.
Proteus vulgaris d. e.
prothipendyl d. e. n.
prothrombin d. e. n.
– time Prothrombinzeit f.
prothrombinopenia Prothrombinopenie f., Prothrombinmangel m.
protide Protein n.
protionamide Protionamid n.
protoactinium Protaktinium n.
protoblast d. e. m.
protocol Protokoll n.
proton d. e. n.; Tripeptid n.; Anlage f.
protoplasm Protoplasma n.
protoplasmic protoplasmatisch
protoporphyrin d. e. n.
prototoxin d. e. n.
prototype Prototyp m.

protoveratrine Protoveratrin n.
protozoon d. e. n.
protrude, to heraustreiben
protrusion d. e. f.
protriptyline Protriptylin n.
protuberance Protuberanz f.
proud flesh wildes Fleisch n.
prove, to beweisen; prüfen
proving of a drug Arzneimittelprüfung f.
provisional vorläufig
provitamin d. e. n.
provocation Provokation f.
provoke, to provozieren
proximad proximalwärts
proximal d. e.
proximobuccal proximobukkal
proximolabial d. e.
proximolingual d. e.
pruriginous pruriginös
prurigo mitis/nodularis d. e.
pruritic juckend
pruritus d. e. m.
prussic acid Acidum prussicum, Hydrozyansäure f.
psammocarcinoma Psammokarzinom n.
psammoma Psammom n.
psammosarcoma Psammosarkom n.
psellism Stottern n.
pseudarthrosis Pseudarthrose f.
pseudoagglutination d. e. f.
pseudoagraphia Pseudoagraphie f.
pseudoangina d. e. f.
pseudobulbar pseudobulbär
pseudocroup d. e. m.
pseudocyesis Scheinschwangerschaft f.
pseudodementia Pseudodemenz f.
pseudodiphtheria Pseudodiphtherie f.
pseudogeusia Pseudogeusie f.
pseudoglioma Pseudogliom n.
pseudoglobulin d. e. n.
pseudogonorrhea (a) Pseudogonorrhöe f.

pseudogonorrhoea (e) Pseudogonorrhöe f.
pseudohallucination Pseudohalluzination f.
pseudohermaphroditism Pseudohermaphroditismus m.
pseudohernia Pseudohernie f.
pseudohypertrophic pseudohypertrophisch
pseudohypertrophy Pseudohypertrophie f.
pseudohypoparathyroidism Pseudohypoparathyreoidismus m.
pseudoisochromatic pseudoisochromatisch
pseudojaundice Pseudoikterus m.
pseudoleukaemia (e) Pseudoleukämie f.
pseudoleukemia (a) Pseudoleukämie f.
pseudologia Pseudologie f.
pseudolymphoma Pseudolymphom n.
pseudomembrane Pseudomembran f.
pseudomembranous pseudomembranös
Pseudomonas aeruginosa d. e., Bazillus pyozyaneus
pseudomyxoma Pseudomyxom n.
pseudoparalysis Pseudoparalyse f.
pseudopod Pseudopodie f.
pseudopregnancy Scheinschwangerschaft f.
pseudorabies, bovine Pseudowut f., Aujeskysche Krankheit f.
pseudoreaction Pseudoreaktion f.
pseudosclerosis Pseudosklerose f.
pseudostructure Pseudostruktur f.
pseudotabes d. e. f.
pseudotuberculosis Pseudotuberkulose f.
pseudouridinuria Pseudouridinurie f.
pseudoxanthoma Pseudoxanthom n.

psicaine Psicain n.
psilocybin d. e. n.
psilosis Psilose f.; Sprue f.
psittacosis Psittakose f., Papageienkrankheit f.
psoas abscess Psoasabszess m.
psora Krätze f.; Psoriasis f.
psoriasis d. e. f.
psoriatic psoriatisch
psychalgia Psychalgie f.
psychalgic psychalgisch
psychasthenia Psychasthenie f.
psychasthenic psychasthenisch
psychataxia Psychataxie f.
psyche d. e. f.
psychedelic psychodelisch, psychedelisch
psychiatric psychiatrisch
psychiatrist Psychiater m.
psychiatry Psychiatrie f.
psychical psychisch
psychics Psychologie f.
psychoanalysis Psychoanalyse f.
psychoanalyst Psychoanalytiker m.
psychoanalytic psychoanalytisch
psychobiology Psychobiologie f.
psychochemistry Psychochemie f.
psychochromaesthesia (e) Psychochromästhesie f.
psychochromesthesia (a) Psychochromästhesie f.
psychodelic psychodelisch, psychedelisch
psychodiagnostics Psychodiagnostik f.
psycho-drug Psychopharmakon n.
psychodynamic psychodynamisch
psychodynamics Psychodynamik f.
psychogenia Psychogenie f.
psychogenic psychogen
psychogenous psychogen
psychological psychologisch
psychologist Psychologe m., Psychologin f.
psychology Psychologie f.
psychomotor psychomotorisch
psychoneurosis Psychoneurose f.
psychoneurotic psychoneurotisch
psychopath Psychopath m., Psychopathin f.
psychopathic psychopathisch
– **personality** psychopathische Persönlichkeit f.
psychopathology Psychopathologie f.
psychopathy Psychopathie f.
psychopharmacology Psychopharmakologie f.
psychophysical psychophysisch
psychoprophylaxis Psychoprophylaxe f.
psychoreaction Psychoreaktion f.
psychosensory psychosensorisch
psychosexual psychosexuell
psychosis Psychose f.
–,**manic-depressive** manisch-depressive Psychose f.
psychosomatic psychosomatisch
psychosurgeon Psychochirurg m.
psychosurgery Psychochirurgie f.
psychosurgical psychochirurgisch
psychotherapeutic psychotherapeutisch
psychotherapeutics Psychotherapie f.
psychotherapy Psychotherapie f.
psychotic psychotisch; psychotische Person f.
psychotropic psychotrop
psychrometer d. e. n.
pteridine Pteridin n.
pterygium d. e. n., Flügelfell n.
pterygomaxillary pterygomaxillär
ptomaine Ptomain n.
ptosis Ptose f.
ptotic ptotisch
ptyalin d. e. n.
ptyalism Ptyalismus m.
ptyalolithiasis d. e. f.
puberty Pubertät f.
–,**precocious** Pubertas praecox
pubescent pubertierend
pubic pubisch

pubiotomy Pubiotomie f., Hebosteotomie f.
Public Health Öffentliches Gesundheitswesen n.
puboprostatic puboprostatisch
puces Krätze f.
puddle sign Pfützenphänomen n.
pudendal d. e.
puerile pueril
puerpera d. e. f.
puerperal d. e. f.
puerperal fever Kindbettfieber n.
– **pyrexia** Kindbettfieber n., Puerperalfieber n.
puerperium Kindbett n., Wochenbett n.
Pulex irritans d. e.
pullet junge Henne f.
pullorum disease Kückenruhr f.
pulmo-aortic pulmo-aortal
pulmonary pulmonal
– **function test** Lungenfunktionsprüfung f.
– **hilar adenopathy** Lungenhiluslymphknotenerkrankung f.
– **valve** Pulmonalklappe f.
– **venous connection, anomalous** Lungenvenentransposition f.
pulmonic pulmonal
– **insufficiency** Pulmonalinsuffizienz f.
– **stenosis** Pulmonalstenose f.
pulmotor d. e. m.
pulp Pulpa f.; Brei m.
– **canal** Pulpenkanal m.
– **cavity** Pulpenhöhle f.
– **chamber** Pulpenkammer f.
–, **devitalized** devitalisierte Pulpa f.
pulpal d. e.
pulpitis d. e. f.
pulpless tooth pulpenloser Zahn m.
pulpotomy Pulpotomie f.
pulsate, to pulsieren
pulsatilla d. e. f.
pulsation d. e. f.

pulse Puls m.
– **deficit** Pulsdefizit n.
pulseless pulslos
– **disease** Aortenbogensyndrom n.
pulsion diverticulum Pulsionsdivertikel n.
pulsus alternans d. e.
pultaceous cataplasm Breiumschlag m.
pulverization Pulverisierung f.
pulverize, to pulverisieren
puma d. e. m.
pump Pumpe f.
–, **filter** Filtrierpumpe f.
– **oxygenator** Pumpoxygenator m.
puna Bergkrankheit f.
punch Locheisen n., Stanze f.; Punsch m.
– **card** Lochkarte f.
punchdrunk Boxerenzephalopathie f.
punched card technique Lochkartenverfahren f.
punctate Punktat n.
puncture Punktion f.
puncture, to punktieren
pupil (of the eye) Pupille f.
pupillary pupillär
pupillatonia Pupillatonie f.
puppy junger Hund m.
pure rein; keusch
purgative purgativ, abführend; Purgativum n., Abführmittel n.
purge, to abführen, purgieren
purification Reinigung f.
purify, to reinigen
purifying the blood blutreinigend
purinase d. e. f.
purine Purin n.
purity Reinheit f.
Purkinje's fiber Purkinjesche Faser f.
puromycin d. e. n.
purpura d. e. f.
–, **thrombocytopenic** Werlhofsche Purpura f.

purpureaglucoside Purpureaglykosid n.
pursestring ligature Umstechung f.
purulent d. e., eiterig
pus Eiter m.
− cell Eiterzelle f.
pushbutton Drucktaste f.
pustulant blasentreibend;
blasentreibendes Mittel n.
pustular pustulär
pustulation Pustelbildung f.
pustule Pustel f.
putrefaction Verwesung f.,
Fäulnis f.
putrefy, to verwesen, faulen
putrescent verwesend
putrescine Putreszin n.
putrid d. e.
putridity Fäulnis f.
PVC-skeleton tablet PVC-Gerüst-
Tablette f.
pyaemia (e) Pyämie f.
pyarthrosis d. e. f.
pyelitic pyelitisch
pyelitis d. e. f.
pyelogram Pyelogramm n.
pyelograph Pyelogramm n.
pyelographical pyelographisch
pyelography Pyelographie f.
−, intravenous intravenöse
Pyelographie f.
−, respiration Veratmungspyelographie f.
−, retrograde retrograde
Pyelographie f.
pyelonephritis d. e. f.
pyeloscopy Pyeloskopie f.
pyelostomy Pyelostomie f.
pyelotomy Pyelotomie f.
pyelovenous pyelovenös
− backflow pyelovenöser
Reflux m.
pyemia (a) Pyämie f.
pyknic pyknisch
pyknolepsy Pyknolepsie f.
pyknosis Pyknose f.
pyknotic pyknotisch

pylephlebitis d. e. f.
pylorectomy Pylorektomie f.
pyloric pylorisch
− insufficiency Pylorusinsuffizienz f.
− stenosis Pylorusstenose f.
pyloromyotomy Pyloromyotomie f.
pyloroplasty Pylorusplastik f.
pylorospasm Pylorospasmus m.
pylorus d. e. m.
pyoderma Pyodermie f.
pyogenesis Eiterbildung f.
pyogenic pyogen
pyometra d. e.
pyometritis d. e. f.
pyonephrosis Pyonephrose f.
pyopneumothorax d. e. m.
pyorrhea (a) Pyorrhöe f.
pyorrhoea (e) Pyorrhöe f.
pyosalpingitis d. e. f.
pyosalpingo-oophoritis d. e. f.
pyosalpinx d. e. f.
pyothorax d. e. m.
pyramidal d. e.
− tract Pyramidenbahn f.
pyran d. e. n.
pyranose d. e. f.
pyrazine Pyrazin n.
pyrazol d. e. n.
pyrazolone Pyrazolon n.
pyretic fiebrig
pyrexia Fieber n.
pyrexial fieberhaft
pyribenzamine Pyribenzamin n.
pyridine Pyridin n.
pyridoxine Pyridoxin n.,
Vitamin B 6 n.
pyrimethamine Pyrimethamin n.
pyrimidine Pyrimidin n.
pyrimidopyrimidine Pyrimidopyrimidin n.
pyrithioxine Pyrithioxin m.
pyrithyldione Pyrithyldion n.
pyroborate Pyroborat n.
pyrocatechin Brenzkatechin n.
pyrogallol d. e. n.
pyrogen d. e. n.

pyrogen free pyrogenfrei
pyrogenic pyrogen
pyroglobulin d. e. n.
pyromania Pyromanie f.
pyronine Pyronin n.
pyrophosphatase d. e. f.
pyrophosphate Pyrophosphat n.
pyrophosphorylase d. e. f.

pyroscope Pyroskop n.
pyroscopic pyroskopisch
pyrosis Sodbrennen n.
pyrotoxin d. e. n.
pyrrolase d. e. f.
pyrrole Pyrrol n.
pyrrolidin d. e. n.
pyruvate Pyruvat n.
pyuria Pyurie f.

Q

Q-fever Q-Fieber n.
QID (= quarter in die) viermal täglich
quack Quacksalber m.
quack, to quacksalbern
quackery Quacksalberei f.
quadrangular viereckig
quadrant d. e. m.
quadrantanopsia Quadrantenanopsie f.
quadricuspid vierzipfelig
quadrigeminal plate Vierhügelplatte f.
quadripara d. e. f.
quadriplegia Quadriplegie f.
quadrivalent vierwertig
quadruplet Vierling m.
quale Qualität f.
qualification Qualifikation f., Befähigung f., Eignung f., Berechtigung f.
qualitative qualitativ
quality Qualität f.
– control Qualitätskontrolle f.
– monitoring Qualitätssicherung f.
quantitative quantitativ
quantity Quantität f.
quantum d. e. n.
– theory Quantentheorie f.
quarantine Quarantäne f.

quarantine, to in Quarantäne legen
quarter evil Rauschbrand m.
quartz Quarz m.
quaternary quaternär
Queckenstedt's phenomenon Queckenstedtsches Zeichen n.
quench, to kühlen; unterdrücken; Durst löschen
querulent Querulant m., Querulantin f.
querulous querulatorisch
quick acting schnellwirkend
quicksilver Quecksilber n.
Quick test Quicktest m.
quiet ruhig
quieting beruhigend
Quincke's disease Quinckesche Krankheit f.
quinethazone Quinethazon n.
quinidine Chinidin n.
quinine Chinin n.
quinine bisulfate (a) Chininbisulfat n.
– bisulphate (e) Chininbisulfat n.
– dihydrochloride Chinindihydrochlorid n.
quinoline Chinolin n.
quinone Chinon n.
quinosol Chinosol n.
quinquivalent fünfwertig

quinsy Halsentzündung f.
quintan fever wolhynisches Fieber n.

quitter Hufknorpelfistel f.
quittor Hufknorpelfistel f.
quote d. e. f.

R

rabbit Kaninchen n.
− **fever** Tularämie f.
rabiate tollwütig
rabies Tollwut f.
− **immunization** Tollwut-Schutzimpfung f.
− **vaccine** Tollwutvakzine f.
rabietic tollwütig
race Rasse f.; Wurzel f.
racemate Razemat n.
racemic razemisch
rachischisis d. e. f.
rachitic rachitisch
− **changes** rachitische Veränderungen f. pl.
rachitis d. e. f.
rachitomy Rachitomie f.
racial rassisch
rack, to recken
−, **film drying** Filmtrockengestell n.
−, **knife** Messerbänkchen n.
rad Rad n. (radiol.)
radiability Bestrahlungsfähigkeit f.; Strahlendurchlässigkeit f.
radiad radialwärts
radial d. e.
− **nerve** Nervus radialis
radian Radiant m.
radiant radioaktive Substanz f.
radiate strahlig
radiate, to strahlen
radiation Strahlung f.; Bestrahlung f.
− **injury** Strahlenschaden m.
− **protection** Strahlenschutz m.
− **sickness** Strahlenkater m.
radical radikal; Radikal n.

radicality Radikalität f.
radicular radikulär
− **syndrome** Wurzelsyndrom n.
radiculitis Radikulitis f.
radiculoneuritis Radikuloneuritis f.
radioactinium Radioaktinium n.
radioactive radioaktiv
− **substance** radioaktive Substanz f.
− **tracer technic** radioaktive Markierung f.
radioactivity Radioaktivität f.
radioanalysis Radioanalyse f.
radioanalytic radioanalytisch
radioautography Autoradiographie f.
radiobiology Radiobiologie f.
radiochemical radiochemisch
radiochemistry Radiochemie f.
radiochromate Radiochromat n.
radiochromium Radiochrom n.
radiocobalt Radiokobalt m.
radiodermatitis Strahlendermatitis f.; Röntgendermatitis f.
radiodiagnosis Röntgendiagnose f.
radiodiagnostic röntgendiagnostisch
radiodiagnostics Röntgendiagnostik f.
radiogen radioaktive Substanz f.
radioglucose Radioglukose f.
radiogram Röntgenbild n.
radiograph Röntgenbild n.
radiographic röntgenographisch; radiographisch

radiography Röntgenographie f.; Radiographie f.
radiohumeral d. e.
radio-immunoassay (RIA) d. e. m.
radioimmunology Radioimmunologie f.
radioiodinate, to mit Radiojod versehen
radioiodine Radiojod n.
radioiron Radioeisen n.
radioisotope Radioisotop n.
radiologic röntgenologisch; radiologisch
radiologic report Röntgenbericht m.
radiologist Röntgenologe m., Röntgenologin f.; Radiologe m., Radiologin f.
radiology Röntgenologie f.; Radiologie f.
radiolucency partielle Strahlendurchlässigkeit f.
radiolucent partiell strahlendurchlässig
radiolysis Radiolyse f.
radiometer d. e. n.
radio-opacity Strahlenundurchlässigkeit f.
radiopacity Strahlenundurchlässigkeit f.
radiopaque strahlenundurchlässig
– **fluid** Kontrastflüssigkeit f.
radioparent strahlendurchlässig
radiophosphorus Radiophosphor m.
radiophotography Radiophotographie f.
radiophysical radiophysikalisch
radioprotective action Strahlenschutzwirkung f.
radioreceptorassay Radiorezeptorassay m.
radioresistance Strahlenresistenz f.
radioresistant strahlenresistent
radioscopic röntgenoskopisch; radioskopisch

radioscopy Röntgendurchleuchtung f.
radiosensibility Strahlenempfindlichkeit f.
radiosensitive strahlenempfindlich
radiosensitiveness Strahlenempfindlichkeit f.
radiosensitivity Strahlenempfindlichkeit f.
radiotherapeutic strahlentherapeutisch
radiotherapeutics Strahlenheilkunde f.
radiotherapy Strahlentherapie f.; Röntgentherapie f.
radiothorium d. e. n.
radiotracer d. e. m., Radioindikator m.
radiotransparent strahlendurchlässig
radium d. e. n.
– **applicator** Radiumträger m.
– **implantation** Radiumspickung f.
radiumization Radiumbestrahlung f.
radon Radiumemanation f.
raffinose d. e. f.
rage Raserei f., Sucht f., krankhafte Begierde f.
râle Rasselgeräusch n.
–, **dry** trockenes Rasselgeräusch n.
–, **moist** feuchtes Rasselgeräusch n.
ram Widder m.
Raman effect Raman-Effekt m.
ramification Verästelung f., Verzweigung f.
ramify, to verästeln, verzweigen
Ramstedt's operation Ramstedt-Webersche Operation f.
rancid ranzig
range Reichweite f., Bereich m.; Reihe f.
rangefinder Entfernungsmesser m.
rankenangioma Rankenangiom n.
ranula d. e. f.
Ranvier's membrane Ranviersche Membran f.

raphe d. e. f.
rapport d. e. m.
Rare Earth Seltene Erde f.
rarefaction Rarefizierung f.
rash Hautausschlag m., flüchtiger Hautausschlag m.
rasp Raspel f.
raspatory Raspatorium n.
rat Ratte f.
− bite fever Rattenbißkrankheit f., Sodoku
rate d. e. f.
Rathke's pouch Rathkesche Tasche f.
ratimeter d. e. n.
ratio Verhältnis n.
ration d. e. f.
rational rational, rationell
rationalization Rationalisierung f.
ratpoison Rattengift n.
rattle Rasselgeräusch
rattle, to rasseln, röcheln
rattlesnake Klapperschlange f.
raucity Heiserkeit f.
rave, to toben, rasen
ravenous appetite Heißhunger m.
raw diet Rohkost f.
ray Strahl m.
−,hard Hartstrahl m.
−,infra-red Infrarotstrahl m.
−,primary Primärstrahl m.
−,roentgen Röntgenstrahl m.
−,soft Weichstrahl m.
−,ultraviolet Ultraviolettstrahl m.
rayage Strahlendosierung f.
raying Strahlenexposition f.
Raynaud's disease Raynaudsche Gangrän f.
razor Rasiermesser n.
R.B.C. (= red blood corpuscles) Erythrozyten m. pl.
R.D. Entartungsreaktion f.
reabsorb, to rückresorbieren
reabsorption Rückresorption f.
reach of sight Schweite f.
react, to reagieren

reaction Reaktion f.
−,arousal Weckreaktion f.
− of degeneration Entartungsreaktion f.
reactivate, to reaktivieren
reactivation Reaktivierung f.
reactive reaktiv
− **depression** reaktive Depression f.
reactivity Reaktionsvermögen n., Ansprechbarkeit f.
readiness Bereitschaft f.; Fertigkeit f.
Read's formula Readsche Formel f.
ready for injection spritzfertig, spritzbereit
reagent Reagens n.
reagin d. e. n.
reality Realität f.
reamer Fräse f.; Nervenkanalerweiterer m.
reamputation d. e. f.
reanimation d. e. f., Wiederbelebung f.
rebleeding Wiederholungsblutung, Blutungsrückfall m.
rebound Nachreflex m.; Rückprall m.
rebreathing Sauerstoffatmung f. während der Narkotisierung f.
recalcification Rekalzifizierung f.
recalcify, to rekalzifizieren
receiver Sammelgefäß n.; Monatsbinde f.
receptor Rezeptor m.
recession Wegziehen n.; Zurückweichen n.
recessive rezessiv
recidivation Rezidivierung f.
recidive Rezidiv n.
recipe Rezept n.
recipe, obtainable only by − rezeptpflichtig
recipient Empfänger m.
reciprocal reziprok
reciprocal ohm Siemens n.

Recklinghausen's disease
Neurofibromatose f.; Ostitis fibrosa
reclination Reklination f.
recognition Erkennung f.
recoil Rückstoß m.
reconditioning Wiederherstellung f.
reconstruction Rekonstruktion f.
record Aufzeichnung f., Eintragung f.; Spitzenleistung f., Rekord m.
record, to aufzeichnen, eintragen
recover, to gesunden, genesen
recovery Genesung f., Gesundung f.
recrudescence Rekrudeszenz f.
rectal rektal
− **tube** Darmrohr n.
rectangular rechteckig
rectification Rektifizierung f., Reinigung f.
rectifier Gleichrichter m.
rectify, to rektifizieren, reinigen, bereinigen
rectocele Rektozele f.
rectostomy Rektostomie f.
rectouterine rektouterin
rectovaginal rektovaginal
rectovesical rektovesikal
rectum Rektum n.
recuperation Wiederherstellung f.
recurrent rekurrierend, rückfällig
− **fever** Rückfallfieber n.
− **nerve** Nervus recurrens
recurvation Rückwärtskrümmung f.
recycling rezirkulierend
red blindness Rotblindheit f.
− **blood cell** rotes Blutkörperchen n.
− **blood count** rotes Blutbild n.
Red Cross Rotes Kreuz n.
redden, to röten, erröten
reddening Erröten n., Rötung f.

red fever Schweinerotlauf m.
− **-green blindness** Rotgrünblindheit f.
redislocation Redislokation f.
redistillation Redestillation f.
redness Röte f.
redox system Redoxsystem n.
redressement d. e. n., Wiedereinrichtung f.
reduce, to reduzieren; einrichten
reductase Reduktase f.
reduction Reduktion f.; Einrichtung f.
redundant überflüssig
− **prepuce** überhängende Vorhaut f.
reel Spule f.
reentry Wiedereintritt m., Wiederinbesitznahme f.
reference Referenz f., Beziehung f.
refine, to raffinieren
reflect, to reflektieren
reflected reflektiert, reflektorisch
reflection Reflexion f.
reflector Reflektor m.
reflectoscope Reflektoskop n.
reflectoscopic reflektoskopisch
reflectoscopy Reflektoskopie f.
reflex d. e. m.
−, **abdominal** Bauchdeckenreflex m.
−, **accommodation** Akkomodationsreflex m.
−, **Achilles tendon** Achillessehnenreflex m.
−, **acquired** erworbener Reflex m.
−, **anal** Analreflex m.
− **arc** Reflexbogen m.
−, **attitudinal** Haltungsreflex m.
−, **axon** Axonreflex m.
−, **Babinski** Babinskireflex m.
−, **Bainbridge** Bainbridgereflex m.
−, **Bechterew's** Bechterewreflex m.
−, **biceps** Bizepsreflex m.
−, **bladder** Blasenreflex m.
−, **bone** Knochenreflex m.

reflex, Brudzinski's Brudzinski-
reflex m.
−, carotid sinus Carotissinus-
reflex m.
− center Reflexzentrum n.
−, chain- Kettenreflex m.
−, conditional bedingter Reflex m.
−, conjunctival Konjunktival-
reflex m.
−, consensual light konsensueller
Lichtreflex m.
−, convulsive Krampfreflex m.
−, coordinated koordinierter
Reflex m.
−, corneal Hornhautreflex m.
−, cremasteric Cremasterreflex m.
−, crossed gekreuzter Reflex m.
−, cutaneous Hautreflex m.
−, delayed verzögerter Reflex m.
−, finger-thumb Mayerscher
Grundreflex m.
−, knee jerk Patellarsehnenreflex m.
−, laryngeal Kehlkopfreflex m.
−, light Lichtreflex m.
−, mass Massenreflex m.
−, Mendel-Bechterew's Mendel-
Bechterewscher Reflex m.
−, Moro embrace Umarmungs-
reflex m.
−, muscular Muskelreflex m.
−, Oppenheim's Oppenheim-
reflex m.
−, palatine Schluckreflex m.
−, paradoxic flexor Gordon-
reflex m.
−, patellar Patellarsehnenreflex m.
−, pathologic pathologischer
Reflex m.
−, perception Wahrnehmungs-
reflex m.
−, periosteal Periostreflex m.
−, pilomotor Gänsehautreflex m.
−, psychogalvanic psycho-
galvanischer Reflex m.
−, pupillary Pupillenreflex m.
−, radial Radiusperiostreflex m.

reflex, reno-renal reno-renaler
Reflex m.
−, Rossolimo's Rossolimoreflex m.
−, sexual Sexualreflex m.
−, Strümpell's Strümpellreflex m.
−, summation Summationsreflex m.
− sympathetic dystrophy
reflektorische sympathische
Dystrophie f.
−, tendon Sehnenreflex m.
−, triceps Trizepsreflex m.
−, vagus Vagusreflex m.
−, visceral viszeraler Reflex m.
reflexogenic reflexogen
reflexotherapy Reflextherapie f.
reflux d. e. m., Rückfluß m.
refraction Refraktion f.
refraction, power of − Brechkraft f.
refractometer Refraktometer n.
refractory refraktär
refracture Refraktur f.
refresh, to erfrischen; aufrauhen
refrigeration Kühlung f.,
Abkühlung f.
refrigeration anaesthesia (e)
Kälteanästhesie f.
− anesthesia (a) Kälteanästhesie f.
refrigerator Kühlschrank m.
regenerate, to regenerieren
regeneration d. e. f.
regenerative regenerativ
regimen Behandlungsvorschrift f.
region d. e. f.
regional d. e.
register d. e. n.
regression d. e. f.
regressive regressiv
regular regulär, regelrecht,
regelmäßig
regulate, to regulieren, regeln
− a diabetes einen Diabetes
einstellen
regulation d. e. f., Regulierung f.
regulatory regulatorisch
regurgitation d. e. f.
rehabilitate, to rehabilitieren

rehabilitation d. e. f., Wiederherstellung f. der Arbeitsfähigkeit
reimplantation d. e. f.
reinfection Reinfektion f.
reinforcement Kraftsteigerung f.
reinfusion d. e. f.
reintubation d. e. f.
reinversion d. e. f.
Reissner's membrane Reißnersche Membran
Reiter's disease Reitersche Krankheit f.
rejection Abstoßung f., Ablehnung f.
rejuvenescence Verjüngung f.
relapse Rückfall m.
relapsing fever Rückfallfieber n.
relation d. e. f., Beziehung f.; Verwandtschaft f.
relationship Beziehung f.; Verwandtschaft f.
relax, to lockern, entspannen
relaxant Entspannungsmittel n.; entspannend
relaxation Erschlaffung f.; Erholung f., Entspannung f.
relaxation of pelvic floor Erschlaffung m. des Beckenbodens
relaxin d. e. n.
release Freigabe f.; Auslöser m.
–, to loslassen, freigeben, freisetzen
relief Nachlassen n., Besserung f.; Relief n.
– area Entlastungszone f.
–, mucosal Schleimhautrelief n.
relieve, to lindern, bessern, nachlassen
reliner Unterfütterungsmaterial n.
remains Überbleibsel n.
Remak's sign Remaksches Zeichen n.
remedy Heilmittel n.
remineralization Remineralisation f.
remission d. e. f.
remittance of a patient Überweisung f. eines Patienten

remit a patient, to... einen Patienten überweisen
remittent remittierend
removal Herausnahme f., Entfernung f.
– of the gastric juice Magenaushebung f.
remove, to entfernen
renal d. e.
– damage Nierenschaden m.
– pelvis Nierenbecken n.
rend, to zerreißen
renew, to erneuern
renewal Erneuerung f.
renin d. e. n.
renography Nephrographie f.
–, radioisotopic Isotopennephrographie f.
re-operate, to nachoperieren
re-operation Nachoperation f.
reoxidation Reoxydation f.
repellent abstoßend; abschwellend
replace, to ersetzen
replacement Ersatz m.
repletion Völle f.
replicase d. e. f.
repolarization Repolarisierung f.
repolarize, to repolarisieren
repopulation Wiederbesiedelung f.
report Bericht m.
–, to berichten
repose, to ruhen, ausruhen
reposition d. e. f.
repressor d. e. m.
reproducibility Reproduzierbarkeit f.
reproducible reproduzierbar
reproduction Fortpflanzung f.
reproductive die Fortpflanzung betreffend, Fortpflanzungs..., reproduktiv
reptil d. e. n., Kriechtier n.
repulse, to verweigern, zurückweisen
repulsion Weigerung f.; Abstoßung f.
request Gesuch n.

request, to nachsuchen, ersuchen
rescinnamine Rescinnamin n.
research Nachforschung f., Forschung f.
resect, to resezieren
resectability Resezierbarkeit f.
resectable resezierbar
resection Resektion f.
resectoscope Resektoskop n.
reserpine Reserpin n.
reserve d. e. f.
– **air** Reserveluft f.
–, **alkali** Alkalireserve f.
– **volume** Reservevolumen n.
reservoir d. e. n.
resident Assistenzarzt m., Assistenzärztin f., behandelnder Krankenhausarzt m., behandelnde Krankenhausärztin f.
residual restlich, zurückbleibend
– **air** Residualluft f.
– **capacity** Residualkapazität f.
– **urine** Restharn m.
– **volume** Residualvolumen n.
residue Überbleibsel n., Rückstand m.
resilient elastisch
resin Harz n.
resist, to widerstehen
resistance Resistenz f., Widerstand m.
resistant resistent
resistant to treatment therapieresistent
resistibility Widerstandsfähigkeit f.
resolve, to auflösen
resolvent auflösend; auflösendes Mittel n.
resolving power Auflösungsvermögen n.
resonance Resonanz f.
resorcinol Resorzin n.
resorption d. e. f.
respiration d. e. f., Atmung f.
–, **absent** aufgehobenes Atmungsgeräusch n.

respiration, amphoric amphorisches Atmungsgeräusch n.
–, **artificial** künstliche Beatmung f.
–, **Biot's** Biotsche Atmung f.
–, **bronchovesicular** Bronchovesikuläratmen n.
–, **Cheyne-Stokes** Cheyne-Stokessche Atmung f.
–, **diminished** abgeschwächtes Atmungsgeräusch n.
–, **indefinite** unbestimmtes Atmungsgeräusch n.
–, **Kussmaul's** Kussmaulsche Atmung f.
–, **puerile** pueriles Atmen n.
–, **tubular** Bronchialatmen n.
–, **vesicular** Bläschenatmen n.
respirator Beatmungsgerät n.
respiratory respiratorisch
– **exercise** Atemübung f.
– **tract** Respirationstrakt m.
respire, to atmen
response Antwort f., Wirkung f., Erfolg m.
responsibility Verantwortlichkeit f.; Zurechnungsfähigkeit f.
rest Ruhe f., Rast f.
rest position Ruhelage f.
rest, to ruhen, rasten
restenosis Re-Stenose f.
resting metabolism Ruhestoffwechsel m.
rest-cure Liegekur f.
restitution d. e. f.
restless ruhelos
restorable wiederherstellbar
restoration Wiederherstellung f.
restore, to wiederherstellen
resuscitation Wiederbelebung f., Wiedererweckung f.
retain, to zurückhalten, verhalten
retardation Verzögerung f., Behinderung f.
retarded verzögert, zurückgeblieben, retardiert
retching Brechreiz m.
retention d. e. f., Verhaltung f.

reticular retikulär
— **lattice fiber** Gitterfaser f.
reticulocyte Retikulozyt m.
reticulocytosis Retikulozytose f.
reticuloendothelial system retikuloendotheliales System n.
reticuloendothelioma Retikuloendotheliom n.
reticuloendotheliosis Retikuloendotheliose f.
reticuloendothelium Retikuloendothel n.
reticulo-filamentary substance Substantia reticulofilamentosa
reticulosarcoma Retikulosarkom n.
reticulosis Retikulose f.
reticulum cell Retikulumzelle f.
— **sarcoma** Retikulumzellsarkom n.
retiform netzförmig, netzartig
retina d. e. f., Netzhaut f.
—, **detachment of** Netzhautablösung f.
retinal d. e.
retinitis d. e. f.
retinoblastoma Retinoblastom n.
retinopathy Retinopathie f.
retinoscopy Skiaskopie f.
retort Retorte f.
retothel sarcoma Retothelsarkom n.
retractile retraktil
retraction Retraktion f.
retractor Retraktor m., Haken m., Wundhaken m.
—, **abdominal** Bauchhaken m.
—, **lid** Lidhalter m.
retroauricular retroaurikulär
retrobulbar retrobulbär
retrocaecal (e) retrozökal
retrocardiac retrokardial
retrocecal (a) retrozökal
retrocoecal (e) retrozökal
retrocolic retrokolisch
retrodisplacement Rückwärtsverlagerung f.

retroflexed retroflektiert
retroflexion d. e. f.
retrograde retrograd
retrogression Rückbildung f.
retrolabyrinthine retrolabyrinthär
retrolental d. e.
retrolabyrinthine retrolabyrinthär
retromammary retromammär
retromandibular retromandibulär
retronasal d. e.
retroperitoneal d. e.
retropharyngeal d. e.
retroplacental retroplazental
retroposed retroponiert
retropubic retropubisch
retropulsion d. e. f.
retrospective retrospektiv
retrosternal d. e.
retrouterine retrouterin
retroversioflexion d. e. f.
retroversion d. e. f.
retroverted retrovertiert
revaccination Zweitimpfung f.
revascularization Revaskularisierung f.
Reverdin's graft Reverdinsche Transplantation f.
reversal Rückverwandlung f., Umkehrung f.
reversibility Reversibilität f.
reversible reversibel
review, bibliographical Literaturübersicht f.
rev./min. (= revolutions per minute) U.p.M. (= Umdrehungen pro Minute)
revivescence Wiederaufleben n.
revolution Umdrehung f.
revolutions per minute Umdrehungen pro Minute
revulsion Blutableitung f.
rewind, to zurückspulen
rhabdomyoma Rhabdomyom n.
rhabdosarcoma Rhabdosarkom n.
rhagade d. e. f.
rhamnose d. e. f.
rhenium d. e. n.

rheobasis Rheobase f.
rheology Rheologie f.
rheoscopy Rheoskopie f.
rheostat d. e. m.
rheostosis Rheostose f.
rheotaxis d. e. f.
rhesus monkey Rhesusaffe m.
rheuma Aufluß m., Katarrh m.
rheumatic rheumatisch
− fever akuter fieberhafter Gelenkrheumatismus m.
− granulomatosis rheumatische Granulomatose f.
− nodule Rheumaknötchen n.
rheumatism Rheumatismus m.
−, articular Gelenkrheumatismus m.
rheumatoid d. e.
− arthritis primär chronischer Gelenkrheumatismus m.
rheumatologist Rheumatologe m., Rheumatologin f.
rheumatology Rheumatologie f.
Rh-factor Rh-Faktor m.
rhinencephalia Rhinenzephalie f.
rhinencephalon Riechhirn n.
rhinitis d. e. f.
rhinoceros Nashorn n.
rhinogenous rhinogen
rhinolalia Rhinolalie f.
rhinological rhinologisch
rhinologist Rhinologe m., Rhinologin f.
rhinology Rhinologie f.
rhinopharyngitis d. e. f.
rhinophyma Rhinophym n.
rhinoplasty Nasenplastik f.
rhinoscopic rhinoskopisch
rhinoscopy Rhinoskopie f.
rhinosporidiosis Rhinosporidiose f.
rhizopoda d. e. n. pl.
rhizotomy Rhizotomie f.
rhodamine Rhodamin n.
rhodane Rhodan n.
rhodium d. e. n.
rhombencephalon Rautenhirn n.
rhubarb Rhabarber m.

rhythm Rhythmus m.
rhythmic rhythmisch
rib Rippe f.
ribitol Adonit n.
riboflavin Laktoflavin n.
ribohexose d. e. f.
ribonuclease Ribonuklease f.
ribonucleotide Ribonukleotid n.
ribose d. e. f.
riboside Ribosid n.
ribosomal d. e.
ribosome Ribosom n.
ribotide Ribotid n.
ribulose d. e. f.
rice Reis m.
− body Reiskörper m.
− polishings Reiskleie f.
− water stools Reiswasserstuhl m.
ricin Rizin n.
ricketic rachitisch
rickets Rachitis f.
Rickettsia burneti Rickettsia Burneti
− prowazeki Rickettsia Prowazeki
ridge Grat m., Wulst m.
ridgling kryptorchides Individuum n.
Riedel's struma Riedel-Struma f.
Rieder's cell Riederzelle f.
rifampicin d. e. n.
Rift Valley fever Rifttalfieber n.
right anterior oblique projection erster Schrägdurchmesser m.
right-handed rechtshändig
right-to-left shunt Rechts-Links-Shunt m.
rigid d. e.
rigidity Rigidität f.
rind Rinde f., Schwarte f.
ring d. e. m.
Ringer's solution Ringerlösung f.
ringworm Mikrosporie f.; Trichophytie f.
Rinne's test Rinnescher Versuch m.
rinse, to spülen, ausspülen
rinsing liquid Spülflüssigkeit f.

rise of the blood pressure
  Blutdruckanstieg m.
rising generation Nachwuchs m.
risk Risiko n.
risk, good gutes Risiko n.
risk, poor schlechtes Risiko n.
Ritgen method Ritgenscher
  Handgriff m.
Rivalta's test Rivaltaprobe f.
Riva-Rocci sphygmomanometer
  Riva-Rocci-Blutdruckmesser m.
RNA Ribonukleinsäure f.
road accident Verkehrsunfall m.
roast, to rösten, braten
robbery with murder Raubmord m.
roborant roborierend;
  Roborans n.
roborating roborierend
Rochelle salt Seignettesalz n.
rock, to wanken
Rocky Mountain fever Rocky-Mountain-Fieber n.
rod Stange f., Stab m.
rodent Nagetier n.
rods and cones, retinal Stäbchen n. pl. und Zapfen m. pl. der Retina
roe Reh n.
roentgen Röntgen n.
Roentgen findings Röntgenbefund m.
Roentgen intoxication Röntgenkater m.
– ray Röntgenstrahl m.
roentgenization Röntgenbestrahlung f.
roentgenize, to röntgenbestrahlen
roentgenkater Röntgenkater m.
roentgenogram Röntgenbild n.
roentgenological röntgenologisch
roentgenologist Röntgenologe m., Röntgenologin f.
roentgenology Röntgenologie f.
roentgenoscopy Röntgendurchleuchtung f.
roentgenotherapy Röntgentherapie f.

roentgenotherapy, deep Röntgentiefentherapie f.
–, high voltage Hochvolt-Röntgentherapie f.
–, low voltage Niedervolt-Röntgentherapie f.
Roger's disease Morbus Roger
rolitetracycline Rolitetracyclin n.
Romberg's sign Rombergsches Zeichen n.
rongeur Hohlmeißelzange f.
room temperature Zimmertemperatur f.
root Wurzel f.
– apex Wurzelspitze f.
– canal Wurzelkanal m.
– elevator Wurzelheber m.
– fragment Wurzelsplitter m.
– screw Wurzelschraube f.
– treatment Wurzelbehandlung f.
Rorschach test Rorschachtest m.
rosacea d. e. f.
rosaniline Rosanilin n.
rosary, rachitic rachitischer Rosenkranz m.
rose Rose f.; Erysipel n.
roseola Roseole f.
Rossolimo's reflex Rossolimo-Reflex m.
rot Verwesung f., Verfall m., Fäulnis f.
rot, to verwesen, verfaulen
rotary joint Radgelenk n.
rotate, to rotieren
rotation d. e. f.
rotation, optic optische Drehung f.
rotatory rotatorisch
roughage unverdauliche Nahrungsbestandteile m. pl.
round cell Rundzelle f.
round off, to abrunden
roundworm Spulwurm m.
roup Geflügelpockendiphtherie f.
Rous' sarcoma Rous-Sarkom n.
routine d. e. f.

Rovsing's sign Rovsingsches Zeichen n.
RP (= referring physician) überweisender Arzt m.
RS (= respiratory system) Respirationstrakt m.
rub, to reiben; frottieren
rub in, to einreiben
rubber Gummi m.
rubber condom Gummischutz m.
− **-dam instrument** Kofferdam-Instrument n.
− **glove** Gummihandschuh m.
− **sponge** Gummischwamm m.
− **tube** Gummischlauch m.
rubefacient hautrötend; hautrötendes Mittel n.
rubella Röteln f. pl.
rubeola Masern f. pl.; Röteln f. pl.
− **scarlatinosa** Vierte Krankheit f.
rubidium d. e. n.
rubidomycin d. e. n.
rudiment d. e. n.
rudimentary rudimentär

rugine Schaber m.
rule Regel f.
− **slide** Rechenschieber m.
ruler Lineal n.
rumbling Gurren n.
ruminant wiederkäuend; Wiederkäuer m.
rumination Wiederkäuen n.; Aufstoßen n.
rump Steiß m.
Rumpel-Leede phenomenon Rumpel-Leedesches Phänomen n.
run, to rennen; rinnen, triefen
running time Laufzeit f.
rupture Ruptur f.
rupture, to rupturieren
rural ländlich
rush Wallung f.; Welle f.
rust Rost m.
rust, to rosten
rut Brunst f.
ruthenium d. e. n.
rutin d. e. n.
rutoside Rutosid n.

S

sabadilla Sabadille f.
Sabin-Feldman test Sabin-Feldman-Test m.
sabinism Sabinismus m., Sabinaölvergiftung f.
sac Tasche f., Sack m.
−, **dental** Zahnsäckchen n.
saccate sackartig, sackförmig
saccharase d. e. f.
saccharate Saccharat n.
saccharate, to zuckern, mit Zucker versetzen
saccharide Saccharid n.
saccharification Verzuckerung f.
saccharimeter d. e. n.

saccharinol Saccharin n.
Saccharomyces d. e. m.
saccharomycosis Saccharomykose f.
saccharose d. e. f.
saccule Säckchen n.
saccus Sack m., Tasche f.
Sachs-Georgi test Sachs-Georgi-Reaktion f.
sacrad sakralwärts
sacral sakral
− **plexus** Plexus sacralis
sacralization Sakralisation f.
sacrococcygeal sakrokokzygeal
sacroiliac joint Sakroiliakalgelenk n.

sacropelvic sakropelvisch
sacroperineal sakroperineal
sacrouterine sakrouterin
sad traurig
saddle Sattel m.
saddle galls Satteldruck m.
saddle joint Sattelgelenk n.
saddle nose Sattelnase f.
sadism Sadismus m.
sadist Sadist m.; Sadistin f.
sadistic sadistisch
sadness Trauer f., Traurigkeit f., Schwermut f.
sadomasochism Sadomasochismus m.
safe sicher
safety Sicherheit f.
safety belt Sicherheitsgurt m.
– pin Sicherheitsnadel f.
sage Salbei m.
sagittal d. e.
Sahli's desmoid reaction Sahlische Desmoidreaktion f.
Saint Vitus's dance Veitstanz m.
salamander d. e. m.
salicyl Salizyl n.
salicylaldehyde Salizylaldehyd m.
salicylamide Salizylamid n.
salicylate Salizylat n.
salicylazosulfapyridine (a) Salizylazosulfapyridin n.
salicylazosulphapyridine (e) Salizylazosulfapyridin n.
salicylic acid Salizylsäure f.
salicyltherapy Salizyltherapie f.
saline salzig, salzhaltig
salipyrin d. e. n.
saliuretic Saliuretikum n.; saliuretisch
saliva Speichel m.
– suction tube Speichelsaugrohr n.
salivary gland Speicheldrüse f.
salivation d. e. f., Speichelfluß m.
salivatory speicheltreibend
Salmonella d. e.
– enteridis Bazillus enteridis Gärtner

Salmonella hirschfeldii Paratyphus-C-Bazillus m.
– infection Salmonellainfektion f.
– parathyphi Paratyphus-A-Bazillus m.
– schottmülleri Paratyphus-B-Bazillus m.
– typhimurium d. e., Bacillus typhi murium
– typhosa d. e., Typhusbazillus m.
salmonellosis Salmonellose f.
salol d. e. n.
salpingectomy Salpingektomie f.
salpingitic salpingitisch
salpingitis d. e. f.
–,eustachian Entzündung f. der Tuba Eustachii
salpingography Salpingographie f.
salpingo-oophoritis d. e. f.
salpingostomy Salpingostomie f.
salpingotomy Salpingotomie f.
salpingoureterostomy Salpingoureterostomie f.
salpinx d. e. f.
salt Salz n.
saltpeter, saltpetre Salpeter m.
salty salzig
salubrious heilbringend, heilsam
salutarium Kurort m.
salutary heilungsfördernd
salvage Bergung f.
salve Salbe f.
salve, to bergen; salben, mit Salbe einreiben
samarium d. e. n.
sample changer Probenwechsler m.
sanatorium d. e. n.
sanatory heilungsfördernd
sandalwood oil Sandelöl n.
sandblast Sandstrahlgebläse n.
sandfly fever Pappatacifieber n.
sane gesund, geistig normal
sanguifacient blutbildend
sanguiferous bluthaltig
sanguineous blutig
sanguinolent d. e.

sanitarian Gesundheitsfürsorger m.
sanitarium Sanatorium n.
sanitary sanitär
− **inspector** Gesundheitsbeamter m.
− **towel** Monatsbinde f.
sanitation Gesundheitspflege f.
sanity Gesundheit f., geistige Gesundheit f.
santalin d. e. n.
santonin d. e. n.
sap Saft m.
saponaceous seifig
saponification Verseifung f.
saponify, to verseifen
sapphism lesbische Liebe f.
sapraemia (e) septische Intoxikation f.
sapremia (a) septische Intoxikation f.
sapropel Faulschlamm m.
saprohyte Saprophyt m.
saprophytic saprophytär
sarcine Sarzine f.
sarcocele Sarkozele f.
sarcoid sarkoid; Sarkoid n.
− **of Boeck** Boecksches Sarkoid n., Morbus Boeck
sarcoidosis Sarkoidose f.
sarcolemma Sarkolemm n.
sarcoma Sarkom n.
−,**giant cell** Riesenzellsarkom n.
−,**round-celled** Rundzellensarkom n.
−,**spindle-celled** Spindelzellensarkom n.
sacromatosis Sarkomatose f.
sarcomatous sarkomatös
sarcoplasm Sarkoplasma n.
Sarcoptes scabiei Krätzemilbe f.
sarcosome Sarkosom n.
sarcosporidiosis Sarkosporidiose f.
sarsaparilla Sarsaparille f.
sardonic sardonisch
sartian Orientbeule f.
satanic bolete Satanspilz m.
satiate, to sättigen

satiation Sättigung f.
satiation, feeling of − Sättigungsgefühl n.
satiety Sattheit f.
satisfactory zufriedenstellend, befriedigend
satisfy, to zufriedenstellen
saturate, to sättigen
saturated gesättigt
saturation Sättigung f.
saturnism Saturnismus m., Bleivergiftung f.
satyriasis d. e. f.
sauna Sauna f.
sausage poisoning Wurstvergiftung f.
savin oil Sabinaöl n.
savor (a) Geschmack m.
savour (e) Geschmack m.
saw Säge f.
−,**amputating** Amputationssäge f.
− **-edged** gezahnt
−,**plaster** Gipssäge f.
scab Schorf m., Kruste f.
scab, to verschorfen
scabies Krätze f., Skabies f.
scabieticide Krätzeheilmittel n.
scabrities Schuppenhaut f.
scald Verbrühung f.
scald, to verbrühen
− **head** Schuppenkopf m.
scale Schuppe f.; Skala f.; Waagschale f.
scalene node biopsy Skalenus-Lymphknotenbiopsie f.
scalenotomy Skalenusdurchtrennung f.
scalenus syndrome Skalenussyndrom n.
scaler Zahnsteinentferner m.
scaling Zahnsteinentfernung f.
scalp behaarte Kopfhaut f.
scalpel Skalpell n.
−,**dissecting** anatomisches Skalpell n.
scaly schuppig
scammony Skammonium n.

scan, to rastern; abtasten; skandieren, zerlegen
scandium Skandium n.
scanning method Abtastmethode f.
scanning speech skandierende Sprache f.
scaphoid kahnförmig; Kahnbein n.
scapular skapular
scapulohumeral skapulohumeral
scar Narbe f.
scarf-skin Epidermis f.
scarification Skarifikation f.
scarlatiniform skarlatiniform, scharlachähnlich
scarlet fever Scharlach m.
Scarpa's triangle Scarpasches Dreieck n.
scarred narbig
scattered rays Streustrahlen m. pl.
Schapiro's sign Schapirosches Zeichen n.
Schauta's operation Schauta-Operation f.
schedule Tabelle f.
schema d. e. n.
schematic schematisch
Scheuermann's disease Scheuermannsche Krankheit f.
Schick's test Schicktest m.
Schiller's test Schillersche Jodprobe f.
Schistosoma haematobium d. e., Distoma haematobium
schistosomiasis d. e. f.
schizogenesis Schizogenese f.
schizogony Schizogonie f.
schizoid d. e.
schizomycete Schizomyzet m.
schizont d. e. m.
schizophrenia Schizophrenie f.
schizophreniac Schizophrener m., Schizophrene f.
schizophrenic schizophren
schizotrichia Schizotrichie f.
Schlange's sign Schlangesches Zeichen n.

Schlatter's disease Schlattersche Krankheit f.
Schlemm's canal Schlemmscher Kanal m.
Schlesinger's test Schlesingersche Probe f.
Schmorl's nodule Schmorlsches Knötchen n.
Schoemaker's operation Schoemakersche Operation f.
school age Schulalter n.
school for backward children Hilfsschule f.
Schreiber's maneuver Schreiberscher Handgriff m.
Schüffner's punctation Schüffnersche Tüpfelung f.
Schultz-Charlton test Schultz-Charltonsches Auslöschphänomen n.
Schwabach test Schwabachscher Versuch m.
schwannoma Schwannom n.
sciatic nerve Nervus ischiadicus
sciatica Neuritis ischiadica
science Wissenschaft f.
scientific wissenschaftlich
scillaridin Szillaridin n.
scillin Szillin n.
scillitoxin Szillitoxin n.
scintillation Szintillation f.
scintillator Szintillator m.
scirrhous szirrhös
scirrhus Szirrhus m.
scission Schnitt m., Abspaltung f.
scissors Schere f.
–, bandage Verbandschere f.
–, bowel Darmschere f.
–, operating Operationsschere f.
–, postmortem anatomische Schere f.
scissure Splitterung f., Spaltung f.
scleral skleral
sclerectomy Sklerektomie f.
sclerema Sklerem n.
scleritic skleritisch

scleritis (anterior/posterior)
  Skleritis f. (anterior/posterior)
scleroconjunctival sklerokonjunktival
sclerocorneal sklerokorneal
scleroderma Sklerodermie f.
scleroma Sklerom n.
sclerophthalmia Sklerophthalmie f.
sclerose, to sklerosieren
sclerosis Sklerose f.
−,amyotrophic lateral amyotrophische Lateralsklerose f.
−,initial Initialsklerose f.
−,multiple multiple Sklerose f.
−,primary lateral spastische Spinalparalyse f.
−,tuberous tuberöse Sklerose f.
sclerotic sklerotisch
sclerotome Sklerotom n.
sclerotomy Sklerotomie f.
scolex Skolex m.
scoliosis Skoliose f.
scoliotic skoliotisch
scoop Löffel m., Schöpflöffel m.
scopolamine Skopolamin n.
scopolamine hydrobromide
  Scopolaminum hydrobromicum
scorbutic skorbutisch
scorch, to versengen, verbrennen
scours, white weiße Kälberruhr f.
scorpion Skorpion m.
scotoma Skotom n.
−,central zentrales Skotom n.
−,flimmer Flimmerskotom n.
scraper Schaber m.
scratch Schramme f.
scratch, to kratzen, ritzen
scratches Fußekzem (veter.)
screen Schirm m., Schranke f; Sieb n.
−,fluorescent Röntgenschirm m.
screening Überprüfung f.; Abschirmung f.; Siebung f.
screening image Schirmbild n.
− test Siebtest m.

screw Schraube f.
− driver Schraubenzieher m.
−,flat Flachschraube f.
− lock Schraubverschluß m.
scrofuloderma (a) Skrofuloderm n.
scrofulosis (a) Skrofulose f.
scrofulous (a) skrofulös
scrophuloderma (e) Skrofuloderm n.
scrophulosis (e) Skrofulose f.
scrophulous (e) skrofulös
scrotal skrotal
scrotum Skrotum n., Hodensack m.
scrub typhus Buschfleckfieber n.
scruff Genick n.
scurvy Skorbut m.
−,infantile Moeller-Barlowsche Krankheit f.
scute Schuppe f.
sea bath Seebad n.
seal Robbe f.
seam Saum m., Naht f.
seamless nahtlos
search, to forschen
seasickness Seekrankheit f.
sea snake Seeschlange f.
seat Sitz m.
seat belt Sitzgurt m.
seatworm Madenwurm m.
sebaceous talgig
− gland Talgdrüse f.
seborrhea (a) Seborrhöe f.
seborrheal (a) seborrhoisch
seborrheic (a) seborrhoisch
seborrhoea (e) Seborrhöe f.
seborrhoeal (e) seborrhoisch
seborrhoic (e) seborrhoisch
secernent sezernierend
secondary sekundär
secretagogue Secretagogum n., sekretagog
secretary Sekretär m., Sekretärin f.
secrete, to abscheiden, absondern
secretin Sekretin n.

secretion Sekretion f., Absonderung f.; Sekret n.
–, **internal** innere Sekretion f.
secretoinhibitory sekretionshemmend
secretomotory sekretionsfördernd
secretory sekretorisch
section Schnitt m.; Sektion f.; Abschnitt m.
–, **frozen** Gefrierschnitt m.
– **lifter** Schnittfänger m.
–, **serial** Serienschnitt m.
sectional roentgenography Schichtaufnahmeverfahren n.
sector Sektor m.
secundines Nachgeburt f.
sedation Sedierung f., Beruhigung f.
sedative sedativ, beruhigend; Beruhigungsmittel n.
sediment d. e. n.
sedimentation Sedimentierung f., Senkung f.
– **rate** Blutsenkungsgeschwindigkeit f.
sedoheptulose d. e. f.
seed Samen m.; Kapsel f.
seeker Finder m.
seethe, to sieden
segment d. e. n.
segmental d. e.
segmentation Segmentierung f.
segmented segmentiert; segmentkernig
segregation d. e. f., Trennung f.
Sehrt's compressor Sehrtsches Kompressorium n.
Seignette's salt Seignettesalz n.
Seitz filter Seitzfilter m.
seizure Anfall m.
selective selektiv
selenite Selenit n.
selenium d. e. n.
self-digestion Selbstverdauung f.
self-mutilation Selbstverstümmelung f.
self-preservation Selbsterhaltung f.
self-purgation Selbstreinigung f.
self-regulation Selbstregulierung f.
Selivanoff's test Seliwanowsche Probe f.
sella turcica d. e., Türkensattel m.
sellar sellär
semantic semantisch
semantics Semantik f.
semeiological semiologisch
semeiology Semiologie f.
semialdehyde Semialdehyd m.
semiautomatic halbautomatisch
semicarbazone Semikarbazon n.
semicircular canal Bogengang m.
semiconductor Halbleiter m.
semilunar halbmondförmig
semimembranous semimembranös
seminal fluid Samenflüssigkeit f.
seminal vesicle Samenblase f.
– **vesiculitis** Samenblasenentzündung f.
seminar Seminar n.
seminoma Seminom n.
semiological semiologisch
semiology Semiologie f.
semipermeable semipermeabel
semiquantitative semiquantitativ, halbquantitativ
semisynthetic halbsynthetisch
semithiocarbazone Semithiokarbazon n.
senescence Seneszenz f., Altern n.
senescent alternd
senile senil
– **dementia** Altersdemenz f.
senility Senilität f.
senna d. e. f.
sensation d. e. f., Sinneseindruck m.
sensation of touch Berührungsempfindung f.
sense Sinn m.
– **of smelling** Geruchsinn m.
sensibility Sensibilität f.
sensibilization Sensibilisierung f.
sensible sensibel
sensitive sensitiv
sensitivity Sensitivität f.

sensitization Sensibilisierung f.
sensitize, to sensibilisieren
sensorial sensorisch
sensory sensorisch
sensory perception Sinneswahrnehmung f.
separate, to separieren, trennen
separating funnel Scheidetrichter m.
separating instrument Separierinstrument n.
separation Trennung f.
sepharose d. e. f.
sepsis d. e. f.
—, puerperal Puerperalsepsis f.
septal defect of the heart Septumdefekt m. des Herzens
septate septiert, durch eine Trennwand geschieden
septic septisch
septicaemia (e) Septikämie f.
septicemia (a) Septikämie f.
septicopyaemia (e) Septikopyämie f.
septicopyemia (a) Septikopyämie f.
septivalent siebenwertig
septostomy Septostomie f.
septum d. e. n.
sequel Folgeerscheinung f.
sequela Folgeerscheinung f.
sequence Sequenz f.
sequestration Sequestrierung f., Sequesterbildung f.; Isolierung f.
sequestrectomy Sequestrektomie f.
sequestrotomy Sequestrotomie f.
sequestrum Sequester m.
— formation Sequesterbildung f.
serial reihenmäßig
series Serie f.
serine Serin n.
serious seriös; ernst, schwerwiegend
serodiagnosis Serodiagnose f.
serofibrinous serofibrinös
serological serologisch
serology Serologie f.
seromembranous seromembranös

seromucous seromukös
seronegative seronegativ
seropneumothorax d. e. m.
seropositive seropositiv
seroprophylaxis Serumprophylaxe f.
seropurulent d. e.
seroreaction Seroreaktion f.
serosanguineous serosanguinös
serotherapy Serumbehandlung f.
serothorax d. e. m.
serotonin d. e. n.
serous serös
serpent Schlange f.
serpentine cording Zopfbildung f.
serpiginous serpiginös
serrefine Gefäßklemme f.
Sertoli's cell Sertolische Zelle f.
serum d. e. n.
—, antilymphocytic Antilymphozytenserum n.
—, bovine Rinderserum n.
— glutamic oxalacetic transaminase Serum-Glutaminsäure-Oxalessigsäure-Transaminase f.
— glutamic pyruvic transaminase Serum-Glutaminsäure-Brenztraubensäure-Transaminase f.
—, horse Pferdeserum n.
— poisoning Serumvergiftung f.
— sickness Serumkrankheit f.
service for the care of veterans militärische Versorgungsbehörde f.
sesamoid bone Sesambein n.
sesquichloride Sesquichlorid n.
sessile breitbasig aufsitzend
session Sitzung f.
set, to (a dislocation) (eine Verrenkung) einrichten
sever, to abtrennen
severance Abtrennung f.
severely wounded schwer verwundet
severity Härte f., Strenge f., Heftigkeit f.
sew, to nähen
sewerage Abwasser n.

sex Geschlecht n.
sex-chromatin body Geschlechtschromatinkörper m.
− **hormone** Sexualhormon n.
− **infantilism with obesity** Dystrophia adiposogenitalis
− **-linked** geschlechtsgebunden
sexivalent sechswertig
sexological sexologisch
sexologist Sexologe m.
sexology Sexologie f., Sexualwissenschaft f.
sexual sexuell, geschlechtlich
− **desire** Geschlechtstrieb m.
− **intercourse** Geschlechtsverkehr m.
− **neurosis** Sexualneurose f.
sexuality Sexualität f.
shadow Schatten m.
shag (zool.) Kormoran m.
shagreen Chagrin n.
shake, to schütteln, erschüttern
shaking chill Schüttelfrost m.
− **palsy** Schüttellähmung f.
shank Schienbein n.
shape Gestalt f.
shaped gestaltet, geformt
sharp scharf
sharpen, to schärfen
shave, to schaben; rasieren
shear, to scheren; wegschneiden
shears Schere f.
sheath Scheide f., Hülle f.
she-camel Kamelstute f.
shed, to verspritzen; schütten, ausbreiten
Sheehan's syndrome Sheehan-Syndrom n.
sheep Schaf n.
sheeting, rubber Gummituch n.
shelf Leiste f.; Brett n.
shellac Schellack m.
shield Schild m.; Hülse f.; Schutzhülle f., Schutzklappe f.
shift Verschiebung f.
shift work Schichtarbeit f.

Shiga's bacillus Shiga-Kruse-Bazillus m.
Shigella dysenteriae Ruhrbazillus m. (Shiga-Kruse)
− **paradysenteriae Flexner** Ruhrbazillus m. (Flexner)
− **paradysenteriae Strong** Ruhrbazillus m. (Strong)
− **sonnei** Ruhrbazillus m. (Sonne)
shin Schienbeinkante f.; Schienbein n.
− **bone fever** wolhynisches Fieber n.
shingles Zoster m.
shiver Schauer m.
shiver, to erschauern, frösteln
shivering fit Schüttelfrost m.
shock Schock m.
shoe boil (veter.) Ellenbogenhygrom n.
Shoemaker's line Shoemakersche Linie f.
shoot, to erschießen, schießen
short-acting kurzwirkend
short breath schweres Atmen n., Kurzatmigkeit f.
− **circuit** Kurzschluß m.
− **-sighted** kurzsichtig
− **-sightedness** Kurzsichtigkeit f.
− **-term therapy** Kurzzeitbehandlung f., Kurzbehandlung f.
− **wave** Kurzwelle f.
shorten, to kürzen, verkürzen
shortening Verkürzung f.
shortness of breath Atemnot f.
short-term memory Kurzzeitgedächtnis n.
short-winded kurzatmig
shoulder Schulter f.
− **blade** Schulterblatt n.
− **girdle** Schultergürtel m.
− **joint** Schultergelenk n.
shower of reticulocytes Retikulozytenkrise f.
Shrapnell's membrane Shrapnellsche Membran f.
shrink, to schrumpfen, abschwellen

shrinkage Schrumpfung f.
shrivel, to schrumpfen
shroud Leichentuch n.
shudder, to erschauern
shunt d. e. m.; Ablenkung f., Umleitung f., Umschaltung f., Nebenschluß m.
shutter Verschluß m.
sialadenitis d. e. f.
sialogram Sialogramm n.
sialographical sialographisch
sialography Sialographie f.
sialolithiasis d. e. f.
sialorrhea (a) Sialorrhöe f.
sialorrhoea (e) Sialorrhöe f.
sibilant zischend
siblings Geschwister pl.
sibship Blutsverwandtschaft f.
sick krank, unwohl, übel; Kranker m., Kranke f.
– **-bed** Krankenbett n.
– **benefit** Krankengeld n.
– **certificate** Krankenschein m.
– **insurance** Krankenversicherung f.
sickle cell Sichelzelle f.
sickly kränklich
sickness Krankheit f., Unwohlsein n.
sickness insurance Krankenkasse f.
sick-sinus-syndrome kranker Sinusknoten-Syndrom n.
side Seite f.
– **-chain** Seitenkette f.
– **effect** Nebenwirkung f.
– **finding** Nebenbefund m.
– **reaction** Nebenreaktion f.
side to end anastomosis Seit-zu-End-Anastomose f.
– **to side anastomosis** Seit-zu-Seit-Anastomose f.
sideramine Sideramin n.
sideroachrestic sideroachrestisch
siderochrome Siderochrom n.
sideropenia Sideropenie f., Eisenmangel m.

sideropenic sideropenisch
siderophilous siderophil
siderosis Siderose f.
siderotic siderotisch
siderous eisenhaltig
siemens d. e. n.
sieve Sieb n.
sigh, to seufzen, stöhnen
sight Sehen n., Sehvermögen n.
sigmoid flexure Sigmoid n.
sigmoidectomy Sigmoidektomie f.
sigmoiditis d. e. f.
sigmoidopexy Sigmoidopexie f.
sigmoidoproctostomy Sigmoidoproktostomie f.
sigmoidoscopy Sigmoidoskopie f.
sigmoidostomy Sigmoidostomie f.
sign Zeichen n.
– **of disease** Krankheitszeichen n., Krankheitserscheinung f.
– **of life** Lebenszeichen n.
signal d. e. n.
signal lamp Signallampe f.
signature Signatur f.
significance Signifikanz f.
significant signifikant
siken, to ekeln
silica Quarz m.
silicate Silikat n.
silicious earth Kieselgur f.
silicon Silizium n.
silicone Silikon n.
silicone rubber Silikongummi m.
silicosiderosis Silikosiderose f.
silicosis Silikose f.
silicotic silikotisch
silicotuberculosis Silikotuberkulose f.
silk Seide f.
silkworm Seidenraupe f.
silkworm-gut Silkwormgut m.
silkworm gut Seidenraupendarm m.
silo-filler's disease Silofüllerkrankheit f.

silver

silver Silber n.
− impregnation Silberimprägnierung f.
− nitrate Silbernitrat n.
Silvester's method Silvestersche künstliche Atmung f.
simian affenartig
similar ähnlich
similarity Ähnlichkeit f.
Simmonds's disease Simmondssche Krankheit f.
Simonart's thread Simonartscher Strang m.
simple einfach
simplification Vereinfachung f.
simplify, to vereinfachen
Sims' speculum Simssches Spekulum n.
simulate, to simulieren
simulation d. e. f.
simultaneous simultan
− phenomenon Begleiterscheinung f.
sinciput Vorderhaupt n.
sine sinus m.
sinew Sehne f.
sinewy sehnig
single carbon unit Einkohlenstoff-Fragment n.
sinistrocardia Sinistrokardie f.
sinistroposed sinistroponiert
sinistroposition d. e. f.
sinistrosis Explosionsschock m.
sinking Senkung f.
sinu-atrial sinuaurikulär
sinu-auricular sinuaurikulär
sinubronchial d. e.
sinus d. e. m.; Nasennebenhöhle f.
− arrhythmia Sinusarrhythmie f.
−, cavernous Sinus cavernosus
− node Sinusknoten m.
− rhythm Sinusrhythmus m.
sinusitis d. e. f.
−, ethmoidal Sinusitis ethmoidalis
−, frontal Sinusitis frontalis
−, maxillary Sinusitis maxillaris
−, sphenoidal Sinusitis sphenoidalis

222

Sippy treatment Sippykur f.
sisomicin d. e. n.
sister (med.) Stationsschwester f.
sitfast (veter.) Druckgeschwulst f.
sitology Ernährungslehre f.
sitosterol Sitosterin n.
sitting Sitzung f.
situation d. e. f., Lage f.
situs inversus d. e.
− transversus d. e.
sitz bath Sitzbad n.
size Umfang m., Größe f.
Sjogren's syndrome Sjögren-Syndrom n.
skatole Skatol n.
skeletal muscle Skelettmuskel m.
skeletization Skelettierung f.
skeletize, to skelettieren
skeleton Skelett n., Knochengerüst n.
Skene's gland Skenesche Drüse f.
skenitis Entzündung f. der Skeneschen Drüse
skeocytosis Linksverschiebung f.
ski accident Schi-Unfall m.
skiagraphy Röntgenographie f.
skiascopy Skiaskopie f.
skid, bone Knochenschaber m.
skim-milk Magermilch f.
skin Haut f.
skin, to häuten
skin test Hauttest m.
skit Lämmerdiarrhöe f.
skull Schädel m.
− base Schädelbasis f.
− holder Schädelhalter m.
shunk Stinktier n.
slack locker, schlaff, schlotternd; Entspannung f., Spielraum m.
slag Schlacke f.
slaughter, to schlachten
slaughterhouse Schlachthaus n.
slaver Speichel m.
sleep Schlaf m.
sleep, to schlafen
sleepiness Verschlafenheit f.

sleeping disease Narkolepsie f.
− **sickness** Schlafkrankheit f.
sleeplessness Schlaflosigkeit f.
sleepwalker Schlafwandler m., Schlafwandlerin f.
sleepy schläfrig
slender schlank
slide Objektträger m.
slime Schleim m.
slimy schleimig
sling Schlinge f.
slit Spalt m., Schlitz m.
− **lamp** Spaltlampe f.
slitter Schlitzer m.
sloth Faultier n.
slough Schorf m.
sludge, blood Kapillarblutentmischung f.
sluice Schleuse f.
small bowel Dünndarm m.
− **bubble** Bläschen n.
− **gut** Dünndarm m.
smallpox Pocken f. pl., Blattern f. pl.
− **vaccine** Pockenvakzine f.
smear Schmiere f.; Ausstrich m.
smear, to schmieren
smegma d. e. n.
smell Geruch m.
smell, to riechen
Smellie's method Veit-Smelliescher Handgriff m.
smog Nebel m. mit Rauch m.
smoke Rauch m.
smoke, to rauchen
− **inhalation** Rauchinhalation f.
smooth glatt
− **muscle** glatter Muskel m.
snail Schnecke f.
snake Schlange f.
− **bite** Schlangenbiß m.
snare Schnürer m., Schlinge f.
−, **nasal** Nasenschlinge f.
−, **tonsil** Tonsillenschlinge f.
sneeze, to niesen
Snellen's test Snellensche Sehprobe f.

sniffing Schnüffeln n.
snore, to schnarchen
snout Schnauze f., Rüssel m.
snow blindness Schneeblindheit f.
−, **carbon dioxide** Kohlensäureschnee m.
snuff Schnupfpulver n.
soap Seife f.
−, **laundry** Wäscheseife f.
−, **soft** Toilettenseife f.
social sozial
− **health insurance** Sozialversicherung f.
− **worker** Fürsorger m., Fürsorgerin f.
socialization Sozialisation f.
sociology Soziologie f.
socket Aussparung f., Höhle f.
−, **eye** Augenhöhle f.
−, **tooth** Zahnalveole f.
soda d. e. f.
− **lime** Natronkalk m.
− **lye** Natronlauge f.
sodium Natrium n.
− **acetate** Natriumazetat n.
− **benzoate** Natriumbenzoat n.
− **bicarbonate** Natriumbikarbonat n.
− **bisphosphate** Natriumbiphosphat n.
− **bisulfate** (a) Natriumbisulfat n.
− **bisulfite** (a) Natriumbisulfit n.
− **bisulphate** (e) Natriumbisulfat n.
− **bisulphite** (e) Natriumbisulfit n.
− **borate** Natriumborat n., Borax m.
− **bromide** Natriumbromid n.
− **cacodylate** Natriumkakodylat n.
− **carbonate** Natriumkarbonat n., Soda f.
− **chloride** Natriumchlorid n.
− **citrate** Natriumzitrat n.
− **fluorescein** Natriumfluoreszein n.
− **hydroxide** Natriumhydroxyd n.

sodium hypochlorite Natriumhypochlorit n.
- **hyposulfite** (a) Natriumhyposulfit n.
- **hyposulphite** (e) Natriumhyposulfit n.
- **indigotindisulfonate** (a) indigodisulfonsaures Natrium n.
- **indigotinsulphonate** (e) indigodisulfonsaures Natrium n.
- **iodide** Natriumjodid n.
- **molybdate** Natriummolybdat n.
- **nitrate** Natriumnitrat n.
- **nitrite** Natriumnitrit n.
- **perborate** Natriumperborat n.
- **phosphate** Natriumphosphat n.
- **pyrophosphate** Natriumpyrophosphat n.
- **salicylate** Natriumsalizylat n.
- **sulfate** (a) Natriumsulfat n.
- **sulphate** (e) Natriumsulfat n.
- **thiosulfate** (a) Natriumthiosulfat n.
- **thiosulphate** (e) Natriumthiosulfat n.

sodokosis Rattenbißfieber n.
sodoku Rattenbißfieber n.
sodomy Sodomie f.
soft weich
- **metal** Weichmetall n.
- **ray method** Weichstrahltechnik f.
- **tissues** Weichteile n. pl.

soften, to erweichen; lindern
softening Erweichung f.
sol d. e. n.
solanin d. e. n.
solanism Solaninvergiftung f.
solar plexus Plexus solaris
solar power Sonnenenergie f.
solarization Besonnung f., Sonnenbestrahlung f.
solarize, to besonnen, der Sonnenbestrahlung aussetzen
solder Lötmittel n.
solder, to löten
sole Sohle f.
solid d. e., fest
solitary solitär
solubilize, to in Lösung bringen
solubility Löslichkeit f., Lösbarkeit f.
soluble löslich, lösbar
soluble, sparingly schwer löslich
solution Lösung f.
solvable löslich, lösbar
solve, to lösen
solvent lösend; Lösungsmittel n.
somatic somatisch
somatogenic somatogen
somatology Somatologie f.
somatostatin d. e. n.
somatotropic somatotrop
- **hormone** Wachstumshormon n.

somatropin Wachstumshormon n.
somite Primitivsegment n.
somnambulism Somnambulismus m.
somnambulist Schlafwandler m., Schlafwandlerin f.
somniferous schlafbringend
somnipathy Schlafstörung f.
somnolence Somnolenz f.
somnolent d. e.
sonicate, to beschallen
sonographical sonographisch
sonography Sonographie f.
sonorous sonor
sonotomography Sonotomographie f.
soothing schmerzlindernd
soporose soporös
soporous soporös
sorbitol Sorbit m.
sorbose d. e. f.
sore wund; rauh; Geschwür n.; Schanker m.
sore throat rauher Hals m.
sorisin d. e. n.
sorrow Sorge f., Gram m., Kummer m.
sort Gattung f., Art f.
sotalol d. e. n.
souffle blasendes Geräusch n.

sound gesund; Sonde f.;
Schall m., Ton m., Laut m.
- **perception** Schallwahrnehmung f.
- **wave** Schallwelle f.

sour sauer, herb

source of infection Ansteckungsquelle f.

soy bean Soyabohne f.

sozoiodolic acid Sozojodolsäure f.

space Raum m., Zwischenraum m.

spaceflight medicine Raumfahrtmedizin f.

space-occupying raumfordernd

space of Disse Dissescher Raum m.

spare Schonung f.; Einsparung f.

spare, to schonen; einsparen

sparganosis Sparganose f.

sparteine Spartein n.

spasm Spasmus m.

spasmoanalgesic spasmoanalgetisch; Spasmoanalgetikum n.

spasmodic spastisch, krampfhaft

spasmolysis Spasmolyse f.

spasmolytic spasmolytisch

spasmophilia Spasmophilie f.

spasmophilic spasmophil

spastic spastisch

spasticity Spastizität f.

spatula Spatel m.

-, **brain** Gehirnspatel m.

spawn Laich m.

spay, to ovarektomieren

special speziell

specialism Spezialismus m.

specialist Spezialist m., Spezialistin f.; Facharzt m., Fachärztin f.

specialize, to spezialisieren

species Gattung f., Art f.

-, **diuretic** Species diureticae

specific spezifisch

- **gravity** spezifisches Gewicht n.
- **pathogen free** frei von spezifisch-pathogenen Erregern m. pl.

specificity Spezifität f.

specificness Spezifität f.

specillum Sonde f.

specimen Probe f.

spectacles Brille f.

spectral spektral

spectrography Spektrographie f.

spectrometer Spektrometer n.

spectrometric spektrometrisch

spectrometry Spektrometrie f.

spectrophotometer Spektrophotometer n.

spectrophotometric spektrophotometrisch

spectrophotometry Spektrophotometrie f.

spectroscope Spektroskop n.

spectroscopic spektroskopisch

spectroscopy Spektroskopie f.

spectrum Spektrum n.

- **analysis** Spektralanalyse f.

speculum Spekulum n.

-, **ear** Ohrtrichter m.

-, **eye** Augenlidhalter m.

-, **vaginal** Scheidenspekulum n.

speech Sprache f.

- **comprehension** Sprachverständnis n.

sperm Sperma n.

spermatic cord Samenstrang m.

spermatin d. e. n.

spermatoblast d. e. m.

spermatocele Spermatozele f.

spermatocidal spermatozid

spermatocystitis Samenblasenentzündung f.

spermatocyte Spermatozyt m.

spermatogenesis Spermatogenese f.

spermatogenic samenbildend

spermatogone Spermatogonium n.

spermatolysis Spermatolyse f.

spermatolytic spermatolytisch

spermatorrhea (a) Spermatorrhöe f.

spermatorrhoea (e) Spermatorrhöe f.

spermatozoon d. e. n.

spermaturia Spermaturie f.

spermicidal spermizid
spermine Spermin n.
spermiogenesis Spermiogenese f.
spew, to speien
sphacelation Absterben n., Brandigwerden n.
sphacelism Absterben n., Brandigwerden n.
sphaerical (e) sphärisch
sphaerocyte (e) Sphärozyt m.
sphaerocytosis (e) Sphärozytose f.
Sphaerophorus d. e. m.
sphagitis Halsentzündung f.
sphenoid keilförmig
− bone Keilbein n.
sphenoidal d. e.
sphenoparietal d. e.
sphenotemporal d. e.
spherical (a) sphärisch
spherocyte (a) Sphärozyt m.
spherocytosis (a) Sphärozytose f.
spheroid joint Kugelgelenk n.
Spherophorus (a) Sphaerophorus m.
sphincter Sphinkter m., Schließmuskel m.
− of Oddi Sphincter Oddi
sphincterectomy Sphinkterektomie f.
sphincteroplasty Sphinkterplastik f.
sphincterotomy Sphinkterotomie f.
sphingolipidosis Fabrysche Krankheit f.
sphingomyelin d. e. n.
sphingosine Sphingosin n.
sphygmobolometer d. e. n.
sphygmogram Sphygmogramm n.
sphygmograph d. e. m.
sphygmographic sphygmographisch
sphygmography Sphygmographie f.
sphygmomanometer d. e. n., Blutdruckapparat m.
sphygmometer d. e. n.
sphygmotonometer d. e. n.
spica Spica f.

spice Gewürz n.
spider Spinne f.
−, poisonous Giftspinne f.
spike (EEG) Spitzenpotential n.
spina bifida d. e.
spinal d. e.
− column Wirbelsäule f.
− cord Rückenmark n.
− fluid protein Liquoreiweiß n.
− paralysis Spinalparalyse f.
− puncture Lumbalpunktion f.
spindle cell Spindelzelle f.
spine Wirbelsäule f.; Rückgrat n.; Knochenvorsprung m.
− saw Wirbelsäulensäge f.
− sign Kniekußzeichen n.
spinobulbar spinobulbär
spinocerebellar spinozerebellär
spinocortical spinokortikal
spiral Spirale f.
spiramycin d. e. n.
spirillolysis Spirillolyse f.
spirillosis Spirillose f.
spirillum Spirille f.
Spirillum buccale d. e.
spirillum fever Rückfallfieber n.
spirit Spiritus m., Geist m.
spirituous spirituös, geistig
− drinks geistige Getränke n. pl.
Spirochaeta berbera d. e.
− bronchialis d. e.
− dentium d. e.
− forans d. e.
− morsus muris d. e.
− novyi d. e.
− obermeieri d. e.
− pallida d. e.
− refringens d. e.
spirochaete (e) Spirochäte f.
spirochaetosis (e) Spirochätose f.
spirochete (a) Spirochäte f.
spirochetosis (a) Spirochätose f.
spirography Spirographie f.
spirolactone Spirolakton n.
spirometer d. e. n.
spirometric spirometrisch
spirometry Spirometrie f.

spironolactone Spironolakton n.
spissate, to eindicken
spit Auswurf m., Sputum n.
spit, to ausspucken, speien
spittle Speichel m.
splanchnic splanchnisch
– nerve Nervus splanchnicus
splanchnicectomy Splanchnikektomie f.
splanchnicotomy Splanchnikotomie f.
splanchnoptosis Splanchnoptose f.
splayfoot Plattfuß m.
spleen Milz f.
splenectomize, to splenektomieren
splenectomy Splenektomie f.
splenic splenisch
splenitis d. e. f.
splenization Splenisation f.
splenogenic splenogen
splenogenous splenogen
splenomegaly Splenomegalie f., Milzvergrößerung f.
splenoportogram Splenoportogramm n.
splenoportographical splenoportographisch
splenoportography Splenoportographie f.
splenoptosis Splenoptose f.
splint Schiene f.
–, Cramer's Cramerschiene f.
–, plaster Gipsschiene f.
–, Volkmann's Volkmannschiene f.
splint, to schienen
splinter Splitter n.
–, to splittern
splinting Schienung f.
split Spalt m., Riß m.
split, to spalten
split product Spaltprodukt n.
split up, to aufspalten
splitting Spaltung f., Aufspaltung f.
splitting of a heart sound Spaltung f. eines Herztones

spondylarthritis d. e. f.
–, hypertrophic Spondylarthrosis deformans
spondylitic spondylitisch
spondylitis d. e. f.
–, ankylosing Spondylitis ankylopoetica, Bechterewsche Krankheit f.
–, hypertrophic Spondylosis deformans
–, tuberculous Spondylitis tuberculosa
spondylolisthesis Spondylolisthese f.
spondylolysis Spondylolyse f.
spondylosis Spondylose f.
sponge Schwamm m.
– kidney Schwammniere f.
spongioblast d. e. m.
spongioblastoma Spongioblastom n.
spongiocyte Spongiozyt m.
spongioplasm Spongioplasma n.
spongy schwammig
spontaneous spontan
spoon Löffel m.
–, sharp scharfer Löffel m.
sporadic sporadisch
sporal residuum Sporenrest m.
spore d. e. f.
– formation Sporenbildung f.
– forming sporenbildend
sporicidal sporizid, sporenabtötend
sporidium Sporidie f.
sporiferous sporenbildend; sporentragend
sporiparous sporenbildend
sporoblast d. e. m.
sporogony Sporogonie f.
sporomycosis Sporomykose f.
sporotrichosis Sporotrichose f.
sporotrichum Sporotrichon n.
sporozoite Sporozoit m.
sporozoon d. e. n.
sporulation d. e. f., Sporenbildung f.

spot Fleck m., Mal n.
spot diagnosis Anhiebsdiagnose f.
spotted fever Fleckfieber n., Flecktyphus m.
− typhus Fleckfieber n., Flecktyphus m.
sprain Verstauchung f., Bänderzerrung f.
sprain, to verstauchen
spray d. e. m.
spread Spreizung f., Ausbreitung f.
spread, to spreizen, ausspreizen, ausbreiten
spreader Spreizer m.
spring Feder f.; Quelle f.; Frühling m.
− clamp Federklemme f.
springhalt Hahnentritt m. (veter.)
sprinkle, to besprengen, bespritzen
sprue d. e. f.
− (dent.) Gußkanal m.
spur Sporn m.
spurious falsch, unecht
sputum d. e. n.
squalene Squalen n.
squamate schuppig
squamoparietal d. e.
squamous squamös
square Quadrat n., Viereck n.; quadratisch, viereckig
− meter Quadratmeter m.
− root Quadratwurzel f.
squeeze, to quetschen, pressen
squid Tintenfisch m.
squill Szilla f.
squint, to schielen
squirrel Eichhörnchen n.
stab Stich m.
− culture Stichkultur f.
−, to stechen, erstechen
stabile stabil
stabilize, to stabilisieren
stabilizer Stabilisator m.
stable stabil
staff Stab m.
− cell stabkerniger Leukozyt m.

staff doctor Belegarzt m., Belegärztin f.
stag Hirsch m.
stage Stadium n.
stagger, to schwanken
stagnation d. e. f.
stain Farbe f., Farbstoff m.
stain, to färben
staining Färben n., Färbung f.
− method Färbetechnik f.
stainless steel rostfreier Stahl m.
stalagmometer d. e. n.
stalk Stiel m., Stengel m.
stallion Hengst m.
stammer, to stottern
stammering Stottern n.
stanazole Stanazol n.
stanch, to abstoppen, unterdrücken
stand Stand m.; Ständer m.
standard d. e. m.
− deviation Standardabweichung f.
standardization Standardisierung f.
standardize, to standardisieren
standstill Stillstand m.
stannate Stannat n.
stannic zinnhaltig (vierwertig)
stanniferous zinnhaltig
stannous zinnhaltig (zweiwertig)
Stannius' ligature Stanniussche Ligatur f.
stapedectomy Stapedektomie f.
stapediotenotomy Stapediotenotomie f.
staphyledema (a) Uvulaödem n.
staphylococcal sepsis Staphylokokkensepsis f.
staphylococcus Staphylokokkus m.
− albus d. e.
− aureus d. e.
− citreus d. e.
− tetragenus d. e.
staphyloedema (e) Uvulaödem n.
staphylolysin d. e. n.
staphyloma Staphylom n.

staphylomatous staphylomatös
staphylomycin d. e. n.
star Stern m.
starch Stärke f., Amylum n.
– agar Stärkeagar m.
– gel Stärkegel n.
starvation Hungerzustand m., Nahrungsentzug m.
– diet Hungerdiät f.
– edema (a) Hungerödem n.
– oedema (e) Hungerödem n.
– treatment Hungerkur f.
stasis Stase f.
state Zustand m.
– of health Gesundheitszustand m.
static statisch
statics Statik f.
station d. e. f.
stationary stationär
statistic statistisch
statistics Statistik f.
statural gestaltlich
stature Gestalt f., Wuchs m., Größe f.
status lymphaticus d. e.
steady state Fließgleichgewicht n.
steal out, to ausschleichen
steal syndrome Anzapfsyndrom n.
steam Dampf m.
– bath Dampfbad n.
steapsin d. e. n.
steapsinogen d. e. n.
stearate Stearat n.
stearin d. e. n.
steatadenoma Steatadenom n.
steatoma Steatom n.
steatorrhea (a) Steatorrhöe f.
steatorrhoea (e) Steatorrhöe f.
steatosis Steatose f.
steeple head Turmschädel m.
steer, to steuern
steerhorn stomach Stierhornmagen m.
steering Steuerung f.
Stein-Leventhal syndrome Stein-Leventhal-Syndrom n.
stellate ganglion Ganglion stellatum

stellite Stellit n.
Stellwag's sign Stellwagsches Zeichen n.
stem Stamm m., Stiel m.
–, to stauen, zurückdrängen, stemmen
– cell Stammzelle f.
stench Gestank m.
stenocardia Stenokardie f.
stenose, to stenosieren
stenosis Stenose f.
stenotic stenotisch
stepless stufenlos
step photometer Stufenphotometer n.
stercobilin Sterkobilin n.
stercolith Sterkolith m., Kotstein m.
stercoral sterkoral
stercorous sterkorös
stereoagnosis Asterognosie f.
stereoauscultation Stereoauskultation f.
stereochemical stereochemisch
stereochemistry Stereochemie f.
stereognosis Stereognosie f.
stereognostic stereognostisch
stereogram Stereogramm n.
stereoisomerism Stereoisomerie f.
stereometry Stereometrie f.
stereomicroscope Stereomikroskop n.
stereomicroscopic stereomikroskopisch
stereomicroscopy Stereomikroskopie f.
stereophotography Stereophotographie f.
stereoroentgenography Stereoröntgenographie f.
stereoscope Stereoskop n.
stereoscopic stereoskopisch
stereoscopy Stereoskopie f.
stereospecific stereospezifisch
stereotactic stereotaktisch
stereotaxic stereotaktisch

stereotypy Stereotypie f.
sterile steril
sterility Sterilität f.
sterilization Sterilisierung f.
sterilize, to sterilisieren
sterilizer Sterilisator m., Sterilisationsapparat m.
sterilizing agent Sterilisationsmittel n.
sternad sternalwärts
sternal d. e.
– **marrow** Sternalmark n.
– **puncture** Sternalpunktion f.
sternoclavicular sternoklavikular
sternocostal sternokostal
sternopericardial sternoperikardial
sternotomy Sternotomie f.
sternum d. e. n., Brustbein n.
steroid d. e. n.
sterol Sterin n.
stertorous stertorös, schnarchend
stetophone Stetophon n.
stethoscope Stetoskop n., Hörrohr n.
stew, to dünsten
stewed fruit Kompott n.
sthenic sthenisch
sthenometer Kraftmesser m.
stibialism Antimonvergiftung f.
stibiated antimonhaltig
stibiation Antimonbehandlung f.
stibosan d. e. n.
stick, to kleben
sticking plaster Heftpflaster n., Klebepflaster n.
Stierlin's symptom Stierlinsches Zeichen n.
stiff steif
stiffen, to versteifen
stiffening Versteifung f.
stiff-neck Nackensteifigkeit f.
– – **fever** epidemische Genickstarre f.
stigma d. e. n.
stigmatic stigmatisch
stigmatization Stigmatisierung f.

stigmatize, to stigmatisieren
stilbene Stilben n.
stilbestrol (a) Stilböstrol n.
stilboestrol (e) Stilböstrol n.
still, to beruhigen
Still's disease Stillsche Krankheit f.
stillbirth Totgeburt f.
stillborn totgeboren
Stiller's sign Stillersches Zeichen n.
Stilling's nucleus Stillingscher Kern m.
stimulant stimulierend; Stimulans n., Reizmittel n.
stimulate, to stimulieren, reizen
stimulation d. e. f., Stimulierung f., Reizung f.
– **therapy** Reiztherapie f.
stimulator d. e. m.
stimulus Reiz m., Reizmittel n.
–, **subliminal** unterschwelliger Reiz m.
–, **supraliminal** überschwelliger Reiz m.
– **threshold** Reizschwelle f.
sting Stich m.
stink, to stinken
Stintzing's table Stintzingsche Tafel f.
stippling Tüpfelung f.
stir, to umrühren
stirrup Steigbügel m.
stitch Seitenstechen n.
stock Stamm m. (bacteriol.)
stoechiometry Stöchiometrie f.
Stoffel's operation Stoffelsche Operation f.
Stokes' reagent Stokes-Reagens n.
Stokes-Adams disease Adams-Stokesscher Symptomenkomplex m.
stomach Magen m.
–, **cascade** Kaskadenmagen m.
stomach, hourglass Sanduhrmagen m.
stomachal d. e.
stomachic Stomachikum n.

stomatitis d. e. f.
—, aphthous Stomatitis aphthosa
—, catarrhal Stomatitis catarrhalis
—, mercurial Stomatitis mercurialis
—, syphilitic Stomatitis syphilitica
—, ulcerative Stomatitis ulcerosa
—, Vincent's Stomatitis fusospirillaris
stomatology Stomatologie f.
stone Stein m.
stool Stuhl m., Stuhlgang m.
—, fatty Fettstuhl m.
—, pea soup Erbensuppenstuhl m.
—, rice water Reiswasserstuhl m.
stop, to anhalten, aufhalten, stoppen
stopper Stöpsel m.
storage Aufbewahrung f.; Speicherung f.
storage disease Speicherkrankheit f.
store Speicher m.
stored blood konserviertes Blut n.
store, to aufbewahren, speichern, lagern
stork Storch m.
strabismus d. e. m.
strabometry Strabometrie f.
strabotomy Strabotomie f.
straddle Spreizschritt m.
straight gerade
strain Überanstrengung f.; Überstreckung f.; Filtrierung f.; Abart f.
—, to anstrengen; überanstrengen; überstrecken; filtrieren
strainer Filter n., Seiher m.
strait Beckenöffnung f.
strait jacket Zwangsjacke f.
stramonium d. e. n.
strangle, to strangulieren, erwürgen, erdrosseln
strangles Druse f. (veter.)
strangulate, to strangulieren
strangulation d. e. f.
stranguria Strangurie f.
strangury Strangurie f.

strap Gurt m.
stratification Schichtung f.
stratigraphy Schichtaufnahmeverfahren n.
Strauss needle Straußsche Kanüle f.
streaked striemig, streifig
stream Strom m.
strength Kraft f.
— of vision Sehkraft f.
strengthen, to kräftigen
streptococcal infection Streptokokkeninfektion f.
streptococcus Streptokokkus m.
Streptococcus acidi lactici d. e.
—, anhaemolytic (e) Streptococcus anhaemolyticus
—, anhemolytic (a) Streptococcus anhaemolyticus
— brevis d. e.
— erysipelatis d. e.
—, haemolytic (e) Streptococcus haemolyticus
—, hemolytic (a) Streptococcus haemolyticus
— longus d. e.
— mitior d. e.
— mutans d. e.
— puerperalis d. e.
— pyogenes d. e.
— salivarius d. e.
— scarlatinae d. e.
— septicus d. e.
— viridans d. e.
streptodornase d. e. f.
streptokinase d. e. f.
streptolysin d. e. n.
streptomycin d. e. n.
streptomycosis Streptomykose f.
streptonigrin d. e. n.
streptotrichosis Streptotrichose f.
streptothrix d. e. f.
Streptothrix bronchitidis d. e.
— leproides d. e.
streptozotocin d. e. n.
stress d. e. m., Druck m.
stress-bearing area Belastungszone f.

stretch, to dehnen, strecken, recken
stretcher Tragbahre f.; Strecker m.
stretch receptor Dehnungsrezeptor m.
strew, to streuen
striate streifig, gestreift
striated streifig, gestreift
– **body** Corpus striatum
– **muscle** quergestreifter Muskel m.
striation streifige Zeichnung f.
stricture Striktur f.
stridor d. e. m.
stridulous stridorös
string galvanometer Saitengalvanometer n.
stringhalt Hahnentritt m. (veter.)
strip, to auspressen; abstreifen
stripe Streifen m.
striped streifig, gestreift
stroboscopy Stroboskopie f.
Stroganoff's treatment Stroganoffsche Behandlung f.
stroke Schlag m., Anfall m.
– **volume** Schlagvolumen n.
stroma d. e. n.
strong kräftig, stark
– **protein silver** Argentum proteinicum
Strongyloides stercoralis d. e.
strontium d. e. n.
strophanthidin d. e. n.
strophanthin d. e. n.
strophulus d. e. m.
structural strukturell
structure Struktur f.
– **of the body** Körperbau m.
Strümpell's disease Strümpellsche Krankheit f.
struma Kropf m.; Skrofeln f. pl.
strumectomy Strumektomie f.
strumiprival strumipriv
strumiprivic strumipriv
strumiprivous strumipriv
strumitis d. e. f.
strychnine Strychnin n.
– **sulfate** (a) Strychninsulfat n.
– **sulphate** (e) Strychninsulfat n.

strychnism Strychninvergiftung f.
stryphnon d. e. n.
student Student m.; Studentin f.
stump Stumpf m., Stummel m.
– **of a tooth** Zahnstumpf m.
stupid d. e., dumm
–, **to become** verdummen (intrans.)
–, **to make** verdummen (trans.)
stupidity Dummheit f.
stupor d. e. m.
stuporous stuporös
sturdy Drehkrankheit f., Coenurose f.
stutter, to stottern
stuttering Stottern n.
Stuttgart dog plague Stuttgarter Hundeseuche f.
sty Liddrüsenentzündung f.
stye Liddrüsenentzündung f.
stylomaxillary stylomaxillär
styptic styptisch, blutstillend; Styptikum n.
styptol d. e. n.
styracol d. e. n.
subacid subazid
subacidity Subazidität f.
subacromial subakromial
subacute subakut
subalimentation Unterernährung f., Mangelernährung f.
subaortic subaortal
subapical subapikal
subarachnoid subarachnoidal
subauricular subaurikulär
subaxillary subaxillär
subcapital subkapital
subcapsular subkapsulär
subcellular subzellulär
subchondral d. e.
subchoroidal subchorioidal
subchronic subchronisch
subclavian subklavikulär
subclavicular subklavikulär
subclinical subklinisch
subconjunctival subkonjunktival

subconscious bewußtseinsgetrübt; unterbewußt
subconsciousness Bewußtseinstrübung f.
subcortical subkortikal
subcorticography Subkortikographie f.
subcostal subkostal
subcutaneous subkutan
subcutis Subkutis f.
subdiaphragmatic subdiaphragmatisch, subphrenisch
subdural d. e.
subendocardial subendokardial
subendothelial d. e.
subepithelial d. e.
subfascial subfaszial
subfebrile subfebril
subfraction Subfraktion f.
subfrontal d. e.
subgingival d. e.
subglottic subglottisch
subgroup Untergruppe f.
subhepatic subhepatisch
subicteric subikterisch
subinfection Subinfektion f.
subintimal d. e.
subinvolution d. e. f.
subject Subjekt n.
subjective subjektiv
sublethal subletal
sublimate Sublimat n.
sublimation d. e. f., Sublimierung f.
sublime, to sublimieren
subliminal unterschwellig
sublingual d. e.
subluxation d. e. f.
submammary submammär
submandibular submandibulär
submarine submarin, unterseeisch, unter dem Flüssigkeitsspiegel gelegen
submaxillary submaxillär
submersion Untertauchen n.; Ertrinken n.
submicroscopical submikroskopisch
submitochondrial d. e.
submucosal submukös
submucous submukös
subnarcotic subnarkotisch
subnormal d. e.
subnutrition Fehlernährung f.
suboccipital subokzipital
suborbital d. e.
subordinate, to unterordnen
subpatellar d. e.
subpericardial subperikardial
subperiosteal subperiostal
subperitoneal d. e.
subphrenic subphrenisch
subpleural d. e.
subscapular subskapulär
subscleral subskleral
subsequent nachfolgend
– **treatment** Weiterbehandlung f.
subserous subserös
subside, to abklingen
subsidence Abklingen n.
subspecies Unterart f.
substance Substanz f.
–, **effective** Wirkstoff m.
substantial substantiell
substernal d. e.
substitute Ersatz m.
substitute, to substituieren
substitution d. e. f.
substrate Substrat n.
substructure Substruktur f.
subtarsal d. e.
subtegumental subkutan
subtemporal d. e.
subtentorial d. e.
subthalamic subthalamisch
subthreshold stimulus unterschwelliger Reiz m.
subtile subtil
subtle subtil
subtotal d. e.
subtrochanteric subtrochanterisch
subtype Subtypus m.
subungual d. e.
suburethral d. e.
subvaginal d. e.

subvalvular subvalvulär
subvolution Umstülpung f.
subwaking halbwach
succedaneous teeth bleibendes Gebiß n.
succenturiate behelfsmäßig
success Erfolg m.
successful erfolgreich
succession Nachfolge f., Aufeinanderfolge f.
successive sukzessiv, aufeinanderfolgend
succinase Sukzinase f.
succinimide Sukzinimid n.
succinyl Sukzinyl n.
sucorrhea (a) Sukorrhöe f.
sucorrhoea (e) Sukorrhöe f.
succusion, hippocratic Succussio Hippocratis
suck, to saugen, einsaugen, aussaugen, absaugen; säugen, stillen
suckle, to säugen, stillen
suckling Säugling m.
sucrase Sukrase f.
sucrose Saccharose f., Rohrzucker m., Sukrose f.
suction Sog m., Saugen n.
– apparatus Saugapparat m.
– biopsy Saugbiopsie f.
– drainage Saugdrainage f.
sudamina Schweißbläschen n.
sudan d. e. n.
sudanophilia Sudanophilie f.
sudarium Schwitzbad n.
sudation Schwitzen n.
sudatoria Hyperhidrose f.
sudatorium Schwitzbad n.
Sudeck's atrophy Sudecksche Atrophie f.
sudoriferous schweißbildend
sudorific schweißtreibend; schweißtreibendes Mittel n.
sudoriparous schweißbildend
sudoriparous gland Schweißdrüse f.
suet Talg m.
suffer, to leiden, klagen, erdulden, kranken

sufficient suffizient
suffocate, to ersticken
suffocation Erstickung f.
suffusion d. e. f.
sugar Zucker m.
– tolerance Zuckertoleranz f.
suggest, to vorschlagen, anregen, andeuten; suggerieren
suggestibility Suggestibilität f.
suggestible suggestibel
suggestion Vorschlag m., Anregung f., Andeutung f.; Suggestion f.
suggestive suggestiv
sugillation d. e. f.
suicidal suizidal, selbstmörderisch
suicide Suizid m., Selbstmord m.
suit, operating Operationskleidung f.
sulcate gefurcht, furchig
sulcated gefurcht
sulfadiazine (a) Sulfadiazin n.
sulfadimethoxine (a) Sulfadimethoxin n.
sulfaguanidine (a) Sulfaguanidin n.
sulfamerazine (a) Sulfamerazin n.
sulfamethazine (a) Sulfamethazin n.
sulfamethoxazole (a) Sulfamethoxazol n.
sulfamethoxydiazine (a) Sulfamethoxydiazin n.
sulfamethoxypyrazine (a) Sulfamethoxypyrazin n.
sulfamethoxypyridazine (a) Sulfamethoxypyridazin n.
sulfamezathine (a) Sulfamezathin n.
sulfanilamide (a) Sulfanilamid n.
sulfaphenazol (a) d. e. n.
sulfapyridine (a) Sulfapyridin n.
sulfapyrimidine (a) Sulfapyrimidin n.
sulfasomidine (a) Sulfasomidin n.
sulfate (a) Sulfat n.
sulfhydrate (a) Sulfhydrat n.
sulfhydryl (a) d. e. n.
sulfide (a) Sulfid n.
sulfite (a) Sulfit n.

sulfmethemoglobin (a) Sulfmethämoglobin n.
sulfo-acid (a) Sulfosäure f.
sulfocysteine (a) Sulfozystein n.
sulfokinase (a) d. e. f.
sulfonamide (a) Sulfonamid n.
− **-resistant** (a) sulfonamidresistent
sulfone (a) Sulfon n.
sulfonyl (a) d. e. n.
sulfonylurea (a) Sulfonylharnstoff m.
sulformethoxine (a) Sulformethoxin n.
sulfo-urea (a) Thioharnstoff m.
sulfoxide (a) Sulfoxid n.
sulfoximine (a) Sulfoximin n.
sulfur (a) Schwefel m.
− **bath** (a) Schwefelbad n.
− **hydride** (a) Schwefelwasserstoff m.
−, **precipitated** (a) Sulfur praecipitatum
−, **sublimed** (a) Sulfur sublimatum
sulfurated (a) schwefelhaltig
sulfuric (a) schwefelhaltig (vierwertig, sechswertig)
− **acid ester** (a) Schwefelsäureester m.
sulfurous (a) schwefelhaltig (zweiwertig)
sulph... (e) look for:/siehe bei: sulf... (a)
sulphmethaemoglobin (e) Sulfmethämoglobin n.
sultam compound Sultam-Verbindung f.
summation d. e. f., Summierung f.
summer cholera Sommerbrechdurchfall m.
summit Scheitel m.
sun bath Sonnenbad n.
sunburn Sonnenbrand m.
superacid superazid
superacidity Superazidität f.
superactivity Superaktivität f., übermäßige Tätigkeit f.

superalimentation Überernährung f.; Mastkur f.
superannuation Überalterung f.
super-ego d. e. n., Über-Ich n.
superfat, to überfetten
superfecundation Superfekundation f.
superfetation (a) Superfötation f.
superficial oberflächlich
superfoetation (e) Superfötation f.
superhuman übermenschlich
superimpose, to überlagern
superinfect, to superinfizieren
superinfection Superinfektion f.
superlethal superletal
supermotility Supermotilität f.
supernormal d. e., übernormal
supernumerary überzählig
supernutrition Überfütterung f., Überernährung f.
superovulation d. e. f.
superphosphate Superphosphat n.
supersaturate, to übersättigen
supersaturation Übersättigung f.
supersecretion Supersekretion f.
supersoft überweich
supersonic speed Überschallgeschwindigkeit f.
supervirulent d. e.
supervision Überwachung f.
− **by X-ray examination** Röntgenüberwachung f., Röntgenkontrolle f.
supinate, to supinieren
supination d. e. f.
supple gelenkig
supplemental supplementär, ergänzend
supplementary supplementär, ergänzend
supplementation Ergänzung f., Vervollständigung f.
supplied with blood (well/poorly) (gut/schlecht) durchblutet
supply Versorgung f.; Vorrat m.; Abhilfe f.
supply area Versorgungsgebiet n.

support Stütze f.
support, to stützen
suppository Suppositorium n., Zäpfchen n.
suppress, to unterdrücken
suppressant unterdrückend; unterdrückendes Mittel n.
suppressible unterdrückbar
suppression Unterdrückung f.
suppurate, to eitern, vereitern
suppuration Eiterung f., Vereiterung f., Eiterbildung f.
supraauricular supraaurikulär
supraaxillary supraaxillär
supraclavicular supraklavikulär
supracondylar suprakondylär
supradiaphragmatic supradiaphragmatisch
supraglottic supraglottisch
suprahisian oberhalb des His-Bündels
suprainguinal d. e.
supraliminal überschwellig
supramalleolar supramalleolär
supramammary supramammär
supramandibular supramandibulär
supramaxillary supramaxillär
supraorbital d. e.
suprapatellar d. e.
suprapubic suprapubisch
suprarenal d. e.
suprarenal cortex Nebennierenrinde f.
suprascapular supraskapulär
suprasellar suprasellär
supraspinal d. e.
supraspinous supraspinal
suprasternal d. e.
supratemporal d. e.
suprathoracic suprathorakal
supratonsillar supratonsillär
supravaginal d. e.
supravalvular supravalvulär
supraventricular supraventrikulär
supravital d. e.
suralimentation Überernährung f.

surdimutism Taubstummheit f.
surdity Taubheit f.
surdomute taubstumm
surexcitation Übererregung f.
surface Oberfläche f.
surface active oberflächenaktiv
–, **grinding** Kaufläche f.
–, **masticatory** Kaufläche f.
–, **occlusal** Okklusalfläche f., Kaufläche f.
– **tension** Oberflächenspannung f.
– **therapy** Oberflächentherapie f.
surgeon Chirurg m.
surgery Chirurgie f.
–, **abdominal** Bauchchirurgie f.
–, **cerebral** Hirnchirurgie f.
–, **cosmetic** kosmetische Chirurgie f.
–, **emergency** Notfallchirurgie f.
–, **general** allgemeine Chirurgie f.
–, **major** große Chirurgie f.
–, **minor** kleine Chirurgie f.
–, **oral** Mundchirurgie f.
–, **plastic** plastische Chirurgie f.
surgery consultation Sprechstundenberatung des praktischen Arztes
surgical chirurgisch
surra d. e. f.
surrenal suprarenal; Nebenniere f.
surrogate Surrogat n., Ersatz m., Ersatzstoff m.
surroundings Umgebung f., Umwelt f., Milieu n.
sursumduction Sursumduktion f.
sursumvergence Sursumvergenz f.
sursumversion d. e. f.
survey Überblick m.
survival Überleben n.
– **rate** Überlebensrate f.
– **time** Überlebenszeit f.
survive, to überleben
survivor Überlebender m., Überlebende f.
susceptibility Empfänglichkeit f., Anfälligkeit f.
susceptible empfänglich, anfällig

suscitation Exzitation f.
suspect, to argwöhnen, in Verdacht haben, vermuten
suspect verdächtig
suspension d. e. f.
suspensory Suspensorium n.
− ligament of lens Linsenaufhängeapparat m.
suspicion Verdacht m.
suspicious verdächtig; mißtrauisch
sustain, to stützen
sustentacular stützend
suturation Nähen n.
suture Naht f.
−, button Knopfnaht f.
− clip Wundklammer f.
− instrument Klammernahtinstrument n.
−, continued fortlaufende Naht f.
−, Gussenbauer's Gussenbauersche Naht f.
−, interrupted Einzelnaht f.
−, lead plate Bleiplattennaht f.
−, Lembert's Lembertnaht f.
−, nerve Nervennaht f.
−, primary Primärnaht f.
−, secondary Sekundärnaht f.
−, sunk versenkte Naht f.
−, tobacco bag Tabakbeutelnaht f.
sutureless nahtlos
suxamethonium d. e. n.
suxethonium d. e. n.
swamp fever Schlammfieber n.
swab Tupfer m.
swallow, to schlucken
sway, to schwanken
sweat Schweiß m.
−, to schwitzen
sweat gland Schweißdrüse f.
sweating Schwitzen n.
sweeny (veter.) Atrophie f. der Schultermuskulatur
swell, to schwellen, aufblähen
swelling Schwellung f., Geschwulst f.
swim, to schwimmen
swimbladder Schwimmblase f.

swine Schwein n.
switch Schalter m.
−, to schalten
− off, to ausschalten
− on, to einschalten
swoon Ohnmacht f.
swooning ohnmächtig
sycose Saccharin n.
sycosis Sykose f.
− vulgaris d. e.
Sydenham's chorea Chorea Sydenham f.
syllable stumbling Silbenstolpern n.
sylviduct Aquaeductus Sylvii
symbiont d. e. m.
symbiosis Symbiose f.
symbiotic symbiotisch
symblepharon d. e. n.
symbol d. e. n.
symbolic symbolisch
symbolic language Symbolsprache f.
symbolism Symbolismus m.
symbolization Symbolisierung f.
symbolize, to symbolisieren
symmetrical symmetrisch
symmetry Symmetrie f.
sympathectomy Sympathektomie f.
sympathetic sympathisch; Sympathikus m.
− block Sympathikusblockade f.
sympathicoblastoma Sympathikoblastom n.
sympathicolytic sympathikolytisch
sympathicotonia Sympathikotonie f.
sympathicotonic sympathikotonisch
sympathicotropic sympathikotrop
sympathin d. e. n.
sympathomimetic sympathikomimetisch
symphysiotomy Symphyseotomie f.
symphysis Symphyse f.

symptom d. e. n.
symptomatic symptomatisch
symptomatology Symptomatologie f.
symptomless symptomlos
symptoms, complex of – Symptomenkomplex m.
synapse d. e. f.
synapsis Synapse f.
synaptic synaptisch
synarthrosis Synarthrose f.
syncardial synkardial
synchondrosis Synchondrose f.
synchrocyclotron Synchrozyklotron n.
synchronia Synchronie f.
synchronize, to synchronisieren
synchronous synchron
synchysis Synchyse f.
synclitic synklitisch
synclitism Synklitismus m.
syncliticism Synklitismus m.
syncopal synkopal
syncope Synkope f.; Ohnmachtsanfall m., Anfall m.
syncytial synzytial
syncytium Synzytium n.
syndactylia Syndaktylie f.
syndactylism Syndaktylie f.
syndactyly Syndaktylie f.
syndesmosis Syndesmose f.
syndesmotome Syndesmotom n.
syndrome Syndrom n.
syndrome of Budd-Chiari Budd-Chiari-Syndrom n.
syndrome of Hamman-Rich Hamman-Rich-Syndrom n.
syndrome of Mallory-Weiss Mallory-Weiss-Syndrom n.
syndrome of Meigs Meigs-Syndrom n.
syndrome of Moschcowitz Moschcowitz-Syndrom n.
syndromic syndromisch
synechia Synechie f.
– anterior vordere Synechie f.
– posterior hintere Synechie f.

synergetic synergetisch
synergic synergisch
synergistic synergistisch
synergy Synergie f.
syngamy Syngamie f.
synkinesis Synkinese f.
synkinetic synkinetisch
synostosis Synostose f.
synovia d. e. f., Gelenkschmiere f.
synovial d. e.
synovial bursa Schleimbeutel m.
synovioma Synoviom n.
synovitis d. e. f.
syntactical syntaktisch
synthesis Synthese f.
synthesize, to synthetisieren
synthetase d. e. f.
synthetic synthetisch
– wool Zellwolle f.
syntonic synton, syntonisch
syphilid d. e. n.
syphilide Syphilid n.
syphilis d. e. f.
–, cardiovascular kardiovaskuläre Syphilis f.
–, cerebrospinal zerebrospinale Syphilis f.
–, congenital angeborene Syphilis f.
–, latent early Frühsyphilis f.
–, mucocutaneous Haut- und Schleimhautsyphilis f.
–, neuro- Neurosyphilis f.
–, ocular Augensyphilis f.
–, primary Syphilis I f.
–, secondary Syphilis II f.
–, tertiary Syphilis III f.
–, visceral viszerale Syphilis f.
syphilitic syphilitisch
– hard chancre syphilitischer Primäraffekt m.
syphiloderm Syphiloderma n.
syphilogenous syphilogen
syphilological syphilologisch
syphilologist Syphilologe m.
syphilology Syphilologie f.
syphiloma Syphilom n.

syphilophobia Syphilophobie f.
syphilosis Syphilose f.
Syrian hamster Goldhamster m.
syringe Spritze f.
–, aural Ohrspritze f.
–, disposable Einmalspritze f.
–, injection Injektionsspritze f.
–, to spritzen
syringitis d. e. f.
syringomyelia Syringomyelie f.

syrup Sirup m.
system d. e. n.
systematic systematisch
systematization Systematisierung f.
systematize, to systematisieren
systematology Systematologie f.
systemic systemisch, systematisch
systole d. e. f.
systolic systolisch

T

tab Lasche f., Klappe f.
tabacosis Tabakose f., Tabakstaubvergiftung f.
tabagism Tabakvergiftung f., Nikotinvergiftung f.
tabes d. e. f.
tabetic tabisch
tabic tabisch
tabid tabisch
table Tafel f.; Tisch m.
–, instrument Instrumententisch m.
tablespoon Eßlöffel m.
tablet Tablette f.
tablier Hottentottenschürze f.
taboo Tabu n.
taboparalysis Taboparalyse f.
taboparesis Taboparalyse f.
tabule Tablette f.
tache Fleck m.
tachetic fleckig
tachistoscopic tachistoskopisch
tachistoscopy Tachistoskopie f.
tachyarrhythmia Tachyarhythmie f.
tachycardia Tachykardie f.
–, paroxysmal paroxysmale Tachykardie f.
–, sinus Sinustachykardie f.
tachycardiac tachykard

tachyphylaxis Tachyphylaxie f.
tachypnea (a) Tachypnoe f.
tachypnoea (e) Tachypnoe f.
tachysterol Tachysterin n.
tachysystoly Tachysystolie f.
tactile taktil
taction Berührung f.; Berührungssinn m.
tactual taktil
taenia Tänie f.; Streifen m., Band n.
Taenia echinococcus d. e.
– saginata d. e.
– solium d. e.
taeniacide (e) bandwurmtötend; bandwurmtötendes Mittel n.
taeniafuge (e) bandwurmtreibend; bandwurmtreibendes Mittel n.
taeniasis (e) Tänienbefall m., Bandwurmerkrankung f.
tag, to anhängen; etikettieren
tail Schwanz m.
Takata-Ara test Takata-Ara-Reaktion f.
Takayam's disease Aortenbogensyndrom n.
talc Talk m.
talent d. e. n.

talipes calcaneovalgus Pes calcaneovalgus
− calcaneovarus Pes calcaneovarus
− calcaneus Pes calcaneus
− cavus Pes cavus
− equinovalgus Pes equinovalgus
− equinovarus Pes equinovarus
− equinus Pes equinus
− planovalgus Pes planovalgus
− planus Pes planus
− valgus Pes valgus
− varus Pes varus
talipomanus Klumphand f.
tallow Talg m.
talon Kralle f., Klaue f.
talotibial d. e.
tamarind Tamarinde f.
tampon d. e. m.
tamponade d. e. f.
tamponing Tamponade f.
tamponment Tamponade f.
tan Sonnenbräune f.
tan, to bräunen, gerben
tank d. e. m.
tannate Tannat n.
tannin d. e. n.
tansy Tanacetum n.
tantalum Tantal n.
tap Pochen n., Klopfen .; Punktion f.; ostindisches Dschungelfieber n.
−, to pochen, klopfen; abzapfen, punktieren
tape Band n., Streifen m.; Pflaster n.
− measure Bandmaß n.
tapeworm Bandwurm n.
tar Teer m.
tarantula Tarantel f.
taraxein d. e. n.
Tardieu's spot Tardieuscher Fleck m.
target Bremsklotz m.; Antikathode f.; Zielscheibe f.
target cell Zielscheibenzelle f., Schießscheibenzelle f.
Tarnier's forceps Tarniersche Zange f.

tarsal d. e.
tarsalgia Tarsalgie f.
tarsitis d. e. f.
tarsus Fußwurzel f.; Lidknorpel m.
tart Torte f., Fruchttorte f.; sauer, herb, schroff
Tart cell Tart-Zelle f.
tartar Zahnstein m.; Weinstein m.
tartrate Tartrat n.
taste Geschmack m.
−, to schmecken
tasteless geschmacklos
tastelessness Geschmacklosigkeit f.
tattoo Tätowierung f.
taurine Taurin n.
taurocholate Taurocholat n.
tautomeral tautomer
tautomeric tautomer
tautomerism Tautomerie f.
Tawara's node Aschoff-Tawara-Knoten m.
Tay-Sachs' disease Tay-Sachssche Krankheit f.
tea Tee m.
tear Träne f.; Riß m.
− sac Tränensack m.
−, to reißen
tease, to zupfen
teaspoon Teelöffel m.
teat Brustwarze f., Zitze f.
technetate Technetat n.
technetium d. e. n.
technic Technik f.
technical technisch
− dentist Zahntechniker m.
technician Techniker m.
technology Technologie f.
tectonic tektonisch
teel oil Sesamöl n.
teeth, (upper/lower) (oberes/unteres) Gebiß n.
−, to zahnen
teething Zahnung f., Dentition f.
Teichmann's crystal Teichmannscher Kristall m.
teichopsia Teichopsie f.
telangiectasia Teleangiektasie f.

telangiectatic teleangiektatisch
telecobalt irradiation Telekobaltbestrahlung f.
telediastolic telediastolisch, enddiastolisch
telegamma therapy Telegamma-Therapie f.
telegony Telegonie f.
telemetering Fernmessung f.
telemetry Fernmessung f.
telencephalon Endhirn n.
teleological teleologisch
teleology Teleologie f.
telepathy Telepathie f.
teleroentgenogram Teleröntgenogramm n.
teleroentgenography Teleröntgenographie f.
telescope Teleskop n.
telesystolic telesystolisch, endsystolisch
television Fernsehen n.
tellurate Tellurat n.
tellurite Tellurit n.
tellurium Tellur n.
telodendron d. e. n.
temper Gemüt n.
temper, to durchmischen; abstimmen; härten
temperament d. e. n.
temperature Temperatur f.
– graphic chart Fieberkurve f., Temperaturkurve f.
temple Schläfe f.
temporal d. e.
– lobe Temporallappen m.
temporary temporär, zeitweilig
– tooth Milchzahn m.
temporoauricular temporoaurikulär
temporofrontal d. e.
temporomandibular temporomandibulär
temporooccipital temporookzipital
temporoparietal d. e.
temulence Trunkenheit f.
tenacious festhaftend

tender empfindlich, zart, schwächlich
tender on pressure druckempfindlich, druckschmerzhaft
tender to the touch berührungsempfindlich
tendinitis d. e. f.
tendinoplasty Sehnenplastik f.
tendinous sehnig
tendon Sehne f.
– sheath Sehnenscheide f.
tendoplasty Sehnenplastik f.
tendosynovitis Tendovaginitis f.
tendovaginitis d. e. f., Sehnenscheidenentzündung f.
tenesmus d. e. m.
tenia (a) Tänie f.
teniacide (a) bandwurmtötend; bandwurmtötendes Mittel n., Bandwurmmittel n.
teniafuge (a) bandwurmtreibend; bandwurmtreibendes Mittel n., Bandwurmmittel n.
teniasis (a) Tänienbefall m., Bandwurmerkrankung f.
Tenon's capsule Tenonsche Kapsel f.
tenosuture Sehnennaht f.
tenosynovitis Tendovaginitis f.
tenotome Tenotom n.
tenotomize, to tenotomieren
tenotomy Tenotomie f.
tense rigid; straff
tension Spannung f.; Streckung f.
– state Spannungszustand m.
tensor Strecker m.
tent Zelt n.
–, laminaria Laminariastift m.
tentorial tentoriell
tepidarium Schwitzbad n.
teratic teratisch
teratism Mißbildung f.
teratoblastoma Teratoblastom n.
teratogenic teratogen
teratogenicity Teratogenität f.
teratological teratologisch
teratology Teratologie f.

teratoma Teratom n.
teratosis Teratose f.
terbium d. e. n.
terchloride Trichlorid n.
terebration Bohren n.
term Termin n.
terminad endwärts
terminal d. e.
termination Endigung f.; Beendigung f.
terminological terminologisch
terminology Terminologie f.
ternary ternär
terpene Terpen n.
terpin d. e. n.
tertiary tertiär
tesla d. e. n.
test d. e. m., Versuch m., Probe f.
— breakfast Probefrühstück n.
— meal Probemahlzeit f.
— paper Reagenzpapier n.
— person Versuchsperson f.
— tube Reagenzglas n.
testicle Hoden m.
testicular testikulär
— hormone männliches Keimdrüsenhormon n.
testosterone Testosteron n.
tetanic tetanisch
tetanus d. e. m., Wundstarrkrampf m.
— antitoxin Tetanusantitoxin n.
tetany Tetanie f.
tetrabasic tetrabasisch, vierbasisch
tetrabenazine Tetrabenazin n.
tetrabutyl d. e. n.
tetrachloride Tetrachlorid n.
tetracosactide Tetracosactid n.
tetracosapeptide Tetracosapeptid n.
tetracycline Tetracyclin n.
tetradecylamine Tetradecylamin n.
tetraethyl lead Tetraäthylblei n.
tetraethylammonium bromide Tetraäthylammoniumbromid n.
tetrafluoroborate Tetrafluoroborat n.

tetrahydrofolate Tetrahydrofolat n.
tetrahydrofurfuryldisulfide (a) Tetrahydrofurfuryldisulfid n.
tetrahydrofurfuryldisulphide (e) Tetrahydrofurfuryldisulfid n.
tetraiodothyronine Tetrajodthyronin n.
tetralogy of Fallot Fallotsche Tetralogie f.
tetranitrol d. e. n.
tetraplegia Tetraplegie f.
tetravalent vierwertig
tetrazolium d. e. n.
tetrose d. e. f.
tetroxide Tetroxid n., Tetroxyd n.
tetter Flechte f., Hautflechte f.
texture Gewebe n.; Struktur f.
thalamic thalamisch
thalamocortical thalamokortikal
thalamolenticular thalamolentikulär
thalamotomy Thalamotomie f.
thalamus d. e. m.
thalassaemia (e) Thalassämie f.
thalassanaemia (e) Cooley-Anämie f.
thalassanemia (a) Cooley-Anämie f.
thalassemia (e) Thalassämie f.
thalassotherapy Thalassotherapie f.
thalidomide Thalidomid n.
thallium d. e. n.
thallotoxicosis Thalliumvergiftung f.
thanatology Thanatologie f.
thebaine Thebain n.
theca cell Thekazelle f.
thecitis Sehnenscheidenentzündung f.
thecoma Thekazellentumor m.
theelin Östron n.
theelol Östriol n.
theine Thein n.
thelitis Brustwarzenentzündung f.
thelytocous thelytokisch
thenar eminence Daumenballen m.

theobromine Theobromin n.
theophylline Theophyllin n.
theorem d. e. n.
theoretical theoretisch
theory Theorie f.
therapeutic therapeutisch
therapeutic range therapeutische Breite f.
therapeutics Therapie f., Heilmethode f., Behandlung f.
therapeutist Therapeut m., Therapeutin f.
therapy Therapie f.
– **aimed** gezielte Therapie f.
–, **deep action** Tiefentherapie f.
–, **occupational** Beschäftigungstherapie f.
therm kleine Kalorie f.
termaesthesia (e) Thermästhesie f.
thermal d. e.
thermalgesia Thermalgesie f.
thermalgia Thermalgie f.
thermanaesthesia (e) Thermanästhesie f.
thermanesthesia (a) Thermanästhesie f.
thermesthesia (a) Thermästhesie f.
thermic thermisch
thermoanalgesia Thermoanalgesie f.
thermocautery Thermokaustik f.
thermochemistry Thermochemie f.
thermocoagulation Thermokoagulation f.
thermodilution d. e. f.
thermodynamic thermodynamisch
thermodynamics Thermodynamik f.
thermoelectric thermoelektrisch
thermogenesis Wärmebildung f.
thermogenetic wärmebildend
thermography Thermographie f.
thermoplacentography Thermoplazentographie f.
thermolabile thermolabil
thermoluminescence Thermolumineszenz f.

thermometer d. e. n.
thermometric thermometrisch
thermometry Thermometrie f., Temperaturmessung f.
thermophil d. e.
thermophilic thermophil
thermophobia Thermophobie f.
thermophore Thermophor m.
thermoprecipitation Thermopräzipitation f.
thermoregulation Thermoregulation f., Wärmeregulation f.
thermoregulatory wärmeregulierend
thermoresistant thermoresistent, hitzebeständig
thermostabile thermostabil
thermostat d. e. m.
thermotropism Thermotropie f.
thesaurismosis Speicherkrankheit f.
thesaurosis Speicherkrankheit f.
thiabutazide Thiabutazid n.
thiadiazole Thiadiazol n.
thiamine Aneurin n.
thiaxanthene Thiaxanthen n.
thiazide Thiazid n.
thiazole Thiazol n.
thick dick; dicht; trüb
thicken, to verdicken, eindicken
Thiersch's graft Thiersch-Transplantation f.
thigenol d. e. n.
thigh Oberschenkel m.
thin dünn
–, **to** verdünnen
thin-layer electrophoresis Dünnschichtelektrophorese f.
thinning Verdünnung f.
thioacetamide Thioacetamid n.
thio acid Thiosäure f.
thiocarbamide Thioharnstoff m.
thiocarlide Thiocarlid n.
thiocyanate Thiozyanat n.
thiodeoxyguanosine Thiodeoxyguanosin n.
thiodeoxyinosine Thiodeoxyinosin n.

thioether Thioäther m.
thioglucose Thioglukose f.
thioguanine Thioguanin n.
thiol d. e. n.
thionin d. e. n.
thiopentone Thiopenton n.
thiophene Thiophen n.
thioridazine Thioridazin n.
thiosemicarbazone Thiosemikarbazon n.
thiosulfate (a) Thiosulfat n.
thiosulphate (e) Thiosulfat n.
thiouracil d. e. n.
thio-urea Thioharnstoff m.
thirst Durst m.
– for pleasure Genußsucht f.
Thoma-Zeiss counting cell Thoma-Zeiß-Zählkammer f.
Thomas' pessary Thomas-Pessar n.
Thomsen's disease Thomsensche Krankheit f.
thoracal thorakal
thoracentesis Thorakozentese f.
thoracic thorakal
– spinal column Brustwirbelsäule f.
– surgery Thoraxchirurgie f.
– vertebra Brustwirbel m.
thoracocautery Thorakokaustik f.
thoracolysis Thorakolyse f.
thoracoscopy Thorakoskopie f.
thoracostomy Thorakostomie f.
thoracotomy Thorakotomie f.
thorax d. e. m.
thorium d. e. n.
Thormählen's test Thormählensche Probe f.
thorter ill Springkrankheit f. (der Schafe)
thought Gedanke m.
– reading Gedankenlesen n.
– transfer Gedankenübertragung f.
thoughtful nachdenklich, tiefsinnig
thoughtfulness Nachdenklichkeit f., Tiefsinn m.

thoughtlessness Zerfahrenheit f., Gedankenlosigkeit f.
thread Faden m.
threadworm Trichocephalus dispar
three-dimensional dreidimensional
three glass test Dreigläserprobe f.
– way stopcock Dreiwegehahn m.
threonine Threonin n.
threose d. e. f.
threshold Schwelle f.
thrill Schwirren n.
thrive, to gedeihen
throat Rachen m., Schlund m.
throb, to pochen
throe Schmerz m.
thrombasthenia Thrombasthenie f.
thrombectomy Thrombektomie f.
thrombelastogram Thrombelastogramm n.
thrombelastographic thrombelastographisch
thrombelastography Thrombelastographie f.
thrombin d. e. n.
thromboangiitis Thrombangiitis f.
– obliterans Endangitis obliterans
thrombocyte Thrombozyt m.
thrombocythaemia (e) Thrombozythämie f.
thrombocythemia (a) Thrombozythämie f.
thrombocytolysis Thrombozytolyse f.
thrombocytopenia Thrombozytopenie f.
thrombocytosis Thrombozytose f.
thromboembolic thromboembolisch
thromboembolism Thromboembolie f.
thrombogenesis Thrombogenese f.
thrombokinase d. e. f.
thrombolysis Thrombolyse f.
thrombolytic thrombolytisch
thrombopathy Thrombopathie f.

thrombopenia Thrombopenie f.
thrombopenic thrombopenisch
thrombophilia Thrombophilie f., Thromboseneigung f.
thrombophlebitic thrombophlebitisch
thrombophlebitis d. e. f.
thromboplastic thromboplastisch
thromboplastin d. e. n.
thrombopoiesis Thrombopoese f.
thrombopoietic thrombopoetisch
thrombose, to thrombosieren
thrombosis Thrombose f.
–, **cerebral** Zerebralthrombose f.
thrombotic thrombotisch
thrombus d. e. m.
throwing back Atavismus m.
thrush Soor m.
thrust Stoß m.; Drang m.
thrust, to stoßen
thulium d. e. n.
thumb Daumen m.
– **sucker** Daumenlutscher m.
thumps (veter.) Singultus m.
thyme Thymian m.
thymectomize, to thymektomieren
thymectomy Thymektomie f., Thymusdrüsenentfernung f.
thymidine Thymidin n.
thymidylate Thymidylat n.
thymine Thymin n.
thymocyte Thymozyt m.
thymol d. e. n.
– **blue** Thymolblau n.
thymol phthalein Thymolphthalein n.
thymoma Thymom n.
thymotropism Thymotropie f.
thymus Thymusdrüse f.
thyroblobulin Thyreoglobulin n.
thyroid gland Schilddrüse f.
thyroid stimulating hormone Thyreotropin n.
thyroidectomy Thyreoidektomie f.
thyroidin Thyreoidin n.
thyroiditis Thyreoiditis f.
thyroprival thyreopriv

thyrotherapy Schilddrüsentherapie f.
thyrotoxic thyreotoxisch
thyrotoxicosis Thyreotoxikose f.
thyrotropic thyreotrop
– **hormone** thyreotropes Hormon n.
thyrotropin Thyreotropin n.
– **releasing factor** thyreotropinfreisetzender Faktor m.
thyroxin d. e. n.
thyroxine Thyroxin n.
tibial d. e.
tibialgia Tibialgie f.
tibiofemoral d. e.
tibiofibular d. e.
tic d. e. m.
– **douloureux** d. e. m.
tick Zecke f.
– **fever** Zeckenfieber n.
– **paralysis** Zeckenlähme f.
tickle, to kitzeln
tickling Kitzeln n., Kitzel m.
TID (= ter in die) dreimal täglich
tidal wave Gezeitenwelle f., Flutwelle f.
tie, to binden
Tietze's syndrome Tietze-Syndrom n.
tiger d. e. m.
tigering Tigerung f.
tight straff
tigroid d. e.
tilidine Tilidin n.
tilt, to kippen
time Zeit f.
– **-consuming** zeitraubend
– **of action** Wirkungsdauer f.
– **saving** zeitsparend
timolol d. e. n.
tin Zinn n.
tinction Färbung f.
tincture Tinktur f.
– **of belladonna** Belladonna-tinktur f.
– **of opium** Opiumtinktur f.
– **of valerian** Baldriantinktur f.

tinea Trichophytie f.
tingible färbbar
tinkling Klingen n.
tinnitus Ohrensausen n.
tip Spitze f.
− **of the nose** Nasenspitze f.
− **of the tongue** Zungenspitze f.
−, **to** tupfen
tire, to ermüden
tissue Gewebe n.
− **bank** Gewebebank f.
− **culture** Gewebskultur f.
− **forceps** chirurgische Pinzette f.
−, **glandular** Drüsengewebe n.
−, **retractor** Wundhaken m.
−, **retractor, self-retaining** Wundsperrer m.
−, **interstitial** Stützgewebe n.
tissular geweblich
titanium Titan n.
titer d. e. m.
titrate, to titrieren
titration d. e. f.
titration, back Rücktitration f.
titre Titer m.
titrimetric titrimetrisch
titrimetry Titrimetrie f.
toad Kröte f.
toadstool Giftpilz m.
tobacco Tabak m.
− **angina** Tabakangina f.
− **bag suture** Tabakbeutelnaht f.
− **mosaic disease** Tabak-Mosaik-Krankheit f.
tobaccoism Tabakvergiftung f.
tobramycin d. e. n.
tocometry Tokometrie f.
tocopherol Tokopherol n.
toddle, to unsicher gehen, schwanken
toe Zehe f.
toenail Zehennagel m.
toilet Toilette f.
tocography Tokographie f.
tokometry Tokometrie f.
tolazamide Tolazamid n.
tolbutamide Tolbutamid n.

tolerable tolerabel, erträglich, verträglich
tolerance Toleranz f., Verträglichkeit f.
tolerant d. e.
toleration Verträglichkeit f.; Duldung f.
toliprolol d. e. n.
Tollen's test Tollens-Probe f.
toluendiamine Toluendiamin n.
toluene Toluol n.
toluidine Toluidin n.
toluidine blue Toluidinblau n.
toluol d. e. n.
toluyl d. e. n.
toluylene Toluylen n.
tolyl d. e. n.
tomogram Tomogramm n.
tomograph d. e. m.
tomographical tomographisch
tomography Tomographie f.
tonality Klangfarbe f.; Tonart f.
tone Ton m.; Tonus m.
− -**control device** Tonblende f.
tongs Zange f.
tongue Zunge f.
−, **black** Melanotrichia linguae
−, **coated** belegte Zunge f.
− **depressor** Zungendrücker m.
−, **geographical** Lingua geographica
− **holding forceps** Zungenzange f.
−, **scrotal** Lingua scrotalis
tonic tonisch; Tonikum n.
tonicity Tonizität f.
tonicize, to tonisieren
tonoclonic tonisch-klonisch
tonofibril Tonofibrille f.
tonometer d. e. n.
tonometrical tonometrisch
tonometry Tonometrie f.
tonsil Tonsille f., Mandel f.
−, **faucial** Gaumenmandel f.
−, **lingual** Zungenmandel f.
−, **pharyngeal** Rachenmandel f.
−, **palatine** Gaumenmandel f.
tonsillar tonsillär

tonsillary tonsillär
tonsillectomy Tonsillektomie f.
tonsillitic tonsillitisch
tonsillitis d. e. f.
tonsillotome Tonsillotom n.
tonsillotomy Tonsillotomie f.
tonus d. e. m.
tool Werkzeug n.
tooth Zahn m.
− angle Zahnwinkel m.
− band Zahnleiste f.
− drawing Zahnziehen n.
−, malposed verlagerter Zahn m.
−, permanent bleibender Zahn m.
− pulp Zahnpulpa f.
− stump Zahnstumpf m.
−, temporary Milchzahn m.
−, wisdom Weisheitszahn m.
toothache Zahnweh n.
top Spitze f.
topectomy Topektomie f.
tophaceous tophusartig
tophus d. e. m.
topic topisch, örtlich
topical topisch, örtlich
topographical topographisch
topography Topographie f.
topology Topologie f.
torment, to quälen
tormentil Tormentille f.
Toronto unit Torontoeinheit f.
torpid d. e.
torpidity Torpidität f.
torque Drehkraft f., Drehung f.
torricelli d. e. n.
torsion d. e. f.
torticollis Schiefhals m., Tortikollis f.
torulosis Torulose f.
total body irradiated ganzkörperbestrahlt
total body irradiation Ganzkörperbestrahlung f.
total protein Gesamteiweiß n.
Toti's operation Totische Operation f.

touch Berührung f.; Berührungssinn m., Tastsinn m., Tasten n.
touch corpuscle Tastkörperchen n.
−, to berühren
tourniquet Staubinde f., Abschnürbinde f., Abklemmvorrichtung f.
towel Handtuch n.
−, sanitary Monatsbinde f.
toxaemia (e) Toxämie f.
toxemia (a) Toxämie f.
toxic toxisch
toxical toxisch
toxicant giftig; Giftstoff m.
toxicity Toxizität f.
toxicogenic giftbildend
toxicologic toxikologisch
toxicologist Toxikologe m., Toxikologin f.
toxicology Toxikologie f.
toxicomania Toxikomanie f.
toxicosis Toxikose f.
toxin d. e. n.
toxoid d. e. n.
toxophorous toxophor
toxoplasma d. e. n.
toxoplasmosis Toxoplasmose f.
trabecular trabekulär
trabs Corpus callosum
trace element Spurenelement n.
−, primitive Primitivstreifen m.
tracer d. e. m.
trachea Luftröhre f., Trachea f.
tracheal d. e.
− catheter Trachealkatheter m.
− stenosis Trachealstenose f.
tracheitic tracheitisch
tracheitis d. e. f.
trachelism Trachelismus m.
trachelobregmatic trachelobregmatisch
trachelopexy Trachelopexie f.
tracheloplasty Tracheloplastik f.
trachelotomy Trachelotomie f.
tracheobronchitis d. e. f.
tracheolaryngeal d. e.

tracheomalacia Tracheomalazie f.
tracheopharyngeal d. e.
tracheoplasty Tracheoplastik f.,
   Luftröhrenplastik f.
tracheoscopic tracheoskopisch
tracheoscopy Tracheoskopie f.
tracheostenosis Trachealstenose f.
tracheostomy Tracheostomie f.
tracheotomize, to tracheotomieren
tracheotomy Tracheotomie f.
− tube Trachealkanüle f.
trachoma Trachom n.
trachomatous trachomatös
tract Strang m., Kanal m.,
   Weg m., Trakt m.
traction Zug m., Ziehen n.
− diverticulum Traktions-
   divertikel n.
tractotomy Traktotomie f.
trade name Handelsname m.
traditional traditionell
traffic Verkehr m.
tragacanth Tragant m.
train, to trainieren, vorbereiten,
   üben
training d. e. n.
trance d. e. f.
tranquilization Beruhigung f.
tranquilize, to beruhigen
tranquilizer d. e. m.
−, major (a) Neurolepticum n.
−, minor (a) Tranquilizer m.
transaminase d. e. f.
transauricular transaurikulär
transbronchial d. e.
transcapillary transkapillär
transcarbamylase Trans-
   karbamylase f.
transcendental transzendent
transconduction Überleitung f.
− time Überleitungszeit f.
transcranial transkranial
transcriptase d. e. f.
transcutaneous transkutan
transdiaphragmatic trans-
   diaphragmatisch

transduce, to überführen
transection Kreuzschnitt m.
transfer Übertragung f.;
   Verlegung f., Überweisung f.
transfer, to transferieren, übertragen, überweisen, verlegen
transferase d. e. f.
transference Übertragung f.;
   Verlegung f., Überweisung f.
transferrin d. e. n.
transform, to transformieren,
   umwandeln
transformation d. e. f., Umwandlung f.
transformer Transformator m.
transformylase d. e. f.
transfuse, to transfundieren
transfusion d. e. f.
transfusion incident Transfusionszwischenfall m.
transglutaminase d. e. f.
transhepatic transhepatisch
transhydrogenase d. e. f.,
   Transhydrase f.
transhydroxymethylase d. e. f.
transient vorübergehend
transillumination d. e. f.,
   Diaphanoskopie f.
transistor d. e. m.
transition cell Übergangszelle f.
transitional vorübergehend,
   transitorisch
− stage Übergangsstadium n.
transjugular transjugulär
transketolase d. e. f.
translucent durchscheinend
transmethylation Transmethylierung f.
transmigration Durchwanderung f.
transmissibility Übertragbarkeit f.
transmissible übertragbar
transmission Übertragung f.
transmission computed tomography
   Transmissionscomputertomo-
   graphie f.
transmit, to übertragen
transmitter Überträger m., d. e. m.

transmural d. e.
transmutation d. e. f.
transorbital d. e.
transpalatal d. e.
transparent d. e., durchsichtig
transpeptidase d. e. f.
transperitoneal d. e.
transpiration d. e. f., Ausdünstung f.
transpire, to transpirieren
transplacental transplazental
transplant Transplantat n.
–, **to** transplantieren
transplantable transplantabel
transplantation d. e. f.
transpleural d. e.
transport form Transportform f.
transposition d. e. f.
transrectal transrektal
transsonic transsonisch
transudate Transsudat n.
transudation Transsudation f.
transumbilical transumbilikal
transurethral d. e.
transuterine transuterin
transvaginal d. e.
transvenous transvenös
transventricular transventrikulär
transverse diameter Querdurchmesser m.
transversotomy Transversotomie f.
transvesical transvesikal
transvestite Transvestit m.
transvestitism Transvestitismus m.
tranylcypromine Tranylcypromin n.
trapeziometacarpal trapeziometakarpal
trapezoid d. e., trapezähnlich
trapped air Blähluft f.
Traube's murmur Galopprhythmus m.
Traube's space Traubescher Raum n.
trauma d. e. n.
traumatic traumatisch
traumatologist Unfallmediziner m.

traumatology Traumatologie f., Unfallheilkunde f.
treadmill Laufband n.
treate, to behandeln
treatment Behandlung f.
– **center** Behandlungszentrum n.
– **for obesity** Entfettungskur f.
–, **to perform initial** – anbehandeln
tree, bronchial Bronchialbaum m.
Treitz's hernia Treitzsche Hernie f.
trematode d. e. f.
tremble, to zittern
tremblement Zittern n.
trembles Milchkrankheit f.
trembling Zittern n.
tremor d. e. m.
trench fever wolhynisches Fieber n.
– **foot** Fußerfrierung f.
trend Neigung f., d. e. m.
Trendelenburg's test Tendelenburgscher Versuch m.
trepan d. e. m., Schädelbohrer m.
trepanation d. e. f.
trephination Trepanation f.
trephine Trepan m., Schädelbohrer m.
trephine, to trepanieren
trepidation Zittern n.; Angstgefühl n.
Treponema pallidum Spirochaeta pallida
– **pertenue** Spirochaeta pertenuis
treponematosis Spirochaetose f.
TRF (thyrotropin releasing factor) thyreotropin-freisetzender Faktor m.
triacetate Triazetat n.
triacetyloleandomycin Triazetyloleandomycin n.
triad dreiwertig; dreiwertiges Element n.; Trias f.
trial Erprobung f., Versuch m., Prüfung f., Probe f.
triamcinolone Triamcinolon n.

triamide Triamid n.
triamine Triamin n.
triamterene Triamteren n.
triangle Dreieck n.; Triangel m.
triangular dreieckig
triarylborane Triarylboran n.
Triatoma magista d. e., Conorrhinus magistus
tribadism Tribadismus m.
tribasic dreibasig
Triboulet's test Tribouletsche Probe f.
tribromethanol Tribromäthylalkohol m.
tribromide Tribromid n.
tributyl d. e. n.
tricellular dreizellig
trichiasis d. e. f.
Trichinella spiralis d. e. f.
trichinosis Trichinose f.
trichinous trichinös
trichloride Trichlorid n.
trichlorphenol d. e. n.
trichoglossia Haarzunge f.
trichomonacide Trichomonadenmittel n.
Trichomonas vaginalis d. e.
trichomycosis Trichomykose f.
trichophytin d. e. n.
Trichophyton acuminatum d. e.
− steroides Trichophyton gypseum
− crateriforme Trichophyton tonsurans
− vilaceum d. e.
trichophytosis barbae Trichophytia barbae
− capitis Trichophytia capitis
− corporis Trichophytia corporis
trichorrhexis nodosa d. e.
trichostrongylosis Trichostrongylose f.
trichromatic trichromatisch
trichromic trichromatisch
Trichuris trichiura Trichocephalus dispar
trickle, to tröpfeln

tricuspid dreizipfelig, dreihöckerig
− insufficiency Trikuspidalinsuffizienz f.
− stenosis Trikuspidalstenose f.
− valve Trikuspidalklappe f.
triethanolamine Triäthanolamin n.
triethylenemelamine Triäthylenmelamin n.
trifacial nerve Nervus trigeminus
trifascicular trifaszikulär
trifluoperazine Trifluoperazin n.
triflupromazine Triflupromazin n.
triglyceride Triglyzerid n.
trigemin d. e. n.
trigeminus nerve Nervus trigeminus
trigone Dreieck n.
trigonitis d. e. f.
trigonometric trigonometrisch
trihydroxymethylaminomethane Trihydroxymethylaminomethan n.
triiodide Trijodid n.
triiodothyroacetic acid Trijodthyroessigsäure f.
triiodotyronine Trijodtyronin n.
trilobate dreilappig
trilobed dreilappig
trilogy of Fallot Fallotsche Trilogie f.
trimeprazine Trimeprazin n.
trimepropimine Trimepropimin n.
trimethoprim d. e. n.
trimethylamine Trimethylamin n.
trimethylendiamine Trimethylendiamin n.
trimmer Putzer m.
trinitrate Trinitrat n.
trinitrobenzene Trinitrobenzol n.
trinucleate dreikernig
triokinase d. e. f.
triose d. e. f.
trioxide Trioxyd n.
trioxypurine Trioxypurin n.
tripara Drittgebärende f.
triparous drittgebärend
tripartite dreigeteilt
triphasic dreiphasig

tripeptid dreiphasig
tripeptidase d. e. f.
tripeptide Tripeptid n.
triphosphate Triphosphat n.
triphosphonucleoside Triphosphonukleosid n.
triple phosphate Tripelphosphat n.
triplegia Triplegie f.
triplet Drilling m.
triploid d. e.
triplopia Triplopie f.
tripod Dreifuß m.
trishydroxymethylaminomethane Trishydroxymethylaminomethan n.
trismaleate Trismaleat n.
trismus d. e. m.
trisomal d. e.
trisulfide (a) Trisulfid n.
trisulphide (e) Trisulfid n.
tritiate, to mit Tritium behandeln, mit Tritium versehen
tritium d. e. n.
triturate, to triturieren, verreiben
trituration d. e. f., Verreibung f.
trivalence Dreiwertigkeit f.
trivalent dreiwertig
trivet Dreifuß m.
trocar Trokar m.
trochanterian trochanterisch
trochanteric trochanterisch
troche Pastille f.
trochlear trochleär
trochoid joint Radgelenk n.
Trommer's test Trommersche Probe f.
tropacocaine Tropakokain n.
tropeine Tropein n.
tropeolin Tropäolin n.
trophic trophisch
trophism Trophik f.
trophoblast d. e. m.
trophoneurosis Trophoneurose f.
trophoneurotic trophoneurotisch
trophonosis Trophonose f.
trophopathy Trophopathie f.

trophoplasm Trophoplasma n.
trophotropic trophotrop
tropical tropisch
– **disease** Tropenkrankheit f.
– **medicine** Tropenmedizin f.
tropine Tropin n.
troubles Beschwerden f. pl.
Trousseau's sign Trousseausches Zeichen n.
true conjugate diameter Conjugata vera
truncate, to amputieren
trunk Rumpf m., Stamm m.
trusion Stoß m.; Fehlhaltung f.
truss Bruchband n.
truthful glaubhaft
trypan blue Trypanblau n.
trypan red Trypanrot n.
Trypanosoma brucei d. e.
– **cruzi** d. e.
– **equiperdum** d. e.
– **gambiense** d. e.
– **rhodesiense** d. e.
trypanosomiasis d. e. f., Schlafkrankheit f.
tryparsamide Tryparsamid n.
trypsin d. e. n.
trypsinogen d. e. n.
tryptamine Tryptamin n.
tryptase d. e. f.
tryptic tryptisch
tryptophan d. e. n.
TSH (thyroid stimulating hormone) Thyreotropin n.
tsetse fly Tsetsefliege f.
tsutsugamushi fever Tsutsugamushifieber n.
tubage Intubation f.
tubal pregnancy Eileiterschwangerschaft f.
tube Tube f., Schlauch m., Rohr n., Röhre f.
–, **aspirating** Aspirationsrohr n.
–, **colon** Darmrohr n.
–, **drainage** Dränagerohr n.
–, **eustachian** Eustachische Röhre f.
–, **fallopian** Eileiter m.

tube, tracheotomy Trachealkanüle f.
- **voltage** Röhrenspannung f.
- **,X-ray** Röntgenröhre f.
tubectomy Tubektomie f.
tubercle Tuberkel m.
tubercular tuberkulär
tuberculation Tuberkelbildung f.
tuberculid Tuberkulid n.
tuberculide Tuberkulid n.
tuberculin Tuberkulin n.
tuberculinization Tuberkulinanwendung f.
tuberculocide tuberkulozid
tuberculofibrosis Tuberkulofibrose f.
tuberculoma Tuberkulom n.
tuberculomania Tuberkulomanie f.
tuberculophobia Tuberkulophobie f.
tuberculosilicosis Tuberkulosilikose f.
tuberculosis Tuberkulose f.
-,**closed** geschlossene Tuberkulose f.
-,**miliary** Miliartuberkulose f.
-,**open** offene Tuberkulose f.
tuberculostatic tuberkulostatisch
tuberculotic Tuberkulöser m., Tuberkulöse f.
tuberculotoxin Tuberkulotoxin n.
tuberculous tuberkulös
tuberosity Tuberosität f.
tuberous tuberös
tubocurarine Tubocurarin n.
tubular tubulär
tubule Röhrchen n.
-,**collecting** Sammelröhrchen n.
-,**connecting** Harnkanälchenschaltstück n.
-,**convoluted renal** gewundenes Harnkanälchen n.
-,**discharging** Ausflußröhrchen n.
-,**renal** Harnkanälchen n.
-,**straight renal** gestrecktes Harnkanälchen n.

Türck's bundle Türcksches Bündel n.
tularaemia (e) Tularämie f.
tularemia (a) Tularämie f.
tumefaction Schwellung f.
tumenol d. e. n.
tumor (a) d. e. m.
tumorous tumorös
tumour (e) Tumor m.
tungsten Wolfram n.
tuning fork Stimmgabel f.
turbellaria d. e. n. pl.
turbid trübe
turbidimeter d. e. n.
turbidimetric turbidimetrisch
turbidimetry Turbidimetrie f.
turbidity Trübung f.
turbinal d. e., Nasenmuschel f.
turbine d. e. f.
Turkish bath Schwitzbad n.
Turnbull's blue Turnbullblau n.
turned-in legs X-Beine n. pl.
Turner syndrome Turner-Syndrom n.
turning Wendung f.
- **point** Wendepunkt m.
turnover Umsatz m.
turnsickness Drehkrankheit f., Coenurose f.
turpentine Terpentin n.
turricephaly Turmschädel m.
turtle Schildkröte f.
tutocain d. e. n.
tweezer Pinzette f.
twilight sleep Dämmerschlaf m.
twin Zwilling m.
- **arch** Zwillingsbogen m.
- **coil kidney** Zwillingsspulenniere f.
twins, binovular zweieiige Zwillinge m. pl.
-,**dichorial** zweieiige Zwillinge m. pl.
-,**dizygotic** zweieiige Zwillinge m. pl.
-,**enzygotic** eineiige Zwillinge m. pl.

twins, fraternal zweieiige
  Zwillinge m. pl.
–, identical eineiige
  Zwillinge m. pl.
–, uniovular eineiige
  Zwillinge m. pl.
twisting of the guts Darmverschlingung f.
two-dimensional zweidimensional
two glass test Zweigläserprobe f.
– way stopcock Zweiwegehahn m.
tyloma Hautschwiele f.
tympanal d. e.
tympanectomy Tympanektomie f.
tympanic tympanal
– membrane Trommelfell n.
tympanism Tympanie f.
tympanites Tympanie f.
tympanitic tympanitisch
tympanomandibular tympanomandibulär
tympanomastoiditis d. e. f.
tympanoplasty Tympanoplastik f.,
  Trommelfellplastik f.
tympanotomy Tympanotomie f.
tympanous tympanitisch
tympanum Mittelohr n.;
  Trommelfell n.
tympany Tympanie f.
Tyndall phenomenon Tyndall-
  Phänomen n.

type Typ m.
typhlatony Typhlatonie f.
typhlitis d. e. f.
typhlostomy Typhlostomie f.
typhlotomy Typhlotomie f.
typhloureterostomy
  Typhloureterostomie f.
typhobacillosis Typhobazillose f.
typhoid typhös; Typhus m.
typhoid fever Typhus abdominalis
typhous fleckfieberartig, fleckfieberförmig
typhus Flecktyphus m., Fleckfieber n., Typhus exanthematicus
– fever Fleckfieber n.
– vaccine Fleckfieberimpfstoff m.
typic typisch
typical typisch
typing of blood Blutgruppenbestimmung f.
typological typologisch
typology Typologie f.
tyramine Tyramin n.
Tyrode's solution Tyrodelösung f.
tyrosinase d. e. f.
tyrosine Tyrosin n.
tyrosinosis Tyrosinose f.
tyrosis Verkäsung f.
tyrothricin d. e. n.
Tyson's gland Tysonsche Drüse
  f.

U

U (= unit) Einheit f.
uberty Fruchtbarkeit f.
udder Euter n.
Uffelmann's test Uffelmannsche
  Probe f.
Uhlenhuth's test Uhlenhuthsches
  Verfahren n.
ula Zahnfleisch n.
ulcer Geschwür n., Ulkus n.

ulcer, decubital Dekubitalgeschwür n.
–, gastric Magengeschwür n.
– of duodenum Zwölffingerdarmgeschwür n.
– of foot, perforating Malum
  perforans pedis
–, secondary jejunal Ulcus jejuni
  pepticum

ulcerate, to ulzerieren
ulcerating granuloma of the pudenda Granuloma venereum
ulceration Ulzeration f., Ulkusbildung f.
ulcerative ulzerativ
ulcerous ulzerös, geschwürig
ulcus hypostaticum d. e.
ulitis Zahnfleischentzündung f.
ulnad ulnarwärts
ulnar d. e.
– **nerve** Nervus ulnaris
ulnoradial d. e.
uloid narbenähnlich
ultimobranchial d. e.
ultracentrifuge Ultrazentrifuge f.
ultra clean ward keimfreie Isoliereinheit f.
ultrafilter d. e. m.
ultrafiltration d. e. f.
ultra-high vacuum Ultrahochvakuum n.
ultramicroscope Ultramikroskop n.
ultramicroscopical ultramikroskopisch
ultrashort wave Ultrakurzwelle f.
ultrasonic examination Ultraschalluntersuchung f.
ultrasonic therapy Ultraschallbehandlung f.
ultrasonic wave Ultraschallwelle f.
ultrasound Ultraschall m.
ultrastructural ultrastrukturell
ultrastructure Ultrastruktur f.
ultraviolet ultraviolett; Ultraviolett n.
ultravirus d. e. n.
ultravisible ultravisibel
umbilical umbilikal
– **band** Nabelbinde f.
– **cord** Nabelschnur f.
– **hernia** Nabelhernie f.
– **rupture** Nabelriß m.
unable unfähig, ungeeignet
– **for work** arbeitsunfähig
unaltered unverändert, unbeeinflußt
unazotized stickstofffrei

unbalance Gleichgewichtsstörung f.
unbreakable unzerbrechlich
unburden, to entlasten
unciform hakenförmig
uncinariasis d. e. f.
unclean unrein
uncleanness Unreinheit f.
unclothe, to entkleiden
uncomfortable unbehaglich, unbequem
uncomplicated unkompliziert
unconcern Teilnahmslosigkeit f.
unconcerned teilnahmlos
unconscious unbewußt, bewußtlos
unconsciousness Bewußtlosigkeit f.
uncontrollable unkontrollierbar
uncooked food Rohkost f.
unction Salbe f.; Salbung f.
unctuous fettig, ölig
uncured ungeheilt
underfed unterernährt
underfeeding Unterernährung f.
undergraduate Student m. / Studentin f. vor dem Examen
underheight unternormale Größe f.
undermine, to unterhöhlen
undernourished unterernährt
underpressure Unterdruck m.
understain, to unterfärben
understand, to verstehen
understanding Verstehen n.; Verstand m.
underwater gymnastics Unterwassergymnastik f.
underwear Leibwäsche f.
underweight Untergewicht n.
undescended testis ausgebliebener Descensus testis
undigested unverdaut
undiluted unverdünnt
undress, to entkleiden
undulant undulierend, wellenförmig
– **fever** Febris undulans, undulierendes Fieber n.

undulation undulierend, wellenförmig
uneasiness Unbehagen n.
uneasy unbehaglich
unesterified unverestert
uneven ungleichmäßig, uneben
unexplored unerforscht
unfavorable (a) ungünstig, infaust
unfavourable (e) ungünstig, infaust
unfreezing Auftauen n.
unfruitful unfruchtbar
ungual d. e.
unguent Salbe f.
unguis incarnatus d. e., eingewachsener Nagel m.
ungulate hufig; Huftier n.
unhurt unverletzt
unicellular einzellig
unification Vereinigung f.
unifocal unifokal
unify, to vereinigen
unigravida d. e. f.
unilateral d. e., einseitig
unilocular unilokulär
uninjured unverletzt, unbeschädigt
uninoculated ungeimpft
union Vereinigung f.; Heilung f.
unioval eineiig
uniovular eineiig
unipara d. e. f.
unipolar d. e.
unipotent d. e.
unipotential unipotent
unit Einheit f.
unite, to vereinigen, verbinden
univalence Univalenz f.
univalent d. e., einwertig
university Universität f.
– **teacher** Universitätslehrer m., Universitätslehrerin f.
unload, to entladen, entlasten
unmedullated marklos
unmixed unvermischt
unnecessary unnötig
unorientation Desorientierung f.
unphysiologic unphysiologisch
unpigmented unpigmentiert

unpleasant unbehaglich; unsympathisch
unpredictable unvorhersehbar
unpsychological unpsychologisch
unrecognized unerkannt
unrounded entrundet
unsafe unsicher, gefährlich
unsalted ungesalzen
unsanitary unhygienisch
unsaturated ungesättigt
unsportsmanlike unsportlich
unstable instabil
unstained ungefärbt
unsteadiness Unstetigkeit f.; Unsicherheit f.
unsteady unstetig; unsicher, ungeschickt
unsuspected unerwartet
unsuspicious unverdächtig
untie, to losbinden
untimely birth Frühgeburt f.
untoward effect unerwünschte Wirkung f.
untreated unbehandelt
unused ungebraucht
unvaccinated ungeimpft
unwell ungut, unpäßlich, unwohl
unwholesome gesundheitsschädlich
unwind, to abspulen, abwickeln
unwomanly unweiblich
update, to aktualisieren
updating Aktualisierung f.
upper abdomen Oberbauch m.
– **jaw** Oberkiefer m.
– **lip** Oberlippe f.
– **part of the body** Oberkörper m.
upperarm Oberarm m.
uptake Aufnahme f.
urachal d. e.
uracil d. e. n.
uracil-mustard Uracil-Lost m.
uraemia (e) Urämie f.
uraemic (e) urämisch
uranist Urning m.
uranium Uran n.
uranoplasty Gaumenplastik f.
urari Pfeilgift n.

urate Urat n.
uratic uratisch
urban städtisch
urbanization Verstädterung f.
urea Harnstoff m.
– **nitrogen** Harnstoffstickstoff m.
ureapoiesis Harnstoffbildung f.
urease d. e. f.
ureide Ureid n.
uremia (a) Urämie f.
uremic (a) urämisch
ureter d. e. m., Harnleiter m.
ureteral d. e.
ureterectomy Ureterektomie f.
ureteric ureteral
ureteritis d. e. f., Harnleiterentzündung f.
ureterocele Ureterozele f.
ureterocolostomy Ureterokolostomie f.
ureterography Ureterographie f.
ureterolithiasis d. e. f.
ureteroplasty Harnleiterplastik f.
ureterostomy Ureterostomie f.
ureterotomy Ureterotomie f.
ureterotubal d. e.
urethane Urethan n.
urethra d. e. f., Harnröhre f.
urethral d. e.
urethritis d. e. f.
urethrocele Urethrozele f.
urethrography Urethrographie f.
urethroplasty Harnröhrenplastik f.
urethroscope Urethroskop n.
urethroscopic urethroskopisch
urethroscopy Urethroskopie f.
urethrostomy Urethrostomie f.
urethrotomy Urethrotomie f.
urge, to drängen
urgency Dringlichkeit f.
urgent dringlich, drängend
uric acid Harnsäure f.
uricolytic harnsäurespaltend
uricosuric harnsäuretreibend; harnsäuretreibendes Mittel n.
uridin d. e. n.
uridinuria Uridinurie f.

urinable harnfähig
urinal Urinflasche f., Harnglas n.
urinalysis Harnanalyse f.
urinary urinär
– **retention** Harnretention f.
– **tract** Harntrakt m.
– **tract infection** Harnweginfektion f.
urinate, to urinieren, harnen, Wasser lassen
urination Urinieren n., Wasserlassen n.
urine Harn m., Urin m.
– **analysis** Urinanalyse f.
– **collection period** Harnsammelperiode f., Urinsammelperiode f.
–, **incontinence of** – Harninkontinenz f.
–, **retention of** – Harnretention f.
– **sugar** Harnzucker m., Urinzucker m.
uriniferous harnleitend
urinific harnbildend
uriniparous harnbildend
urinometer Urometer n.
urinous urinös
urnism Homosexualität f.
urobilin d. e. n.
urobilinaemia (e) Urobilinämie f.
urobilinemia (a) Urobilinämie f.
urobilinicterus Urobilinikterus m.
urobilinogen d. e. n.
urobilinogenuria Urobilinogenurie f.
urobilinuria Urobilinurie f.
urochrome Urochrom n.
uroerythrin d. e. n.
urogenital d. e.
urography Urographie f.
urokinase d. e. f.
urolithiasis d. e. f.
urological urologisch
urologist Urologe m.
urology Urologie f.
uropepsin d. e. n.
uropepsinogen d. e. n.
uropoiesis Harnbildung f.

uroporphyrin Harnbildung f.
urosepsis d. e. f.
ursotherapy Ursotherapie f.
urticaria Urtikaria f.
urticarial urtikariell
urticarious urtikariell
use Gebrauch m.
–, to gebrauchen, benützen
useful brauchbar, nützlich
useless unbrauchbar
utensil Gerät n.
uterine uterin
– **segment** Uterinsegment n.
uteroabdominal d. e.
uterofixation Uterusfixation f.
uterography Uterographie f.
uteroovarian uteroovariell
uteroplacental uteroplazental, uteroplazentar
uteroplasty Gebärmutterplastik f.
uterosacral uterosakral
uterovaginal d. e.
uterovesical uterovesikal

uterus d. e. m., Gebärmutter f.
utilization Verwertung f., Ausnutzung f.
utilize, to verwerten, ausnutzen
utricle Utrikulus m.
utriculosaccular utrikulosakkulär
uvea d. e. f.
uveal d. e.
uveitis d. e. f.
uveoparotid uveoparotisch
– **fever** Heerfordtsche Krankheit f.
uveoparotitis d. e. f.
uveoplasty Uveaplastik f.
uviol Ultraviolettlampe f.
uviolize, to ultraviolett bestrahlen
uvioresistant ultraviolettresistent
uviosensitive ultraviolettempfindlich
uvula d. e. f., Zäpfchen n.
uvulitis d. e. f.
uzara d. e. f.
uzarin d. e. n.

V

vacant leer, leerstehend
vaccinable impffähig
vaccinal vakzinal
vaccinate, to impfen
vaccinating pen Impffeder f.
– – **holder** Impffederhalter m.
– **set** Impfbesteck n.
vaccination Impfung f., Vakzination f.
– **register** Impfliste f.
–, **typhoid** Typhusimpfung f.
vaccinator Impfarzt m.
vaccine Vakzine f.
– **matter** Impfstoff m.
vaccinia Kuhpocken f. pl.
vaccinid Impfpusteln f. pl., Vakzinid n.

vaccinide Impfpusteln f. pl., Vakzinid n.
vacciniform vakziniform
vaccinotherapy Vakzinebehandlung f.
vacuolar vakuolär
vacuolate, to vakuolisieren
vacuolation Vakuolisierung f.
vacuole Vakuole f.
vacuolization Vakuolisierung f.
vacuum Vakuum n.
– **extraction** Vakuumextraktion f.
– **pump** Vakuumpumpe f.
vagabond Vagabund m.
vagal d. e.
vagina d. e. f., Scheide f.
vaginal d. e.

vaginismus d. e. m.
vaginitis d. e. f.
vaginolabial d. e.
vaginoperineal d. e.
vaginoplasty Scheidenplastik f.
vagotomy Vagotomie f.
vagotonia Vagotonie f.
vagotonic vagotonisch
vagotony Vagotonie f.
vagotropic vagotrop
vagrant wandernd; Vagabund m.
vagus d. e. m.
valamin d. e. n.
valence Valenz f., Wertigkeit f.
valency Valenz f., Wertigkeit f.
valent wertig, gültig
valerian Baldrian m.
valerianate Valerianat n.
valine Valin n.
vallecular vallekulär
Valleix's point Valleixscher Punkt m.
Valsalva's experiment Valsalvascher Versuch m.
valuation Bewertung f., Auswertung f.
value Wert m.
valve Klappe f.
– **bulb** Ventilball m.
valvotomy Valvotomie f.
valvula Klappe f., Kläppchen n.
valvular valvulär
– **murmur** Klappengeräusch n.
valvuloplasty Klappenplastik f.
valvulotome Valvulotom n.
valvulotomy Valvulotomie f.
valyl d. e. n.
vanadium d. e. n.
vancomycin d. e. n.
vanillin d. e. n.
vapor (a) Dampf m.
vaporization Verdampfung f.
vaporize, to verdampfen
vapour (e) Dampf m.
Vaquez's disease Vaquez-Oslersche Krankheit f.
variable variabel

variation d. e. f.
varication Varizenbildung f.
varicella Varizellen f. pl., Windpocken f. pl.
varicocele Varikozele f.
varicose varikös
varicose vein Krampfader f.
varicose veins, sclerosing treatment of – Krampfaderverödung f.
varicosis Varikose f.
varicosity Varikosität f.
varicotomy Varikotomie f.
variety Abart f., Varietät f.
variola Pocken f. pl.
variolar variolär
varioliform d. e.
varioloid Variolois f.
variolous variolös
varix Blutgefäßknoten m.
vasal d. e.
vascular vaskulär
vascular resistance Gefäßwiderstand m.
vascular tree Gefäßbaum m.
vascular wall Gefäßwand f.
vascularization Vaskularisierung f.
vascularize, to vaskularisieren
vasectomize, to vasektomieren
vasectomy Vasektomie f.
vaselin d. e. n.
vasoconstriction Vasokonstriktion f., Gefäßverengerung f.
vasoconstrictive vasokonstriktiv, gefäßverengernd
vasodilatation d. e. f., Gefäßerweiterung f.
vasodilating gefäßerweiternd
vasodilative gefäßerweiternd
vasodilator Gefäßerweiterer m., Vasodilatator m.
vasography Vasographie f.
vasomotor vasomotorisch
vasomotorial vasomotorisch
vasomotory vasomotorisch
vasoneurosis Vasoneurose f.
vasoneurotic vasoneurotisch
vasoparalysis Gefäßlähmung f.

vasopressin d. e. n.
vasospasm Vasospasmus m., Gefäßkrampf m.
vasospastic vasospastisch
vasostomy Vasostomie f.
vasotomy Vasotomie f.
Vater's papilla Papilla Vateri, Vatersche Papille f.
vault Gewölbe n.
V.D. (venereal disease) Geschlechtskrankheit f.
vection Übertragung f.
vector Vektor m.; Träger m.
vectorcardiography Vektorkardiographie f.
vectorial vektoriell
vegetable pflanzlich
– oil Pflanzenöl n.
vegetal pflanzlich
vegetarian Vegetarier m., Vegetarierin f.
vegetation d. e. f.
vegetative vegetativ
vehicle Vehikel n.
vein Vene f.
–, basilic Vena basilica
–, epigastric Vena epigastrica
–, femoral Vena femoralis
–, intercostal Vena intercostalis
–, jugular Vena jugularis
–, pulmonary Vena pulmonalis
–, saphenous Vena saphena
–, thyroid Vena thyreoidea
–, umbilical Vena umbilicalis
Veit-Smellie maneuver Veit-Smelliescher Handgriff m.
velamentous velamentös
velocity Schnelligkeit f., Geschwindigkeit f.
– of light Lichtgeschwindigkeit f.
– of sound Schallgeschwindigkeit f.
velvet Samt f.
velvety samten, samtartig
venectasia Venektasie f.
venenation Vergiftung f.
venenific giftbildend

venenous giftig
venereal venerisch
– disease (V.D.) Geschlechtskrankheit f.
venereologist Venerologe m.
venereology Venerologie f.
venerological venerologisch
venerology Venerologie f.
venery Geschlechtsverkehr m.
venesection Venensektion f.
venipuncture Venenpunktion f.
venoarterial venoarteriell
venographic venographisch
venography Venographie f.
venom Gift n.
venomous giftig
venose venös, venenhaltig
venous venös
venous hum Nonnensausen n.
vent Ausgang m., Öffnung f.
ventilate, to ventilieren
ventilation Ventilation f., Lüftung f.
ventilation, demand – Abrufbeatmung f.
ventilation, maximal voluntary maximale willkürliche Ventilation f.
ventrad ventralwärts
ventral d. e.
ventricle Ventrikel m.
–, fourth vierter Ventrikel m.
–, lateral Seitenventrikel m.
–, left linker Ventrikel m.
–, right rechter Ventrikel m.
–, third dritter Ventrikel m.
ventricular ventrikulär
ventriculoatrial ventrikuloatrial
ventriculographical ventrikulographisch
ventriculography Ventrikulographie f.
ventriculostomy Ventrikulostomie f.
ventrodorsal d. e.
ventroinguinal d. e.
ventrolateral d. e.

ventromedial d. e.
venule Venole f.
verapamil d. e. n.
veratrine Veratrin n.
Veratrum album d. e.
– **viride** d. e.
verbal d. e.
Verbascum thapsus d. e.
verbenone Verbenon n.
verbigeration d. e. f.
verbomania Geschwätzigkeit f., Verbomanie f.
verify, to verifizieren
vermicidal wurmtötend
vermicide wurmtötendes Mittel n., Wurmmittel n.
vermicular wurmartig
vermiform wurmförmig
vermifugal wurmtreibend
vermifuge wurmtreibendes Mittel n., Wurmmittel n.
vermin Ungeziefer n.
vermination Verwurmung f., Wurmbefall m.
verminosis Wurmbefall m.
verruca peruviana Verruga peruviana, Peruwarze f.
– **plana** flache Warze f.
– **vulgaris** gewöhnliche Warze f.
verrucose warzig
verrucous warzig
verruga peruana Peruwarze f.
version Wendung f.
–, **abdominal** äußere Wendung f.
–, **Braxton Hick's** Wendung f. nach Braxton Hicks
–, **cephalic** Wendung f. auf den Kopf
–, **internal** innere Wendung f.
vertebra Wirbel m.
–, **cervical** Halswirbel m.
–, **lumbar** Lendenwirbel m.
–, **thoracic** Brustwirbel m.
vertebral d. e.
– **body** Wirbelkörper m.
– **column** Wirbelsäule f.
vertebrata d. e. n. pl.

vertebrate mit Wirbelsäule; Wirbeltier n.
vertebrosternal d. e.
vertebrotomy Vertebrotomie f.
vertex Scheitel m.
vertical vertikal
vertiginous vertiginös
vertigo d. e. f., Schwindel m.
verumontanitis Colliculitis seminalis
verumontanum Colliculus seminalis
vesical vesikal
vesicant blasenziehend; blasenziehendes Mittel n.
vesication Blasenbildung f.
vesicatory blasenziehend; blasenziehendes Mittel n.
vesicle Bläschen
vesicoabdominal vesikoabdominal
vesicocele Vesikozele f.
vesicoprostatic vesikoprostatisch
vesicopubic vesikopubisch
vesicorectal vesikorektal
vesikorenal vesikorenal
vesicosigmoidostomy Vesikosigmoidostomie f.
vesicotomy Vesikotomie f.
vesicoumbilical vesikoumbilikal
vesicoureteral vesikoureteral
vesicourethral vesikourethral
vesicouterine vesikouterin
vesicovaginal vesikovaginal
vesicular vesikulär
– **breath sounds** Bläschenatmen n.
vesiculation Bläschenbildung f.
vesiculectomy Vesikulektomie f.
vesiculitis Vesikulitis f.
vesiculobronchial vesikulobronchial
vesiculography Vesikulographie f.
vesiculotomy Vesikulotomie f.
vessel Gefäß n.
vessignon (veter.) Gallen f. pl.
vestibular vestibulär
vestibule Vestibulum n.

vestibulocerebellar vestibulozerebellar
vestibulotomy Vestibulotomie f.
vestibulourethral d. e.
vestige Spur f.
veterinarian Veterinär m.
veterinary science Tierheilkunde f.
— **surgeon** Tierchirurg m.
— **surgery** Tierchirurgie f.
viability Lebensfähigkeit f.
viable lebensfähig
vial Fläschchen n., Kolben m.
vibrate, to vibrieren
vibration d. e. f.
Vibrio comma d. e.
Viburnum prunifolium d. e.
vicarious vikariierend
vicious fehlerhaft
Vicq d' Azyr's bundle Vicq d'Azyrsches Bündel n.
victuals Lebensmittel n. pl.
video display Sichtanzeigegerät n.
Vidian canal Canalis pterygoideus
vigil Nachtwache f.
villose villös
villous villös
vinblastine Vinblastin n.
vincaleukoblastine Vincaleukoblastin n.
Vincent's infection fusospirilläre Infektion f.
vincristine Vincristin n.
vinegar Essig m.
vinyl d. e. n.
violate, to verletzen; schänden
viomycin d. e. n.
viosterol d. e. n., bestrahltes Ergosterin n.
viper d. e. f.
viral infection Virusinfektion f.
viral scratch lymphadenitis Katzenkratzkrankheit f.
virgin Jungfrau f.
virginal jungfräulich, virginell
virginity Jungfräulichkeit f.
virile viril, männlich, mannbar
virilism Virilismus m.
virility Virilität f., Männlichkeit f., Mannbarkeit f.
virilize, to vermännlichen, virilisieren
virological virologisch
virologist Virologe m., Virologin f.
virology Virologie f.
virosis Viruskrankheit f.
virtual virtuell
virulence Virulenz f.
virulent d. e.
virus d. e. n.
virus, adeno- Adenovirus n.
—,**cat-scratch** Katzenkratzvirus n.
—,**chickenpox** Varizellenvirus n.
—,**coxsackie** Coxsackievirus n.
—,**ECHO** ECHO-Virus n.
—,**encephalitis** Enzephalitisvirus n.
—,**entero-** Enterovirus n.
—,**hepatitis** Hepatitisvirus n.
—,**herpes** Herpesvirus n.
—,**influenza** Influenzavirus n., Grippevirus n.
—,**measles** Masernvirus n.
—,**oncorna** Oncorna-Virus n.
—,**picorna** Picorna-Virus n.
—,**poliomyelitis** Poliomyelitisvirus n.
—,**polyoma** Polyomavirus n.
—,**rabies** Tollwutvirus n.
—,**respiratory syncytial** respiratorisches Synzytium-Virus n.
—,**smallpox** Pockenvirus n.
—,**yellow fever** Gelbfiebervirus n.
visceral viszeral
visceromotor viszeromotorisch
visceroparietal viszeroparietal
visceropleural viszeropleural
visceroptosis Viszeroptose f.
viscerosensory viszerosensorisch
viscoelastic viskoelastisch
viscosimetry Viskosimetrie f.
viscosity Viskosität f.
viscous viskös
visibility Sichtbarkeit f.
visible sichtbar

vision Sehen n., Sehvermögen n.; Sicht f.; Vision f.
—, **blurred** verschwommenes Sehen n.
— **discorder** Sehstörung f.
— **test** Sehprüfung f.
visit Besuch m.
visiting time Besuchszeit f.
visual visuell
— **acuity** Sehschärfe f.
— **field** Gesichtsfeld n.
visualize, to sichtbar machen
vital d. e.
— **capacity** Vitalkapazität f.
— —, **forced** forcierte Vitalkapazität f.
— **granulation** Vitalgranulation f.
— **staining** Vitalfärbung f.
vitalism Vitalismus m.
vitalistic vitalistisch
vitality Vitalität f.
vitals lebenswichtige Körperteile m. pl.
vitamin d. e. n.
— **B complex** Vitamin-B-Komplex m.
— **carrier** Vitaminträger m.
vitaminology Vitaminologie f.
vitellin d. e. n.
vitiliginous vitiliginös
vitiligo d. e. f.
vitious circle Circulus vitiosus
vitreous glasig; Glaskörper m.
— **body** Glaskörper m.
—, **opacity of** Glaskörpertrübung f.
vitriol d. e. m.
vivisection Vivisektion f.
vixen Füchsin f.
Vleminckx's solution Vlemnickxsche Lösung f.
vocal vokal
vocal cord Stimmband n.
vocal fremitus Stimmfremitus m.
vocational beruflich
Vögtlin unit Vögtlineinheit f.
voice Stimme f.
voiced stimmhaft

voiceless stimmlos
void leer; zwecklos
volar d. e.
volatile flüchtig, volatil
—, **easily** leicht flüchtig
—, **sparingly** schwer flüchtig
volatilization Verdampfung f., Verflüchtigung f.
volatilize, to verdampfen, verflüchtigen
vole Wühlmaus f.
Volhard's test Volhardsche Nierenfunktionsprüfung f.
Volhynia fever wolhynisches Fieber n.
volition Wille m., Wollen n.
volitional willensmäßig, willentlich
Volkmann's splint Volkmannschiene f.
volt d. e. n.
voltage elektrische Spannung f.
—, **low** Niederspannung f.
voltmeter d. e. n.
volume Volumen n.
—, **blood** Blutvolumen n.
—, **minute** Minutenvolumen n.
volume of red blood corpuscles Erythrozytenvolumen n.
—, **stroke** Schlagvolumen n.
volumetric volumetrisch
volumetry Volumetrie f.
voluminous voluminös
voluntary freiwillig
volunteer, healthy freiwillige gesunde Versuchsperson f., gesunder Proband m.
voluptuous wollüstig
voluptuousness Wollüstigkeit f.
volupty Wollust f.
volvulus d. e. m.
vomeronasal d. e.
vomicose ulzerös
vomit, to sich übergeben, erbrechen
vomiting Erbrechen n.
vomitive Brechmittel n.

vomiturition Brechreiz m.
vucin Vuzin n.
vulcanite Hartgummi m.
vulcanize, to vulkanisieren
vulnerability Verwundbarkeit f.
vulnerable verwundbar, vulnerabel
vulnerate, to verwunden
vulval vulvär
vulvar vulvär
vulvectomy Vulvektomie f.
vulvitis d. e. f.
vulvovaginal d. e.
vuzin d. e. n.

W

wad Polster n.
—, **to** polstern
wadding Watte f.
waddle, to watscheln
waddling watschelig
Wahl's sign Wahlsches Zeichen
waist Taille f.
waiting list Warteliste f.
waiting room Wartezimmer n.
wakefulness Wachheit
Walcher's position Walchersche Hängelage f.
Waldeyer's tonsillar ring Waldeyerscher Rachenring m.
wale Striemen m.
walking calliper Gehschiene f.
— **chair** Fahrstuhl m.
— **machine** Gehwagen m.
wall Wand f.
wall, colonic Dickdarmwand f.
wall, vascular Gefäßwand f.
Wallenberg's syndrome Wallenbergsches Syndrom n.
wallerian degeneration Wallersche Degeneration f.
walleyed auswärtsschielend
walrus Walroß n.
wambles Milchkrankheit f.
wandering wandernd
wandering cell Wanderzelle f.
wandering kidney Wanderniere f.
want Mangel m., Bedarf m.
—, **to** benötigen, bedürfen

Warburg's yellow enzyme Warburgsches Atmungsferment n.
ward Krankensaal m., Krankenstation f.
ward, isolation Isolierstation f.
ward patient stationär liegender Patient m.
warm d. e.
—, **to** wärmen, erwärmen
warm-blooded warmblütig
warming bath Überwärmungsbad n.
— **bottle** Wärmflasche f.
warmth Wärme f.
warping seuchenhafter Abortus m. (veter.)
wart Warze f.
Wartenberg's sign Wartenbergsches Zeichen n.
warty warzig
war veterans, service for the care of — militärische Versorgungsbehörde f.
wash Waschen n., Wäsche f., Spülung f.; Spülflüssigkeit f.
—, **to** waschen, spülen
— **cannula** Spülkanüle f.
— **catheter** Spülkatheter m.
washable waschbar
wash off, to abspülen, abwaschen
washout method Auswaschmethode f.
wasp Wespe f.

Wassermann's test Wassermannsche Reaktion f.
waste Verschwendung f.; Abfall m., Schlacke f.; Schwund m.
waste-dressing pail Verbandstoffeimer m.
waste gas Abgas n.
waste water Abwasser n.
wasting palsy progressive Muskelatrophie f.
water Wasser n.
–, **to** verwässern
– **bath** Wasserbad n.
–, **distilled** destilliertes Wasser n.
–, **heavy** schweres Wasser n.
–, **potable** Trinkwasser n.
– **proof** wasserdicht
– **-closet** Toilette f., Wasserklosett n.
Waterhouse-Friderichsen syndrome Waterhouse-Friderichsen-Syndrom n.
water-soluble wasserlöslich
watt d. e. n.
wave Welle f.
–, **decimeter** Dezimeterwelle f.
– **length** Wellenlänge f.
–, **sharp (EEG)** steile Welle f.
wax Wachs n.
– **bath** Wachsbad n.
– **model** Wachsabdruck m.
– **molding spoon** Wachsfließer m.
waxy wächsern
WBC (= white blood count) weißes Blutbild n.
weak schwach
weaken, to schwächen
weakening Schwächung f.
weak-minded schwachsinnig
weakness Schwäche f.
weal Wohl n., Wohlfahrt f.
wean, to entwöhnen
wear Tragen n.; Abnutzung f.; Ermüdung f.
wear, to tragen; abnutzen; ermüden

weasand Luftröhre f.
weasel Wiesel n.
web Gewebe n., Netzwerk n.; Schwimmhaut f.
web, spider's Spinnwebe f.
webbed fingers Fingerverwachsung f., Syndaktylie f.
webbed penis Penis palmatus
webbed toes Zehenverwachsung f., Syndaktylie f.
weber d. e. n.
Weber's syndrome Webersches Syndrom n.
Weber's test Weberscher Versuch m.
wedge Keil m.
– **pressure** Verkeilungsdruck m.
wedging of a vertebra Keilwirbelbildung f.
wedlock Ehe f.
Wegener's granulomatosis Wegenersche Granulomatose f.
Weichbrodt's reaction Weichbrodtsche Reaktion f.
Weigert's method Weigertsche Methode f.
weight Gewicht n.
weight gain Gewichtszunahme f.
weightless schwerelos
weightlessness Schwerelosigkeit f.
weight loss Gewichtsverlust m., Gewichtsabnahme f.
weight reduction Gewichtsverminderung f.
Weil's disease Weilsche Krankheit f.
Weil-Felix reaction Weil-Felixsche-Reaktion f.
weld, to schweißen
welfare Wohlfahrt f.
wellbeing Wohlbefinden n.
Wenckebach's period Wenckebachsche Periode f.
Werdnig-Hoffmann type Werdnig-Hoffmannscher Typ m.
Werlhof's disease Werlhofsche Purpura f.

Werner's syndrome Wernersches Syndrom n.
Wertheim's operation Wertheimsche Operation f.
Westphal's sign Westphalsches Zeichen n.
wet naß, feucht
– **-brain** Gehirnödem n.
– **-nurse** Amme f.
– **-pack** feuchte Packung f., Wickel m.
wet, to nässen, benetzen
wether Hammel m.
Wharton's jelly Whartonsche Sulze f.
wheal Striemen m., Hautverdickung f.
wheat germ oil Weizenkeimöl n.
Wheatstone's bridge Wheatstonesche Brücke f.
wheel Rad n.
wheel, to drehen, sich drehen
wheel-chair Rollstuhl m.
wheeze, to keuchen
whelk Hautverdickung f.
whey Molke f.
Whipple's disease Whipplesche Krankheit f.
whipworm Trichocephalus dispar
whirl Wirbel m., Strudel m.
whisky d. e. m.
whisper, to flüstern
whistle Pfeife f.
whistle, Galton's Galtonsche Pfeife f.
white blood cell weißes Blutkörperchen n.
– **blood count** weißes Blutbild n.
– **of egg** Eiweiß n.
whites weißer Fluß m.
whitlow Panaritium n.
whole body computed tomography Ganzkörper-Computertomographie f.
wholesome bekömmlich, heilsam
whoop Keuchhustenanfall m.
whooping cough Keuchhusten m.

widow Witwe f.
widower Witwer m.
wife Ehefrau f., Gattin f.
Wigand's maneuver Wigandscher Handgriff m.
Wilkinson's ointment Wilkinsonsche Salbe f.
will Wille m.
Wilson's disease Wilsonsche Krankheit f.
wind, broken (veter.) paroxysmale Dyspnoe f.; Dämpfigkeit f.
wind gall (veter.) Gallen f. pl.
winding Windung f.
windpipe Luftröhre f.
wind up, to aufwickeln, aufspulen
wing Flügel m.
– **of the nose** Nasenflügel m.
wink, to blinzeln
Wintrich's sign Wintrichscher Schallwechsel m.
wipe, to wischen, abwischen, reinigen, trocknen
wire Draht m.
– **arch** Drahtbogen m.
– **saw** Drahtsäge f.
wire traction Drahtzug m.
wiring Drahtnaht f.
wisdom tooth Weisheitszahn m.
wither, to welken, austrocknen
withdraw, to entziehen
withdrawal Entzug m., Entziehung f.
– **bleeding** Abbruchblutung f.
– **method** Entziehungsmethode f.
– **pains** Entziehungsbeschwerden f. pl.
withers Widerrist m.
Witte's peptone Wittepepton n.
Witzel's fistula Witzelfistel f.
Wohlgemuth's test Wohlgemuthsche Probe f.
wolf d. e. m.
Wolff-Parkinson-White syndrome Wolff-Parkinson-White-Syndrom n.
Wolframium Wolfram n.

woman doctor Ärztin f.
womb Gebärmutter f.
women's disease Frauenkrankheit f.
wood pulp Zellstoff m.
wool fat Adeps lanae anhydricus
− fat, hydrous Adeps lanae
word blindness Wortblindheit f.
word deafness Worttaubheit f.
working through Verarbeitung f.
worm Wurm n.
wormseed Wurmsamen m.
wormwood Wermut m.
wormy wurmig
worker bee Arbeitsbiene f.
work table Arbeitstisch m.
worry Quälerei f.; Aufregung f.
worry, to quälen; sich sorgen, sich aufregen
wound Wunde f.
−, blowing offener Pneumothorax m.
wound clip Wundklammer f.
−, contused Quetschwunde f.
−, incised Schnittwunde f.
−, lacerated Rißwunde f.
−, punctured Stichwunde f.
− fever Wundfieber n.
wounding Verwundung f.
wrap, to wickeln
wrench Verrenkung f.
wrick Verrenkung f.
wrinkle Runzel f.
wrinkled runzelig
wrist Handgelenk n., Handwurzel
wristdrop Fallhand f.
wrought bearbeitet, geschmiedet; schmiedbar
wryneck Schiefhals m.
Wuchereria bancrofti Filaria bancrofti

X

xanthelasma d. e. n.
xanthene Xanthen n.
xanthine Xanthin n.
xanthinoxidase Xanthinoxydase f.
xanthinuria Xanthinurie f.
xanthochromatic xanthochrom
xanthochromia Xanthochromie f.
xanthochromic xanthochrom
xanthoma Xanthom n.
xanthomatosis Xanthomatose f.
xanthomatous xanthomatös
xanthoprotein d. e. n.
xanthopsia Xanthopsie f.
xanthosarcoma Xanthosarkom n.
xanthosine Xanthosin n.
xanthosis Xanthose f.
xenon d. e. n.
xeroderma d. e. n.
xerographic xerographisch
xerography Xerographie f.
xerophthalmia Xerophthalmie f.
xeroradiographical xeroradiographisch
xeroradiography Xeroradiographie f.
xerosis Xerose f.
xiphoid process Schwertfortsatz m.
x-ray apparatus Röntgenapparat m.
x-ray processor Film-Entwicklungsmaschine f.
x-ray tube Röntgenröhre f.
x-rays Röntgenstrahlen m. pl.
x-ray sickness Röntgenkater m.
xylene Xylol n.
xylidine Xylidin n.
xylitol d. e. n.
xylometazoline Xylometazolin n.
xylose d. e. f.
xylulose d. e. f.

Y

yam Yamwurzel f.
yarn Garn n.
yaw Frambösie-Exanthem n.
yawn, to gähnen
yaws Frambösie f.
year of birth Geburtsjahr n.
yeast Hefe f.
yellow fever Gelbfieber n.

yield, to tragen, ertragen, gewähren, sich fügen
yoghurt Yoghurt f.
yogurt Yoghurt f.
yohimbine Yohimbin n.
yolk Eigelb n.; Wollfett n.
ytterbium d. e. n.
yttrium d. e. n.

Z

Zander apparatus Zanderapparat m.
Zangemeister's maneuver Zangemeisterscher Handgriff m.
zebra d. e. n.
zebu d. e. m.
Zenker's diverticulum Zenkersches Divertikel n.
zero null
zest Würze f.
Ziehl-Neelsen's method Ziehl-Neelsen-Färbung f.
zinc Zink n.
− acetate Zinkazetat n.
− chloride Zinkchlorid n.
− oxide Zinkoxyd n.
− ointment Zinksalbe f.
− paste Zinkpaste f.
− sulfate (a) Zinksulfat n.
− sulphate (e) Zinksulfat n.
zincalism Zinkvergiftung f.
Zinn's zonule Zonula Zinni
zirconium Zirkonium n.
Zollinger-Ellison syndrome Zollinger-Ellison-Syndrom n.
zona Gürtel m.; Gürtelrose f.
zonal d. e.
zonation Zonierung f.
zone d. e. f.
−, Head's Headsche Zone f.
zonography Zonographie f.

zonule of Zinn Zonula Zinni
zonulolysis Zonulolyse f.
zoogony Zoogonie f.
zoological zoologisch
zoologist Zoologe m.; Zoologin f.
zoology Zoologie f.
zoonosis Zoonose f.
zoopathology Tierpathologie f.
zoopsychology Tierpsychologie f.
zoster d. e. m.
zosteriform zosterartig
zoxazoleamine Zoxazolamin n.
Zuckerkandl's organ Zuckerkandlsches Organ n.
zygoma Jochbogen m.
zygomatic process Processus zygomaticus
zygomaticofacial zygomatikofazial
zygomaticofrontal zygomatikofrontal
zygomaticoorbital zygomatikoorbital
zygomaxillary zygomaxillär
zygotic zygot
zymase d. e. f.
zymogen Proferment n.
zymogenic fermentativ
zymogenous fermentativ
zymology Fermentlehre f.
zymolysis Zymolyse f.
zymosis Gärung f.

ZWEITER TEIL

Deutsch-Englisch

SECOND PART

German-English

A

A.A. (= Anonyme Alkoholiker) Alcoholics Anonymous
Abadiesches Zeichen Abadie's sign
abakteriell abacterial
Abart variety
Abasie abasia
abaxial e. e.
Abbau degradation, dissimilation
abbauen to degrade, to dissimilate
Abbiegung deflection, deviation
abbinden to tie, to ligate
Abbindung deligation, ligation
abblättern to exfoliate
Abblassen fading
Abblassung, bitemporale bitemporal pallor
Abbruchblutung withdrawal bleeding
Abdampfschale evaporating dish
Abdecker horse-knacker
Abderhalden-Fanconisches Syndrom cystine storage disease
Abderhaldensche Reaktion Abderhalden's reaction
Abdomen e. e.
abdominal e. e.
Abdominalgie abdominalgia
abdominoanterior e. e.
abdominogenital e. e.
abdominoperineal e. e.
abdominoposterior e. e.
Abdominoskop abdominoscope
Abdominoskopie abdominoscopy
abdominoskopisch abdominoscopical
abdominoskrotal abdominoscrotal
abdominothorakal abdominothoracic
abdominovaginal e. e.
abdominovesikal abdominovesical
Abdominozentese abdominocentesis
abdominozystisch abdominocystic
Abdruck (dent.) impression
Abdrucklöffel impression tray
Abdruck nehmen, einen to take an impression
Abduktion abduction
Abduktionsschiene abduction splint
Abduktor abductor
abduzieren to abduct
Aberration e. e.
aberrierend aberrant
Abfall (= Abstieg) descent
– (= Überbleibsel) waste
abfallen (= absteigen) to descend
– (= übrig bleiben) to be lost
abflachen to bevel
Abfluß flowing off
abführen to purge
abführend purgative, laxative
Abführmittel purgative, laxative
Abgas waste gas
abgehen to be discharged
abgemagert emaciated
abgestorben mortified, dead
abgewöhnen to leave off
abgrenzen to bound
Abgrenzung delimitation, bound, boundary
abhängig dependent
Abhängigkeit dependence
abhärten to harden
abhobeln to plane
abhorchen to listen, to auscultate
Abiogenese abiogenesis
abiogenetisch abiogenetic

Abiose abiosis
abiotisch abiotic
Abiotrophie abiotrophy
abiotrophisch abiotrophic
abiuretisch abiuretic
Abkauung attrition
abklemmen to clamp
Abklemmvorrichtung tourniquet
abklingen to subside
Abklingen subsidence
Abklingquote disappearance rate
abkochen to decoct
Abkochung decoction, concoction
Abkühlung refrigeration
Abkürzung abbreviation
Ablagerung deposit
Ablagerungsvorgang deposal
Ablaktation ablactation
Ablatio ablation
Ablatio mammae mastectomy
Ablehnung rejection
ableiten to derive
ableiten (Flüssigkeit) to draw off
ableitend derivative
ableitendes Mittel derivative
Ableitung derivation
– **(EKG)** lead, circuit
Ablenkung deflection; shunt
ablösen to ablate
Ablösung (= Loslösung) ablation, detachment
abmagern to get thin
Abmagerung emaciation
Abnahme (= Verringerung) decrease
abnehmen to decrease
– **(= abmagern)** to get thin
abnorm abnormal
Abnormität abnormity
Abnutzung wearing out
Abokklusion abocclusion
aboral e. e.
Abort (= Fehlgeburt) abortion
abortieren to abort
abortiv abortive
Abortivum abortive, aborticide
Abortus arteficialis artificial abortion
Abortus completus complete abortion
– **criminalis** criminal abortion
– **febrilis** febrile abortion
– **imminens** imminent abortion
– **incompletus** incomplete abortion
–**, seuchenhafter (veter.)** warping
Abortuszange ovum forceps
Abprall rebound
Abrachie abrachia
Abrachiozephalie abrachiocephalia
abradieren to abrade
Abrasio abrasion
Abrasion e. e.
Abreagieren abreaction
Abreaktion abreaction
Abreibung friction, ablution
Abriß avulsion
Abrufbeatmung demand ventilation
Abrufprogramm calling program
abrunden to round off
abrupt e. e.
absaugen to suck
abschaben to abrade
abscheiden to secrete
abschilfern to shed in scales, to defurfurate
Abschirmung screening
Abschlußkontrolle final check
Abschnürbinde tourniquet
abschrägen to bevel
Abschürfung abrasion
abschuppen to desquamate
Abschuppung desquamation
abschwellen to shrink
abschwellend shrinking; decongestant
abschwellendes Mittel decongestant
Abschwellung detumescence, shrinkage
absetzen, eine Behandlung to discontinue a treatment
absetzen, ein Glied to amputate a limb

Absetzen einer Therapie discontinuation of a therapy
Absicht intention
absichtlich intentional
absolut absolute
absondern (= ausscheiden) to excrete, to secrete
— (= isolieren) to isolate, to separate
Absonderung (= Ausscheidung) secretion
— (= Isolierung) isolation, separation
Absorbens absorbent
absorbieren to absorb
absorbierend absorptive
Absorption e. e.
Absorptionsfähigkeit absorbability
Abspaltung scission
absplittern to splinter
abspülen to wash off
abspulen to unwind
abstammen to descend
Abstammung descent
Abstand distance
absteigen to descend
absterben to mortify
Absterben mortification, sphacelation
absterben (= gefühllos werden) to get numb
Abstieg descent
Abstillen delactation
abstinent e. e.
Abstinenz abstinence
abstoßend repellent
Abstoßung repulsion, rejection
abstrakt abstract
Abstraktion abstraction
Abstrich microscopic preparation
Abszeß abscess, gathering
—, **Brodiescher** Brodie's abscess
—, **heißer** hot abscess
—, **kalter** cold abscess
Abszeßmesser abscess lancet
Abszisse abscissa

Abtastmethode scanning method
Abulie abulia
abulisch abulic
Abulomanie abulomania
abwaschen to wash off
Abwaschung ablution
Abwasser sewerage, waste water
Abwehr defence (e), defense (a)
Abwehrmechanismus defence mechanism
Abweichung aberration; deviation; deflection
abwenden to avert
abwerten to degrade
abwischen to wipe
abzapfen to tap
Abzweigung shunt
Acanthosis nigricans e. e.
Accretio accretion
Acetabuloplastik acetabuloplasty
Acetanilid e. e.
Acetat acetate
Acetazolamid acetazoleamide
Aceton acetone
Acetophenetidin e. e.
Acetylcholin acetylcholine
Achalasie achalasia
Achat agate
Acheilie acheilia
Achillessehne Achilles tendon
Achillessehnenreflex Achilles reflex, ankle jerk
Achillodynie achillodynia
Achillorrhaphie achillorrhaphy
Achillotomie achillotomy
Achlorhydrie achlorhydria
achlorhydrisch achlorhydric
Acholie acholia
acholisch acholic
Acholurie acholuria
acholurisch acholuric
Achondroplasie achondroplasia
Achorese achoresis
achrestisch achrestic
Achromat e. e.
achromatisch achromatic
Achromatopsie achromatopsia

Achromie achromia
Achse axis
Achselhöhle axilla, armpit
Achsenverschiebung axial shift
Achsenzugzange axis-traction forceps
Achsenzylinder axis cylinder
Achsenzylinderfortsatz neuraxon
achteckig octagonal
achtwertig octavalent
Achylie achylia
achylisch achylic
Achymie achymia
Acidimeter e. e.
Acidose acidosis
acidotisch acidotic
Acne e. e.
Aconitin aconitine
Acrocyanose acrocyanosis
Acrodermatitis e. e.
Acrylamid acrylamide
Acrylat acrylate
ACTH-freisetzender Faktor corticotropin releasing factor
Actinid actinide
Actinomycin e. e.
Actinomycosis e. e.
Acylguanidin acylguanidine
Acylureidomethylpenicillin e. e.
adäquat adequate
Adamantin adamantine
Adamantinom adamantinoma
Adamantoblast e. e.
Adamsapfel Adam's apple
Adams-Stokessches Syndrom Adams-Stokes disease
Adamsit adamsite
Adaptation e. e.
Adapter e. e.
Addisonismus addisonism
Addisonsche Krankheit Addison's disease
Adduktion adduction
Adduktor adductor
Adduktorenkanal Hunter's canal
adduzieren to adduct
adelomorph adelomorphous

Adenin adenine
Adenitis e. e.
adenitisch adenitic
Adenoakanthom adeno-acanthoma
Adenoangiosarkom adeno-angiosarcoma
Adenoblast e. e.
Adenochondrom adenochondroma
Adenochondrosarkom adenochondrosarcoma
Adenofibrom adenofibroma
Adenohypophyse adenohypophysis
adenoid e. e.
adenoide Vegetationen hypertrophy of adenoids
Adenoidektomie adenoidectomy
Adenokarzinom adenocarcinoma
Adenolipomatose adenolipomatosis
Adenom adenoma
– **des Inselgewebes** adenoma of insular tissue
Adenoma sebaceum e. e.
– **sudoriferum** e. e.
adenomatös adenomatous
Adenomatose adenomatosis
Adenomyom adenomyoma
Adenosin adenosine
Adenosintriphosphat adenosine triphosphate
Adenosklerose adenosclerosis
Adenotom adenotome
Adenotomie adenotomy
Adenovirus e. e.
Adenovirusinfektion adenoviral infection
Adenozele adenocele
Adenylat adenylate
Adeps lanae hydrous wool fat
– **lanae anhydricus** wool fat
Ader (= Vene) vein
– **lassen, zur** to let blood
Aderhaut choroid membrane
Aderlaß bloodletting, bleeding
Adermin e. e.

Adhäsion adhesion
adiabatisch adiabatic
Adiadochokinese adiadokokinesis
Adiaphorese adiaphoresis
Adiesches Syndrom Adie's syndrome
adipös adipose
Adipositas adiposis
Adipositas dolorosa adiposis dolorosa, Dercum's disease
adiposogenital e. e.
Adipsie adipsia
adjustieren to adjust
Adjuvans adjuvant
Adnexanheftung adnexopexy
Adnexitis e. e.
adnexitisch adnexitic
Adnexopexie adnexopexy
Adoleszent adolescent
Adoleszenz adolescence
Adonidin e. e.
Adonit adonitol, ribitol
adrenal e. e.
Adrenalektomie adrenalectomy
adrenalektomieren to adrenalectomize
Adrenalin epinephrine
adrenergisch adrenergic
adrenogenital e. e.
adrenokortikotrop adrenocorticotropic
adrenokortikotropes Hormon adrenocorticotropic hormone
adrenolytisch adrenolytic
Adrenorezeptor adrenoreceptor
adrenotrop adrenotropic
Adriamycin e. e.
adsorbieren to adsorb
Adsorption e. e.
Adstringens astringent
adstringierend astringent
Adventitia e. e.
Adynamie adynamia
ächzen to sigh, to groan
Ägophonie aegophony (e), egophony (a)
ähnlich similar

Äquilibrierung equilibration
Äquilibriometrie equilibriometry
äquimolekular equimolecular
Äquivalenz equivalence
aerob aerobic, aerobical
Aerobier aerobe
Aerogramm aerogram
Aerographie aerography
aerographisch aerographic
Aeroneurose aeroneurosis
Aerophagie aerophagy
Aerosol e. e.
Aerozystoskopie aerocystoscopy
aerozystoskopisch aerocystoscopic
Ärztemuster physician sample
Ärztetasche physician's bag
Ärzteverein medical society
Ärztin lady doctor
ärztlich medical
ärztliche Berufsordnung code of medical ethics
Äsculin aesculin (e), esculin (a)
ästhetisch aesthetical (e), esthetical (a)
Äthambutol ethambutol
Äthan ethane
Äther ether
Äthinyl ethinyl
Äthionamid ethionamide
Äthyl ethyl
Äthylalkohol ethanol
Äthylen ethylene
Äthylendiamin ethylenediamine
Äthylenimino-Gruppe ethyleneimino group
Äthylierung ethylation
Äthylismus ethylism
Äthylmorphinhydrochlorid ethylmorphine hydrochloride
Ätiandiolon etiandiolone
Ätianolon etianolone
Ätiologie aetiology (e), etiology (a)
ätiologisch aetiologic (e), etiologic (a)
Ätioporphyrin aetioporphyrin
ätzen corrode, to

ätzend escharotic, corrosive
ätzendes Mittel escharotic, corrosive
Ätzkali potassium hydroxide
Affe monkey
Affe, schwanzloser ape
Affekt affect
Affektepilepsie affect epilepsy
Affektion affection
Affektlabilität affective instability
affektiv affective
Affektschwäche affective instability
affenartig simian
Affenhand monkey paw
Affenspalte ape fissure
afferent e. e.
Afferenz afference
Affinität affinity
affizieren to affect
Afflux e. e.
Afibronogenämie afibrinogenaemia (e), afibrinogenemia (a)
Aflatoxin e. e.
After anus
Afterklaue dew-claw
Agalaktie agalactia
Agammaglobulinämie agammaglobulinaemia (e), agammaglobulinemia (a)
Aganglionose aganglionosis
Agar e. e.
−, Ascites- ascitic fluid agar
−, Blut- blood agar
−, Brillantgrün- brilliant green agar
−, Dextrose- dextrose agar
−, Dieudonné- Dieudonné's agar
−, Drigalski- Drigalski's agar
−, Fuchsin- fuchsin agar
−, Gallensalz- bile salt agar
−, Gelatine- gelatin agar
−, Glukose- glucose agar
−, Kartoffel-Blut- potato-blood agar
−, Löffler- Löffler's agar

Agar, Serum- serum agar
−, Tellurit- tellurite agar
Agarizin agaricin
agastrisch agastric
Agenitalismus agenitalism
Agens agent
Ageusie ageusia
Agglomerat agglomerate
agglutinabel agglutinable
Agglutination e. e.
agglutinieren to agglutinate
Agglutinin e. e.
Agglutinogen e. e.
Aggravation e. e.
aggravieren to aggravate
Aggregat aggregate
Aggregation e. e.
Aggression e. e.
aggressiv aggressive
Agitation e. e.
Aglukon aglucone
Aglykon aglucone
Agnosie agnosia
agonal e. e.
Agonie agony
Agonist e. e.
Agoraphobie agoraphobia
Agrammatismus agrammatism
agranulozytär agranulocytic
Agranulozytose agranulocytosis
Agraphie agraphia
Agrypnie agrypnia
Ahlfeldsches Zeichen Ahlfeld's sign
Ahorn maple
Ajmalin ajmaline
Akademie academy
Akademiker academic
Akademikerin academic
akademisch academic
Akalkulie acalculia
Akanthom acanthoma
Akanthose acanthosis
Akapnie acapnia
Akardie acardia
Akinästhesie akinaesthesia (e), akinesthesia (a)
Akinesie akinesia

akinetisch akinetic
akklimatisieren to acclimatize
Akklimatisierung acclimation, acclimatization
Akkommodation accommodation
akkommodieren to accommodate
Akkommodometer accommodometer
Akkretion accretion
Akkumulator accumulator
Akne acne
Akonit aconite
Akonitin aconitine
Akridin acridine
Akrodynie acrodynia
Akrohyperhidrose acrohyperhidrosis
akromegal acromegalic
Akromegalie acromegaly
akromioklavikulär acromioclavicular
akromioskapulär acromioscapular
akromiothorakal acromiothoracic
Akropachie acropachy
Akroparästhesie acroparaesthesia (e), acroparesthesia (a)
akroparästhetisch acroparaesthetic (e), acroparesthetic (a)
Akrozyanose acrocyanosis
akrozyanotisch acrocyanotic
Akrylamid acrylamide
Akrylat acrylate
Aktinid actinide
Aktinium actinium
Aktinobazillose actinobacillosis
Aktinomykose actinomycosis
aktinomykotisch actinomycotic
Aktinomycin actinomycin
Aktinotherapie actinotherapy
aktiv active
Aktivator activator
aktivieren to activate
Aktivierung activation
Aktivierungssystem, retikuläres alerting system
Aktivität activity

Aktomyosin actomyosin
aktualisieren to update
Aktualisierung updating
Akuität acuity
Akupunktur acupuncture
Akustik acoustics
Akustikusneurinom acoustic neurinoma
akustisch acoustic
akut acute
akute gelbe Atrophie acute yellow atrophy
Akzent accent
Akzentuation accentuation
akzentuieren to accentuate
Alabamin alabamine
Alanin alanine
Alarm e. e.
Alastrim e. e.
Alaun alum
Albers-Schönbergsche Marmorknochenkrankheit marble bones disease
Albinismus albinism
Albino e. e.
albinotisch albinotic
Albrightsches Syndrom Albright's disease
Albuginea e. e.
Albugineotomie albugineotomy
Albumin e. e.
Albuminimeter e. e.
Albuminurie albuminuria
albuminurisch albuminuric
Albumose e. e.
Alcianblau alcian blue
Aldehyd aldehyde
Aldohexose e. e.
Aldokortikosteron aldocorticosterone
Aldol e. e.
Aldolase e. e.
Aldose e. e.
Aldosteron aldosterone
Aldosteronismus aldosteronism
Aldrin e.e.

Aleukämie aleukaemia (e),
aleukemia (a)
aleukämisch aleukaemic (e),
aleukemic (a)
Aleukie aleukia
Alexander-Adams-Operation
Alexander-Adams operation
Alexie alexia
Alexin e. e.
Algebra e. e.
Alginat alginate
alimentär alimentary
aliphatisch aliphatic
Alizarin e. e.
Alizaringelb alizarin yellow
alizyklisch alicyclic
Alkali e. e.
Alkaligehalt alkalinity
Alkalinität alkalinity
Alkalireserve alkali reserve
Alkalisation alkalization, alkalinization
alkalisch alkaline
alkalisieren to alkalify, to alkalize
Alkalisierung alkalization, alkalinization
Alkaloid e. e.
Alkalose alkalosis
alkalotisch alkalotic
Alkapton e. e.
Alkaptonurie alkaptonuria
Alkohol alcohol
–, **absoluter** absolute alcohol
–, **Äthyl-** ethyl alcohol
–, **Allyl-** allyl alcohol
–, **Amyl-** amyl alcohol
–, **aromatischer** aromatic alcohol
–, **Butyl-** butyl alcohol
–, **Cetyl-** cetyl alcohol
–, **dehydrierter** dehydrated alcohol
–, **Methyl-** methyl alcohol
–, **primärer** primary alcohol
–, **Propyl-** propyl alcohol
–, **sekundärer** secondary alcohol
–, **tertiärer** tertiary alcohol
–, **ungesättigter** unsaturated alcohol

Alkohol, verdünnter diluted alcohol
–, **vergällter** embittered alcohol
Alkoholblockade alcohol block
Alkoholiker alcoholic
Alkoholiker, anonyme
alcoholics anonymous
Alkoholikerin alcoholic
alkoholisch alcoholic
Alkoholismus alcoholism
Alkoholsucht alcohol addiction
Alkyl e. e.
Alkylamin alkylamine
alkylieren to alkylate
Allantoin e. e.
Allantois e. e.
allelomorph allelomorphic
Allelomorphie allelomorphism
Allen-Doisy-Test Allen-Doisy test
Allergen e. e.
Allergie allergy
allergisch allergic
allergisieren to allergize
Allergisierung allergization
Allergose allergosis
Allerweltsmittel panchrest
Alles-oder-Nichts-Gesetz
all or none law
Allgemeinbefinden general state of health
Allgemeinpraktiker general practitioner
Allgemeinpraxis general practice
Alligator e. e.
Allobiose allobiosis
allobiotisch allobiotic
Allopath allopathist
Allopathie allopathy
Allopathin allopathist
allopathisch allopathic
Allopregnan allopregnane
Allopregnandiol e. e.
Allopregnanolon allopregnanolone
Allopsychose allopsychosis
allopsychotisch allopsychotic
Allopurinol e. e.
Allorhythmie allorhythmia
allorhythmisch allorhythmic

allotypisch allotypic
Alloxan e. e.
Alloxazin alloxazine
Alloxin e. e.
Allyl e. e.
Allzweckmaschine general-purpose machine
Aloe e. e.
Aloin e. e.
Alopecia areata e. e., porrigo decalvans, pelade
Alopezie alopecia
—,seborrhoische alopecia furfuracea, dandruff
Alpdrücken nightmare
alphabetisch alphabetic
Alpha-Globulin alpha globulin
— -Methyldopa alpha-methyl-dopa
— -Rezeptor alpha receptor
— -Strahl alpha ray
— -Strahler alpha emitter
—,Welle alpha wave
— -Zelle alpha cell
Alprenolol e. e.
Alter age
Alter, höheres advanced age
Alteration e. e.
altern to grow old
Altern senescence, insenescence, ageing, aging
alternd senescent
alternierend alternating
altersabhängig age-dependent
Altersdemenz senile dementia
Altersgrenze age-limit
Altersheim old people's home
altersschwach age-worn
alterssichtig presbyopic
Alterssichtigkeit presbyopia
Altersveränderungen age changes
Alttuberkulin old tuberculin
Aluminat aluminate
Aluminium e.e., aluminum (a)
Aluminiumoxyd alumina
Aluminose aluminosis
Alveobronchiolitis e. e.
alveolär alveolar

Alveolarabszeß alveolar abscess
Alveolarluft alveolar air
Alveolarpyorrhöe pyorrhea alveolaris (a), pyrrhoea alveolaris (e)
Alveole alveolus
Alveolektomie alveolectomy
Alveolitis e. e.
alveoloarteriell alveoloarterial
alveolodental e. e.
alveolokapillär alveolocapillary
Alveoloklasie alveoloclasia
Alveoloplastik alveoloplasty
Alveolotomie alveolotomy
alveolovenös alveolovenous
Alveolyse alveolysis
Alymphie alymphia
Alzheimersche Krankheit Alzheimer's disease
Amalgam e. e.
amalgamieren to amalgamate
Amalgamlöffel amalgam spoon
Amalgammischer amalgamator
Amalgamstopfer amalgam plugger
Amalgamträger amalgam carrier
Amastie amastia
Amaurose amaurosis
amaurotisch amaurotic
ambivalent e. e.
Ambivalenz ambivalence
Amblyopie amblyopia
Amboß anvil
ambulant e. e., ambulatory
ambulante Patientin out-patient
ambulanter Patient out-patient
Ambulanz outpatient department
Ambulatorium outpatient department; outpatient clinic
Ameisenlaufen formication
Ameisensäure formic acid
Amelie amelia
Ameloblast e. e.
Ameloblastom ameloblastoma
amelodentinal e. e.
Amenorrhöe amenorrhea (a), amenorrhoea (e)

amenorrhoisch amenorrheal (a), amenorrhoic (e)
Ametropie ametropia
Amid amide
Amidase e. e.
Amilorid amiloride
Amimie amimia
Amin amine
Aminase e. e.
Aminochinolin aminoquinoline
Aminopeptidase e. e.
Aminophenazol aminophenazole
Aminophyllin aminophylline
Aminoprotease e. e.
Aminopyrin aminopyrine
Aminosäure amino acid
Aminothiazol aminothiazole
Aminotransferase e. e.
amitotisch amitotic
Amitriptylin amitriptyline
Amme wet-nurse
Ammoniak ammonia
ammoniakhaltig ammoniacal
Ammonium e. e.
Ammoniumazetat ammonium acetate
Ammoniumchlorid ammonium chloride
Ammoniumkarbonat ammonium carbonate
Ammoniumsalizylat ammonium salicylate
Ammonshorn Ammon's horn
Amnesie amnesia
amnestisch amnestic
Amniographie amniography
amniographisch amniographic
Amnion e. e.
Amöbe ameba (a), amoeba (e)
Amöbenruhr amebic dysentery (a), amoebic dysentery (e)
amöboid ameboid (a), amoeboid (e)
amorph amorphous
Amoxicillin e. e.
Ampere e. e.
Amphetamin amphetamine
Amphiarthrosis amphiarthrosis
Amphibie amphibium
amphibol amphibolic
amphorisch amphoric
amphoter amphoteric
Amphotericin e. e.
Ampicillin e. e.
Amplitude e. e.
ampullär ampullar
Ampulle (anat.) ampulla
– (pharm.) ampoule, ampule
ampullieren to ampoulate
Amputation e. e.
Amputationsmesser amputation knife
Amputationssäge amputation saw
Amputationsstumpf amputation stump
amputieren to amputate
Amputierter amputee
Amusie amusia
amusisch amusic
Amygdalin e. e.
Amyl e. e.
Amylase e. e.
Amylen amylene
Amylenhydrat amylene hydrate
Amylnitrit amyl nitrite
amyloid e. e.
Amyloid e. e.
Amyloidnephrose amyloid nephrosis
Amyloidose amyloidosis
Amylomaltase e. e.
Amylopektin amylopectin
Amylose e. e.
amyostatisch amyostatic
Amyotrophie amyotrophia
amyotrophisch amyotrophic
amyotrophische Lateralsklerose amyotrophic lateral sclerosis
Anabiose anabiosis
Anabolikum anabolic
anabolisch anabolic
Anacholie anacholia
Anachorese anachoresis
anachoretisch anachoric

Anämie anaemia (e), anemia (a)
—, **aplastische** aplastic anaemia (e), aplastic anemia (a)
—, **perniziöse** pernicious anaemia (e), pernicious anemia (a)
anämisch anaemic (e), anemic (a)
anaerob anaerobical
Anaerobier anaerobe
Anästhesie anaesthesia (e), anesthesia (a)
Anästhesienadel anaesthesia needle (e), anesthesia needle (a)
anästhesieren to anaesthetize (e), to anesthetize (a)
Anästhesiologie anaesthesiology (e), anesthesiology (a)
anästhesiologisch anaesthesiologic (e), anesthesiologic (a)
anästhetisch anaesthetic (e), anesthetic (a)
anaklitisch anaclitic
anal e. e.
Analbuminämie analbuminaemia (e), analbuminemia (a)
Analeptikum analeptic
analeptisch analeptic
analeptisches Mittel analeptic
Analfissur fissure of anus
Analfistel fistula of anus
Analgesie analgesia
Analgetikum analgesic
analgetisch analgesic
analgetisches Mittel analgesic
analog analog (a), analogue (e)
Analogie analogy
Analyse analysis
analysieren to analyse, to analyze
analytisch analytic
Anamnese anamnesis
anamnestisch anamnestic
Anaphase e. e.
Anaphorese anaphoresis
anaphylaktisch anaphylactic
Anaphylaxie anaphylaxis
Anaplasie anaplasia
Anaplasmose anaplasmosis, gall-sickness, galziekte

anaplastisch anaplastic
Anastigmat e. e.
anastigmatisch anastigmatic
Anastomose anastomosis
anastomosieren to anastomose
anastomotisch anastomotic
Anatom anatomist
Anatomie anatomy
anatomisch anatomic
Anatoxin e. e.
anazid anacid
Anazidität anacidity
anbehandeln to perform initial treatment
andeuten tu suggest
Ancrod e. e.
Andeutung suggestion
Andradiol e. e.
androgen androgenic
Androgen e. e.
Androgynie androgynism
Andrologie andrology
Androstan androstane
Androstandiol e. e.
Androstandion e. e.
Androstendion e. e.
Androstenolon androstenolone
Androsteron androsterone
Anenzaphalie anencephaly
Anergie anergy
anergisch anergic
Aneurin thiamine
Aneurysma aneurysm
aneurysmatisch aneurysmal
anfällig susceptible
Anfälligkeit susceptibility, propensity
Anfall onset, fit, attack, seizure
Anfangsstadium initial stage
anfeuchten to moisten
Anfeuchtung madefaction
angeboren connatal, inborn
angeerbt inherited
Angelhakenmagen fishhook stomach
angenehm agreeable
angewandte Biologie applied biology

Angiektasie angiectasis
Angiektomie angiectomy
Angiitis e. e.
angiitisch angiitic
Angina e. e.
− **agranulocytica** agranulocytic angina
− **follicularis** follicular angina
− **lacunaris** lacunar angina
− **Ludovici** Ludwig's angina
− **pectoris** e. e.
− **Plaut-Vincent** Vincent's angina
anginös anginous
Angioblastom angioblastoma
Angioendotheliom angioendothelioma
Angiofibrom angiofibroma
Angiogliomatose angiogliomatosis
Angiographie angiography
angiographisch angiographic
Angiokardiogramm angiocardiogram
Angiokardiographie angiocardiography
angiokardiographisch angiocardiographic
Angiokeratose angiokeratosis
Angiologie angiology
angiologisch angiologic
Angiolymphom angiolymphoma
Angiolyse angiolysis
Angiom angioma
Angioma serpiginosum e. e.
Angiomatose angiomatosis
Angiomyom angiomyoma
Angiomyoneurom angiomyoneuroma
Angiomyosarkom angiomyosarcoma
Angioneurose angioneurosis
angioneurotisch angioneurotic
Angioplastik angioplasty
Angiosarkom angiosarcoma
Angiospasmus angiospasm
angiospastisch angiospastic
Angiostomie angiostomy

Angiotensin e. e.
Angiotensinase e. e.
Angiotomie angiotomy
Angiotonin e. e.
Angleichung habituation; adaptation
angreifen to affect
Angriffspunkt point of action
Angst anxiety
Angstgefühl trepidation
angstlösend anxiolytic
angstlösendes Mittel anxiolytic
Angstneurose anxiety neurosis
Angström-Einheit Angström unit
Angstzustand anxiety state
Anhängsel appendage
Anhäufung accumulation
anhaften to adhere
Anhangsgebilde appendage
anheben to elevate
anhepatisch anhepatic
Anhiebsdiagnose spot diagnosis
Anhydrämie anhydraemia (e), anhydremia (a)
anhydrämisch anhydraemic (e), anhydremic (a)
Anhydrase e. e.
Anhydrid anhydride
anhydrisch anhydrous
anikterisch anicteric
Anilin aniline
animalisch animal
Anion e. e.
Aniridie aniridia
Anis anise
Anisin anisine
Anisochromasie anisochromasia
anisochromatisch anisochromatic
Anisokorie anisocoria
Anisometropie anisometropia
anisotonisch anisotonic
Anisozytose anisocytosis
Anker anchor
Ankyloblepharon e. e.
ankylopoetisch ankylopoietic
Ankylose ankylosis
ankylosierend ankylosing

Ankylostoma duodenale Ancylostoma duodenale
Ankylostomiasis ancylostomiasis
ankylotisch ankylotic
Anlage (= angeborene Eigenschaft) proton
− (= Konstruktion) construction
− (= Talent) talent, disposition
anlagebedingt protonic
Anlegung application
Annäherung approach
Annahme (= Zulassung) admission
Annuloplastik annuloplasty
Anode e. e.
Anodenöffnungszuckung anodal opening contraction
Anodenschließungszuckung anodal closure contraction
Anodontie anodontia
anomal anomalous
Anomalie anomaly
anomer anomeric
anonym anonymous
anoperineal e. e.
Anopheles e. e.
Anophthalmie anophthalmia
Anopsie anopsia
Anorchismus anorchism, absence of testis
anorektal anorectal
Anorexie anorexia
anorganisch anorganic, inorganic
Anosmie anosmia
anovesikal anovesical
anovulatorisch anovulatory
Anoxämie anoxaemia (e), anoxemia (a)
anoxämisch anoxaemic (e), anoxemic (a)
Anoxie anoxia
anpassen to adjust, to adapt
Anpassung adjustment, adaptation
anregen (= reizen) to stimulate
− (= vorschlagen) to suggest
Anregung (= Reizung) stimulation

Anregung (= Vorschlag) suggestion
anreichern to enrich
Anreicherung enrichment
ansäuern to acidify
anschwellen to swell
Anschwellung intumescence
Anspannungszeit pre-ejection period
Ansprechbarkeit reactivity
anstecken to infect
ansteckend infectious, contagious
Ansteckung infection, contagion
ansteckungsfähig infectible
Ansteckungsfähigkeit infectivity, contagiosity
Ansteckungsquelle source of infection
Anstrengung effort
antacid e. e.
Antacidum antacid
Antagonismus antagonism
Antagonist e. e.
antagonistisch antagonistic
antazid antacid
Anteflexion e. e.
Antefixation e. e.
antegrad antegrade
antenatal e. e.
Antenne antenna
Anteposition e. e.
anterodorsal e. e.
anteroinferior e. e.
anteroposterior e. e.
anterosuperior e. e.
Anteversion e. e.
antevertiert anteverted
Anthelminthikum anthelminthic
anthelminthisch anthelminthic
Anthrachinon anthraquinone
Anthrakose anthracosis
Anthramin anthramine
Anthrarobin e. e.
Anthrax e. e.
Anthrazen anthracene
Anthropologe anthropologist
Anthropologie anthropology
Anthropologin anthropologist

anthropologisch anthropological
Antiallergikum antiallergic
antiallergisch antiallergic
antianämisch antianaemic (e), antianemic (a)
antiarhythmisch antiarrhythmic
antiarthritisch antiarthritic
Antiasthmatikum antiasthmatic, antasthmatic
antiasthmatisch antiasthmatic, antasthmatic
Antibabypille oral contraceptive, oral ovulation inhibitor
antibakteriell antibacterial
antibiliös antibilious
Antibiotikum antibiotic
antibiotisch antibiotic
Anticholinergicum anticholinergic
anticholinergisch anticholinergic
Anticholinesterase e. e.
antidepressiv antidepressant
Antidepressivum antidepressant
Antidiabetikum antidiabetic
antidiabetisch antidiabetic
antidiabetogen antidiabetogenic
antidiphtherisch antidiphtheritic
Antidiuretikum antidiuretic
antidiuretisch antidiuretic
Antidot antidote
antidrom antidromic
Antiemetikum antiemetic
antiemetisch antiemetic
Antienzym antienzyme
Antiepileptikum antiepileptic
antiepileptisch antiepileptic
antifebril antifebrile
Antiferment e. e.
antigen antigenic
Antigen e. e.
Antigenität antigenicity
Antiglobulin e. e.
antigonorrhoisch antiblennorrhagic
antihämolytisch antihaemolytic (e), antihemolytic (a)
antihämophil antihaemophilic (e), antihemophilic (a)

antihämorrhagisch antihaemorrhagic (e), antihemorrhagic (a)
Antihistaminikum antihistaminic
antihistaminisch antihistaminic
antihypertonisch antihypertensive
antikariös anticariogenic
antikarzinogen anticarcinogenic
antikatarrhalisch anticatarrhal
Antikathode anticathode; target
antiketogen antiketogenic
Antikoagulans anticoagulant
antikoagulierend anticoagulant, anticoagulative
Antikörper antibody
Antikörpermangel antibody deficiency
Antikomplement anticomplement
antikomplementär anticomplementary
antikonvulsiv anticonvulsive
antikonzeptionell anticonceptional
Antikonzipiens contraceptive
Antilope antelope
antilipolytisch antilipolytic
Antiluetikum antiluetic
antiluetisch antiluetic
antilymphozytär antilymphocytic
Antilymphozytenserum antilymphocyte serum
Antimetabolit antimetabolite
antimikrobiell antimicrobial
Antimon antimony
Antimonbehandlung stibiation
antimonhaltig stibiated
Antimonvergiftung stibialism
Antimykotikum antimycotic
antimykotisch antimycotic
antineoplastisch antineoplastic
Antineuralgikum antineuralgic
antineuralgisch antineuralgic
antineuritisch antineuritic
Antiöstrogen antiestrogen (a), antioestrogen (e)
antiparasitär antiparasitic
Antipathie antipathy
Antiperistaltik antiperistalsis
antiperistaltisch antiperistaltic

Antiphlogistikum antiphlogistic
antiphlogistisch antiphlogistic
Antiplasmin e. e.
antipruriginös antipruriginous
Antipyretikum antipyretic
antipyretisch antipyretic
Antipyrin antipyrine
antirachitisch antirachitic
Antirheumatikum antirheumatic
antirheumatisch antirheumatic
Anti-Rh-Serum anti-Rh-serum
Antisepsis e. e.
Antiseptikum antiseptic
antiseptisch antiseptic
Antiserotonin e. e.
Antiserum e. e.
Antispastikum antispasmodic
antispastisch antispasmodic
Antistaphylolysin e. e.
Antistreptolysin e. e.
Antisyphilitikum antisyphilitic
antisyphilitisch antisyphilitic
antitetanisch antitetanic
Antithrombin e. e.
antithromboplastisch antithromboplastic
Antithrombotikum antithrombotic
antithrombotisch antithrombotical
Antitoxin e. e.
antitoxisch antitoxic
Antitrypsin e. e.
antituberkulös antituberculotic
Antivirusmittel antiviral agent
Antivitamin e. e.
antixerophthalmisch antixerophthalmic
antizellulär anticellular
Antizytolysin anticytolysin
Antrektomie antrectomy
antronasal e. e.
Antroskop antroscope
Antroskopie antroscopy
antroskopisch antroscopical
Antrostomie antrostomy
Antrotomie antrotomy

antrotympanisch antrotympanic
Antwort response
Anurie anuria, anuresis
anurisch anuric
Anus praeternaturalis praeternatural anus (e), preternatural anus (a)
anwenden to adhibit, to apply, to use
Anwendung application, use
Anwendungsart manner of application
Anzapfsyndrom steal syndrome
anzeigen to indicate
Anzeigestellung indication
anziehen to attract
– (= ankleiden) to dress
Anziehung attraction
Aorta e. e.
Aortenbogen aortic arch
Aortenbogensyndrom pulseless disease
Aortenerweiterung dilatation of aorta
Aorteninsuffizienz aortic insufficiency
Aortenisthmusstenose coarctation of aorta
Aortenklappe aortic valve
Aortenstenose aortic stenosis
Aortitis e. e.
Aortographie aortography
aortoiliakal aortoiliac
aparalytisch aparalytic
Apareunie apareunia
Apathie apathy
apathisch apathic
Apatit apatite
Apertur aperture
Apexkardiogramm apicogram
Aphakie aphakia
Aphasie aphasia
aphasisch aphasic
Aphonie aphonia
aphonisch aphonic
Aphrodisiakum aphrodisiac
Aphthe aphtha

Apikogramm apicogram
apikal apical
Apikolyse apicolysis
Apikostomie apicostomy
Apiol e. e.
Apizitis apicitis
Aplanat e. e.
aplanatisch aplanatic
Aplasie aplasia
aplastisch aplastic
Apnoe apnea (a), apnoea (e)
apnoisch apneic (a), apnoic (e)
Apoenzym apoenzyme
Apoferritin e. e.
apokrin apocrine
Apomorphin ampormorphine
Aponeurose aponeurosis
apophysär apophysary
Apophyse apophysis
Apophysitis e. e.
apoplektiform apoplectiform
apoplektisch apoplectic
Apoplexie apoplexy
Apoprotein e. e.
Apotheke chemist's shop (e), drug store (a), pharmacy
—,**Krankenhaus-** dispensary, hospital pharmacy
—,**Zweig-** satellite pharmacy
Apotheker pharmaceutical chemist, pharmacist, druggist
Apothekerin pharmaceutical chemist, pharmacist, druggist
Apotoxin e. e.
Apparat apparatus
Appendektomie appendectomy
Appendix e. e.
Appendizitis appendicitis
appendizitisch appendicitic
Apperzeption apperception
apperzeptiv apperceptive
Appetit appetite
Appetitlosigkeit want of appetite, inappetence
Appetitzügler appetite depressant
Apposition e. e.
approximal e. e.

apraktisch apractic
Apraxie apraxia
Aptyalismus asialia
Aqua destillata distilled water
Aquaeductus Sylvii sylviduct
Aquokobalamin aquocobalamine
Arabinosid arabinoside
Arabinose e. e.
Arabinosurie arabinosuria
Arachnida e. e.
Arachnitis e. e.
Arachnodaktylie arachnodactylia
arachnoidal e. e.
Arachnoidea arachnoid
Arachnoiditis e. e.
Arbeit work
—,**geistige** brain work
Arbeitsbiene worker bee
arbeitsfähig able for work
Arbeitsfähigkeit ability for work
—,**Wiederherstellung der** rehabilitation
Arbeitsmedizin industrial medicine
Arbeitstisch work-table
arbeitsunfähig unable for work
Arbeitsunfähigkeit unability for work
Arborisation arbosisation, arborization
Arbutin e. e.
archaisch archaic
Archetyp archetype
Architektonik architectonic
architektonisch architectonic
Archiv archive
Arcus senilis e. e.
Arecolin arecaline
Areflexie areflexia
aregenerativ aregenerative
areolär areolar
argentaffin argentaffine
Argentaffinom argentaffinoma
Argentamin argentamine
argentophil e. e.
Argentum proteinicum strong protein silver
Arginase e. e.

Arginin arginine
Argininosukzinase argininosuccinase
Argon e. e.
Argyrie argyria
argyrophil e. e.
Arhythmie arrhythmia
arhythmisch arrhythmic
Ariboflavinose ariboflavinosis
Arithmomanie arithmomania
Arkade arcade
Arkansasabziehstein Arkansas oil stone
Arm e. e.
Armbad arm bath
Armtrageschlinge armsling
Armut poverty
Arndt-Schulzsches Gesetz Arndt-Schulz law
Arningsche Tinktur Arning's tincture
Aroma e. e.
aromatisch aromatic
Arretierung locking
Arrhenoblastom arrhenoblastoma
Arrhythmie arrhythmia
arrhythmisch arrhythmic
Arrosion e. e.
Arsen arsenic
Arsenbehandlung arsenotherapy
arsenhaltig (dreiwertig) arsenous
arsenhaltig (fünfwertig) arsenic
Arsenit arsenite
Arsenik arsenic trioxide
Arsin arsine
Arsonat arsonate
Art kind, species
Artefakt artefact
artefiziell artificial
Arteria anonyma innominate artery
– **basilaris** basilar artery
– **brachialis** brachial artery
– **carotis communis** common carotid artery
– **carotis externa** external carotid artery

Arteria carotis interna internal carotid artery
– **centralis retinae** artery of Zinn
– **cerebelli** cerebellar artery
– **cerebri** cerebral artery
– **circumflexa femoris** femoral circumflex artery
– **communicans** communicating artery
– **coronaria** coronary artery
– **epigastrica** epigastric artery
– **femoralis** femoral artery
– **fibularis** peroneal artery
– **frontalis** frontal artery
– **gastrica** gastric artery
– **gastroepiploica** gastroepoploic artery
– **haemorrhoidalis** haemorrhoidal artery (e), hemorrhoidal artery (a)
– **hepatica** hepatic artery
– **hypogastrica** hypogastric artery
– **ileocolica** ileocolic artery
– **iliaca** iliac artery
– **infraorbitalis** infraorbital artery
– **intercostalis** intercostal artery
– **labialis** labial artery
– **lacrimalis** lacrimal artery
– **laryngea** laryngeal artery
– **lienalis** splenic artery
– **lingualis** lingual artery
– **mammaria** mammary artery
– **maxillaris** maxillary artery
– **meningica** meningeal artery
– **mesenterica** mesenteric artery
– **obturatoria** obturator artery
– **occipitalis** occipital artery
– **ophthalmica** opthalmic artery
– **ovarica** ovarian artery
– **palatina** palatine artery
– **pancreaticoduodenalis** pancreaticoduodenal artery
– **perinealis** perineal artery
– **peronea** peroneal artery
– **phrenica** phrenic artery
– **poplitea** popliteal artery

Arteria profunda femoris deep femoral artery
- **pudendalis** pudendal artery
- **pulmonalis** pulmonary artery
- **radialis** radial artery
- **renalis** renal artery
- **spermatica** spermatic artery
- **subclavia** subclavian artery
- **supraorbitalis** supraorbital artery
- **temporalis** temporal artery
- **thoracalis** thoracic artery
- **thyreoidea** thyroid artery
- **tibialis** tibial artery
- **umbilicalis** umbilical artery
- **uterina** uterine artery
- **vertebralis** vertebral artery

arterialisieren to arterialize
Arterialisierung arterialization
arteriell arterial
Arterienklemme artery forceps
Arteriennaht arteriorrhaphy
Arteriitis arteritis
Arteriogramm arteriogram
Arteriographie arteriography
arteriographisch arteriographical
arteriokapillär arteriocapillary
arteriolär arteriolar
Arteriole e. e.
Arteriolosklerose arteriolosclerosis
arteriolosklerotisch arteriolosclerotic
Arteriosklerose arteriosclerosis
arteriosklerotisch arteriosclerotic
arteriovenös arteriovenous
Arthralgie arthralgia
arthralgisch arhralgic
Arthrektomie arthrectomy
Arthritis e. e.
arthritisch arthritic
Arthritismus arthritism
Arthrodese arthrodesis
Arthrolyse arthrolysis
Arthropathie arthropathy
–,**klimakterische** climacteric arthropathy
Arthropoda e. e.

Arthrosis deformans hypertrophic arthritis, degenerative arthritis, osteoarthritis, osteoarthrosis
Arthrotomie arthrotomy
Arthus-Phänomen Arthus's phenomenon
artikulär articular
Artikulation articulation
Artikulator articulator
artikulieren to articulate
aryepiglottisch aryepiglottic
Aryknorpel arytaenoid cartilage (e), arytenoid cartilage (a)
Aryl e. e.
Arylamidase e. e.
Arylierung arylation
Arznei medicament, remedy
Arzneibuch pharmacopeia (a), pharmacopoeia (e)
Arzneimittel drug, medicament
–,**verschreibungspflichtiges** prescription-only medicine
arzneimittelbedingt drug induced
Arzneimittelabhängigkeit drug dependence
Arzneimittelprüfung proving of drug
– **am lebenden Tier** bioassay
Arzneimittelreaktion drug reaction
Arzneimittelresistenz drug resistance
Arzneimittelspezialität proprietary
Arzneimittelsucht drug addiction, pharmacomania
Arzneimitteltherapie drug therapy
Arzneiwaage analytical balance
Arzneiware drug
Arzt physician, doctor
–,**beratender** consultant
–,**diensttuender** doctor in attendance
–,**praktischer** practitioner
–,**überweisender** referring physician
Arztpraxis doctor's office
Arzttasche physician's bag

Asa foetida asafetida (a), asafoetida (e)
Asbest asbestos
Asbestose asbestosis
Asche ash
Aschheim-Zondek-Test Aschheim-Zondek test
Aschoffsches Knötchen Aschoff's nodule
Aschoff-Tawara-Knoten atrioventricular node, Aschoff-Tawara node
Ascites e. e.
Ascorbinsäure ascorbic acid
Asemie asemia
Asepsis e. e.
aseptisch aseptic
Asialie asialia
Asiatische Grippe Asian influenza
Asiderose asiderosis
Askaridiasis ascariasis
Askaris ascaris
Askorbat ascorbate
Askorbinsäure ascorbic acid
asozial asocial
Asparagin asparagine
Asparaginase e. e.
Asparaginat asparaginate
Aspergillose aspergillosis
Aspermatismus aspermatism
Aspermie aspermia
asphyktisch asphyctic
Asphyxie asphyxia
Aspidinol e. e.
Aspiration e. e.
Aspirationspneumonie aspiration pneumonia
Aspirationsrohr aspirating tube
Aspirator e. e.
aspirieren to aspirate
ASS (Azetylsalizylsäure) ASA (acetylsalicylic acid)
Assimilation e. e.
Assimilationsbecken assimilation pelvis
assimilieren to assimilate
Assistent assistant
Assistenz assistance
Assistenzärztin resident
Assistenzarzt resident
assistieren to assist
Assoziation association
Astasie astasia
Asteatose asteatosis
Astereognosie astereognosis, stereoagnosis
Asthenie asthenia
asthenisch asthenic
Asthenopie asthenopia
Asthma e. e., aasmus
– **bronchiale** bronchial asthma
– **cardiale** cardiac asthma
asthmatisch asthmatic
astigmatisch astigmatic
Astigmatismus astigmatism
Astronautik astronautics
Astrozyt astrocyte
Astrozytom astrocytoma
Asyl asylum
Asymmetrie asymmetry
asymmetrisch asymmetrical
Asymmetrogammagramm asymmetrogammagram
asymptomatisch asymptomatic
asymptotisch asymptotical
asynchron asynchronous
Asynergie asynergy
asynergisch asynergic
asynklitisch asynclitic
Asynklitismus asynclitism
Asystolie asystolia
aszendierend ascending
Aszites ascites
ataktisch ataxic
Ataraktikum ataractic
ataraktisch ataractic
Ataraxie ataraxy
Atavismus atavism, throwing back
atavistisch atavistic
Ataxie ataxia
Atelektase atelectasis
atelektatisch atelectatic
Atem breath
–**, schwerer** short breath

Atemgeräusch breath sounds
Atemgrenzwert maximal breathing capacity
atemlos breathless
Atemlosigkeit breathlessness
Atemnot shortness of breath
Atemstromstärke, exspiratorische expiratory flow rate
—, **inspiratorische** inspiratory flow rate
Atemübung respiratory exercise
Atenolol e. e.
atherogen atherogenic
Atherom atheroma
atheromatös atheromatous
Atheromatose atheromatosis
Atherosklerose atherosclerosis
atherosklerotisch atherosclerotic
Athetose athetosis
athetotisch athetosic
Athletenfuß athlete's foot
athletisch athletic
Athyreose athyreosis
atlantookzipital atloidooccipital
atmen to breathe
Atmen breathing, respiration
—, **abgeschwächtes** diminished respiration
—, **amphorisches** amphoric respiration
—, **aufgehobenes** absent respiration
—, **Biotsches** Biot's respiration
—, **Bläschen-** vesicular respiration
—, **Bronchial-** tubular respiration
—, **bronchoveskuläres** bronchovesicular respiration
—, **Cheyne-Stokessches** Cheyne-Stokes respiration
—, **Kußmaulsches** air hunger
—, **pueriles** puerile respiration
—, **unbestimmtes** indefinite respiration
Atmokausis atmocausis
Atmosphäre atmosphere
atmosphärisch atmospheric
Atmung respiration
—, **künstliche** artificial respiration

Atmung, Kußmaulsche Kussmaul's respiration
Atmungsgeräusch breath sounds
Atom e. e.
atomar atomic
Atomgewicht atomic weight
Atomisierung atomization
Atonie atony
atonisch atonic
Atoxyl e. e.
Atransferrinämie atransferrinaemia (e), atransferrinemia (a)
Atresie atresia
atresisch atresic
atrial e. e.
Atrichie atrichia
atrioventrikulär atrioventricular
Atrophie atrophy
atrophisch atrophic
Atropin atropine
Atropinisierung atropinization
Attacke bout, attack
Attest e. e., certificate
attestieren to attest
Atypie atypia
atypisch atypical
Audiometrie audiometry
audiometrisch audiometric
audiovisuell audiovisual
auditorisch auditory
Auerbachscher Plexus Auerbach's plexus
Aufbewahrung storage
Aufblasung inflation
Aufbrauch consumption
Aufeinanderfolge succession
aufeinanderfolgend successive
auffällig striking
aufflackern to flare up
Aufflackern flare up
aufgeregt sein to be excited
aufhalten to arrest
aufhellen to clear
Aufhellschirm brightening screen
Aufhellung clearing
aufhören to cease, to finish
Aufhören cessation

auflösen to dissolve, to resolve
Auflösung dissolution
Auflösungsvermögen resolving power
Aufmerksamkeit attention
Aufnahme intake, uptake
Aufnahme (ins Krankenhaus) admission
Aufnahmebefund findings on admission
–,**Röntgen-** roentgenogram
aufputschen to dope
Aufputschen doping
Aufputschmittel dope
aufrauhen to refresh
Aufrechterhaltung maintenance
aufregen, sich to worry
Aufregung excitement
aufreizend irritant
aufrichten to erect
aufschneiden to cut open
aufspalten to split up
Aufspaltung splitting, scissure
Aufsplitterung splitting
aufsteigend ascending
aufsteigendes aktivierendes System alerting system
aufstoßen (= rülpsen) to belch
Aufstoßen eructation
Auftauen unfreezing
Aufwand expenditure
aufwecken to awaken
aufwickeln to wind up
aufzeichnen to record
Aufzeichnung record; note, notice
Aufzucht breeding
Augapfel eyeball
Auge eye
Augenärztin ophthalmologist, oculist
Augenarzt ophthalmologist, oculist
Augenbindehautentzündung conjunctivitis
–,**epidemische mukopurulente** pink-eye
augenblicklich instantaneous
Augenbraue eyebrow

Augenchirurgie ophthalmologic surgery
Augendiagnose iridodiagnosis
Augenhintergrund fundus of the eye
Augenhöhle eye socket
Augeninnendruck intraocular pressure
Augenkammer, hintere posterior chamber of the eye
–,**vordere** anterior chamber of the eye
Augenklappe eye shield
Augenlid eyelid
–,**Fehlen des –** ablepharon
Augenlidhalter eye speculum
Augenmagnet eye magnet
Augenmuskel ocular muscle
Augensalbe ophthalmic ointment
Augenspezialist eye specialist
Augenspezialistin eye specialist
Augenspülflüssigkeit collyrium
Augentrübung caligo
Augenwasser eyewater
Augenwimper eyelash
Aujeszkysche Krankheit bovine pseudorabies, mad itch
Aura e. e.
aurikulär auricular
aurikuloventrikulär auriculoventricular
Aurothiomalat aurothiomalate
Ausagieren acting out
ausatmen to expire
Ausatmung expiration
ausbleiben to fail
ausbluten to exsanguinate
ausbreiten to spread
Ausbreiter spreader
Ausbreitung spread
Ausbruch outburst; eruption
Ausbruch (einer Krankheit) outbreak (of a disease)
ausbrüten to hatch
Ausdehnung distention, expansion
ausdrücken to express
Ausdrücken expression
Ausdruck expression

ausdünsten to transpire, to perspire
Ausdünstung transpiration
außersinnlich extrasensory
Ausfallquote failure rate
Ausflockung flocculation
Ausfluß discharge, drainage, outflow
Ausflußröhrchen discharging tubule
Ausgang issue, vent
Ausgangspunkt level
ausgeblutet exsanguinated
ausgedehnt patulous
ausglühen to anneal
Ausgußkörper cast
Auskleidung lining, covering
Auskratzung erasement
Auskultation auscultation
auskultatorisch auscultatory
auskultieren to auscultate
auslöschen to extinguish
Auslöser release
ausnutzen to utilize
Ausnutzung utilization
auspressen to strip, to express
Ausräucherung fumigation
ausrenken to dislocate
ausrotten to eradicate
Ausrottung eradication
Ausrüstung equipment
aussaugen to suck
ausschaben to abrade
Ausschabung abrasion
Ausschälung enucleation
ausschalten to switch off; to exclude
Ausschaltung switching off; exclusion
ausscheiden to excrete
Ausscheidung excretion
Ausscheidungsurographie excretion urography
Ausschlag exanthema, rash
ausschleichen to steal out
Ausschluß exclusion
Ausschlußprinzip exclusion principle

Ausschneidung excision; ectomy
ausschütten to pour out
Ausschüttung pouring out
Ausschuhen exungulation
Ausschwitzung exudation
außerehelich extramarital
Aussparung socket
ausspritzen to syringe
ausspülen to cleanse, to irrigate
Ausspülung irrigation
ausspucken to spit; to expectorate
Ausstattung outfit
ausstopfen to plug
Ausstopfung plugging
ausstoßen to eliminate, to dump
Ausstoßung output
Ausstrahlung radiation
Ausstülpung evagination
Austausch exchange
Austauscher exchanger
Austauschtransfusion exchange transfusion
Austreibungszeit ejection time
Austrittsdosis exit dose
austrocknen to desiccate, to exsiccate
Austrocknung desiccation, exsiccation
Auswärtsdrehung eversion
Auswahlfragen-Examen multiple choice examination
Auswaschmethode washout method
auswechselbar interchangeable, exchangeable
Auswechseloptik exchangeable lenses
auswerfen to dump
auswerten to value, to evaluate
Auswertung valuation, evaluation
auswischen to efface
Auswuchs excrescence
Auswurf spit, sputum
Auszählung enumeration
Auszehrung consumption, emaciation
Autismus autism

autistisch autistic
autistisches Denken autistic thinking
Autoagglutination e. e.
Auto-Antikörper auto-antibody
autochthon autochthonous
autogen autogenous
Autohämolyse autohaemolysis (e), autohemolysis (a)
Autohämolysin autohaemolysin (e), autohemolysin (a)
autohämolytisch autohaemolytic (e), autohemolytic (a)
Autohypnose autohypnosis
autoimmum autoimmune
Autoinfektion autoinfection
Autointoxikation autointoxication
Autoisolysin e. e.
Autokannibalismus autocannibalism
Autoklav autoclave
Autokrankheit car sickness, motion sickness
autolog autologous
Autolysat autolysate
Autolyse autolysis
autolysieren to autolyze
Autolysin e. e.
autolytisch autolytic
Automatisation automatization
automatisch automatical
Automatisierung automatization
Automatismus automatism
autonom autonomic
Autonomie autonomy
Autoplastik autoplasty
autoplastisch autoplastic
Autopräzipitin autopraecipitin (e), autoprecipitin (a)
Autor author
Autorin author
Autoradiographie radioautography, autoradiography
Autoregulation e. e.
Autosom autosome
autosomal e. e.
Autosuggestion e. e.

Autotransfusion e. e.
Autotransplantation e. e.
Autotoxin e. e.
Autovakzination autovaccination
Autovakzine autovaccine
auxiliär auxiliary
Auxin e. e.
A.V. (= **atrioventrikulär**) atrioventricular
avirulent e. e.
Avitaminose avitaminosis
Avogadrosches Gesetz Avogadro's law
Axanthopsie axanthopsia
axial e. e.
Axillarlinie, vordere anterior axillary line
axiobukkogingival axiobuccogingival
axiobukkolingual axiobuccolingual
axiobukkozervikal axiobuccocervical
axiodistal e. e.
axiodistogingival e. e.
axiodistoinzisal axiodistoincisal
axiodistookklusal axiodistoocclusal
axiodistozervikal axiodistocervical
axiogingival e. e.
axioinzisal axioincisal
axiomesial e. e.
axiomesiodistal e. e.
axiomesiozervikal axiomesiocervical
axiopulpal e. e.
Axolotl e. e.
Axonreflex axon reflex
Axoplasma axoplasm
Ayerzasche Krankheit Ayerza's disease
Azaadenin azaadenine
Azahypoxanthin azahypoxanthine
Azathioprin e. e.
Azauracil e. e.
Azauridin azauridine
Azephalie acephalia

Azetabulektomie acetabulectomy
Azetabuloplastik acetabuloplasty
Azetaldehyd acetaldehyde
Azetamid acetamide
Azetamidin acetamidine
Azetaminofluoren acetaminofluorene
Azetanilid acetanilid
Azetazolamid acetazoleamide
Azetarson acetarsone
Azetat acetate
Azetessigsäure diacetic acid
Azetidin acetidin
Azetobromanilid acetobromanilide
Azetobutolol acetobutolol
Azetol acetol
Azetolase acetolase
Azeton acetone
Azetonämie acetonaemia (e), acetonemia (a)
azetonämisch acetonaemic (e), acetonemic (a)
Azetonaphthon acetonaphthone
Azetonglykosurie acetonglycosuria
Azetonid acetonide
Azetonitrat acetonitrate
Azetonitril acetonitrile
Azetonkörper acetone body
Azetonresorzin acetonoresorcinol
Azetonurie acetonuria
Azetonyl acetonyl
Azetophenetidin acetophenetidin
Azetophenon acetophenone
Azetopyrin acetopyrine
Azetosal acetylsalicylic acid
Azetylazeton acetylacetone
Azetylcholin acetylcholine

Azetylcholinesterase acetylcholinesterase
Azetylen acetylene
Azetylglukosamin acetylglucosamine
azetylieren to acetylate
Azetylierung acetylation
Azetylphenylhydrazin acetylphenylhydrazine
Azetylsalizylamid acetylsalicylamide
Azetylsalizylsäure (ASS) acetylsalicylic acid, acetosal (ASA)
Azetyltannin acetyltannin
Azetylthymol acetylthymol
Azidämie acidaemia (e), acidemia (a)
azidämisch acidaemic (e), acidemic (a)
Azidalbumin acidalbumin
Azidimeter acidimeter
azidophil acidophil
Azidose acidosis
—,Laktat- lactic acidosis
azidotisch acidotic
azinös acinous
azinotubulär acinotubular
Azol azole
Azolitmin e. e.
Azoospermie azoospermia
Azorubinprobe azorubin test
Azotämie azotaemia (e), azotemia (a)
azotämisch azotaemic (e), azotemic (a)
Azo-Verbindung azo-compound
Azur azure
azurophil azurophilic
Azurophilie azurophilia
azyklisch acyclic

B

Babesiose babesiosis
Babinskisches Zeichen Babinski's sign

Bacillus look also for:/siehe auch unter: Bazillus
— **anthracis** e. e.

Bacillus botulinus
   Clostridium botulinum
- **coli communis** Escherichia coli
- **enteridis Gärtner** Salmonella enteridis
- **faecalis alcaligenes** Alcaligenes faecalis
- **lactis aerogenes** Aerobacter aerogenes
- **oedematis maligni** Clostridium oedematis maligni
- **pneumoniae** Klebsiella pneumoniae
- **putrificus** Clostridium putrificum
- **pyocyaneus** Pseudomonas aeruginosa
- **tetani** Clostridium tetani
- **,typhi murium** Salmonella typhimurium

Bacitracin e. e.
Backe cheek
backen to bake
Backentasche cheek pouch
Backenzahn bicuspid tooth
Bacterium look also for:/siehe auch unter: Bakterium
- **granulosis** Noguchia granulosis
- **ozaenae** Klebsiella ozaenae
- **tularense** Pasteurella tularensis

Bacteroides e. e.
Bad bath
baden to bathe
Badetuch bath towel
Badewanne bathing-tub
Bäderabteilung balneary
Bändererschlaffung relaxation of ligaments
Bänderriß tear of ligaments
Bär bear
Bahnung facilitation
Bakelit bakelite
Bakteriämie bacteriaemia (e), bacteriemia (a)
bakteriämisch bacteriaemic (e), bacteriemic (a)
bakteriell bacterial
bakterizid bactericidal
bakterizides Mittel bacericide
Bakteriocholie bacteriocholia
Bakteriologe bacteriologist
Bakteriologie bacteriology
Bakteriologin bacteriologist
bakteriologisch bacteriological
Bakteriolyse bacteriolysis
bakteriolytisch bacteriolytic
Bakteriophage bacteriophage
Bakteriophagie bacteriophagia
Bakteriophobie bacteriophobia
bakteriostatisch bacteriostatic
bakteriotrop bacteriotropic
Bakterium bacterium
Bakteriurie bacteriuria
Balanitis e. e.
balanitisch balanitic
Balanoposthitis e. e.
Balantidiasis e. e.
Balantidium coli e. e.
Baldrian valerian
Baldriantinktur tincture of valerian
Ballen (= Paket) pack
Ballen, Hand- ball of the thumb
Ballismus ballism
Ballistokardiogramm ballistocardiogram
Ballistokardiographie ballistocardiography
ballistokardiographisch ballistocardiographic
Ballon balloon
Ballonkatheter balloon catheter
Ballottement e. e.
Balneologie balneology
balneologisch balneologic
Balneotherapie balneotherapy
Balsam balsam
Band e. e.; ligament
bandagieren to bandage
Bandagist bandager
Bandlsche Furche Bandl's ring
Bandmaß tape measure
Bandscheibe intervertebral disk

Bandscheibenprolaps herniation of intervertebral disk
Bandwurm tapeworm
—,**Fisch-** fish tapeworm
—,**Hunde-** dog tapeworm
—,**Rinder-** beef tapeworm
—,**Schweine-** pork tapeworm
Bandwurmbefall taeniasis (e), teniasis (a)
Bandwurmglied proglottis
Bandwurmmittel taeniacide (e), taeniafuge (e), teniacide (a), teniafuge (a)
bandwurmtötend taeniacide (a), teniacide (a)
bandwurmtötendes Mittel taeniacide (e), teniacide (a)
bandwurmtreibend taeniafuge (e), teniafuge (a)
bandwurmtreibendes Mittel taeniafuge (e), teniafuge (a)
Bangsche Krankheit abortus fever
Banisterin banisterine
Banthin banthine
Bantisches Syndrom Banti-syndrome
Bàrànyscher Versuch Bàràny's test
Barbiturat barbiturate
Barium e. e.
Bariumsulfat barium sulfate (a), barium sulphate (e)
Barorezeptor baroreceptor
Barriere bar
Bart beard
Bartholinsche Drüse Bartholin's gland
Bartholinitis e. e.
Bartonella e. e.
Bartonelliasis e. e.
basal e. e.
Basalmembran basement membrane
Basal-Zelle basal cell
Basalzellenepitheliom basal epithelioma
Base (chem.) base

Basedowsche Krankheit exophthalmic goiter, Graves' disease, Basedow's disease
Basis e. e., base
basisch basic
Basisnarkose basal anaesthesia (e), basal anesthesia (a)
Basisplatte base plate
basophil e. e.
Basophilie basophilia
Bassini-Operation Bassini's operation
Bastard e. e.
bathmotrop bathmotropic
Batterie battery
Bau construction, frame, framework
Bauch abdomen, belly
Bauchbinde abdominal bandage
Bauchchirurgie abdominal surgery
Bauchfell peritoneum
Bauchhalter abdominal retractor
Bauchhöhlenschwangerschaft abdominal pregnancy
Bauchspeicheldrüse pancreas
Bauchspeicheldrüsenentzündung pancreatitis
Bauchwand abdominal wall
Bauhinsche Klappe Bauhin's valve
Baumwolle cotton
Baumwollbinde cotton bandage
Bayonett bayonet
Bazillämie bacillaemia (e), bacillemia (a)
bazillär bacillary
bazilliform bacilliform
bazillogen bacillogenic
Bazillophobie bacillophobia
Bazillose bacillosis
Bazillurie bacilluria
Bazillus bacillus
BCG-Impfung BCG vaccination
BCG-Vakzine BCG vaccine
beabsichtigt intentional
Beatin e. e.

Beatmung respiration, ventilation
Beatmung, künstliche artificial respiration
Beatmungsgerät respirator
Becherglas beaker
Becherzelle goblet cell
Bechterewsche Krankheit Bechterew's disease, ankylosing spondylitis
Bechterewscher Reflex Bechterew's reflex
Becken basin
Becken (anat.) pelvis
—,**allgemein erweitertes** pelvis justo major
—,**allgemein verengtes** pelvis justo minor
—,**Assimilations-** assimilation pelvis
—,**Nägele-** Nägele's pelvis
—,**plattes** flat pelvis
—,**rachitisches** rachitic pelvis
—,**trichterförmiges** funnel-shaped pelvis
Beckenachse pelvic axis
Beckenausgang outlet of pelvis
Beckenboden floor of the pelvis
Beckendurchmesser pelvic diameter
Beckenebene pelvic plane
Beckeneingang inlet of the pelvis
Beckenmessung pelvimetry
Beckenobliquität obliquity of pelvis
Beckenöffnung pelvic strait
Beckenzirkel pelvimeter
Becquerel e. e.
Bedarf want
bedeckt coated
Bedeckung coat
Bedingung condition
Bedrängnis distress
beendigen to end
Beendigung termination
Befähigung qualification
Befall affection, involvement, infestation
befallen to affect, to involve, to strike
befallen sein to be affected
Befestigung attachment
befeuchten to damp, to moisten
Befeuchtung madefaction
Befinden state of health
befriedigend satisfactory
befruchten to fertilize
Befruchtung fertilization, fecundation, impregnation
Befund finding
Begehrungsneurose compensation neurosis
begleitend concomitant
Begleiterscheinung simultaneous phenomenon
begrenzen to bound
Begrenzung limitation
begutachten to give an expert view
Behälter container
behandeln to treat
Behandlung treatment
Behandlungsstation infirmary
Behandlungsvorschrift medical regimen
Behandlungszentrum treatment center (a), treatment centre (e)
Behçet-Syndrom Behçet's syndrome
behelfsmäßig succenturiate
behindern to handicap, to impede
behindert handicapped
Beikost additional food
Beil hatchet
Beimischung admixture
Bein (= Extremität) leg
Beine, O- bandy legs
Beine, X- knock-knees
Beinhalter leg-holder
Beinverkürzung shortening of leg
Beinverstümmelung deformity of leg
Beißblock bite block
beißen to bite
Beitrag contribution
Beklemmung oppression
bekömmlich wholesome

beladen to load
Belag coat, fur
belasten to burden
Belastung burdening
—, **körperliche** physical exercise
Belastungsdyspnoe dyspnea on exertion (a), dyspnoea on exertion (e)
Belastungszone stress-bearing area
beleben to animate
Belegärztin staff doctor
Belegarzt staff doctor
belegt (= bedeckt) coated
Belegzelle delomorphous cell, parietal cell
beleuchten to illuminate
Beleuchtung illumination
Belichtung exposure
Belichtungsspielraum exposure latitude
Belladonna e. e., nightshade
Bellocqsche Röhre Bellocq's cannula
Bellsches Phänomen Bell's phenomenon
belüften to aerate
Belüftung aeration
benachbart neighbouring
Benazin benazine
Bence-Jonesscher Eiweißkörper Bence-Jones protein
Benedictsche Probe Benedict's test
Benehmen behaviour
Benfotiamin benfotiamine
Benorylat benorylate
Bentyl e. e.
Benzaldehyd benzaldehyde
Benzanilid benzanilide
Benzanthren benzanthrene
Benzidin benzidine
Benzin benzine
Benzoat benzoate
Benzochinon benzoquinone
Benzodiazepin benzodiazepine
Benzodioxan benzodioxane
Benzoë benzoin
Benzol benzene

Benzothiadizin benzothiadizine
Benzoyl e. e.
Benzpyren benzpyrene
Benzyl e. e.
Benzylorange benzyl orange
Beobachtung observation
Beratungsstelle advisory center (a), advisory centre (e)
Beraubung deprivation
berauschen to intoxicate
Berechnung calculation
Bereich range
bereinigen to rectify
Bereitschaft readiness
Bergkrankheit mountain sickness, hypobaropathy
bergen to salve
Bergung salvage
Beriberi e. e.
Bericht report, information
Berkefeldfilter Berkefeld filter
Berlinerblau Berlin blue
Bernstein amber
berühren to touch
Berührung touch, taction
berührungsempfindlich tender to the touch
Berührungssinnn sense of touch
Beruf occupation
beruflich occupational, vocational
berufsbedingt occupational
Berufskrankheit occupational disease
Berufsordnung, ärztliche code of medical ethics
beruhigen to appease, to tranquilize
beruhigend sedative
Beruhigung sedation, tranquilization
Beruhigungsmittel sedative
Beryllium e. e.
Besamung insemination
beschädigen to hurt
Beschäftigung occupation
Beschäftigungsneurose occupation neurosis

Beschäftigungstherapie occupational therapy
Beschälseuche dourine, mal de coit
beschallen to sonicate
beschleunigen to accelerate
Beschleunigung acceleration
Beschneidung circumcision
beschreiben to describe
Beschreibung description
Beschwerden complaints, troubles
beschwerdefrei free of complaints
Besinnung consciousness
besonnen (= bestrahlen) to solarize
Besonnung solarization, heliation
bessern to improve
Besserung improvement, amelioration; relief
Bestandteil ingredient
Bestimmung determination; estimation
bestrahlen to irradiate
Bestrahlung irradiation, radiation; exposure
Bestrahlungsdosis exposure dose
Besuch visit
Besuchszeit visiting time
beta-adrenergic beta-adrenergic
Betaglobulin beta globulin
Betain betaine
Betalactamase e. e.
Betamethason betamethasone
Betaoxybuttersäure betaoxybutyric acid
Betarezeptor beta receptor
Betarezeptorenblocker beta blocker
Betastrahl beta ray
Betastrahler beta emitter
Betatron e. e.
– -Therapie betatron therapy
Betawelle beta wave
Beta-Zelle beta cell
Beteiligung participation
Betelnuß betel nut
Betrachtungsweise approach

Betriebsmaterial equipment
Betriebsamkeit activity
betrunken drunken
Bett bed
bettlägerig bedridden
Bettruhe bed rest
Bettwanze bedbug
Beule boil
Beulenpest bubonic plague
Beuteltier marsupial
bewegen to move
beweglich mobile
Beweglichkeit motility, mobility
Bewegung movement, motion
Bewegungsapparat locomotor system, locomotorium
Bewegungsbestrahlung moving field irradiation
Bewegungstherapie kinesitherapy
Bewegungsunschärfe movement blurring
Bewerber applicant
Bewerberin applicant
Bewerbung application
Bewertung valuation
bewirken to cause
bewußtlos unconscious
Bewußtlosigkeit unconsciousness
Bewußtsein consciousness
bewußtseinsgetrübt subconscious
Bewußtseinstrübung subconsciousness
Beziehung relation, relationship, interrelationship, reference
Beziehungswahn delusion of reference
Bezirk area
Bezoldsche Mastoiditis Bezold's mastoiditis
Biber beaver
Bibliothek library
Bichlorid bichloride
Bienenstich bee's sting
Biermersche perniziöse Anämie
    Biermer's anaemia (e),
    Addison's anaemia (e),
    Biermer's anemia (a),
    Addison's anemia (a)

bifaszikulär bifascicular
bifokal bifocal
Bifurkation bifurcation
Bigeminie bigeminy
Biguanid biguanide
Bikarbonat bicarbonate
bilateral e. e.
Bild image
Bild, klinisches clinical picture
bildgebendes System, medizinisches medical imaging
Bildung (= Entstehung) formation
Bildverstärker image intensifier
Bildwinkel angle of view
Bilharziose bilharziasis
biliär biliary
Biliflavin e. e.
Bilifuszin bilifuscin
biliös bilious
Bilirubin e. e.
−, **direkt reagierendes** direct reacting bilirubin
−, **indirekt reagierendes** indirect reacting bilirubin
Bilirubinämie bilirubinaemia (e), bilirubinemia (a)
Bilirubinurie bilirubinuria
Biliverdin e. e.
Billroth I/II-Operation Billroth I/II-operation
Billrothbatist oiled rayon
bilophodont e. e.
bimanuell bimanual
bimaxillär bimaxillary
binär binary
binaural e. e.
Binde bandage; belt
Bindegewebe bindweb, connective tissue
Bindehaut conjunctiva
Bindehautentzündung conjunctivitis
Bindehautplastik conjunctivoplasty
Bindenwickler bandage roller
Bindung binding, linkage, fixation
Bindungskapazität binding capacity

Binet-Simon-Test Binet-Simon test
binokulär binocular
Biochemie biochemistry
Biochemiker biochemist
Biochemikerin biochemist
biochemisch biochemical
bioelektrisch bioelectric
biogen biogenous
Biogenese biogenesis
biogenetisch biogenetic
Bioklimatologie bioclimatology
Biologe biologist
Biologie biology
Biologin biologist
biologisch biological
Biomedizin biomedicine
Biometeorologie biometeorology
biometeorologisch biometeorological
Bionik bionics
Biopharmazie biopharmaceutics
Biophysik biophysics
Biopsie biopsy
Biopsiezange biopsy forceps
bioptisch bioptic
Bioskopie bioscopy
Biosphäre biosphere
Biosynthese biosynthesis
Biotelemetrie biotelemetry
Biotin e. e.
Biotransformation e. e.
biotrop biotropic
Biotropie biotropism
Biotsche Atmung Biot's respiration
biparietal e. e.
biphasisch biphasic
bipolar e. e.
bisexuell bisexual, ambosexual
Biskuit biscuit
Bismarckbraun Bismarck brown
Bismutum subgallicum subgallic bismuth
− **subnitricum** subnitric bismuth
− **subsalicylicum** bismuth subsalicylate
Bison e. e.
Biß bite

Biß, offener open bite, apertognathia
Bißanalyse (dent.) bite analysis
Bißnahme bite-taking, checkbite
bistabil bistable
Bistouri bistoury, folding knife
Bisulfat bisulfate (a), bisulphate (e)
Bisulfid bisulfide (a), bisulphide (e)
Bisulfit bisulfite (a), bisulphite (e)
Bitartrat bitartrate
bitemporal e. e.
bitter e. e.
Biuret e. e.
Biuretprobe biuret test
bivalent e. e.
Bivalenz bivalence
Blähdruck distending pressure
blähend flatulent
Blähluft trapped air
Blähung flatulence
blähungswidrig carminative
blähungswidriges Mittel carminative
Bläschen vesicle, pustule, small bubble
Bläschenatmen vesicular breath sounds
Bläschenausschlag vesicular exanthema
Bläschenbildung vesiculation
Blässe pallescence, paleness, pallor
Blase bladder; bubble
Blasenbildung vesication
Blasenbruch vesical hernia
Blasenfixation cystopexy
Blasenhals vesical neck
Blasenmole hydatidiform mole
Blasennaht cystorrhaphy
Blasenplastik cystoplasty
Blasenscheidenplastik colpocystoplasty
Blasenschnitt cystotomy
Blasenstein vesical calculus
blasentreibend pustulant
blasentreibendes Mittel pustulant
blasenziehend vesicant

blasenziehendes Mittel vesicant
blaß pale, pallid
Blastoderm e. e.
Blastom blastoma
blastomatös blastomatous
Blastomatose blastomatosis
Blastomykose blastomycosis
Blastulation e. e.
Blatter pock
Blattern smallpox
Blatternvakzine smallpox vaccine
blau blue
Blaudsche Pillen Blaud's pills
Blechschere plate shears
Blei lead
Bleiazetat lead acetate
bleich pale
Bleichmittel bleaching agent
bleichsüchtig chlorotic
bleihaltig plumbic
Bleihandschuh lead glove
Bleisaum (am Zahnfleisch) Burton's line
Bleischürze lead apron
Bleivergiftung saturnism, plumbism
Blende diaphragm
blenden to dazzle, to glare
Blendung glare
Blennorhagie blennorrhagia
blennorrhagisch blennorrhagic
Blennorrhöe blennorrhea (a), blennorrhoea (e)
Blepharitis e. e.
Blepharoplastik blepharoplasty
Blepharoptose blepharoptosis
Blepharospasmus blepharospasm
Blickwinkel angle of view
blind e. e.
Blinddarm blindgut
Blindenschrift braille
blinder Fleck blindspot
Blindheit blindness
Blindversuch, einfacher/doppelter simple/double blind study
blinzeln to wink, to nictitate
blitzartig fulgurant

Blitzschlag lightning shock
Block e. e.
Block, His-Bündel hisian block
Block, tri-faszikulärer bilateral bundle branch block
Blockade e. e., blocking, block
blockieren to block
Blockieren blocking
blockierendes Mittel blocker
blond e. e., fair
Blumbergsches Zeichen Blumberg's sign
Blut blood
—, **konserviertes** stored blood
Blutableitung revulsion of blood
Blutalkoholbestimmung blood-alcohol testing
Blutandrang congestion
blutarm poor-blooded
Blutarmut lack of blood
Blutausstrich blood smear
Blutaustausch exchange transfusion
Blutaustritt extravasation of blood
Blutbank blood bank
Blutbild haemogram (e), hemogram (a), blood count, blood picture
—, **rotes** red blood count
—, **weißes** white blood count
blutbildend haemapoietic (e), hemapoietic (a), blood forming
Blutbildung haemapoiesis (e), hemapoiesis (a)
Blutblase blood blister
Blutdruck blood pressure
Blutdruckabfall blood pressure drop
Blutdruckanstieg rise of blood pressure
Blutdruckapparat sphygmomanometer
Blutegel leech
Bluteindickung haemoconcentration (e), hemoconcentration (a)
Blutempfänger donee

Blutempfängerin donee
bluten to bleed
Blutentnahmekanüle blood collecting needle
Blutentnahmelanzette blood lancet
Bluter haemophiliac (e), hemophiliac (a), bleeder
Bluterguß effusion of blood
Blutersatz blood substitute
Blutgift haemotoxin (e), hemotoxin (a)
Blutgruppe blood group
Blutgruppenbestimmung blood grouping, typing of blood
bluthaltig sanguiferous
Blutharnstoff blood urea
blutig (= blutbefleckt) bloody
blutig (med.) sanguineous
Blutkonserve blood preserve
Blutkreislauf blood circulation
Blutkultur blood culture
blutleer bloodless
blutleer machen to exsanguinate
Blut-Liquorschranke haematoencephalic barrier (e), hematoencephalic barrier (a)
Blutmole blood mole
Blutplättchen blood platelet, plastocyte
Blutprobe blood test
blutreich plethoric
blutreinigend purifying the blood
Blutschande incest
Blutsenkung sedimentation of blood, erythrocyte sedimentation
Blutsenkungsgeschwindigkeit erythrocyte sedimentation rate
Blutserum blood serum
Blutspender blood donor
Blutspenderin blood donor
Blut stillen to stanch the blood
blutstillend blood-stanching, styptic
blutstillendes Mittel styptic
blutstrotzend sanguineous

Blutsturz bursting of a blood vessel
Blutsverwandtschaft consanguinity, relationship by blood
Bluttransfusion blood transfusion
—, Apparat zur indirekten indirect blood transfusion apparatus
Bluttransfusionsreaktion reaction following blood transfusion
Blutung bleeding, haemorrhage (e), hemorrhage (a)
Blutungsrückfall rebleeding
Blutungszeit bleeding time
Blutuntersuchung examination of the blood
Blutvergiftung blood poisoning
Blutversackung pool of blood
Blutversorgung blood supply
Blutvolumen blood volume
Blutzucker blood sugar
Bock buck
Boecksches Sarkoid Boeck's sarcoid
Böhler-Schiene Böhler's splint
bösartig malignant
Bogen arc
Bogen (= Gewölbe) arch
Bogengang semicircular canal
bohren to bore
Bohren boring, terebration
Bohrer drill, bur drill
Bohrmaschine, zahnärztliche dental engine
Bohrstaub buring dust
Bolometer e. e.
Boltonscher Punkt Bolton point
Bolus e. e.
bombardieren to bombard
Bombardierung bombardment
Bombesin bombesine
Bor boron
Borat borate
Borax e. e., sodium borate
Bordetella e. e.

Bordet-Gengouscher Keuchhustenbazillus Haemophilus pertussis (e), Hemophilus pertussis (a)
Borke (botan.) bark
Borke (med.) crust
Bornasche Krankheit Borna disease, equine encephalomyelitis
Borneol e. e.
Bornholmkrankheit Bornholm disease
Bornyval e. e.
Borsalbe ointment of boric acid
Botallischer Gang arterial duct
Botanik botany
Botaniker botanist
Botanikerin botanist
botanisch botanic
Bothriocephalus latus Diphyllobothrium latum
Botryomykose botryomycosis
Botulismus botulism
Bougie e. e.
Bougierung bouginage
Bouillon e. e.
bovin bovine
Bowmansche Kapsel Bowman's capsule
Boxerenzephalopathie punchdrunk
Brachialgie brachialgia
brachiozephal brachiocephalic
Brachydaktylie brachydactyly
Brachymetropie brachymetropia
Bradsot e. e.
bradykard bradycardic
Bradykardie bradycardia
Bradykinesie bradykinesia
bradykinetisch bradykinetic
Bradykinin e. e.
Bradylalie bradylalia
Bradyphrasie bradyphrasia
Bradyphrenie bradyphrenia
Bradyteleokinese bradyteleokinesis
bradytroph bradytrophic
Bradytrophie bradytrophia
Bradyurie bradyuria

Bräune brownness
bräunen to tan
branchiogen branchiogenous
Brandblase burn blister
brandig gangrenous
Brandigwerden sphacelation, gangrene
Branntwein brandy
braten to roast
Braue brow
braun brown
Braune (veter.) bay horse
Braunsche Anastomose Braun's anastomosis
Brausepulver effervescent powder
Brechkraft power of refraction
Brechmittel emetic, vomitive
Brechreiz vomiturition, retching
Brechschale emetic bowl
Brechwurzel ipecac
Brei pap, pulp
breitbasig aufsitzend sessile
Breite breadth
Breitspektrum broad spectrum
Breiumschlag poultice
Bremse brake
Bremse (= Fliege) gadfly
Brenner burner
Brenner-Tumor Brenner tumor (a), Brenner tumour (e)
Brennpunkt focal spot
Brennstoff fuel
Brenzkatechin pyrocatechin, brenzcatechin, catechol
Brenzkatechinamin catecholamine
Brenztraubensäure pyruvic acid
Brett board, shelf
brettharte Bauchdeckenspannung board-like rigidity of the abdominal wall
Bretyliumtosylat bretylium tosylate
brillantgrün brilliant green
Brillantgrün brilliant green
Brille spectacles, glasses
Brillenanpassen fitting of spectacles

Brillenhämatom haematoma of orbit (e), hematoma of orbit (a)
Brillsche Krankheit Brill's disease
Brill-Symmerssche Krankheit Brill-Symmer's disease
Brittle-Diabetes brittle diabetes
Broadbentsches Zeichen Broadbent's sign
Brocasches Zentrum Broca's center (a), Broca's centre (e)
Brocqsche Krankheit Brocq's disease
Brodiescher Abszeß Brodie's abscess
Brom bromine
Bromat bromate
Bromazeton bromacetone
Brombenzol bromobenzene
Bromelin e. e.
bromhaltig bromic
Bromid bromide
Bromismus bromism
Bromkresolgrün bromcresol green
Bromkresolpurpur bromcresol purple
Bromocriptin e. e.
Bromoform e. e.
Bromphenolblau bromphenol blue
Bromphenolrot bromphenol red
Bromsulfaleintest bromsulfalein test (a), bromsulphalein test (e)
Bromthymolblau bromthymol blue
Bronchadenitis e. e.
bronchial e. e.
Bronchialasthma bronchial asthma
Bronchialatmen bronchial breath sounds
Bronchialbaum bronchial tree
Bronchialkarzinom bronchogenic carcinoma
Bronchialkatarrh bronchial catarrh
Bronchialspasmus bronchospasm
Bronchialstenose bronchostenosis
Bronchiektasie bronchiectasis
bronchiektatisch bronchiectatic
Bronchiloquie bronchiloquy
bronchiolär bronchiolar

Bronchiole e. e.
Bronchiolitis e. e.
Bronchitis e. e.
bronchitisch bronchitic
Bronchoadenitis e. e.
Bronchoblenorrhöe bronchoblennorrhea (a), bronchoblennorrhoea (e)
bronchogen bronchogenic
Bronchogramm bronchogram
Bronchographie bronchography
bronchographisch bronchographic
Bronchokonstriktion bronchoconstriction
Broncholithiasis e. e.
Bronchologie bronchology
bronchologisch bronchological
Bronchoplastik bronchoplasty
Bronchopleuropneumonie bronchopleuropneumonia
Bronchopneumonie bronchopneumonia
bronchopneumonisch bronchopneumonic
Bronchoskop bronchoscope
Bronchoskopie bronchoscopy
bronchoskopisch bronchoscopic
Bronchospirometrie bronchospirometry
Bronchotomie bronchotomy
bronchovesikulär bronchovesicular
Bronzediabetes bronzed diabetes
Broschüre brochure
Brown-Séquardsche Halbseitenlähmung Brown-Séquard's disease
Brucella abortus e. e.
– **melitensis** e. e.
Brucellose brucellosis
Bruch (= Fraktur) fracture
Bruch (= Hernie) hernia
Bruchband truss
Bruchsack hernial sac
Brudzinskisches Zeichen Brudzinski's sign
brüchig fragile

Brüchigkeit fragility
Brücke (dent.) bridge
Brückenpfeiler (dent.) bridge abutment
Brühe broth
brüten to hatch
Brunnen (= Mineralwasser) mineral waters
Brunnersche Drüse Brunner's gland
Brunst heat (veter.), rut
Brust breast
Brustabtragung mastectomy
Brustbein breastbone
Brustdrüse mammary gland
Brustfell pleura
Brustfellentzündung pleurisy
Brusthalter breast support
Brustkasten chest
Brustkind breast-fed baby
Brustpulver pectoral powder
Brustwand chest wall
Brustwandelektrokardiogramm precordial electrocardiogram
Brustwarze nipple, mammilla, mamilla
Brustwarzenentzündung mammillitis, thelitis
Brustwirbel thoracic vertebra
Brustwirbelsäule thoracic spinal column
Brut hatch
Brutapparat incubator
Bryantsches Dreieck Bryant's triangle
BSG (= Blutsenkungsgeschwindigkeit) ESR (= erythrocyte sedimentation rate)
Bubo e. e.
Bubonenpest bubonic plague
Buchweizenvergiftung fagopyrism
Buckyblende Bucky diaphragm
Budd-Chiari-Syndrom syndrome of Budd-Chiari, Chiari disease
Budinsche Regel Budin's rule
Bücherei library

Büffel buffalo
Bügel bar
Bülausche Drainage Bülau's treatment
Bündel bundle
–,Hissches bundle of His
Bürette burette
Bürgersche Krankheit Bürger's disease
Büste bust
bukkal buccal
bukkoaxial buccoaxial
bukkoaxiozervikal buccoaxiocervical
bukkogingival buccogingival
bukkolabial buccolabial
bukkolingual buccolingual
bukkomesial buccomesial
bukkopharyngeal buccopharyngeal
bukkopulpal buccopulpal
bulbär bulbar
Bulbärparalyse, progressive progressive bulbar paralysis
Bulbitis e. e.
Bulbogastron bulbogastrone
Bulboskop bulboscope
Bulboskopie bulboscopy
bulboskopisch bulboscopic
bulbourethral e. e.
Bulimie bulimia
bullös bullous

bursektomieren to bursectomize
Bursitis e. e.
Buschfleckfieber scrub typhus
Busen bosom
Butadien butadiene
Butalamin butalamine
Butan butane
Butandiol e. e.
Buttermilch buttermilk
Butyl e. e.
Butylakohol butanol
Butylbiguanid butyl biguanide
Butylen butylene
Butyramid butyramide
Butyrat butyrate
Butyrophenon butyrophenone
Byssinose byssinosis
Bullose bullosis
Bunitrolol e. e.
bunodont e. e.
bunolophodont e. e.
bunoselenodont e. e.
Bunsenbrenner Bunsen burner
Buphthalmus e. e.
Bupranolol e. e.
Burimamid burimamide
Burkitt-Tumor Burkitt's lymphoma
burning feet-Syndrom burnig feet
Burritusche Burri's stain
Bursa e. e.
Bursektomie bursectomy

C
(siehe auch:/look also for: Z, K)

Cabotscher Ring Cabot's ring
Cadmium e. e.
Caissonkrankheit caisson disease
Calabarbohne Calabar bean
calcaneoplantar e. e.
Calciferol e. e.
Calcinose calcinosis

Calcitonin e. e.
Calcium e. e.
Calciumcarbonat calcium carbonate
Calciumchlorid calcium chloride
Calciumglukonat calcium gluconate
Calciumhydroxyd calcium hydroxide

Calciumlaktat calcium lactate
Caldwell-Luc-Operation Caldwell-Luc operation
Callositas e. e.
Calorose e. e.
Camazepam e. e.
Canadabalsam Canada balsam
Canalis pterygoideus Vidian canal
Candela e. e.
Cannabin cannabine
Capistrum Barton's bandage
Capreomycin e. e.
Caproat caproate
Caprylat caprylate
Caprylsäure caprylic acid
Capsicum e. e.
Captodiamin captodiamine
Caput femoris head of femur
– **humeri** head of humerus
– **medusae** e. e., cirsomphalos
Carbamazepin carbamazepine
Carbamazin carbamazine
Carbamidsäure carbamic acid
Carbenicillin e. e.
Carbenoxolon carbenoxolone
Carbo medicinalis activated charcoal
Carboanhydrase carbonic anhydrase
Carboanhydrasehemmer carbonic anhydrase inhibitor
Carbomycin e. e.
Carbonyl e. e.
Carboxamid carboxamide
Carboxylase e. e.
Carbutamid carbutamide
carcinoembryogenes Antigen carcinoembryogenic antigen
Cardiolipin e. e.
Cardiospasmus cardiospasm
Carinamid carinamide
Carindacillin e. e.
Carisoprodol e. e.
carminativ carminative
Carminativum carminative
Carrageen e. e., Irish moss

Cascara Sagrada-Extrakt cascara sagrada extract
Castle-Faktor Castle's factor
Catalase e. e.
Cataracta cataract
Catechin e. e.
Catgut e. e.
Cavographie cavography
Cefamandol e. e.
Cefazolin e. e.
Cefoxitin e. e.
Cefuroxim cefuroxime
Cephalalgie cephalalgia
Cephalexin e. e.
Cephalhämatom cephalhaematoma (e), cephalhematoma (a)
Cephalin e. e.
Cephaloridin cephaloridine
Cephalosporin e. e.
Cephalosporinase e. e.
Cephalothin e. e.
Cephalozin e. e.
Cephradin cephradine
Cer cerium
cerebral e. e.
Cerebralthrombose cerebral thrombosis
Cervix e. e.
Cestode e. e.
Chagaskrankheit Chagas disease
Chagrin shagreen
Chalazion e. e.
Chalazionpinzette chalazion forceps
Chalikose chalicosis
Champagner champagne
Chaoulsche Nahbestrahlung Chaoul therapy
Charakter character
charakterisieren to characterize
charakteristisch characteristical
Charakterkunde characterology
Charcot-Leydenscher Kristall Charcot-Leyden crystal
Charriéresche Skala Charriére scale
Chaulmoograöl chaulmoogra oil

Chediaksche Reaktion Chediak's test
Cheilitis e. e.
Chelat chelate
Chelatbildner chelating agent
Chelidonium celandine
Chelometrie chelometry
Chemie chemistry
—,**physiologische** physiologic chemistry
Chemikalie chemical
Chemiker chemist
Chemikerin chemist
chemisch chemical
Chemismus chemism
Chemodektom chemodectoma
Chemoprophylaxe chemoprophylaxis
chemoresistent chemoresistant
Chemoresistenz chemoresistance
Chemosis e. e.
chemotaktisch chemotactic
Chemotaxis e. e.
chemotherapeutisch chemotherapeutical
Chemotherapie chemotherapy
Chenotherapie chenotherapy
Cheyne-Stokessche Atmung Cheyne-Stokes respiration
Chiasma chiasm
Chilaiditi-Syndrom subphrenic displacement of colon
Chinarinde Cinchona, Peruvian bark
Chinidin quinidine
Chinin quinine
Chininbisulfat quinine bisulfate (a), quinine bisulphate (e)
Chininhydrochlorid quinine hydrochloride
Chininsulfat quinine sulfate (a), quinine sulphate (e)
Chinolin quinoline
Chinon quinone
Chinosol e. e.
Chiropraktiker chiropractor
chiropraktisch chiropractic
Chiropraxis e. e.
Chirurg surgeon
Chirurgie surgery
—,**allgemeine** general surgery
—,**große** major surgery
—,**kleine** minor surgery
—,**kosmetische** cosmetic surgery
—,**plastische** plastic surgery
chirurgisch surgical
Chitin e. e.
Chlamydia e. e.
Chloasma e. e.
Chlor chlorine
Chloräthyl ethyl chloride
Chlorakne chloracne
Chloral e. e.
Chloralhydrat chloral hydrate
Chloralose e. e.
Chlorambucil e. e.
Chloramin chloramine
Chloramphenicol e. e.
Chlorat chlorate
Chlordiazepoxid chlordiazepoxide
Chlorid chloride
chlorieren to chlorinate
Chlorit chlorite
Chlorkalium potassium chloride
Chlorkalzium calcium chloride
Chlormadinon chlormadinone
Chlorochin chloroquine
Chloroform e. e.
Chloroformierung chloroformization
Chlorolymphosarkom chlorolymphosarcoma
Chlorom chloroma
Chloropercha e. e.
Chlorophyll e. e.
Chloropurin chloropurine
Chloroquin chloroquine
Chlorose chlorosis
Chlorothiazid chlorothiazide
chlorotisch chlorotic
Chlorphenol e. e.
Chlorphenolrot chlorphenol red
Chlorpromazin chlorpromazine
Chlorpropamid chloropropamide

Chlorprothixen chlorprothixene
Chlortetracyclin chlortetracycline
Chlorthalidon chlorthalidone
Chlumskysche Lösung
　Chlumsky's solution
Choane choana
Cholämie cholaemia (e),
　cholemia (a)
cholämisch cholaemic (e),
　cholemic (a)
cholagog cholagogue
Cholagogum cholagogue
Cholangiogramm cholangiogram
Cholangiographie cholangio-
　graphy
cholangiographisch cholangio-
　graphic
Cholangiolitis e. e.
Cholangiom cholangioma
Cholangiopankreatikographie
　cholangiopancreaticography
Cholangioskopie cholangioscopy
Cholangiostomie cholangiostomy
Cholangiotomie cholangiotomy
Cholangitis e. e.
cholangitisch cholangitic
Cholanthren cholanthrene
Cholat cholate
Choledochektomie choledoch-
　ectomy
Choledochoduodenostomie
　choledochoduodenostomy
Choledochoenterostomie
　choledochoenterostomy
Choledocholithiasis e. e.
Choledochorrhaphie
　choledochorrhaphy
Choledochostomie
　choledochostomy
Choledochotomie choledochotomy
Choledochusplastik
　choledochoplasty
Cholelithiasis e. e.
Cholera asiatica Asiatic cholera
Cholerese choleresis
Choleretikum choleretic
choleretisch choleretic

cholerisch choleric
Cholestase cholestasis
cholestatisch cholestatic
Cholesteatom cholesteatoma
Cholesterase e. e.
Cholesterin cholesterol
Cholestyramin cholestyramine
Cholezystektomie cholecystectomy
Cholezystitis cholecystitis
cholezystitisch cholecystitic
Cholezystoduodenostomie
　cholecystoduodenostomy
Cholezystogastrostomie
　cholecystogastrostomy
Cholezystogramm cholecystogram
Cholezystographie cholecysto-
　graphy
cholezystographisch cholecysto-
　graphic
Cholezystoileostomie
　cholecystoileostomy
Cholezystojejunostomie
　cholecystojejunostomy
Cholezystokinin cholecystokinin
Cholezystopathie cholecystopathy
Cholezystopexie cholecystopexy
Cholezystostomie cholecystostomy
Cholezystotomie cholecystotomy
Cholin choline
cholinergisch cholinergic
Cholinesterase e. e.
cholinesterasehemmend
　cholinesterase-inhibiting
Cholostase cholestasis
cholostatisch cholestatic
Cholurie choluria
Chondrin e. e.
Chondritis e. e.
Chondroadenom chondroadenoma
Chondroangiom chondroangioma
Chondroblast e. e.
Chondroblastom chondroblastoma
Chondrodysplasie chondrodysplasia
Chondrodystrophie chondro-
　dystrophia
Chondrogenese chondrogenesis
Chondroitin e. e.

Chondrokalzinose chondrocalcinosis
Chondroklast chondroclast
Chondrolyse chondrolysis
Chondrom chondroma
Chondromalazie chondromalacia
Chondromatose chondromatosis
Chondromyxom chondromyxoma
Chondroosteodystrophie chondroosteodystrophy
chondroplastisch chondroplastic
Chondrosarkom chondrosarcoma
Chondrotomie chondrotomy
Chondrozyt chondrocyte
Chopartsche Amputation Chopart's amputation
Chorda e. e., cord
Chordata e. e.
Chorditis e. e.
Chordoblastom chordoblastoma
Chordotomie chordotomy
Chorea Huntington hereditary chorea
— **minor** Sydenham's chorea
choreatisch choreatic
choreiform e. e.
choreoathetoid e. e.
Choreoathetose choreoathetosis
Choreomanie choreomania
chorial e. e.
Chorioangiom chorioangioma
chorioidal choroidal
Chorioidea choroid
Chorioidektomie choroidectomy
Chorioiditis choroiditis
Choriom chorioma
Choriomeningitis e. e.
Chorion e. e.
Chorionepitheliom chorioepithelioma
Choriongonadotropin chorionic gonadotropin, pregnancy urine hormone
Chorionkarzinom choriocarcinoma
Chorioptesräude chorioptic itch
Chorioretinitis e. e.
Christmas-Faktor Christmas factor

Chrom chromium
chromaffin e. e.
Chromaffinom chromaffinoma
chromargentaffin e. e.
Chromat chromate
Chromatin e. e., caryotin, chromoplasm
chromatisch chromatic
chromatogen chromatogenous
Chromatographie chromatography
chromatographisch chromatographic
chromatophil chromatophilic
Chromatophilie chromatophilia
Chromatopsie chromatopsia
Chromatoskiameter e. e.
Chromhidrose chromidrosis
chromogen chromogenic
chromogen e. e.
chromophil e. e.
chromophob chromophobic
Chromoskop chromoscope
Chromoskopie chromoscopy
chromoskopisch chromoscopical
Chromosom chromosome
chromotrop chromotropic
Chromozystoskopie chromocystoscopy
chromozystoskopisch chromocystoscopic
Chromsäure chromium trioxide, chromic acid
Chronaxie chronaxia
Chronaximeter e. e.
Chronaximetrie chronaximetry
chronaximetrisch chronaximetric
chronisch chronic
Chronizität chronicity
chronotrop chronotropic
Chrysarobin e. e.
Chrysoidin e. e.
Chrysotoxin e. e.
Chvosteksches Zeichen Chvostek's sign
chylös chylous
Chylomicron e. e.
Chyloperikard chylopericardium

Chyloperitoneum e. e.
Chylothorax e. e.
Chylurie chyluria
Chylus chyle
Chymase e. e.
chymös chymous
Chymotrypsin e. e.
Chymus chyme
Ciliarkörper ciliary body
Ciliata e. e.
Cimetidin cimetidine
Cimex lectularius e. e.
Cinnarizin cinnarizine
Circulus arteriosus circle of Willis
Circulus vitiosus vitious circle
Cirrhose cirrhosis
cirrhotisch cirrhotic
Citochol-Reaktion citochol reaction
Citrovorum-Faktor citrovorum factor
Citrullin citrulline
Citrullinurie citrullinuria
Cladosporiose cladosporiosis
Cladotrichose cladothricosis
Clarkesche Säule Clarke's column
Claubergscher Nährboden Clauberg's culture medium
Claudicatio intermittens intermittent claudication
Claustrophilie claustrophilia
Claustrophobie claustrophobia
Clavicepsin e. e.
claviculär clavicular
Clavisepsin e. e.
Clavus e. e., corn
Clindamycin e. e.
Clofenapat clofenapate
Clofibrat clofibrate
Clonidin clonidine
Clonorchiose clonorchiosis
Clonorchis sinensis e. e.
Clotrimazol clotrimazole
Cloxacillin e. e.
Cobalamin cobalamine
Cobalt e. e.
Cobamid cobamide

Cocain cocaine
Cocarboxylase e. e.
Coccidioidomykose coccidioidomycosis
Coccidiose coccidiosis
Coccygodynie coccygodynia
cochleär cochlear
Cochleitis e. e.
Cochleographie cochleography
Code e. e.
Codehydrogenase e. e.
Codein codeine
Codierung coding
Coecum caecum (e), cecum (a)
Coelenterata e. e.
Cöliakie intestinal infantilism, idiopathic steatorrhea (a), idiopathic steatorrhoea (e)
Coenurose coenurosis, turnsickness
Coenzym coenzyme
Coeruloplasmin ceruloplasmin (a), coeruloplasmin (e)
Coffein caffeine
Coffeinum citricum citrated caffeine
– -Natrium benzoicum caffeine with sodium benzoate
Cohydrogenase e. e.
Coitus e. e., coition
Colchizin colchicine
Colibazillus Escherichia coli
Colica mucosa e. e.
Colipyelitis e. e.
Colitis e. e.
colitisch colitic
Colliculitis seminalis verumontanitis
Colliculus seminalis verumontanum
Collip-Einheit Collip unit
Collodium collodion
Colloid e. e.
colloidal e. e.
Colocynthe colocynth
Colopexie colopexy
Coloptose coloptosis
Coloradozeckenfieber Colorado tick fever
Coloskop coloscope

Coloskopie coloscopy
coloskopisch coloscopic
Colostomie colostomy
Colotomie colotomy
Coma e. e.
comatös comatose
Commotio cerebri concussion of the brain
Computer e. e.
Computer-Tomographie computed tomography
Conchotom conchotome
Conchotomie conchotomy
Concretio pericardii pericardial concretion
Condurango e. e.
Condyloma acuminatum e. e.
– **latum** e. e.
Coniin coniine
Conjugata diagonalis diagonal conjugate diameter
Conjugata externa external conjugate diameter
Conjugata vera true conjugate diameter
conjunctival e. e.
Conjunctivitis e. e.
Conn-Syndrom Conn's syndrome
Conorrhinus magistus Triatoma magista
Contrecoup e. e.
Contusio cerebri contusion of the brain
Convallamarin e. e.
Convallarin e. e.
Convallatoxin e. e.
Cooleysche Anämie Cooley's anaemia (e), Cooley's anemia (a), thalassanaemia (e), thalassanemia (a)
Cordotomie cordotomy
Corepressor e. e.
Cor nervosum cardiac neurosis
Cornutin cornutine
coronar coronary
Coronarinfarkt coronary infarction

Coronarsklerose coronary arteriosclerosis
Coronarthrombose coronary thrombosis
Coronarverschluß coronary occlusion
Corpus callosum trabs
Corpus luteum e. e.
– **luteum-Hormon** corpus luteum hormone, progesterone
– **striatum** striated body
Cortexolon cortexolone
Cortexon cortexone
Corticosteroid e. e.
Corticosteron corticosterone
Corticotropin e. e., adrenocorticotropic hormone
corticotropin-freisetzender Faktor corticotropin releasing factor
Cortin e. e.
Cortisches Organ Corti's organ
Cortisol e. e.
Cortison cortisone
Costa fluctuans floating rib
Cotarnin cotarnine
Co-trimoxazol e. e.
Coulomb e. e.
Courvoisiersches Zeichen Courvoisier's sign
Cowperitis e. e.
Cowpersche Drüse bulbourethral gland, Cowper's gland
Coxa valga e. e.
– **vara** e. e.
Coxitis e. e.
coxitisch coxitic
Coxsackievirus Coxsackie virus
Cozymase e. e.
Cramer-Schiene Cramer's splint
Crataegin e. e.
Crataegus oxyacantha e. e.
C-reaktives Protein C-reactive protein
Crédéscher Handgriff Crédé's method
Crescendo e. e.
Crepitatio crepitation

Cristothermographie cristothermography
cristothermographisch cristothermographical
Crohnsche Krankheit Crohn's disease
Croup e. e.
croupös croupous
Cruorgerinnsel cruor clot
Crush-Syndrom crush syndrome
Crustacea e. e.
Cryoglobulin e. e.
Culdoskopie culdoscopy
Cumarin coumarin
Cunnilingus e. e.
Cuprein cupreine
Curarin curarine
Curarisierung curarization
Curettage e. e.
Curette curet
Curie e. e.
Curschmannsche Spirale Curschmann's spiral
Cushingsche Krankheit Cushing's disease
Cyanamid cyanamide
Cyanoacrylat cyanoacrylate
Cyanose cyanosis

cyanotisch cyanotic, cynosed
Cyclamat cyclamate
Cyclase e. e.
Cyclazocin cyclazocine
Cyclitis e. e.
Cyclopenthiazid cyclopenthiazide
Cycloserin cycloserine
Cyclotron e. e.
Cyproheptadin cyproheptadine
Cystadenom cystadenoma
Cyste cyst
Cystenniere cystic kidney
Cysticercosis e. e.
cystisch cystic
Cystitis e. e.
cystitisch cystitic
Cystocele e. e.
Cystom cystoma
Cystoskop cystoscope
Cystoskopie cystoscopy
cystoskopisch cystoscopic
Cytidin e. e.
Cytidylat cytidylate
Cytochalasin e. e.
Cytochrom cytochrome
Cytoglobin e. e.
Cytoplasma cytoplasm
Cytosin cytosine

D

Dacry... siehe bei:/look for: Dakry...
Dactylolysis spontanea ainhum
Dämmerschlaf twilight sleep
Dämpfigkeit (veter.) broken wind
Dämpfung dulness
Dakinsche Lösung Dakin's solution
Dakryoadenitis dacryadenitis
Dakryokanalikulitis dacryocanaliculitis
Dakryolithiasis dacryolithiasis

Dakryozystektomie dacryocystectomy
Dakryozystitis dacryocystitis
Damm (anat.) perineum
Dammnaht suture of perineum, episiorrhaphy
Dammplastik episioplasty
Dammriß perineal rupture
Dammschnitt episiotomy
Dampf steam, vapor (a), vapour (e)
Dampfbad steam bath

Darm intestine, gut, bowel
Darmbein ilium
Darmbeinkamm iliac crest
Darmblutung intestinal haemorrhage (e), intestinal hemorrhage (a)
Darmfaßzange intestinal forceps
Darmgeräusch bowel sound
Darmgrimmen gripe
Darmklemme intestinal clamp
Darmkolik intestinal colic
Darmnaht enterorrhaphy
Darmreizung irritation of the intestines
Darmrohr rectal tube, colon tube
Darmschere bowel scissors
Darmverschlingung twisting of the intestines
Dasein entity
Dasselfliege botfly
Datei data file
Datenverarbeitung data processing
Dauer duration
Dauerausscheider chronic carrier
Dauerbad permanent bath
dauerhaft durable
Dauerkatheter permanent catheter
Dauerspülkatheter permanent irrigation catheter
Dauertropfinfusion, intravenöse intravenous drip
Daumen thumb
Daumenballen thenar eminence
Daumenlutscher thumb sucker
Daunorubicin e. e.
Decanoat decanoate
Decidua e. e.
− **basalis** basal decidua
− **capsularis** capsular decidua
− **graviditatis** decidua of pregnancy
− **marginalis** marginal decidua
− **menstruationis** menstrual decidua
− **parietalis** parietal decidua
decidual e. e.
Decke cover
Deckglas cover glass

Deckglaspinzette cover glass forceps
Deckzellenepitheliom squamous epithelioma
Decrescendo e. e.
Defäkation defaecation (e), defecation (a)
defäkieren to defaecate (e), to defecate (a)
defensiv defensive
Deferentitis e. e.
Deferveszenz defervescence
Defibrillation e. e.
Defibrillator e. e.
defibrillieren to defibrillate
Defibrillierung defibrillation
defibrinieren to defibrinate
Defibrinierung defibrination
Definition e. e.
Defizit deficit
Deflexion deflection
Defloration e. e.
Deformität deformity
Degeneration e. e.
degenerativ degenerative
degenerieren to degenerate
degradieren to degrade
Degradierung degradation
Degranulation e. e.
Dehiszenz dehiscence
Dehnbarkeit compliance
dehnen to extend, to stretch
Dehnungsrezeptor stretch receptor
Dehnungsschraube jackscrew
Dehydrase dehydrogenase
Dehydrierung dehydration
Dehydroemetin dehydroemetine
Dehydrogenase e. e.
Dehydrokortikosteron dehydrocorticosterone
Dehydropeptidase e. e.
Dehydroxylierung dehydroxylation
Deitersscher Kern Deiters' nucleus
déjà vu e. e.
Dejerinesches Zeichen Dejerine's sign
Dekantierung decantation

Dekapeptid decapeptide
Dekapitation decapitation
Dekapsulation decapsulation
Dekarboxylase decarboxylase
Dekarboxylierung decarboxylation
Deklination declination
Dekompensation decompensation
dekompensieren to decompensate
Dekompression decompression
Dekrudeszenz decrudescence
Dekubitalgeschwür decubital ulcer
Dekubitus decubitus
deletär deleterious
delirant delirious
Delirium e. e.
– **tremens** e. e.
Délormesche Operation
 Délorme's operation
Delphin dolphin
Demarkation demarcation
Demarkationslinie line of demarcation
dement e. e.
demente Person dement
Dementia paralytica general paralysis of the insane, general paresis
Demenz dementia
Demethylchlortetrazyklin demethylchlortetracycline
demethylieren to demethylate
Demethylimipramin desmethylimipramine
Demineralisation demineralization
Demodexausschlag demodicosis
demodulieren to demodulate
Demonstration e. e.
demonstrieren to demonstrate
denaturieren to denature
Denaturierung denaturation
Dendrit dendrite
Dengue e. e., breakbone fever
Densiographie densography
Densiometrie densiometry
dental e. e.
Dentaldepot dental depot
Dentimeter e. e.

Dentin e. e., ivory
Dentinoblast e. e.
Dentinom dentinoma
dentinozemental dentinocemental
Dentist e. e.
Dentistin dentist
Dentition e. e.
–,**erste** primary dentition
–,**zweite** secondary dentition
dentoalveolär dentoalveolar
Depersonalisation depersonalization
dephosphorylieren to dephosphorylate
Depersonalisationssyndrom Alice in wonderland syndrome
Depolarisation depolarization
depolarisieren to depolarize
Depolymerase e. e.
depolymerisieren to depolymerize
Depot e. e.
Depotform eines Arzneimittels delayed action drug, slow release drug
Depotinsulin depot insulin
Depotpenicillin depot penicillin
Depression e. e.
depressiv depressive
Dercumsche Krankheit adiposis dolorosa
Derivat derivative
Dermatitis e. e.
– **actinica** e. e.
– **exfoliativa** e. e.
– **herpetiformis** e. e.
dermatitisch dermatitic
Dermatologe dermatologist
Dermatologie dermatology
Dermatologin dermatologist
dermatologisch dermatological
Dermatom dermatome
Dermatomykose dermatomycosis
Dermatomyositis e. e.
Dermatophytid dermatophytide
Dermatophytie dermatophytosis
Dermatose dermatosis
dermatotrop dermatotropic

Dermographismus dermographism, dermographia
Dermoid e. e.
Dermoidzyste dermoid cyst
Desamidase deamidase
Desamidierung deamidization
Desaminase deaminase
Desaminierung deamination, deamidation
Desault-Verband Desault's bandage
Desazylase deacylase
Descemetitis e. e.
Descemetsche Membran Descemet's membrane
Descensus testis descent of the testicle
Deschamps-Nadel Deschamps' needle
desensibilisieren to desensitize
Desensibilisierung desensitization
Deserpidin deserpidine
Desferrioxamin desferrioxamine
Desinfektion disinfection
Desinfektionsmittel disinfectant
desinfizieren to disinfect
desinfizierend disinfectant
Desintegration disintegration
desmodontal e. e.
Desmolase e. e.
Desmologie desmology
Desobliteration e. e.
desodorieren to deodorize
desodorierend deodorant
desodorierendes Mittel deodorant
Desodorierung deodorization
Desorganisation disorganization
desorientiert disoriented
Desorientierung disorientation
Desoxydation deoxidation
desoxydieren to deoxidize
Desoxykortikosteron desoxycorticosterone, cortexone
Desoxyribonuklease desoxyribonuclease
Desoxyribose e. e.

d'Espinesches Zeichen d'Espine's sign
Desquamation e. e.
desquamativ desquamative
Destillat distillate
Destillation distillation
Destillierapparat distilling apparatus
destillieren to distil
deszendierend descending
Detritus e. e.
Deuteranopie deuteranopia
Deuterium e. e.
Deuteron e. e.
devaskularisieren to devascularize
Deviation e. e.
devitalisieren to devitalize
Dexamethason dexamethasone
Dextran e. e.
Dextrin e. e.
Dextroamphetamin dextroamphetamine
Dextrokardie dexiocardia
dextroponiert dextroposed
Dextroposition e. e.
Dextrose e. e.
Dextroversion e. e.
dextrovertiert dextroverted
Dezibel decibel
Dezidua decidua, caduca
dezidual decidual
Dezimeterwelle decimeter wave
Diabetes insipidus e. e.
—, **Insulinmangel-** insulin-deficient diabetes
— **mellitus** e. e.
— **renalis** e. e.
Diabetiker diabetic
Diabetikerin diabetic
diabetisch diabetic
diabetogen diabetogenic
Diadochokinese diadochokinesia, diadokokinesia
Diät diet
—, **eiweißarme** low protein diet
—, **eiweißreiche** high protein diet
—, **glutenarme** low gluten diet

Diät, glutenfreie gluten-free diet
—, kalziumreiche high calcium diet
—, vitaminreiche high vitamin diet
Diätbehandlung dietotherapy
Diätetik dietetics
Diätetiker dietitian
Diätetikerin dietitian
diätetisch dietetic
Diätfehler faulty diet
Diäthylamid diethylamide
Diäthylbarbitursäure barbital (a), barbitone (e)
Diäthylkarbamazin diethylcarbamazine
Diäthylpropion diethylpropion
Diätschema dietary
Diagnose diagnosis
—, endgültige final diagnosis
—, vorläufige tentative diagnosis
Diagnostiker diagnostician
Diagnostikerin diagnostician
diagnostisch diagnostic
diagnostizieren to diagnose
Diagramm diagram
Diakon deacon
Diakonissin deaconess
Diallyl e. e.
Dialysat dialysate
Dialysator dialyzer
Dialyse dialysis
dialysieren to dialyze
Diamid diamide
Diamidomonoester diamidomonoester
Diamin diamine
Diaminodiphosphatid diaminodiphosphatide
Diaminokapronsäure lysine
Diaminomonophosphatid diaminomonophosphatide
Dianisidin dianisidine
Diapedese diapedesis
Diaphanoskopie diphanoscopy
Diaphorase e. e.
Diaphorese diaphoresis
Diaphoretikum diaphoretic
diaphoretisch diaphoretic

diaphragmatisch diaphragmatic
diaphysär diaphyseal
Diaphyse diaphysis
diaplazental diaplazental
Diarginyl e. e.
Diarrhöe diarrhea (a), diarrhoea (e)
Diarthrose diarthrosis
Diaskopie diascopy
Diastase (anat.) diastasis
Diastase (enzymol.) amylopsin
Diastole e. e.
diastolisch diastolic
Diathermie diathermy
Diathese diathesis
diathetisch diathetic
Diazepam e. e.
Diazepin diazepine
Diazepoxid diazepoxide
Diazetat diacetate
Diazetyl diacetyl
Diazetylmorphin diacetylmorphine
Diazin diazine
Diazoreaktion diazo reaction
Diazoverbindung diazo compound
Diazoxid diazoxide
Diazoxyd diazoxide
Dibenamin dibenamine
Dibenzanthracen dibenzanthracene
Dibenzazepin dibenzazepine
Dibromid dibromide
Dibutyl e. e.
Dibutyryladenosinmonophosphat dibutyryladenosinemonophosphate
Dichloramin dichloramine
Dichlorid dichloride
Dichotomie dichotomy
Dichromatopsie dichromatopsia
dicht dense
Dichte density
Dichtegradientelektrophorese density-gradient electrophoresis
Dickdarm large intestine, colon
Dickdarmwand colonic wall
dickleibig abdominous

Dick-Test Dick test
Diclofenac e. e.
Dicumarin dicoumarin
Dicyandiamid dicyandiamide
didaktisch didactic
Dieldrin e. e.
dielektrisch dielectric
Dien diene
dienzephal diencephalic
Diester e. e.
different e. e.
differential e. e.
Differentialdiagnose differential diagnosis
Differenz difference
differenzieren to differentiate
Differenzierung differentiation
diffundieren to diffuse
diffus diffuse
Diffusion e. e.
Diffusionskapazität diffusion capacity
digestiv digestive
Digestivum digestive
digital e. e.
Digitalanzeige digital display
Digitalin e. e.
Digitalis e. e.
digitalisieren to digitalize
Digitalisierung digitalization
Digitaloid e. e.
Digitalose e. e.
Digitogenin e. e.
Digitonin e. e.
Digitoxin e. e.
Digitoxose e. e.
Dignität dignity
Diguanidin diguanidine
Dihydrat dihydrate
Dihydroergotamin dihydroergotamine
Dihydrofolat dihydrofolate
Dihydrokodeinon dihydrocodeinone
Dihydrophenylalanin dihydrophenylalanine
Dihydrostreptomycin e. e.

Dihydrotachysterin dihydrotachysterol
Dijodid diiodide
Dijodtyronin diiodotyronin
Dijodtyrosin diiodotyrosine
dikrot dicrotic
Dikrotie dicrotism
diktieren to dictate
Diktiergerät dictating machine
Dikumarin dicoumarin
Dilatation e. e.
Dilatator dilatator
Dimethylamin dimethylamine
Dimethylaminoazobenzol dimethylamino-azobenzene
Dimethylaminophenazon aminopyrine
Dimethylbiguanid dimethylbiguanide
Dimethylguanidin dimethylguanidine
Dimethylsulfoxid dimethyl sulfoxide (a), dimethyl sulphoxide (e)
Dinatriumsalz disodium salt
Dinitrat dinitrate
Dinitrophenol e. e.
Dinukleotid dinucleotide
Diode e. e.
Dioptrie diopter, dioptry
Dioxan dioxane
Dioxyd dioxide
Dipeptid dipeptide
Dipeptidase e. e.
diphasisch diphasic
Diphenicillin e. e.
Diphenyl e. e.
Diphenylamin diphenylamine
Diphenylhydantoin e. e.
Diphenylmethan diphenylmethane
Diphosphat diphosphate
Diphosphatase e. e.
Diphosphonukleosid diphosphonucleoside
Diphtherie diphtheria
Diphtherieantitoxin diphtheria antitoxin

Diphtheriebazillus Corynebacterium diphtheriae
diphtherisch diphtheric, diphtherial
diphtheroid e. e.
Diphyridamol e. e.
Dipikrylamin dipicrylamine
Diplegie diplegia
diplegisch diplegic
Diplobazillus diplobacillus
diploid e. e.
Diplokokkus diplococcus
— **Morax-Axenfeld** Morax-Axenfeld diplococcus
Diplopie diplopia
Dipsomanie dipsomania
Dipyridamol dipyridamole
direkt direct
Disaccharid disaccharide
Disaccharidase e. e.
Diskrepanz discrepancy
diskret discrete
Diskussion discussion
Dislokation dislocation
Dismutase e. e.
Disopyramid disopyramide
Dispensarium dispensary
dispensieren to dispense
dispers disperse
Dispersion e. e.
Disposition e. e.
disproportional e. e.
disseminiert disseminated
Disseminierung dissemination
Dissertation e. e.
Dissescher Raum space of Disse
Dissimilation e. e., disassimilation
dissimilieren to dissimilate, to disassimilate
Dissoziation dissociation
dissoziieren to dissociate
distal e. e.
distalwärts distad
Distanz distance
distoangulär distoangular
distobukkal distobuccal
distobukkookklusal distobuccoocclusal
distobukkopulpal distobuccopulpal
Distokklusion distocclusion
distolabial e. e.
distolingual e. e.
Distomiasis e. e.
distomolar e. e.
Distomum haematobium Schistosoma haematobium
— **hepaticum** Fasciola hepatica
— **pulmonale** Paragonismus westermani
Distorsion distortion
Distoversion e. e.
Disulfat disulfate (a), disulphate (e)
Disulfid disulfide (a), disulphide (e)
Diszission discission
Dithiokarbamoylhydrazin dithiocarbamoylhydrazine
Dithiol e. e.
Dithizon dithizone
Dittrichscher Pfropf Dittrich's plug
Diurese diuresis
Diuretikum diuretic
diuretisch diuretic
divergent e. e.
Divergenz divergence
Divertikel diverticulum
Divertikulitis diverticulitis
Divertikulose diverticulosis
Dizyandiamid dicyandiamide
DL (= dosis letalis) LD (= lethal dose)
Döderleinscher Bazillus Döderlein's bacillus
Döhlesches Einschlußkörperchen Döhle's inclusion body
dogmatisch dogmatic
Doldscher Test Dold's test
Doktor doctor
dolichozephal dolichocephalic

dominant e. e.
Dominanz dominance
Donath-Landsteinerscher Test Donath-Landsteiner test
Dopa e. e.
Dopamin dopamine
Dopaoxydase dopaoxidase
Doppelblindversuch double blind study, double blind trial
Doppelinstrument double-ended instrument
Doppellappenverschluß double Collin's lock
Doppelmembranstethoskop phonendoscope
doppelseitig bilateral
doppelt double
doppeltbrechend birefractive, birefringent
dorsal e. e.
dorsalwärts dorsad
dorsoanterior e. e.
dorsoposterior e. e.
Dosierung dosage
—,**erhöhte** increased dosage
—,**erniedrigte** reduced dosage
—,**hohe** high dosage
—,**niedrige** low dosage
Dosimeter e. e.
Dosimetrie dosimetry
dosimetrisch dosimetric
Dosis dose
dosisabhängig dose-dependent, dose-related
Douglasscher Raum Douglas' cul-de-sac
Doversches Pulver Dover's powder
Doxepin e. e.
Doxycyclin doxycycline
Dozent university teacher
Dozentin university teacher
Drän drain
Dränage drainage
Dränageklammer drainage clip
Dränagerohr drainage tube
drängen to urge

drängend urgent
Dragée e. e.
Draht wire
Drahtbogen wire arch
Drahtnaht wiring
Drahtsäge wire saw
Drahtschiene wire ladder splint
Drahtschneider wire cutter
Drahtspannzange wire twisting forceps
Drahtzug wire traction
Drain e. e.
Drainage e. e.
Drainageklammer drainage clip
Drainagerohr drainage tube
dramatisch dramatic
drastisch drastic
drastisches Mittel drastic
drehen to turn
—,**sich** to wheel
Drehkraft torque
Drehkrankheit staggers, coenurosis, turnsickness
Drehkurbel revolving crank
Drehung rotation, turning
—,**optische** optic rotation
dreibasig tribasic
dreidimensional three-dimensional
Dreieck triangle, trigone
dreieckig triangular
Dreifuß trivet
dreigeteilt tripartite
Dreigläserprobe three glass test
dreikernig trinucleate
dreilappig trilobate
dreiphasig triphasic
Dreiwegehahn three way stopcock
dreiwertig triad, trivalent
dreiwertiges Element triad
Dreiwertigkeit trivalence
dreizellig tricellular
dreizipfelig tricuspid
Drepanozyt drepanocyte
Dreuwsche Paste Dreuw's paste
Drigalski-Nährboden Drigalski medium
Drilling triplet

dringlich urgent, emergent
Dringlichkeit urgency, emergency
drittgebärend triparous
Drittgebärende tripara
Droge drug
Drogist druggist
Drogistin druggist
drohend (= bevorstehend) imminent
Dromedar dromedary
dromotrop dromotropic
Drossel (techn.) choke
drosseln to choke
Drosselung chocking
Drostanolon drostanolone
Druck compression, pressure, stress
druckempfindlich tender on pressure
Druckgeschwulst (veter.) sitfast
Druckklemme angiotribe forceps
druckschmerzhaft tender on pressure
Drucksensibilität piesaesthesia (e), piesesthesia (a)
Drucktaste pushbutton
Druckverband pressure bandage
Drückeberger malingerer
Drüse gland
Drüsenepithel glandular epithelium
Drüsengewebe glandular tissue
drüsig glandular
Druse (med.) e. e.
Druse (veter.) strangles
dual e. e., binary
Dualismus dualism
dualistisch dualistic
Dubin-Johnson-Syndrom Dubin-Johnson syndrome
Ductus arteriosus arterial duct
− **choledochus** common bile duct
− **cysticus** cystic duct
− **hepaticus** hepatic duct
− **thoracicus** thoracic duct
− **thyreoglossus** thyroglossal duct
− **wirsungianus** pancreatic duct
Dünndarm small intestine, small bowel

Dünnschichtelektrophorese thin-layer electrophoresis
dünsten to stew
Düse nozzle
dulden to tolerate
dumm dull, stupid
Dummheit stupidity
Dumpingsyndrom dumping syndrome
Dunkelanpassung darkadaptation
Dunkelfeld darkfield, darkground
Dunkelkammer darkroom
Dunst haze
duodenal e. e.
Duodenalgeschwür duodenal ulcer
Duodenitis e. e.
duodenobiliär duodenobiliary
Duodenocholedochotomie duodenocholedochotomy
Duodenocholezystostomie duodenocholecystostomy
duodenojejunal e. e.
Duodenostomie duodenostomy
Duodenum e. e.
Dupuytrensche Kontraktur contracture of the palmar fascia, Dupuytren's contraction
dural e. e.
Duraplastik duraplasty
durchblutet (gut/schlecht) (well/poorly) supplied with blood
Durchblutung blood supply
durchbohren to perforate
Durchbruch breakthrough
Durchdringung pervasion
Durchflußelektrophorese continuous flow electrophoresis
durchgängig pervious
Durchgang passage, duct
Durchlässigkeit permeability
Durchleuchtung, röntgenologische fluoroscopy
Durchmesser diameter
durchmischen to temper
durchscheinend translucent

durchschlagend effective
Durchschnitt (= Mittelwert) average
durchsichtig transparent
durchstechen to pierce
Durchsteckverschluß box lock
Durchtrennung division
Durchwanderung transmigration
Duroziezsches Doppelgeräusch
 Duroziez's sign
Durst thirst
durstig thirsty
Dusche douche
Dynamik dynamics
dynamisch dynamic
Dynamo e. e.
Dynamometer e. e.
Dysakusis dysacousia
Dysarthrie dysarthria
Dysbasia intermittens
 intermittent claudication
Dysbasie dysbasia
Dyschezie dyschezia
Dysdiadochokinese dysdiadokokinesia
Dysenterie dysentery
dysenterisch dysenteric
Dysergie dysergia
dysergisch dysergic
Dysfunktion dysfunction
Dysgenesie dysgenesia
Dysgerminom dysgerminoma
Dyshidrose dyshidrosis
dyshidrotisch dyshidrotic
Dyskeratose dyskeratosis
Dyskinesie dyskinesia
dyskinetisch dyskinetic
Dyskrasie dyscrasia
dyskrasisch dyscrasic
Dyslalie dyslalia
Dyslexie dyslexia
Dysmenorrhöe dysmenorrhea (a),
 dysmenorrhoea (e)

Dysostose dysostosis
Dysovarismus dysovarism
Dyspareunie dyspareunia
Dyspepsie dyspepsia
dyspeptisch dyspeptic
Dysphagie dysphagia
Dysphasie dysphasia
Dysplasie dysplasia
dysplastisch dysplastic
Dyspnoe dyspnea (a),
 dyspnoea (e)
Dyspnoe, paroxysmale (veter.)
 heaves, broken wind
dyspnoisch dyspneic (a),
 dyspnoic (e)
Dyspraxie dyspraxia
Dysprosium e. e.
Dysproteinämie dysproteinaemia
 (e), dysproteinemia (a)
dysrhythmisch dysrhythmic
Dyssynergie dyssynergia
Dysthymie dysthymia
Dysthyreose dysthyreosis
dysrhaphisch dysrhaphic
Dysrhythmie dysrhythmia
Dystonie dystonia
–,vegetative imbalance of the
 autonomic nervous system,
 autonomic nervous disorder
dystonisch dystonic
Dystonie dystonia
dystonisch dystonic
Dystrophia adiposogenitalis
 sex infantilism with obesity,
 adiposogenital syndrome
– musculorum progressiva (Erb)
 progressive muscular
 dystrophy
Dystrophie dystrophy
dystrophisch dystrophic
Dysurie dysuria
dysurisch dysuric

E

eben even, plane
Ebene plane
ebnen to plane
Ebsteinsche Anomalie Ebstein's anomaly
Echinococcus cysticus e. e.
– multilocularis e. e.
Echinokokkenkrankheit echinococcosis
Echinuriose echinuriosis
Echo e. e.
Echoenzephalographie echoencephalography
Echographie echography
echographisch echographic
Echokardiographie echocardiography
echokardiographisch echocardiographic
Echoskopie echoscopy
echoskopisch echoscopic
echosonisch echosonic
Echo-Tomographie echotomography
ECHO-Virus ECHO virus
eckig angular
Ecksche Fistel Eck's fistula
Eckzahn canine tooth, canine
Ecthyma e. e.
Ectopie ectopy
Eczema vaccinatum Kaposi's varicelliform eruption
Edelgas noble gas
Edelmetall noble metal
Edetat edetate
Edingerscher Kern Edinger's nucleus
efferent e. e.
Effloreszenz efflorescence
Effort-Syndrom irritable heart
egozentrisch egocentric
Ehe marriage, matrimony
Eheberatung marriage counselling, marriage guidance
ehelich conjugal, marital
Ehrlichsche Reaktion Ehrlich's reaction
Ei egg
Ei (med.) ovum
Eichel (med.) glans, head of the penis
eichen to gauge
Eichhörnchen squirrel
Eid des Hippokrates hippocratic oath
eidetisch eidetical
Eierstock ovary
Eierstockentfernung ovariectomy
Eifersucht jealousy
Eigelb yolk
Eigenblut autoblood
Eigenschaft quality, peculiarity
eigentümlich peculiar
Eigentümlichkeit peculiarity, property
Eigentum property
Eileiter fallopian tube, oviduct
Eileiterschwangerschaft tubal pregnancy
Eimer bucket
Einäscherung cremation
einäugig one-eyed
einarmig one-armed
einatmen to inspire, to inhale
Einatmung inspiration, inhalation
einbalsamieren to embalm
Einbalsamierung embalming
einbetten to embed; to invest (dent.)
Einbettung embedding
Einbeziehung implication
einbilden, sich to imagine, to fancy
Einbildung imagination
einblasen to blow in
Einblasung inflation
eindicken to thicken, to spissate
eindimensional one-dimensional

eindringen to penetrate; to invade
Eindringungsvermögen invasiveness
Eindruck impression
eineiig uniovular
Einengung coarctation
einfach simple, uncomplicated
Einfallsdosis incident dose
Einfassung framework
einfetten to grease
einführen to introduce
Einführung introduction
Eingabe input
eingeben to give in
eingedrückt depressed
eingekeilt impacted
eingeklemmt impacted, incarcerated
Eingeschlafensein obdormition
eingewachsen ingrown
Eingeweide viscera; intestines
Eingeweideparasit visceral parasite
Eingeweidewurm helminth
Eingriff gearing; operation; surgical intervention
Einheit unit
einhüllen to invest
einimpfen to inoculate
einkapseln to encapsulate
Einkapselung encapsulation
Einkeilung impaction
Einklemmung impaction, incarceration
Einkohlenstoff-Fragment single carbon unit
Einlage (= Stütze) support
Einlage (= Zahneinlage) temporary filling
Einlauf enema
Einmalspritze disposable syringe
Einmündung abouchement
Einnahme intake
einnehmen to intake
einreiben to rub in, to inunct
Einreibung infriction, embrocation

einrenken to set
einrichten to reduce
einrichten (z.B. eine Verrenkung) to set (e. g. a dislocation)
Einrichtung reduction; setting
einsaugen to suck in
einschalten to switch on
Einschichtkultur monolayer culture
einschlafen to fall asleep
einschleifen to mill in
Einschleifen milling-in
Einschluß inclusion
–, **zytomegaler** cytomegalic inclusion
Einschlußkörperchen inclusion body
Einschmelzung colliquation
einschneiden to cut in
Einschneiden (obstetr.) crowning
Einschnitt cut, incision
Einschnürung strangulation; coarctation
einseitig unilateral
einsparen to spare
Einsparung spare
einspritzen to inject
einstechen to puncture
einstellen, einen Diabetes – to regulate a diabetes
Einstich paracentesis, tapping, puncture
einträufeln to drop in
eintragen to record
Eintragung charting, record
einverleiben to incorporate
Einverleibung incorporation
einwandern to immigrate
Einweisung, stationäre stationary assignment
einwertig univalent, monovalent
einwickeln to wrap
einzählig single
einzellig unicellular
Eis ice
Eisbeutel ice bag
Eisen iron

Eisenammoniumsulfat ferric ammonium sulfate (a), ferric ammonium sulphate (e)
Eisenbahnkrankheit car sickness, motion sickness
Eisenbindungskapazität ironbinding capacity
Eisendraht iron wire
eisenhaltig siderous
− **(dreiwertig)** ferric
− **(zweiwertig)** ferrous
Eisenmangel sideropenia, iron deficiency
Eisenmengerkomplex Eisenmenger complex
Eisensulfat ferrous sulfate (a), ferrous sulphate (e)
Eisentherapie ferrotherapy
Eisenverbindung, dreiwertige ferric compound
−**, zweiwertige** ferrous compound
Eisessig glacial acetic acid
Eiteil, vorangehender presentation
Eiter pus, matter
Eiterbildung pyogenesis, suppuration
eiterig purulent, suppurative
eitern to suppurate, to fester
Eiterung suppuration
Eiterzelle pus cell
Eiweiß white of an egg
Eiweiß (med.) protein
eiweißarme Kost low protein diet
Eiweißfraktion protein fraction
eiweißfrei protein-free
eiweißgebunden protein-bound
Eiweißharnen proteinuria
eiweißspaltend protein splitting
Eiweißstoffwechsel proteometabolism
Eizelle egg cell
Ejakulat ejaculate
Ejakulation ejaculation
Ekchondrom ecchondroma
Ekchymose ecchymosis
Ekel disgust
ekelhaft offensive, disgusting

ekeln to disgust, to siken
EKG (= Elektrokardiogramm) e.c.g. (= electrocardiogram)
Ekgonin ecgonine
ekkrin eccrine
Eklampsie eclampsia
eklamptisch eclamptic
Ekstase ecstasy
Ektasie ectasy
Ektebin e. e.
Ekthym ecthyma
Ektoderm ectoderm
ektodermal ectodermal
Ektoglia ectoglia
Ektomie ectomy
Ektoparasit ectoparasite
Ektopie ectopy
ektopisch ectopic
Ektoplasma ectoplasm
Ektropion ectropion
ektropionieren to ectropionize
Ekzem eczema
−**, allergisches** allergic eczema, atopic dermatitis
Ekzematisierung eczematization
ekzematös eczematous
ekzentrisch eccentric
Elaidin e. e.
elaidinisieren to elaidinize
Elastase e. e.
Elastin e. e.
Elastinase e. e.
elastisch elastic
elastisches Gewebe elastic tissue
Elastizität elasticity
Elastogenese elastogenesis
Elastolysat elastolysate
Elastomer e. e.
Elastoproteinase e. e.
Elastose elastosis
Elefant elephant
elektiv elective
elektrisch electric
elektrisieren to electrize
Elektrisierung electrization
Elektrizität electricity
Elektroanalyse electroanalysis

elektroanalytisch electroanalytic
Elektrobiologie electrobiology
elektrobiologisch electrobiological
Elektrochirurgie electrosurgery
elektrochirurgisch electrosurgical
Elektrode electrode
Elektroenterographie electroenterography
Elektroenzephalogramm electroencephalogram
Elektroenzephalograph electroencephalograph
Elektroenzephalographie electroencephalography
elektroenzephalographisch electroencephalographic
Elektrokardiogramm electrocardiogram
Elektrokardiograph electrocardiograph
Elektrokardiographie electrocardiography
   Ableitung I, II, III lead I, II, III
   P-Zacke P wave
   QRS-Komplex QRS complex
   T-Zacke T wave
elektrokardiographisch electrocardiographic
Elektrokardiophonographie electrocardiophonography
Elektrokaustik electric cautery
Elektrokauter electric cauter
Elektrokauterisation electric cauterization
Elektrokoagulation electrocoagulation
Elektrolyse electrolysis
Elektrolyt electrolyte
elektrolytisch electrolytic
Elektromagnet electromagnet
elektromagnetisch electromagnetic
Elektromassage electromassage
Elektrometer electrometer
Elektromyographie electromyography
elektromyographisch electromyographical
Elektron electron
—,**schnelles** fast electron
Elektronarkose electronarcosis
elektronegativ electronegative
Elektronengehirn electronic computer
Elektronenmikroskop electron microscope
Elektroneurolyse electroneurolysis
elektronisch electronic
Elektronystagmographie electronystagmography
Elektrophorese electrophoresis
elektrophoretisch electrophoretic
Elektrophotometer electrophotometer
Elektrophotometrie electrophotometry
Elektrophysiologie electrophysiology
elektrophysiologisch electrophysiologic
elektropositiv electropositive
Elektroretinographie electroretinography
Elektroschock electric shock, electroconvulsion
Elektrospektrographie electrospectrography
elektrostatisch electrostatic
Elektrotherapeut electrotherapeutist
elektrotherapeutisch electrotherapeutical
Elektrotherapie electrotherapy
Elektrothermometer electrothermometer
elektrotonisch electrotonic
Elektrotonus electrotonus
Elektuarium electuary
Element e. e.
elementar elementary
Elephantiasis e. e.
elephantiastisch elephantiasic
Elevator e. e.

Elfenbein ivory
Eliminase e. e.
eliminieren to eliminate
Elixier elixir
Ellenbogen elbow
Ellenbogenhygrom (veter.) shoe boil
Ellipsoidgelenk ellipsoid joint
elliptisch elliptical
Elliptozyt elliptocyte
Elliptozytose elliptocytosis
Ellis-Garlandsche Linie Ellis-Garland line
elterlich parenteral
Eltern parents
eluieren to elute
Elution e. e.
Emanation e. e.
Embolektomie embolectomy
Embolie embolism
embolisch embolic
Embolus e. e.
Embryogenese embryogeny
Embryokardie embryocardia
Embryologie embryology
embryologisch embryological
Embryom embryoma
embryonal embryonary
Embryotomie embryotomy
Emesis e. e.
Emetin emetine
Emission e. e.
Emissionscomputertomographie emission computed tomography
emmetrop emmetropic
Emmetropie emmetropia
Emodin e. e.
emotionell emotional
Empfänger donee, recipient
empfänglich susceptible
Empfänglichkeit susceptibility
Empfängnis conception
empfängnisfähig conceptive
empfängnisverhütend contraceptive, anticoncipient
empfängnisverhütendes Mittel contraceptive

Empfängnisverhütung contraception
empfinden to feel
empfindlich sensible, delicate, tender
empfindsam sensitive
Empfindung sensation
Emphysem emphysema
emphysematös emphysematous
Empirie empiricism
Empiriker empiric
Empirikerin empiric
empirisch empirical
Empyem empyema
emulgieren to emulsify
Emulsion e. e.
Emulsionssalbe emulsifying ointment
Enanthem enanthema
enanthematös enanthematous
enantiomorph enantiomorphic
Enarthrose enarthrosis
en bloc e. e.
Encephal... look for:/siehe unter: Enzephal...
Enchondrom enchondroma
Endangiitis e. e.
endangiitisch endangiitic
Endangiitis obliterans thromboangiitis obliterans
Endarterektomie endarterectomy
Endarterie endartery
enddiastolisch telediastolic, end diastolic
Endemie endemic
endemisch endemic
endexspiratorisch end expiratory
Endhirn telencephalon
Endigung ending
Endkontrolle final check
Endoantitoxin e. e.
Endocard... look for:/siehe unter: Endokard...
Endodontie endodontia
Endoenzym endoenzyme
endogen endogenous
Endognathion e. e.

Endokard endocardium
endokardial endocardial
Endokarditis endocarditis
– **lenta** subacute bacterial endocarditis
endokarditisch endocarditic
endokochleär endocochlear
endokranial endocranial
endokrin endocrine
Endokrinologie endocrinology
endokrinologisch endocrinologic
Endolabyrinthitis e. e.
endolaryngeal e. e.
endolumbal endolumbal
Endolymphe endolymph
endometrial e. e.
Endometriose endometriosis
Endometritis e. e.
Endometrium e. e.
Endomyokarditis endomyocarditis
Endonährboden Endo's medium
endonasal e. e.
endoneural e. e.
endoperitoneal e. e.
Endoperoxid endoperoxide
Endophlebitis e. e.
Endophthalmitis e. e.
Endophyt endophyte
Endoplasma endoplasm
endoplasmatisch endoplasmic
Endorgan end-organ
Endosalpingitis e. e.
Endoskop endoscope
Endoskopie endoscopy
endoskopisch endoscopic
Endosmose endosmosis
Endosteom endosteoma
Endostitis endosteitis
Endothel endothelium
endothelial e. e.
Endotheliitis e. e.
Endothelioblastom endothelioblastoma
Endotheliom endothelioma
Endotheliose endotheliosis
Endotoxin e. e.
endotoxisch endotoxic

endotracheal e. e.
Endotrachealnarkose
 endotracheal anaesthesia (e),
 endotracheal anesthesia (a)
endourethral e. e.
endouterin endouterine
endovesikal endovesical
endozervikal endocervical
Endozytose endocytosis
Endplatte end-plate
endsystolisch telesystolic
endwärts terminad
End- zu Endanastomose
 end to end anastomosis
End- zu Seitanastomose
 end to side anastomosis
energetisch energetic
Energie energy
Energielehre energetics
energiereiches Phosphat
 high energy phosphate
eng narrow
engbrüstig narrow-chested
Englische Krankheit rachitis
Engramm engram
Enkopresis encopresis
Enol e. e.
Enolase e. e.
Enophthalmus enophthalmos
Enostose enostosis
Entamoeba histolytica
 Endamoeba histolytica
entarten to despeciate,
 to degenerate
Entartung despeciation,
 degeneration
Entartungsreaktion reaction of degeneration
entbinden to deliver
Entbindung delivery, accouchement
Entbindungsanstalt maternity hospital
entbleien to delead
entblocken to deblock
entbluten to exsanguinate
Entblutung exsanguination
Entchlorung dechloridation

entcholesterinisieren to decholesterolize
Entdeckung discovery
entdifferenzieren to dedifferentiate
Entdifferenzierung dedifferentiation
Ente duck
Entelechie entelechy
enteral e. e.
Enteritis e. e.
enteritisch enteritic
Enteroanastomose enteroanastomosis
enterobiliär enterobiliary
Enterocholezystostomie enterocholecystostomy
Enterocholezystotomie enterocholecystotomy
Enteroglukagon enteroglucagon
enterohepatisch enterohepatic
Enterohepatitis e. e.
Enterohormon enterohormone
Enterokinase e. e.
Enterokokkus enterococcus
Enterokolitis enterocolitis
Enterokolostomie enterocolostomy
Enterolithiasis e. e.
Enterologie enterology
Enteropathie enteropathy
—, **eiweißverlierende** protein-losing enteropathy
Enteropexie enteropexy
Enteroptose enteroptosis
Enterostomie enterostomy
Enterotomie enterotomy
Enterotoxin e. e.
Enterovirus e. e.
Enterozele enterocele
entfärben to decolorize
entfermentieren to dezymotize
entfernen to remove
Entfernung (= Abstand) distance
Entfernung (= Beseitigung) removal
entfettet defatted
Entfettungskur treatment for obesity
Entfremdung estrangement
Entgasung degassing
entgegengesetzt opposite
entgiften to detoxicate, to detoxify
Entgiftung detoxification
Entgranulierung degranulation
enthaaren to depilate
Enthaarung depilation
Enthaarungsmittel depilatory
enthalten to contain
—, **sich** to abstain
enthaltsam abstinent
Enthaltsamkeit abstinence
enthaupten to decapitate
Enthauptung decapitation, decollation
Enthemmung disinhibition
enthirnen to excerebrate, to decerebrate
Enthirnung excerebration, decerebration
Entität entity
entkalken to decalcify
Entkalkung decalcification
entkleiden to unclothe, to undress
entkräften to enfeeble, to debilitate
entladen to unload
entlassen to dismiss, to discharge
Entlassung dismissal, discharge
Entlassungsschein dismissal slip
entlasten to unburden
Entlastung exoneration
Entlastungszone relief area
Entlausung delousing
Entlausungsmittel pediculicide
entleeren to deplete
Entleerung depletion, evacuation
entleiben, sich to commit suicide
entmannen to castrate
Entmannung castration, eviration
entmarken to emedullate
Entmarkung emedullation
entmyelinisieren to demyelinize
Entmyelinisierung demyelinization
entnerven to enervate, to denervate

Entnervung enervation, denervation
Entoderm e. e.
Entokon entocone
Entokonid entoconid
Entomologie entomology
Entpersönlichung dispersonalization, depersonalization
Entropion e. e.
Entropionpinzette entropion forceps
entrunded unrounded
entsäuern to desacidify, to deacidify
Entsäuerung deacidification
Entsalzung desalination
Entschädigungsneurose compensation neurosis
entspannend relaxant
Entspannung relaxation
Entspannungsmittel relaxant
entstellen to disfigure
Entstörung debugging
entvaskularisieren to devascularize
entwässern to dehydrate
Entwässerung dehydration
Entweiblichung defemination
entwickeln to develop
Entwickler developer
Entwicklung development; evolution
entwicklungsmäßig developmental
entwöhnen to disaccustom
entziehen to withdraw
Entziehung withdrawal
Entziehungsbeschwerden withdrawal pains
Entziehungsmethode withdrawal method
entzünden, sich to become inflamed
entzündlich inflammatory
Entzündung inflammation
entzündungshemmend antiinflammatory
entzündungswidrig antiinflammatory

Entzug deprivation, withdrawal
Enukleation enucleation
enukleieren to enucleate
Enuresis e. e.
Enzephalitis encephalitis
– **lethargica** lethargic encephalitis
enzephalitisch encephalitic
Enzephaloarteriographie encephaloarteriography
Enzephalogramm encephalogram
Enzephalograph encephalograph
Enzephalographie encephalography
enzephalographisch encephalographic
Enzephalomalazie encephalomalacia
Enzephalomeningitis encephalomeningitis
Enzephalomyelitis encephalomyelitis
– **disseminata** disseminated encephalomyelitis
Enzephalopathie encephalopathy
Enzephalose encephalosis
enzephalotrigeminal encephalotrigeminal
enzootisch enzootic
Enzym enzyme
Enzymologie enzymology
Enzymolyse enzymolysis
Enzymregulation enzymic regulation
Eosin e. e.
Eosinopenie eosinopenia
eosinophil eosinophile, eosinophilic, eosinophilous
eosinophiler Leukozyt eosinophil
Eosinophilie eosinophilia
Ependym ependyma
ependymal e. e.
Ependymitis e. e.
Ependymom ependymoma
Ephedrin ephedrine
ephemer ephemeral
Ephetonin ephetonine

Epicanthus e. e.
Epicardia e. e.
Epicillin e. e.
Epicondylitis e. e.
Epidemie epidemic
Epidemiologie epidemiology
epidemiologisch epidemiological
epidemisch epidemic
epidermal e. e.
Epidermis e. e.
Epidermolysis bullosa e. e.
Epidermophytid e. e.
Epidermophytie epidermophytosis
Epidiaskop epidiascope
Epididymitis e. e.
Epididymoorchitis e. e.
epidural e. e.
epigastrisch epigastric
Epiglottis e. e.
epiglottisch epiglottic
Epignathus e. e.
Epikantus epicanthus
Epikard epicardium
Epikardia epicardia
epikardial epicardial
Epikardiektomie epicardiectomy
Epikarin epicarin
Epikondylitis epicondylitis
Epikrise epicrisis
epikritisch epicritic
Epikutantest patch test
Epilation e. e.
Epilepsie epilepsy
–, genuine idiopathic epilepsy
–, Jacksonsche jacksonian epilepsy
epileptiform e. e.
epileptisch epileptic
epileptisches Äquivalent epileptic equivalent
epileptogen epileptogenic
epileptoid e. e.
epineural e. e.
Epipharyngitis e. e.
Epiphora e. e.
Epiphyse (endocrinol.) pineal gland
Epiphyse (osteol.) epiphysis

Epiphysenlinie epiphyseal line
Epiphysenlösung epiphyseal separation, epiphyseolysis
Epiphysitis e. e.
Epiploon e. e., caul
Epiplopexie epiplopexy
Epiplozele epiplocele
Episiotomie episiotomy
episkleral episcleral
Episkleritis episcleritis
Episkop episcope
Epispadie epispadias
Epistaxis e. e.
episternal e. e.
Epitestosteron epitestosterone
epithalamisch epithalamic
Epithel epithelium
–, kubisches cubical epithelium
–, mehrschichtiges stratified epithelium
epithelial e. e.
Epitheliose epitheliosis
Epithelisierung epithelization
Epithelkörperchen parathyroid, parathyroid gland
Epithelkörperchenüberfunktion hyperparathyroidism
Epithelkörperchenunterfunktion hypoparathyroidism
Epituberkulose epituberculosis
epizootisch epizootic
Epulis e. e.
equin equine
Erbgang inheritance
Erbgrind favus
Erbium e. e.
erblich hereditary
Erblichkeit heredity
erblinden to grow blind
erbrechen to vomit
Erbrechen vomiting
Erbsche Lähmung Erb's paralysis
Erbscher Punkt Erb's point
Erbsches Zeichen Erb's sign
Erbsensuppenstuhl pea soup stool

ERCP (= endoskopische retrograde Cholangiopankreatikographie)
endoscopic retrograde cholangiopancreaticography (ERCP)
Erde, Seltene Rare Earth
erden to earth
erdrosseln to strangle
erdulden to suffer
Erdung earth connection
Erektion erection
Erepsin e. e.
erethisch erethistic
Erethismus erethism
erfahren expert
Erfahrung experience
Erfolg success; response
erfolglos unsuccessful
erfolgreich successful
Erforschung exploration, investigation
erfrieren to freeze to death, to perish from cold
Erfrierung congelation
erfrischen to refresh
erfroren frostbitten
Erg e. e.
ergänzend supplementary
Ergänzung supplementation
ergiebig productive, efficient
Ergobasin ergometrine (e), ergonovine (a)
Ergochrysin e. e.
Ergoclavin ergoclavine
Ergocornin ergocornine
Ergocristin ergocristine
ergograph e. e.
Ergographie ergography
ergographisch ergographic
Ergokryptin ergocryptine
Ergometer e. e.
Ergometrie ergometry
Ergometrin ergometrine (e), ergonovine (a)
Ergometrinin ergometrinine
ergometrisch ergometric
Ergomonamin ergomonamine
Ergonomie ergonomics
Ergosin ergosine
Ergosinin ergosinine
Ergospirometrie ergospirometry
ergospirometrisch ergospirometric
Ergosterin ergosterol
—, bestrahltes viosterol
Ergotamin ergotamine
Ergotaminin ergotaminine
Ergothionein ergothioneine
Ergotin ergotine
Ergotinin ergotinine
Ergotismus ergotism
Ergotoxin ergotoxine
ergotrop ergotropic
Erguß effusion
Erhaltung maintenance
Erhaltungsdosis maintenance dose
erhitzen to heat
erhöhen to elevate, to enhance
Erholung recovery
erkälten, sich to catch a cold
Erkältung chill
Erkältungsinfekt common cold
Erkenntnis cognition
Erkenntniskritik epistemology
Erkenntnistheorie epistemology
Erkennung recognition
Erkrankung illness
Erleichterung alleviation; facilitation
Erlenmeyerkolben Erlenmeyer flask
Ermattung defatigation
Ermüdbarkeit fatigability
ermüden to fatigue
Ermüdung fatigue, defatigation
ernähren to nourish, to feed
Ernährung nutrition, alimentation
Ernährungslehre sitology
ernährungsmäßig nutritional
Ernährungswissenschaftler nutritionist
Ernährungswissenschaftlerin nutritionist
erneuern to renew
Erneuerung renewal

erogen erogenous
Erosion e. e.
erotisch erotic
Erotomanie erotomania
Erprobung test, trial, assay
erregbar excitable
Erregbarkeit excitability
erregen to excite
erregend excitatory
Erregung excitation
Erregungsleitungssystem conduction system (of the heart)
Erregungsmittel excitant
erröten to redden
Erröten reddening
Ersatz replacement; substitute, surrogate; prosthesis
Ersatzschlag escape beat
Ersatzstoff surrogate
erschlaffen to languish
Erschlaffung relaxation
erschöpft exhausted
Erschöpfung exhaustion, prostration
erschüttern to shake
Erschütterung concussion
erschweren to impede
ersetzen to replace
erstarken to grow strong
erstechen to pierce, to stab
erstgebärend primiparous
Erstgebärende primipara
ersticken to suffocate, to choke
Erstickung asphyxiation, suffocation
Erstickungsanfall choke
erträglich tolerable
ertränken to drown
ertragen to bear; to tolerate
Ertragen bearing; toleration
ertrinken to be drowned
Ertrinken drowning
Eruption e. e.
eruptiv eruptive
erwachen to awake
erwachsen adult
erwachsene Person adult

Erwartungsneurose expectation neurosis
Erweiterer dilator
erweitern to dilate
Erweiterung dilatation
erweiterungsfähig dilatable
erworben acquired
erwürgen to choke, to strangle
Erysipel erysipelas
Erysipeloid e. e.
Erysipelothrix insidiosa e. e.
Erythem erythema
Erythema induratum e. e.
– infectiosum e. e.
– exsudativum multiforme erythema multiforme
– nodosum e. e.
erythematös erythematous
Erythrämie erythraemia (e), erythremia (a)
erythrämisch erythraemic (e), erythremic (a)
Erythroblast e. e.
Erythroblastenanämie erythroblastic anaemia (e), erythroblastic anemia (a)
erythroblastisch erythroblastic
Erythroblastose erythroblastosis
Erythrodermie erythroderma
erythrokinetisch erythrokinetic
Erythroleukämie erythroleukaemia (e), erythroleukemia (a)
Erythroltetranitrat erythroltetranitrate
Erythromelalgie erythromelalgia
Erythromelie erythromelia
Erythromycin e. e.
Erythrophagozytose erythrophagocytosis
Erythropoese erythropoiesis
erythropoetisch erythropoietic
Erythrose (chem.) e.e.
Erythrose (dermatol.) erythrosis
Erythrozyanose erythrocyanosis
Erythrozyt erythrocyte, red blood corpuscle
erythrozytär erythrocytic

Erythrozytenvolumen volume of red blood corpuscles
Erythrozytose erythrocytosis
Erythrulose e. e.
Erythrurie erythruria
Esbachs Reagens Esbach's reagent
Esel donkey
Eserinum sulfuricum eserine sulfate (a), eserine sulphate (e)
Esmarchsche Binde Esmarch's bandage
esoterisch esoteric
essen to eat
essentiell essential
essentielle Hypertonie essential hypertension, benign hypertension
– **Thrombopenie** thrombopenic purpura
Essenz essence
Essig vinegar
Essigsäure acetic acid
essigsaure Tonerde aluminium acetate (e), aluminum acetate (a)
eßbar edible, esculent
Eßlöffel tablespoon
BSG (= Blutsenkungsgeschwindigkeit) ESR (= erythrocyte sedimentation rate)
Ester e. e.
Esterase e. e.
Esterolyse esterolysis
esterolytisch esterolytic
ethmoidal e. e.
Ethmoiditis e. e.
Ethnographie ethnography
ethnographisch ethnographic
Ethnologie ethnology
ethnologisch ethnologic
etikettieren to tag, to label
Euchinin euchinine
Eugenik eugenics
eugenisch eugenic
Eugenol e. e.
Eugenolat eugenolate
Euglobulin e. e.
Eukain eucaine

Eukalyptusöl eucalyptus oil
Eukapnie eucapnia
eumetabolisch eumetabolic
Eumydrin eumydrine
Eunuch e. e.
eunuchoid e. e.
Eunuchoidismus eunuchoidism
eupeptisch eupeptic
Euphorie euphoria
euphorisch euphoric
euphorisierend euphoristic
Europium e. e.
Eurhythmie eurhythmia
eurhythmisch eurhythmic
Eustachische Röhre eustachian tube
eutektisch eutectic
Euter udder
Euthanasie euthanasia
Evan-Blau Evan's blue
Eventration e. e.
Eviszeration evisceration
Evolution e. e.
evolutiv evolutive
Ewaldsches Probefrühstück Ewald's test meal
Ewing-Tumor Ewing's tumor (a), Ewing's tumour (e)
exakt exact
Exaltiertheit exaltation
examinieren to examine
Examinierung examination
Exanthem exanthema
exanthematisch exanthematous
Exanthema vesiculosum vesicular exanthema
Exartikulation exarticulation
Exazerbation exacerbation
Exenteration e. e.
Exerzierknochen exercise bone
Exfoliation e. e.
Exhairese exeresis
Exhalation e. e.
exhumieren to exhume
Exhumierung exhumation
existentiell existential
Exkavation excavation

Exkavator excavator
exkavieren to excavate
Exkochleation excochleation
Exkoriation excoriation
Exkret excrete
Exkretion excretion
exkretorisch excretory
Exkursion excursion
exogen exogenous
exokrin exocrine, exacrinous
Exophthalmus exophthalmos
Exostose exostosis
exotisch exotic
Exotoxin e. e.
Exozytose exocytosis
Expander e. e.
Expansion e. e.
expansiv expansive
Expektorans expectorant
Expektoration expectoration
expektorieren to expectorate
Experiment e. e.
experimentell experimental
experimentieren to experiment
Explantat explant
Explantation e. e.
explantieren to explant
explodieren to explode
Exploration e. e.
exploratorisch exploratory
Explosion e. e.
Explosionsschock explosion shock, sinistrosis
explosiv explosive
Exponent e. e.
Expression e. e.
exprimieren to express
Exspiration expiration
Exspirationsvolumen expiratory volume
exspiratorisch expiratory
exspirieren to expire
Exstirpation extirpation
exstirpieren to extirpate
Exsudat exudate
Exsudation exudation
Extension e. e.

Extensionsbügel extension stirrup
Extensionsvorrichtung extension apparatus
extern external
Extinktion extinction
extraartikulär extraarticular
extrabulbär extrabulbar
Extractum Filicis oleoresin of aspidium
– Secalis cornuti fluidum fluidextract of ergot
extradural e. e.
extrafaszial extrafascial
extragastral extragastric
extragenital e. e.
extrahepatisch extrahepatic
extrahierbar extractable
extrahieren to extract
extrakapsulär extracapsular
extrakardial extracardial
extrakorporal extracorporeal
extrakranial extracranial
Extrakt extract
Extraktion extraction
Extraktor extractor
extramaxillär extramaxillary
extramedullär extramedullary
extramural e. e.
extraoral e. e.
extraossär extraosseous
extravariell extraovarian
extrapankreatisch extrapancreatic
extraperitoneal e. e.
extrapleural e. e.
extrapulmonal extrapulmonary
extrapyramidal e. e.
extrarenal e. e.
Extrasystole e. e., ectopic beat
extratracheal e. e.
extrauterin extrauterine
extravaginal e. e.
Extravasat extravasation
extravaskulär extravascular
extraventrikulär extraventricular
extrazellulär extracellular
extrem extreme
Extremität extremity

extrinsic factor e. e.
Extroversion e. e.
Extubation e. e.
extubieren to extubate

exzentrisch excentric
Exzeß excess
exzidieren to excise, to cut out
Exzision excision

F

Fabrysche Krankheit
 sphingolipidosis
Facette facet, facing
facettiert faceted
Fachärztin specialist
Facharzt specialist
Facharzt für Anästhesie
 anaesthetist (e), anesthetist (a)
− **Anatomie** anatomist
− **Augenkrankheiten** ophthalmologist
− **Bakteriologie** bacteriologist
− **Chirurgie** surgeon
− **Frauenkrankheiten** specialist for women's diseases
− **Geschlechtskrankheiten** venereologist
− **Gynäkologie** gynaecologist (e), gynecologist (a)
− **Hals-Nasen-Ohrenleiden** oto-rhino-laryngologist
− **Hautkrankheiten** dermatologist
− **Hygiene** hygienist
− **Innere Medizin** internist
− **Kinderkrankheiten** paediatrician (e), pediatrician (a)
− **Neurologie** neurologist
− **Orthopädie** orthopaedist (e), orthopedist (a)
− **Pathologie** pathologist
− **Physiologie** physiologist
− **Psychiatrie** psychiatrist
− **Psychologie** psychologist
− **Röntgenologie** roentgenologist
− **Urologie** urologist
Faden thread, filament

Fadenabschneider ligature cutter
fadenförmig filiform
fähig able
Fähigkeit ability, aptitude, faculty
fäkal faecal (e), fecal (a)
fäkulent faeculent (e), feculent (a)
fällen to precipitate
färbbar tingible
Färbeindex color index (a), colour index (e)
färben to stain
Färben staining
Färbetechnik staining method
Färbung staining, tinction
Fäulnis putrefaction
Fahrrad-Ergometrie bicycle ergometry
Fahrstuhl (med.) walking chair
Fahrtauglichkeit driving ability
Faktor factor
Fakultät faculty
fakultativ facultative
Fallhand wristdrop
Fallotsche Pentalogie pentalogy of Fallot
− **Tetralogie** tetralogy of Fallot
− **Trilogie** trilogy of Fallot
fallsüchtig epileptic
Fallsucht falling sickness, epilepsy
falsch false, spurious
Falte fold
familiär familial
Familienplanung family planning
Fango e. e.
Farad e. e.

Faradisation faradization
faradisieren to faradize
faradisch faradic
Farbe color (a), colour (e); stain, dye
farbenblind color blind (a), colour blind (e)
farbenblinde Person achromate
Farbenblindheit daltonism, color blindness (a), colour blindness (e)
Farbstoff dye, stain
Farbstoffverdünnungskurve dye-dilution curve
Farmerlunge farmer's lung
Farn fern
Fasciola hepatica e. e.
Faser fiber
Faserknorpel fibrocartilage
Fasernetz network
Faserwerk network
faßförmiger Thorax barrel chest
Fassungsvermögen capacity
Faßzange grasping forceps
fasten to fast
Faszie fascia
Faszienplastik fasciaplasty
faszikulär fascicular
Fasziotomie fasciotomy
Faulbrut (veter.) foul brood
Faulecke perlèche
faulen to putrefy
faulig putrid
Faulschlamm sapropel
Faultier sloth
Fauna e. e.
Faust fist
Favismus favism
Favus e. e., porrigo favosa
Fazialislähmung facial paralysis, Bell's palsy
Fazialis-Nerv facial nerve
Febris undulans undulant fever
Feder (z.B. Uhrfeder) spring
Federklemme spring clamp
Feersche Krankheit Feer's disease, pink disease
Fehlbehandlung malpractice

Fehlen absence; poverty; deprival
Fehlentwicklung maldevelopment
Fehler fault, defect
Fehlerbereich error range
fehlerhaft vicious, faulty, malformed, defective
Fehlernährung subnutrition, malnutrition
Fehlgeburt abortion, miscarriage
—, **drohende** threatened abortion
—, **künstliche** artificial abortion, abaction
—, **septische** septic abortion
—, **verhaltene** missed abortion
Fehlhaltung trusion
Fehlingsche Lösung Fehling's solution
Fehlingsche Probe Fehling's test
Feigwarze fig wart
Feile file
Feinstruktur fine structure
Feldarzt army surgeon
Feldlazarett field hospital
Feldnephritis war nephritis
Fell hide, fell
Felty-Syndrom Felty's syndrome
femoral e. e.
Fenchel fennel
fenstern to fenestrate
Fensterung fenestration
Ferkel pig
Ferment e. e., enzyme
fermentativ fermental, zymogenous
Fermentlehre zymology, enzymology
Fernmessung telemetering
Fernsehen television
fernsichtig longsighted
Ferratazelle Ferrata's cell
Ferrioxamin ferrioxamine
Ferrit ferrite
Ferritin e. e.
Ferrizyanid ferricyanide
Ferrum reductum reduced iron
Ferse heel
Fessel (veter.) fetlock

Fesselgelenk fetlock joint, pastern joint
fest fast
festhaftend adhesive; tenacious
Fetischismus fetishism
Fetischist fetishist
Fetoprotein e. e.
fett fat
Fett fat
Fettembolie fat embolism
Fettgewebe fatty tissue
Fettgewebeentzündung panniculitis
fettig fatty
fettleibig obese
Fettleibigkeit obesity, corpulence
fettlöslich fat-soluble
fettspaltend fat splitting
Fettstuhl fatty stool
Fettsucht adiposis, adiposity fatness, obesity, pimelosis
fettsüchtig adipose
Fettzelle fat cell
feucht moist, wet
Feuchtigkeit moisture, dampness
Feuchtigkeitsgrad humidity
feuerfest fireproof
feuergefährlich highly inflammable
Fiberskop fiberscope
fibrillär fibrillary
Fibrille fibril
fibrillieren to fibrillate
Fibrillieren fibrillation
Fibrin e. e.
fibrinös fibrinous
Fibrinogen e. e.
fibrinogen fibrinogenic
Fibrinogenopenie fibrinogenopenie
fibrinoid e. e.
Fibrinokinase e. e.
Fibrinolyse fibrinolysis
Fibrinolysin e. e.
Fibrinolysokinase e. e.
fibrinolytisch fibrinolytic
Fibrinopenie fibrinopenia
Fibroadenie fibroadenia

Fibroadenom fibroadenoma
Fibroblast e. e.
Fibroelastose fibroelastosis
fibrös fibrous
Fibrogliom fibroglioma
fibroid e. e.
Fibrokarzinom fibrocarcinoma
Fibrolipom fibrolipoma
Fibrolysin e. e.
Fibrom fibroma
fibromatös fibromatous
Fibromatose fibromatosis
Fibromyom fibromyoma
Fibromyxom fibromyxoma
Fibromyxosarkom fibromyxosarcoma
Fibroplasie fibroplasia
Fibroplastin e. e.
fibroplastisch fibroplastic
Fibrosarkom fibrosarcoma
Fibrose fibrosis
Fibrositis e. e.
Fibrozyt fibrocyte
fibular e. e.
Fichtennadelbad pine bath
Fieber fever, pyrexia
Fieber der Mittelmeerländer, familiär gehäuft auftretendes familial Mediterranean fever
Fieber, hitziges ague
Fieberanfall attack of fever
fiebererzeugend febrifacient
fieberhaft febrile, pyrexial
Fieberhitze fever heat
fieberkrank feverish
Fieberkurve temperature graphic chart
Fiebermittel febrifuge
fiebern to be in fever
fiebersenkend febrifugal
Fiebertherapie fever therapy
Fieberthermometer clinical thermometer
Fiebertraum feverish dream
fiebrig febrile
Filaria bancrofti Wuchereria bancrofti, Filaria bancrofti

Filaria loa Loa loa
Filariasis e. e.
filiform e. e.
Filmaron e. e.
Film e. e.
Filmentwicklungsmaschine x-ray processor
Filmhalter film holder
Filmtrockengestell film drying rack
Filter e. e., strainer
Filterpapier filter paper
filtrabel filtrable
Filtrat filtrate
Filtration e. e.
filtrierbar filtrable
filtrieren to filter, to strain
Filtrierpumpe filter pump
Filtrierung filtration, strain
Filz felt
Filzlaus crab louse
Filzlausbefall phthiriasis inguinalis
Fimbrie fimbria
final e. e.
Finder seeker
Finger e. e.
Fingerabdruck fingerprint, dactylogram
Fingergelenk finger joint
Fingerling finger stall
Fingernägelbeißen nail biting
Fingernasenversuch finger-nose test
Fingerschützer finger protector
Fingerspitze finger tip
Fingerverwachsung webbed fingers
fingieren to feign
Finierfeile finishing file
Finierinstrument finishing instrument
Finne larva
Finkelsteinsche Eiweißmilch Finkelstein's albumin milk
Fisch fish
Fischbandwurm fish tapeworm
Fissur fissure

Fistel fistula
—,**arteriovenöse** arteriovenous fistula
Fistelbildung fistulization
fistulös fistulous
Fixierbad fixing bath
fixieren to fix
Fixiermittel fixative, fixing agent
Fixierpinzette fixation forceps
Fixierung fixation
Fixpunkt breakpoint
Flachmeißel chisel
Flachschraube flat screw
Fläche area
Fläschchen vial
Flagellata e. e.
Flamingo e. e.
Flammenphotometrie flame photometry
flammig flamelike
Flanellbinde flannel bandage
Flasche bottle
Flaschenkind bottle-fed infant
Flattern flutter
Flatulenz flatulence
Flavin e. e.
Flavon e. e.
Flavonoid e. e.
Flavoprotein e. e.
Flechte tetter
Fleck spot, patch, tache, dot
Fleckfieber typhus fever
fleckfieberartig typhous
fleckfieberförmig typhous
Flecktyphus typhus fever
fleckig spotted, tachetic
Fledermaus bat
Fleisch flesh
—,**wildes** proud flesh
Fleischbeschauer inspector of butcher's meat
Fleischbrühe broth
fleischig carneous
Fleischkost meat diet
Fleischmole carneous mole
Flexner-Bazillus Flexner's bacillus
Flexur flexure

Fliege fly
Fliegenpilz fly agaric
Fliegerkrankheit plane sickness, aviator's disease
fliegertauglich airing worthy
Fließeigenschaft flow property
Fließgleichgewicht steady state
Fließpapier blotting paper
Flimmerepithel ciliated epithelium
flimmern to fibrillate, to glimmer
Flimmern fibrillation, glimmering
Flimmerskotom flimmer scotoma
Flintsches Geräusch Flint's murmur
Flocke flake
flockig flaky
Flockung flocculation
Flockungsreaktion flocculoreaction
Floh flea
Flora e. e.
Flotation e. e.
Flucloxapenicillin e. e.
flüchtig volatile
–, leicht easily volatile
–, schwer sparingly volatile
Flügel wing
Flügelbißfilm bitewing
Flügelfell pterygium
flüssig liquid, fluid
Flüssigkeit liquid, fluid, humor (a), humour (e)
Flüssigkeitsersatz fluid substitution
Flüssigkeitsspiegel level of fluid
flüstern to whisper
Fluidextrakt fluidextract (a), liquid extract (e)
Fluktuation fluctuation
fluktuieren to fluctuate
fluktuierend fluctuant
Flumethiazid flumethiazide
Flunitrazepam e. e.
Fluocinolon fluocinolone
Fluocortolon fluocortolone
Fluor fluorine
Fluor albus leukorrhea (a), leukorrhoea (e)

Fluorenylazetamid fluorenylacetamide
Fluoreszenz fluorescence
Fluoreszin fluorescein
fluorieren to fluorinate
Fluorohydrocortison fluorohydrocortisone
Fluoroprednisolon fluoroprednisolone
Fluoropyrimidin fluoropyrimidine
Fluorose fluorosis
Fluoroskopie fluoroscopy
fluoroskopisch fluoroscopic
Fluorvergiftung fluorosis
Flurazepam e. e.
Fluß flow, fluxion
Flußmesser flowmeter
Flußmittel flux
Flutamid flutamide
Flutwelle tidal wave
Förstersche Operation Förster's operation
fötal fetal (a), foetal (e)
fötid fetid (a), foetid (e)
Fötoprotein fetoprotein
Fötor fetor (a), foetor (e)
Fötus fetus (a), foetus (e)
Fohlen foal
fohlen to foal
fokal focal
Fokalinfektion focal infection
Fokaltoxikose focal toxicosis
Fokus focus
Folat folate
Folgeerscheinung sequela
Folgerung implication
Folie foil
Folinerin e. e.
Folliculitis decalvans e. e.
Follikel follicle
Follikelhormon follicular hormone
Follikelreifungshormon follicle-stimulating hormone
follikulär follicular
Follikulitis folliculitis
Fominoben e. e.
Fontanelle fontanel, fontanelle

forciert forced
forcierte Vitalkapazität forced vital capacity
forensisch forensic
Form e. e., pattern
Formaldehyd formaldehyde
Format e. e.
Formel formula
Formelsammlung formulary
Formolgelreaktion formolgel reaction
Formyl e. e.
forschen to search, to inquire
Forscher investigator
Forschung investigation, research
Fortbewegung locomotion
Fortbildung perfecting
fortdauernd perpetual
fortpflanzen to propagate
Fortpflanzung propagation, reproduction
Fortpflanzungs... reproductive
Fortsatz process
fortschreiten to advance, to progress
Fortschritt progress
Fovea e. e.
Fowlersche Lösung Fowler's solution
Fox-Fordycesche Krankheit Fox-Fordyce disease
Fränkelscher Bazillus Diplococcus pneumoniae
Fräse reamer
Fragment e. e.
Fragmentation e. e.
Fraktion fraction
fraktionieren to fractionate
fraktioniert fractional
Fraktionierung fractionation
Fraktur fracture
—,**einfache** simple fracture
—,**Ermüdungs-** fatigue fracture
—,**Grünholz-** greenstick fracture
—,**komplizierte** compound fracture
—,**komplizierte Splitter-** compound comminuted fracture
Fraktur, Marsch- march fracture
—,**Splitter-** comminuted fracture
Frambösie frambesia (a), framboesia (e), pian, buba, yaws
Frambösie-Exanthem yaw
Frankenhäusersches Ganglion Frankenhäuser's ganglion
Fraß caries
Frauenarzt specialist for women's diseases
Frauenkrankheit women's disease
Fraunhofersche Linie Fraunhofer's line
freigeben to release
Freilegung denudation
Freiluft open air
Freische Probe Frei test
freisetzen to liberate, to release
Freisetzung liberation, release
freiwillig voluntary
Fremdkörper foreign body
Fremdkörperzange foreign body removing forceps
Fremdstoff alien substance
Fremitus e. e.
frequent e. e.
Frequenz frequency
Frettchen ferret
Friedländerscher Bazillus Klebsiella pneumoniae, Friedländer's bacillus
Friedreichsche Ataxie Friedreich's ataxia
frieren to be cold, to feel cold
frigid e. e.
Frigidität frigidity
Frischblut fresh blood
Fröhlichsches Syndrom adiposogenital syndrome
frösteln to shiver, to feel chilly
Frösteln chill
fröstelnd chilly
frontal e. e.
frontobasal e. e.
frontonasal e. e.
frontookzipital frontooccipital

frontoparietal e. e.
frontotemporal e. e.
frontozygomatisch frontomalar
Frosch frog
Froschbauch frog belly
Frostbeule chilblain, congelation
frottieren to rub
Frucht fruit
fruchtbar fruitful; fertile
fruchtbar machen to fertilize
Fruchtbarkeit fruitfulness; fertility, fecundity
Fruchttötung aborticide
Fruchtwasser liquor amnii
Fruchtzucker fructose
früh early
Frühentdeckung early detection
Früherkennung early detection
Frühgeburt premature birth
Frühjahrskonjunktivitis vernal conjunctivitis
frühreif precocious
Frühreife precociousness
Fruktokinase fructokinase
Fruktose fructose
Fruktosurie fructosuria
frustran frustrane
Fuadin e. e.
Fuchs fox
Fuchs (= Pferd) sorrel horse
Fuchsin e. e.
fuchsinophil fuchsinophilous
Fucosamin fucosamine
Fucose e. e.
Füchsin vixen
fühlen to feel
füllen to fill
Füllung filling
Füllungsdefekt filling defect
Füllungsdruck filling pressure
Fünftagefieber trench fever
fünfwertig pentavalent
Fürsorge care
Fürsorger social worker
Fürsorgerin social worker

Fütterung feeding
fulminant e. e.
Fumarat fumarate
Fundament e. e.
fundamental e. e.
Fundus e. e.
fungös fungous
Fungus e. e.
Funiculus spermaticus spermatic cord
funikulär funicular
funikuläre Myelose funicular myelosis
Funikulitis funiculitis
Funikulus funiculus
Funktion function
funktionell functional
Funktionsprüfung function test
Furan e. e.
Furanose e. e.
Furazon furazone
Furche furrow, groove
furchig sulcate
Furcht fear
Furunkel furuncle
furunkulös furuncular
Furunkulose furunculosis
Furylalanin furylalanine
Fuscin e. e.
fusiform e. e.
Fusobacterium fusiforme e. e.
fusospirillär fusospirillary
Fuß foot
Fuß- und Handpflege chiropody
Fuß verstauchen, den − to sprain the foot
Fußbad footbath
Fußekzem (veter.) scratches
Fußgelenk ankle
Fußklonus ankle clonus
Fußpuder foot powder
Fußsohle sole (of the foot)
Fußwurzel tarsus (of the foot)
Futter (dent.) chuck
Futter (veter.) fodder
Futurologie futurology

G

Gabel fork
Gadolinium e. e.
gähnen to yawn
Gärtner-Bazillus Salmonella enteritidis, Gärtner's bacillus
Gärung fermentation, zymosis
Gärungsprobe fermentation test
galaktagog galactagogue
Galaktagogum galactagogue
Galaktokinase galactokinase
Galaktorrhöe galactorrhea (a), galactorrhoea (e)
Galaktosamin galactosamine
Galaktose galactose
Galaktosebelastungsprobe galactose tolerance test
Galaktosetoleranz galactose tolerance
galaktosid galactoside
Galaktosidase galactosidase
Galaktosurie galactosuria
Galenik galenics
galenisch galenic
Gallat gallate
Galle gall, bile
Gallen (veter.) wind gall, vessignon
Gallenbildung cholopoiesis
Gallenblase gallbladder
Gallenfieber bilious fever
Gallenfistel biliary fistula
Gallengang biliferous duct
Gallenpulver bile powder
Gallensäure bile acid
Gallenstein gallstone
Gallentrakt biliary tract
Gallenwege biliary ducts
Gallerte jelly
Gallium e. e.
Gallone gallon
Galmei calamine
Galopprhythmus gallop rhythm
Galtonsche Pfeife Galton's whistle
galvanisch galvanic

Galvanisierbad electroplating bath
galvanisieren to galvanize
Galvanisierung galvanization
Galvanometer e. e.
Galvanokaustik galvanocautery
galvanotaktisch galvanotactic
Gambiafieber Gambian horse sickness
Gamet gamete
Gametogonie gametogony
Gametozyt gametocyte
Gammaglobulin gamma globulin
Gammastrahl gamma ray
Gammastrahler gamma emitter
Gammatron e. e.
Gang (Durchgang) duct
Gang (Gehen) gait
Gangart gait
Gangliektomie gangliectomy
Ganglienblocker ganglionic blocking agent
Ganglienzelle ganglion cell
Gangliom ganglioma
Ganglion e. e.
– **Gasseri** gasserian ganglion
– **stellatum** stellate ganglion
Gangliogliom ganglioglioma
Ganglionektomie ganglionectomy
Ganglioneurom ganglioneuroma
Ganglionitis e. e.
Ganglioplegikum ganglioplegic
ganglioplegisch ganglioplegic
Gangliosid ganglioside
Gangrän gangrene
gangränös gangrenous
Gans goose
ganzkörperbestrahlt total body irradiated
Ganzkörperbestrahlung total-body irradiation
Ganzkörper-Computertomographie whole body computed tomography
Gargoylismus gargoylism

Garlandsches Dreieck Garland's triangle
Garn yarn
Gas e. e.
Gas-Analyse gas analysis
gasartig gaseous
Gasbazillus Clostridium welchii
Gasbrand gas gangrene
Gas-Chromatographie gas chromatography
gasförmig gaseous
Gasgangrän gas gangrene
Gasgangränantitoxin gas gangrene antitoxin
gasgefüllt gas-filled
Gassersches Ganglion gasserian ganglion
Gastralgie gastralgia
gastralgisch gastralgic
Gastrektasie gastrectasis
Gastrektomie gastrectomy
Gastrin e. e.
gastrisch gastric
Gastritis e. e.
gastritisch gastritic
gastroduodenal e. e.
Gastroduodenitis e. e.
Gastroduodenostomie gastroduodenostomy
Gastroenteritis e. e.
gastroenteritisch gastroenteritic
Gastroenterokolitis gastroenterocolitis
Gastroenterologe gastroenterologist
Gastroenterologie gastroenterology
gastroenterologisch gastroenterological
Gastroenteroptose gastroenteroptosis
Gastroenterostomie gastroenterostomy
gastrogen gastrogenic
gastrokardial gastrocardiac
Gastrokolostomie gastrocolostomy
gastrolienal e. e.
Gastropathie gastropathy
gastropathisch gastropathic
Gastrophiliasis e. e.
Gastroplegie gastroplegia
Gastroptose gastroptosis
Gastroskop gastroscope
Gastroskopie gastroscopy
gastroskopisch gastroscopic
Gastrostomie gastrostomy
Gastrosukkorrhöe gastrosuccorrhea (a), gastrosuccorrhoea (e)
Gastrotomie gastrotomy
Gastrula e. e.
Gastrulation e. e.
Gatte husband, consort, mate
Gattin wife, consort, mate
Gattung species, sort, kind
Gauchersche Krankheit Gaucher's disease
Gaultheriaöl oil of gaultheria
Gaumen palate
Gaumengeschwulst (veter.) lampas, lampers, inflamed gums
Gaumenmandel faucial tonsil
Gaumenplastik palatoplasty, uranoplasty
Gaumenplatte (eines künstlichen Gebisses) base (of an artificial denture)
Gaumenspalte cleft palate
Gay-Lussacsches Gesetz Gay-Lussac's law
Gazelle e. e.
Gebärde gesture
gebären to give birth
Gebären childbirth, accouchement, labor (a), labour (e)
gebärend parturient
Gebärende parturient
Gebärmutter uterus, womb
Gebärmutterhals neck of the womb
Gebärmutterplastik uteroplasty
Gebiet area
Gebilde formation
Gebiß, bleibendes permanent teeth
—, künstliches artificial teeth, denture

Gebiß, Milch- milk teeth
—, natürliches teeth
Gebläse blower
gebogen curved
Gebrechen fault, defect
gebrechlich frail
Gebühr fee
Geburt childbirth, parturition, delivery, birth
—, schmerzlose anodinia
Geburtenhäufigkeit natality
Geburtsakt childbirth, labor (a), labour (e)
Geburtsbeginn engagement
Geburtshelfer obstetrician
Geburtshilfe obstetrics, midwifery
geburtshilflich obstetrical
Geburtsjahr year of birth
Geburtslähmung birth palsy
Geburtstrauma birth trauma
Geburtsvorgang parturition
Geburtswehe pain in labor (a), pain in labour (e)
Geburtszange midwifery forceps
Gedächtnis memory, recollection
Gedächtnisverlust lethe, amnesia
Gedanke thought, idea
Gedankenflucht flight of ideas
Gedankenlesen thought reading
Gedankenlosigkeit thoughtlessness
Gedankenübertragung thought transfer
gedeihen to thrive
gedrückt depressed
Geduld patience
Gefäß vessel
Gefäßbaum vascular tree
Gefäßerweiterer vasodilator
gefäßerweiternd vasodilative
Gefäßerweiterung vasodilatation
Gefäßklemme haemostatic forceps (e), hemostatic forceps (a), serrefine, artery clamp
Gefäßkrampf vasospasm, angiospasm
Gefäßlähmung vasoparalysis
Gefäßplastik angioplasty

Gefäßschwäche vascular insufficiency
Gefäßspasmus angiospasm
gefäßverengernd vasoconstrictive
Gefäßwand vascular wall
Gefäßwiderstand vascular resistance
Gefäßzerreißung angiorrhexis
Geflecht network
Geflügel fowl
Geflügelcholera chicken cholera
Geflügelpockendiphtherie roup
geformt shaped
Gefrierapparat freezing apparatus
gefrieren to freeze
— lassen to freeze
Gefrierplasma frozen plasma
Gefrierpunkt freezing point
Gefrierschnitt frozen section
Gefriertrocknung freeze-drying
Gefüge frame
Gefühl feeling
—, brennendes burning
gefühllos numb, insensible
Gefühllosigkeit insensibility
gefurcht sulcate
Gegenanzeige contraindication
Gegenextension counterextension
Gegengift counterpoison
Gegeninzision contraincision, contraaperture
Gegenlicht counterlight
Gegenöffnung counteropening
Gegenregulation counterregulation
gegenseitig mutual; contralateral
Gegenstrom countercurrent
gegenüberliegend opposite
Gegenzug countertraction, counterextension
gegliedert articulated
Gehalt content; level
Gehen gait
Gehgipsverband plaster dressing allowing the patient to walk
Gehilfe assistant
Gehilfin assistant
Gehirn brain

Gehirnerschütterung concussion of brain
Gehirnerweichung softening of brain
Gehirnprellung contusion of brain
Gehirnschlag apoplexy of brain
Gehirnspatel brain spatula
Gehirnwindung convolution
Gehör hearing, audition
Gehörgang auditory passage
Gehschiene walking calliper
Gehwagen walking machine
Geiger-Zählrohr Geiger counter
Geist spirit; intellect, mind
geistesgestört abalienated, mentally deranged
Geistesgestörtheit abalienation, derangement of mind
geisteskrank insane, mentally ill
Geisteskranke mentally ill
Geisteskranker mentally ill
Geisteskrankheit insanity, mental disease
geistesschwach weak in mind
Geistesschwäche weakness in mind
Geistesstörung (ab)alienation
Geistesverwirrung mental disturbance
geistig mental
Gekröse mesentery
Gel e. e.
gelähmt paralytic
gelähmte Person paralytic
gelappt lobate
Gelatine gelatin
gelatinieren to gelatinize
gelatinös gelatinous
gelb yellow
Gelbblindheit axanthopsia
Gelbfieber yellow fever
Gelbkörper corpus luteum
Gelbkörperhormon progesterone
Gelbkörperphase progestational phase
Gelbsucht jaundice
gelbsüchtig jaundiced
gelegentlich occasional

Gelenk joint
Gelenkerguß, blutiger haemarthrosis (e), hemarthrosis (a)
gelenkig pliable, supple, flexible
Gelenkigkeit suppleness, flexibility
Gelenkkontraktur contracture of joint
Gelenkmaus loose body in the joint
Gelenkrheumatismus articular rheumatism
—, **akuter** rheumatic fever
—, **primär chronischer** rheumatoid arthritis
—, **sekundär chronischer** chronic articular rheumatism
Gelenkschmerz arthralgia
Gelenkschmiere synovia
Gelenktuberkulose tuberculosis in a joint
Gelose gelosis
Gelotripsie gelotripsy
Gelsemin gelsemine
Gemeindeschwester community nurse
Gemeinschaftsarbeit, wissenschaftliche, mehrerer Kliniken multicentre study, multicenter study
Gemenge conglomerate
Gemüt mind, temper
Gemütsbewegung emotion
gemütskrank diseased in mind
Gemütskrankheit mental disorder
Gemütsverfassung, ausgeglichene emotional stability
Gemütsverstimmung mental derangement; cafard, blues
Gen gene
genau exact
Genauigkeit precision
Genauigkeitsprüfung accuracy check
generalisiert generalized
Generation e. e.
Generator e. e.
generell general

Genese genesis
genesen to recover
genesende **Person** convalescent
Genesung recovery, recuperation
Genetik genetics
Genetiker geneticist
Genetikerin geneticist
genetisch genetic
Genick scruff
Genickstarre stiff-neck fever
genital e. e.
Genitalien genitals
Genoblast e. e.
Genom genome
Genosse mate
Genossin mate
Genotyp genotype
genotypisch genotypic
Gentamycin e. e.
Gentianaviolett gentian violet
Genu recurvatum e. e.
– valgum e. e.
– varum e. e.
Genuß enjoyment
Genußmittel mean of enjoyment
Genußsucht thirst for pleasure
genußsüchtig pleasure-seeking
Geomedizin geomedicine
geomedizinisch geomedical
Geometrie geometry
geometrisch geometrical
gepaart conjugate, paired, coupled
gerade straight, even
Gerät utensil, device, appliance
Geräusch bruit, noise
–, blasendes souffle
–, Herz- cardiac murmur
gerben to tan
Gerbsäure tannid acid
gereinigt depurated
Gerhardtsche Probe Gerhardt's reaction
Geriatrie geriatrics
geriatrisch geriatric
Gerichtsmedizin forensic medicine
gerichtsmedizinisch medicolegal
geringgradig low-grade

gerinnen to coagulate
Gerinnsel clot
Gerinnung coagulation, clotting
Gerinnungsmeßgerät clotting timer
Gerinnungszeit clotting time
Gerippe skeleton
Germanium e. e.
germinativ germinative
Gerontologe gerontologist
Gerontologie gerontology
gerontologisch gerontological
Gerson-Hermannsdorfersche Diät Gerson-Hermannsdorfer diet
Geruch odor (a), odour (e)
geruchlos odorless (a), odourless (e)
Geruchsinn sense of smelling
Geruchsvermögen faculty of smelling
Gerüst frame
Gesäß buttock
gesättigt saturated
Gesamtazidität total acidity
Gesamteiweiß total protein
Geschiebe (dent.) attachment
Geschlecht sex
geschlechtlich sexual
Geschlechtschromatinkörper sex-chromatin body
Geschlechtsdrüse gonad
geschlechtsgebunden sex-linked
Geschlechtskrankheit venereal disease
Geschlechtsteile genitals
Geschlechtstrieb sexual desire
Geschlechtsverkehr sexual intercourse, copulation, venery
geschlossen closed
Geschmack gustation, taste; savor (a), savour (e)
geschmacklich gustatory
geschmacklos tasteless
Geschmacklosigkeit tastelessness
Geschmacksinn gustation
geschmackswidrig contrary to taste
geschmiedet wrought

Geschwätzigkeit verbomania
Geschwindigkeit velocity
Geschwister (biol.) siblings
Geschwür ulcer
geschwürig ulcerous
Geschwulst tumor (a), tumour (e), swelling
Geschwulstbildung oncogenesis
Gesicht face
Gesichtsausdruck physiognomy
Gesichtsfarbe complexion
Gesichtsfeld visual field
Gesichtskreis horizon
Gesichtslähmung prosopoplegia
Gesichtsmaske face mask
Gesichtsmuskel facial muscle
Gesichtsplastik facioplasty
Gesichtsrötung flush
Gesichtszug feature
Gestagen e. e.
Gestalt form, stature, shape
gestaltlich statural; formal
Gestank stench, stink
Gestation e. e.
gestielt pedunculated
Gestose gestosis
gestreift striated
gesund healthy, sound, sane
gesunden to recover
Gesundheit health, soundness, sanity
Gesundheitsbeamter sanitary inspector
Gesundheitsbehörde public health service
Gesundheitsfürsorger sanitarian
Gesundheitsfürsorgerin sanitarian
Gesundheitsministerium ministry of health
Gesundheitspflege sanitation
Gesundheitspolizei sanitary police
gesundheitsschädlich unwholesome, injurious to health
Gesundheitswesen, öffentliches public health
Gesundheitszustand state of health

Gesundung recovery
Getränk drink, beverage
—,geistiges spirituous drink
Gewebe tissue
—,interstitielles interstitial tissue
Gewebebank tissue bank
Gewebe-Klebstoff histoadhesive
geweblich tissular
Gewebskultur tissue culture
Gewebslappen flap
Gewerbemedizin industrial medicine
Gewicht weight, gravity
—,spezifisches specific gravity
Gewichtsabnahme loss in weight, weight loss
Gewichtsverlust loss in weight
Gewichtsverminderung weight reduction
Gewichtszunahme increase in weight, weight gain
gewissenhaft painstaking
gewöhnen to accustom
gewöhnen, sich to become accustomed
Gewöhnung habituation
Gewölbe vault, fornix, arch
Gewohnheit habit
Gewürz spice
gezackt pronged
gezahnt saw-edged
Gezeitenwelle tidal wave
Ghonscher Tuberkel Ghon tubercle
Gibbus e. e.
Gicht gout
gichtig gouty
Giemsafärbung Giemsa's staining
Gier eagerness, greediness
gierig eager, greedy
Gießen casting
Gift venom, poison
giftbildend venenific, toxicogenic
Giftgas poisongas
giftig venomous, poisonous
Giftigkeit poisonousness
Giftmord murder by poisoning

Giftpflanze poisonous plant
Giftspinne poisonous spider
Giftzahn venom tooth
Gigantismus gigantism
Gigantoblast e. e.
Gigantozyt gigantocyte
Giglische Säge Gigli's saw
gingival e. e.
Gingivektomie gingivectomy
Gingivitis e. e.
gingivitisch gingivitic
Gipfel peak
Gips gypsum; plaster of paris
Gipsabdruck plaster cast
Gipsbett plaster bed
Gipsbohrer plaster trephine
gipsen to plaster
Gipsmesser plaster knife
Gipsraum plaster room
Gipssäge plaster saw
Gipsschere plaster shear
Gipsschiene plaster splint
Gipsspreizer plaster spreader
Gipsverband plaster bandage
Gitalin e. e.
Gitogenin e. e.
Gitoxigenin e. e.
Gitoxin e. e.
Gitter lattice
Gitterfaser reticular lattice fiber
glandulär glandular
Glanzauge glossy eye
Glas glass
glasig glassy, vitreous
Glaskörper vitreous
Glaskörpertrübung opacity of vitreous
Glasspatel pleximeter
Glasstange glass rod
Glastrichter glass funnel
Glasur glaze
glatt smooth
Glatze baldpate
Glaubersalz Glauber's salt
glaubhaft truthful
Glaukom glaucoma
glaukomatös glaucomatous

Gleichgewicht equilibrium, balance
Gleichgewichtsstörung disequilibrium, imbalance, unbalance
gleichmäßig even, regular, equable, equal
Gleichrichter rectifier
gleichseitig ipsilateral
gleichzeitig simultaneous
Gleichung equation
Glenardsche Krankheit visceroptosis
Glibenclamid glibenclamide
Glied member, limb
Glied, männliches penis
gliedern to joint
Gliederung memberment
Gliedmaßen extremities, limbs
Glioblastom glioblastoma
Gliom glioma
Gliomatose gliomatosis
Gliosarkom gliosarcoma
Gliose gliosis
Glisoxepid glisoxepide
Glissonsche Kapsel Glisson's capsule
Glissonsche Schlinge Glisson's sling
global e. e.
Globin e. e.
Globulin e. e.
Glomangiose glomangiosis
glomerulär glomerular
Glomerulitis e. e.
Glomerulonephritis e. e.
Glomerulosklerose glomerulosclerosis
Glossektomie glossectomy
Glossina morsitans e. e.
– palpalis e. e.
Glossitis e. e.
glossitisch glossitic
Glossodynie glossodynia
Glossolalie glossolalia
Glossoplegie glossoplegia
Glottis e. e.
glottisch glottic

Glotzauge exophthalmus
Glühlampe light bulb
Glukagon e. e., glucagon, hyperglycaemic glycogenolytic factor (e), hyperglycemic glycogenolytic factor (a)
Glukokinase glucokinase
Glukokortikoid glucocorticoid
Glukonat gluconate
Glukoprotein glucoprotein
Glukosamin glucosamine
Glukose glucose
Glukosebelastung glucose load
Glukosid glucoside
Glukosidase glucosidase
Glukosurie glucosuria
Glukuronat glucuronate
Glukuronidase glucuronidase
Glutamat glutamate
Glutamin glutamine
Glutaminase e. e.
Glutaminsäure glutamic acid
— **-Brenztraubensäure-Transaminase** glutamic pyruvic transaminase
— **-Oxalessigsäure-Transaminase** glutamic oxalacetic transaminase
Glutarat glutarate
Glutathion glutathione
Gluten e. e.
glutenfrei gluten-free
Glutethimid glutethimide
Glycin glycine
Glycodiazin glycodiazine
Glykämie glycaemia (e), glycemia (a)
glykämisch glycaemic (e), glycemic (a)
Glykodiazin glycodiazine
Glykogen glycogen
Glykogenase glycogenase
Glykogenese glycogenesis
Glykogenie glycogeny
Glykogenolyse glycogenolysis
glykogenolytisch glycogenolytic
Glykogenspeicherkrankheit glycogenosis

Glykokoll glycocoll, glycine, aminoacetic acid, glycocine
Glykolipid glycolipid
Glykolyse glycolysis
glykolytisch glycolytic
Glykoneogenese glyconeogenesis
glykopriv glycoprivous
Glykoprotein glycoprotein
Glykosid glycoside
Glykosidase glucosidase, glycosidase
Glykozyamin glycocyamine
Glyoxalase e. e.
Glyoxalat glyoxalate
Glyoxalylharnstoff glyoxalyl urea
Glyzerat glycerate
Glyzerid glyceride
Glyzerin glycerol
Glyzerinaldehyd glyceric aldehyde
Glyzerit glycerite
Glyzerokinase glycerokinase
Glyzerophosphat glycerophosphatase
Glyzerophosphatid glycerophosphatide
Glyzeryl glyceryl
Glyzin glycine
Glyzinamid glycinamide
Glyzyl glycyl
Glyzyrrhizin glycyrrhizin
Gmelinsche Probe Gmelin's test
gnotobiotisch gnotobiotic
Gold e. e.
Goldbehandlung chrysotherapy
Goldblat-Hypertonie Goldblat hypertension
Goldhamster Syrian hamster
Goldsolreaktion gold sol test
Golgi-Apparat Golgi's apparatus
Golgi-Körper Golgi's corpuscle
Gon grade
Gonadektomie gonadectomy
Gonadendysgenesie gonadal dysgenesis
Gonadorelin e. e.
gonadotrop gonadotropic
Gonadotropin e. e.

Gonarthritis e. e.
Goniometer e. e.
Gonioskop gonioscope
Gonioskopie gonioscopy
gonioskopisch gonioscopical
Gonitis e. e.
Gonoblennorhöe gonoblennorrhea (a), gonoblennorrhoea (e)
Gonokokkeninfektion gonococcal infection
Gonokokkus Neisseria gonorrhoeae, gonococcus
Gonorrhöe gonorrhea (a), gonorrhoea (e)
gonorrhoisch gonorrheal (a), gonorrhoic (e)
Goodpasture-Syndrom Goodpasture's syndrome
Gordonsches Zeichen Gordon's sign
Gorilla e. e.
Graafscher Follikel graafian follicle
Grad degree
Gradenigo-Syndrom Gradenigo's syndrome
Gradient e. e.
Gradierung gradation
graduell gradual
graduieren to graduate
Graduierung graduation
Graefesches Zeichen Graefe's sign
Gramfärbung Gram's staining method
Gramicidin e. e.
Graminol e. e.
Gramm gram
Grammäquivalent gram equivalent
gramnegativ gram-negative
grampositiv gram-positive
granulär granular
Granularatrophie granular atrophy
Granulation e. e.
Granulationsgewebe granulation tissue
Granulom granuloma

Granuloma annulare e. e.
— **venereum** ulcerating granuloma of the pudenda
granulomatös granulomatous
Granulomatose granulomatosis
Granulose granulosis
Granulozyt granulocyte
Granulozytopenie granulocytopenia
granulozytopenisch granulocytopenic
Granulozytopoese granulocytopoiesis
granulozytopoetisch granulocytopoietic
graphisch graphic
graphische Darstellung graph
Graphologie graphology
graphologisch graphological
Graskrankheit grass disease
Grat ridge
Gratioletsche Sehstrahlung Gratiolet's optic radiation
grau gray, grey
graue Salbe mercurial ointment
graue Substanz des Nervensystems nervous gray
grauhaarig grey-haired
Grauhaarigkeit canities
Gravimeter e. e.
Gravimetrie gravimetry
gravimetrisch gravimetric
Gravitation e. e.
Grawitztumor Grawitz's tumor (a), Grawitz's tumour (e)
grazil gracile
Greifzange grasping forceps
Grenze limit, bound, boundary
Grenzgebiet borderland
Grenzlinie borderline
Grenzstrahl grenz ray
Griesingersches Zeichen Griesinger's sign
Grieß grit
Grieß, Nieren- gravel
Griff grip; grasp
grippal e. e.

Grippe e. e., influenza
Griseofulvin e. e.
Grittische Amputation Gritti's amputation
Grocco-Rauchfußsches Dreieck Grocco's triangle
Größe size, tallness
Grube pit
Gruber-Widalsche Reaktion Gruber-Widal reaction
Grünblindheit deuteranopia
Grundangst basic anxiety
Grundlinie baseline
Grundsubstanz ground substance
Grundumsatz basal metabolic rate
Gruppe group
Gruppenpsychotherapie group psychotherapy
gruppenspezifisch group specific
Gruppierung pattern, grouping
Guaiakol guaiacol
Guanase e. e.
Guanethidin guanethidine
Guanidase e. e.
Guanidin guanidine
Guanin guanine
Guanosin guanosine
Guanoxan guanoxane
Guarnierisches Körperchen Guarnieri's corpuscle
günstig favorable (a), favourable (e), opportune
Günzburgsche Probe Günzburg's test
Gürtel girdle
Gürtelrose zoster, shingles, zona
Guillain-Barré-Syndrom Guillain-Barré syndrome
Gullstrandsche Spaltlampe Gullstrand's lamp
Gumma e. e.
Gummi rubber
– **arabicum** acacia
Gummihandschuh rubber glove
Gummischlauch rubber tube
Gummischutz rubber condom
Gummischwamm rubber sponge
Gummistöpsel rubber stopper

Gummituch rubber sheeting
gummös gummous, gummy
Gummose e. e.
Gumprechtsche Scholle Gumprecht's shadow
Gunnsches Zeichen Gunn's syndrome
Gurgel gorge
gurgeln to gargle
Gurgelwasser gargarism, gargle
Gurren rumbling
Guß (nach Kneipp) affusion (acc. to Kneipp)
Gußform mold (a), mould (e), die
Gußfüllung inlay
Gußkanal (dent.) sprue
Gußkrone cast crown
Gußmaschine casting machine
Gustometer e. e.
Gustometrie gustometry
Gutachten, ärztliches medical opinion, medical evidence
– – **abgeben** to give a medical opinion
– – **einholen** to call in a medical opinion
Gutachter expert
Gutachterin expert
Gutachtertätigkeit expertise
gutachtlich expert
gutartig benign
Gutartigkeit benignness
Guttapercha guttapercha
guttural e. e.
Gymnastik gymnastics
gymnastisch gymnastic
Gynäkologe gynaecologist (e), gynecologist (a)
Gynäkologie gynaecology (e), gynecology (a)
Gynäkologin gynaecologist (e), gynecologist (a)
gynäkologisch gynaecological (e), gynecological (a)
Gynäkomastie gynaecomastia (e), gynecomastia (a)
Gynandroblastom gynandroblastoma
Gynatresie gynatresia

H

Haar hair
Haarausfall loss of hair, alopecia
Haarbalg hair follicle
haarentfernend epilatory
Haarentfernung epilation
Haarentfernungsmittel epilatory
Haargefäß capillary
haarlos hairless
Haarschneidemaschine hair clippers
Haarschuppenkrankheit dandruff
Haarzelle hairy cell
Haarzunge trichoglossia
Habichtschnabel hawk's bill
habituell habitual
Hacke (= Ferse) heel
Hacke (instrum.) hoe
Hähnchen cockerel
Häm haeme (e), heme (a)
Hämagglutination haemagglutination (e), hemagglutination (a)
Hämagglutinin haemagglutinin (e), hemagglutinin (a)
Hämangioendotheliom haemangioendothelioma (e), hemangioendothelioma (a)
Hämangiom haemangioma (e), hemangioma (a)
Hämarthrose haemarthrosis (e), hemarthrosis (a)
Hämatemesis haematemesis (e), hematemesis (a)
Hämatin haematin (e), hematin (a)
Hämatinurie haematinuria (e), hematinuria (a)
Hämatoblast haematoblast (e), hematoblast (a)
Hämatocele haematocele (e), hematocele (a)
hämatogen haematogenous (e), hematogenous (a)
Hämatogonie haematogone (e), hematogone (a)

Hämatoidin haematoidin (e), hematoidin (a)
Hämatokolpos haematocolpos (e), hematocolpos (a)
Hämatokrit haematocrit (e), hematocrit (a)
Hämatologe haematologist (e), hematologist (a)
Hämatologie haematology (e), hematology (a)
Hämatologin haematologist (e), hematologist (a)
hämatologisch haematological (e), hematological (a)
Hämatom haematoma (e), hematoma (a)
Hämatomyelie haematomyelia (e), hematomyelia (a)
Hämatoporphyrin haematoporphyrin (e), hematoporphyrin (a)
Hämatothorax haematothorax (e), hematothorax (a)
hämatotoxisch hematotoxic (e), hematotoxic (a)
Hämatoxylin haematoxylin (e), hematoxylin (a)
Hämatozele haematocele (e), hematocele (a)
Hämatozyturie haematocyturia (e), hematocyturia (a)
Hämaturie haematuria (e), hematuria (a)
Hämazytometer haemacytometer (e), hemacytometer (a)
Hämin haemin (e), hemin (a)
Hämoblast haemoblast (e), hemoblast (a)
Hämoblastose haemoblastosis (e), hemoblastosis (a)
Hämochromatose haemochromatosis (e), hemochromatosis (a)
Hämochromometer haemochromometer (e), hemochromometer (a)

Hämodialyse haemodialysis (e), hemodialysis (a)
Hämodynamik haemodynamics (e), hemodynamics (a)
hämodynamisch haemodynamic (e), hemdoynamic (a)
Hämoglobin haemoglobin (e), hemoglobin (a)
Hämoglobinometer haemoglobinometer (e), hemoglobinometer (a)
Hämoglobinolyse haemoglobinolysis (e), hemoglobinolysis (a)
Hämoglobinurie haemoblobinuria (e), hemoglobinuria (a)
Hämolysat haemolyzate (e), hemolyzate (a)
Hämolyse haemolysis (e), hemolysis (a)
hämolysieren to haemolyze (e), to hemolyze (a)
Hämolysierung haemolyzation (e), hemolyzation (a)
Hämolysin haemolysin (e), hemolysin (a)
hämolytisch haemolytic (e), hemolytic (a)
Hämometer haemometer (e), hemometer (a)
Hämoperfusion haemoperfusion (e), hemoperfusion (a)
Hämoperikard haemopericardium (e), hemopericardium (a)
hämophil haemophilic (e), hemophilic (a)
hämophile Person haemophiliac (e), hemophiliac (a)
Hämophilie haemophilia (e), hemophilia (a)
Hämophthalmus haemophthalmos (e), hemophthalmos (a)
Hämopoese haemopoiesis (e), hemopoiesis (a)
hämopoetisch haemopoietic (e), hemopoietic (a)

Hämoptoe haemoptysis (e), hemoptysis (a)
Hämoptyse haemoptysis (e), hemoptysis (a)
Hämopyrrol haemopyrrol (e), hemopyrrol (a)
Hämorrhagie haemorrhage (e), hemorrhage (a)
hämorrhagisch haemorrhagic (e), hemorrhagic (a)
hämorrhoidal haemorrhoidal (e), hemorrhoidal (a)
Hämorrhoide haemorrhoid (e), hemorrhoid (a)
Hämosiderin haemosiderin (e), hemosiderin (a)
Hämosiderose haemosiderosis (e), hemosiderosis (a)
Hämostase haemostasis (e), hemostasis (a)
Hämostatikum haemostatic (e), hemostatic (a)
hämostatisch haemostatic (e), hemostatic (a)
Hämostyptikum haemostyptic (e), hemostyptic (a)
hämostyptisch haemostyptic (e), hemostyptic (a)
Hämothorax haemothorax (e), hemothorax (a)
Hämotoxin haemotoxin (e), hemotoxin (a)
hämotoxisch haemotoxic (e), hemotoxic (a)
Hängebauch pendulous abdomen
Hängebrust mastoptosis, pendulous breast
hängen to hang
hängender Tropfen hanging drop
Härte hardness
härten to harden
Härten hardening
Häufigkeitsquote incidence
häuslich domiciliary
Häutchen pellicle, membrane, film
Hafermehl oatmeal

Haferschleim gruel
Haffkrankheit Haff disease
Hafnium e. e.
Haftschale contact lens
Hageman-Faktor Hageman factor
hager lean
Hahn (veter.) cock
Hahnentritt (veter.) stringhalt
Haken hook, retractor; clasp
—, **scharfer** sharp hook
hakenförmig unciform
Hakenpinzette tissue forceps
Hakenwurm hookworm
Hakenzange tenaculum forceps
halbautomatisch semiautomatic
Halbbad half bath
Halbleiter semi-conductor
Halbmilch 50% diluted milk
halbmondförmig semilunar
halbquantitativ semiquantitative
Halbseitenchorea hemichorea
Halbseitenepilepsie hemiepilepsy
Halbseitenlähmung hemiparesis
halbsynthetisch semisynthetic
halbwach subwaking
Halbwelle half wave
Halbwertzeit half-life-period
Halid halide
Halisterese halisteresis
Hallervorden-Spatzsche Krankheit Hallervorden-Spatz disease
Hallux valgus e. e.
— **varus** e. e.
Halluzination hallucination
halluzinogen hallucinogenic
Halluzinose hallucinosis
Halogen e. e.
halogenieren to halogenate
Halometer e. e.
Halometrie halometry
halometrisch halometric
Haloperidol e. e.
Halothan halothane
Hals neck
—, **rauher** sore throat
Halsentzündung sphagitis, quinsy
Halsmark cervical spinal cord

Hals-Nasen-Ohrenärztin otorhinolaryngologist
hals-nasen-ohrenärztlich otorhinolaryngological
Hals-Nasen-Ohrenarzt otorhinolaryngologist
Hals-Nasen-Ohrenheilkunde otorhinolaryngology
Halsrippe cervical rib
Halstedsche Operation Halsted's operation
Halsvenenstauung neck vein congestion
Halswirbel cervical vertebra
Halswirbelsäule cervical spinal column
Halteapparat attachment apparatus
Halter holder, clamp
Haltung gait, bearing, posture, position
haltungsbedingt postural
haltungsmäßig postural
Hamamelin e. e.
Hamamelis e. e.
Hamartom hamartoma
Hamman-Rich-Syndrom syndrome of Hamman-Rich
Hammarstensche Probe Hammarsten's test
Hammel wether
Hammer mallet, hammer
Hammerzehe hammer toe
Hamster e. e.
Hamycin e. e.
Hand e. e.
Handbuch handbook
Handelsname trade name
Handgelenk wrist
Handgriff handle
— (= **Manipulation**) maneuver
Handlungsweise procedure
Hand-Schüller-Christiansche Krankheit Hand-Schüller-Christian disease
Handstück handpiece
Handteller palm
Hand- und Fußpflege chiropody

Handverkaufsmedikament
free sale drug
Handwaschbecken hand basin
Handwurzel wrist, carpus
Hanganutziu-Deicher-Test Paul-Bunnell test
Hanotsche Zirrhose Hanot's cirrhosis
haplodont e. e.
haploid e. e.
Hapten e. e.
Haptoglobin e. e.
Haptophor haptophore
Harmin harmine
Harnanalyse urinalysis
Harnausscheidung urinary excretion
harnbildend uriniparous
Harnbildung uropoiesis
Harnblase urinary bladder
harnen to urinate
harnfähig urinable
Harnglas urinal
Harngrieß gravel
Harninkontinenz incontinence of urine
Harnkanälchen renal tubule
—, **gestrecktes** straight renal tubule
—, **gewundenes** convoluted renal tubule
— **Schaltstück-** connecting renal tubule
harnleitend uriniferous
Harnleiter ureter
Harnleiterplastik ureteroplasty
Harnretention urinary retention
Harnröhre urethra
Harnröhrenplastik urethroplasty
Harnsäure uric acid
harnsäurespaltend uricolytic
harnsäuretreibend uricosuric
harnsäuretreibendes Mittel uricosuric
Harnsammelperiode urine collection period
Harnstoff urea, carbamide
Harnstoffbildung ureapoiesis
Harnstoffclearance urea clearance
Harnstoffstickstoff urea nitrogen
Harntrakt urinary tract
Harn- und Geschlechtsorgane genito-urinary organs
Harnwegsinfektion urinary tract infection
Harnzucker urine sugar
Harnzwang strangury
Harpune harpoon
Hartgummi vulcanite
Hartleibigkeit constipation
Hartstrahltechnik hard ray method
Harz resin
Haschisch hashish
Hase hare
Haselmaus dormouse
Hasenscharte harelip
Haupt head
Hauptverbandplatz base hospital
Hauptzelle adelomorphous cell, chief cell, peptic cell, principal cell
Hausarzt family doctor
Haustrierung haustration
Haut skin, integument
Hautärztin dermatologist
Hautarzt dermatologist
Hautatrophie dermatrophy
Hautausschlag exanthema, skin eruption
—, **flüchtiger** rash
Hautinnervationsbezirk, sementaler dermatome
Hautkrankheit skin disease
Hautleishmaniose leishmaniasis of skin
Hautplastik dermatoplasty
Hautreaktion cutireaction
hautrötend rubefacient
hautrötendes Mittel rubefacient
Hautschaden durch Kälte perniosis
Hautschwiele tyloma, callosity
Hauttest skin test
Haverssches Kanälchen Haver's canal

Hautverträglichkeit cutaneous tolerance
Hayemsche Lösung Hayem's solution
Headsche Zone Head's zone
Hebamme midwife
Hebel lever
heben to lift, to elevate
hebephren hebephrenic
Hebephrenie hebephrenia
Heber lifter
Heberdenscher Knoten Heberden's node
Hebosteotomie hebosteotomy, pubiotomy
Hebrasche Salbe Hebra's ointment
Heerfordtsche Krankheit uveoparotid fever
Hefe yeast
Heftigkeit severity
Heftpflaster sticking plaster
Hegarstift Hegar's dilator
Heilanstalt medical establishment
heilbar curable
Heilbarkeit curableness
heilbringend salutary, salubrious
heilen (transitiv) to cure
heilen (intransitiv) to heal
Heilgymnastik medical gymnastics
Heilkraft healing power
Heilkunde art of therapeutics, physic
Heilmittel medicine, remedy, medicament
Heilquelle medicinal spring
heilsam salutary
Heilserum antitoxic serum
Heilung healing
Heilung per primam intentionem healing by first intention
Heilung per secundam intentionem healing by second intention
heilungsfördernd salutary
Heilverfahren medical treatment
Heimdialyse home dialysis
Heimweh homesickness, nostalgia

Heinzsches Innenkörperchen Heinz body
heiser hoarse
Heiserkeit hoarseness
Heißhunger ravenous appetite
Heißluft hot air
Heizstrom heating current
hektisch hectic
Helferin, zahnärztliche dental assistant
Heliotherapie heliotherapy
Helium e. e.
hell clear, bright
Helleborus hellebore
Helligkeitsumfang brightness contrast
Helmholtzsche Theorie Helmholtz's theory
Helminthiasis e. e.
Helminthologie helminthology
helminthologisch helminthological
Hemeralopie hemeralopia
Hemiachromatopsie hemiachromatopsia
Hemialbumose e. e.
Hemialgie hemialgia
Hemiamblyopie hemiamblyopia
Hemianästhesie hemianaesthesia (e), hemianesthesia (a)
Hemianopsie hemianopsia
–,**binasale** binasal hemianopsia
–,**bitemporale** bitemporal hemianopsia
–,**heteronyme** heteronymous hemianopsia
–,**homonyme** homonymous hemianopsia
–,**Quadranten-** quadrantic hemianopsia
hemianoptisch hemianoptic
Hemiapraxie hemiapraxia
Hemiataxie hemiataxia
Hemiathetose hemiathetosis
Hemiatrophie hemiatrophy
Hemiballismus hemiballism
Hemiblock e. e.
Hemichorea e. e.

Hemikorporektomie hemicorporectomy
Hemiepilepsie hemiepilepsy
Hemigastrektomie hemigastrectomy
Hemihydrat hemihydrate
Hemihyperhidrose hemihyperhidrosis
Hemiparästhesie hemiparaesthesia (e), hemiparesthesia (a)
Hemiparese hemiparesis
hemiparetisch hemiparetic
Hemipelvektomie hemipelvectomy
Hemiplegie hemiplegia
hemiplegisch hemiplegic
Hemisphäre hemisphere
Hemisphärektomie hemispherectomie
Hemisukzinat hemisuccinate
Hemizellulase hemicellulase
Hemizellulose hemicellulose
hemmen to inhibit
hemmend inhibitory, colytic
Hemmer inhibitor
Hemmung inhibition
Hemmungsmißbildung fusion defect
Hengst stallion
Henlesche Schleife Henle's loop
Henne hen
—, **junge** pullet
Henry e. c.
Heparin e. e.
heparinisieren to heparinize
Heparinisierung heparinization
Hepatargie hepatargy
Hepatikoduodenostomie hepaticoduodenostomy
Hepatikostomie hepaticostomy
Hepatikotomie hepaticotomy
Hepatisation hepatization
hepatisch hepatic
hepatisiert hepatized
Hepatitis e. e.
Hepatitis epidemica infectious hepatitis (a), infective hepatitis (e)
Hepatocholangioduodenostomie hepatocholangioduodenostomy
Hepatocholangitis e. e.
hepatogastrisch hepatogastric
hepatogen hepatogenous
Hepatographie hepatography
hepatolentikulär hepatolenticular
hepatolienal e. e.
Hepatomegalie hepatomegaly
Hepatopathie hepatopathy
hepatorenal e. e.
Hepatose hepatosis
Hepatosplenomegalie hepatosplenomegaly
hepatotoxisch hepatotoxic
hepatotrop hepatotropic
Hepatozyt hepatocyte
Heptan heptane
Heptose e. e.
Heptulose e. e.
heraustreiben to protrude
herb sour
Herd (med.) focus
Herdinfektion focal infection
Herdnephritis focal nephritis
Herkunft origin
Hermaphroditismus hermaphroditism
hermetisch hermetical
Hernie hernia
—, **direkte** direct hernia
—, **eingeklemmte** strangulated hernia
—, **Hiatus-** hiatal hernia
—, **indirekte** indirect hernia
—, **irreponible** irreducible hernia
—, **Leisten-** inguinal hernia
—, **Nabel-** umbilical hernia
—, **Narben-** cicatricial hernia
—, **reponible** reducible hernia
—, **Schenkel-** femoral hernia
—, **skrotale** scrotal hernia
—, **Treitzsche** Treitz's hernia
—, **unvollständige** incomplete hernia
—, **vollständige** complete hernia
—, **Zwerchfell —** diaphragmatic hernia

Hernienbildung herniation
Herniotomie herniotomy
Herpangina e. e.
Herpes e. e., dartre
– **labialis** labial herpes, cold sore
– **progenitalis** progenital herpes
– **simplex** e. e.
– **tonsurans** tinea tonsurans
– **zoster** e. e.
herpetiform e. e.
herpetisch herpetic
Herpetismus herpetism
Herter-Heubnersche Krankheit intestinal infantilism
Hertz cycle per second
hervorrufen to cause, to induce
Herxheimersche Reaktion Herxheimer's reaction
Herz heart
Herzaneurysma aneurysm of heart
Herzasthma cardiac asthma
Herzbehandlung cardiotherapy
Herzbeklemmung oppression of heart
Herzbeutel pericardium
Herzbeutelerguß pericardial effusion
Herzblock heart block
Herzchirurgie cardiosurgery
Herzdilatation cardiac dilatation
Herzerkrankung heart disease
Herzerweichung cardiomalacia
Herzfehler organic heart defect
Herzfehlerzelle heart-disease cell, heart-lesion cell
herzförmig heart-shaped, cordiform
Herzfrequenz heart rate
Herzfunktionsprüfung heart function test
Herzgegend cardiac region
Herzgeräusch cardiac murmur
Herzgrube pit of the heart
Herzhypertrophie cardiac hypertrophy
Herzinfarkt cardiac infarction

Herzinsuffizienz cardiac insufficiency
–, **dekompensierte** congestive heart failure
–, **muskuläre** myocardial insufficiency
Herzkatheter cardiac catheter
Herzkatheterisierung cardiac catheterization
Herzklappenerkrankung valvular heart disease
Herzklappenfehler valvular heart defect
Herzklappengeräusch valvular cardiac murmur
Herzklopfen palpitation of the heart
Herzkrankheit heart disease, cardiopathy
–, **hyperthyreotische** hyperthyroid heart disease
–, **rheumatische** rheumatic heart disease
Herzleiden heart disease, heart disorder
Herz-Lungenmaschine heart-lung machine
Herzmassage cardiac massage
–, **äußere** closed chest cardiac massage
–, **direkte** open chest cardiac massage
Herzminutenvolumen cardiac minute output
Herzmuskel heart muscle, myocardium
Herzmuskelinfarkt myocardial infarction
Herzmuskelinsuffizienz myocardial insufficiency
Herzmuskelschaden myocardial damage
Herzneurose cardiac neurosis
Herzohr atrial appendage of the heart
Herzruptur rupture of the heart
Herzschallschreibung phonocardiography

Herzschatten heart shadow
Herzschlag apoplexy of the heart
Herzschlagen heart beat
Herzspezialist cardiologist
herzstärkend cordial
Herzstillstand cardiac arrest
Herzton heart sound
—,gespaltener split heart sound
Herz- und Kreislaufkrankheit cardiovascular disease
Herzuntersuchung examination of the heart
Herzversagen heart failure
Herzvorhof atrium of the heart, auricle of the heart
Hesperidin e. e.
Hetacillin e. e.
Heteroautoplastik heteroautoplasty
heterochrom heterochromous
Heterochromie heterochromia
Heterochromosom heterochromosome
heterodont e. e.
heterogen heterogenous
Heteroinfektion heteroinfection
Heteroinokulation heteroinoculation
Heterointoxikation heterointoxication
Heterokinese heterokinesis
Heterokomplement heterocomplement
heterolog heterologous
Heterologie heterology
heteronom heteronomous
heteronym heteronymous
Heterophagie heterophagy
heterophil heterophilic
heterophon heterophonic
Heterophorie heterophoria
Heteroplasie heteroplasia
Heteroplastik heteroplasty
heteroplastisch heteroplastic
heteroploid e. e.
heterosexuell heterosexual
Heteroskopie heteroscopy

Heterosuggestion e. e.
heterotop heterotopic
Heterotopie heterotopy
Heterotoxin e. e.
Heterotransplantation e. e.
heterozentrisch heterocentric
heterozygot heterozygous
heterozyklisch heterocyclic
Heubnersche Krankheit Heubner's disease
Heufieber hay fever
Hexahydrat hexahydrate
Hexamethonium e. e.
Hexamethoniumbromid hexamethonium bromide
Hexamethylen hexamethylene, cyclohexane
Hexamethylendiamin hexamethylendiamine
Hexamethylentetramin hexamethylenetetramine, methenamine (a), hexamine (e), hexamethylenamine
Hexan hexane
Hexanikotinat hexanicotinate
Hexanoat hexanoate
Hexapeptid hexapeptide
Hexazonium e. e.
Hexenschuß lumbago
Hexetidin hexetidine
Heximid heximide
Hexokinase e. e.
Hexopeptidase e. e.
Hexosamin hexosamine
Hexose e. e.
Hexosediphosphat hexose diphosphate
Hexosemonophosphat hexose monophosphate
Hexosephosphatase e. e.
Hexuronat hexuronate
Hexyl e. e.
Hexylamin hexylamine
Hexylresorzin hexylresorcinol
Hiatushernie hiatal hernia
Hidradenitis e. e.
Hidradenom hidradenoma

Hidrose hidrosis
hidrotisch hidrotic
hilär hilar
Hilfsschule school for backward children
hilfsweise auxiliary, assistant
Hilitis e. e.
Hilus e. e.
Hiluslymphknotenerkrankung hilar adenopathy
hindern to impede, to hinder
hinken to go lame, to limp
Hinken claudication
Hinterhauptshaltung, hintere occiput posterior position
—,vordere occiput anterior position
Hinterhirn metencephalon
Hinterkopf back of the head
Hinterteil buttock, back part
Hinterwand posterior wall
Hippokrates, Eid des — hippocratic oath
Hippurat hippurate
Hippursäure hippuric acid
Hirn brain
Hirnblutung cerebral haemorrhage (e), cerebral hemorrhage (a)
Hirnchirurgie cerebral surgery
Hirnforschung brain research
hirngeschädigt brain injured
Hirnhaut meninge
Hirnhautentzündung meningitis
Hirnmantel brain mantle
Hirnmasse cerebral substance
Hirnrinde cerebral cortex
Hirnrindenatrophie cortical atrophy of the brain
Hirnschale, knöcherne skull
Hirnstamm brain stem
Hirnstromkurve current curve of the brain
Hirntätigkeit cerebration
His-Bündels, oberhalb des suprahisian
His-Bündels, unterhalb des infrahisian
Hisssches Bündel bundle of His

Hirsch stag
Hirschkalb fawn
Hirschkuh hind
Hirschsprungsche Krankheit Hirschsprung's disease
Hirsutismus hirsutism
Hirudin e. e.
Hirudinea e. e.
Hissches Bündel His' bundle
Histamin histamine
Histaminase e. e.
Histidase e. e.
Histidin histidine
Histidinase e. e.
Histidyl e. e.
Histioblast e. e.
histiotrop histiotropic
Histiozyt histiocyte
histiozytär histiocytic
Histiozytose histiocytosis
Histochemie histochemistry
histochemisch histochemical
Histogenese histogenesis
Histologe histologist
Histologie histology
Histologin histologist
histologisch histological
Histolyse histolysis
histolytisch histolytic
Histomorphologie histomorphology
histomorphologisch histomorphological
Histon histone
Histopathologie histopathology
histopathologisch histopathological
Histoplasmose histoplasmosis
histotrop histotropic
Hitze heat
hitzebeständig heat-stable, heat-resisting, thermoresistant
Hitzekoagulation thermocoagulation
Hitzschlag heat prostration
HNO (= Hals, Nase, Ohren) ENT (= ear, nose, throat)
Hochdruck hypertension, high pressure

Hochdruck, blasser pale hypertension
—,roter red hypertension
Hochfrequenz high frequency
hochgradig high-grade
hochlagern to elevate
Hochlagerung elevation
hochmolekular high molecular
hochschwanger far advanced in pregnancy
Hochsingersches Zeichen Hochsinger's phenomenon
Hochspannung (elektr.) high voltage
Hochspannungselektrophorese high voltage electrophoresis
Hoden testicle
Hodenentfernung orchiectomy
Hodensack scrotum
Hodge-Pessar Hodge's pessary
Höhenkrankheit altitude sickness
Höhenkurort high altitude health resort
Höhepunkt climax
Höhle cavity; pouch; sinus
Höhlenbildung cavitation
Höllenstein nitrate of silver
Hörapparat hearing aid
Hörbrille combined spectacles and hearing aid
hören to hear
Hören hearing, audition
Hörrohr stethoscope
Hörsturz hearing precipitation
Hörvermögen hearing, audition
hohl hollow, concave
hohläugig hollow-eyed
Hohlfuß pes cavus
Hohlmeißel gouge
Hohlmeißelzange rongeur, rongeur forceps
Hohlspiegel concave mirror
Holmium e. e.
Holographie holography
holokrin holocrine
Holzknechtscher Raum Holzknecht space

Holzkohle wood charcoal
Homalographie homalography
Homatropin homatropine
Homescher Lappen Home's lobe
Homöopath homeopathist (a), homoeopathist (e)
Homöopathie homeopathy (a), homoeopathy (e)
Homöopathin homeopathist (a), homoeopathist (e)
homöopathisch homeopathic (a), homoeopathic (e)
Homöostase homeostasis (a), homoeostasis (e)
Homöotherapie homeotherapy (a), homoeotherapy (e)
Homöotransplantation homeotransplantation (a), homoeotransplantation (e)
homoerotisch homoerotic
homogen homogeneous
Homogenat homogenate
homogenisieren to homogenize
Homogenisierung homogenization
Homogenität homogeneity
homolateral e. e.
homolog homologous
Homolog homologue
homologe Serumhepatitis homologous serum hepatitis
Homologie homology
homonom homonomous
homonym homonymous
Homoplastik homoplasty
homoplastisch homoplastic
Homoserin homoserine
Homosexualität homosexuality
homosexuell homosexual
Homotransplantation e. e.
homozentrisch homocentric
homozygot homozygous
Homozygotie homozygosis
homozyklisch homocyclic
Homozystin homocystine
Honig honey
Honigbiene honey bee
Honorar fee, honorarium

honorieren (= Honorar bezahlen) to pay fees
Hopfen hop
Hordeolum e. e., sty
Horizont horizon
horizontal e. e.
Hormon hormone
Hormonbehandlung hormonotherapy
hormonell hormonal
Horn e. e.
hornartig horny
Hornersches Syndrom Horner's syndrome
Hornhaut (der Oberhaut) horny layer of the cuticle
Hornhaut (des Auges) cornea
Hornhautgeschwür corneal ulcer
Hornhautstaphylom staphyloma of the cornea
Hornhauttrübung opacity of the cornea, achlys
hornig horny
Hospitalismus hospitalism
Hottentottenschürze Hottentot apron, tablier
Hüfte hip
Hüftgelenk hip joint
Hüftknochen hip bone
Hühnerauge clavus, corn
Hühnerpest fowl plague, chickenpest
Hülle sheath
Hülse shield
Hündin bitch
hüsteln to cough slightly
Huf hoof
Hufeisen horseshoe
Hufeisenniere horseshoe kidney
Hufgeschwür fetlow
Hufhaar fetlock
Hufknorpelfistel quittor, quitter
Hufkrebs verrucose pododermatitis
Hufkrone coronet (veter.)
Hufrehe founder (veter.)
Hufrollenentzündung podotrochilitis

Hufschlag hoof-beat
Hufstrahl frog (veter.)
Huftier ungulate, hoofed animal
Huhn hen
humeroskapulär humeroscapular
humoral e. e.
humpeln to hubble
Hund dog
—, junger puppy
Hundebiß dog-bite
Hunger e. e.
Hungerkur starvation treatment
Hungerödem starvation edema (a), starvation oedema (e)
Hungerzustand starvation
hungrig hungry
Huntersche Glossitis Hunter's glossitis
Huntingtonsche Chorea Huntington's chorea
Hunt-Test Hunt's test
Hurler-Syndrom Hurler's syndrome
husten to cough
Husten cough
hustenlindernd antitussive
hustenstillend antibechic, paregoric
hustenstillendes Mittel antibechic, paregoric
Hutchinsonsche Trias Hutchinson's triad
Hyäne hyena
hyalin hyaline
Hyalin e. e.
hyaliner Zylinder hyaline cast
Hyalitis e. e.
Hyaloplasma hyaloplasm
Hyaluronat hyaluronate
Hyaluronidase e. e.
Hybridation hybridization
Hybride hybrid
Hydantoin e. e.
Hydatide hydatid
Hydatidenschwirren hydatid fremitus
Hydrämie hydraemia (e), hydremia (a)

hydrämisch hydraemic (e), hydremic (a)
Hydralazin hydralazine
Hydramin hydramine
Hydramnion e. e.
Hydrargyrum oxydatum flavum yellow precipitate
– **praecipitatum album** white precipitate
Hydrase hydrogenase
Hydrastin hydrastine
Hydrastinin hydrastinine
Hydrat hydrate
Hydration e. e.
hydraulisch hydraulic
Hydrazid hydrazide
Hydrazin hydrazine
Hydrazinophthalazin hydrazinophthalazine
Hydrazon hydrazone
hydrieren to hydrate
Hydroa vacciniforme e. e.
Hydrobilirubin e. e.
Hydrobromat hydrobromate
Hydrobromid hydrobromide
Hydrocele e. e.
Hydrocephalus externus e. e.
– **internus**
Hydrochinon hydroquinone
Hydrochlorid hydrochloride
Hydrochlorothiazid hydrochlorothiazide
Hydrocholesterin hydrocholesterol
Hydrocortison hydrocortisone, cortisol
Hydrocuprein hydrocupreine
Hydrodynamik hydrodynamics
hydrodynamisch hydrodynamic
Hydroflumethiazid hydroflumethiazide
Hydrogenase e. e.
Hydrokuprein hydrocupreine
Hydrolase e. e.
Hydrolysat hydrolysate
Hydrolyse hydrolysis
hydrolysieren to hydrolyze
hydrolytisch hydrolytic

Hydronephrose hydronephrosis
Hydropathie hydropathy
hydropathisch hydropathic
hydrophil hydrophilous
Hydrophilie hydrophilia
Hydrophobie hydrophobia
Hydrophthalmus hydrophthalmos
hydropisch hydropic
Hydrops e. e.
Hydrorrhöe hydrorrhea (a), hydrorrhoea (e)
Hydrosalpinx e. e.
hydrostatisch hydrostatic
hydrotherapeutisch hydrotherapeutical
Hydrotherapie hydrotherapeutics, hydrotherapy
Hydrothorax e. e.
Hydroxyäthylstärke hydroxyethyl starch
Hydroxybutyrat hydroxybutyrate
Hydroxychlorochin hydroxychloroquine
Hydroxyd hydroxide
Hydroxykobalamin hydroxycobalamine
Hydroxykodein hydroxycodeine
Hydroxykortikosteroid hydroxycorticosteroid
Hydroxyl e. e.
Hydroxylamin hydroxylamine
Hydroxylase e. e.
hydroxylieren to hydroxylate
Hydroxyprolin hydroxyproline
Hydroxysteroid e. e.
Hydroxytryptamin hydroxytryptamine
Hydroxytryptophan e. e.
Hygiene e. e., hygienics
Hygieniker hygienist
Hygienikerin hygienist
hygienisch hygienic, sanitary
Hygrom hygroma
Hygrometer e. e.
Hygrometrie hygrometry
hygrometrisch hygrometric
hygroskopisch hygroscopic

Hymen e. e.
Hymenektomie hymenectomy
Hymenitis e. e.
Hymenolepiasis e. e.
Hyoscyamin hyoscyamine
Hyoscyamus e. e.
Hypästhesie hypaesthesia (e), hypesthesia (a)
hypästhetisch hypaesthetic (e), hypesthetic (a)
Hypalbuminämie hypalbuminosis
Hypalgesie hypalgesia
hypalgetisch hypalgesic
hypazid hypacid
Hypazidität hypacidity
Hyperadrenalismus hyperadrenalism
Hyperämie hyperaemia (e), hyperemia (a)
hyperämisch hyperaemic (e), hyperemic (a)
Hyperästhesie hyperaesthesia (e), hyperesthesia (a)
hyperästhetisch hyperaesthetic (e), hyperesthetic (a)
Hyperaktivität hyperactivity
Hyperakusis hyperacousia (e), hyperacusis (a)
Hyperalbuminämie hyperalbuminosis
Hyperaldosteronismus hyperaldosteronism
Hyperalgesie hyperalgesia
hyperalgetisch hyperalgesic
Hyperalgie hyperalgia
hyperazid hyperacid
Hyperazidität hyperacidity
hyperbar hyperbaric
Hyperbel hyperbola
Hyperbilirubinämie hyperbilirubinaemia (e), hyperbilirubinemia (a)
hyperbilirubinämisch hyperbilirubinaemic (e), hyperbilirubinemic (a)
Hyperchlorämie hyperchloraemia (e), hyperchloremia (a)

hyperchlorämisch hyperchloraemic (e), hyperchloremic (a)
Hyperchlorhydrie hyperchlorhydria
hyperchlorhydrisch hyperchlorhydric
Hypercholesterinämie hypercholesteraemia (e), hypercholesteremia (a)
hyperchrom hyperchromic
Hyperchromasie hyperchromatism, hyperchromatosis
hyperchromatisch hyperchromatic
Hypercuprämie hypercupraemia (e), hypercupremia (a)
hyperdens hyperdense
Hyperdikrotie hyperdicrotism
Hyperemesis e. e.
Hypereosinophilie hypereosinophilia
Hyperergie hyperergy
hyperergisch hyperergic
Hyperextension e. e.
Hyperfibrinolyse hyperfibrinolysis
hyperfibrinolytisch hyperfibrinolytic
Hyperflexion e. e.
Hyperfunktion hyperfunction
Hypergalaktie hypergalactia
Hypergenitalismus hypergenitalism
Hyperglobulie hyperglobulia
Hyperglobulinämie hyperglobulinaemia (e), hyperglobulinemia (a)
Hyperglykämie hyperglycaemia (e), hyperglycemia (a)
hyperglykämisch hyperglycaemic (e), hyperglycemic (a)
Hyperhidrose hyperhidrosis
Hyperinsulinismus hyperinsulinism
Hyperkaliämie hyperpotassaemia (e), hyperpotassemia (a)
Hyperkalzämie hypercalcaemia (e), hypercalcemia (a)
hyperkalzämisch hypercalcaemic (e), hypercalcemic (a)
Hyperkapnie hypercapnia
Hyperkeratose hyperkeratosis
Hyperkinesie hyperkinesia

hyperkinetisch hyperkinetic
Hyperkuprämie hypercupraemia (e), hypercupremia (a)
Hyperleukozytose hyperleukocytosis
Hyperlipämie hyperlipaemia (e), hyperlipemia (a)
Hyperlipoproteidämie hyperlipoproteidaemia (e), hyperlipoproteidemia (a)
Hyperluteinisierung hyperluteinization
Hypermagnesiämie hypermagnesaemia (e), hypermagnesemia (a)
Hypermenorrhöe hypermenorrhea (a), hypermenorrhoea (e)
hypermetrop hypermetropic
Hypermetropie hypermetropia
Hypermotilität hypermotility
Hypernephrom hypernephroma
hypernormal e. e.
Hyperopie hyperopia
hyperopisch hyperopic
Hyperostose hyperostosis
Hyperovarie hyperovaria
Hyperoxalurie hyperoxaluria
hyperoxalurisch hyperoxaluric
Hyperoxie hyperoxia
Hyperpathie hyperpathia
Hyperperistaltik hyperperistalsis
Hyperphagie hyperphagia
Hyperpigmentation e. e.
Hyperplasie hyperplasia
hyperplastisch hyperplastic
Hyperpnoe hyperpnea (a), hyperpnoea (e)
Hyperproinsulinämie hyperproinsulinaemia (e), hyperproinsulinemia (a)
Hyperproteinämie hyperproteinaemia (e), hyperproteinemia (a)
hyperpyretisch hyperpyretic
Hyperpyrexie hyperpyrexia
Hyperreflexie hyperreflexia
hypersegmentiert hypersegmented
Hypersekretion hypersecretion
hypersekretorisch hypersecretory
hypersensibel hypersensitive
Hypersensibilität hypersensitiveness
Hypersomnie hypersomnia
Hypersplenie hypersplenia, hypersplenism
Hypersthenurie hypersthenuria
Hypersystole e. e.
Hypertensin angiotonin
Hypertension e. e.
hypertensiv hypertensive
Hyperthermie hyperthermia
hyperthym hyperthymic
Hyperthymie hyperthymia
Hyperthyreose hyperthyroidism, hyperthyreosis
hyperthyreotisch hyperthyroid
Hypertonie hypertonia
—,essentielle essential hypertension, neurogenic hypertension
—,nephrogene renal hypertension
hypertonisch hypertonic
Hypertrichose hypertrichosis
Hypertriglyzeridämie hypertriglyceridaemia (e), hypertriglyceridemia (a)
Hypertrophie hypertrophy
hypertrophisch hypertrophic
Hyperurikämie hyperuricaemia (e), hyperuricemia (a)
Hyperventilation e. e.
Hypervitaminose hypervitaminosis
Hypervolämie hypervolaemia (e), hypervolemia (a)
Hyperzementose hypercementosis
Hyphäma hyphaemia (e), hyphemia (a)
Hypinose hypinosis
Hypnoanalyse hypnoanalysis
hypnoanalytisch hypnoanalytic
Hypnose hypnosis
hypnotisch hypnotic
Hypnotiseur hypnotist
hypnotisieren to hypnotize
Hypnotisierung hypnotization

Hypnotismus hypnotism
Hypobromit hypobromite
Hypochlorämie hypochloraemia (e), hypochloremia (a)
hypochlorämisch hypochloraemic (e), hypochloremic (a)
Hypochlorhydrie hypochlorhydria
hypochlorhydrisch hypochlorhydric
Hypochlorit hypochlorite
Hypocholesterinämie hypocholesteraemia (e), hypocholesteremia (a)
Hypochonder hypochondriac
Hypochondrie hypochondriasis
hypochondrisch hypochondriacal
hypochrom hypochromic
Hypochromasie hypochromasia
hypochromatisch hypochromatic
Hypochromie hypochromia
hypodens hypodense
hypodynamisch hypodynamic
Hypofibrinogenämie hypofibrinogenaemia (e), hypofibrinogenemia (a)
Hypofunktion hypofunction
Hypogalaktie hypogalactia
Hypogammaglobulinämie hypogammaglobulinaemia (e), hypogammaglobulinemia (a)
hypogastrisch hypogastric
Hypogenitalismus hypogenitalism
Hypoglykämie hypoglycaemia (e), hypoglycemia (a)
hypoglykämisch hypoglycaemic (e), hypoglycemic (a)
Hypokaliämie hypopotassaemia (e), hypopotassemia (a)
Hypokalzämie hypocalcaemia (e), hypocalcemia (a)
hypokalzämisch hypocalcaemic (e), hypocalcemic (a)
Hypokapnie hypocapnia
Hypokinese hypokinesis
hypokinetisch hypokinetic
Hypokonid hypoconid
Hypokonulid hypoconulid

Hypomagnesiämie hypomagnesaemia (e), hypomagnesemia (a)
Hypomanie hypomania
hypomanisch hypomanic
Hypomenorrhöe hypomenorrhea (a), hypomenorrhoea (e)
Hyponatriämie hyponatraemia (e), hyponatremia (a)
hypopharyngeal e. e.
Hypopharynx e. e.
Hypophosphat hypophosphate
Hypophosphit hypophosphite
hypophysär hypophysial
Hypophyse pituitary gland, hypophysis
Hypophysektomie hypophysectomy
hypophysektomieren to hypophysectomize
Hypophysenfunktionsstörung dyspituitarism
Hypophysenhinterlappen posterior lobe of the pituitary gland, posthypophysis
Hypophysenhinterlappenextrakt posterior pituitary extract
Hypophysenhinterlappenhormon hypophamine
Hypophysenhinterlappenüberfunktion posterior pituitary hyperfunction
Hypophysenhinterlappenunterfunktion posterior pituitary hypofunction
Hypophysenüberfunktion hyperpituitarism
Hypophysenunterfunktion hypopituitarism
Hypophysenvorderlappen anterior lobe of the pituitary gland, prehypophysis
Hypophysenvorderlappenextrakt anterior pituitary extract
Hypophysenvorderlappenhormon, laktotropes prolactin
Hypophysenvorderlappenüberfunktion anterior pituitary hyperfunction

**Hypophysenvorderlappenunter-
funktion** anterior pituitary hypofunktion
Hypophysin e. e.
Hypophysitis e. e.
Hypopion e. e.
Hypoplasie hypoplasia
hypoplastisch hypoplastic
Hypoproteinämie hypoproteinaemia (e), hypoproteinemia (a)
Hypoprothrombinämie hypoprothrombinaemia (e), hypoprothrombinemia (a)
Hyporeflexie hyporeflexia
Hypospadie hypospadia, hypospadias
Hypostase hypostasis
hypostatisch hypostatic
Hyposthenurie hyposthenuria
Hypotension e. e.
hypotensiv hypotensive
hypothalamisch hypothalamic
Hypothermie hypothermia
Hypothese hypothesis
hypothetisch hypothetical
Hypothyreose hypothyroidism, hypothyreosis
hypothyreotisch hypothyroid
Hypotonie hypotonia
hypotonisch hypotonic
Hypotrichose hypotrichosis
Hypoventilation e. e.
Hypovitaminose hypovitaminosis
Hypovolämie hypovolaemia (e), hypovolemia (a)

Hypoxämie hypoxaemia (e), hypoxemia (a)
hypoxämisch hypoxaemic (e), hypoxemic (a)
Hypoxanthin hypoxanthine
Hypoxie hypoxia
Hypsarhythmie hypsarrhythmia
hypsodont e. e.
Hypsophobie hypsophobia
Hysterektomie hysterectomy
—, **abdominale** abdomino-hysterectomy
Hysterese hysteresis
Hysterie hysteria
Hysterieanfall hysterics
Hysteriker hysteriac
Hysterikerin hysteriac
hysterisch hysterical
Hysteroepilepsie hysteroepilepsy
Hysterographie hysterography
hysterographisch hysterographical
Hysteronarkolepsie hysteronarcolepsy
Hysteroptose hysteroptosis
Hysterosalpingographie hysterosalpingography
Hysterosalpingostomie hysterosalpingostomy
Hysterosalpingotomie hysterosalpingotomy
Hysterotomie hysterotomy
—, **abdominale** abdomino-hysterotomy
Hysterotonin e. e.
Hysterozervikotomie hysterocervicotomy

I

i.a. (= intraarteriell) IA (= intraarterial)
iatrogen iatrogenic
Ibuprofen e. e.
Ichthyose ichthyosis
ichthyotisch ichthyotic
Ideal e. e.
ideal e. e.

Ideation e. e.
Idee idea
identifizieren to identify
Identifizierung identification
identisch identical
Identität identity
ideomotorisch ideomotor
Idioisoagglutinin e. e.
Idioisolysin e. e.
idiokratisch idiocratic
Idiolysin e. e.
idiopathisch idiopathic
Idiosynkrasie idiosyncrasy
idiosynkratisch idiosyncratic
Idiot e. e.
Idiotie idiocy
Idiotyp idiotype
idiotypisch idiotypic
Ignipunktur ignipuncture
ikterisch icteric
Ikterus jaundice, icterus
Ileitis e. e.
– terminalis terminal ileitis
Ileo-Ileostomie ileo-ileostomy
ileokolisch ileocolic
Ileokolitis ileocolitis
Ileokolostomie ileocolostomy
Ileokolotomie ileocolotomy
Ileoproktostomie ileoproctostomy
Ileosigmoidostomie ileosigmoidostomy
Ileostomie ileostomy
Ileotomie ileotomy
Ileotransversostomie ileotransversostomy
ileozökal ileocecal (a), ileocaecal (e)
Ileum e. e.
Ileus e. e.
iliopubisch iliopubic
Illusion e. e.
illusionär illusional
i.m. (= intramuskulär) intramuscular
imaginär imaginary
Imbibition e. e.
Imid imide
Iminazol iminazole

Iminodibenzyl e. e.
Iminostilben iminostilbene
Imipramin imipramine
immatrikulieren to enrol
immobil immobile
immobilisieren to immobilize
Immobilität immobility
immun immune
Immunchemie immunochemistry
immunchemisch immunochemical
Immunelektrophorese immunoelectrophoresis
Immunglobulin immunoglobulin
immunisieren to immunizate
Immunisierung immunization
Immunität immunity
Immunitätslehre immunology
immunoblastisch immunoblastic
Immunochromatographie immunochromatography
Immunodiffusion e. e.
Immunofluoreszenz immunofluorescence
Immunologie immunology
immunologisch immunological
Immunoreaktion immunoreaction
Immunotherapie immunotherapy
Immunosuppression e. e.
Immunreaktionsfähigkeit immunoreactivity
immunreaktiv immunoreactive
Immunreaktivität immunoreactivity
immunsuppressiv immunosuppressive
Impedanz impedance
Impetiginisierung impetiginization
impetiginös impetiginous
Impetigo e. e.
Impfarzt vaccinator
Impfbesteck vaccinating set
impfen to vaccinate
impffähig vaccinable
Impffeder vaccinating pen
Impffederhalter vaccinating pen holder
Impfgegner antivaccinationist
Impfgegnerin antivaccinationist

Impfliste vaccination register
Impfpustel vaccinide
Impfstoff vaccine matter
Impfung vaccination, immunization
Implantat implant
Implantation e. e.
implantieren to implant
Implantologie implantology
impotent e. e.
Impotenz impotence
Imprägnation impregnation
imprägnieren to impregnate
Impression e. e.
Impuls impulse
Inadäquanz inadequacy
inadäquat inadequate
inaktiv inactive
inaktivieren to inactivate
Inaktivierung inactivation
Inanition e. e.
Inappetenz inappetence
Index e. e.
indifferent e. e.
Indifferenz indifference
Indigestion e. e.
Indigo e. e.
Indigoblau indigo blue
Indigokarmin indigo carmine
Indikan indican
Indikanurie indicanuria
Indikation indication
Indikator indicator
indirekt indirect
Indium e. e.
individualisieren to individualize
individuell individual
indizieren to indicate
Indol indole
Indolamin indolamine
indolent e. e.
Indolenz indolence
Indomethacin e. e.
Indophenol e. e.
Indoxyl e. e.
Indozyaningrün indocyanine green
Induktion induction
Induktor inductor

Induration e. e.
indurativ indurative
indurieren to indurate
induzieren to induce
ineinandergreifen to interlock
infantil infantile
Infantilismus infantilism
Infarkt infarct
Infarktpneumonie pneumonia due to pulmonary infarction
Infarzierung infarction
–, **stumme** silent infarction
infaust infavorable (a), infavourable (e)
Infektanämie anaemia due to infection (e), anemia due to infection (a)
Infektarthritis infectional arthritis
infektiös infectious, infective
Infektion infection
Infektionskrankheit infectious disease, infective disease
Infektiosität infectiosity
Infiltrat infiltrate
Infiltration e. e.
infiltrieren to infiltrate
infinitesimal e. e.
infizieren to infect
Influenza e. e.
Influenzabazillus Haemophilus influenzae (e), Hemophilus influenzae (a)
infraaxillär infraaxillary
infraglottisch infraglottic
infraklavikulär infraclavicular
Infraktion infraction
inframammär inframammary
inframandibulär inframandibular
inframaxillär inframaxillary
Infraokklusion infraocclusion
infraorbital e. e.
infrapatellar e. e.
Infrarot infra-red
infrarot infra-red
Infrarotstrahl infra-red ray
Infrarotthermographie infra-red thermography

infrasellär infrasellar
infraskapular infrascapular
infraspinal e. e.
infravalvulär infravalvular
infundibulär infundibular
Infusion e. e.
Infusionspumpe infusion pump
Infusorien infusoria
inguinal e. e.
Inguinalring inguinal ring
Inhalation e. e.
Inhalationsapparat inhaler
Inhalationsnarkose inhalation anaesthesia (e), inhalation anesthesia (a)
inhalieren to inhale
Inhalt content
Inhibin e. e.
Inhibitor e. e.
inhomogen inhomogenous
initial e. e.
Initialstadium initial stage
Injektion injection
Injektionsspritze injection syringe
injizieren to inject
Inkarzeration incarceration
inkarzerieren to incarcerate
Inklination inclination
inkohärent incoherent
inkompatibel incompatible
Inkompatibilität incompatibility
inkontinent incontinent
Inkontinenz incontinence
Inkorporation incorporation
inkorporieren to incorporate
inkretorisch incretory
Inkubation incubation
Inkubationszeit incubation
Inkubator incubator
inkubieren to incubate
Inlay e. e.
—,**mit Stift verankertes** pinledge
Innenohr inner ear
Innere Medizin internal medicine
Inneres interior
innerlich internal

innersekretorisch endosecretory
Innervation e. e.
innervieren to innervate
Inokulation inoculation
Inokulationshepatitis homologous serum jaundice
inokulieren to inoculate
inoperabel inoperable
Inosin inosine
Inosit inositol
inotrop inotropic
Insekt insect
Insektenpulver insect powder
Insektenvernichtung disinsectization
Insektenvertilgungsmittel insecticide
insektizid insecticide
Insel, Langerhanssche island of Langerhans
Inselgewebe insular tissue
Insemination e. e.
Insertion e. e.
Inskription inscription
Inspektion inspection
Inspiration inspiration
inspiratorisch inspiratory
inspirieren to inspire
instabil instabile, unstable
Instabilität instability
Instillation e. e.
Instinkt instinct
instinktiv instinctive
Institut institute
Instrument e. e.
instrumentell instrumental
Instrumentenhalter instrument holder
Instrumententisch instrument table
Instrumentierung instrumentation
insuffizient insufficient
Insuffizienz insufficiency
Insufflation e. e.
insulär insular
Insulin e.e.
—,**Depot-** depot insulin

Insulin, Rinder- bovine insulin
–,Schweine- porcine insulin
Insulinase e. e.
insulinbedürftig insulin-dependant
Insulinbehandlung insulinization
insulinisieren to insulinizate
Insulinisierung insulinization
Insulinmangeldiabetes insulin-deficient diabetes
insulinotrop insulinotropic
Insulin-Zinksuspension insulin-zinc suspension
Insulom insuloma
integral e. e.
Integration e. e.
integrieren to integrate
Integrität integrity
Intellekt intellect
intelligent e. e.
Intelligenz intelligence
Intelligenzversuch intelligence test
Intensität intensity
intensiv intensive
Intensivbehandlung intensive therapy
intensivieren to intensify
Intensivierung intensification
Intensivpflege intensive care, intensive nursing
Intensivpflegestation intensive care unit
Intensivstation, Herzinfarkt – coronary care unit
interaural e. e.
interdental e. e.
Interdentalraum embrasure
interdigital e. e.
Interferenz interference
interferieren to interfere
Interferometer e. e.
Interferometrie interferometry
Interferon e. e.
interindividuell interindividual
interkondylär intercondylar
interkostal intercostal
Interkostalneuralgie intercostal neuralgia

interkurrent intercurrent
Interkuspidation intercuspidation
interlobär interlobar
interlobulär interlobular
intermaxillär intermaxillary
intermediär intermediary
Intermedin e. e.
Intermenstruum e. e.
Intermission e. e.
intermittieren to intermit
intermittierend intermittent
intern internal
Internist e. e.
Internistin internist
internodal e. e.
interokklusal interocclusal
interpolieren to interpolate
Interposition e. e.
interproximal e. e.
interradikulär interradicular
Interrenalismus interrenalism
Intersex e. e.
Intersexualität intersexuality
intersexuell intersexual
interstitiell interstitial
Interstitium interstice
intertrabekulär intertrabecular
intertriginös intertriginous
Intertrigo e. e.
intertrochanterisch intertrochanteric
Intervall interval
interventrikulär interventricular
intervertebral e. e.
intervillös intervillous
interzellulär intercellular
intestinal e. e.
intimal e. e.
Intimitis e. e.
intolerant e. e.
Intoleranz intolerance
Intoxikation intoxication
–,septische septic intoxication, sapraemia (e), sapremia (a)
intraabdominell intraabdominal
intraarteriell intraarterial
intraartikulär intraarticular

intraazinös intraacinous
intrabronchial e. e.
intradermal e. e.
intraduodenal e. e.
intradural e. e.
intragastral intragastric
intraglandulär intraglandular
intrahepatisch intrahepatic
intraindividuell intraindividual
intrakanalikulär intracanalicular
intrakapsulär intracapsular
intrakardial intracardiac
intrakraniell intracranial
intrakutan intracutaneous
intralaryngeal e. e.
intralienal intrasplenic
intralingual e. e.
intralobär intralobar
intralobulär intralobular
intralumbal intralumbar
intramammär intramammary
intramaxillär intramaxillary
intramedullär intramedullary
intrameningeal e. e.
intramural e. e.
intramuskulär intramuscular
intranasal e. e.
intraneural e. e.
intranukleär intranuclear
intraokulär intraocular
intraoral e. e.
intraossär intraosseous
intraossal e. e.
intrapankreatisch intrapancreatic
intraperitoneal e. e.
intraplazental intraplacental
intrapleural e. e.
intrapulmonal intrapulmonary
intrarektal intrarectal
intrarenal e. e.
intraskrotal intrascrotal
intraspinal e. e.
intrasplenisch intrasplenic
intrasternal e. e.
intrasynovial e. e.
intrathekal intrathecal
intrathorakal intrathoracic

intrathyreoidal intrathyroid
intratracheal e. e.
intraurethral e. e.
intrauterin intrauterine
Intrauterinspirale intrauterine device
intravaginal e. e.
intravaskulär intravascular
intravenös intravenous, endovenous
intraventrikulär intraventricular
intravesikal intravesical
intravital e. e.
intrazellulär intracellular, endocellular
intrazerebral intracerebral
intrazervikal intracervical
intrazisternal intracisternal
intrinsic factor e. e.
Introduktion introduction
Introversion e. e.
introvertieren to introvert
Intrusion e. e.
Intubation e. e., tubage
Intubationsnarkose endotracheal anaesthesia (e), endotracheal anesthesia (a)
intubieren to intubate
Intumeszenz intumescence
Intussuszeption intussusception
Inulase e. e.
Inulin e. e.
Inunktion inunction
Invagination e. e.
invalid e. e.
Invalide invalid
Invasion e. e.
Invasionsvermögen invasiveness
invasiv invasive
Inversion e. e.
Invertzucker invert sugar, invertose
in vitro e. e.
in vivo e. e.
Involution e. e.
involutionell involutional
Inzest incest
Inzision incision

Inzisur incisure
Inzucht inbreeding
Ion e. e.
ionisieren to ionize
Ionisierung ionization
Ionogramm ionogram
Ionometer e. e.
Ionometrie ionometry
ionometrisch ionometric
Iontophorese iontophoresis
iontophoretisch iontophoretical
Ipratropiumbromid ipratropiumbromide
Iproniazid e. e.
ipsilateral e. e.
Iridektomie iridectomy
Iridektomiemesser iridectomy knife
iridektomieren to iridectomize
Iridium e. e.
Iridochorioiditis iridochoroiditis
Iridodialyse iridodialysis
Iridodonesis e. e.
Iridoplegie iridoplegia
Iridosklerotomie iridosclerotomy
Iridoskop iridoscope
Iridoskopie iridoscopy
iridoskopisch iridoscopical
Iridotomie iridotomy
Iridozele iridocele
Iridozyklitis iridocyclitis
Iris e. e.
Irisdiagnose iridodiagnosis
Irispinzette iris forceps
Irisprolaps prolapse of iris
Irisschlottern iridodonesis
Iritis e. e.
irre insane
irregulär irregular
Irregularität irregularity
Irrenanstalt lunatic asylum, mental hospital, bedlam
irreversibel irreversible
Irrigation e. e.
Irrigator e. e.
Irrigoskopie irrigoscopy
Irritation e. e.
irritieren to irritate

irritierend irritant
Irrsinn insanity, madness
irrtümlich mistakenly
Ischämie ischaemia (e), ischemia (a)
ischämisch ischaemic (e), ischemic (a)
Ischiasneuritis sciatica
ischiopubisch ischiopubic
ischiorektal ischiorectal
Ischuria paradoxa e. e.
Isoagglutination e. e.
Isoagglutinin e. e.
Isoalloxazin isoalloxazine
Isoantikörper isoantibody
Isocarboxazid isocarboxazide
isochromatisch isochromatic
isochron isochronous
Isochronie isochronia
isodens isodense
isodont e. e.
Isodosis e. e.
isodynamisch isodynamic
isoelektrisch isoelectric
isoenergetisch isoenergetic
isogam isogamous
Isohämolysin isohaemolysin (e), isohemolysin (a)
Isohydrie isohydria
Isoimmunisation isoimmunization
Isoliereinheit, keimfreie pathogen-free room, ultra-clean ward
isolieren to isolate
Isolierstation isolation ward
Isolierung isolation
Isolysin e. e.
Isomaltase e. e.
Isomaltose e. e.
Isomer e. e.
isomer isomeric
Isomerase e. e.
Isomerie isomerism
isometrisch isometric
Isometropie isometropia
isomorph isomorphous
Isoniazid e. e.
Isopren isoprene
Isoprenalin isoprenaline

Isopropamid isopropamide
Isopropyl e. e.
Isopropylarterenol e. e.
Isopropylhydrazin isopropylhydrazine
Isopropylnoradrenalin isoproterenol
isosexuell isosexual
Isosorbiddinitrat isosorbide dinitrate
Isospora belli e. e.
Isospora hominis e. e.
Isosthenurie isosthenuria
isosthenurisch isosthenuric
Isothiazol isothiazole
Isothiozyanat isothiocyanate
Isotonie isotonia
isotonisch isotonic

Isotop isotope
Isotopennephrographie radio-isotopic renography
Isotransplantation e. e.
isotrop isotropic
isovolumetrisch isovolumetric
Isoxazol isoxazole
Isoxazolidon isoxazolidone
Isoxazolyl e. e.
Isozym isozyme
Isozytose isocytosis
isthmisch isthmic
Isthmus e. e.
i.v. (= intravenös) IV (= intravenous)
Ixodes e. e.
Ixodiasis e. e.

J

Jaborin jaborine
Jacketkrone jacket crown
Jacksonepilepsie jacksonian epilepsy
Jacobsonsche Anastomose Jacobson's anastomosis
Jaguar e. e.
Jalapin e. e.
Janusgrün Janus green
Jarisch-Herxheimersche Reaktion Jarisch-Herxheimer phenomenon
Javal-Ophthalmometer Javal's ophthalmometer
jejunal e. e.
Jejunitis e. e.
Jejunoileostomie jejunoileostomy
Jejunojejunostomie jejunojejunostomy
Jejunokolostomie jejunocolostomy
Jejunostomie jejunostomy
Jejunum e. e.
Jendrassikscher Handgriff Jendrassik's maneuver

Jochbogen zygoma
Jod iodine
Jodat iodate
Jodid iodide
jodieren to iodize
Jodöl iodized oil
Jodoform iodoform
Jodometrie iodometry
jodometrisch iodometric
Jodtinktur tincture of iodine
Johimbin johimbine
Jollykörper Jolly's body, Howell's body
Joule e. e.
jucken to itch
Jucken itch
juckend pruritic
Juckreiz itch
juckreizstillend antipruritic
Jünglingsalter adolescence
Jünglingsche Krankheit Jüngling's disease
jugendlich juvenile

jugendlicher Leukozyt
juvenile leukocyte
jugulär jugular
jungfräulich virginal
Jungfräulichkeit virginity
Jungfrau virgin

Junggeselle bachelor
juvenil juvenile
juxtaartikulär juxtaarticular
juxtaglomerulär juxtaglomerular
Juxtaposition e. e.
juxtapylorisch juxtapyloric

K
(siehe auch:/look also for: C)

Kabel cable, cord
Kabelgriff cord handle
Kabine cabin
kachektisch cachectic
Kachexie cachexia
Kadaverin cadaverine
Kälberruhr, weiße white scours
Kälteagglutination cold agglutination
Kälteagglutinin cold agglutinin
Kälteanästhesie refrigeration anaesthesia (e), refrigeration anesthesia (a)
Kälteanwendung crymotherapy, cryotherapy
Kältegrad degree of cold
Känguruh kangaroo
käsig caseous, cheesy
Kätzchen kitten
Kaffee coffee
Kafka-Reaktion Kafka's reaction
kahl bald
Kahlersche Krankheit multiple myeloma
kahlköpfig baldheaded
Kahnbauch scaphoid abdomen
Kahlkopf baldhead
Kahnbein scaphoid bone
kahnförmig scaphoid
Kahnsche Reaktion Kahn's test
Kaiserschnitt caesarean section (e), cesarean section (a)
Kakao cacao, cocoa

Kakaobutter cocoa butter
Kakodyl cacodyl
Kakodylat cacodylate
Kala-Azar e. e.
Kalb calf (veter.)
kalben to calve
Kaliber caliber, gauge
Kalium potassium
Kaliumazetat potassium acetate
Kaliumbikarbonat potassium bicarbonate
Kaliumbitartrat potassium bitartrate
Kaliumbromid potassium bromide
Kaliumchlorid potassium chloride
kaliumhaltig potassic
Kaliumhydroxyd potassium hydroxide, caustic potash
Kaliumjodid potassium iodide
Kaliumkarbonat potassium carbonate
Kaliumnatriumtartrat potassium and sodium tartrate
Kaliumnitrat potassium nitrate, niter (a), nitre (e), saltpeter (a), saltpetre (e)
Kaliumpermanganat potassium permanganate
Kaliumsulfat potassium sulphate (e), potassium sulfate (a)
Kaliurese kaliuresis
Kalk lime, chalk
kalkarme Kost low calcium diet

Kalkmangel acalcerosis
kalkreiche Kost high calcium diet
Kalkwasser lime water
Kallidin e. e.
Kallikrein e. e.
kallös callous
Kallus callus
Kallusbildung callus formation
Kalomel calomel
Kalorie, große large calorie
–, **kleine** small calorie
kalorigen calorigenic
Kalorimeter calorimeter
Kalorimetrie calorimetry
kalorimetrisch calorimetric
kalorisch caloric
kalt cold
Kaltwasserbehandlung cold water treatment
kalzipriv calciprivic
Kalzium calcium
Kalziumkarbonat calcium carbonate, chalk
Kalziumchlorid calcium chloride
Kalziumglukonat calcium gluconate
Kalziumhydroxyd calcium hydroxide
Kalziumlaktat calcium lactate
Kalziumoxyd calcium oxide, lime, calcarea
Kalziurie calciuria
Kamel camel
Kamelstute she-camel
Kamille chamomile
Kammer chamber; ventricle
Kammerflimmern ventricular fibrillation
Kammerwinkel des Auges angle of chamber of the eye
Kampfer camphor
Kampferöl camphorated oil
Kanal channel, canal; tract
kanalikulär canalicular
Kanalisation canalization
Kanamycin e. e.
Kanarienvogel canary
Kaninchen rabbit
kankroid cankroid
Kankroid cancroid
Kanne pot, jug
Kannibalismus cannibalism
Kantharide cantharide
Kanüle cannula
Kanülenentfernung decannulation
kanzerogen cancerogenic
kanzerotoxisch cancerotoxic
Kaolin e. e.
Kapaun capon
Kapazität capacity
kapillär capillary
Kapillare capillary
Kapillarmikroskopie capillaroscopy
kapillarmikroskopisch capillaroscopical
Kaproat caproate
Kaprylat caprylate
Kapsel capsule
Kapselfärbung capsule staining
Karbamat carbamate
Karbamazepin carbamazepine
Karbamazin carbamazine
Karbamoyltransferase carbamoyltransferase
Karbamyl carbamyl
Karbamylase carbamylase
Karbazon carbazone
Karbenicillin carbenicillin
Karbenoxolon carbenoxolone
Karbid carbide
Karboanhydrase carbonic anhydrase
Karboanhydrasehemmer carbonic anhydrase inhibitor
Karbohydrase carbohydrase
Karbolfuchsin carbolfuchsin
Karbolsäure carbolic acid
Karbonat carbonate
Karbonyl carbonyl
Karborund carborundum
Karboxamid carboxamide
Karboxyl carboxyl
Karboxylierung carboxylation

Karbunkel carbuncle
Karbutamid carbutamide
Kardia cardia
kardial cardiac
kardinal cardinal
Kardiogramm cardiogram
Kardiographie cardiography
kardiographisch cardiographic
Kardiologe cardiologist
Kardiologie cardiology
Kardiologin cardiologist
kardiologisch cardiologic
Kardiolyse cardiolysis
Kardiomalazie cardiomalacia
Kardiomyopathie cardiomyopathy
Kardiopathie cardiopathy
kardiopathisch cardiopathic
kardioportal cardioportal
Kardiotokographie cardiotocography
kardiovaskulär cardiovascular
Kardioversion cardioversion
Karditis carditis
Karellkur Karell's treatment
Karies caries
kariös carious
Karlsbader Salz Carlsbad salt
Karmin carmine
Karnifikation carnification
karnifizieren to carnify
Karotin carotene
karpal carpal
Karpaltunnelsyndrom carpal tunnel syndrome
karpopedal carpopedal
Kartagenersches Syndrom Kartagener's syndrome
Kartei card index
Kartoffelkultur potato culture
Kartothek card file
Karyolyse karyolysis
karyolytisch karyolytic
Karyoplasma karyoplasm
karzinoembryogenes Antigen carcinoembryogenic antigen
Karzinogen carcinogen

karzinogen carcinogenic, carcinogenous
Karzinoid carcinoid
Karzinolyse carcinolysis
karzinolytisch carcinolytic
Karzinom carcinoma
karzinomatös carcinomatous
Karzinomatose carcinomatosis
Karzinophobie carcinophobia
Karzinosarkom carcinosarcoma
Karzinose carcinosis
Kasein casein
Kaskadenmagen cascade stomach
Kassenärztin panel doctor
Kassenarzt panel doctor
Kassette (roentgenol.) cassette, plate holder
Kastanie chestnut
Kastrat castrate
Kastration castration
kastrieren to castrate, to geld
Kasuistik casuistics
kasuistisch casuistic
Katabiose catabiosis
katabiotisch catabiotic
Katabolikum catabolic
katabolisch catabolic
katabolisieren to catabolize
Katabolismus catabolism
Katalase catalase
Katalepsie catalepsy
kataleptisch cataleptic
Katalog catalog
Katalysator catalyzer
Katalyse catalysis
katalysieren to catalyze
katalytisch catalytic
Katamnese catamnesis, follow-up
katamnestisch catamnestic
Kataphorese cataphoresis
kataphoretisch cataphoretic
Kataplasie cataplasia
Kataplasma cataplasm
kataplastisch cataplastic
Kataplexie cataplexy
Katarakt cataract
Katarrh catarrh

katarrhalisch catarrhal
Katatonie catatony
katatonisch catatonic
Katechin catechin
Katecholamin catecholamine
Katechu catechu
Kategorie category
Kater (= Tier) tom-cat
Kater (= schlechtes Befinden) hangover
Katgut catgut
Katharsis catharsis, abreaction
kathartisch cathartic
Kathepsin cathepsin
Katheter catheter
—,**Bozemanscher** Bozeman's catheter
—,**Dauer-** permanent catheter
—,**Harnleiter-** ureteral catheter
—,**Herz-** cardiac catheter
—,**Mercierscher** Mercier's catheter
—,**Nélatonscher** Nélaton's catheter
—,**Pezzerscher** de Pezzer catheter
—,**Spül-** irrigation catheter
Katheterspanner catheter introducer
katheterisieren to catheterize
Katheterisierung catheterization
Katheterismus catheterism
Kathode cathode
Kathodenöffnungszuckung cathodal opening contraction
Kathodenschließungszuckung cathodal closure contraction
Kathodenstrahl cathode ray
Kation cation
Kationenaustausch cation exchange
Katze cat
Katzenkratzkrankheit viral scratch lymphadenitis
Kauapparat masticatory apparatus
kaudal caudal
kaudalwärts caudad
kauen to masticate, to chew
Kauen mastication
Kaufläche grinding surface, masticatory surface, occlusal surface
Kaufmannscher Versuch Kaufmann's test
Kaulquappe polliwog
kausal causal
Kausalgie causalgia
kausalgisch causalgic
Kaustik cautery
Kaustikum caustic
kaustisch caustic
Kauter cauter
Kauterisation cauterization
kauterisieren to cauterize
Kautschuk caoutchouc
Kautüchtigkeit masticatory efficiency
Kaverne cavern
Kavernisierung cavitation
kavernös cavernous
Kavernom cavernoma
Kavernosographie cavernosographie
Kavität cavity
Kavitätenschutzlack cavity liner
Kavographie cavography
Kefir e. e.
Kehlkopf larynx
Kehlkopflähmung laryngoplegia
Kehlkopfplastik laryngoplasty
Kehlkopfspiegel laryngoscope
Kehlkopfstenose laryngostenosis
Keil wedge, cone
Keilbein sphenoid bone
Keilbeinhöhlenentzündung sphenoidal sinusitis
keilförmig cuneiform, wedge-shaped, sphenoid
Keilwirbelbildung wedging of a vertebra
Keim germ
—,**Pflanzen-** cotyledon
Keimdrüse gonad
Keimdrüsenentfernung gonadectomy

Keimdrüsenhormon, männliches
   testicular hormone
—, weibliches ovarian hormone
Keimdrüsenüberfunktion
   hypergonadism
Keimdrüsenunterfunktion
   hypogonadism
keimen to germinate
Keimepithel germinal epithelium
keimfrei sterile, germfree
keimfrei machen to sterilize
Keimgehalt germ content
Keimplasma germ plasm
Keimschicht germinal layer
keimtötend germicidal
keimtötendes Mittel germicide
Keimträger germ carrier
Keimzelle germ cell
Keith-Flackscher Knoten
   Keith-Flack node
Kelch calix
Keloid e. e.
Kelotomie kelotomy
Kelvin e. e.
Kennzeichen criterion, sign
kennzeichnend significant
Kentsches Bündel Kent's bundle
Kephalhämatom cephalhaematoma (e), cephalhematoma (a)
Kephalometer cephalometer
Kephalotripsie cephalotripsy
Keramik ceramics
Keramisch ceramic
Kerasin e. e.
Keratin e. e.
Keratinisierung keratinization
Keratitis e. e.
– **interstitialis** interstitial keratitis
– **neuroparalytica** neuroparalytic keratitis
– **phlyctaenulosa**
   phlyctaenular keratitis (e),
   phlyctenular keratitis (a)
keratitisch keratitic
Keratodermie keratodermia
keratohyalin keratohyaline

Keratoiritis e. e.
Keratokonjunktivitis
   keratoconjunctivitis
Keratokonus keratoconus, conical cornea
Keratolyse keratolysis
keratolytisch keratolytic
Keratom keratoma
Keratomalazie keratomalacia
Keratose keratosis
Keratoskop keratoscope
Keratoskopie keratoscopy
keratoskopisch keratoscopical
Keratozentese keratocentesis
Kerion Celsi kerion of Celsus
Kerkringsche Falte
   Kerkring's fold
Kern core, nucleus
kerngesund thoroughly sound
kernhaltig nucleated
Kernigsches Zeichen Kernig's sign
Kernikterus kernicterus
kernlos acaryote
Kernphysik nuclear physics
Kernreaktor nuclear reactor
Ketobutyrat ketobutyrate
ketogen ketogenic
Ketoglutarat ketoglutarate
Ketohexose e. e.
ketolytisch ketolytic
Keton ketone
Ketonämie ketonaemia (e), ketonemia (a)
Ketonkörper ketone body
Ketonurie ketonuria
Ketose ketosis
Ketose (= Ketozucker) ketose
Ketosteroid e. e.
Ketoverbindung keto compound
Ketozucker ketose
Kette chain
Kettenhaken chain hook
Kettensäge chain saw
keuchen to wheeze, to gasp
Keuchhusten whooping cough, pertussis
Keuchhustenanfall whoop

Khellidin khellidine
Khellin khelline
Khellinin khellinine
Kiefer jaw
Kieferchirurgie maxillary surgery
Kieferplastik gnathoplasty
Kieferspalte gnathoschisis
Kieferwinkel jaw angle
Kienböcksche Krankheit
 Kienböck's disease
Kieselgur kieselguhr, silicious earth
Kiesselbachscher Ort
 Kiesselbach's area
Killiansche Operation
 Killian's operation
Kilogramm kilogram
Kilohertz e. e.
Kiloliter e. e.
Kilometer e. e.
Kilovolt e. e.
Kilowatt e. e.
Kinästhesie kinaesthesia (e),
 kinesthesia (a)
kinästhetisch kinaesthetic (e),
 kinesthetic (a)
Kinase e. e.
Kindbett childbed
Kindbettfieber childbed fever,
 puerperal pyrexia
Kinderärztin paediatrician (e),
 pediatrician (a)
Kinderarzt paediatrician (e),
 pediatrician (a)
Kinderkrankenschwester
 child's nurse
Kinderlähmung infantile
 paralysis; poliomyelitis
Kinderpflegerin child's nurse
Kindesalter childhood
Kindheit childhood
kindisch childish
kindlich infantile
Kindslage presentation
  Beckenendlage
   pelvic presentation
  Fußvorlagerung
   footling presentation

Kindslage
  Gesichtslage face presentation
  Hinterhauptslage
   vertex presentation
  Kopflage head presentation
  Nabelschnurvorlagerung
   funis presentation
  Querlage transverse presentation
  Schädellage cephalic presentation
  Schulterlage
   shoulder presentation
  Steißlage breech presentation
  Stirnlage brow presentation
Kindsmißhandlungsfolgen
 battered child syndrome
Kindsvernachlässigungsfolgen
 battered child syndrome
Kinematographie cinematography
Kineradiographie cineradiography
Kineröntgenographie cine-
 roentgenography
Kinetik kinetism, kinetics
kinetisch kinetic
Kinetose motion sickness
Kinin e. e.
Kininase e. e.
Kininogen e. e.
Kininogenase e. e.
Kinn chin
Kinnstütze chin holder
kippen to tilt
Kissen cushion, pillow
kitzeln to tickle
Kitzeln tickling
Kjeldahlverfahren
 Kjeldahl's method
Kjellandzange Kjelland's forceps
Kladosporiose cladosporiosis
Kladotrichose cladothricosis
klären to clear, to clarify
Klärung clarification, clearance
klagen über to complain of,
 to suffer from
Klammer clamp, clasp, clip
Klammernahtinstrument suture
 clip instrument
Klang sound

Klangfarbe tonality
Klappe valve, valvula
Klappenplastik valvuloplasty
Klapperschlange rattlesnake
Klappsche Kriechbehandlung
 Klapp's creeping treatment
klar clear
Klarzelle clear cell
Klasse class
Klassifikation classification
klassifizieren to classify
klassisch classical
klastisch clastic
Klaue claw, hoof
Klauenfuß clawfoot
Klauengeschwür fetlow
Klauenhand clawhand
Klaustrophilie claustrophilia
Klaustrophobie claustrophobia
Klebepflaster sticking plaster, adhesive tape
Klebsiella e. e.
Kleiderlaus body louse
Kleidotomie cleidotomy
Kleine-Levinsches Syndrom
 Kleine-Levin syndrome
Kleinhirn cerebellum
Kleinhirnbrückenwinkel
 cerebello-pontine angle
Klemme forceps
klemmen to clamp
Kleptomane kleptomaniac
Kleptomanie kleptomania
Kleptomanin kleptomaniac
kleptomanisch kleptomanic
Klient client
Klientin client
Klima climate
Klimabehandlung climatotherapy
klimakterisch climacteric
Klimakterium climacterium
klimatisch climatic
Klimatologie climatology
klimatologisch climatological
Klinefelter-Syndrom
 Klinefelter's syndrome
Klinge blade

Klingen tinkling
Klinik clinic
Kliniker clinician
Klinikerin clinician
klinisch clinical
klinischer Verlauf clinical course
Klippel-Feilsche Krankheit
 Klippel-Feil disease
Klistier enema
Kloake cloaca
kloakogen cloakogenic
klonisch clonic
klonisch-tonisch clonicotonic
Klonus clonus
Klumpfuß clubfoot
Klumpkesche Lähmung
 Klumpke's paralysis
Kneippbehandlung kneippism
kneten to knead
Knick kink
Knie knee
Kniebeuge knee-crooking
Kniegelenk knee joint
Kniegelenkentzündung
 gonarthritis
Knie-Hackenversuch heel-knee test
Kniekehle hollow of the knee
knien to kneel
Kniescheibe patella
knirschen to grind
Knirschen grinding
Knoblauch garlic
Knochen bone
Knochenbank bone bank
knochenbildend ossiferous
Knochenbildung bone formation
Knochenbohrer bone drill
Knochenbruch fracture of bone
Knochengerüst skeleton
Knochenhörer bone-conduction hearing aid
Knochenleitung bone conduction
 – **des Schalls** bone conduction of sound waves
Knochenmark bone marrow
Knochenmarksinsuffizienz
 bone marrow insufficiency

Knochenmarkskultur medulloculture
Knochenmeißel bone chisel
Knochenplastik bone plasty
Knochenplatte bone plate
Knochenschaber bone skid
Knochenschraube bone screw
Knochensplitter bone fragment
Knochenvorsprung spine
Knochenwachs bone wax
Knochenzange bone cutting forceps
knochig bony
Knöchel, äußerer lateral malleolus
—, innerer medial malleolus
knöchern osseous
Knötchen nodule
Knollenblätterpilz deadly amanita, death-cup
Knopf knob
Knorpel cartilage, gristle
Knorpelbildung chondrification, gristle formation
knorpelig cartilaginous, gristly
Knorpelmesser cartilage knife
Knorpelplastik chondroplasty
Knorpelverkalkung calcification of the cartilage
Knospe bud
Knoten node, kink
Knotenrhythmus nodal rhythm
Koagglutinin coagglutinin
Koagel coagulum, clot, curd
Koagulabilität coagulability
Koagulans coagulant
Koagulase coagulase
Koagulation coagulation
Koagulationselektrode coagulation electrode
koagulativ coagulative
koagulieren to coagulate
koagulierend coagulant
Koagulopathie coagulopathy
Kobalamin cobalamine
Kobalt cobalt
Kobaltbestrahlung cobalt irradiation

Kobra cobra
Kobragift cobra venom
kochen to cook
Kocherrinne grooved probe after Kocher
Kochersche Operation Kocher's operation
Kochfleisch meat
Kochkessel boiling pan
kochleär cochlear
Kochprobe coagulation test
Kochsalz common salt
kochsalzähnlich halide
Kochsalzlösung, physiologische normal saline solution
Kochscher Bazillus Koch's bacillus
Koch-Weeks-Bazillus Koch-Weeks bacillus, Haemophilus conjunctivitidis (e), Hemophilus conjunctivitidis (a)
Kodehydrase codehydrase
Kodehydrogenase codehydrogenase
Köcherfliege caddis fly
Koeffizient coefficient
Köhlersche Krankheit Köhler's disease
Königswasser nitrohydrochloric acid, nitromuriatic acid
Koenzym coenzyme
Körnchen granule
Körper body
körperbehindert physically handicapped
körperbehinderte Person physically handicapped person
Körperbeschaffenheit structure of the body
Körperchen corpuscle
Körperflüssigkeit body fluid
Körpergewicht body weight
körperlich bodily, physical, corporeal, corporal
Körperpflegemittel body culture agent
Körperschwäche bodily weakness

Körperteile, edle vital parts of the body, vitals
Körperverfassung habit
Körperwärme body heat
Ko-Faktor co-factor
Koferment coferment
Koffein caffeine
Kofferdam-Instrument rubber-dam instrument
Kohabitation cohabitation
kohärent coherent
Kohäsion cohesion
Kohlehydrat carbohydrate
Kohlenbogenlampe carbon arc lamp
Kohlendioxid carbon dioxide
Kohlendioxydbad carbon dioxide bath
Kohlenmonoxyd carbon monoxide
Kohlensäure carbonic acid
Kohlensäureschnee carbon dioxide snow
Kohlenstoff carbon
Kohlenwasserstoff hydrocarbon
Kohlrauschsche Falte Kohlrausch's fold
Koinzidenz coincidence
Koitus coitus, coition
Kokain cocaine
kokainisieren to cocainize
Kokainisierung cocainization
Kokainismus cocainism
Kokainist cocainist
Kokainistin cocainist
Kokon cocoon
Kokosnuß coconut
Kola e. e.
Kolation colation
Kolchizin colchicine
Kolibazillus Escherichia coli
Kolik colic
Kolipyelitis colipyelitis
kollagen collagenic, collagenous
Kollagen collagen
Kollagenose collagenosis
Kollaps collapse
Kollapstherapie collapsotherapy
kollateral collateral
Kollateralkreislauf collateral circulation
Kollege collegue
Kollegin collegue
Kolliquation colliquation
kolliquativ colliquative
Kollmanndilatator Kollmann's dilator
Kollodium collodion
Kolloid colloid
kolloidal colloidal
Kolloidchemie collochemistry
Kolloidkropf colloid goiter
kolloidosmotisch colloid osmotic
Kolobom coloboma
Kolocynthe colocynth
Kolonie colony
Kolopexie colopexy
Kolophonium colophony
Koloptose coloptosis
Kolorimeter colorimeter
Kolorimetrie colorimetry
kolorimetrisch colorimetric
Koloskop coloscope
Koloskopie coloscopy
koloskopisch coloscopic
Kolostomie colostomy
Kolotomie colotomy
Kolpeurynter colpeurynter
Kolpitis colpitis
kolpitisch colpitic
Kolporrhaphie colporrhaphy
Kolposkop colposcope
Kolposkopie colposcopy
kolposkopisch colposcopical
Kolpozystozele colpocystocele
Koma coma
komatös comatose
Komedo comedo
Komitee committee
Kommissur commissure
Kommissurotomie commissurotomy
Kommunikation communication
kommunizieren to communicate

kompakt compact
kompatibel compatible
Kompatibilität compatibility
Kompensation compensation
kompensatorisch compensatory
kompensieren to compensate
kompetitiv competitive
Komplement complement
komplementär complementary, complemental
Komplementärluft complemental air
Komplementbindung complement fixation
komplex complex
Komplex complex
Komplexbildner complexing agent
Komplexometrie complexometry
komplexometrisch complexometric
Komplikation complication
kompliziert complicated
Komponente component
Kompott stewed fruit
Kompresse compress
Kompression compression
Kompressionsfraktur compression fracture
Kompressionslähmung paralysis from compression
Kompressor compressor
Kompressorium compressorium
komprimieren to compress
Konchotom conchotome
Konchotomie conchotomy
Kondensat condensate
Kondensation condensation
Kondensor condenser
Kondition condition
Kondom condom
Konduktion conduction
Kondylom condyloma
kondylomatös condylomatous
Kondylomatose condylomatosis
Konfabulation confabulation
konfabulieren to confabulate
Konferenz conference

Konfiguration configuration
– des fötalen Kopfes sub partu moulding
konfigurieren to configurate
Konflikt conflict
konfluierend confluent
Konfusion confusion
kongenital congenital
Kongestion congestion
kongestiv congestive
Konglomerat conglomerate
Kongorot Congo red
Koniin coniine
Koniotomie coniotomy
konisch conical
Konjugase conjugase
Konjugat conjugate
Konjugata conjugate
konjugiert conjugate
Konjunktiva conjunctiva
konjunktival conjunctival
Konjunktivalsack conjunctival sac
Konjunktivitis conjunctivitis
konjunktivitisch conjunctivitic
konkav concave
Konkavität concavity
Konkrement concrement, calculus
konkret concrete
Konkretion concretion
konsensuell consensual
konservativ conservative
Konserve preserve
Konservierung preservation
Konservierungsmittel preservative agent
konsolidieren to consolidate
Konsolidierung consolidation
Konsonant consonant
konstant constant
Konstante constant
Konstitution constitution
konstitutionell constitutional
Konstriktion constriction
Konstriktor constrictor
konstriktorisch constrictive
konstruktiv constructive
Kontakt contact

Kontaktfläche contact area
Kontaktlinse contact lens
Kontiguität contiguity
kontinuierlich continuous
Kontinuität continuity
kontrahieren to contract
Kontraindikation contraindication
kontraindiziert contraindicant
kontrainsulär contrainsular
kontraktil contractile
Kontraktilität contractility
Kontraktion contraction
Kontraktur contracture
kontralateral contralateral
Kontrast contrast
Kontrasteinlauf barium enema
Kontrastflüssigkeit radiopaque fluid
kontrastgebend opacifying
Kontrastmittel contrast medium
Kontrolle control, check up (a)
kontrollieren to control
Kontrollperson control subject
kontrovers controversial
Kontur contour
konturiert contoured
Kontusion contusion
Konus cone
konvergent convergent
Konvergenz convergence
Konversion conversion
konvex convex
Konvexität convexity
Konzentrat concentrate
Konzentration concentration
Konzentrationsvermögen concentrating ability
Konzentrationsversuch concentration test
konzentrieren to concentrate
konzentrisch concentric
Koordination coordination
koordinieren to coordinate
Kopf head
Kopfbiß (dent.) edge-to-edge bite
Kopfhaut, behaarte scalp
Kopflaus head louse

Kopflicht headlight
Kopfschmerzen headache
kopiös copious
Koplikschhe Flecken Koplik's spots
Koprämie copraemia (e), copremia (a)
koprophil coprophilous
Koprophilie coprophilia
Koproporphyrin coproporphyrin
Koprosterin coprostanol
korakoakromial coracoacromial
korakoklavikular coracoclavicular
Korkzieherarterie corkscrew artery
Kormoran shag (zool.)
Kornutin cornutine
Kornzange dressing forceps
koronar coronary
Koronaritis coronaritis
korpulent corpulent
Korpulenz corpulency
Korpuskel corpuscle
korpuskulär corpuscular
Korrelation correlation
korrelativ correlative
Korrigens corrigent
korrigierend corrigent
Korrosion corrosion
korrosiv corrosive
Korsakoffsche Psychose Korsakoff's psychosis
Korsett corset
kortikal cortical
kortikomedullär corticomedullary
kortikospinal corticospinal
Kortikosteroid corticosteroid
Kortikosteron corticosterone
kortikotrop corticotropic
Kortikotropin adrenocorticotropic hormone
Kosmetik cosmetics, cosmesis
kosmetisch cosmetic
kosmetisches Mittel cosmetic
kosmisch cosmic
Kost food, nourishment
kostovertebral costovertebral
Kot faeces (e), feces (a), excrement

Kotarnin cotarnine
Koteinklemmung impacted faeces (e), impacted feces (a)
Kotfistel bowel fistula
kotig miry
Kotstein stercolith, coprolith
Kozymase cozymase
kräftig strong
kräftigen to strengthen
kränkeln to be sickly
kränklich sickly
Krätze scabies, itch
Krätzeheilmittel scabieticide
Krätzemilbe Sarcoptes scabiei
Krätzephobie acarophobia
Kräuterbuch herbal
Kraft force, strength
Kraftmesser sthenometer
Kraftsteigerung reinforcement
Kraftstoff fuel
Kralle claw, talon
Krallenheber claw elevator
Kramerschiene wire ladder
Krampf cramp, convulsion, spasm
Krampfader varicose vein
Krampfaderverödung cirsenchysis, sclerosing treatment of varicose veins
Krampfanfall convulsive attack
krampfauslösend convulsant
krampfhaft convulsive, spasmodic
krampflösend spasmolytic
Krampfmittel convulsant
Krampusneurose crampus neurosis
kranial cranial
Kraniektomie craniectomy
kraniokaudal craniocaudal
Kranioklast cranioclast
kraniopharyngeal craniopharyngeal
Kraniopharyngiom craniopharyngioma
Kraniotabes craniotabes
Kraniotomie craniotomy
kraniozerebral craniocerebral
krank sick
krank (prädikativ) ill
krank (von Körperteilen) diseased
krank fühlen, sich to feel ill
krank sein to be ill (e), to be sick (a)
krank sein an to suffer from
Kranke sick, patient
kranken to suffer
Krankenabteilung clinical department
Krankenanstalt hospital
Krankenbericht doctor's report
Krankenbett sick-bed
Krankenblatt clinical history
Krankenfahrstuhl invalid wheel chair
Krankengeld sick-benefit
Krankengeschichte case history
Krankenhaus hospital
Krankenhausärztin, behandelnde resident
Krankenhausarzt, behandelnder resident
Krankenhausaufnahme hospitalization, admission to the hospital
Krankenhaus, aufnehmen in ein – to hospitalize
Krankenhausbelegärztin extern
Krankenhausbelegarzt extern
Krankenhaushilfsärztin intern
Krankenhaushilfsarzt intern
Krankenhaus, einliefern in ein to hospitalize
Krankenpflege nursing
Krankenpflegeperson nurse
Krankenpflegerin nurse
Krankenpflegeschule school of nursing
Krankensaal ward
Krankenschein sick certificate
Krankenschwester nurse
Krankenstation ward
Krankenversicherung sick insurance
Krankenwagen ambulance
Krankenwärter orderly
Kranker sick, patient

kranker Sinusknoten-Syndrom
  sick sinus syndrome
Krankheit (= fehlende Gesundheit) illness
Krankheit (mit näherer Bezeichnung) disease
Krankheit (= Gebrechen, Siechtum) sickness
Krankheit (= leichte Gesundheitsstörung) ailment
Krankheitsbericht doctor's report
Krankheitserreger morbific agent
Krankheitserscheinung sign of the disease
Krankheit, sich eine – zuziehen
  to contract a disease
Krankheitsstoff morbid matter
Krankheitsverlauf clinical course
Krankheitszeichen sign of disease
krankmachend morbific
krank werden to fall ill
Krater crater
kratzen to scratch
Kraurose kraurosis
Kraut herb
Kreatin creatine
Kreatinin creatinine
kreativ creative
Kreativität creativity
Kreatur creature
Krebs (med.) carcinoma, cancer
krebsartig cancerous
krebserzeugend carcinogenic
Kreide chalk
Kreis circle
kreisförmig circinate
Kreiskrankenhaus regional hospital
Kreislauf circulation
–, großer systemic circulation, greater circulation
–, kleiner pulmonary circulation, lesser circulation
kreißen to be in labor (a), to be in labour (e)
Kreißsaal birth room
Krematorium crematory
Kreosol creosol

Kreosot creosote
Krepitation crepitation
krepitierend crepitant
Kresol cresol
Kresolphthalein cresol phthalein
Kresolpurpur cresol purple
Kresolrot cresol red
Kresolseifenlösung saponated solution of cresol
Kresyl cresyl
Kretin cretin
Kretinismus cretinism
kreuzen to cross
kreuzlahm lame in the hip
Kreuzotter vipera berus
Kreuzprobe cross typing
Kreuzreaktion cross reaction
Kreuzschmerz low back pain, sacralgia
Kreuzschnitt cross section, transection
Kreuzung crossing; decussation
Kriechtier reptil
Krikoidektomie cricoidectomy
krikopharyngeal cricopharyngeal
Krikotomie cricotomy
kriminell criminal
Krise crisis
Krisis crisis
Kristall crystal
kristallisch crystalline
Kristallurie crystalluria
Kristellerscher Handgriff
  Kristeller's technic
Kritik critique
kritisch critical
Krönleinsche Operation
  Krönlein's operation
Kröte toad
Krokodil crocodil
Kromayerlampe Kromayer's lamp
Krone crown
–, Zahn- dental crown
Kronensetzer crown pusher
Kropf goitre, goiter, struma
–, Adoleszenten- adolescent goiter
–, Knoten- nodular goiter

kropferzeugend goitrogenous
kropfig goitrous
Krotonöl croton oil
Krücke crutch
Krümmung curve
Krüppel cripple
Krukenbergarm Krukenberg's arm
Krupp croup
kruppös croupous
Kruste crust, scab
Krustenbildung incrustation
Krustenentfernung decrustation
kryogen cryogenic
Krypte crypt
kryptisch cryptic
kryptogenetisch cryptogenetic
Kryptokokkose cryptococcosis
Krypton e. e.
Kryptorchismus cryptorchidism
Kubikmeter cubic meter
Kubikwurzel cube root
kubital cubital
Kübel bucket
Kücken chicken
Kückenruhr bacillary white diarrhea (a), bacillary white diarrhoea (e)
Kügelchen globule
kühl cool
Kühle cool
kühlen to cool
Kühlschrank refrigerator
Kühlung cooling, refrigeration
künstlich factitious, artificial
Kürette curet, curette
Küstersche Operation Küster's operation
Küstnersches Zeichen Küstner's sign
Kugelgelenk spheroid joint, diarthrosis
Kuh cow
Kuhhornschnabel cow horn beak
Kuhnsche Maske Kuhn's mask
Kuhpocken vaccinia
Kultivierung cultivation

Kultur culture
—,**bakteriologische** bacteriological culture
kulturell cultural
Kumarin coumarin
Kumulation cumulation
kumulativ cumulative
kumulieren to cumulate
Kumyß koumiss
Kunstglied artificial limb
Kunstprodukt artefact
Kunststoff plastics; resin
Kunstzahn pontic
Kupfer copper
Kupferdraht copper wire
Kupferdrahtarterie copper wire artery
Kupfersulfat cupric sulfate (a), cupric sulphate (e)
Kupffersche Sternzelle Kupffer's cell
Kuprein cupreine
Kur cure
Kurare curare
Kurarin curarine
Kurarisierung curarization
Kurmittel curative medium
Kurort health resort, salutarium
Kurs course
Kurvatur, große greater curvature
—,**kleine** lesser curvature
kurzatmig short-winded
Kurzatmigkeit short breath
Kurzbehandlung short-term therapy
Kurzschluß short circuit, shunt
kurzsichtig nearsighted, short-sighted
Kurzsichtigkeit shortsightedness
Kurzwelle short wave
kurzwirkend short-acting
Kurzzeitbehandlung short-term therapy
Kurzzeitgedächtnis short-term memory
Kußmaulsche Atmung Kußmaul-Kien respiration

Kwashiorkor e.e.
kybernetisch cybernetic
Kymogramm kymogram
Kymograph e.e.
Kymographie kymography
kymographisch kymographic

Kyphose kyphosis
Kyphoskoliose kyphoscoliosis
kyphoskoliotisch kyphoscoliotic
kyphotisch kyphotic
Kystadenom cystadenoma
Kystom cystoma

L

Labferment lab ferment
labial e.e.
labil labile
Labilität lability
labiodental e.e.
labionasal e.e.
Laborant laboratorian
Laborantin laboratorian
Laboratorium laboratory
Laborbefund laboratory report
Labung refreshment
Labyrinth e.e.
labyrinthär labyrinthine
Labyrinthektomie labyrinthectomy
Labyrinthitis e.e.
Labyrinthstörung labyrinthine disturbance
Lachen laugh
lachen to laugh
Lachgas laughing gas
Lackmus litmus
Lactam e.e.
Lactamase e.e.
Lactam e.e.
Lactobacillus acidophilus e.e.
– bifidus e.e.
– bulgaricus e.e.
laden to load
Ladung load, loading
lähmen to paralyze
Lähmung paralysis, palsy
ländlich rural
Laennecsche Zirrhose Laennec's cirrhosis

Läppchen lobule
Läppchenprobe patch test
Lärchenschwamm larch agaric
Lärm noise
Lärmapparat noise apparatus
Läsion lesion
Lävallorphan lacvallorphan (e), levallorphan (a)
Lävulose laevulose (e), levulose (a)
Lävulosurie laevulosuria (e), levulosuria (a)
Lage situation
Lagophthalmus lagophthalmos
lahm lame, paralytic
Laich spawn
Laie layman
laienhaft laical
Lakritze licorice (a), liquorice (e)
laktagog galactogogue
Laktagogum galactogogue
Laktalbumin lactalbumin
Laktat lactate
Laktatazidose lactic acidosis
Laktation lactation
Laktationshormon prolactin hormone, mammotropin
Laktazidogen lactacidogen
Laktobionat lactobionate
Laktoflavin riboflavin
laktogen lactogenic
Lakton lactone
Laktose lactose, milk sugar
laktotrop lactotropic
Laktulose lactulose

lakunär lacunar
Lakune lacuna
Lallen lalling
Lalophobie lalophobia
Laloplegie laloplegia
Lambdanaht lambdoid suture
Lamblia intestinalis e. e., Giardia lamblia
Lambliasis e. e.
lamellär lamellar
Lamelle lamella
Lamellenluftstrom laminar air flow
laminar e. e.
Laminariastift laminaria tent
Laminektomie laminectomy
Laminotomie laminotomy
Lamm lamb
lammen to lamb
Lampe lamp
Lamziekte e. e.
Landrysche Paralyse Landry's paralysis
langdauernd long-lasting
Langenbecksche Operation Langenbeck's operation
Langerhanssche Insel Langerhans' island
Langhanssche Zelle Langhans' cell
Langlebigkeit longevity
langsam wachsend growing slowly
Langwelle long wave
langwirkend long-acting
Langzeitbehandlung long-term therapy
Langzeitgedächtnis long-term memory
Lanolin e. e.
Lanolol e. e.
Lanthan lanthanum
Lanthanid lanthanide
Lanzette lancet
lanzinierend lancinating
Laparoskop laparoscope
Laparoskopie laparoscopy
laparoskopisch laparoscopical

Laparotomie laparotomy
laparotomieren to laparotomize
Lappen lobe, flap
Lappenmesser lobe knife
Lappenverschluß Collin's lock
Lappung lobulation
Larva migrans e. e.
Larve larva
Larvenvertilgungsmittel larvicide
larvieren to larvate
laryngeal e. e.
Laryngektomie laryngectomy
Laryngitis e. e.
laryngitisch laryngitic
Laryngographie laryngography
laryngographisch laryngographic
Laryngologe laryngologist
Laryngologie laryngology
Laryngologin laryngologist
laryngologisch laryngological
laryngopharyngeal e. e.
Laryngoskop laryngoscope
Laryngoskopie laryngoscopy
laryngoskopisch laryngoscopical
Laryngospasmus laryngospasm
Laryngostomie laryngostomy
Laryngotomie laryngotomy
Laryngotracheoskopie laryngotracheoscopy
Larynx e. e.
Larynxspasmus laryngospasm
Lasche tab
Lasèquesches Zeichen Lasèque's sign
LASER-Strahl LASER ray
Lassarsche Paste Lassar's paste
Last burden
latent e. e.
Latenz latency
Latenzzeit latency period, lag
Lateroposition e. e.
lateroventral e. e.
Latex-Tropfentest latex drop test
Lathyrismus lathyrism, lupinosis
Latrine e. e.
Latrodectismus latrodectism
Latwerge lincture

Laufzeit running time
Lauge lye
Lauryl e. e.
Laus louse, lice
Lavendel lavender
Laxans laxative
Laxativum laxative
laxierend laxative
Lazarett hospital
Lazarettzug ambulance train
Leben life
leben to live
lebend living
Lebensalter age
lebensbedrohlich life-threatening
Lebensdauer life span
Lebenserwartung expectation of life
lebensfähig viable
Lebensfähigkeit viability
Lebensgefahr danger to life
Lebensmittel food, victual
Lebensmittelvergiftung food poisoning
Lebensverlängerung lengthening of life
Lebensversicherung assurance
Lebensweise mode of living
Lebenszeichen sign of life
Leber liver
Leberabszeß liver abscess
Leberbiopsie liver biopsy
Leberegel liver fluke
Leberegelbefall clonorchiosis
Leberextrakt liver extract
Leberextraktinjektion liver injection
Leberfleck freckle
Leberfunktionsprüfung liver function test
leberkrank suffering from hepatic disease
Lebertherapie hepatotherapy
Lebertran cod liver oil
Leber- und Gallenwege hepatic and biliary ducts
Leberzirrhose, atrophische Laennec's cirrhosis
Leberzirrhose, hypertrophische hypertrophic cirrhosis of liver
leblos lifeless
Leblosigkeit lifelessness
Lecksein leakage
Lederersche Anämie Lederer's anaemia (e), Lederer's anemia (a)
Lederhaut corium
Lederhaut des Hufs pododerm
leer empty
Leerversuch blank test
Legalsche Probe Legal's test
Legierung alloy
Leguan iguana
leguminös leguminous
Lehrling apprentice
Leib body
Leibarzt physician in ordinary
Leibbinde belt, body bandage, body pad
Leibesbeschaffenheit constitution of the body
Leibesfrucht fetus (a), foetus (e)
Leibesgestalt stature
Leibesgröße stature
Leibesübung physical exercise
Leibschmerzen colic, stomachache
Leibwäsche underwear, body linen
Leichdorn clavus, corn
Leiche dead body, corpse, cadaver
Leichenbeschauer coroner
Leichenblut cadaver blood
Leichengeruch cadaverous smell
Leichengift poison of dead bodies
Leichennadel postmortem needle
Leichenöffnung postmortem examination
Leichenschau necropsy, autopsy
Leichenstarre cadaveric rigidity
Leichentuch shroud
Leichenverbrennung cremation
Leichenwachs adipocere, gravewax
leichtfertig frivolous
Leichtfertigkeit frivolity
leiden to suffer, to endure, to complain, to bear

Leiden suffering, complaint
Leinöl linseed oil
Leinsamen linseed
Leiomyom leiomyoma
Leiomyosarkom leiomyosarcoma
Leishmania donovani e. e.
Leishmaniose leishmaniasis
Leiste crest; shelf
Leiste (med.) groin
Leistenhernie inguinal hernia
Leistung performance; effect; output
leistungsfähig efficient
Leiter conductor
Leitfähigkeit conductivity
Leitgeschwindigkeit conduction velocity
Leitmaterial conducting matter
Leitungsanästhesie conduction anaesthesia (e), conduction anesthesia (a)
Lembertnaht Lembert's suture
Lemure lemur
Lende loin
Lendengegend lumbar region
Lendenwirbel lumbar vertebra
Lendenwirbelsäule lumbar spinal column
Lentigo e. e.
lentikulothalamisch lenticulo-thalamic
Leopard e. e.
Lepra leprosy
Lepra anaesthetica anaesthetic leprosy (e), anesthetic leprosy (a)
Lepra tuberosa nodular leprosy
Leprabazillus Mycobacterium leprae
leprös leprous
Leprom leproma
Leprosorium leprosary
Leptomeningitis e. e.
–,Staphylokokken- staphylococcic leptomeningitis
leptomeningitisch leptomeningitic
leptosom leptosomatic

Leptospira autumnalis e. e.
– canicola e. e.
– grippotyphosa e. e.
– icterogenes Leptospira icterohaemorrhagiae
Leptospirose leptospirosis
Leptothrix e. e.
lesbisch lesbian
lesbische Liebe lesbianism, sapphism
letal lethal
Letalität lethality
Lethargie lethargy
Letterer-Siwesche Krankheit Letterer-Siwe disease
Leucin leucine
Leucin-Aminopeptidase leucine aminopeptidase
Leukämie leukaemia (e), leukemia (a)
–,lymphatische lymphoblastic leukaemia (e), lymphoblastic leukemia (a)
–,myeloische myeloid leukaemia (e), myeloid leukemia (a)
leukämisch leukaemic (e), leukemic (a)
leukämoid leukaemoid (e), leukemoid (a)
Leukanämie leukanaemia (e), leukanemia (a)
Leukodermie leukoderma
Leukoenzephalitis leukoencephalitis
Leukom leukoma
Leukopenie leukopenia
leukopenisch leukopenic
Leukoplakie leukoplakia
Leukopoese leukopoiesis
leukopoetisch leukopoietic
Leukorrhöe leukorrhea (a), leukorrhoea (e)
Leukose leukosis
Leukotomie leukotomy
leukotoxisch leukotoxic
Leukotrichie leukotrichia
Leukozyt leukocyte, white blood cell

Leukozyt, basophiler basophil leukocyte
–, **eosinophiler** eosinophil leukocyte
–, **granulierter** granular leukocyte
–, **jugendlicher** juvenile leukocyte
–, **neutrophiler** neutrophil leukocyte
–, **polymorphkerniger** polymorphonuclear leukocyte
–, **segmentkerniger** segmented leukocyte
–, **stabkerniger** staff cell leukocyte
–, **ungranulierter** nongranular leukocyte
leukozytär leukocytic
Leukozytopenie leukocytopenia
Leukozytose leukocytosis
Levallorphan e. e.
Leydigsche Zwischenzelle Leydig's cell
L.E.-Zelle L.E. cell
Lezithin lecithin
Lezithinase lecithinase
libidinös libidinous
Libido e. e.
Libmann-Sacks-Syndrom Libmann-Sacks syndrome
Lichen e. e.
– **chronicus simplex** e. e.
– **nitidus** e. e.
– **ruber planus** e. e.
– **scrofulosus** lichen scrofulosus (a), lichen scrophulosus (e)
Lichenifizierung lichenification
lichenoid e. e.
Licht light
Lichtbad light bath
Lichtgeschwindigkeit velocity of light
Lichtkoagulation photocoagulation
Lichtscheu heliophobia
Lichtschwelle light threshold
lichtundurchlässig opaque
Lid e. e.
Liddrüsenentzündung sty, stye
Lidhalter lid retractor

Lidknorpel tarsus (of the lid)
Lidoflazin lidoflazine
Liebensche Probe Lieben's test
Lieberkühnsche Krypte Lieberkühn's crypt
Liegekur rest cure
lienal e. e.
Ligament e. e.
Ligamentum Gimbernati Gimbernat's ligament
Ligase e. e.
Ligatur ligature
Ligaturmesser ligature knife
ligieren to ligate
limbisch limbic
Lincomycin e. e.
Lindenblütentee lime-blossom tea
lindern to mitigate, to alleviate, to relieve
Linderung mitigation, alleviation, relief
Linderungsmittel lenitive
linear e. e.
Lingua geographica geographical tongue
– **scrotalis** scrotal tongue
lingual e. e.
Linguatula serrata e. e.
Linie line
Liniment e. e.
Linitis e. e.
linksdrehend laevorotatory (e), levorotatory (a), sinistrorotatory
Linksdrehung laevorotation (e), levorotation (a)
linkshändig left-handed
Linkshändigkeit left-handedness
Links-Rechts-Shunt left-to-right shunt
Linksverschiebung deviation to the left
Linoleat linoleate
Linolein e. e.
Linolensäure linolenic acid
Linolsäure linolic acid, linoleic acid
Linse lens

Linsenaufhängeapparat suspensory ligament of lens
Linsenerweichung phacomalacia
Linsentrübung phacoscotasmus, clouding of the lens
Liothyronin liothyronine
Lipämie lipaemia (e), lipemia (a)
lipämisch lipaemic (e), lipemic (a)
Lipid e. e.
Lipocaic-Faktor lipocaic factor
Lipochrom lipochrome
Lipodystrophie lipodystrophy
Lipofuscin e. e.
lipogen lipogenic
Lipogranulomatose lipogranulomatosis
Lipoid e. e.
lipoidal lipoid
Lipoidnephrose lipoid nephrosis
Lipoidose lipoidosis
Lipoidurie lipoiduria
Lipolyse lipolysis
lipolytisch lipolytic
Lipom lipoma
lipomatös lipomatous
Lipomatose lipomatosis
Lipomyom lipomyoma
Lipomyxom lipomyxoma
Lipopexie lipopexia
Lipophagie lipophagy
Lipophagozytose lipophagocytosis
lipophil e. e.
Lipoprotein e. e.
Liposarkom liposarcoma
Lipurie lipuria
lipurisch lipuric
Lippe (obere/untere) (upper/lower) lip
Lippenhalter lip retractor
Lippenplastik cheiloplasty, labioplasty
Liquor cerebrospinalis cerebrospinal fluid
Liquoreiweiß cerebrospinal fluid protein
Liquorrhöe liquorrhea (a), liquorrhoea (e)
Lisfrancsches Gelenk Lisfranc's joint
Listeria monocytogenes Listerella monocytogenes
Listeriose listerellosis
Literatur literature
Literaturübersicht bibliographical review
Literaturquelle literature source
Lithium e. e.
Lithiumoxalat lithium oxalate
Lithocholat lithocholate
Lithotripsie lithotripsy
Littlesche Krankheit Little's disease
Littresche Hernie Littre's hernia
Litzmannsche Obliquität Litzmann's obliquity
livid e. e.
Lizenz licence
lobär lobar
Lobärpneumonie lobar pneumonia
Lobektomie lobectomy
Lobelin lobeline
Lobotomie lobotomy
lobulär lobular
Loch hole
Locheisen punch
lochial e. e.
Lochien lochia
Lochiometra e. e.
Lochkarte punch card
Lochkartenverfahren punched card technique
locker slack
löchrig full of holes
Löffel spoon, ladle
—, scharfer sharp spoon, bone curette
Löffelzange scoop forceps
Löfflerfärbung Löffler's staining
Löschung cancellation
lösen to solve, to dissolve
lösend solvent

löslich soluble
Löslichkeit solubility
Lösung solution
Lösung, in − bringen
  to solubilize
Lösungsmittel solvent
löten to solder
Lötmittel solder
Löwe lion
Löwin lioness
Logarithmus logarithm
logisch logical
Logorrhöe logorrhea (a),
  logorrhoea (e)
lokal local
Lokalanästhesie local
  anaesthesia (e),
  local anesthesia (a)
Lokalisation localization
lokalisieren to localize
lokomotorisch locomotor
longitudinal e. e.
Longuette long compress
Lorazepam e. e.
Lordose lordosis
lordotisch lordotic
Loschmidtsche Konstante
  Avogadro's constant
loslösen to ablate, to detach
Luchs lynx
Lücke gap, breach
lüften to ventilate
Lüftung ventilation
Lues e. e.
Luetiker luetic
Luetikerin luetic
luetisch luetic
Luft air
Luftbad air bath
luftdicht air tight
Luftdruck air pressure
Lufteinblasung air inflation
Luftembolie air embolism
Luftfahrtmedizin aviation
  medicine
luftfahrtmedizinisch aeromedical
luftgekühlt air-cooled

Luftkissen air cushion
Luftröhre trachea, windpipe,
  weasand
Luftröhrenplastik tracheoplasty
Luftschlucken inructation
Luftweg airway
Lugolsche Lösung Lugol's solution
Lumbago e. e.
lumbal e. e.
Lumbalpunktion spinal puncture
Lumbalpunktionsnadel
  spinal puncture needle
lumbodorsal e. e.
lumbosakral lumbosacral
Lumen e. e.
Lumineszenz luminescence
Lunge lung
Lungenabszeß abscess of lung
Lungenblutung pulmonary
  haemorrhage (e), pulmonary
  hemorrhage (a)
Lungenegel Paragonimus
  westermani
Lungenemphysem pulmonary
  emphysema
Lungenentzündung pneumonia
Lungenfeld lung field
Lungenfunktionsprüfung
  pulmonary function test
Lungengangrän gangrene of the
  lung
Lungeninfarkt pulmonary
  infarction
Lungenlappen lobe of the lung
Lungenmalaria pneumopaludism
Lungenödem pulmonary edema
  (a), pulmonary oedema (e)
Lungenpest pneumonic plague
Lungenschwindsucht phthisis of
  the lungs
Lungentuberkulose tuberculosis of
  the lungs
Lungenvenentransposition
  anomalous pulmonary venous
  connection
Lungenvolumen lung volume
Lupe loupe, magnifying lens

lupoid e. e.
Lupus e. e.
– erythematodes lupus erythematosus
– erythematodes, generalisierter systemic lupus erythematosus
– pernio e. e.
– vulgaris e. e.
Lutein e. e.
luteinisieren to luteinize
Luteinisierung luteinization
Luteinisierungshormon luteinizing hormone
Lutembachersyndrom Lutembacher's syndrome
Luteohormon progesterone
Lutetium lutecium
Lux e. e.
Luxation e. e.
luxieren to luxate
Lycopodium e. e.
Lymphadenitis e. e.
lymphadenitisch lymphadenitic
Lymphadenom lymphadenoma
Lymphadenose lymphadenosis
–, aleukämische aleukaemic lymphadenosis (e), aleukemic lymphadenosis (a)
–, leukämische leukaemic lymphadenosis (e), leukemic lymphadenosis (a)
Lymphangiektasie lymphangiectasis
Lymphangioendotheliom lymphangioendothelioma
Lymphangiom lymphangioma
Lymphangiosarkom lymphangiosarcoma
Lymphangitis e. e.
lymphangitisch lymphangitic
lymphatisch lymphatic
Lymphatismus lymphatism
Lymphe lymph
Lymphgang lymphatic duct
Lymphgefäß lymphatic vessel
Lymphknoten lymph node
Lymphknotenerkrankung lymphadenopathy

Lymphoblast e. e.
lymphoblastisch lymphoblastic
Lymphoblastom lymphoblastoma
lymphogen lymphogenous
Lymphogranulom lymphogranuloma
Lymphogranuloma inguinale venereal lymphogranuloma
Lymphogranulomatose lymphogranulomatosis
lymphoid e. e.
Lymphoidozyt lymphoidocyte
Lymphologie lymphology
Lymphom lymphoma
Lymphom, nicht lymphogranulomatöses non Hodgkin lymphoma
lymphomatös lymphomatous
Lymphomatose lymphomatosis
Lymphopenie lymphopenia
lymphopenisch lymphopenic
Lymphopoese lymphopoiesis
lymphopoetisch lymphopoietic
Lymphorrhöe lymphorrhea (a), lymphorrhoea (e)
Lymphosarkom lymphosarcoma
Lymphosarkomatose lymphosarcomatosis
Lymphozyt lymphocyte
lymphozytär lymphocytic
Lymphozytopenie lymphocytopenia
Lymphozytopoese lymphocytopoiesis
Lymphozytose lymphocytosis
Lymphspalte lymphatic scissure
lyophil lyophile, lyophilic
lyophilisieren to lyophilize
Lyophilisierung lyophilization
lyophob lyophobe
lyotrop lyotropic
Lyse lysis
Lysin e. e.
Lysis e. e.
Lysoform e. e.
Lysosom lysosome
Lysozym lysozyme
lytisch lytic

M

Made maggot
Madelungscher Fetthals Madelung's neck
Madenwurm seatworm, pinworm
madig maggotty
Madurafuß maduromycosis, mycetoma
Mähne (veter.) mane
Männchen male
männlich masculine, virile, male
Männlichkeit masculinity
mäßig moderate
Mäßigkeit frugality
Magen stomach
Magenatonie atony of stomach, stomachal atony
Magenaushebung removal of gastric juice
—, **fraktionierte** fractional removal of gastric juice
Magenbeschwerden indigestion
Magendarmallergie gastro-intestinal allergy
Magendrücken pressure on the stomach
Magenfistel gastric fistula
Magenfistelernährung gastrogavage
Magenfunktionsprüfung gastric function test
Magengeschwür gastric ulcer, ulcer of stomach
Magengrube pit of the stomach
Mageninhalt content of the stomach
Magenkrampf spasm of the stomach
Magenleiden stomach complaint
Magenneurose gastric neurosis
Magenpararauschbrand bradsot
Magensäure gastric acid
Magensaft gastric juice
Magenspülung gastric lavage
Magentropfen stomachic, digestive tonic
Magenverträglichkeit gastric tolerance
Magenverwachsung adhesion of stomach
mager meagre, lean
Magerkeit meagreness
Magermilch skim-milk
magistral e. e.
Magnesia e. e.
Magnesiamilch magma of magnesia
Magnesium e. e.
Magnesiumkarbonat magnesium carbonate
Magnesiumoxyd magnesium oxide
Magnesiumperoxyd hopogan
Magnesiumsulfat magnesium sulfate (a), magnesium sulphate (e)
Magnet e. e.
magnetisch magnetic
magnetisieren to magnetize
Magnetsonde magnet probe
Mahl meal
Mahlersches Zeichen Mahler's sign
Mahlzahn molar
Mahlzeit meal
Maische mash
Makroblast macroblast
Makrodontie macrodontia
Makroglobulin macroglobulin
Makroglobulinämie macroglobulinaemia (e), macroglobulinemia (a)
Makromelie macromelia
Makromolekül macromolecule
makromolekular macromolecular
makroskopisch macroscopic
Makrosomie macrosomy
makrozephal macrocephalous
Makrozyt macrocyte
makrozytär macrocytic
makulär macular

makulopapulös maculopapular
Mal mark, spot
Malachit malachite
Malaria e. e.
– **quartana** quartan malaria
– **quotidiana** quotidian malaria
– **subtertiana** subtertian malaria
– **tertiana** tertian malaria
– **tropica** tropical malaria
Malariafieber malarial fever, ague
Malariakachexie malarial cachexia, impaludism
Malariatherapie malariotherapy
Malat malate
Malazie malacia
malazisch malacic
Mal de Caderas mal de caderas
Maleat maleate
Maleimid maleimide
Malgaignesche Fraktur Malgaigne's fracture
Malgaignesche Hernie Malgaigne's hernia
maligne malignant
Malignität malignancy
Malignolipin e. e.
Malignom malignoma
Mallein e. e.
malleolär malleolar
Malleolus e. e.
Malleus e. e., glanders
Mallory-Weiss-Syndrom syndrome of Mallory-Weiss
Malokklusion malocclusion
Malonyl e. e.
Malpighisches Körperchen malpighian corpuscle
Maltafieber Malta fever
Maltase e. e.
Maltose e. e.
Malthusianismus malthusianism
Malum perforans pedis perforating ulcer of foot
Malum Pottii Pott's disease
Malz malt
Malzzucker maltose, malt sugar
mamillär mammillary

Mamille mammilla
Mamma e. e.
Mamma-Abtragung mastectomy
mammär mammary
Mammographie mammography
Mammotropin e. e.
Mandel (med.) tonsil
Mandelabszeß tonsillar abscess
Mandelat mandelate
Mandibula mandible
mandibulär mandibular
Mandlsche Lösung Mandl's solution
Mandrin e. e.
Mangan manganese
Mangansäure manganic acid
Mangel deficiency, lack, want
Mangelernährung subalimentation, malnutrition
Mangelkrankheit deficiency disease
mangeln to lack, to be wanting
Manie mania
manieriert affected
Manieriertheit affectedness
Manifestation e. e.
Manipulation e. e.
manisch manic
manisch-depressives Irresein manic-depressive psychosis
Mann man, male
mannbar virile
Mannbarkeit virility
Mannit mannitol
Mannokinase e. e.
Mannose e. e.
Manometer e. e.
manometrisch manometric
Manschette cuff
Mantoux-Probe Mantoux test
manuell manual
marantisch marantic, marasmic
Marasmus e. e.
Marfan-Syndrom Marfan syndrome
Margarine e. e.
marginal e. e.
Marihuana e. e.

Mark marrow, medulla
Marke mark
Markfibrose myelofibrosis
markieren to label
Markknochen marrow bone
Markkultur medulloculture
marklos unmedullated
Marmorisierung marmoration
Marmorknochenkrankheit marble bones disease
Marsupialisation marsupialization
Masche mesh
Masern measles
MASER-Strahl MASER ray
Maske mask
maskieren to mask
maskiert masked
maskulinisieren to masculinize
Masochismus masochism
Masochist e. e.
Masochistin masochist
masochistisch masochistic
Maß measure
Massage e. e.
Masse mass; bulk
massenhaft numerous
Massenwirkungsgesetz law of mass action
Masseur e. e.
Masseuse e. e.
massieren to massage
massiv massive
Maßlosigkeit intemperance
Mastdarm rectum
Mastdarmbiopsie rectal biopsy
Mastdarmbiopsiezange rectal biopsy forceps
Mastektomie mastectomy
mastikatorisch masticatory
Mastitis e. e.
mastitisch mastitic
Mastix mastic
Mastixreaktion mastic test
Mastkur gavage, superalimentation
Mastodynie mastodynia
Mastoid e. e.
mastoidal e. e.

Mastoidektomie mastoidectomy
Mastoiditis e. e.
Mastoidotomie mastoidotomy
Mastoidotympanektomie mastoidotympanectomy
Mastopathie mastopathy
Mastoptose mastoptosis
Mastose mastosis
Mastotomie mastotomy
Mastozyt mastocyte
Mastozytose mastocytosis
Masturbation e. e.
masturbieren to masturbate
Mastzelle mast cell
Material e. e.
materiell material
Mathematiker mathematician
Mathematikerin mathematician
mathematisch mathematical
Matrize matrix
matt feeble
Mattigkeit exhaustion
Mauke malanders
Maultier mule
Maul- und Klauenseuche foot- and mouth disease
Maulwurf mole
Maus mouse
Mauserung molting
Maxilla e. e.
maxillär maxillary
maxillofazial maxillofacial
maxillomandibulär maxillomandibular
maximal e. e.
maximal zulässige Konzentration maximal allowable concentration
Maximum e. e.
Mazeration maceration
mazerieren to macerate
McBurneyscher Punkt McBurney's point
Mebanazin mebanazine
Mechanik mechanics
mechanisch mechanical
Mechanismus mechanism

Mechanotherapie mechanotherapy
Meckelsches Divertikel Meckel's diverticulum
Meclizin meclizine
medial e. e.
medialwärts mediad
median e. e.
medianwärts mesad
mediastinal e. e.
Mediastinitis e. e.
Mediastinoperikarditis mediastinopericarditis
Mediastinoskopie mediastinoscopy
Mediastinum e. e.
Medikation medication
medikolegal medicolegal
medikomechanisch medicomechanical
mediokarpal midcarpal
Medioklavikularlinie midclavicula line
mediolateral e. e.
Medium e. e.
Medizin medicine
Medizinalassistent intern
Medizinalassistentin intern
Medizinalbad medicated bath
Medizingeschichte history of medicine
medizinisch medicinal
medizinisch-technisch medicotechnical
Medroxyprogesteron medroxyprogesterone
Medulla e. e.
medullär medullary
Medulloblast e. e.
Medulloblastom medulloblastoma
Meerrettich horseradish
Meerschweinchen guinea-pig
Megabulbus justo-major bulb
Megahertz e. e.
Megakaryoblast e. e.
Megakaryozyt megakaryocyte
Megakolon megacolon

Megaloblast e. e.
Megaloblastenanämie megaloblastic anaemia (e), megaloblastic anemia (a)
Megaloblastose megaloblastosis
Megalozyt megalocyte
megalozytär megalocytic
Megalozytose megalocytosis
Mehl flour, farina
mehlig farinaceous
Mehltau mildew
Mehrgebärende multipara
Mehrkanalsystem multi-channel system
mehrkernig multinuclear
mehrphasig multiphasic
Mehrzweck multipurpose
Meibomsche Drüse meibomian gland
Meigs-Syndrom syndrome of Meigs
Meile mile
Meinickereaktion Meinicke reaction
Meißel chisel
Meißnerscher Plexus Meissner's plexus
Mekamylamin mecamylamine
Mekonium meconium
Melaena melaena (e), melena (a)
Melancholie melancholia
melancholisch melancholiac
Melanin e. e.
Melanoblast e. e.
Melanoblastom melanoblastoma
Melanodermie melanoderma
Melanogen e. e.
melanogen melanogenic
Melanokarzinom melanocarcinoma
Melanom melanoma
Melanosarkom melanosarcoma
Melanose melanosis
melanotisch melanotic
Melanotrichia linguae black tongue
Melanotrichie melanotrichia
Melanozyt melanocyte
Melanurie melanuria

Melasma e. e.
meldepflichtig certifiable
Melisse melissa
Melorheostose melorheostosis
Membran membrane
membranös membranous
Menadion menadione
Menarche e. e.
Mendel-Bechterewscher Reflex
 Mendel's reflex
Mendel-Mantouxprobe
 Mendel-Mantoux test
mendeln to mendelize
Mendelsches Gesetz
 Mendel's law
Menge multitude; quantity
Menge-Pessar Menge's pessary
Ménièrescher Symptomenkomplex
 Ménière's syndrome
meningeal e. e.
Meningeom meningioma
Meningismus meningism
Meningitis e. e.
 —, **akute aseptische** acute aseptic meningitis
 —, **eitrige** purulent meningitis
 —, **epidemische** epidemic cerebrospinal meningitis
 —, **lymphozytäre** lymphocytic meningitis
 —, **seröse** serous meningitis
 —, **tuberkulöse** tuberculous meningitis
 —, **Virus-** virus meningitis
meningitisch meningitic
Meningoenzephalitis
 meningoencephalitis
Meningoenzephalomyelitis
 meningoencephalomyelitis
Meningokokkenserum
 antimeningococcic serum
Meningokokkus Neisseria intracellularis, meningococcus
meningovaskulär meningovascular
Meningozele meningocele
Meniskotomie meniscotomy

Meniskusdislokation am Knie
 dislocation of articular cartilage of the knee
Meniskusmesser meniscotomy knife
Meniskusoperation meniscotomy
Menometrorrhagie
 menometrorrhagia
Menopause e. e.
Menorrhagie menorrhagia
menschlich human
Menschlichkeit humanity
Mensingapessar Mensinga diaphragm
Menstruation e. e.
menstruell menstrual
menstruieren to menstruate
mental e. e.
Mentalität mentality
Menthol e. e.
mentoanterior e. e.
mentolabial e. e.
mentoposterior e. e.
Mepazin mepazine
Meperidin meperidine
Mephenesin e. e.
Meprobamat meprobamate
Mepyramin mepyramine
Meralgia paraesthetica e. e.
Meralgie meralgia
Meridian e. e.
meridional e. e.
Merkaptan mercaptan
Merkaptopurin mercaptopurine
Merkmal mark
Merkurialismus mercurialism
Merkurisalizylat
 mercuric salicylate
Merkurochlorid
 mercurous chloride
merokrin merocrine
Merseburger Trias Merseburg triad
Merzbacher-Pelizaeussche Krankheit
 Merzbacher-Pelizaeus disease
Mesaortitis e. e., mesoaortitis
Mesenchym mesenchyma

mesenchymal e. e.
mesenterisch mesenteric
Mesenterium mesentery
mesenzephal mesencephalic
Mesenzephalitis mesencephalitis
mesial e. e.
mesioangulär mesioangular
mesiobukkal mesiobuccal
mesiodistal e. e.
mesiolingual e. e.
mesiookklusal mesioocclusal
Meskalin mezcaline
Mesobilirubin e. e.
Mesobilirubinogen e. e.
Mesoblast e. e.
Mesoderm e. e.
mesodermal e.e.
mesodiastolisch mesodiastolic
mesodienzephal mesodiencephalic
Mesoinosit mesoinositol
Mesometritis e.e.
mesosystolisch mesosystolic
Mesotheliom mesothelioma
Mesothelium e. e.
Mesoxalylharnstoff mesoxalyl urea
messen to measure
Messer knife
Messerbänkchen knife rack
Messerstich stab wit a knife
Meßstelle measuring point
Messung measurement, mensuration
Mesterolon mesterolone
metabolisch metabolic
Metabolit metabolite
Metachromasie metachromasia
metachromatisch metachromatic
Metahexamid metahexamide
metakarpal metacarpal
Metall metal
Metallfüllung, gegossene (dent.) inlay
metallisch metallic
Metalloid e. e.
Metallständer metal rack
Metallurgie metallurgy
Metamorphose metamorphosis

Metamyelozyt metamyelocyte
Metanilgelb metaniline yellow
Metaphyse metaphysis
Metaplasie metaplasia
metaplastisch metaplastic
metapneumonisch metapneumonic
Metastase metastasis
metastasieren to metastasize
metastatisch metastatic
Metasyphilis e. e.
metasyphilitisch metasyphilitic
metatarsal e. e.
Metatarsalgie metatarsalgia
Meteorologie meteorology
meteorologisch meteorological
Metformin e. e.
Methadon methadone
Methämoglobin methaemoglobin (e), methemoglobin (a)
Methaminodiazepoxid methaminodiazepoxide
Methamphetamin methamphetamine
Methan methane
Methandrostenolon methandrostenolone
Methanthelin methantheline
Methaqualon methaqualone
Methicillin e. e.
Methionin methionine
Methode method
Methodologie methodology
Methonium e. e.
Methopterin methopterine
Methopyrapon methopyrapone
Methotrexat methotrexate
Methoxamin methoxamine
Methylalkohol methanol
Methylase e. e.
Methylat methylate
Methylcholin methylcholine
Methyldimethoxyamphetamin methyldimethoxyamphetamine
Methyldopa methyl dopa
Methylen methylene
Methylenblau methylene blue, methylthionine chloride

Methylhydrocortison
  methylhydrocortisone
methylieren to methylate
Methylierung methylation
Methyljodid methyliodide
Methylorange methyl orange
Methylphenidylat
  methylphenidylate
Methylphenylhydrazin
  methylphenylhydrazine
Methylprednisolon methyl-
  prednisolone
Methylrosanilin e. e.
Methylrot methyl red
Methylthiouracil methyl thiouracil
Methyltransferase e. e.
Methylviolett methyl violet
Metiamid metiamide
Metoclopramid metoclopramide
Metoprolol e. e.
Metrazol e. e.
Metreurynter e. e.
metrisch metric
Metritis e. e.
Metropathia haemorrhagica
  haemorrhagic metropathia (e),
  hemorrhagic metropathia (a)
Metropathia metropathia
metropathisch metropathic
Metrorrhagie metrorrhagia
Metrosalpingographie
  metrosalpingography
Metypranol e. e.
Mezlocillin e. e.
Michaelissche Raute
  Michaelis rhomboid
Migräne migraine
Mikroanalyse microanalysis
mikroanalytisch microanalytic
Mikroaneurysma microaneurysm
Mikrobe microbe
Mikrobestimmung micro-
  determination
mikrobiell microbial
Mikrobiologie microbiology
mikrobiologisch microbiological
Mikrobulbus justo-minor bulb

Mikrochemie microchemistry
mikrochemisch microchemical
Mikrococcus micrococcus
Mikrocurie microcurie
Mikrodontie microdontia
Mikroelektrode microelectrode
Mikroelektrophorese micro-
  electrophoresis
Mikroelement microelement
Mikroflockung microflocculation
Mikroglia microglia
Mikrogliomatose microgliomatosis
Mikrogramm microgram
Mikroheiztisch microheating
  table apparatus
Mikroinjektion microinjection
Mikrokörper microbody
Mikrokokkus micrococcus
– **tetragenus** Gaffkya tetragena
Mikroliter microliter
Mikromelie micromelia
Mikrometer micrometer
Mikromethode micromethod
Mikromolekül micromolecule
mikromolekular micromolecular
Mikron micron
Mikroorganismus microorganism
Mikrophon microphone
Mikrophthalmie microphthalmia
Mikrophysik microphysics
Mikropinozytose micropinocytosis
Mikropsie micropsia
Mikropunktion micropuncture
Mikroquantität microquantity
Mikroradiologie microradiology
mikroradiologisch microradio-
  logical
Mikroreaktion microreaction
**Mikroskop (binokuläres/
  monokuläres)** (binocular/
  monocular) microscope
Mikroskopie microscopy
Mikroskopiebesteck
  microscopic set
mikroskopisch microscopic
mikroskopisch untersuchen
  to examine by the microscope

Mikrosom microsom
mikrosomal microsomal
Mikrosporon Audouini Microsporon audouini
— **furfur** Microsporon furfur
— **mentagrophytes** Microsporon mentagrophytes
— **minutissimum** Microsporon minutissimum
Mikrotubulus microtubule
mikrozephal microcephalic
Mikrozephalie microcephalia
Mikrozirkulation microcirculation
Mikrozyt mikrocyte
mikrozytär microcytic
Mikrozytose microcytosis
Miktion miction, micturition
Miktionsstörung micturition disorder
Mikuliczsche Krankheit Mikulicz's disease
Mikuliczsche Zelle Mikulicz's cell
Milbe mite
Milbenseuche der Biene Isle of Wight disease
Milch milk
Milch-Alkali-Syndrom burnett syndrome
milchbildend lactigenous
Milchbrustgang thoratic duct
Milchgangentzündung galactophoritis
Milchgebiß milk teeth
milchig milky
Milchkrankheit trembles
Milchpumpe breast pump
Milchstauung galactostasis
milchtreibend lactogenic, galactogogue
milchtreibendes Mittel galactogogue
Milchzahn temporary tooth
Milchzucker milk sugar
miliar miliary
Miliaria cristallina miliaria crystallina
Miliaria rubra e. e.

Miliartuberkulose miliary tuberculosis
Milieu surroundings, environment, peristasis
Milium e. e.
Milkman-Syndrom Milkman's syndrome
Miller-Abbottsonde Miller-Abbott tube
Milliampère milliampere
Millibar e. e.
Millicurie e. e.
Milligramm milligram
Milliliter e. e.
Millimikron millimicron
Millimol e. e.
Millivolt e. e.
Millonsche Probe Millon's test
Milz spleen
Milzbrand anthrax
Milzruptur rupture of spleen
mimetisch mimetic
Mineral e. e.
Mineralbad mineral bath
mineralisch mineral
Mineralisierung mineralization
Mineralöl mineral oil
Mineralokortikoid mineralocorticoid
Mineralsalz mineral salt
minimal e. e.
Minimum e. e.
Minocyclin e. e.
Minoxidil e. e.
Minutenvolumen minute volume
Miosis e. e.
Miotikum miotic
miotisch miotic
Miraculin e. e.
mischbar miscible
Mischbarkeit miscibility
mischen to mix
Mischinfektion mixed infection
Mischung mixture; medley
Mißbildung malformation, deformity; teratism, monster
Mißbrauch abuse, misuse

Mißerfolg failure
Mißgeburt monster
mißhandeln to maltreat
Mißhandlung maltreatment
mißtrauisch suspicious
Mißverhältnis disproportion
Mistel mistletoe
Mitarbeiter coworker
Mitarbeiterin coworker
Mitella e. e.
Mitesser blackhead
mitochondrial e. e.
Mitochondrien mitochondria
Mitose mitosis
mitotisch mitotic
Mitralinsuffizienz mitral insufficiency
Mitralklappe mitral valve
Mitralstenose mitral stenosis
Mitteilung, persönliche personal communication
Mittelbauch middle abdomen
Mittelfinger middle finger
Mittelhirn midbrain
Mittellage middle position
Mittelmeeranämie erythroblastic anaemia (e), erythroblastic anemia (a)
Mittelohr middle ear
Mittelpunkt middle point, center
Mittelschmerz midpain
Mittelstrahlharn midstream urine
Mittelwert mean
Mixtur mixture
Miyagawanella e. e.
Mnemotechnik mnemonics
mobil mobile
mobilisieren to mobilize
Mobilisierung mobilization
Mobilität mobility
Modalität modality
Modell, anatomisches manikin
Modellierinstrument modelling instrument, carver
Modifikation modification
modifizieren to modify
Modulation e. e.

modulieren to modulate
Möbiussches Zeichen Möbius' sign
Moeller-Barlowsche Krankheit Moeller-Barlow disease, infantile scurvy
Mönckebergsche Sklerose Mönckeberg's sclerosis
Mörser mortar
Mol e. e.
Molalität molality
Molar e. e.
molar e. e.
Molarität molarity
Mole e. e.
—, Blasen- hydatid mole
—, Blut- blood mole
—, Fleisch- fleshy mole
Molekül molecule
molekular molecular
Molekulargewicht molecular weight
Molke whey
Mollsche Drüse Moll's gland
Mollusca e. e.
Molluscum contagiosum e. e.
molluskizid molluscicidal
Molsidomin molsidomine
Molybdän molybdenum
molybdänhaltig (dreiwertig) molybdous
molybdänhaltig (sechswertig) molybdic
Molybdat molybdate
momentan instantaneous
Monakowsches Bündel Monakow's fasciculus
Monaldidrainage Monaldi's drainage
Monamid monamide
Monamin monamine
Monaminoxydase amine oxidase
monamniotisch monamniotic
Monarthritis e. e.
monartikulär monarticular
monatlich monthly, mensual
Monatsbinde receiver, sanitary towel

Monatsblutung monthlies, menses
mondförmig moonshaped
Mondorsche Krankheit
  Mondor's disease
mondsüchtig moonstruck
Mongolismus mongolism
mongoloid e.e.
Monilia albicans e.e.
Moniliasis e.e.
Monitor e.e.
monobasisch monobasic
Monoblast e.e.
monochromatisch monochromatic
monochromatophil e.e.
monofaszikulär monofascicular
Monojodtyrosin monoiodotyrosine
monokulär monocular
Monomanie monomania
mononukleär mononuclear
Mononukleose mononucleosis
Mononukleotid mononucleotide
monophasisch monophasic
Monophosphat monophosphate
monoplasmatisch monoplasmatic
Monoplegie monoplegia
Monorchismus monorchidism,
  monorchism
Monosaccharid monosaccharide
monosomal e.e.
Monospeziesinsulin monospecies
  insulin
monosymptomatisch mono-
  symptomatic
monovalent e.e.
Monoxyd monoxide
monozygot monozygotic
Monozyt monocyte
monozytär monocytic
Monozytenleukämie
  monocytic leukaemia (a),
  monocytic leukemia (a)
Monozytose monocytosis
Monro-Richtersche Linie
  Monro-Richter line
Montgomeryesche Drüse
  Montgomery's gland
Moorbad moor bath

Moos moss
—,**Irländisches** Irish moss,
  carrageen
—,**Isländisches** Iceland moss,
  Cetraria islandica
moralisch ethical
Morax-Axenfeldscher Bazillus
  Haemophilus lacunatus (e),
  Hemophilus lacunatus (a)
Moraxella e.e.
morbid e.e.
Morbidität morbidity
Morbus abortus Bang
  abortus fever
— **Addison** Addison's disease
— **Basedow** Grave's disease
— **Boeck** sarcoid of Boeck
— **Crohn** Crohn's disease
— **Hodgkin** Hodgkin's disease
— **maculosus Werlhofi**
  thrombopenic purpura
— **Parkinson** Parkinson's disease
— **Roger** Roger's disease
Morchel morel
Mord murder
Morgagnisches Syndrom
  Morgagni's syndrome
morgendlich matutinal
moribund e.e.
Moroprobe Moro's test
Morphin morphine
Morphinbehandlung
  morphinization
Morphinismus morphinism
Morphinsucht morphinomania
Morphium morphine
Morphogenese morphogenesis
morphogenetisch morphogenetic
Morphologie morphology
morphologisch morphological
morphometrisch morphometric
Mortalität mortality
Morula e.e.
Morulation e.e.
Moschcowitz-Syndrom
  syndrome of Moschcowitz
Moskito mosquito

Moskitoklemme mosquito forceps
Motilität motility
Motivierung motivation
Motor e. e.
motorisch motorial
Mottenfraßnekrose piecemeal necrosis
Mucilago mucilage
Mucin e. e.
Mucinose mucinosis
Mucosa e.e.
Mucosa-Block mucosal block
Mückenvertilgungsmittel culicide
mündlich oral
Mündung orifice
münzenförmig nummiform
münzenförmige Lungenverschattung coin lesion of the lung
mütterlich maternal
mukös mucous
Mukopeptid mucopeptide
Mukopolysaccharid mucopolysaccharide
Mukoprotein mucoprotein
Mukosa mucous membrane, mucosa
Mukosa-Block mucosal block
Mukosaccharid mucosaccharide
mukostatisch mucostatic
Mukoviskidose mucoviscidosis
Mukozele mucocele
Mull e. e.
Mullbinde gauze bandage
multiartikulär multiarticular
multidisziplinär multidisciplinary
multifokal multifocal
multiglandulär multiglandular
multikapsulär multicapsular
multilobulär multilobular
multilokulär multilocular
multinukleär multinuclear
Multipara e. e., multiparous patient
multipel multiple
multiphasisch multiphasic
multiple Sklerose multiple sclerosis
multipolar e.e.
multivalent e.e.
Multivitamin e.e.

multizellulär multicellular
multizentrisch multicentric
multizentrische wissenschaftliche Arbeit multicenter study, multicentre study
multizystisch multicystic
Mumifizierung mummification
Mumps e. e., epidemic parotitis
Mund mouth
Mundatmung mouth breathing
Mundchirurgie oral surgery
Mundhöhle mouth cavity
Mundkeil oral wedge
Mundlampe mouth lamp
Mundpflege care of the mouth
Mundschutztuch mouth protection cloth
Mundsperrer mouth gag
Mundspiegel mouth mirror
Mundspülwasser gargle
Mundstück mouth piece
Mundtrockenheit mouth dryness
Mundulzeration canker
Mundwinkel labial angle
Mund-zu-Mund-Beatmung mouth-to-mouth insufflation
Mund-zu-Nase-Beatmung mouth-to-nose insufflation
mural e. e.
Muramidase e. e.
Murexid murexide
Murexidprobe murexide test
muriatisch muriatic
musikalisch musical
Muskarin muscarine
Muskatnuß nutmeg
Muskel muscle
—,**glatter** smooth muscle
—,**quergestreifter** striated muscle
Muskelatrophie muscular atrophy
Muskeldystrophie myodystrophy
muskelelektrisch myoelectric
Muskelflimmern muscular fibrillation
Muskelhaken hook retractor
Muskelhernie muscular hernia
Muskelkraft muscular strength

Muskelplastik myoplasty
Muskelrheumatismus
  muscular rheumatism
Muskelspannung muscular tension
Muskelspasmus myospasm
muskulär muscular
Muskulatur musculature
 –,**glatte** smooth musculature
 –,**quergestreifte** striated
  musculature
muskulös musculous
muskulokutan musculocutaneous
muskulomembranös musculo-
  membranous
Musselin muslin
Musselinbinde muslin bandage
Mutagenese mutagenesis
Mutase e. e.
Mutation e. e.
Mutter mother
 –,**werdende** expectant mother
Mutterkuchen maza
Muttermal mother's mark
Muttermilch mother's milk
Mutterschaft maternity
Muzinose mucinosis
Myalgie myalgia
Myasthenia gravis pseudoparalytica
  myasthenia gravis
myasthenisch myasthenic
Myatonie myatonia
Myatrophie myatrophy
myatrophisch myatrophic
Mycobacterium leprae e. e.
 – **smegmatis** e. e.
 – **tuberculosis** e. e.
 – – **avium** e. e.
 – – **bovis** e. e.
Mycoplasma e. e.
Mycosis fungoides e. e.
Mydriasis e. e.
Mydriatikum mydriatic
mydriatisch mydriatic
Myektomie myectomy
Myelin e. e.
Myelinisierung myelinization
Myelitis e. e.

myelitisch myelitic
Myeloblast e. e.
Myeloblastose myeloblastosis
Myelodysplasie myeolodysplasia
myelogen myelogenous
Myelogenese myelogenesis
Myelogramm myelogram
Myelographie myelography
myelographisch myelographical
myeloid e. e.
Myelom myeloma
Myelomalazie myelomalacia
Myelomatose myelomatosis
Myelopathie myelopathy
Myelophthise myelophthisis
Myelosarkom myelosarcoma
Myelose myelosis
 –,**aleukämische**
  aleukaemic myelosis (e),
  aleukemic myelosis (a)
 –,**funikuläre** funicular myelosis
 –,**leukämische** leukaemic myelosis
  (e), leukemic myelosis (a)
Myelosklerose myelosclerosis
Myelotomie myelotomy
Myelozele myelocele
Myelozyt myelocyte
Mykologe mycologist
Mykologie mycology
Mykologin mycologist
mykologisch mycological
Mykose mycosis
mykotisch mycotic
Mykotoxin mycotoxin
myoarchitektonisch myo-
  architectonic
Myoblast e. e.
Myodegeneration e. e.
Myofibrille myofibril
Myofibrom myofibroma
Myofibrose myofibrosis
Myogelose myogelosis
myogen myogenous
Myoglobin e. e.
Myoglobinurie myoglobinuria
Myoglobulin e. e.
Myographie myography

Myohämoglobin myohaemoglobin (e), myohemoglobin (a)
Myokard myocardium
myokardial myocardial
Myokarditis myocarditis
myokarditisch myocarditic
Myokardschaden myocardial damage
Myoklonie myoclonia
myoklonisch myoclonic
Myoklonusepilepsie myoclonus epilepsy
Myolipom myolipoma
Myologie myology
Myolyse myolysis
Myom myoma
Myomalazie myomalacia
myomatös myomatous
Myomektomie myomectomy
Myometritis e. e.
Myomheber myoma screw
myoneural e. e.
Myoneurom myoneuroma
Myopathie myopathy
myopathisch myopathic
Myopie myopia
myopisch myopic
Myoplasma myoplasm
Myosarkom myosarcoma
Myosin e. e.
Myositis e. e.
– **ossificans** ossifying myositis
Myotomie myotomy
Myotonia congenita (Thomsen) myotonia congenita
Myotonie myotonia
myotonisch myotonic
Myringitis e. e.
Myringotomie myringotomy
Myristicin e. e.
Myrrhe myrrh
Myxadenom myxadenoma
Myxoblastom myxoblastoma
Myxochondrofibrosarkom myxochondrofibrosarcoma
Myxochondrom myxochondroma
Myxochondrosarkom myxochondrosarcoma
Myxolipom myxolipoma
Myxom myxoma
myxomatös myxomatous
Myxomatose myxomatosis
Myxomyom myxomyoma
Myxoneurom myxoneuroma
Myxoneurose myxoneurosis
Myxosarkom myxosarcoma
Myxovirus e. e.
Myxödem myxedema (a), myxoedema (e)
myxödematös myxedematous (a), myxoedematous (e)
Myxoendotheliom myxoendothelioma
Myxofibrom myxofibroma
Myxofibrosarkom myxofibrosarcoma
Myxogliom myxoglioma
Myzel mycelium

N

Nabel navel
Nabelbinde umbilical band
Nabelbruch umbilical hernia
Nabelschnur umbilical cord
Nabelschnurblut cord blood
Nachbarorgan adjacent organ
Nachbehandlung aftertreatment
Nachbelastung afterload
Nachbild after-image

Nachblutung posthaemorrhage (e), posthemorrhage (a), after-bleeding
nachdenklich thoughtful
Nachdenklichkeit thoughtfulness
Nacherregung after-discharge
Nachfolge succession
nachfolgend subsequent
Nachgeburt after-birth
Nachgeburtsblutung post-partum haemorrhage (e), post-partum hemorrhage (a)
Nachhinken lagging
Nachhirn myelencephalon, after-brain
Nachkomme descendant
Nachkommenschaft offspring
Nachkondensation after-condensation
Nachkur completion of a cure
Nachlassen abatement, relief
Nachoperation re-operation
nachoperieren to re-operate
Nachprüfung after-examination
Nachreflex rebound
Nachtarbeit night work
Nachtblindheit nyctalopia, night blindness
Nachtessersyndrom night eating syndrome
Nachtschmerz nyctalgia
Nachtschweiß nightsweats
Nachtwache night watch, vigil
nachuntersuchen to post-examine
Nachuntersuchung after-examination
Nachwehen after-pains
Nachwirkung after-effect
Nachwuchs after-growth
Nachwuchserzeugung procreation
Nacken nape
nackt nude, naked
Nacktheit nudity
Nadel needle
Nadelbiopsie needle biopsy
Nadel, chirurgische suture needle
Nadelhalter needle holder

Nadel, Unterbindungs- ligature needle
nächtlich nocturnal
Nägelebecken Nägele's pelvis
Nägelesche Obliquität Nägele's obliquity
Nähen suturation
nähen to sew
Nährboden culture medium
nähren to nourish
nährend nutrient
Nährkraft nutritive power
Nährstoff nutritive material
Nährwert nutritive quality
nässen to wet, to moisten
Naevus naevus (e), nevus (a)
Nagana e. e.
Nagel nail
—,eingewachsener ingrowing nail
Nagelbett nail bed
Nagelfalz nail fold
Nagelfeile nail file
nageln to nail
Nagelreiniger nail cleaner
Nagelschere nail scissors
Nageltritt (veter.) picked-up nail
Nagelwall nail wall
Nagelwurzel nail root
Nagelzange nail clipper
Nagelzieher nail extractor
nagen to nibble
Nagetier rodent
Nahbestrahlung short distance irradiation
nahrhaft nourishing, nutritious, nutritive
Nahrhaftigkeit nutritiousness
Nahrung food, nourishment
Nahrungsaufnahme ingestion
Nahrungsmittel food
Nahrungsmittelallergie food allergy
Nahrungsmittelentzug starvation
Naht suture, seam
—,Bleiplatten- lead plate suture
—,Einzel- interrupted suture
—,fortlaufende continued suture

Naht, Gussenbauersche Gussenbauer's suture
—, **Knopf-** button suture
—, **Lembert-** Lembert's suture
—, **Nerven-** nerve suture
—, **Primär-** primary suture
—, **Sekundär-** secondary suture
—, **Tabaksbeutel-** tobacco bag suture
—, **versenkte** sunk suture
nahtlos sutureless
Naloxon naloxone
Nandrolon nandrolone
Nanogramm nanogram
Naphthalin naphthalene
Naphthidin naphthidine
Naphthochinon naphthoquinone
Naphtholphthalein e. e.
Naphtholviolett naphthol violet
Naphthyl e. e.
Naproxen e. e.
Narbe scar
narbenähnlich uloid
Narbenbildung cicatrization
Narbenkontraktur cicatricial contracture
Narbenverunstaltung cicatricial deformity
narbig scarred, cicatricial
Narcotin narcotine
Narcylen e. e.
Narkoanalyse narcoanalysis
Narkolepsie narcolepsy
narkoleptisch narcoleptic
Narkose narcosis
—, **endotracheale** endotracheal anaesthesia (e), endotracheal anesthesia (a)
Narkoseäther ether for anaesthesia (e), ether for anesthesia (a)
Narkoseapparat anaesthetic apparatus (e), anesthetic apparatus (a)
Narkosemaske anaesthetic inhaler (e), anesthetic inhaler (a)
Narkosetubus anaesthesia tube (e), anesthesia tube (a)

Narkotikum narcotic
narkotisch narcotic
Narkotiseur anaesthetist (e), anesthetist (a)
narkotisieren to narcotize, to anaesthetize (e), to anesthetize (a)
Narzißmus narcissism
narzißtisch narcissistic
nasal e. e.
Nase nose
Nasenbein nasal bone
Nasenbluten nosebleed
Nasendeformität deformity of the nose
Nasenflügel wing of the nose
Nasenknochenhautelevator nasal periosteal elevator
Nasenloch nostril
Nasenmuschel turbinal, turbinated bone
Nasennebenhöhle paranasal sinus
Nasenplastik rhinoplasty
Nasenschleim nasal mucus
Nasenschleimhautpolyp mucous polypus of the nose
Nasenschlinge nasal snare
Nasenspitze tip of the nose
Nasentamponpinzette nasal dressing forceps
Nashorn rhinoceros
nasoalveolär nasoalveolar
nasolabial e. e.
nasopalatinal nasopalatine
nasopharyngeal e. e.
Nasopharyngitis e. e.
nasotracheal e. e.
naß wet
Natamycin e. e.
Natrium sodium
Natriumbenzoat sodium benzoate
Natriumbikarbonat sodium bicarbonate
Natriumbiphosphat sodium biphosphate
Natriumbisulfat sodium bisulfate (a), sodium bisulphate (e)

Natriumbisulfit sodium bisulfite (a), sodium bisulphite (e)
Natriumborat sodium borate
Natriumbromid sodium bromide
Natriumchlorid sodium chloride
Natriumfluoreszein sodium fluorescein
Natriumhydroxyd sodium hydroxide
Natriumhypochlorit sodium hypochlorite
Natriumhyposulfit sodium hyposulfite (a), sodium hyposulphite (e)
Natrium, indigodisulfonsaures sodium indigotindisulfonate (a), sodium indigotindisulphonate (e)
Natriumjodid sodium iodide
Natriumkakodylat sodium cacodylate
Natriumkarbonat sodium carbonate
Natriummolybdat sodium molybdate
Natriumnitrat sodium nitrate
Natriumnitrit sodium nitrite
Natriumperborat sodium perborate
Natriumphosphat sodium phosphate
Natriumpyrophosphat sodium pyrophosphate
Natriumsalizylat sodium salicylate
Natriumsulfat sodium sulfate (a), sodium sulphate (e)
Natriumthiosulfat sodium thiosulfate (a), sodium thiosulphate (e)
Natriumzitrat sodium citrate
Natriurese natriuresis
Natron, doppeltkohlensaures bicarbonate of soda
Natronkalk soda lime
Natronlauge soda lye
natürlich natural
naturgemäß corresponding to nature
Naturgesetz natural law

Naturheilkunde naturopathy
Naturheilkundige naturopath
Naturheilkundiger naturopath
Naturwissenschaft natural science
Nausea e. e.
Nebel mist
—, **dichter** fog
— **mit Rauch** smog
Nebenbefund side finding
Nebenhoden epididymis
Nebenhöhle, Nasen- paranasal sinus
Nebenniere suprarenal body, adrenal gland
Nebennierenblutung suprarenal haemorrhage (e), suprarenal hemorrhage (a)
Nebennierenentfernung adrenalectomy
Nebenniereninsuffizienz adrenal insufficiency
Nebennierenmark adrenal medulla, adrenal marrow
Nebennierenrinde adrenal cortex
Nebennierenrindenhormon adrenal cortical hormone
Nebennierenrindenüberfunktion adrenal cortical hyperfunction
Nebennierenrindenunterfunktion adrenal cortical hypofunction, hypocorticalism
Nebenreaktion side reaction
Nebenschilddrüse parathyroid gland
Nebenschilddrüsenextrakt parathyroid extract
Nebenschluß shunt
Nebenwirkung side effect
Necator americanus e. e.
Nefopam e. e.
negativ negative
Negativismus negativism
Negrisches Körperchen Negri's body
Neigung inclination; trend
Nekrobiose necrobiosis
nekrobiotisch necrobiotic
nekrophil necrophilous
Nekrophilie necrophilism

Nekropsie necropsy
Nekrose necrosis
Nekrospermie necrospermia
nekrotisch necrotic
nekrotisieren to necrose, to necrotize
Nekrotomie necrotomy
Nélatonkatheter Nélaton's catheter
Nélatonsche Linie Nélaton's line
Nelkenöl oil of cloves
Nematode nema
Nematodenbefall nematodiasis
Neodym neodymium
Neomycin e. e.
Neon e. e.
Neoplasma neoplasm
neoplastisch neoplastic
Neophelometrie nephelometry
nephelometrisch nephelometric
Nephrektomie nephrectomy
Nephritis e. e.
 – mit **nephrotischem Einschlag** nephrosonephritis
nephritisch nephritic
nephrogen nephrogenous
Nephrographie renography
Nephrolithiasis e. e.
Nephrologe nephrologist
Nephrologie nephrology
Nephrologin nephrologist
nephrologisch nephrological
Nephropathie nephropathy
Nephroptose nephroptosis
Nephrose nephrosis
Nephrosklerose nephrosclerosis
nephrosklerotisch nephrosclerotic
Nephrostomie nephrostomy
nephrotisch nephrotic
Nephrotomie nephrotomy
nephrotoxisch nephrotoxic
Nerv nerve
nerval e. e.
Nervenbahn path, nervous pathway
Nervenfieber nervous fever
Nervenkanalerweiterer reamer
nervenkrank neuropathic

Nervenkrankheit nervous disease, neuropathy
Nervenleiden neuropathy
nervenleidend neuropathic
Nervennaht neurorrhaphy
Nervenplastik neuroplasty
Nervenschmerz neuralgia
Nervenschock nervous shock
Nervenschwäche neurasthenia, nervous debility
Nervensystem nervous system
Nervenwachstumsfaktor nerve growth factor
Nervenzusammenbruch nervous breakdown
Nervnadel nerve broache
nervös nervous
Nervosität nervosity
Nervus abducens abducens nerve
 – **accelerans** accelerans nerve
 – **acusticus** acoustic nerve
 – **cochlearis** cochlear nerve
 – **facialis** facial nerve
 – **femoralis** femoral nerve
 – **genitofemoralis** genitofemoral nerve
 – **glossopharyngeus** glossopharyngeal nerve
 – **hypoglossus** hypoglossal nerve
 – **iliohypogastricus** iliohypogastric nerve
 – **ilioinguinalis** ilioinguinal nerve
 – **infraorbitalis** infraorbital nerve
 – **intercostalis** intercostal nerve
 – **intermedius** intermediary nerve
 – **ischiadicus** sciatic nerve
 – **medianus** median nerve
 – **obturatorius** obturator nerve
 – **oculomotorius** oculomotor nerve
 – **olfactorius** olfactory nerve
 – **opticus** optic nerve
 – **peronaeus** peroneal nerve
 – **phrenicus** phrenic nerve
 – **radialis** radial nerve
 – **recurrens** recurrent nerve
 – **splanchnicus** splanchnic nerve
 – **sympathicus** sympathetic nerve

Nervus tibialis tibial nerve
- **trigeminus** trifacial nerve
- **trochlearis** trochlear nerve
- **ulnaris** ulnar nerve
- **vagus** vagus nerve, pneumogastric nerve

Nerz mink
Nesselsucht urticaria, nettle rash
Netz (med.) omentum
Netzanheftung omentopexy, epiplopexy
netzartig retiform
netzförmig retiform
Netzhaut retina
Neubildung neoformation
neugeboren new born
Neugeborenenperiode neonatal period
Neugeborenes new born, neonate
Neugrad grade
neural e. e.
Neuralgie Neuralgia
neuralgiform e. e.
neuralgisch neuralgic
Neuraminidase e. e.
Neurasthenie neurasthenia
Neurastheniker neurastheniac
Neurasthenikerin neurastheniac
neurasthenisch neurasthenic
Neurektomie neurectomy
Neurin e. e.
Neurinom neurinoma
Neurit neurite
Neuritis e. e.
-, **alkoholische** alcoholic neuritis
-, **diphtherische** diphtheric neuritis
- **nervi optici** optic neuritis
-, **retrobulbäre** retrobulbar neuritis
neuritisch neuritic
Neuroblast e. e.
Neuroblastom neuroblastoma
Neurochirurg neurosurgeon
Neurochirurgie neurosurgery
neurochirurgisch neurosurgical
Neurodermatitis e. e.
Neurodermatose neurodermatosis

neuroepithelial e. e.
Neuroepitheliom neuroepithelioma
Neuroepithel neuroepithelium
neurofibrillär neurofibrillar
Neurofibrille neurofibril
Neurofibrom neurofibroma
Neurofibromatose neurofibromatosis
neurogen neurogenic
Neuroglia e. e.
Neurogliom neuroglioma
Neurogliomatose neurogliomatosis
Neurogliozytom neurogliocytoma
neurohormonal e. e.
neurohumoral e. e.
neurohypophysär neurohypophyseal
Neurohypophyse neurohypophysis
Neurokinin e. e.
Neuroleptanalgesie neuroleptanalgesia
Neuroleptikum neuroleptic, major tranquilizer (a)
neuroleptisch neuroleptic
Neurologe neurologist
Neurologie neurology
Neurologin neurologist
neurologisch neurological
Neurolues e. e.
Neurolyse neurolysis
Neurom neuroma
neuromuskulär neuromuscular
Neuron e. e.
neuronal e. e.
Neuronophagie neuronophagy
Neuroparalyse neuroparalysis
neuroparalytisch neuroparalytic
Neuropath e. e.
Neuropathie neuropathy
Neuropathin neuropath
neuropathisch neuropathic
Neuropathologie neuropathology
neuropathologisch neuropathologic
Neurophysiologie neurophysiology
neurophysiologisch neurophysiologic

Neuropile e. e.
Neuroplegikum neuroplegic
neuroplegisch neuroplegic
Neuropsychopharmakologie neuropsychopharmacology
Neuroretinitis e. e.
Neurose neurosis
Neurosekretion neurosecretion
Neurosyphilis e. e.
neurosyphilitisch neurosyphilitic
Neurotiker neurotic
Neurotikerin neurotic
neurotisch neurotic
Neurotomie neurotomy
neurotoxisch neurotoxic
neurotrop neurotropic
Neurotropie neurotropism
neurovaskulär neurovascular
neurovegetativ neurovegetative
neurozirkulatorisch neurocirculatory
neutral e. e.
Neutralfett neutral fat
neutralisieren to neutralize
Neutralisierung neutralization
Neutralrot neutral red
Neutron e. e.
Neutropenie neutropenia
neutropenisch neutropenic
neutrophil neutrophil, neutrophilic
neutrophiler Leukozyt neutrophil leukocyte, neutrophil
Neutrophilie neutrophilia
Neusilber German silver
Newton (physikal. Maß) e. e.
Newtonscher Ring Newton's ring
Nialamid nialamide
nichtinvasiv noninvasive
Nichtmetall nonmetal
nichtmetallisch nonmetallic
nichtspezifisch nonspezific
nicht unterdrückbar nonsuppressible
nichtverestert nonesterified
Nickel e. e.
Nicolsches Prisma Nicol prism
Nidation e. e.

Niederfrequenz low frequency
Niederkunft accouchement, delivery, parturition, confinement
niedermolekular low molecular
niederschlagen to precipitate
Niederspannung low voltage
Niemann-Picksche Krankheit Niemann-Pick disease
Niere kidney
—,**künstliche** artificial kidney
Nierenbecken renal pelvis
Nierenbiopsie kidney biopsy
Nierendekapsulation nephrocapsectomy
Nierenentfernung nephrectomy
Nierenfunktionsprüfung kidney function test
Nierenkrankheit renal disease
Nierenschaden renal damage
Nierenschale kidney dish
Nierenstein renal calculus
Nierentuberkulose renal tuberculosis
niesen to sneeze
Nifedipin nifedipine
nigrostriatal e. e.
Nihilismus nihilism
Nikotin nicotin
Nikotinamid nicotinamide
Nikotinat nicotinate
Nikotinsäure nicotinic acid
Nikotinsäureamid nicotinamide
Nikotinsäuresalz nicotinate
Nikotinvergiftung nicotine poisoning
Ninhydrin e. e.
Niob niobium
Nische niche
Nisse nit
Nisslsches Körperchen Nissl's body
Niträmie nitraemia (e), nitremia (a)
Nitramin nitramine
Nitrat nitrate
Nitrid nitride
Nitril nitrile

Nitrit nitrite
Nitrobenzol nitrobenzene
Nitrofurantoin e. e.
Nitrofurazon nitrofurazone
Nitroglyzerin glyceryl trinitrate
Nitrophenol e. e.
Nitroprussid nitroprusside
Nitrosamin nitrosamine
Niveau level
Nobelpreis Nobel prize
Nocardia e. e.
Nocardiose nocardiasis
nocizeptiv nociceptive
nodal e. e.
nodulär nodular
Noguchia e. e.
Nomenklatur nomenclature
Nomogramm nomogram
nomotop nomotopic
Nonne-Apeltsche Reaktion Nonne-Apelt reaction
Nonnensausen venous hum
Noradrenalin norepinephrine
Noräthandrolon norethandrolone
Norandrostenolon norandrostenolone
Norephedrin norephedrine
Norethisteron norethisterone
Norgestrel e. e.
Norleucin norleucine
Norm e. e.
normal e. e.
normalisieren to normalize
Normalisierung normalization
normergisch normergic
Normoblast e. e.
Normothermie normothermia
normothermisch normothermic
normoton normotensive
Normozyt normocyte
Norprogesteron norprogesterone
Nortestosteron nortestosterone
Nosematose nosematosis

Nosologie nosology
nosologisch nosological
Not distress, emergency
Notatin e. e.
Notenblindheit note blindness
Notfallchirurgie emergency surgery
Notfallendoskopie emergency endoscopy
Notlage emergency
Notverband emergency dressing
Novobiocin e. e.
nuchal e. e.
nüchtern sober
Nüchternblutzucker fasting blood glucose
Nuhnsche Drüse Nuhn's gland
nukleär nuclear
nuklearmedizinisch nuclearmedical
Nuklease nuclease
Nuklein nuclein
Nukleoalbumin nucleoalbumin
nukleolär nucleolar
Nukleophosphatase nucleotidase
Nukleoproteid nucleoprotein
Nukleosid nucleoside
Nukleosidase nucleosidase
Nukleotid nucleotide
Nukleotidase nucleotidase
Nuklid nuclide
Null zero
Nullipara e. e., nulliparous patient
Nußgelenk ball-and socket joint
nutritionell nutritional
nutritiv nutritive
Nux vomica e. e.
Nykturie nycturia
Nylandersche Probe Nylander's test
Nyphomanie nymphomania
nystagmogen nystagmogenic
Nystagmograph e. e.
Nystagmographie nystagmography
Nystagmus e. e.

O

Obduktion obduction, medicolegal autopsy
Obduktionsbesteck postmortem set
obduzieren to make a postmortem examination
Oberärztin head physician, chief resident
Oberarm upperarm
Oberarzt head physician, chief resident
Oberbauch upper abdomen
Oberfläche surface
oberflächenaktiv surface active
Oberflächenanästhesie surface anaesthesia (e), surface anesthesia (a)
Oberflächenspannung surface tension
Oberflächentherapie surface therapy
oberflächlich superficial
Oberhaut epidermis, scarf skin, cuticle
Oberin matron
Oberkiefer superior maxilla, upper jaw bone
Oberkörper upper of the body
Oberlippe upperlip
Obermayersche Probe Obermayer's test
Oberpfleger head nurse
Oberschenkel thigh
Oberschenkelbruch fracture of the femur
Oberschwester head nurse
Objekt object
objektiv objective
Objektiv objective
Objektträger micro slide
Objektträgerpinzette slide holding forceps
obligat obligate
Obliquität obliquity
Obliteration e. e.

obliterieren to obliterate
Oblongata e. e.
obsolet obsolete
Obst fruits
Obstipation constipation, costiveness
obstipiert costive
Ochronose ochronosis
Ochse ox
Odontoblast e. e.
Odontoblastom odontoblastoma
Odontograph e. e.
Odontoklast odontoclast
Odontom odontoma
Ödem edema (a), oedema (e)
—,**Quinckesches** angioneurotic edema (a), angioneurotic oedema (e)
ödematös edematous (a), oedematous (e)
Ödipuskomplex Oedipus complex
Öffentliche Gesundheitspflege public health nursing
Öffentliches Gesundheitswesen Public Health
Öffnung opening, orifice, vent
Öffnungston opening snap
Öhr eye
Ökologie ecology (a), oecology (e)
Ökonomie economy
Öl oil
Ölbad oil bath
Öldiffusionspumpe oil diffusion pump
örtlich local; topical
Öse loop
Ösophagektasie esophagectasia (a), oesophagectasia (e)
Ösophagoduodenostomie esophagoduodenostomy (a), oesophagoduodenostomy (e)
Ösophagogastrostomie esophagogastrostomy (a), esophagogastrostomy (e)

Ösophagojejunogastrostomie esophagojejunogastrostomy (a), oesophagojejunogastrostomy (e)
Ösophagoskop esophagoscope (a), oesophagoscope (e)
Ösophagoskopie esophagoscopy (a), oesophagoscopy (e)
ösophagoskopisch esophagoscopical (a), oesophagoscopical (e)
Ösophagostomie esophagostomy (a), oesophagostomy (e)
Ösophagus esophagus (a), oesophagus (e)
Ösophagusvarizen esophageal varicosis (a), oesophageal varicosis (e)
Östradiol dihydrotheelin, estradiol (a), oestradiol (e)
Östran estrane (a), oestrane (e)
Östriol estriol (a), oestriol (e)
östrogen estrogenic (a), oestrogenic (e)
Östrogen estrogen (a), oestrogen (e)
Östron estrone (a), oestrone (e)
offen open, patent
Offenstehen patency
offiziell official
offizinell official
Ohm e. e.
Ohnmacht faint, swoon
Ohnmachtsanfall fainting fit
ohnmächtig fainting, swooning
– **werden** to faint, to swoon
Ohr ear
–, **abstehendes** prominent ear
Ohrenarzt otologist
Ohrenfluß otorrhea (a), otorrhoea (e)
Ohrenklappe ear-cap
Ohrenleiden ear complaint
Ohrensausen buzzing in the ear
Ohrenschmalz ear wax
Ohrläppchen lobule of the ear, earlap
Ohrloch ear hole
Ohrlöffel ear picker

Ohrmuschel auricle
Ohrschmalz ear wax, cerumen
Ohrschmalzpfropf impacted cerumen
Ohrspeicheldrüse parotid gland
Ohrspritze aural syringe
Ohrtoilette aural toilet
Oidiomykose oidiomycosis
Oidium albicans e. e., Monilia albicans
Oikologie oikology
okklusal occlusal
Okklusalfläche occlusal surface
Okklusion occlusion
okklusiv occlusive
Okklusivverband occlusive dressing
Oktan octane
okulär ocular
Okular ocular, eyepiece
okulomotorisch oculomotor
okzipital occipital
okzipitoanterior occipitoanterior
okzipitofrontal occipitofrontal
okzipitomental occipitomental
okzipitoparietal occipitoparietal
okzipitoposterior occipitoposterior
okzipitotemporal occipitotemporal
okzipitozervikal occipitocervical
Oleander e. e.
Oleandomycin e. e.
Oleandrin e. e.
Oleat oleate
Oleoresin e. e.
Oleothorax e. e.
Oleum Chenopodii anthelmintici oil of chenopodium
Oleum Ricini castor oil
Olfaktometer olfactometer
olfaktorisch olfactory
Oligämie oligaemia (e), oligemia (a)
oligämisch oligaemic (e), oligemic (a)
Oligodendroblastom oligodendroblastoma
Oligodendroglia e. e.

Oligodendrozyt oligodendrocyte
oligodynamisch oligodynamic
Oligomenorrhöe oligomenorrhea (a), oligomenorrhoea (e)
oligomorph oligomorphic
Oligophrenie oligophrenia
Oligozoospermie oligozoospermatism
Oligozythämie oligocythaemia (e), oligocythemia (a)
Oligurie oliguria
Olive e. e.
Olivenöl olive oil
Oliver-Cardarellisches Zeichen Oliver-Cardarelli sign
Olivomycin e. e.
Olmersche Krankheit exanthematous Mediterranean fever
Omarthritis e. e.
Ombrédanne-Maske Ombrédanne's mask
Omphalitis e. e.
Omphalocele e. e.
Onanie onanism
Onchozerkiasis onchocerciasis
Onkogenese oncogenesis
Onkologie oncology
onkologisch oncological
Onkolyse oncolysis
onkolytisch oncolytic
onkotisch ancotic
Ontogenese ontogenesis
ontogenetisch ontogenetic
Onychogrypose onychogryposis
Onychomykose onychomycosis
Ooblast e. e.
Oophorektomie oophorectomy
Oophoritis e. e.
Oosporose oosporosis
Oozyt oocyte
Opaleszenz opalescence
opaleszierend opalescent
Operateur operator, operating surgeon
Operation e. e.
Operationsanzug operating suit
Operationsbesteck operating set

Operationsbesteckkasten operating case
Operationsgebiet field of operation
Operationshandschuhe surgeon's gloves
Operationskleid operating gown
Operationsmütze operating cap
Operationsnarbe postoperative scar
Operationssaal operating theatre
Operationsschere operating scissors
operativ operative
Operator-Gen operator gene
operieren, einen Patienten to operate upon a patient
– **wegen Appendizitis** to operate for appendicitis
–, **einen Patienten wegen Appendizitis** to operate upon a patient for appendicitis
Operon e. e.
Ophthalmie ophthalmia
Ophthalmitis e. e.
Ophthalmologe ophthalmologist
Ophthalmologie ophthalmology
Ophthalmologin ophthalmologist
ophthalmologisch ophthalmological
Ophthalmometer e. e.
Ophthalmoplegie ophthalmoplegia
ophthalmoplegisch ophthalmoplegic
Ophthalmoskop ophthalmoscope
Ophthalmoskopie ophthalmoscopy
Opiat opiate
Opipramol e. e.
Opisthotonus opisthotonus
Opium e. e.
Opiumsucht paregorism
Opiumtinktur tincture of opium
Opodeldok camphor and soap liniment
Opossum e. e.
Oppenheimsches Zeichen Oppenheim's sign

Opsonin e. e.
Opsonozytophagie opsonocytophagy
opsonozytophagisch opsonocytophagic
Optik optics
Optiker optician
Optikerin optician
Optikusatrophie optic atrophy
optimal e. e.
optimieren to optimize
optimistisch optimistic
Optimum e. e.
optisch optic
oral e. e.
Orange e. e.
Orangenblüte orange flower
Orbita e. e.
orbital e. e.
Orchiektomie orchectomy, orchiectomy
Orchitis e. e.
Ordinate e. e.
Organ e. e.
Organelle organella
Organisation organization
organisch organic
organisieren to organize
Organismus organism
Organophosphat organophosphate
Organotherapie organotherapy
organotrop organotropic
Orgasmus orgasm
Orientbeule oriental boil
Orientierung orientation
Ornipressin e. e.
Ornithin ornithine
Ornithodorus moubata e. e.
orofazial oro-facial
Orotidyldekarboxylase orotidyldecarboxylase
Orotidylpyrophosphorylase e. e.
Oroyafieber Oroya fever, Carrión's disease
Orphenadrin orphenadrine
orthochromatisch orthochromatic
Orthodontie orthodontia
orthodontisch orthodontic
orthodrom orthodromic
Orthopäde orthopaedist (e), orthopedist (a)
Orthopädie orthopaedics (e), orthopedics (a)
Orthopädin orthopaedist (e), orthopedist (a)
orthopädisch orthopaedic (e), orthopedic (a)
Orthophosphat orthophosphate
Orthopnoe orthopnea (a), orthopnoea (e)
orthorhythmisch orthorhythmic
Orthoskop orthoscope
Orthoskopie orthoscopy
orthoskopisch orthoscopic
orthostatisch orthostatic
orthotonisch orthotonic
Ortung location
Orzein orcein
Orzin orcin
Orziprenalin orciprenaline
Osazon Osazone
Osgood-Schlattersche Erkrankung Osgood-Schlatter's disease
Oslersche Krankheit Osler's disease
Osmium e. e.
Osmolalität osmolality
Osmolarität osmolarity
Osmometer e. e.
Osmose osmosis
osmotisch osmotic
osseofibrös osseofibrous
Ossifikation ossification
ossifizieren to ossify
Ostektomie ostectomy
Osteoarthritis e. e.
Osteoarthropathie osteoarthropathy
Osteoarthrosis interspinalis kissing spine
Osteoblast e. e.
osteoblastisch osteoblastic
Osteoblastom osteoblastoma
Osteochondritis e. e.

Osteochondrofibrom
osteochondrofibroma
Osteochondrom osteochondroma
Osteochondromatose osteochondromatosis
Osteochondrosarkom osteochondrosarcoma
Osteochondrose osteochondrosis
Osteofibrom osteofibroma
Osteogenese osteogenesis
Osteogenesis imperfecta
e. e., brittle bones
osteoid e. e.
Osteoklast osteoclast
osteoklastisch osteoclastic
Osteologie osteology
osteologisch osteologic
Osteolyse osteolysis
–, **kryptogenetische progressive**
disappearing bone disease
osteolytisch osteolytic
Osteomalazie osteomalacia
osteomalazisch osteomalacic
Osteomyelitis e. e.
osteomyelitisch osteomyelitic
Osteopathie osteopathy
Osteopetrosis e. e.
Osteophyt osteophyte
osteoplastisch osteoplastic
Osteoporose osteoporosis
osteoporotisch osteoporotic
Osteopsathyrose osteopsathyrosis
Osteosarkom osteosarcoma
Osteosklerose osteosclerosis
osteosklerotisch osteosclerotic
Osteosynthese osteosynthesis
Osteotom osteotome
Osteotomie osteotomy
Ostitis osteitis
Ostitis deformans osteitis
deformans
Oszillation oscillation
Oszillator oscillator
Oszillogramm oscillogram
Oszillograph oscillograph
Oszillographie oscillography
oszillographisch oscillographic

Oszillometer oscillometer
Oszillometrie oscillometry
oszillometrisch oscillometric
Otalgie otalgia
Othämatom othaematoma (e),
othematoma (a)
Otiatrie otiatrics
otiatrisch otiatric
Otitis e. e.
– **externa** e. e.
– **interna** e. e.
– **media** e. e.
otogen otogenous
Otologe otologist
Otologie otology
Otologin otologist
otologisch otological
Otomykose otomycosis
Oto-Rhino-Laryngologie
oto-rhino-laryngology
Otosklerose otosclerosis
Otoskop otoscope, auriscope
Otoskopie otoscopy
otoskopisch otoscopic
ototoxisch ototoxic
Ovalozyt ovalozyte
Ovalozytose ovalocytosis
Ovarektomie ovariectomy,
oophorectomy
ovarektomieren to spay,
to ovariectomize
Ovarialgeschwulst ovarian
neoplasm
Ovarialzyste ovarian cyst
ovariell ovarian, oaric
Ovariosalpingektomie ovariosalpingectomy
Ovariotomie ovariotomy
ovaripriv ovariprival
Ovarium ovary
Ovulation e. e.
Ovulationshemmer ovulation
inhibitor
ovulatorisch ovulatory
Ovulum ovule
Oxacillin e. e.
Oxalat oxalate

Oxalazetat oxalacetate
Oxalosis oxalosis
Oxalsäure oxalic acid
Oxazin oxazine
Oxazol e. e.
Oxazon oxazone
Oxi... look for:/siehe bei: Oxy...
Oxprenolol e. e.
Oxyd oxide
Oxydase oxidase
oxydasenegativ oxidase-negative
oxydasepositiv oxidase-positive
Oxydation oxidation
oxydativ oxidative
oxydieren to oxidize
Oxydoreduktase oxidoreductase

Oxyfedrin oxyfedrine
Oxygenase e. e.
Oxyhämoglobin oexyhaemoglobin (e), oxyhemoglobin (a)
Oxymetrie oxymetry
oxymetrisch oxymetrical
oxyphil oxyphilous
Oxypurin oxypurine
Oxytetracyclin oxytetracycline
Oxytocin e. e.
Oxyuriasis e. e.
Oxyuris vermicularis e. e., Enterobius vermicularis
Ozaena ozaena (e), ozena (a)
Ozelot ocelot
Ozon ozone

P

Paardenziekte horse sickness
Paarung mating
Pacchionisches Grübchen pacchionian depression
Pachydermie pachydermia
Pachymeningitis e. e.
Packung pack
–, feuchte wet pack
–, heiße hot pack
Päderastie paederasty (e), pederasty (a)
Pädiater paediatrician (e), paediatrist (e), pediatrician (a), pediatrist (a)
Pädiatrie paediatrics (e), pediatrics (a)
Pädiatrin paediatrician (e), paediatrist (e), pediatrician (a), pediatrist (a)
pädiatrisch paediatric (e), pediatric (a)
Pagetsche Krankheit Paget's disease
Paket pack, packet

paläokinetisch palaeokinetic (e), paleokinetic (a)
Paläontologie palaeontology (e), paleontology (a)
Paläopathologie palaeopathology (e), paleopathology (a)
palatal e. e.
palatin palatine
palatomaxillär palatomaxillary
palatonasal e. e.
palatopharyngeal e. e.
palindromisch palindromic
Palisade e. e.
Palladium e. e.
Pallästhesie pallaesthesia (e), pallesthesia (a)
Pallanästhesie pallanaesthesia (e), pallanesthesia (a)
palliativ palliative
Palliativum palliative
Pallidektomie pallidectomy
palmar e. e.
Palmitat palmitate
Palmitin e. e.

palpabel palpable
Palpation e. e.
palpebral e. e.
palpieren to palpate
Panästhesie panaesthesia (e), panesthesia (a)
panagglutinabel panagglutinable
Panagglutination e. e.
Panagglutinin e. e.
Panaritium panaris, whitlow, felon
Panarteriitis panarteritis
Pancoasttumor Pancoast's neoplasm
Pancreatographie pancreatography
Pandemie pandemic
pandemisch pandemic
Pandysche Probe Pandy's test
Panik panic
panisch panic
Pankarditis pancarditis
Pankreas pancreas
Pankreaskopf head of pancreas
Pankreasschwanz pancreatic tail
Pankreasstein pancreatic calculus
Pankreatektomie pancreatectomy
pankreatektomieren to pancreatectomize, to depancreatize
Pankreatikocholezystostomie pancreaticocholecystostomy
Pankreatikoduodenostomie pancreaticoduodenostomy
Pankreatikographie pancreaticography
pankreatisch pancreatic
Pankreatitis pancreatitis
pankreatitisch pancreatitic
Pankreatoenterostomie pancreatoenterostomy
Pankreatographie pancreatography
pankreatotrop pancreatotropic
Pankreozymin pancreozymin
Panmyelophthise panmyelophthisis
Panophthalmitis e. e.
panoptisch panoptic
Panotitis e. e.
Pansen paunch
Pansinusitis e. e.
Panther e. e.
pantoskopisch pantoscopic
Pantothenat pantothenate
Pantothensäure pantothenic acid
Panzerherz armour heart
Panzytopenie pancytopenia
Papagei parrot
Papageienkrankheit parrot fever, psittacosis
Papain e. e.
Papaverin papaverine
Papayotin e. e.
Papel papule
Papier paper
Papierelektrophorese filter paper electrophoresis
Papilla Vateri Vater's papilla
papillär papillary
Papille papilla
Papillektomie papillectomy
Papillennekrose papillary necrosis
Papillenödem papilledema (a), papilloedema (e)
Papillitis e. e.
Papillom papilloma
papillomakulär papillomacular
papillomatös papillomatous
Papillomatose papillomatosis
Papillosphinkterotomie papillosphincterotomy
Pappatacifieber sandly fever, pappataci fever
Pappenheimfärbung Pappenheim's staining
Pappschiene cardboard splint
papulär papular
papuloerythematös papuloerythematous
papulös papular
papulopustulär papulopustular
papulosquamös papulosquamous
papulovesikulär papulovesicular
Paraaminobenzoesäure para-aminobenzoic acid
Paraaminosalizylsäure para-aminosalicylic acid

Parabel parabola
Parabiose parabiosis
parabiotisch parabiotic
Parablastom parablastoma
Paracentese paracentesis
Parachloromercuribenzoat
 parachloromercuribenzoate
Parachromatin e. e.
paradental e. e.
Paradentitis e. e., parodontitis
Paradentopathie paradentopathy
Paradentose paradentosis
paradox paradoxical
Paradoxon paradox
paraduodenal e. e.
Parästhesie paraesthesia (e),
 paresthesia (a)
parästhetisch paraesthetic (e),
 paresthetic (a)
Paraffin e. e.
Paraffinom paraffinoma
Paraform e. e.
Paragangliom paraganglioma
Paraganglion e. e.
Parageusie parageusia
Paragglutination e. e.
Paraglobulin e. e.
Paragonimiasis e. e.
Paragonimus ringeri
 Paragonimus Ringeri
 — westermani
 Paragonimus Westermani
Paragraphie paragraphia
Parahämophilie parahaemo-
 philia (e), parahemophilia (a)
parahepatisch parahepatic
Parahypnose parahypnosis
parainfektiös parainfectious
Parainfektion parainfection
Parainfluenza e. e.
Parakeratose parakeratosis
Parakinese parakinesis
parakinetisch parakinetic
Parakusis paracusis, paracusia
Paralalie paralalia
Paraldehyd paraldehyde
Paralexie paralexia

Parallaxe parallax
parallel e. e.
Parallergie parallergy
parallergisch parallergic
Paralogie paralogia
Paralyse paralysis
—,progressive paretic
 dementia, general paralysis of
 the insane, general paresis
paralysieren to paralyze
Paralysis agitans e. e.
Paralytiker paralytic
Paralytikerin paralytic
paralytisch paralytic
paramagnetisch paramagnetic
Paramastitis e. e.
Paramastoiditis e. e.
Parameter e. e.
Paramethason paramethasone
Parametritis e. e.
parametritisch parametritic
Parametrium e. e.
Paramnesie paramnesia
paramolar e. e.
Paramyelin e. e.
Paramyeloblast e. e.
paramyeloblastisch paramyelo-
 blastic
Paramyoklonus multiplex
 paramyoclonus multiplex
Paramyotonie paramyotonia
paraneoplastisch paraneoplastic
Paranephritis e. e.
paranephritisch paranephritic
paraneural e. e.
Paranoia e. e.
paranoid e. e.
Paranoiker paranoiac
Paranoikerin paranoiac
paranoisch paranoic
paranormal e. e.
parapankreatisch parapancreatic
Paraparese paraparesis
paraparetisch paraparetic
Paraphasie paraphasia
paraphasisch paraphasic
Paraphimose paraphimosis

Paraphrenie paraphrenia
paraphrenisch paraphrenic
Paraplegie paraplegia
paraplegisch paraplegic
Paraprostatitis e. e.
Paraprotein e. e.
Paraproteinämie paraproteinaemia (e), paraproteinemia (a)
Paraproteinurie paraproteinuria
Parapsoriasis e. e.
Parapsychologie parapsychology
parapsychologisch parapsychological
pararektal pararectal
parasagittal e. e.
Parasalpingitis e. e.
Parasit parasite
parasitär parasitic
Parasitologie parasitology
parasitologisch parasitological
parasitotrop parasitotropic
Paraspadie paraspadia
paraspezifisch paraspecific
parasternal e. e.
parasympathikolytisch parasympatholytic
parasympathikomimetisch parasympathomimetic
Parasympathikus parasympathetic
parasympathisch parasympathetical
Parasyphilis e. e.
parasyphilitisch parasyphilitic
Parasystole e. e.
Parathion e. e.
Parathymie parathymia
parathyreoidal parathyroidal
parathyreopriv parathyroprival
parathyreotrop parathyrotropic
paratuberkulös paratuberculous
Paratuberkulose paratuberculosis
Paratyphlitis e. e.
paratyphlitisch paratyphlitic
Paratyphus paratyphoid
Paratyphus-A-Bazillus
 Salmonella paratyphi
Paratyphus-B-Bazillus
 Salmonella schottmülleri
Paratyphus-C-Bazillus Salmonella hirschfeldii
paraurethral e. e.
paravaginal e. e.
paravenös paravenous
paravertebral e. e.
Parazentese paracentesis
– **des Trommelfells**
 paracentesis tympani
parazentral paracentral
parazervikal paracervical
Parazystitis paracystitis
Parenchym parenchyma
parenchymatös parenchymatous
parenteral e. e.
Parese paresis
paretisch paretic
parietal e. e.
parietofrontal e. e.
parietookzipital parietooccipital
parietotemporal e. e.
parietoviszeral parietovisceral
Parkinsonismus parkinsonism
Parkinson-Patient parkinsonian patient
Parkinson-Patientin parkinsonian patient
Parkinsonsche Krankheit
 Parkinson's disease
parodontal e.e.
Parodontose parodontosis
Paromomycin e. e.
Paronychie paronychia
Paroophoritis e. e.
Parophthalmie parophthalmia
Parotidektomie parotidectomy
Parotis parotid gland
Parotitis e. e.
paroxysmal e. e.
paroxysmale Tachykardie
 paroxysmal tachycardia
Paroxysmus paroxysm
Parrotsches Zeichen Parrot's sign
Parthenogenese parthenogenesis
Partialdruck partial pressure

Partikel particle
Partner e. e.
Partnerin female partner
Parulis e. e.
Pascal e. e.
Paschensches Körperchen Paschen's body
Passavantscher Wulst Passavant's bar
passierbar pervious
passiv passive
Passivität passivity
Paste e. e.
pasteurisieren to pasteurize
Pasteurisierung pasteurization
Pastille troche
patellar e. e.
Patellarklonus patella clonus
Patellarsehnenreflex patellar reflex
Patent e. e.
patentiert patented
Pathergie pathergy
pathergisch pathergic
pathetisch pathetic
pathoanatomisch pathoanatomical
Pathobiologie pathobiology
pathobiologisch pathobiological
pathogen pathogenic
Pathogenese pathogenesis
pathogenfrei pathogen free
pathogenetisch pathogenetic
pathognomonisch pathognomonic
Pathographie pathography
Pathologe pathologist
Pathologie pathology
Pathologin pathologist
pathologisch pathological
Patient e. e.
Patient, stationär liegender ward patient
Patientin patient
Paul-Bunnell-Test Paul-Bunnell test
Pause e. e.
–, **kompensatorische** compensatory pause

Pavian baboon
Pawlowscher Reflex Pavlov's reflex
Payrsches Darmkompressorium Payr's clamp
Péansche Klemme Péan's forceps
Pech pitch
Pechblende pitchblende
pedal e. e.
Pediculosis capitis e. e.
– **corporis** e. e.
– **palpebrarum** e. e.
– **pubis** e. e.
Pedikulose pediculosis
pedunkulär peduncular
Pektin pectin
Pektinase pectinase
pektoral pectoral
Pektoriloquie pectoriloquy
Pel-Ebsteinsche Krankheit Pel-Ebstein disease
Pelgersche Kernanomalie Pelger's nuclear anomaly
Peliosis rheumatica rheumatic purpura
Pelizaeus-Merzbachersche Krankheit Pelizaeus-Merzbacher disease
Pellagra e. e.
pellagrös pellagrous
Pelletierin pelletierine
peloid e. e.
Pelveoperitonitis e. e.
Pelveostomie pelviostomy
Pelveotomie pelviotomy
Pelvigraphie pelvigraphy
Pelvimetrie pelvimetry
pelvimetrisch pelvimetric
Pemphigus e. e.
Pendeltherapie pendulum therapy
Penetration e. e.
penetrieren to penetrate
Penicillamin penicillamine
Penicillanat penicillanate
Penicillin e. e.
Penicillinase e. e.
Penis e. e.

Penisklemme penis clamp
Penis palmatus webbed penis
Pentaborat pentaborate
Pentabromid pentabromide
Pentachlorid pentachloride
Pentachlorophenol e. e.
Pentagastrin e. e.
Pentan pentane
Pentazocin pentazocine
Pentdyopent e. e.
Pentetat pentetate
Pentosan e. e.
Pentosazon e. e.
Pentose e. e.
Pentosid pentoside
Pentosurie pentosuria
Pentoxyd pentoxide
Pentylentetrazol pentylene tetrazole
Pepsin e. e.
Pepsinogen e. e.
Peptase e. e.
Peptid peptide
Peptidase e. e.
Peptidyl e. e.
peptisch peptic
Pepton peptone
Peptonurie peptonuria
perakut peracute
Perazetat peracetate
Perazin perazine
Perchlorat perchlorate
Perchlorid perchloride
Perforation e. e.
perforieren to perforate
Perfusion e. e.
Perhexilin perhexiline
perianal e. e.
periapikal periapical
Periappendizitis periappendicitis
periarteriell periarterial
periarterielle Sympathektomie Leriche's operation
Periarteriitis nodosa polyarteritis nodosa
Periarthritis e. e.
– humeroscapularis peritendinitis calcarea of shoulder joint
periazinös periacinous
peribronchial e. e.
peribronchiektatisch peribronchiectatic
Peribronchitis e. e.
peribronchiolär peribronchiolar
Pericholangitis e. e.
Pericholezystitis pericholecystitis
pericholezystitisch pericholecystitic
Perichondritis e. e.
peridental e. e.
Peridivertikulitis peridiverticulitis
Periduodenitis e. e.
periduodenitisch periduodenitic
peridural e. e.
perifokal perifocal
perifollikulär perifollicular
Perifollikulitis perifolliculitis
perigastrisch perigastric
Perigastritis e. e.
periglandulär periglandular
perihepatisch perihepatic
Perihepatitis e. e.
perikanalikulär pericanalicular
perikapillär pericapillary
perikapsulär pericapsular
Perikard pericardium
perikardial pericardial
Perikardiektomie pericardiectomy
Perikardiolyse pericardiolysis
Perikarditis pericarditis
perikarditisch pericarditic
Perikolitis pericolitis
Perikolpitis pericolpitis
perikorneal pericorneal
Perilabyrinthitis e. e.
perilaryngeal e. e.
Perilaryngitis e. e.
perilobär perilobar
Perilymphe perilymph
Perimetritis e. e.
perimetritisch perimetritic
perimuskulär perimuscular

perimysial e. e.
Perimysium e. e.
perineal e. e.
Perinephritis e. e.
perinephritisch perinephritic
Perineum e. e.
perineural e. e.
Perineuritis e. e.
perinukleär perinuclear
Periode period
periodisch periodical
Periodizität periodicity
periodontal e. e.
Periodontitis e. e.
Periodontoklasie periodontoclasia
periokulär periocular
perioral e. e.
periorbital e. e.
Periorchitis e. e.
Periost periosteum
Periostitis e. e.
periostitisch periostitic
Periostose periostosis
peripankreatisch peripancreatic
Peripankreatitis peripancreatitis
peripapillär peripapillary
peripharyngeal e. e.
peripher peripheral
Peripherie periphery
Periphlebitis e. e.
peripleural e. e.
Peripleuritis e. e.
periportal e. e.
periproktisch periproctic
Periproktitis periproctitis
periproktitisch periproctitic
Periprostatitis e. e.
peripylorisch peripyloric
periradikulär periradicular
perirenal e. e.
perirenale Lufteinblasung perirenal air insufflation
Perisalpingitis e. e.
Perisigmoiditis e. e.
Perisinusitis e. e.
Perisplenitis e. e.
perisplenitisch perisplenitic

Peristaltik peristalsis
peristaltisch peristaltic
Peristase peristasis
peristatisch peristatic
Peristole e. e.
peristolisch peristolic
Peritendinitis e. e.
peritoneal e. e.
Peritonealdialyse peritoneal dialysis
Peritoneoskopie peritoneoscopy
Peritoneum e. e.
Peritonismus peritonism
Peritonitis e. e.
—,gallige choleperitonitis
peritonitisch peritonitic
peritonsillär peritonsillar
Peritonsillarabszeß peritonsillar abscess
Peritonsillitis e. e.
peritracheal e. e.
Perityphlitis e. e.
perityphlitisch perityphlitic
periurethral e. e.
perivaginal e. e.
perivaskulär perivascular
perivenös perivenous
perizellulär pericellular
Perizementitis pericementitis
Perizementoklasie pericementoclasia
perizentral pericentral
Perizystitis pericystitis
Perkolation percolation
Perkolator percolator
perkolieren to percolate
Perkussion percussion
Perkussionshammer percussion hammer
perkutan percutaneous
perkutieren to percuss
Perle pearl
perlingual e. e.
Perlsucht pearl disease
permanent e. e.
Permanenz permanence
permeabel permeable

Permeabilität permeability
pernasal e. e.
Perniosis e. e.
perniziös pernicious
peroral e. e.
Peroxyd peroxide
Peroxydase peroxidase
Perphenazin perphenazine
Perseveration e. e.
Persönlichkeit personality
Persönlichkeitsveränderung personality change
Person e. e.
Persulfat persulfate (a), persulphate (e)
Perthessche Krankheit Perthes disease
pertrochanter pertrochanteric
Pertubation e. e.
Pertussis e. e., whooping cough
Perubalsam balsam of Peru
Peruvosid peruvoside
Peruwarze verucca peruviana
pervers perverse
Perversion e. e.
Perversität perversity
Pes calvaneovalgus talipes calcaneovalgus
- calcaneovarus talipes calcaneovarus
- calcaneus talipes calcaneus
- cavus talipes cavus
- equinovalgus talipes equinovalgus
- equinovarus talipes equinovarus
- equinus talipes equinus
- planovalgus talipes planovalgus
- planus talipes planus
- valgus talipes valgus
- varus talipes varus
Pessar pessary
Pessimismus pessimism
Pest plague
pestartig pestilential
Pestbazillus Pasteurella pestis
Pestbeule plague boil
Pestsepsis septic plague

petechial e. e.
Petechie petechia
petit mal e. e.
Petrischale Petri dish
Petroleum e. e.
Petruschkysche Lackmusmolke Petruschky's litmus whey
Peyerscher Lymphfollikelhaufen Peyer's patch
Pfählung impalement
Pfannengelenk ball and socket joint
Pfannenstielscher Querschnitt Pfannenstiel's incision
Pfaundler-Hurlersche Krankheit gargoylism
Pfeffer pepper
Pfefferminze peppermint
Pfeife whistle
-, Galtonsche Galton's whistle
Pfeiffersches Drüsenfieber infectious mononucleosis
Pfeilgift arrow poison
Pferd horse
Pferdeegel horseleech
Pferdepest horse sickness
Pferdeserum horse serum
Pflanze plant
Pflanzenkeim cotyledon
Pflanzenschutzmittel plant protective
Pflanzenöl vegetable oil
pflanzlich vegetable
Pflaster plaster
Pflasterepithel pavement epithelium
Pflasterspatel plaster spatula
Pflasterzelle pavement cell
Pflege care
Pflegeanstalt hospital for incurables
Pflegeheim nursing home
pflegen to take care
Pflegeperson nurse
Pflegepersonal nursing personnel
Pfleger nurse
pflegerisches Hilfspersonal auxiliary nursing personnel

Pfortader portal vein
Pfortaderkreislauf portal circulation
Pfortaderthrombose portal vein thrombosis
Pfote claw
Pfropf plug
Pfützenphänomen puddle sign
Phänomen phenomenon
Phänotyp phaenotype (e), phenotype (a)
phänotypisch phaenotypic (e), phenotypic (a)
Phäochromozytom phaeochromocytoma (e), pheochromocytoma (a)
Phagolyse phagolysis
Phagozyt phagocyte
phagozytär phagocytic
phagozytieren to phagocytize
Phagozytolyse phagocytolysis
Phagozytose phagocytosis
Phakitis e. e.
Phakoskopie phakoscopy, phacoscopy
phalangeal e. e.
Phalanx e. e.
phallisch phallic
Phallitis e. e.
Phantasie phantasy
Phantom e. e.
Phantomglied phantom limb
Phantomschwangerschaft phantom pregnancy
Pharmakochemie pharmacochemistry
Pharmakochemiker pharmaceutical chemist
Pharmakochemikerin pharmaceutical chemist
pharmakochemisch pharmacochemical
Pharmakodynamik pharmacodynamics
pharmakodynamisch pharmacodynamic
Pharmakognosie pharmacognosy
Pharmakokinetik pharmacokinetics
pharmakokinetisch pharmacokinetic
Pharmakologe pharmacologist
Pharmakologie pharmacology
Pharmakologin pharmacologist
pharmakologisch pharmacological
Pharmakopöe pharmacopeia (a), pharmacopoeia (e)
pharmakotherapeutisch pharmacotherapeutic
Pharmakotherapie pharmacotherapy, drug therapy
Pharmazeut pharmacist
Pharmazeutin pharmacist
pharmazeutisch pharmaceutical
Pharmazie pharmacy, pharmaceutics
Pharyngitis e. e.
pharyngitisch pharyngitic
pharyngolaryngeal e. e.
Pharyngoskop pharyngoscope
Pharyngoskopie pharyngoscopy
pharyngoskopisch pharyngoscopic
Pharyngospasmus pharyngospasm
Pharyngotomie pharyngotomy
Pharynx e. e.
Phase e. e.
Phasenkontrastmikroskop phase contrast microscope
Phasenkontrastmikroskopie phase contrast microscopy
Phenanthren phenanthrene
Phenanthrolin phenanthroline
Phenazin phenazine
Phenazon phenazone
Phenelzin phenelzine
Phenethicillin e. e.
Phenetidin e. e.
Phenformin e. e.
Phenmetrazin phenmetrazine
Phenol e. e.
Phenolase e. e.
Phenolat phenolate
phenolieren to phenolate
Phenolphthalein e. e.
Phenothiazin phenothiazine

Phenoxybenzamin
  phenoxybenzamine
Phenprocoumon e. e.
Phentolamin phentolamine
Phenyl e. e.
Phenyläthylamin phenylethylamine
Phenyläthylbarbitursäure
  phenobarbitone, phenylethylbarbituric acid, phenobarbital
Phenyläthylbiguanid phenethylbiguanide
Phenyläthylhydrazin phenylethylhydrazine
Phenylalanin phenylalanine
Phenylbutazon phenylbutazone
Phenylchinolin phenylchinoline
Phenylchinolinkarbonsäure
  cinchophen
Phenylhydrazin phenylhydrazine
Phenylen phenylene
Phenylendiamin phenylenediamine
Phenylketonurie phenylketonuria
Phenylzyklopropylamin phenylcyclopropylamine
Philosophie philosophy
philosophisch philosophical
Phimose phimosis
Phlebektasie phlebectasia
Phlebektomie phlebectomy
Phlebitis e. e.
phlebitisch phlebitic
Phlebogramm phlebogram
Phlebographie phlebography
phlebographisch phlebographic
Phlebolith e. e.
Phlebotomie phlebotomy
Phlebotomus papatasii e. e.
phlegmatisch phlegmatic
Phlegmone cellulitis
phlogistisch phlogistic
Phloridzin phlorhizin
Phorhizin phlorhizin
Phlorogluzin phloroglucin
Phloxin phloxine
Phlyktäne phyctaena (c),
  phlyctena (a)

Phobie phobia
phobisch phobic
Phokomelie phocomelia
Phon e. e.
Phonangiographie phonangiography
Phonation e. e.
phonatorisch phonatory
Phonetik phonetics
phonetisch phonetic
Phonokardiogramm phonocardiogram
Phonokardiographie phonocardiography
phonokardiographisch phonocardiographical
Phosgen phosgene
Phosphagen e. e.
Phosphamid phosphamide
Phosphat phosphate
Phosphatase e. e.
phosphatbildend phosphagenic
phosphathaltig phosphatic
Phosphatid phosphatide
Phosphatidyl e. e.
Phosphatin phosphatine
Phosphaturie phosphaturia
Phosphid phosphide
Phosphin e. e.
Phosphit phosphite
Phosphoadenosin phosphoadenosine
Phosphodiesterase e. e.
Phosphoglukose phosphoglucose
Phosphoglyzerat phosphoglycerate
Phosphokinase e. e.
Phospholipase e. e.
Phospholipid e. e.
Phosphomannoisomerase e. e.
Phosphoprotein e. e.
Phosphopyridin phosphopyridine
Phosphor phosphorus
Phosphoreszenz phosphorescence
phosphorhaltig (dreiwertig)
  phosphorous
– **(fünfwertig)** phosphoric

Phosphoribosylpyrophosphat
  phosphoribosylpyrophosphate
phosphorieren to phosphorate
Phosphoryl e. e.
Phosphorylase e. e.
phosphorylieren to phosphorylate
Phosphorylierung phosphorylation
Phosphosulfat phosphosulfate (a),
  phosphosulphate (e)
Phot phote
Photobiologie photobiology
photochemisch photochemical
Photodermie photodermia
photoelektrisch photoelectric
Photographie photography
photographisch photographical
Photokoagulation photocoagulation
Photometer e. e.
Photometrie photometry
photometrisch photometric
Photooxidation e. e.
Photophosphorylierung photophosphorylation
Photorezeptor photoreceptor
Photosynthese photosynthesis
Photozelle photocell
Phrenikusexairese phrenicoexairesis
Phrenologe phrenologist
Phrenologie phrenology
Phrenologin phrenologist
phrenologisch phrenological
phrygische Mütze Phrygian cap
Phthalamidin phthalamidine
Phthalanilid phthalanilide
Phthalat phthalate
Phthalein e. e.
Phthalidolon phthalidolone
Phthalylsulfathiazol
  phthalylsulfathiazole (a),
  phthalylsulphathiazole (e)
Phthiriasis inguinalis e.e.
Phthise phthisis
Phthisiogenese phthisiogenesis
phthisisch phthisic
Phylogenese phylogenesis
phylogenetisch phylogenetic

Physik physics
physikalisch physical
– -chemisch physicochemical
Physiker physicist
Physikerin physicist
Physiologe physiologist
Physiologie physiology
Physiologin physiologist
physiologisch physiological
– -chemisch physiochemical
physiologische Chemie physiochemistry
physiopsychisch physiopsychic
Physiotherapie physiotherapy
physisch physical
Physostigmin physostigmine
Phytat phytate
Phytin e.e.
Phytoagglutinin e. e.
Phytoglobulin e. e.
Phytohämagglutinin phytohaemagglutinin (e), phytohemagglutinin (a)
Phytotherapie phytotherapy
Phytotoxin e. e.
phytotoxisch phytotoxic
Picksche Atrophie Pick's atrophy
Pickwick-Syndrom Pickwick syndrome
Picofarad e. e.
Piezochemie piezochemistry
piezoelektrisch piezoelectric
Pigment e. e.
pigmentieren to pigment
pigmentiert pigmented
Pigmentierung pigmentation
Pigmentzelle pigment cell
Pikrin picrin
Pikrinsäure picric acid
Pikrotoxin picrotoxin
Pillchen pellet, pillet
Pille pill
Pilojektion pilojection
Pilokarpin pilocarpine
pilomotorisch pilomotor
Pilz fungus
–,Blätter- agaric

Pilz, eßbarer mushroom
—,Schimmel- mold, mould
—,ungenießbarer toadstool
Pindolol e. e.
Pinealektomie pinealectomy
Pinealom pinealoma
Pinguecula e. e.
Pinguin penguin
Pinozytose pinocytosis
Pinzette forceps; tweezer
—,anatomische dissecting forceps
—,chirurgische tissue forceps
Piperazin piperazine
Piperidin piperidine
Piperin piperine
Pipette pipet
Pirogoffsche Amputation
 Pirogoff's amputation
Piroplasmose piroplasmosis
Pirquetsche Probe Pirquet's
 reaction
Piskaceksche Ausladung
 Piskacek's sign
Pityriasis rosea/rubra/versicolor
 e. e.
Pivampicillin e. e.
Pix liquida pine tar
Placebo e. e.
Placenta praevia placenta praevia
 (e), placenta previa (a)
Placidosche Scheibe Placido's disk
Plättchenaggregationstest lamina
 aggregation test
plantar e. e.
Plasma e. e.
Plasmaeiweiß plasma protein
Plasmakinin e. e.
Plasmal e. e.
Plasmalogen e. e.
Plasmapherese plasmapheresis
plasmatisch plasmatic
Plasmazelle plasma cell
Plasmazellenvermehrung
 plasmacytosis
Plasmin e. e.
Plasminogen e. e.
plasmodientötend plasmodiocidal

Plasmodium falciparum e. e.
— **immaculatum** e. e.
— **malariae** e. e.
— **vivax** e. e.
Plasmolyse plasmolysis
plasmolytisch plasmolytic
Plasmozytom plasmocytoma
Plastik plastics
Plastikbeutel plastic bag
plastisch plastic
plastisches Material plastics
Plastizität plasticity
Plastogamie plastogamy
Plathelminth platyhelminth
Platin platinum
Platinat platinate
Platinöse platinum loop
Platte plate
Plattenepithel squamous
 epithelium
Plattfuß splayfoot, flatfoot
Plattfußeinlage instep raiser,
 foot easer
Plattwurm platyhelminth
Platzangst agoraphobia
Plazenta placenta
plazental placental
Plazenta-Laktationshormon,
 menschliches human placenta
 lactogen
Plazentaschranke placental barrier
Plazentation placentation
Plazentitis placentitis
Plazentographie placentography
Plazentom placentoma
Plazentotoxin placentotoxin
Pleiochromie pleiochromia
pleomorph pleomorphic
Pleomorphie pleomorphism
Pleozytose pleocytosis
Plessimeter pleximeter
Plethora e. e.
plethorisch plethoric
Plethysmogramm plethysmogram
Plethysmograph e. e.
Plethysmographie plethysmo-
 graphy

plethysmographisch plethysmographical
Pleura e. e.
Pleuraadhäsion pleural adhesion
pleural e. e.
Pleurektomie pleurectomy
Pleuritis pleurisy
pleuritisch pleuritic
Pleurodynie pleurodynia
Pleuroperikarditis pleuropericarditis
pleuroperitoneal e. e.
Pleuroperitoneostomie pleuroperitoneostomy
Pleuropneumolyse pleuropneumolysis
Pleuropneumonie pleuropneumonia
Pleuroskopie pleuroscopy
Pleurotomie pleurotomy
pleuroviszeral pleurovisceral
Plexus e. e.
- brachialis brachial plexus
- cervicalis cervical plexus
- sacralis sacral plexus
- solaris solar plexus
Plikotomie plicotomy
Plombierung plugging
Plummer-Vinson-Syndrom Plummer-Vinson syndrome
pluriglandulär pluriglandular
Pluripara e. e.
pluripolar e. e.
pluripotent e. e.
pneumatisch pneumatic
pneumatisieren to pneumatize
Pneumatisierung pneumatization
Pneumatose pneumatosis
Pneumaturie pneumaturia
Pneumektomie pneumectomy
Pneumenzephalographie pneumencephalography
Pneumobazillus Friedländer Klebsiella pneumoniae
Pneumographie pneumography
pneumokardial pneumocardial
Pneumokokkus pneumococcus
Pneumokolon pneumocolon

Pneumokoniose pneumoconiosis
Pneumolyse pneumolysis
Pneumomediastinum e. e.
Pneumonektomie pneumonectomy
Pneumonie pneumonia
-, akute interstitielle acute interstitial pneumonitis
-, biliäre bilious pneumonia
-, Broncho- bronchopneumonia
-, chronische fibröse interstitial pneumonia, cirrhosis of the lung
-, croupöse lobar pneumonia
-, hypostatische hypostatic pneumonia
-, käsige cheesy pneumonia
pneumonisch pneumonic
Pneumoperikard pneumopericardium
Pneumoperitoneographie pneumoperitoneography
Pneumoperitoneum e. e.
Pneumopyelographie pneumopyelography
Pneumotachograph e. e.
Pneumothorax e. e.
Pneumothoraxapparat pneumothorax apparatus
pneumotrop pneumotropic
Pneumozystose pneumocystosis
Pneumozyt pneumocyte
pochen to throb
Pocken variola, smallpox
Podagra e. e.
Podophyllin e. e.
Podophyllotoxin e. e.
Podotrochlitis podotrochilitis
Poikiloderma e. e.
Poikilozyt poikilocyte
Poikilozytose poikilocytosis
Poiseuillesches Gesetz Poiseuille's law
Pol pole
polar e. e.
Polarimeter e. e.
Polarimetrie polarimetry
polarimetrisch polarimetric
Polarisation polarization

polarisieren to polarize
Polarisierung polarization
Polariskopie polariscopy
Polarität polarity
Polarographie polarography
polarographisch polarographic
polieren to polish
Polierinstrument burnisher
Poliermittel polishing agent
Poliklinik policlinic, outpatient clinic
Polioenzephalitis polioencephalitis
Poliomyelitis anterior acuta acute anterior poliomyelitis
poliomyelitisch poliomyelitic
Poliomyelitis-Impfstoff polio vaccine
politzern to politzerize
Politzerverfahren politzerization
Pollakisurie pollakiuria
Pollen e. e.
Pollenkrankheit pollinosis
Pollinose pollinosis
Pollution e. e.
Polonium e. e.
Polster bolster
polstern to bolster
Polyacrylamid polyacrylamide
Polyadenitis e. e.
Polya-Operation Polya's operation
Polyästhesie polyaesthesia (e), polyesthesia (a)
Polyäthylen polyethylene
Polyakrylamid polyacrylamide
Polyalgesie polyalgesia
Polyarteriitis polyarteritis
Polyarthritis e. e.
– rheumatica acuta rheumatic fever, acute articular rheumatism
– –, primär chronische rheumatoid arthritis
–, sekundär chronische chronic articular rheumatism
polyarthritisch polyarthritic
polyartikulär polyarticular
Polyavitaminose polyavitaminosis

polybasisch polybasic
Polycholie polycholia
Polychromasie polychromasia
polychromatisch polychromatic
polychromatophil 0olychromatophilic
Polychromatophilie polychromatophilia
Polydaktylie polydactylism
Polydipsie polydipsia
polyergisch polyergic
Polygalaktie polygalactia
Polygalakturonase polygalacturonase
polyglandulär polyglandular
Polyglobulie polyglobulism
Polyhypermenorrhöe polyhypermenorrhea (a), polyhypermenorrhoea (e)
Polyhypomenorrhöe polyhypomenorrhea (a), polyhypomenorrhoea (e)
Polymenorrhöe polymenorrhea (a), polymenorrhoea (e)
polymer polymeric
Polymerase e. e.
Polymerie polymerism
polymerisieren to polymerize
Polymerisierung polymerization
Polymethylen polymethylene
polymorph polymorphic, polymorphous
Polymorphie polymorphism
polymorphkernig polymorphonuclear
polymorphkerniger Leukozyt polymorphonuclear leukocyte, polymorph
Polymyositis e. e.
Polymyxin e. e.
polyneural e. e.
Polyneuritis e. e.
polyneuritisch polyneuritic
polynukleär polynuclear
Polynukleotid polynucleotide
Polyol e. e.
Polyopsie polyopsia

Polyp polypus
Polypenzange polypus forceps
Polypeptid polypeptide
Polypeptidase e. e.
polyphasisch polyphasic
Polyphosphat polyphosphate
polyploid e. e.
polypös polypous
Polypose polyposis
Polypragmasie polypragmasy
Polypropylen polypropylene
Polyradikulitis polyradiculitis
Polyradikuloneuritis polyradiculoneuritis
Polyribosom polyribosome
Polysaccharid polysaccharide
Polyserositis e. e.
Polysom polysome
Polystyrol polystyrene
Polythiazid polythiazide
Polytopie polytopy
polytopisch polytopical
Polyurie polyuria
polyvalent e. e.
Polyvinyl e. e.
polyzentrisch polycentric
polyzyklisch polycyclic
polyzystisch polycystic
Polyzythämie polycythaemia (e), polycythemia (a)
Pomade pomatum
Poncetsches Rheumatoid Poncet's disease
pontin pontine
pontozerebellar pontocerebellar
Pony e. e.
popliteal e. e.
Population e. e.
Poradenitis e. e.
Pore e. e.
Porenzephalie porencephalia
Poriomanie poriomania
porös porous
Porphin e. e.
Porphobilinogen e. e.
Porphyrie porphyria
Porphyrin e. e.

Porphyrinurie porphyrinuria
Porro-Operation Porro's operation
portal e. e.
Portion e. e.
Portographie portography
portokaval portacaval
portokavale Anastomose portacaval shunt
Porzellan porcelain
Position e. e.
positiv positive
Positron e. e.
Positrozephalogramm positrocephalogram
Positrozephalographie positrocephalography
positrozephalographisch positrocephalographical
Posologie posology
postabortal e. e.
postapoplektisch postapoplectic
postdiphtherisch postdiphtheric
postenzephalitisch postencephalitic
postepileptisch postepileptic
posteroinferior e. e.
posterolateral e. e.
posteroparietal e. e.
posterotemporal e. e.
postfebril postfebrile
postganglionär postganglionic
postgrippal e. e.
postherpetisch postherpetic
Posthitis e. e.
posthum posthumous
posthypnotisch posthypnotic
postklimakterisch postmenopausal, postclimacteric
Postkommisurotomie-Syndrom postcommisurotomy syndrome
Postkommotionssyndrom postconcussion syndrome
Postkontusionssyndrom postcontusion syndrome
Postmastektomiesyndrom postmastectomy syndrome
Postmenstruum postmenstrua

postmortal e. e.
postnatal e. e.
postoperativ postoperative
postpartual postpartum
postpneumonisch postpneumonic
postpoliomyelitisch postpoliomyelitic
postprandial e. e.
poststenotisch poststenotic
posttraumatisch posttraumatic
postvakzinal postvaccinal
Potainscher Apparat Potain's apparatus
potent e. e.
Potential potential
potentiell potential
Potentiometer e. e.
Potentiometrie potentiometry
potentiometrisch potentiometric
Potenz potency
potenzieren to potentize, to potentiate
Potenzierung potentiation
Pottasche potash
Poupartsches Band Poupart's ligament
Practolol e. e.
präagonal preagonal
Präalbumin prealbumin
Prädiabetes prediabetes
prädiabetisch prediabetic
prädiastolisch prediastolic
prädisponierend predisposing
Prädisposition predisposition
Präeklampsie preeclampsia
Präformation preformation
präformieren to preform
präfrontal prefrontal
präganglionär preganglionic
präkanzerös precancerous
Präkanzerose precancerosis
präkapillär precapillary
Präkapillare precapillary
präkariös precarious
präkarzinomatös precarcinomatous
präklimakterisch premenopausal, preclimacteric

praeklinisch preclinical
Präkoma precoma
präkomatös precomatose
präkordial precordial
Prämedikation premedication
prämenstruell premenstrual
prämitotisch premitotic
Prämolar premolar, bicuspid tooth
prämonitorisch premonitory
prämorbid premorbid
pränatal prenatal
präneoplastisch preneoplastic
präoperativ preoperative
präparalytisch preparalytic
Präparat preparation
—,zusammengesetztes multicomponent preparation
Präparation preparation
— (anatom.) dissection
Präparierbesteck dissecting set
präparieren to preparate
— (anatom.) to dissect
präpatellar prepatellar
präperitoneal preperitoneal
Präpubertät prepuberty
präpylorisch prepyloric
präsakral presacral
präsenil presenile
Präservativ preservative
Präsklerose presclerosis
präsklerotisch presclerotic
prästenotisch prestenotic
präsystolisch presystolic
prätibial pretibial
präzentral precentral
Präzipitat precipitate
Präzipitation precipitation
Präzipitin precipitin
Prager Handgriff Prague maneuver
pragmatisch pragmatic
Pragmatismus pragmatism
praktisch practical
praktischer Arzt general practitioner
Praseodym praseodymium
Pravazsche Spritze Pravaz's syringe

Praxis practice
Praxisführung, unkorrekte malpractice
Praxisräume des Arztes doctor's office
Prazosin e.e.
Prednisolon prednisolone
Prednison prednisone
Preglsche Lösung Pregl's solution
Pregnan pregnane
Pregnandiol e.e.
Pregnandion e.e.
Pregnanol e.e.
Pregnanolon pregnanolone
Pregnen pregnene
Preisträger laureate
Preisträgerin laureate
Prellung contusion
Prenylamin prenylamine
presbyop presbyopic
Presbyophrenie presbyophrenia
Presbyopie presbyopia
Pressorsubstanz pressor substance
pressorezeptiv pressosensitive
Priapismus priapism
Price-Jonessche Kurve Price-Jones curve
Priessnitzwickel Priessnitz's bandage
primär primary
Primäreffekt, syphilitischer syphilitic hard chancre
Primärstrahl primary ray
Primat primate
Primipara e.e., primiparous patient
Primitivsegment somite
Primitivstreifen primitive streak, primitive trace
primordial e.e.
Prindolol e.e.
Prinzip principle
Priorität priority
Prisma prism
privat private
Proaccelerin e.e.

Proband, gesunder freiwilliger healthy volunteer
Probe specimen
Probeexzision exploratory excision
Probeexzisionszange specimen forceps
Probefrühstück test breakfast
Probelaparotomie exploratory laparotomy
Probemahlzeit test meal
Probenwechsler sample changer
Processus coracoideus coracoid process
– mastoideus mastoid process
– zygomaticus zygomatic process
Prochlorperazin prochlorperazine
Prodrom prodrome
prodromal e.e.
Prodromalstadium prodromal period
Produkt product
Produktion production; output
produktiv productive
Proerythroblast e.e.
Pro-Esterase proesterase
Proferment e.e., zymogen
professionell professional
Professor e.e.
Professorin professor
Profil profile
profus profuse
Progenie prognathism
Progesteron progesterone
Progestogen e.e.
Prognathie prognathism
Prognose prognosis
Prognostiker prognostician
Prognostikerin prognostician
prognostisch prognostic
prognostizieren to prognosticate
programmgesteuert program controlled
programmiert programmed
Programmierung programming
Progression e.e.
progressiv progressive

progressive Bulbärparalyse
  progressive bulbar paralysis
- **Muskelatrophie** wasting palsy
- **Paralyse** paralytic dementia, general paresis

Proinsulin e. e.
Projektion projection
Prokain procaine
Prokainhydrochlorid procaine hydrochloride
Prokonvertin proconvertin
Prokteuryse procteurysis
Proktitis proctitis
proktitisch proctitic
proktogen proctogenic
Proktologe proctologist
Proktologie proctology
proktologisch proctological
Proktoskopie proctoscopy
proktoskopisch proctoscopic
Proktostomie proctostomy
Proktotomie proctotomy
Proktozystotomie proctocystotomy
Prolaktin prolactin
Prolamin e. e.
Prolan e. e.
Proliferation e. e.
proliferativ proliferative
proliferieren to proliferate
Prolin proline
Prolinase e. e.
prolongieren to prolong
Promazin promazine
Promethazin promethazine
Promethium e. e.
Prominenz prominence
Promonozyt promonocyte
Promontorium promontory
Promotion graduation
promovierte Person graduate
prompt e. e.
Promyelozyt premyelocyte, promyelocyte
Pronation e. e.
Propädeutik propaedeutics (e), propedeutics (a)

propädeutisch propaedeutic (e), propedeutic (a)
Propamid propamide
Propan propane
Propandiol e. e.
Propanol e. e.
Propanolol e. e.
Properdin e. e.
prophylaktisch prophylactic
Prophylaxe prophylaxis
Propicillin e. e.
Propion e. e.
Propionat propionate
Propionsäure propionic acid
Propionyl e. e.
Proportion e. e.
proportional e. e.
Propoxyphen propoxyphene
Propranolol e. e.
propriozeptiv proprioceptive
Propulsion e. e.
Propyl e. e.
Propylamin propylamine
Propylen propylene
Propylrot propyl red
Propylthiouracil e. e.
Prosekretin prosecretin
Prosektor prosector
Prosopoplegie prosopoplegia
Prostaglandin e. e.
Prostata prostate
Prostataadenom adenoma of prostate
Prostatahypertrophie hypertrophy of prostate
Prostatakarzinom carcinoma of prostate
Prostatektomie prostatectomy
prostatikovesikal prostaticovesical
prostatisch prostatic
Prostatitis e. e.
prostatitisch prostatitic
Prostatorrhöe prostatorrhea (a), prostatorrhoea (e)
Prostatotomie prostatotomy
prosthetisch prosthetic
Prostitution e. e.

Protaktinium protoactinium
Protamin protamine
Protaminase e. e.
Protease e. e.
Proteid e. e.
Protein e. e.
–,**C-reaktives** C-reactive protein
Proteinase e. e.
proteingebundenes Jod protein-bound iodine
Proteinkörpertherapie proteinotherapy
Proteinose proteinosis
Proteohormon proteohormone
Proteolyse proteolysis
proteolytisch proteolytic
Proteose e. e.
Proteus vulgaris e. e.
Prothese prosthesis
Prothese (dent.) denture
Prothesenhaftung (dent.) denture adhesion
prothesenstützend (dent.) denture supporting
prothetisch prosthetic
Prothipendyl e. e.
Prothrombin e. e.
Prothrombinmangel prothrombinopenia
Prothrombinopenie prothrombinopenia
Prothombinzeit prothrombin time
Protionamid protionamide
Protoblast e. e.
Protokoll protocol
Proton e. e.
Protoplasma protoplasm
protoplasmatisch protoplasmic
Protoporphyrin e. e.
Prototoxin e. e.
Prototyp prototype
Protoveratrin protoveratrine
Protozoon e. e.
Protrusion e. e.
Protriptylin protriptyline
Protuberanz protuberance
Provitamin e. e.

Provokation provocation
provozieren to provoke
proximal e. e.
proximalwärts proximad
proximobukkal proximobuccal
proximolabial e. e.
proximolingual e. e.
Prozedur procedure
Prozent percent
Prozentsatz percentage
Prozeß process
prüfen to examine
Prüfer examiner
Prüferin examiner
Prüfling examinee
Prüfung examination
pruriginös pruriginous
Prurigo mitis e. e.
– **nodularis** e. e.
Pruritus e. e.
– **ani** e. e.
Psammokarzinom psammocarcinoma
Psammom psammoma
Psammosarkom psammosarcoma
Pseudarthrose pseudarthrosis
Pweudoagglutination e. e.
Pseudoagraphie pseudoagraphia
Pseudoangina e. e.
pseudobulbär pseudobulbar
Pseudocroup e. e.
Pseudodemenz pseudodementia
Pseudodiphtherie pseudodiphtheria
Pseudodiphtheriebazillus Corynebacterium pseudodiphtheriae
Pseudogeusie pseudogeusia
Pseudogliom pseudoglioma
Pseudoglobulin e. e.
Pseudogonorrhöe pseudogonorrhea (a), pseudogonorrhoea (e)
Pseudographie pseudographia
Pseudohalluzination pseudohallucination
Pseudohermaphroditismus pseudohermaphroditism

Pseudohernie pseudohernia
Pseudohypertrophie pseudohypertrophy
pseudohypertrophisch pseudohypertrophic
Pseudohypoparathyreoidismus pseudohypoparathyroidism
Pseudoikterus pseudojaundice
pseudoisochromatisch pseudoisochromatic
Pseudoleukämie pseudoleukaemia (e), pseudoleukemia (a)
Pseudologie pseudologia
Pseudolymphom pseudolymphoma
Pseudomembran pseudomembrane
pseudomembranös pseudomembranous
Pseudomonas aeruginosa e. e.
Pseudomyxom pseudomyxoma
Pseudoparalyse pseudoparalysis
Pseudopodie pseudopod
Pseudoreaktion pseudoreaction
Pseudosklerose pseudosclerosis
Pseudostruktur pseudostructure
Pseudotabes e. e.
Pseudotuberkulose pseudotuberculosis
Pseudouridinurie pseudouridinuria
Pseudowut mad itch, bovine pseudorabies
Pseudoxanthom pseudoxanthoma
Psicain psicaine
Psilocybin e. e.
Psilose psilosis
Psoasabszeß psoas abscess
Psoriasis e. e.
psoriatisch psoriatic
Psychalgie psychalgia
psychalgisch psychalgic
Psychasthenie psychasthenia
psychasthenisch psychasthenic
Psychataxie psychataxia
Psyche e. e.
psychedelisch psychodelic, psychedelic
Psychiater psychiatrist
Psychiatrie psychiatry

psychiatrisch psychiatric
psychisch psychic
psychoaktiv psychoactive
Psychoanalyse psychoanalysis
Psychoanalytiker psychoanalyst
psychoanalytisch psychoanalytic
Psychobiologie psychobiology
Psychochemie psychochemistry
Psychochirurg psychosurgeon
Psychochirurgie psychosurgery
psychochirurgisch psychosurgical
Psychochromästhesie psychochromaesthesia (e), psychochromesthesia (a
psychodelisch psychodelic, psychedelic
Psychodiagnostik psychodiagnostics
Psychodynamik psychodynamics
psychodynamisch psychodynamic
psychogen psychogenic
Psychogenie psychogenia
Psychologe psychologist
Psychologie psychology
Psychologin psychologist
psychologisch psychological
psychomotorisch psychomotor
Psychoneurose psychoneurosis
psychoneurotisch psychoneurotic
Psychopath e. e.
Psychopathie psychopathy
Psychopathin psychopath
psychopathisch psychopathic
psychopathische Persönlichkeit psychopathic personality
Psychopharmakologie psychopharmacology
psychopharmakologisch psychopharmacological
Psychopharmakon psycho-drug
psychophysisch psychophysical
Psychoprophylaxe psychoprophylaxis
Psychoreaktion psychoreaction
Psychose psychosis
—,**manisch-depressive** manic-depressive psychosis
—,**schizophrene** schizophrenic psychosis

psychoseimitierend psychotomimetic
psychosensorisch psychosensory
psychosexuell psychosexual
psychosomatisch psychosomatic
psychotherapeutisch psychotherapeutic
Psychotherapie psychotherapy
psychotisch psychotic
psychotomimetisch psychotomimetic
psychotrop psychotropic
Psychrometer e. e.
Pteridin pteridine
Pterygium e. e.
pterygomaxillär pterygomaxillary
Ptomain ptomaine
Ptose ptosis
ptotisch ptotic
Ptyalin e. e.
Ptyalismus ptyalism
Ptyalolithiasis e. e.
Pubertät puberty
Pubertas praecox precocious puberty
pubertierend pubescent
Pubiotomie pubiotomy
pubisch pubic
puboprostatisch puboprostatic
pudendal e. e.
Puder powder
pudern to powder
pueril puerile
Puerpera e. e.
puerperal e. e.
Puerperalfieber puerperal pyrexia
Puerperalsepsis puerperal sepsis
Puerperium e. e.
Puffer buffer
puffern to buffer
Pufferung buffering
Pufferungsvermögen buffer value
Pulex irritans e. e.
pulmoaortal pulmo-aortic
pulmonal pulmonary, pulmonic
Pulmonalinsuffizienz pulmonic insufficiency

Pulmonalklappe pulmonary valve
Pulmonalstenose pulmonic stenosis
Pulpa pulp
pulpal e. e.
Pulpenhöhle pulp cavity
Pulpenkammer pulp chamber
Pulpenkanal pulp canal
Pulpitis e. e.
Pulpotomie pulpotomy
Puls pulse
Pulsatilla e. e.
Pulsdefizit pulse deficit
pulsieren to pulsate
Pulsionsdivertikel pulsion diverticulum
pulslos pulseless
Pulsschlag pulsation
Pulsus alternans e. e.
 – bigeminus bigeminal pulse
 – paradoxus e. e.
Pulver powder
Pulverbläser powder blower
pulverisieren to pulverize
Pulverisierung pulverization
Pulvis Ipecacuanhae opiatus ipecac and opium powder
Puma e. e.
Pumpe pump
Pumpoxygenator pump oxygenator
Punctum maximum point of maximum
Punkt point
Punktat punctate
punktieren to punctate, to tap
Punktion puncture
pupillär pupillary
Pulillatonie pupillatonia
Pupille pupil (of the eye)
Purin purine
Purinase e. e.
Purkinjesche Faser Purkinje's fiber
Puromycin e. e.
Purpura e. e.
 –, thrombopenische thrombocytopenic purpura

Purpureaglykosid purpureaglucoside
Pustel pustule
Pustelbildung pustulation
Pustula maligna malignant
 pustule
pustulär pustular
Putreszin putrescine
Putzer trimmer
PVC-Gerüst-Tablette PVC-
 skeleton tablet
Pyämie pyaemia (e), pyemia (a)
pyämisch pyaemia (e), pyemia (a)
Pyarthrosis e. e.
Pyelitis e. e.
pyelitisch pyelitic
Pyelogramm pyelogram
Pyelographie pyelography
–, **intravenöse** intravenous
 pyelography
–, **retrograde** retrograde
 pyelography
pyelographisch pyelographic
Pyelonephritis e. e.
pyelonephritisch pyelonephritic
Pyeloskopie pyeloscopy
Pyelostomie pyelostomy
Pyelotomie pyelotomy
pyelovenös pyelovenous
pyelovenöser Reflux pyelovenous
 backflow
pyknisch pyknic
Pyknolepsie pyknolepsy
Pyknose pyknosis
pyknotisch pyknotic
Pylephlebitis e. e.
Pylorektomie pylorectomy
pylorisch pyloric
Pyloromyotomie pyloromyotomy
Pylorospasmus pylorospasm
Pylorus e. e.
Pylorusinsuffizienz pyloric
 insufficiency
Pylorusplastik pyloroplasty
Pylorusstenose pyloric stenosis
Pyodermie pyodermia

pyogen pyogenic
Pyometra e. e.
Pyometritis e. e.
Pyonephrose pyonephrosis
Pyopneumothorax e. e.
Pyorrhöe pyorrhea (a),
 pyorrhoea (e)
Pyosalpingitis e. e.
Pyosalpingo-Oophoritis e. e.
Pyosalpinx e. e.
Pyothorax e. e.
pyramidal e. e.
Pyramidenbahn pyramidal tract
Pyran e. e.
Pyranose e. e.
Pyrazin pyrazine
Pyrazol e. e.
Pyrazolon pyrazolone
Pyribenzamin pyribenzamine
Pyridin pyridine
Pyridoxin pyridoxine
Pyrimethamin pyrimethamine
Pyrimidin pyrimidine
Pyrimidopyrimidin pyrimido-
 pyrimidine
Pyrithioxin pyrithioxine
Pyrithyldion pyrithyldione
Pyrogallol e. e.
Pyrolgallussäure pyrogallic
 acid
Pyrogen e. e.
pyrogen pyrogenic
pyrogenfrei pyrogen free
Pyroglobulin e. e.
Pyromanie pyromania
Pyronin pyronine
Pyrophosphat pyrophosphate
Pyrophosphatase e. e.
Pyrophosphorylase e. e.
Pyrotoxin e. e.
Pyrrol pyrrole
Pyrrolase e. e.
Pyrrolidin e. e.
Pyruvat pyruvate
Pyurie pyuria
pyurisch pyuric

Q

Q-Fieber Q-fever
Quacksalber quack
Quacksalberei quackery
Quacksalberin quack
quacksalbern to quack
Quadrant e. e.
Quadrantenanopsie quadrantanopsia
Quadrat square
Quadratmeter square meter
Quadratwurzel square root
Quadripara e. e.
Quadriplegie quadriplegia
quälen to torment
Quälerei worry
Qualität quale, quality
Qualitätskontrolle quality control
Qualitätssicherung quality monitoring
qualitativ qualitative
Quantentheorie quantum theory
Quantität quantity
quantitativ quantitative
Quantum e. e.
Quarantäne quarantine
Quarantäne, in – legen to quarantine
Quarz quartz
quaternär quaternary
Queckenstedtsches Zeichen Queckenstedt's phenomenon
Quecksilber mercury, quicksilver
Quecksilberbehandlung mercurialization
Quecksilberchlorid mercury bichloride, mercuric chloride
Quecksilberchlorür mercurous chloride
Quecksilberdampfquarzlampe mercury quartz lamp
quecksilberhaltig (einwertig) mercurous
– (zweiwertig) mercuric
Quecksilberoxyd mercuric oxide
quellen to gush
Querdurchmesser transverse diameter
Querschnitt cross-section
Querschnittslähmung paraplegia
Querulant querulent
Querulantin querulent
querulatorisch querulous
quetschen to crush
Quetschhahn pinchcock clamp
Quetschklemme crushing forceps
Quetschung crushing
Quicktest Quick test
Quinckesche Krankheit Quincke's disease
Quinethazon quinethazone
Quote e. e.
Quotient e. e.

R

Rabies e. e.
Rachen throat, pharynx
Rachenmandel pharyngeal tonsil
Rachitis rickets, rachitis
rachitisch ricketic, rachitic
rachitischer Rosenkranz rachitic rosary
Rad wheel
Rad (radiol.) e. e.
Radgelenk rotary joint
radial e. e.

radialwärts radiad
Radiant radian
radikal radical
Radikal radical
Radikalität, radicality
radikulär radicular
Radikulitis radiculitis
Radikuloneuritis radiculoneuritis
Radioaktinium radioactinium
radioaktiv radioactive
radioaktive Markierung radioactive tracer technic
radioaktive Substanz radioactive substance, radiant
Radioaktivität radioactivity
Radioanalyse radioanalysis
radioanalytisch radioanalytic
Radiobiologie radiobiology
Radiochemie radiochemistry
radiochemisch radiochemical
Radiochrom radiochromium
Radiochromat radiochromate
Radioeisen radioiron
Radioglukose radioglucose
Radiographie radiography
radiohumeral e. e.
Radio-Immunoassay (RIA) e. e.
Radioimmunologie radioimmunology
Radioindikator radiotracer
Radioisotop radioisotope
Radiojod radioiodine
Radiojod, mit − versehen to radioiodinate
Radiokobalt radiocobalt
Radiologie radiology
radiologisch radiological
Radiolyse radiolysis
Radiometer e. e.
Radiophosphor radiophosphorus
Radiophotographie radiophotography
radiophysikalisch radiophysical
Radiorezeptorassay radioreceptorassay
Radiothorium e. e.
Radiotracer e. e.

Radium e. e.
Radiumbestrahlung radiumization
Radiumemanation radon, radium emanation, niton
Radiumspickung radium implantation
Radiumträger radium applicator
Radix Althaeae marshmallow root
räuchern to fumigate
Räude mange
räudig mangy
raffinieren to refine
Raffinose e. e.
Rahm cream
Rahmen frame
Raman-Effekt Raman effect
Ramstedt-Webersche Operation Ramstedt's operation
Rand margin
Randwulstbildung lipping
Rankenangiom rankenangioma
Ranula e. e.
Ranviersche Membran Ranvier's membrane
ranzig rancid
Raphe e. e.
Rappe black horse
Rapport e. e.
Rarefizierung rarefaction
rasen to rave
Raserei rage
rasieren to shave
Rasiermesser razor
Raspatorium raspatory
Raspel rasp
Rasse race
Rasselgeräusch rale
−, **feuchtes** moist rale
−, **trockenes** dry rale
rasseln to rattle
rassisch racial
Raster grid
Rastlosigkeit restlessness
Rat advice
Rate e. e.
raten to advise
Rathkesche Tasche Rathke's pouch

Ratimeter e. e.
Ration e. e.
rational e. e.
Rationalisierung rationalization
rationell rational
Ratte rat
Rattenbißkrankheit rat bite fever, sodoku
Rattengift ratpoison
Raubmord robbery with murder
Rauch smoke
rauchen to smoke
Rauchfuß-Groccosches Dreieck Grocco's triangle
Rauchinhalation smoke inhalation
Raumfahrtmedizin spaceflight medicine
raumfordernd space-occupying
Raumluft ambient air
Rausch drunkenness; intoxication
Rauschbrand symptomatic anthrax
Rauschgift dope, narcotic
Rautenhirn rhombencephalon
Raynaudsche Gangrän Raynaud's disease
Razemat racemate
razemisch racemic
Readsche Formel Read's formula
Reagens reagent
Reagenzglas test tube
Reagenzpapier test paper
reagieren to react
Reagin e. e.
Reaktion reaction
Reaktionsfähigkeit reactivity
Reaktionsvermögen reactivity
reaktiv reactive
reaktive Depression reactive depression
reaktivieren to reactivate
Reaktivierung reactivation
Realität reality
Reamputation e. e.
Reanimation e. e.
Rechenmaschine computer
rechteckig rectangular

rechtsdrehend dextrorotatory
Rechtsdrehung dextrorotation
rechtshändig dextromanual, right-handed
Rechts-Links-Shunt right-to-left shunt
Recklinghausensche Krankheit neurofibromatosis; osteitis fibrosa osteoplastica
Redestillation cohobation, redistillation
Redislokation redislocation
Redoxsystem redox system
Redressement e. e.
Reduktase reductase
Reduktion reduction
reduzieren to reduce
Referat report
Referenz reference
reflektieren to reflect
Reflektor reflector
reflektorisch reflected
reflektorische sympathische Dystrophie reflex sympathetic dystrophy
Reflektoskop reflectoscope
Reflektoskopie reflectoscopy
reflektoskopisch reflectoscopic
Reflex e. e.
–,**Achillessehnen-** Achilles tendon reflex
–,**Akkomodations-** accommodation reflex
–,**Anal-** anal reflex
–,**Axon-** axon reflex
–,**Babinski-** Babinski reflex
–,**Bainbridge-** Bainbridge reflex
–,**Bauchdecken-** abdominal reflex
–,**Bechterewscher** Bechterew's reflex
–,**bedingter** conditional reflex
–,**Bizeps-** biceps reflex
–,**Blasen-** bladder reflex
–,**Cremaster-** cremasteric reflex
–,**erworbener** acquired reflex
–,**Gänsehaut-** pilomotor reflex
–,**gekreuzter** crossed reflex

Reflex, Gordonscher paradoxic flexor reflex
–, **Haltungs-** attitudinal reflex
–, **Haut-** cutaneous reflex
–, **Hornhaut-** corneal reflex
–, **Karotissinus-** carotid sinus reflex
–, **Kehlkopf-** laryngeal reflex
–, **Ketten-** chain reflex
–, **Konjunktival-** conjunctival reflex
–, **konsensueller Licht-** consensual light reflex
–, **koordinierter** coordinated reflex
–, **Krampf-** convulsive reflex
–, **Licht-** light reflex
–, **Massen-** mass reflex
–, **Mayerscher Grund-** finger-thumb reflex
–, **Mendel-Bechterewscher** Mendel-Bechterew's reflex
–, **Muskel-** muscular reflex
–, **Oppenheimscher** Oppenheim's reflex
–, **Patellarsehnen-** patellar reflex
–, **pathologischer** pathological reflex
–, **Periost-** periosteal reflex
–, **psychogalvanischer** psychogalvanic reflex
–, **Pupillen-** pupillary reflex
–, **Radiusperiost-** radial reflex
–, **renorenaler** reno-renal reflex
–, **Rossolimo-** Rossolimo's reflex
–, **Schluck-** palatine reflex
–, **Sehnen-** tendon reflex
–, **Sexual-** sexual reflex
–, **Strümpellscher** Strümpell's reflex
–, **Summations-** summation reflex
–, **Trizeps-** triceps reflex
–, **Umarmungs-** Moro embrace reflex
–, **Vagus-** vagus reflex
–, **verzögerter** delayed reflex
–, **viszeraler** visceral reflex
–, **Wahrnehmungs-** perception reflex

Reflexbewegung reflex action
Reflexbogen reflex arc
Reflexion reflection
reflexogen reflexogenic
Reflextherapie reflexotherapy
Reflexzentrum reflex center (a), reflex centre (e)
Reflux e. e., backflow
refraktär refractory
Refraktion refraction
Refraktometer refractometer
Refraktur refracture
Regel rule
regelmäßig regular
regelrecht regular
regelwidrig irregular
Regeneration e. e.
regenerativ regenerative
regenerieren to regenerate
Region e. e.
regional e. e.
Register e. e.
Regression e. e.
regressiv regressive
regulär regular
Regulation e. e.
regulatorisch regulatory
regulieren to regulate
Regulierung regulation
regungslos motionless
Regurgitation e. e.
Reh roe
Rehabilitation e. e.
rehabilitieren to rehabilitate
Rehe (veter.) founder
Rehkalb fawn
reiben to rub
Reibung friction
Reichmannsche Krankheit gastrosuccorrhea (a), gastrosuccorrhoea (e)
Reichweite range
reif mature
Reife maturity
Reifung maturation
Reifungshemmung maturation inhibition

Reifungsstillstand maturation arrest
reihenmäßig serial
Reimplantation e. e.
rein pure, clean
Reinfektion reinfection
Reinfusion e. e.
Reinheit purity
reinigen to clear, to purify, to rectify, to clarify, to clean
Reiniger cleanser
Reinigung purification, clarification, clearance
Reintubation e. e.
Reis rice
Reisekrankheit motion sickness
Reiskleie rice polishings
Reiskörper rice body
reißen to tear
Reißnersche Membran Reissner's membrane
Reiswasserstuhl rice water stool
Reitersche Krankheit Reiter's disease
Reiz stimulus
reizbar irritable
Reizbarkeit irritability
reizen to stimulate, to irritate
Reizerscheinung irritation symptom
Reizhusten dry cough
Reizleitungssystem conduction system of the heart
reizmildernd abirritant
Reizmittel stimulant
Reizschwelle stimulus threshold
Reiztherapie stimulation therapy
Reizung stimulation, irritation
rekalzifizieren to recalcify
Rekalzifizierung recalcification
Reklination reclination
Rekonstruktion reconstruction
Rekonvaleszent convalescent
Rekonvaleszentin convalescent
Rekonvaleszenz convalescence
Rekord record
Rekrudeszenz recrudescence

rektal rectal
rektifizieren to rectify
Rektifizierung rectification
Rektoromanoskop proctosigmoidoscope
Rektoromanoskopie proctosigmoidoscopy
Rektostomie rectostomy
rektoureteral rectoureteral
Rektoureteralfistel rectoureteral fistula
rektouterin rectouterine
rektovaginal rectovaginal
rektovesikal rectovesical
Rektozele rectocele
Rektum rectum
Rektumstriktur stricture of rectum
Rektusdiastase diastasis recti abdominis
rekurrierend recurrent
Relaxin e. e.
Relief e. e.
Remaksches Zeichen Remak's sign
Remineralisation remineralization
Remission e. e.
remittierend remittent
Renin e. e.
Renographie renography
Reoxydation reoxidation
Replicase e. e.
repolarisieren to repolarize
Repolarisierung repolarization
Reposition e. e.
Repressor e. e.
reproduktiv reproductive
reproduzierbar reproducible
Reproduzierbarkeit reproducibility
Reptil e. e.
Rescinnamin rescinnamine
Resektion resection
Resektoskop resectoscope
Reserpin reserpine
Reserve e. e.
Reserveluft reserve air

Reservevolumen reserve volume
Reservoir e. e.
resezierbar resectable
Resezierbarkeit resectability
resezieren to resect
residual e.e.
Residualkapazität residual capacity
Residualluft residual air
Residualvolumen residual volume
resistent resistant
Resistenz resistance
—,gekreuzte cross-resistance
Resonanz resonance
resorbieren to absorb
Resorption absorption, resorption
Resorptionsstörung, intestinale malabsorption
Resorzin resorcinol
Respiration e. e.
Respirationstrakt respiratory tract
respiratorisch respiratory
respirieren to respire
Rest e. e.
Re-Stenose restenosis
Restharn residual urine
Restitution e. e.
restlich residual
Reststickstoff nonprotein nitrogen
Retard-Arzneimittel delayed action drug, slow release drug
retardiert retarded
Retention e. e.
retikulär reticular
Retikuloendothel reticuloendothelium
retikuloendothelial reticuloendothelial
retikuloendotheliales System reticuloendothelial system
Retikuloendotheliom reticuloendothelioma
Retikuloendotheliose reticuloendotheliosis
Retikulosarkom reticulosarcoma
Retikulose reticulosis
Retikulozyt reticulocyte

Retikulozytenkrise shower of reticulocytes
Retikulozytose reticulocytosis
Retikulumzelle reticulum cell
Retina e. e.
retinal e. e.
Retinalarterie retinal artery
Retinitis e. e.
Retinoblastom retinoblastoma
Retinopathie retinopathy
Retorte retort
Retothelsarkom retothel sarcoma
retraktil retractile
Retraktion retraction
Retraktor retractor
retroaurikulär retroauricular
retrobulbär retrobulbar
retroflektiert retroflexed
Retroflexion e. e.
retrograd retrograde
retrokardial retrocardiac
retrokolisch retrocolic
retrolabyrinthär retrolabyrinthine
retrolental e.e.
retromammär retromammary
retromandibulär retromandibular
retronasal e. e.
retroperitoneal e. e.
retropharyngeal e. e.
retroplazental retroplacental
retroponiert retroposed
retropubisch retropubic
Retropulsion e.e.
retrospektiv retrospective
retrosternal e. e.
retrouterin retrouterine
Retroversioflexion e. e.
Retroversion e. e.
retrovertiert retroverted
retrozökal retrocecal (a), retrocoecal (e)
Revaskularisation revascularization
Reverdinsche Transplantation Reverdin's graft
reversibel reversible
Reversibilität reversibility

Rezept recipe, prescription
Rezeptor receptor
rezeptpflichtig obtainable only by recipe
Rezeptur dispensing
Rezepturarznei magistery
rezessiv recessive
Rezidiv recidive, relapse
Rezidivierung recidivation
reziprok reciprocal
rezirkulierend recycling
Rh-Faktor Rh factor
Rhabarber rhubarb
Rhabdomyom rhabdomyoma
Rhabdosarkom rhabdosarcoma
Rhagade e. e.
Rhamnose e. e.
Rhenium e. e.
Rheobase rheobasis
Rheologie rheology
Rheoskopie rheoscopy
Rheostat e. e.
Rheostose rheostosis
Rheotaxis e. e.
Rhesusaffe rhesus monkey
Rheumaknötchen rheumatic nodule
rheumatisch rheumatic
rheumatische Granulomatose rheumatic granulomatosis
Rheumatismus rheumatism
—, **fieberhafter akuter** rheumatic fever
rheumatoid e. e.
Rheumatoid e. e.
Rheumatologe rheumatologist
Rheumatologie rheumatology
Rheumatologin rheumatologist
rheumatologisch rheumatological
Rhinenzephalie rhinencephalia
Rhinitis e. e.
— **atrophicans** atrophic rhinitis
— **membranacea** membranous rhinitis
— **vasomotoria** vasomotor rhinitis
rhinogen rhinogenous
Rhinolalie rhinolalia
Rhinologe rhinologist
Rhinologie rhinology
Rhinologin rhinologist
rhinologisch rhinological
Rhinopharyngitis e. e.
Rhinophym rhinophyma
Rhinosklerom rhinoscleroma
Rhinosklerombazillus Klebsiella rhinoscleromatis
Rhinosporidiose rhinosporidiosis
Rhizoma filicis rhizome of aspidium
Rhizopoda e. e.
Rhizotomie rhizotomy
Rhodamin rhodamine
Rhodan rhodane
Rhodium e. e.
rhythmisch rhythmic
Rhythmus rhythm
Riboflavin e. e.
Ribohexose e. e.
Ribonuklease ribonuclease
Ribonukleinsäure ribonucleic acid
Ribonukleotid ribonucleotide
Ribose e. e.
Ribosid riboside
Ribosom ribosome
ribosomal e. e.
Ribotid ribotide
Ribulose e. e.
Ricke e. e.
Rickettsia Burneti Rickettsia burneti
— **Prowazeki** Rickettsia prowazeki
Rickettsie rickettsia
riechen to smell
Riechhirn rhinencephalon
Riechsalz smelling salt
Riedel-Struma Riedel's struma
Riederzelle Rieder's cell
Riese giant
Riesenwuchs gigantism
Riesenzelle giant cell
Riesenzellensarkom giant cell sarcoma
Rifampicin e. e.

Rifttalfieber Rift Valley fever
rigid e. e.
Rigidität rigidity
Rind neat
Rinde bark; cortex
Rindergalle oxgall
Rinderpest cattle plague
Rinderserum bovine serum
Rindvieh cattle
Ring e. e.
Ringerlösung Ringer's solution
ringförmig annular
Rinne groove
rinnen to run, to flow
Rinnescher Versuch Rinne's test
Rippe rib
Rippenschere rib shear
Risiko risk
–,**gutes** good risk
–,**schlechtes** poor risk
Riß tear, rent
rissig full of rents
Rißwunde laceration
Rist instep
Ritgenscher Handgriff Ritgen method
Ritze fissure, crevice
ritzen to scratch
Rivaltaprobe Rivalta's test
Riva-Rocci-Blutdruckmesser Riva-Rocci spygmomanometer
Rizin ricin
Rizinusöl castor oil
Robbe seal
Roborans roborant
roborierend roborant
Rocky-Mountain-Fieber black fever, Rocky mountain fever
röcheln to rattle
Röhrchen tubule
Röhre tube
Röhrenspannung tube voltage
Röntgenapparat x-ray-apparatus
Röntgenaufnahme x-ray-picture
Röntgenaufnahme, eine – anfertigen to take a x-ray picture
Röntgenbefund Roentgen findings

Röntgenbehandlung Roentgen treatment
Röntgenbericht x-ray report
röntgenbestrahlen to roentgenize
Röntgenbestrahlung roentgenization
Röntgenbild x-ray picture, roentgenogram
Röntgenbrille x-ray goggles
Röntgendermatitis radiodermatitis
Röntgendiagnose x-ray diagnosis, radiodiagnosis
Röntgendiagnostik x-ray diagnostics, radiodiagnostics
röntgendiagnostisch radiodiagnostic
Röntgendurchleuchtung roentgenoscopy
Röntgenfilm x-ray film
Röntgenfilm-Entwicklungsmaschine x-ray processor
Röntgenkater x-ray sickness
Röntgenkontrolle supervision by x-ray examination
Röntgenographie roentgenography
Röntgenologe roentgenologist
Röntgenologie roentgenology
Röntgenologin roentgenologist
röntgenologisch roentgenological
Röntgenphotographie roentgenphotography
Röntgenreihenuntersuchung mass radiography
Röntgenröhre x-ray tube
Röntgenschirm fluorescent screen
Röntgenstrahlen x-rays
Röntgentherapie roentgenotherapy
–,**Hochvolt-** high voltage roentgenotherapy
–,**Niedervolt-** low voltage roentgenotherapy
Röntgentiefenbestrahlung deep roentgen therapy
Röntgenüberwachung supervision by x-ray examination

rösten to roast
Röte redness
Röteln German measles
röten to redden
Rötung reddening
roh crude, raw
Rohkost uncooked food, raw diet
Rohr tube
Rohrzucker sucrose
Rolitetracyclin rolitetracycline
Rollstuhl wheel-chair
Rombergsches Zeichen Romberg sign
Rorschachtest Rorschach test
Rosacea e. e.
Rosanilin rosaniline
Rose e. e.
Rosenkranz, rachitischer rachitic rosary
Roseole roseola
Roßkastanie horse chestnut
Rossolimo-Reflex Rossolimo's reflex
Rost rust
Rotation e. e.
rotatorisch rotatory
Rotblindheit red blindness
Rotes Kreuz Red Cross
Rotgrünblindheit red-green blindness
rotieren to rotate
Rotkreuzarmbinde brassard
Rotsehen erythropia
Rotwild deer
Rotz glanders, malleus
Rotzbazillus Actinobacillus mallei
Rous-Sarkom Rous' sarcoma
Routine e. e.
Rovsingsches Zeichen Rovsing's sign
Rubeola scarlatinosa fourth disease
Rubidium e. e.
Rubidomycin e. e.
Rudiment e. e.

rudimentär rudimentary
Rückbildung involution; improvement; retrogression
Rückbildungsmelancholie involutional melancholia
Rücken back
Rückenmark spinal cord
Rückenschmerz backache
rückfällig recurrent, relapsing
Rückfall relapse
Rückfallfieber relapsing fever, recurrent fever
Rückfluß reflux, backflow
Rückgrat spine
Rückkopplung feedback
Rückprall rebound
rückresorbieren to reabsorb
Rückresorption reabsorption
Rückschritt regression
Rückstand residue
Rückstoß recoil
Rücktitration back titration
Rückverwandlung reversal
Rückwärtskrümmung recurvation
Rückwärtsverlagerung retro-displacement
Rührei battered egg
rülpsen to belch
Rülpsen belching, eructation
Rüssel snout, proboscis
Ruhe rest
Ruhelage rest position
ruhen to rest, to repose
Ruhestadium dormancy
Ruhestoffwechsel resting metabolism
ruhigstellen (= fixieren) to fix
ruhigstellen (= sedieren) to calm, to allay excitement
Ruhr dysentery
—, Amöben- entamebic dysentery (a), entamoebic dysentery (e)
—, Bazillen- bacillary dysentery
Ruhrbazillus (Flexner) Shigella paradysenteriae Flexner
— (Shiga-Kruse) Shigella dysenteriae

Ruhrbazillus (Sonne) Shigella Sonnei
– **(Strong)** Shigella paradysenteriae Strong
Rumination e. e.
Rumpel-Leedesches Phänomen Rumpel-Leede phenomenon
Rumpf trunk
Rundzelle round cell

Rundzellensarkom round celled sarcoma
Runzel wrinkle
runzelig wrinkled
Ruptur rupture
rupturieren to rupture
Ruthenium e. e.
Rutin e. e.
Rutosid rutoside

S

Sabadille sabadilla
Sabin-Feldmantest Sabin-Feldman test
Sabinaöl savin oil
Sabinaölvergiftung sabinism
Sabinismus sabinism
Saccharase e. e.
Saccharat saccharate
Saccharid saccharide
Saccharimeter e. e.
Saccharomyces e. e.
Saccharomykose saccharomycosis
Saccharose e. e., sucrose
Sacharin gluside, sycose
Sachs-Georgireaktion Sachs-Georgi test
sachverständig expert
Sachverständiger expert
Sack sac
sackartig saccate
sackförmig saccate
Sadismus sadism
Sadist e. e.
Sadistin sadist
sadistisch sadistic
Säckchen saccule
Säge saw
sättigen to saturate, to satiate
Sättigung saturation, satiation
Sättigungsgefühl feeling of satiation
säuerlich acescent

säuern to acidify
säugen to suckle
Säugen lactation
Säugetier mammal
Säugetier... mammalian
Säugling suckling
Säuglingsalter infancy
Säuglingsfürsorge infant welfare
Säuglingsheim baby nursery
Säuglingspflegerin dry nurse
Säule column, pillar
Säulenchromatographie column chromatography
Säure acid
–, **Abietin-** abietinic acid
– **Absinth-** absinthic acid
– **Adenosinphosphor-** adenosine phosphoric acid
– **Adenyl-** adenylic acid
– **Äthacryn-** ethacrynic acid
– **Äthylendiamintetraessig-** ethylenediamine tetraacetic acid
– **Aetian-** aetianic acid (e), etianic acid (a)
– **Agarizin-** agaricic acid
– **Akonit-** aconitic acid
– **Akryl-** acrylic acid
– **Aldon-** aldonic acid
– **aliphatische** aliphatic acid
– **Alloxan-** alloxanic acid
– **Ameisen-** formic acid

Säure, Amido- amido acid
- **Amino-** amino acid
- **Aminoessig-** aminoacetic acid
- **Aminoisobutter-** aminoisobutyric acid
- **Aminokapron-** aminocaproic acid
- **Anthranil-** anthranilic acid
- **Arachidin-** arachidic acid
- **Arachidon-** arachidonic acid
- **aromatische** aromatic acid
- **Arsen-** arsenic acid
- **arsenige** arsenous acid
- **Arsin-** arsinic acid
- **Arson-** arsonic acid
- **Aryloxyessig-** aryloxyacetic acid
- **Askorbin-** ascorbic acid
- **Asparagin-** asparaginic acid
- **Azetessig-** diacetic acid
- **Azetylen-** acetylenic acid
- **Azetylgerb-** acetyltannic acid
- **Azetylsalizyl-** acetylsalicylic acid
- **Baldrian-** valerianic acid
- **Barbitur-** barbituric acid
- **Behen-** behenic acid
- **Benzoe-** benzoic acid
- **Bernstein-** succinic acid
- **Betaoxybutter-** betaoxybutyric acid
- **Blau-** hydrocyanic acid, prussic acid
- **Bor-** boric acid
- **Brenzschleim-** pyromucic acid
- **Brenztrauben-** pyruvic acid
- **Bromwasserstoff-** hydrobromic acid
- **Butter-** butyric acid
- **Butyläthylbarbitur-** butylethylbarbituric acid
- **Caprin-** capric acid
- **Capron-** caproic acid
- **Capryl-** caprylic acid
- **Carbamid-** carbamic acid
- **Cephalin-** cephalinic acid
- **Cerebron-** cerebronic acid
- **Cerotin-** cerotinic acid
- **Chaulmoogra-** chaulmoogric acid

Säure, Chelidon- chelidonic acid
- **Chenodesoxychol-** chenodeoxycholic
- **China-** quinic acid
- **Chlor-** chloric acid
- **Chloressig-** chloracetic acid
- **chlorige** chlorous acid
- **Chol-** cholic acid
- **Cholesterin-** cholesterinic acid
- **Chondroitin-** chondroitic acid
- **Chondroitinschwefel-** chondroitin-sulfuric acid (a), chondroitin-sulphuric acid (e)
- **Chrom-** chromic acid
- **Chrysophan-** chrysophanic acid
- **Cytidyl-** cytidylic acid
- **Decen-** decenoic acid
- **Dehydrochol-** dehydrocholic acid
- **Deltaaminolävulin-** deltaaminolaevulinic acid (e), deltaaminolevulinic acid (a)
- **Desoxychol-** desoxycholic acid
- **Desoxyribonuklein-** desoxyribonucleic acid
- **Diäthylbarbitur-** diethylbarbituric acid
- **Diäthylentriaminpentaessig-** diethylene triamine pentaacetic acid
- **Diaminoessig-** diaminoacetic acid
- **Diaminokapron-** lysine
- **Dichloressig-** dichloracetic acid
- **Dihydrofol-** dihydrofolic acid
- **dreibasige** tribasic acid
- **einbasige** monobasic acid
- **Epsilon-Aminokapron-** epsilon aminocaproic acid
- **Ergotin-** ergotinic acid
- **Essig-** acetic acid
- **Etacryn-** ethacrynic acid
- **Fett-** fatty acid
- **Fluorwasserstoff-** hydrofluoric acid
- **Fol-** folic acid
- **Folin-** folinic acid

Säure, Formiminoglutamin-
formiminoglutaminic acid
- **Fumar-** fumaric acid
- **Galakturon-** galacturonic acid
- **Gallen-** bile acid
- **Gallus-** gallic acid
- **Gerb-** tannic acid
- **Glukon-** gluconic acid
- **Glukuron-** glucuronic acid
- **Glutamin-** glutaminic acid
- ,**Glutar-** glutaric acid
- **Glykochol-** glycocholic acid
- **Glyzerin-** glyceric acid
- **Glyzerophosphor-** glycerophosphoric acid
- **Gold-** auric acid
- **Guanyl-** guanylic acid
- **Harn-** uric acid
- **Helvella-** helvellic acid
- **Heptacosan-** heptacosanic acid
- **Hexosediphosphor-** hexosediphosphoric acid
- **Hexuron-** hexuronic acid
- **Hippur-** hippuric acid
- **Homogentisin-** homogentisic acid
- **Homopiperidin-** homopiperidinic acid
- **Hyaluron-** hyaluronic acid
- **Hydrakryl-** hydracrylic acid
- **Hydroxy-** hydroxy acid
- **Indolessig-** indolacetic acid
- **Inosin-** inosinic acid
- **Isovalerian-** isovalerianic acid
- **Jod-** iodic acid
- **Jodgorgo-** iodogorgic acid
- **Kakodyl-** cacodylic acid
- **Kampfer-** camphoric acid
- **Kamphoglukuron-** camphoglycuronic acid
- **Kantharidin-** cantharidic acid
- **Kaprin-** capric acid
- **Kapron-** caproic acid
- **Kapryl-** caprylic acid
- **Karbamid-** carbamic acid
- **Karbol-** carbolic acid
- **Keto-** keto acid

Säure, Ketoisokapron- ketoisocaproic acid
- **Kiesel-** silicic acid
- **Klee-** oxalic acid
- **Kohlen-** carbonic acid
- **Kresyl-** cresylic acid
- **Kroton-** crotonic acid
- **Lävulin-** laevulinic acid (e), levulinic acid (a)
- **Laurin-** lauric acid
- **Lignocerin-** lignoceric acid
- **Linol-** linolic acid, linoleic acid
- **Linolen-** linolenic acid
- **Lithochol-** lithocholic acid
- **Lyserg-** lysergic acid
- **Magen-** gastric acid
- **Mandel-** mandelic acid
- **Mangan-** manganic acid
- **Margarin-** margaric acid
- **Melissin-** melissic acid
- **Merkaptur-** mercapturic acid
- **Metaphosphor-** metaphosphoric acid
- **Milch-** lactic acid
- **Monochloressig-** monochloracetic acid
- **Montan-** octacosanic acid
- **Mukoitinschwefel-** mucoitinsulfuric acid (a), mucoitinsulphuric acid (e)
- **Myristin-** myristic acid
- **Nalidixin-** nalidixic acid
- **Neuramin-** neuraminic acid
- **Nikotin-** nicotinic acid
- **Nonacosan-** nonacosanic acid
- **Nuklein-** nucleinic acid
- **Öl-** oleic acid
- **Oktan-** octanoic acid
- **Orot-** orotic acid
- **Orthoaminosalizyl-** orthoaminosalicylic acid
- **Orthophosphor-** orthophosphoric acid
- **Osmium-** osmic acid
- **Oxal-** oxalic acid
- **Oxybernstein-** malic acid
- **Palmitin-** palmitic acid

Säure, Pantothen- pantothenic acid
- **Paraaminobenzoe-** paraaminobenzoic acid
- **Paraaminohippur-** paraaminohippuric acid
- **Paraaminosalizyl-** paraaminosalicylic acid
- **Paraffin-** paraffinic acid
- **,Pelargon-** pelargonic acid
- **Penicillan-** penicillanic acid
- **Pentacosan-** pentacosanic acid
- **Perbor-** perboric acid
- **Peressig-** peracetic acid
- **Permangan-** permanganic acid
- **Phenyläthylbarbitur-** phenylethylbarbituric acid
- **Phenylchinolinkarbon-** phenylcinchoninic acid
- **Phenylessig-** phenylacetic acid
- **Phosphatid-** phosphatidic acid
- **Phosphor-** phosphoric acid
- **Phosphoribosylimidazolessig-** phosphoribosylimidazole-acetic acid
- **phosphorige** phosphorous acid
- **Phosphorwolfram-** phosphotungstic acid
- **Phthal-** phthalic acid
- **Pikrin-** picric acid
- **Piperidin-** piperidinic acid
- **Propion-** propionic acid
- **Prostan-** prostanic acid
- **Pyrogallus-** pyrogallic acid
- **Pyrophosphor-** pyrophosphoric acid
- **rauchende Salpeter-** nitrosonitric acid, fuming nitric acid
- **rauchende Schwefel-** pyrosulfuric acid (a), pyrosulphuric acid (e)
- **Rhodan-** rhodanic acid
- **Ribonuklein-** ribonucleic acid
- **Rizinol-** ricinolic acid
- **Rosol-** rosolic acid
- **Salizyl-** salicylic acid
- **salizylige** salicylous acid
- **Salpeter-** nitric acid

Säure, salpetrige nitrous acid
- **Salz-** hydrochloric acid, muriatic acid
- **Santalin-** santalinic acid
- **Santonin-** santoninic acid
- **Schleim-** mucic acid
- **schwache** weak acid
- **Schwefel-** sulfuric acid (a), sulphuric acid (e)
- **schweflige** sulfurous acid (a), sulphurous acid (e)
- **Selen-** selenic acid
- **Sorbin-** sorbic acid
- **Sozojodol-** sozoiodolic acid
- **Stearin-** stearic acid
- **Sulfanil-** sulfanilic acid (a), sulphanilic acid (e)
- **Sulfo-** sulfo acid (a), sulpho acid (e)
- **Sulfosalizyl-** sulfosalicyclic acid (a), sulphosalicyclic acid (e)
- **Taurochol-** taurocholic acid
- **Tetracosan-** tetracosanic acid
- **Tetrahydrofol-** tetrahydrofolic acid
- **Thio-** thio acid
- **Thioaminopropion-** thioaminopropionic acid
- **Thioessig-** thioacetic acid
- **Thiokt-** thioctic acid
- **Thymidyl-** thymidylic acid
- **Tranexam-** tranexamic acid
- **Trichloressig-** trichloracetic acid
- **Tricosan-** tricosanic acid
- **Trijodthyroessig-** triiodothyroacetic acid
- **Triphosphor-** triphosphoric acid
- **Tropa-** tropic acid
- **unterphosphorige** hypophosphorous acid
- **Ursodesoxychol-** ursodeoxycholic acid
- **Valerian-** valerianic acid
- **Vanadin-** vanadic acid
- **Vanille-** vanillic acid

Säure, Vanillinmandel- vanillinmandelic acid
- **vierbasige** tetrabasic acid
- **Wein-** tartaric acid
- **Zimt-** cinnamic acid
- **Zitronen-** citric acid
- **zweibasige** dibasic acid

Säure-Basen-Gleichgewicht acid-base equilibrium
säurebeständig acid-resisting
säurebildend acid-forming
säurefest acidoresistant, acid-fast
säurefestes Stäbchen acid-fast bacillus
säureresistent acidoresistant, acid-resisting
Säureresistenz acidoresistance
Saft sap, juice
sagittal e. e.
Sahlische Desmoidreaktion Sahli's desmoid reaction
Sahne cream
Saitengalvanometer string galvanometer
sakral sacral
Sakralisation sacralization
sakralwärts sacrad
sakroiliakal sacroiliac
Sakroiliakalgelenk sacroiliac joint
sakrokokzygeal sacrococcygeal
sakropelvisch sacropelvic
sakroperineal sacroperineal
sakrouterin sacrouterine
Salamander e. e.
Salbe ointment, anointment, salve
Salbe, einreiben mit – to salve, to anoint
Salbei sage
salben to anoint, to salve
Salbenanwendung unction
Salbengrundlage ointment base
Salipyrin e. e.
Saliuretikum saliuretic
saliuretisch saliuretic
Salizyl salicyl
Salizylaldehyd salicylaldehyde
Salizylamid salicylamide
Salizylat salicylate
Salizylazosulfapyridin salicylazosulfapyridine (a), salicylazosulphapyridine (e)
Salizylsäure salicylic acid
Salizyltherapie salicyltherapy
Salmiak ammonia
Salmiakgeist ammonia water
Salmonella e. e.
Salmonelleninfektion salmonella infection
Salol e. e.
Salpeter saltpeter (a), saltpetre (e), niter (a), nitre (e)
Salpetersäure nitric acid
Salpingektomie salpingectomy
Salpingitis e. e.
salpingitisch salpingitic
Salpingographie salpingography
Salpingo-Oophoritis e. e.
Salpingostomie salpingostomy
Salpingotomie salpingotomy
Salpingoureterostomie salpingoureterostomy
Salpinx e. e.
Salz salt
–, kohlensaures carbonate
salzhaltig saline
salzig salty
Salzmangelsyndrom low salt syndrome
Salzsäure hydrochloric acid
–, freie free hydrochloric acid
Samarium e. e.
Samen (botan.) seed
Samen (med.) semen
samenbildend spermatogenic
Samenblase seminal vesicle
Samenblasenentzündung seminal vesiculitis, spermatocystitis
Samenflüssigkeit seminal fluid
Samenstrang spermatic cord
Sammelgefäß receiver
sammeln to pool, to collect
Sammelröhrchen, renales collecting renal tubule

Sanatorium e. e., sanitarium
Sandelöl sandalwood oil
Sandfliegenfieber sandfly fever
Sandsack sand bag
Sandstrahlgebläse sandblast
Sanduhrmagen hourglass stomach
sanguinolent e. e.
sanitär sanitary
Sanitäter first aid man
Sanitätseinrichtung infirmary
Sanitätspolizei sanitary police
Santalin e. e.
Santonin e. e.
Saprophyt saprophyte
saprophytär saprophytic
sardonisch sardonic
Sarg coffin
Sarkoid sarcoid
Sarkoidose sarcoidosis
Sarkolemm sarcolemma
Sarkom sarcoma
sarkomatös sarcomatous
Sarkomatose sarcomatosis
Sarkoplasma sarcoplasm
Sarkosom sarcosome
Sarkosporidiose sarcosporidiosis
Sarkozele sarcocele
Sarsaparille sarsaparilla
Sarzine sarcine
Satanspilz satanic bolete
satt satisfied, saturated
Sattel saddle
Satteldruck (veter.) saddle galls
Sattelgelenk saddle joint
Sattelnase saddle nose
Sattheit satiety
Saturnismus saturnism
Satyriasis e. e.
sauer acid
— machen to acidify
Sauermilch curdled milk
Sauerstoff oxygen
Sauerstoffatmung oxygen breathing
Sauerstoffbad oxygen bath
Sauerstoffbeladung oxygenation

Sauerstoffentladung deoxygenation
Sauerstoffflasche oxygen cylinder
sauerstoffhaltig oxygenic
Sauerstoffsättigung oxygenation
Sauerstoffverbrauch oxygen consumption
Saugapparat suction apparatus
Saugbiopsie suction biopsy
Saugdrainage suction drainage
saugen to suck
Saugen suction
Saum seam
Sauna sauna
s.c. (= subcutan) subcutaneous
Scabies e. e.
Scarpasches Dreieck Scarpa's triangle
Schaber scraper, rugine
Schaden damage, injury
Schädel skull
Schädelbasis skull base
Schädelbohrer trephine
Schädelbruch fracture of skull
Schädelhalter skull holder
Schädelimpressionsfraktur depressed fracture of skull
Schädelmessung craniometry, cephalometry
Schädelplastik cranioplasty
Schädelzange skull forceps
schädlich noxious, hurtfull
schänden to violate
schälen to peel
schärfen to sharpen
Schätzung estimation
Schaf sheep
Schafbock ram
Schakal jackal
Schale (= Gefäß) dish
Schale (= Rinde) peel
Schall sound
Schallgeschwindigkeit velocity of sound
Schalleitung conduction of sound waves

Schallwahrnehmung sound perception
Schallwelle sound wave
schalten to switch
Schalter switcher
Schalttisch control desk
Schambein pubic bone
Schamteile privy parts
Schanker chancre
—, **weicher** chancroid
Schapirosches Zeichen Schapiro's sign
Scharlach scarlet fever
scharlachähnlich scarlatiniform
Scharnier hinge
Scharniergelenk ginglymus, hinge joint
Schatten shadow
schattengebend opacifying
Schauer shiver
schauern to shiver
Schaum foam
Schaumbad foam bath
schaumbildend foam-forming
Schaumgummi foam rubber
Schaumzelle foam cell
Schauta-Operation Schauta's operation
Scheibe disk
Scheide vagina; sheath
Scheiden-Dammplastik colpoperineoplasty
Scheidenplastik colpoplasty
Scheidenspekulum vaginal speculum
Scheidenvorfall coleoptosis, prolapse of vagina
Scheidetrichter separating funnel
Scheidewand diaphragm, dividing wall, septum
Scheinschwangerschaft pseudopregnancy, pseudocyesis, false pregnancy, spurious pregnancy
Scheintod apparent death
Scheitel vertex
Schellack shellac

Schema e. e.
schematisch schematic
Schenkel thigh, leg
Schenkelblock, linksseitiger left bundle branch block
—, **rechtsseitiger** right bundle branch block
Schenkelhals neck of femur
Schenkelhernie femoral hernia
Schere scissors, shears
—, **anatomische** postmortem scissors
—, **chirurgische** operating scissors
Scheuermannsche Krankheit Scheuermann's disease
Schicht layer
Schichtarbeit shift work
Schichtaufnahmeverfahren sectional roentgenography, planigraphy, stratigraphy tomography
Schichtung lamination, stratification
Schicktest Schick test
Schiebedeckel sliding lid
schief oblique
Schiefhals wryneck, torticollis
Schielbrille louchettes
schielen to squint
schielend, auswärts- wall-eyed
—, **einwärts-** cross-eyed
Schielpinzette strabismus forceps
Schienbein shank, tibia
Schienbeinkante shin
Schiene splint
schienen to splint
Schienung splinting
Schießscheibenzelle target cell
Schild shield
Schilddrüse thyroid gland
Schilddrüsenadenom adenoma of thyroid gland
Schilddrüsentherapie thyrotherapy
Schildkröte turtle
Schillersche Jodprobe Schiller's test
Schimmel (= Pferd) white horse

Schimmel (= Pilz) mold, mould, mildew
Schimmelpilz mold, mould
Schimpanse chimpanzee
Schirmbild screening image
Schirm, Röntgen- fluorescent screen
Schistosoma haematobium e. e.
Schistosomiasis e. e.
Schi-Unfall ski accident
Schizogonie schizogony
schizoid e. e.
schizophren schizophrenic
Schizophrene schizophreniac
Schizophrener schizophreniac
Schizophrenie dementia praecox (e), dementia precox (a), schizophrenia
   Hebephrenie hebephrenic type
   Katatonie catatonic type
   Paranoid paranoid type
Schizotrichie schizotrichia
schlachten to slaughter
Schlachten slaughtering
Schlachthaus slaughterhouse
Schlacke cinder, slag
Schläfe temple
schläfrig sleepy
Schläfrigkeit sleepiness
Schlaf sleep
schlafbringend somniferous
schlafen to sleep
schlaff flaccid, slack
Schlaffheit laxity
Schlafkrankheit sleeping sickness; trypanosomiasis
—,**afrikanische** Congo trypanosomiasis, African sleeping sickness
—,**amerikanische** Chagas' disease
schlaflos sleepless
Schlaflosigkeit sleeplessness, insomnia
Schlafmittel hypnotic
Schlafmohn poppy
Schlafstörung somnipathy
Schlafsucht hypersomnia

Schlafwandeln somnambulism
Schlafwandler sleep walker, somnambulist
Schlafwandlerin sleep walker, somnambulist
Schlag beat, stroke
Schlaganfall apoplectic fit
schlagen to beat, to stroke
Schlagen beat, stroke
Schlagvolumen stroke volume
Schlamm mud
Schlammbad mud bath
Schlammfieber mud fever
Schlange snake, serpent
Schlangenbiß snake bite
Schlangenserum, antitoxisches antivenin
Schlangesches Zeichen Schlange's sign
schlank slender
Schlattersche Krankheit Schlatter's disease
Schlauch tube
Schleife loop, fillet
Schleifen grinding
Schleim slime, phlegm, mucus
Schleimbeutel synovial bursa
Schleimbeutelentzündung bursitis
schleimbildend mucigenous
Schleimbildung formation of mucus
Schleimfaden mucus thread
Schleimhaut mucous membrane, mucosa
Schleimhautrelief mucosal relief
schleimig slimy, mucous
schleimlösend mucolytic
Schleimsuppe gruel
Schlemmscher Kanal Schlemm's canal
Schlesingersche Probe Schlesinger's test
Schleuse sluice
Schließmuskel sphincter
Schlinge sling, snare
Schlitzer slitter
schlotternd slack
Schluckbeschwerden acataposis

Schlucken deglutition
schlucken to swallow
Schlüsselbein clavicle
Schmalz grease
Schmarotzer sponger
schmecken to taste
Schmecken gustation, degustation
Schmeißfliege blowfly
Schmelz enamel
Schmelzbereich melting range
schmelzen to melt
Schmelzmeißel enamel chisel
Schmelzmesser enamel hatchet
Schmelzpunkt melting point
Schmelzspalter enamel cleaver
Schmerz pain, ache
schmerzen painful
Schmerzhaftigkeit painfullness
schmerzlindernd soothing, anodyne
schmerzlos indolent
Schmerzlosigkeit indolency, anodynia
schmerzstillend anodyne, pain-deadening
schmerzstillendes Mittel anodyne, analgesic drug
Schmetterlingswirbel butterfly vertebra
schmiedbar wrought
Schmierblutung, uterine silent menstruation
Schmiere smear
schmieren to smear
Schmirgel emery
schmoren to fry
Schmorlsches Knötchen Schmorl's nodule
Schmutz filth, dirt
Schnabel beak
schnarchen to snore
schnarchend stertorous
Schnauze snout
Schnecke snail
Schneeblindheit snowblindness
Schneidezahn incisor
Schnellbestimmung rapid determination

Schnelligkeit velocity
schnellwachsend rapidly growing
schnellwirkend quick acting
schneuzen to blow the nose
Schnitt cut, scission, section
Schnittfänger section lifter
Schnittwunde incised wound
Schnüffeln sniffing
Schnürer snare
Schnupfen coryza
Schnupfpulver snuff
Schock shock
Schoemakersche Operation Schoemaker's operation
Schöpflöffel scoop
Schokoladenzyste chocolate cyst
schonen to spare
Schonung spare
Schorf scab, eschar, slough
schorfig scurvy
schräg bias
Schrägdurchmesser, erster right anterior obligue projection
Schrägdurchmesser, zweiter left anterior obligue projection
Schramme scratch
Schranke barrier
Schraube screw
Schraubengelenk cochlear joint
Schraubenzieher screw driver
Schraubverschluß screw lock
Schrecken fright
Schreiberscher Handgriff Schreiber's maneuver
Schrittmacher pacemaker
Schrittmacherbehandlung des Herzens cardiac pacing
schröpfen to cup
Schröpfkopf cupping glass
schroff tart
schrumpfen to shrink
Schrumpfung shrinkage
Schub, schizophrener schizophrenic episode
Schüffnersche Tüpfelung Schüffner's punctation
Schürfwunde excoriation

Schürze apron
Schüttelfrost shaking chill
Schüttellähmung shaking palsy
schütten to shed
Schulalter school age
Schulter shoulder
Schulterblatt scapula, shoulder blade
Schultergelenk shoulder joint
Schultergürtel shoulder girdle
Schultz-Charltonsches Auslöschphänomen Schultz-Charlton test
Schuppe scale, scute
Schuppenausschlag lepidosis
Schuppenhaut scabrities
schuppig scaly
Schurz apron
Schußwunde gunshot wound
Schusterbrust cobbler's chest
Schutz protection
Schutzdosis protective dose
Schutzfilm protective film
Schutzhülle shield
Schutzimpfung protective immunization
Schutzklappe shield
Schutzverband protective bandage
Schutzwirkung protective effect
Schwabachscher Versuch Schwabach test
schwach weak, faint, debile
– **werden** to faint
Schwachsinn feebleness of mind, mental deficiency
schwachsinnig weak-minded, feebleminded
Schwäche weakness, feebleness, debility
schwächen to weaken, to debilitate
schwächlich feeble, weakly
Schwächung weakening
schwängern to impregnate
Schwamm sponge
schwammig spongy
Schwammniere sponge kidney
Schwammschale sponge basin

Schwan swan
schwanger pregnant, enceinte, gravid
Schwangerschaft pregnancy, gravidity
Schwangerschaftsblutung haemorrhage of pregnancy (e), hemorrhage of pregnancy (a)
Schwangerschaftstest pregnancy test
Schwangerschaftstoxikose toxaemia of pregnancy (e), toxemia of pregnancy (a)
schwanken to sway, to stagger
Schwannom schwannoma
Schwannsche Scheide neurilemma
Schwanz tail
Schwarte rind
Schwarzwasserfieber blackwater fever
Schwefel sulfur (a), sulphur (e)
Schwefelbad sulfur bath (a), sulphur bath (e)
Schwefelblüte sublimed sulfur (a), sublimed sulphur (e)
schwefelhaltig sulfurated (a), sulphurated (e)
– **(sechswertig, vierwertig)** sulfuric (a), sulphuric (e)
– **(zweiwertig)** sulfurous (a), sulphurous (e)
Schwefelleber potassa sulfurata (a), potassa sulphurata (e)
Schwefelmilch precipitated sulfur (a), precipitated sulphur (e)
Schwefelsäure sulfuric acid (a), sulphuric acid (e)
Schwefelsäureester sulfuric acid ester (a), sulphuric acid ester (e)
Schwefelwasserstoff sulfur hydride (a), sulphur hydride (e)
schweflige Säure sulfurous acid (a), sulphurous acid (e)
Schweigepflicht duty of secrecy, professional discretion
Schwein swine, pig, hog
Schweinebandwurm pork tapeworm

Schweinefett lard
Schweinepest hog cholera
Schweinerotlauf red fever
Schweinfurter Grün Paris green
Schweinsberger Krankheit
Bottom disease
Schweiß sweat
Schweißabsonderung perspiration
schweißbildend sudoriparous
Schweißbläschen sudamina
Schweißdrüse sweat gland
Schweißdrüsenabszeß sudoriparous abscess
schweißen to weld
schweißtreibend sudorific, diaphoretic
schweißtreibendes Mittel sudorific, diaphoretic
Schweißzyste hydrocyst
Schwelle threshold
schwellen to swell
Schwellstrom swelling current
Schwellung tumefaction, gathering, swelling
schwer heavy
– (= ernst) serious
schwerelos weightless
Schwerelosigkeit weightlessness
schweres Wasser heavy water
schwerhörig hard of hearing
schwerlöslich sparingly soluble
Schwermetall heavy metal
Schwermut sadness
Schwertfortsatz xiphoid process
Schwesternausbildung nursing education
Schwesternschülerin student nurse
Schwesternschule school of nursing
Schwiele callosity
schwimmen to swim
Schwimmblase swimbladder
Schwimmhaut web
Schwindel (med.) vertigo
–, **leichter** dizziness
–, **otogener** auditory vertigo
Schwindelanfall attack of dizziness

Schwindelgefühl giddiness
Schwindsucht phthisis
schwindsüchtig phthisic
schwingen to vibrate, to swing
Schwingung vibration
Schwirren thrill
Schwitzbad sweat bath; sudatorium, tepidarium
schwitzen to sweat
Schwitzen sweating, sudation
Schwitzmittel sudorific
Schwund waste
Scilla squill
Scirrhus e. e.
Scopolaminum hydrobromicum scopolamine hydrobromide
Seborrhöe seborrhea (a), seborrhoea (e)
seborrhoisch seborrheic (a), seborrhoic (e)
Secale cornutum ergot
sechseckig hexagonal
sechswertig sexivalent
Secretagogum secretagogue
sedativ sedative
Sedativum sedative
Sedierung sedation
Sediment e. e., deposit
Sedimentierung sedimentation
Sedoheptulose e. e.
Seebad sea bath
Seehund seal
Seekrankheit pelagism, seasickness
Seele mind
Seelenblindheit mindblindness, mental blindness
Seelentaubheit minddeafness, mental deafness
seelisch mental
seelische Störung mental disturbance
Seemeile nautical mile
Seeschlange sea snake
Segment e. e.
segmental e. e.
segmentiert segmented
Segmentierung segmentation

Segregation e. e.
sehen to see
Sehen sight, vision
–, **verschwommenes** blurred vision
Sehkraft strength of vision
Sehne sinew, tendon
Sehnennaht tendosuture
Sehnenplastik tendoplasty
Sehnenscheide tendon sheath
Sehnenscheidenentzündung tendovaginitis
Sehnervpapille optic disk
sehnig tendinous, sinewy
Sehprüfung vision test
Sehrtsches Kompressorium Sehrt's compressor
Sehschärfe visual acuity
Sehstörung vision disorder
Sehvermögen vision
Sehweite reach of sight
Seide, chirurgische surgical silk
Seidenraupe silkworm
Seife soap
seifig saponaceous
Seignettesalz Rochelle salt
Seiher strainer
Sein entity
Seit- zu Endanastomose side to end anastomosis
Seit- zu Seitanastomose side to side anastomosis
Seite side
Seitenkette side chain
Seitenstechen stitch
Seitenventrikel lateral ventricle
seitlich lateral
Seitzfilter Seitz filter
Sekret secretion
Sekretär secretary
Sekretärin secretary
sekretagog secretagogue
Sekretin secretin
Sekretion secretion
–, **innere** internal secretion
sekretionsfördernd secretomotory
sekretionshemmend secretoinhibitory

sekretorisch secretory
Sektion section
– **(anatom.)** dissection, autopsy
Sektionsbesteck postmortem instruments
Sektionshandschuhe autopsy gloves
Sektionsnadel postmortem needle
Sektor sector
sekundär secondary
Selbsterhaltung self-preservation
Selbstimmunisierung auto-immunization
Selbstinduktion inductance
Selbstmord suicide
– **verüben** to commit suicide
Selbstregulierung autoregulation
Selbstreinigung self-purgation
Selbstschutz autoprotection
Selbstverdauung autodigestion
Selbstverstümmelung self-mutilation
selektiv selective
Selen selenium
Selenit selenite
Seliwanowsche Probe Selivanoff's test
Sella turcica e. e.
sellär sellar
Semantik semantics
semantisch semantic
Semialdehyd semialdehyde
Semikarbazon semicarbazone
semimembranös semimembranous
Seminar seminar
Seminom seminoma
Semiologie semiology
semiologisch semiological
semipermeabel semipermeable
semiquantitativ semiquantitative
Semithiokarbazon semithiocarbazone
Seneszenz senescence
Senföl oil of mustard, allyl isothiocyanate
Senfpapier mustard paper
senil senile

Senilität senility
Senkfuß splayfoot
Senkfußeinlage arch support, instep raiser
Senkung sinking
Senna e. e.
sensibel sensible
sensibilisieren to sensitize
Sensibilisierung sensitization
Sensibilität sensibility, sensitivity
sensitiv sensitive
Sensitivität sensitivity
sensorisch sensory
Separierinstrument separating instrument
Separiermittel separating medium
Sepharose e. e.
Sepsis e. e.
septiert septate
Septikämie septicaemia (e), septicemia (a)
Septikopyämie septicopyaemia (e), septicopyemia (a)
septisch septic
Septostomie septostomy
Septum e. e.
Septumdefekt, kardialer septal defect of the heart
Septumdeviation deflection of septum
Sequenz sequence
Sequester sequestrum
Sequesterbildung sequestration, sequestrum formation
Sequestrektomie sequestrectomy
Sequestrotomie sequestrotomy
Serie series
Serienschnitt serial section
Serin serine
Serodiagnose serodiagnosis
Serologie serology
serologisch serological
seromembranös seromembranous
seromukös seromucous
seronegativ seronegative
Seropneumothorax e. e.
seropositive seropositive
seropurulent e. e.
Seroreaktion seroreaction
serosanguinolent serosanguineous
Serothorax e. e.
Serotonin e. e.
serpiginös serpiginous
Sertolische Zelle Sertoli's cell
Serum e. e.
Serumbehandlung serotherapy
Serum-Glutaminsäure-Brenztraubensäure-Transaminase serum glutamic pyruvic transaminase
Serum-Glutaminsäure-Oxalessigsäure-Transaminase serum glutamic oxalacetic transaminase
Serumkrankheit serum sickness
Serumprophylaxe seroprophylaxis
Serumvergiftung serum poisoning
Sesambein sesamoid bone
Sesamöl teel oil
Sesquichlorid sesquichloride
Seuche epidemic; pestilence
Seuchenherd center of an epidemic (a), centre of an epidemic (e)
Sexologe sexologist
Sexologie sexology
Sexologin sexologist
sexologisch sexological
Sexualhormon sex hormone
Sexualität sexuality
Sexualneurose sexual neurosis
Sexualwissenschaft sexology
sexuell sexual
sezernierend secernent
sezieren to dissect
Sheehan-Syndrom Sheehan's syndrome
Shiga-Kruse-Bazillus Shiga's bacillus
Shoemakersche Linie Shoemaker's line
Shrapnellsche Membran Shrapnell's membrane
Shunt e. e.
Sialadenitis e. e.
Sialogramm sialogram

Sialographie sialography
sialographisch sialographic
Sialolithiasis e. e.
Sialorrhöe sialorrhea (a), sialorrhoea (e)
Sichelzelle sickle cell
Sicherheit safety
Sicherheitsgurt safety belt
sichern to assure, to secure
Sicherung assurance
Sichtanzeigegerät video display
sichtbar visible
– **machen** to visualize
Sichtbarkeit visibility
Sickerblutung microhaemorrhage (e), microhemorrhage (a)
Sideramin sideramine
sideroachrestisch sideroachrestic
Siderochrom siderochrome
Sideropenie sideropenia
sideropenisch sideropenic
siderophil siderophilous
Siderose siderosis
siderotisch siderotic
Sieb sieve; screen; riddle
Siebbein ethmoid bone
siebenwertig septivalent
Siebtest screening test
siechen to pine away, to be sickly
Siechenhaus hospital for incurables
sieden to seethe, to boil
Siedepunkt boiling point
Siemens e. e.
Sigmoid sigmoid flexure
Sigmoidanheftung sigmoidopexy
Sigmoidektomie sigmoidectomy
Sigmoiditis e. e.
Sigmoidoproktostomie sigmoidoproctostomy
Sigmoidoskopie sigmoidoscopy
Sigmoidostomie sigmoidostomy
Signal e. e.
Signallampe signal lamp
Signatur signature
signifikant significant

Signifikanz significance
Silbenstolpern syllable stumbling
Silber silver
Silberimprägnation silver impregnation
Silberimprägnierung silver impregnation
Silbernitrat silver nitrate
Silikat silicate
Silikon silicone
Silikongummi silicone rubber
Silikose silicosis
Silikosiderose silicosiderosis
silikotisch silicotic
Silikotuberkulose silicotuberculosis
Silizium silicon
Siliziumdioxyd silica
Silkwormgut silkworm-gut
Silofüllerkrankheit silo-filler's disease
Silvestersche künstliche Atmung Silvester's method
Simmondssche Krankheit Simmonds' disease
Simonartscher Strang Simonart's thread
Simssches Spekulum Sims' speculum
Simulant malingerer
Simulantin malingerer
Simulation malingering, simulation
simulieren to simulate
simultan simultaneous
Sinistrokardie sinistrocardia
sinistroponiert sinistroposed
Sinistroposition e. e.
Sinn sense
Sinneswahrnehmung sensory perception
sinuaurikulär sinu-auricular
sinubronchial e. e.
Sinus e. e.
Sinusarhythmie sinus arrhythmia
Sinus cavernosus cavernous sinus
Sinusitis ethmoidalis ethmoidal sinusitis

Sinusitis frontalis frontal sinusitis
- **maxillaris** maxillary sinusitis
- **sphenoidalis** sphenoidal sinusitis

Sinusknoten sinus node
Sinusrhythmus sinus rhythm
Sinustachykardie sinus tachycardia
Sippykur Sippy treatment
Sirup syrup
Sisomicin e. e.
Sitosterin sitosterol
Sittich parakeet
sittlich ethical
Situation e. e.
Situs e. e.
- **inversus** e. e.
- **transversus** e. e.

Sitzbad sitz bath
Sitzgurt seat belt
Sitzung session, sitting
Sjögren-Syndrom Sjogren's syndrome
Skabies scabies
Skala scale
Skalenusdurchtrennung scalenotomy
Skalenus-Lymphknotenbiopsie scalene node biopsy
Skalenussyndrom scalenus syndrome
Skalpell scalpel
- **,anatomisches** dissecting scalpel
- **,Operations-** operating knife

Skammonium scammony
skandieren to scan
skandierende Sprache scanning speech
Skandium scandium
skapular scapular
skapulohumeral scapulohumeral
Skarifikation scarification
skarlatiniform scarlatiniform
Skatol skatole
Skelett skeleton
skelettieren so skeletize
Skelettierung skeletization
Skelettmuskel skeletal muscle
Skenesche Drüse Skene's gland

Skiaskopie skiascopy, retinoscopy
skleral scleral
Sklerektomie sclerectomy
Sklerem sclerema
Skleritis anterior scleritis anterior
- **posterior** scleritis posterior

skleritisch scleritic
Sklerodermie scleroderma
sklerokonjunktival scleroconjunctival
sklerokorneal sclerocorneal
Sklerom scleroma
Sklerophthalmie sclerophthalmia
Sklerose sclerosis
-, **multiple** multiple sclerosis
-, **tuberöse** tuberous sclerosis

sklerosieren to sclerose
Sklerosierung sclerosing
sklerotisch sclerotic
Sklerotom sclerotome
Sklerotomie sclerotomy
Skolex scolex
Skoliose scoliosis
skoliotisch scoliotic
Skopolamin scopolamine
Skorbut scurvy
skorbutisch scorbutic
Skorpion scorpion
Skotom scotoma
-, **Flimmer-** flimmer scotoma
-, **zentrales** central scotoma

Skrofeln scrofula (a), scrophula (e)
Skrofuloderm scrofuloderma (a), scrophuloderma (e)
skrofulös scrofulous (a), scrophulous (e)
Skrofulose scrofulosis (a), scrophulosis (e)
skrotal scrotal
Smegma e. e.
Smegmabazillus Mycobacterium smegmatis
Snellensche Sehprobe Snellen's test
Soda e. e.
Sodbrennen pyrosis, heartburn

Sodoku e. e., rat-bite fever
Sodomie sodomy
Sofortmaßnahme emergency measure
Sog suction
sogenannt so-called
Sohlengänger plantigrade
Sol e. e.
Solanin e. e.
Solaninvergiftung solanism
solid e. e.
solitär solitary
somatisch somatic
somatogen somatogenic
Somatologie somatology
Somatostatin e. e.
somatotrop somatotropic
Sommerbrechdurchfall summer cholera
Sommersprosse freckle, lentigo
somnolent e. e.
Somnolenz somnolence
Sonde probe, explorer, specillum, sound
Sondenernährung gavage
sondieren to probe
Sonne sun
Sonnenbad sun bath
Sonnenbestrahlung heliation, insolation
—,**der — aussetzen** to solarize
Sonnenbräune tan
Sonnenbrand sunburn
Sonnenenergie solar power
Sonnenstich sunstroke
Sonographie sonography
sonographisch sonographical
sonor sonorous
Sonotomographie sonotomography
Soor thrush
Soorpilz Monilia albicans
soporös soporous
Sorbit sorbitol
Sorbose e. e.
sorgen, sich to worry
Sortiment assortment

Sotalol e. e.
Soyabohne soy bean
sozial social
Sozialisation socialization
Sozialversicherung social health insurance
Soziologie sociology
Sozojodolsäure sozoiodolic acid
spät late
Spätergebnis after-result
Spätgeburt postterm birth
Spätresultat after-result, late result
Spätschaden late damage
Spalt slit, cleft, fissure
spaltbar fissionable
Spalte slit, cleft, fissure
Spaltlampe slit lamp
Spaltprodukt fission product, split product
Spaltung splitting, fission, scissure
Spaltung eines Herztones splitting of a heart sound
Span splinter
Spange clasp
Spannung tension
—,**elektrische** voltage
Spannungszustand tension state
Sparganose sparganosis
Spartein sparteine
Spasmoanalgetikum spasmoanalgesic
spasmoanalgetisch spasmoanalgesic
Spasmolyse spasmolysis
Spasmolytikum antispasmodic
spasmolytisch spasmolytic, antispasmodic
spasmophil spasmophilic
Spasmophilie spasmophilia
Spasmus spasm
spastisch spastic
Spastizität spasticity
Spatel spatula
Species diureticae diuretic species
Speckhaut buffy coat
Speichel spittle, saliva
Speicheldrüse salivary gland

Speicheldrüsenentzündung sialadenitis
Speicheldurchmischung insalivation
Speichelfluß salivation
speichelhemmend antisialogogue
Speichelsaugrohr saliva suction tube
speicheltreibend salivatory
Speicher store
Speicherkrankheit storage disease, thesaurosis
speichern to store up
Speicherung storage
speien to spit, to spew
Speise food, nourishment
Speiseröhre esophagus (a), oesophagus (e), gullet
Speiseröhrenektasie esophagectasia (a), oesophagectasia (e)
Speisenröhrenentzündung esophagitis (a), oesophagitis (e)*
Speiseröhrenplastik esophagoplasty (a), oesophagoplasty (e)
spektral spectral
Spektralanalyse spectrum analysis
Spektrographie spectrography
Spektrometer spectrometer
Spektrometrie spectrometry
spektrometrisch spectrometric
Spektrophotometer spectrophotometer
Spektrophotometrie spectrophotometry
spektrophotometrisch spectrophotometric
Spektroskop spectroscope
Spektroskopie spectroscopy
spektroskopisch spectroscopic
Spektrum spectrum
Spekulum speculum
Spender donor
Sperma sperm
Spermatin e. e.
Spermatoblast e. e.
Spermatogenese spermatogenesis
Spermatogonium spermatogone

Spermatolyse spermatolysis
spermatolytisch spermatolytic
Spermatorrhöe spermatorrhea (a), spermatorrhoea (e)
Spermatozele spermatocele
spermatozid spermatocidal
Spermatozoon e. e.
Spermatozystitis spermatocystitis
Spermatozyt spermatocyte
spermaturie spermaturia
Spermin spermine
Spermiogenese spermiogenesis
spermizid spermicidal
spezialisieren to specialize
Spezialismus specialism
Spezialist specialist
Spezialistin specialist
speziell special
spezifisch specific
spezifisches Gewicht specific gravity
Spezifität specificity
sphärisch sphaerical (e), spherical (a)
Sphaerophorus e. e.
Sphärozyt sphaerocyte (e), spherocyte (a)
Sphärozytose sphaerocytosis (e), spherocytosis (a)
sphenoidal e. e.
sphenoparietal e. e.
sphenotemporal e. e.
Sphincter Oddi sphincter of Oddi
Sphingomyelin e. e.
Sphingosin sphingosine
Sphinkter sphincter
Sphinkterektomie sphincterectomy
Sphinkterotomie sphincterotomy
Sphinkterplastik sphincteroplasty
Sphygmobolometer e. e.
Sphygmogramm sphygmogram
Sphygmograph e. e.
Sphygmographie sphygmography
sphygmographisch sphygmographic
Sphygmomanometer e. e.
Sphygmometer e. e.

Sphygmotonometer e. e.
Spica spica bandage
Spiegel mirror
– **(z.B. einer Flüssigkeit)** level (e. g. of a fluid)
Spielraum slack
Spina bifida e. e.
spinal e. e.
Spinalerkrankung, funikuläre funicular myelosis
Spinalparalyse, spastische primary lateral sclerosis of the spinal cord
Spindelzelle spindle cell
Spindelzellensarkom spindle cell sarcoma
Spinne spider
Spinngewebe spider's web
spinobulbär spinobulbar
spinokortikal spinocortical
spinozerebellar spinocerebellar
Spirale spiral
Spiramycin e. e.
Spirille spirillum
Spirillose spirillosis
Spirillolyse spirillolysis
Spirillum buccale e. e.
– **morsus muris** Spirillum minus
– **Vincenti** Borrelia vincenti
spirituös spirituous
Spiritus ethyl alcohol
Spirochaeta berbera e. e.
– **bronchialis** e. e.
– **dentium** e. e.
– **Duttoni** Borrelia duttoni
– **forans** e. e.
– **morsus muris** e. e., Spirillum minus
– **Novyi** Borrelia novyi
– **Obermeieri** Borrelia recurrentis
– **pertenuis** Treponema pertenue
– **refringens** e. e.
Spirochäte spirochaete (e), spirochete (a)
Spirochätose spirochaetosis (e), spirochetosis (a)
Spiroergometrie spiroergometry

Spirographie spirography
spirographisch spirographic
Spirolakton spirolactone
Spirometrie spirometry
spirometrisch spirometric
Spironema Duttoni Borrelia duttoni
– **Kochi** Borrelia kochi
– **Novyi** Borrelia novyi
– **recurrentis** Borrelia recurrentis
Spironolakton spironolactone
Spitze tip, top, peak, apex
Spitzenpotential (EEG) spike
Spitzenstoß apex beat
–**,hebender** heaving apex beat
Splanchnikektomie splanchnicectomy
Splanchnikotomie splanchnicotomy
splanchnisch splanchnic
Splanchnoptose splanchnoptosis
Splenektomie splenectomy
splenektomieren to splenectomize
Splenisation splenization
splenisch splenic
Splenitis e. e.
splenogen splenogenous
Splenomegalie splenomegaly
–**,tropische** dumdum fever
Splenoportogramm splenoportogram
Splenoportographie splenoportography
splenoportographisch splenoportographic
Splenoptose splenoptosis
Splitter splinter
Splitterpinzette splinter forceps
Splitterung splitting
Spondylarthritis e. e.
– **ankylopoetica** ankylosing spondylarthritis
Spondylarthrose spondylarthrosis
Spondylarthrosis deformans hypertrophic spondylarthritis
Spondylitis e. e.
– **ankylopoetica** ankylosing spondylitis

Spondylitis tuberculosa tuberculous spondylitis
spondylitisch spondylitic
Spondylolisthese spondylolisthesis
Spondylolyse spondylolysis
Spondylose spondylosis
Spondylosis deformans hypertrophic spondylitis
Spongioblast e. e.
Spongioblastom spongioblastoma
Spongioplasma spongioplasm
Spongiozyt spongiocyte
spontan spontaneous
Spontanhypothermie accidental hypothermia
Spore e. e.
sporenabtötend sporicidal
sporenbildend spore forming, sporiferous
Sporenbildung spore formation, sporogeny, sporulation
Sporenrest sporal residuum
sporentragend sporiferous
sporenvernichtend sporicidal
Sporidie sporidium
sporizid sporicidal
Sporn spur
Sporoblast e. e.
Sporogonie sporogony
Sporomykose sporomycosis
Sporotrichon sporotrichum
Sporotrichose sporotrichosis
Sporozoit sporozoite
Sporozoon e. e.
Sportherz athlete's heart
Sporulation e. e.
Sprache speech
Sprachfehler defect of speech
Sprachstörung dysphasia, speech disorder, language disturbance
Sprachverständnis speech comprehension
Spray e. e.
Sprechstunde consultation hour
Sprechzimmer consulting room
Spreizschritt straddle

Springkrankheit der Schafe thorter ill
spritzbereit ready for injection
Spritze syringe
spritzen to syringe
spritzfertig ready for injection
Sprue e. e.
spülen to rinse, to wash, to irrigate
Spülflüssigkeit rinsing liquid, collutory, wash
Spülinstrument irrigation instrument
Spülkanüle wash cannula
Spülkatheter wash catheter, irrigation catheter
Spüllösung lavage solution
Spülung irrigation, lavation, lavement
Spule coil, reel
—,**Induktions-** induction coil
Spulenniere coil kidney
Spulwurm eelworm, roundworm
Spurenelement trace element
Sputum e. e.
Squalen squalene
squamös squamous
squamoparietal e. e.
Stab staff
stabil stable
Stabilisator stabilizer
stabilisieren to stabilize
stabkerniger Leukozyt staff cell
Stachel prick
Stacheldrahtkrankheit barbed wire disease
Stachelschwein porcupine
Stachelzelle prickle cell
Stadium stage
Stäbchen (bakteriol.) bacillus
Stäbchen und Zapfen der Netzhaut des Auges retinal rods and cones
städtisch urban
Stärke (chem.) starch
Ständer stand
Stärkeagar starch agar
Stärkebinde starch bandage

Stärke-Gel starch gel
Stärkeverband starch bandage
Stagnation e. e.
Stahl steel
—, **rostfreier** stainless steel
Stalagmometer e. e.
Stalagmometrie stalagmometry
Stamm (anatom.) trunk
Stamm (bacteriol.) stock
Stammbaum family tree
Stammbaum (biol.) pedigree
Stammzelle stem cell
Stanazol stanazole
Standard e. e.
Standardabweichung standard deviation
standardisieren to standardize
Standardisierung standardization
Standeskunde deontology
Stannat stannate
Stanniussche Ligatur Stannius' ligature
Stanze punch
Stapedektomie stapedectomy
Stapediotenotomie stapediotenotomy
Staphylococcus albus e. e.
— **aureus** e. e.
— **citreus** e. e.
— **tetragenus** e. e.
Staphylokokkus staphylococcus
Staphylolysin e. e.
Staphylom staphyloma
staphylomatös staphylomatous
Staphylomycin e. e.
Star (med.) cataract
—, **grüner** glaucoma
Starmesser cataract knife
Stase stasis
Statik statics
Station e. e.
— **(im Krankenhaus)** ward
stationär stationary
Stationsschwester sister
statisch static
Statistik statistics
statistisch statistic

Status e. e.
— **lymphaticus** e. e.
Staub dust
Staubinde tourniquet
stauen to stem
Staupe, Hunde- distemper
—, **Pferde-** strangles
Stauung congestion
Stauungshyperämie Bier's hyperaemia (e), Bier's hyperemia (a)
Stauungsinsuffizienz, kardiale congestive heart failure
Stauungspapille choked disk
Stauungszirrhose congestive cirrhosis
Steapsin e. e.
Steapsinogen e. e.
Stearat stearate
Stearin e. e.
Steatadenom steatadenoma
Steatom steatome
Steatorrhöe steatorrhea (a), steatorrhoea (e)
Steatose steatosis
Stechmücke gnat
Steigbügel stapes, stirrup
steigern to increase
Steigerung increase, rise
Stein stone
Steinkohlenteer coal tar
Stein-Leventhal-Syndrom Stein-Leventhal syndrome
Steinmole stone mole
Steinschnitt lithotomy
Steinschnittlage lithotomy position
Steiß breech, coccyx
Steißlage breech presentation
Stellenwert place value
Stellit stellite
Stellung position, situation, posture
Stellwagsches Zeichen Stellwag's sign
stemmen to stem
Stengel stalk
stenographieren to write shorthand

Stenokardie stenocardia
Stenose stenosis
stenosieren to stenose
stenotisch stenotic
sterben to die
sterblich mortal
Sterblichkeit mortality
Sterblichkeitsquote death rate
Stereoauskultation stereoauscultation
Stereochemie stereochemistry
stereochemisch stereochemical
Stereognosie stereognosis
stereognostisch stereognostic
Stereogramm stereogram
Stereoisomerie stereoisomerism
Stereometrie stereometry
Stereomikroskop stereomicroscope
Stereomikroskopie stereomicroscopy
stereomikroskopisch stereomicroscopic
Stereophotographie stereophotography
Stereoröntgenographie stereoroentgenography
Stereoskop stereoscope
Stereoskopie stereoscopy
stereoskopisch stereoscopic
stereospezifisch stereospecific
stereotaktisch stereotactic
Stereotypie stereotypy
steril sterile
Sterilisation sterilization
Sterilisationsapparat sterilizer
Sterilisationsmittel sterilizing agent
Sterilisator sterilizer
sterilisieren to sterilize
Sterilisierpinzette sterilizing forceps
Sterilität sterility
Sterin sterol
Sterkobilin stercobilin
sterkoral stercoral
sterkorös stercorous
Stern star
sternal e. e.

Sternalmark sternal marrow
Sternalpunktion sternal puncture
sternalwärts sternad
sternoklavikular sternoclavicular
sternokostal sternocostal
sternoperikardial sternopericardial
Sternotomie sternotomy
Sternum e. e.
Steroid e. e.
stertorös stertorous
Stethophon stethophone
Stethoskop stethoscope
steuern to steer, to check, to control
Steuerung steering, checking, control
sthenisch sthenic
Stibosan e. e.
Stich sting, stab, prick
–,**giftiger** venomous sting
Stichkultur stab culture
Stichwunde stab wound
Stickstoff nitrogen
stickstofffrei unazotized
stickstoffhaltig nitrogenous
– **(dreiwertig)** nitrous
– **(fünfwertig)** nitric
Stickstofflost nitrogen mustard
Stiel stalk, peduncle
Stier bull
–,**junger** bullock
Stierhornmagen steerhorn stomach
Stierlinsches Zeichen Stierlin's symptom
Stift pin, peg
Stifthülse pin and tube
Stiftzahn dowel crown
Stiftzieher post puller
Stigma e. e.
stigmatisch stigmatic
stigmatisieren to stigmatize
Stigmatisierung stigmatization
Stilben stilbene
Stilböstrol stilbestrol (a), stilboestrol (e)

stillen (= beruhigen) to appease
- (= an der Brust ernähren) to suckle
Stillersches Zeichen Stiller's sign
Stillingscher Kern Stilling's nucleus
Stillperiode nursing period
Stillsche Krankheit Still's disease
Stillstand standstill
-, zum - bringen to arrest
Stimmband vocal cord
Stimme voice
Stimmfremitus vocal fremitus
Stimmgabel tuning fork
stimmhaft voiced
stimmlos voiceless
Stimmung mood
Stimulans stimulant
Stimulation e. e.
Stimulator e. e.
stimulieren to stimulate
stimulierend stimulant
Stimulierung stimulation
stinken to stink
Stinktier skunk
Stintzingsche Tafel Stintzing's table
Stirn front
Stirnader frontal vein
Stirnlampe head lamp
Stirnreflektor headband mirror
Stockschnupfen chronic cold in the nose
Stöchiometrie stoechiometry
stöhnen to groan
Stöpsel stopper, plug
stören to disturb
Störung disorder, disturbance, impairment
Stoffelsche Operation Stoffel's operation
Stoffwechsel metabolism
stoffwechselgesund eumetabolic
stoffwechselmäßig metabolic
Stoffwechselprodukt metabolite
Stokes-Reagens Stokes' reagent
Stollbeule (veter.) shoe boil

stomachal e. e.
Stomachikum stomachic
Stomatitis e. e.
- **aphthosa** aphthous stomatitis
- **catarrhalis** catarrhal stomatitis
- **fusospirillaris** Vincent's stomatitis
- **mercurialis** mercurial stomatitis
- **syphilitica** syphilitic stomatitis
- **ulcerosa** ulcerative stomatitis
stomatitisch stomatitic
Stomatologie stomatology
stopfen, den Stuhlgang - to cause constipation
Stopfer plugger
Stoppuhr stop watch
Storch stork
Stoß trusion, shove, push
stottern to stutter
Stottern stuttering
Strabismus e. e.
Strabometrie strabometry
Strabotomie strabotomy
straff tight
Straffheit tightness
Strahl ray, beam
- (veter.) frog
Strahlbeinlahmheit podotrochilitis
strahlen to radiate, to beam
Strahlenbehandlung actinotherapy
Strahlenbiologie radiobiology
Strahlenbrechung refraction of rays
Strahlendermatitis radiodermatitis
Strahlendosierung rayage
strahlendurchgängig, partiell radiolucent
Strahlendurchgängigkeit, partielle radiolucency
strahlendurchlässig radioparent
Strahlendurchlässigkeit radioparency
strahlenempfindlich radiosensitive
Strahlenempfindlichkeit radiosensibility, radiosensitiveness
Strahlenexposition raying
Strahlenheilkunde radiotherapeutics

Strahlenkater radiation sickness
Strahlenkunde actinology
strahlenkundlich actinological
strahlenresistent radioresistant
Strahlenresistenz radioresistance
Strahlenschaden radiation injury
Strahlenschutz radiation protection
Strahlenschutzwirkung radioprotective action
Strahlentherapie radiotherapy, actinotherapy
strahlenundurchlässig radiopaque
Strahlenundurchlässigkeit radiopacity
strahlig radiate
Strahlung radiation
Stramonium e. e.
Strang cord; tract
Strangulation e. e.
strangulieren to strangulate, to strangle
Strauß (Vogel) ostrich
Straußsche Kanüle Strauss needle
Streckbett orthopaedic bed (e), orthopedic bed (a)
strecken to stretch, to extend
Strecker tensor
Streckmuskel extensor
Streckung extension, tension
Streifen stripe
Streifenzeichnung striation
streifig striped
Streifschuß grazing shot
Streitfrage point of controversy
Strenge severity
Streptobacillus Ducrey-Unna Haemophilus of Ducrey (e), Hemophilus of Ducrey (a)
Streptobacterium ulceris mollis Haemophilus of Ducrey (e), Hemophilus of Ducrey (a)
Streptococcus acidi lactici e. e.
– **anhaemolyticus** anhaemolytic streptococcus (e), anhemolytic streptococcus (a)
– **brevis** e. e.

Streptococcus erysipelatis e. e.
– **haemolyticus** haemolytic streptococcus (e), hemolytic streptococcus (a)
– **longus** e. e.
– **mitior** e. e.
– **mutans** e. e.
– **puerperalis** e. e.
– **pyogenes** e. e.
– **salivarius** e. e.
– **scarlatinae** e. e.
– **septicus** e. e.
– **viridans** e. e.
Streptodornase e. e.
Streptokinase e. e.
Streptokokkus streptococcus
Streptolysin e. e.
Streptomycin e. e.
Streptomykose streptomycosis
Streptonigrin e. e.
Streptothrix e. e.
Streptothrikose streptothricosis
Streptotrichose nocardiasis, streptothricosis
Streptozotocin e. e.
Stress e. e.
streuen to strew
Streustrahlen scattered rays
Stridor e. e.
stridorös stridulous
Striemen wheal
Striktur stricture
Stroboskopie stroboscopy
Stroganoffsche Behandlung Stroganoff's treatment
Strom stream, flow
–, **elektrischer** electric current
  Drehstrom three phase current
  faradischer Strom faradic current
  galvanischer Strom galvanic current
  Gleichstrom continuous current
  Wechselstrom alternating current
Stroma e. e.
Stromkreis circuit

Strongyloides stercoralis e. e.
Strontium e. e.
Strophanthidin e. e.
Strophanthin (g-Stroph.) ouabain
– **(k-Stroph.)** strophanthin
Strophulus e. e.
Strümpellsche Krankheit
   Strümpell's disease
Struktur structure
strukturell structural
Strukturformel structural
   formula
Struma goitre, goiter, struma
Strumektomie strumectomy
strumigen goitrigenous,
   goitrogenic
strumipriv strumiprivous
Strumitis e. e.
Strychnin strychnine
Strychninsulfat
   strychnine sulfate (a),
   strychnine sulphate (e)
Strychninvergiftung strychnism
Student e. e.
Studentin student
stündlich every hour
Stütze support, pillar, sustainment,
   prop
stützen to sustain, to support,
   to prop
Stützgewebe interstitial tissue
Stufe level; step; grade
stufenlos stepless
Stufenphotometer step
   photometer
Stuhlgang stool
Stuhlinkontinenz incontinence
   of stool, encopresis
Stuhlverstopfung constipation
stumm mute, dumb
Stummel stump
Stummheit mutism
Stumpf blunt, stump
stumpf blunt, obtuse
Stumpfheit bluntness
Stupor e. e.
stuporös stuporous

Sturge-Webersches Syndrom
   encephalotrigeminal angiomatosis
Sturzanfall drop seizure
Stute mare
Stuttgarter Hundeseuche
   Stuttgart dog plague
stylomaxillär stylomaxillary
Styptikum styptic
styptisch styptic
Styptol e. e.
Styracol e. e.
subacid e. e.
Subacidität subacidity, hypacidity
subakromial subacromial
subakut subacute
subaortal subaortic
subapikal subapical
subarachnoidal subarachnoid
Subarachnoidalblutung
   subarachnoid haemorrhage (e),
   subarachnoid hemorrhage (a)
subaurikulär subauricular
subaxillär subaxillary
Subazetat subacetate
subazid subacid
Subazidität subacidity, hypacidity
subchondral e. e.
subchorioidal subchoroidal
subchronisch subchronic
subcutan subcutaneous,
   hypodermic
Subcutis e. e.
subdiaphragmatisch
   subdiaphragmatic
subdural e. e.
subdurales Hämatom
   subdural haematoma (e),
   subdural hematoma (a)
subendokardial subendocardial
subendothelial e. e.
subepithelial e. e.
subfaszial subfascial
subfebril subfebrile
Subfraktion subfraction
subfrontal e. e.
subgingival e. e.

Subgingivalspalt gingival crevice
subglottisch subglottic
subhepatisch subhepatic
subikterisch subicteric
Subinfektion subinfection
subintimal e. e.
Subinvolution e. e.
Subjekt subject
subjektiv subjective
subkapital subcapital
subkapsulär subcapsular
subklavikulär subclavicular
subklinisch subclinical
subkortikal subcortical
Subkortikographie subcorticography
subkostal subcostal
subkutan subcutaneous, hypodermic
Subkutis subcutis
subletal sublethal
Sublimat sublimate
Sublimation e. e.
sublimieren to sublime
Sublimierung sublimation
sublingual e. e.
Subluxation e. e.
submammär submammary
submandibulär submandibular
submarin submarine
submaxillär submaxillary
submikroskopisch submicroscopical
submitochondrial e. e.
submukös submucous
subnarkotisch subnarcotic
subnormal e. e.
subokzipital suboccipital
Subokzipitalpunktion cisternal puncture
suborbital e. e.
subpatellar e. e.
subperikardial subpericardial
subperiostal subperiosteal
subperitoneal e. e.
subphrenisch subphrenic, subdiaphragmatic

subpleural e. e.
subserös subserous
subskapulär subscapular
subskleral subscleral
Substantia reticulofilamentosa reticulo-filamentary substance
substantiell substantial
Substanz substance; matter
substernal e. e.
substituieren to substitute
Substitution e. e.
Substrat substrate
Substruktur substructure
subtarsal e. e.
subtemporal e. e.
subtentorial e. e.
subthalamisch subthalamic
subtil subtile, subtle
subtotal e. e.
subtrochanterisch subtrochanteric
Subtypus subtype
subungual e. e.
suburethral e. e.
subvaginal e. e.
subvalvulär subvalvular
subzellulär subcellular
Succinase e. e.
Succinat succinate
Succussio Hippocratis hippocratic succussion
Sucht, Arzneimittel- drug addiction
Sucht (= krankhafte Begierde) passion, mania
Sucht (= Krankheit) disease
Sudan e. e.
Sudanophilie sudanophilia
Sudecksche Atrophie Sudeck's atrophy
süchtig addict
süßen to edulcorate, to sweeten
Süßholzwurzel Licorice root (a), Liquorice root (e)
suffizient sufficient
Suffusion e. e.
suggerieren to suggest

suggestibel suggestible
Suggestibilität suggestibility
Suggestion e. e.
suggestiv suggestive
Suggillation e. e.
Suizid suicide
suizidal suicidal
Sukkorrhöe succorrhea (a), succorrhoea (e)
Sukrase sucrase
Sukrose sucrose
Sukzinase succinase
Sukzinat succinate
Sukzinimid succinimide
Sukzinyl succinyl
Sulfadiazin sulfadiazine (a), sulphadiazine (e)
Sulfadimethoxin sulfadimethoxine (a), sulphadimethoxine (e)
Sulfaguanidin sulfaguanidine (a), sulphaguanidine (e)
Sulfamerazin sulfamerazine (a), sulphamerazine (e)
Sulfamethoxazol sulfamethoxazole (a), sulphamethoxazole (e)
Sulfamethoxydiazin sulfamethoxydiazine (a), sulphamethoxydiazine (e)
Sulfamethoxypyrazin sulfamethoxypyrazine (a), sulphamethoxypyrazine (e)
Sulfamethoxypyridazin sulfamethoxypyridazine (a), sulphamethoxypyridazine (e)
Sulfamezathin sulfamezathine (a), sulphamezathine (e)
Sulfanilamid sulfanilamide (a), sulphanilamide (e)
Sulfaphenazol sulfaphenazol (a), sulphaphenazol (e)
Sulfapyridin sulfapyridine (a), sulphapyridine (e)
Sulfapyrimidin sulfapyrimidine (a), sulphapyrimidine (e)
Sulfasomidin sulfasomidine (a), sulphasomidine (e)

Sulfat sulfate (a), sulphate (e)
Sulfhydrat sulfhydrate (a), sulphhydrate (e)
Sulfhydryl sulfhydryl (a), sulphhydryl (e)
Sulfid sulfide (a), sulphide (e)
Sulfit sulfite (a), sulphite (e)
Sulfmethämoglobin Sulfmethemoglobin (a), sulphmethaemoglobin (e)
Sulfokinase sulfokinase (a), sulphokinase (e)
Sulfon sulfone (a), sulphone (e)
Sulfonamid sulfonamide (a) sulphonamide (e)
sulfonamidresistent sulfonamideresistant (a), sulphonamideresistant (e)
Sulfonyl sulfonyl (a), sulphonyl (e)
Sulfonylharnstoff sulfonylurea (a), sulphonylurea (e)
Sulformethoxin sulformethoxine (a), sulphormethoxine (e)
Sulfosäure sulfo-acid (a), sulpho-acid (e)
Sulfoxid sulfoxide (a), sulphoxide (e)
Sulfoximin sulfoximine (a), sulphoximine (e)
Sulfozystein sulfocysteine (a), sulphocysteine (e)
Sulfur praecipitatum precipitated sulfur (a), precipitated sulphur (e)
Sulfur sublimatum sublimed sulfur (a), sublimed sulphur (e)
Sultam-Verbindung sultam compound
Summation e. e.
Summierung summation
Superaktivität superactivity
superazid superacid
Superazidität superacidity
Super-Ego e. e.
Superfekundation superfecundation

Superfötation superfetation (a), superfoetation (e)
Superinfektion superinfection
superinfizieren to superinfect
superletal superlethal
Supermotilität supermotility
supernormal e. e.
Superovulation e. e.
Superphosphat superphosphate
Supersekretion supersecretion
supervirulent e. e.
Supination e. e.
supinieren to supinate
supplementär supplementary
Suppositorium suppository
supraaurikulär supraauricular
supraaxillär supraaxillary
supradiaphragmatisch supradiaphragmatic
supraglottisch supraglottic
suprainguinal e. e.
supraklavikulär supraclavicular
suprakondylär supracondylar
supramalleolär supramalleolar
supramammär supramammary
supramandibulär supramandibular
supramaxillär supramaxillary
supraorbital e. e.
suprapatellär suprapatellar
suprapubisch suprapubic
suprarenal e. e., surrenal
Suprarenin epinephrine
suprasellär suprasellar
supraskapulär suprascapular
supraspinal e. e.
suprasternal e. e.
supratemporal e. e.
suprathorakal suprathoracic
supratonsillär supratonsillar
supravaginal e. e.
supravalvulär supravalvular
supraventrikulär supraventricular
supravital e. e.
Surra e. e.
Surrogat surrogate
Sursumduktion sursumduction
Sursumvergenz sursumvergence
Sursumversion e. e.
Suspension e. e.
Suspensorium suspensory
Suxamethonium e. e.
Suxethonium e. e.
Sycosis vulgaris e. e.
Sykose sycosis
Symbiont e. e.
Symbiose symbiosis
symbiotisch symbiotic
Symblepharon e. e.
Symbol e. e.
symbolisch symbolic
symbolisieren to symbolize
Symbolisierung symbolization
Symbolismus symbolism
Symbolsprache symbolic language
Symmetrie symmetry
symmetrisch symmetrical
Sympathektomie sympathectomy
Sympathikoblastom sympathicoblastoma
sympathikolytisch sympathicolytic
sympathikomimetisch sympathicomimetic, sympathomimetic
Sympathikotonie sympathicotonia
sympathikotonisch sympathicotonic
sympathikotrop sympathicotropic
Sympathikus sympathetic nerve, sympathetic system
Sympathikusblockade sympathetic block
Sympathin e. e.
sympathisch (anat.) sympathetical
Symphyse symphysis
Symphyseotomie symphysiotomy
Symptom e. e.
symptomatisch symptomatic
Symptomatologie symptomatology
Symptomenkomplex complex of symptoms
symptomlos symptomless
Synapse e. e.

synaptisch synaptic
Synarthrose synarthrosis
Synchondrose synchondrosis
synchron synchronous
Synchronie synchronia
synchronisieren to synchronize
Synchroton synchrotone
Synchrozyklotron synchrocyclotron
Synchyse synchysis
Syndaktylie syndactylia
Syndesmose syndesmosis
Syndesmotom syndesmotome
Syndrom syndrome
syndromisch syndromic
Synechie, hintere
 posterior synechia
Synechie, vordere
 anterior synechia
synergetisch synergetic
Synergie synergy
synergisch synergic
synergistisch synergistic
Syngamie syngamy
synkardial syncardial
Synkinese synkinesis
synkinetisch synkinetic
synklitisch synclitic
Synklitismus synclitism, syncliticism
synkopal syncopal
Synkope syncope
Synostose synostosis
Synovia e. e.
synovial e. e.
Synoviom synovioma
Synovitis e. e.
syntaktisch syntactical
Synthese synthesis
Synthetase e. e.
synthetisch synthetic
synthetisieren to synthesize

synton syntonic
syntonisch syntonic
synzytial syncytial
Synzytium syncytium
Syphilid syphilid
Syphilis e. e.
–, **konnatale** connatal syphilis
–, **latente Früh-** latent early syphilis
–, **primäre** primary syphilis
–, **sekundäre** secondary syphilis
–, **tertiäre** tertiary syphilis
syphilitisch syphilitic
Syphiloderma syphiloderm
syphilogen syphilogenous
Syphilologe syphilologist
Syphilologie syphilology
Syphilologin syphilologist
syphilologisch syphilological
Syphilom syphiloma
Syphilophobie syphilophobia
Syphilose syphilosis
Syringitis e. e.
Syringomyelie syringomyelia
System e. e.
–, **retikuläres Aktivierungs-** alerting system
systematisch systematic
systematisieren to systematize
Systematisierung systematization
Systematologie systematology
systemisch systemic
Systole e. e.
systolisch systolic
Szilla squill
Szillaridin scillaridin
Szillin scillin
Szillitoxin scillitoxin
Szintillation scintillation
Szintillator scintillator
szirrhös scirrhous
Szirrhus scirrhus

T

Tabak tobacco
Tabakangina tobacco angina
Tabakbeutelnaht tobacco bag suture
Tabak-Mosaikkrankheit tobacco-mosaic disease
Tabakose tabacosis
Tabakstaubvergiftung tabacosis
Tabakvergiftung tabagism, tobaccoism
Tabelle schedule, table
Tabes dorsalis locomotor ataxia
– **mesaraica** e. e.
Tabiker tabetic
Tabikerin tabetic
tabisch tabetic
Tablette tablet, tabule, lozenge
Taboparalyse taboparesis
Tabu taboo
Tachistoskopie tachistoscopy
tachistoskopisch tachistoscopic
Tachyarhythmie tachyarrhythmia
tachykard tachycardiac
Tachykardie tachycardia
Tachyphylaxie tachyphylaxis
Tachypnoe tachypnea (a), tachypnoea (e)
Tachysterin tachysterol
Tachysystolie tachysystoly
Täfelchen tablet
Taenia echinococcus e. e.
– **saginata** e. e.
– **solium** e. e.
Tänie taenia
Tätigkeit action, activity
Tätowierung tattoo, tatoo
täuschen to feign
Tafel table
Taille waist
taktil tactile
Talg tallow
Talgdrüse sebaceous gland
talgig sebaceous
Talk talc

talotibial e. e.
Tamarinde tamarind
Tampon e. e.
Tamponade e. e.
Tamponstopfer gauze packer
Tanacetum tansy
Tank e. e.
Tannat tannate
Tannin e. e.
Tantal tantalum
Tarantel tarantula
Taraxein e. e.
Tardieuscher Fleck Tardieu's spot
Tarniersche Zange Tarnier's forceps
tarsal e. e.
Tarsalgie tarsalgia
Tarsitis e. e.
Tartarus stibiatus antimony and potassium tartrate
Tartrat tartrate
Tart-Zelle Tart cell
Tasche pocket
Tasche (anat.) pouch
Taschenbesteck pocket set
Taschenformat pocket size
Tascheninhalator pocket inhaler
tastbar palpable
Tastbarkeit palpability
tasten to palpate; to touch
Tasten palpation; touch
Tasterzirkel caliper
Tastkörperchen touch corpuscle
Tastsinn touch
taub deaf
Taube pigeon
Taubheit deafness, surdity
taubstumm surdomute, deaf and dumb
Taubstummheit surdomutism, deaf-mutism
Taucher diver
taumeln to reel
Taurin taurine

Taurocholat taurocholate
tautomer tautomeric
Tautomerie tautomerism
Tay-Sachssche-Krankheit
 Tay-Sachs' disease
Technetat technetate
Technetium e. e.
Technik technic, technique
Techniker technician
technisch technical
Technologie technology
Tee tea
Teelöffel teaspoon
Teer tar
Teeröl oil of tar
Teichmannscher Kristall
 Teichmann's crystal
Teichopsie teichopsia
Teil part
Teilbad partial bath
Teilchen particle
Teilnehmer participant
Teilnehmerin participant
Teilung division
tektonisch tectonic
Teleangiektasie teleangiectasia
teleangiektatisch teleangiectatic
telediastolisch telediastolic
Telegamma-Therapie
 telegamma therapy
Telegonie telegony
Telekobaltbestrahlung telecobalt
 irradiation
Telemetrie telemetry
Teleologie teleology
teleologisch teleological
Telepathie telepathy
Teleröntgenogramm tele-
 roentgenogram
Teleröntgenographie tele-
 roentgenography
Teleskop telescope
telesystolisch telesystolic
Tellur tellurium
Tellurat tellurate
Tellurit tellurite
Telodendron e. e.

Temperament e. e.
Temperatur temperature
Temperaturmessung thermometry
temporär temporary
temporal e. e.
Temporallappen temporal lobe
temporoaurikulär temporoauri-
 cular
temporofrontal e. e.
temporomandibulär temporo-
 mandibular
temporookzipital temporooccipital
temporoparietal e. e.
Tendinitis e. e.
tendinös tendinous
Tendovaginitis e. e.
Tenesmus e. e.
Tenonsche Kapsel
 Tenon's capsule
Tenotom tenotome
Tenotomie tenotomy
tenotomieren to tenotomize
tentoriell tentorial
teratisch teratic
Teratoblastom teratoblastoma
teratogen teratogenic
Teratogenität teratogenicity
Teratologie teratology
teratologisch teratological
Teratom teratoma
Teratose teratosis
Terbium e. e.
Termin term
terminal e. e.
Terminologie terminology
terminologisch terminological
ternär ternary
Terpen terpene
Terpentin turpentine
Terpentinöl oil of turpentine
tertiär tertiary
Tesla e. e.
Test e. e.
testieren to testify
Testikel testicle
testikulär testicular
Testosteron testosterone

Tetanie tetany
tetanisch tetanic
Tetanus e. e.
Tetanusantitoxin tetanus antitoxin
Tetanusserum antitetanic serum
Tetanustoxoid tetanus toxoid
Tetraäthylammoniumbromid tetraethylammonium bromide
Tetraäthylblei tetraethyl lead
tetrabasisch tetrabasic
Tetrabenazin tetrabenazine
Tetrabutyl e. e.
Tetrachlorid tetrachloride
Tetrachlorkohlenstoff carbon tetrachloride
Tetracosactid tetracosactide
Tetracosapeptid tetracosapeptide
Tetracyclin tetracycline
Tetradecylamin tetradecylamine
Tetrafluoroborat tetrafluoroborate
Tetrahydrofolat tetrahydrofolate
Tetrahydrofurfuryldisulfid tetrahydrofurfuryldisulfide (a), tetrahydrofurfuryldisulphide (e)
Tetrajodthyronin tetraiodothyronine
Tetranitrol e. e.
Tetraplegie tetraplegia
Tetrazolium e. e.
Tetrose e. e.
Tetroxid tetroxide
Tetroxyd tetroxide
thalamisch thalamic
thalamokortikal thalamocortical
thalamolentikulär thalamolenticular
Thalamotomie thalamotomy
Thalamus e. e.
Thalassämie thalassaemia (e), thalassemia (a)
Thalassanämie thalassanaemia (e) thalassanemia (a)
Thalassotherapie thalassotherapy
Thalidomid thalidomide
Thallium e. e.

Thalliumvergiftung thallotoxicosis
Thanatologie thanatology
Thebain thebaine
Thein theine
Thekazelle theca cell
Thekazellentumor thecoma
thelytokisch thelytocous
Theobromin theobromine, cacaine
Theophyllin theophylline
Theorem e. e.
theoretisch theoretical
Theorie theory
Therapeut therapeutist
Therapeutin therapeutist
therapeutisch therapeutical
Therapie therapy; therapeutics
Therapie, gezielte aimed therapy
therapieresistent resistant to treatment
Thermästhesie thermaesthesia (e), thermesthesia (a)
thermal e. e.
Thermalgesie thermalgesia
Thermalgie thermalgia
Thermanästhesie thermanaesthesia (e), thermanesthesia (a)
thermisch thermic
Thermoanalgesie thermoanalgesia
Thermochemie thermochemistry
Thermodilution e. e.
Thermodynamik thermodynamics
thermodynamisch thermodynamic
thermoelektrisch thermoelectric
Thermographie thermography
Thermoplazentographie thermoplacentography
Thermokaustik thermocautery
Thermokoagulation thermocoagulation
thermolabil thermolabile
Thermolumineszenz thermoluminescence
Thermometer e. e.
Thermometrie thermometry
thermometrisch thermometric

thermophil thermophilic
Thermophobie thermophobia
Thermophor thermophore
Thermopräzipitation thermoprecipitation
Thermoregulation e. e.
thermoregulatorisch thermoregulatory
thermoresistent thermoresistant
thermostabil thermostabile
Thermostat e. e.
Thermotropie thermotropism
Thiabutazid thiabutazide
Thiadiazol thiadiazole
Thiamin thiamine
Thiaxanthen thiaxanthene
Thiazid thiazide
Thiazol thiazole
Thiersch-Transplantation
   Thiersch's graft
Thigenol e. e.
Thiocetamid thiocetamide
Thioäther thioether
Thiocarlid thiocarlide
Thiodeoxyguanosin thiodeoxyguanosine
Thiodeoxyinosin thiodeoxyinosine
Thioglukose thioglucose
Thioguanin thioguanine
Thioharnstoff thio-urea
Thiol e. e.
Thionin e. e.
Thiopenton thiopentone
Thiophen thiophene
Thioridazin thioridazine
Thiosäure thio acid
Thiosemikarbazon thiosemicarbazone
Thiosulfat thiosulfate (a), thiosulphate (e)
Thiouracil e. e.
Thiozyanat thiocyanate
Thoma-Zeiss-Zählkammer
   Thoma-Zeiss counting cell
Thomas-Pessar Thomas' pessary
Thomsensche Krankheit
   Thomsen's disease

thorakal thoracic, thoracal
Thorakokaustik thoracocautery
Thorakolyse thoracolysis
Thorakoplastik thoracoplasty
Thorakoskopie thoracoscopy
Thorakostomie thoracostomy
Thorakotomie thoracotomy
Thorakozentese thoracentesis
Thorax e. e.
Thorax, faßförmiger
   barrel chest
Thorium e. e.
Thormählensche Probe
   Thormählen's test
Threonin threonine
Threose e. e.
Thrombangitis thromboangiitis
Thrombangitis obliterans
   thromboangiitis obliterans
thrombangitisch thromboangiitic
Thrombasthenie thrombasthenia
Thrombektomie thrombectomy
Thrombelastogramm
   thrombelastogram
Thrombelastographie
   thrombelastography
thrombelastographisch
   thrombelastographic
Thrombin e. e.
Thromboembolie thromboembolism
thromboembolisch thromboembolic
Thrombogenese thrombogenesis
Thrombokinase e. e.
Thrombolyse thrombolysis
thrombolytisch thrombolytic
Thrombopathie thrombopathy
Thrombopenie thrombopenia
thrombopenisch thrombopenic
Thrombophilie thrombophilia
Thrombophlebitis e. e.
thrombophlebitisch thrombophlebitic
Thromboplastin e. e.
thromboplastisch thromboplastic
Thrombopoese thrombopoiesis

thrombopoetisch thrombopoietic
Thrombose thrombosis
Thromboseneigung thrombophilia
thrombosieren to thrombose
thrombotisch thrombotic
Thrombozyt thrombocyte
Thrombozythämie thrombocythaemia (e), thrombocythemia (a)
Thrombozytolyse thrombocytolysis
Thrombozytopenie thrombocytopenia
Thrombozytose thrombocytosis
Thrombus e. e.
Thujaöl oil of thuja
Thulium e. e.
Thymektomie thymectomy
thymektomieren to thymectomize
Thymian thyme
Thymidin thymidine
Thymidylat thymidylate
Thymin thymine
Thymol e. e.
Thymolblau thymol blue
Thymolphthalein thymolphthalein
Thymom thymoma
Thymotropie thymotropism
Thymozyt thymocyte
Thymus thymus gland
Thymusdrüse thymus gland
Thymusdrüsenentfernung thymectomy
Thymusdrüsenüberfunktion hyperthymization
Thymushyperplasie hyperplasia of thymus gland
Thyreoglobulin thyroglobulin
Thyreoidea thyroid gland
Thyreoidektomie thyroidectomy
Thyreoidin thyroidin
Thyreoiditis thyroiditis
thyreopriv thyroprival
Thyreotoxikose thyrotoxicosis
thyreotoxisch thyrotoxic
thyreotrop thyrotropic

thyreotropes Hormon thyrotropic hormone
Thyreotropin thyrotropin
thyreotropin-freisetzender Faktor thyrotropin releasing factor
Thyroxin e. e.
tibial e. e.
Tibialgie tibialgia
tibiofemoral e. e.
tibiofibular e. e.
Tic e. e.
tief deep
Tiefbiß close bite
Tiefdruck low pressure
Tiefensensibilität bathyaesthesia (e), bathyesthesia (a)
Tiefentherapie deep action therapy
Tiefenwirkung deep action
Tiefsinn thoughtfulness
tiefsinnig thoughtful, pensive
tiefsitzend deep-seated
Tiegel crucible
Tierarzt veterinary doctor
Tierchirurg veterinary surgeon
Tierchirurgie veterinary surgery
Tierexperiment animal experiment, bioassay
Tierheilkunde veterinary science
Tierkohle animal charcoal
Tierpathologie animal pathology, zoopathology
Tierpsychologie zoopsychology
Tierreich animal kingdom
Tierstall animal cage
Tierversuch animal experiment
Tietze-Syndrom Tietze's syndrome
Tiger e. e.
Tigerung tigering
tigroid e. e.
Tilidin tilidine
Timolol e. e.
Tinctura Belladonnae tincture of belladonna
– **Benzoes** tincture of benzoin
– **Opii** tincture of opium
– **Opii camphorata** paregoric elixir

trichromatisch trichromatic, trichromic
Trichter funnel
Trichterbrust funnel chest
trichterförmig funnel-shaped
Trichuris trichiura e. e.
trifaszikulär trifascicular
Triefauge blear-eye
Trifluoperazin trifluoperazine
Trifluopromazin triflupromazine
Trigeminus, Nervus- trifacial nerve, trigeminus nerve
Trigeminusneuralgie trigeminal neuralgia
Triglyzerid triglyceride
Trigonitis e. e.
trigonometrisch trigonometric
Trihydroxymethylaminomethan trihydroxymethylaminomethane
Trijodid triiodide
Trijodthyroessigsäure triiodothyroacetic acid
Trijodtyronin triiodotyronine
Trikuspidalinsuffizienz tricuspid insufficiency
Trikuspidalklappe tricuspid valve
Trikuspidalstenose tricuspid stenosis
Trimeprazin trimeprazine
Trimepropimin trimepropimine
Trimethoprim e. e.
Trimethylamin trimethylamine
Trimethylendiamin trimethylendiamine
Trinitrat trinitrate
Trinitrobenzol trinitrobenzene
trinkbar potable
Trinkwasser potable water
Triokinase e. e.
Triose e. e.
Trioxyd trioxide
Trioxypurin trioxypurine
Tripelphosphat triple phosphate
Tripeptid tripeptide
Triphosphat triphosphate

Tinctura Strychni tincture of nux vomica
– Valerianae tincture of valerian
Tinktur tincture
Tinte ink
Tintenfisch squid
Titan titanium
Titer titer (a), titre (e)
Titration e. e.
titrieren to titrate
Titrimetrie titrimetry
titrimetrisch titrimetric
toben to rave
Tobramycin e. e.
Tobsucht frenzy
Tod death
todbringend deadly
Todesangst fear of death
Todesart manner of death
Todesfall case of death
Todesgefahr deadly peril
Todeskampf death struggle
Todesstunde hour of death
todkrank dangerously ill
tödlich deadly, mortal
tödliches Ende fatal end
töten to kill
töten (= abtöten) to deaden
Tötung killing
Toilette toilet
– (= Klosett) closet, water closet, lavatory
Tokographie tocography
Tokometrie tocometry
Tokopherol tocopherol
Tolazamid tolazamide
Tolbutamid tolbutamide
tolerant e. e.
Toleranz tolerance
Toliprolol e. e.
Tollens-Probe Tollens' test
Tollkirsche deadly nightshade
tollwütig rabietic
Tollwut rabies, lyssa
Tollwut-Schutzimpfung rabies immunization
Tolubalsam balsam of Tolu

Toluendiamin toluendiamine
Toluidin toluidine
Toluidinblau toluidine blue
Toluol toluene
Toluyl e. e.
Toluylen toluylene
Tolyl e. e.
Tomogramm tomogram
Tomograph e. e.
Tomographie tomography
tomographisch tomographical
Ton (= Laut) tone, sound
Tonblende tone-control device
Tonerde argillaceous earth
Tonikum tonic
tonisch tonic
tonisch-klonisch tonoclonic
tonisieren to tonicize
Tonizität tonicity
Tonofibrille tonofibril
Tonometer e. e.
Tonometrie tonometry
tonometrisch tonometric
Tonsilla lingualis lingual tonsil
– palatina faucial tonsil, palatine tonsil
– pharyngea pharyngeal tonsil
tonsillär tonsillary, tonsillar
Tonsille tonsil
Tonsillektomie tonsillectomy
Tonsillenschlinge tonsil snare
Tonsillitis e. e.
tonsillitisch tonsillitic
Tonsillotom tonsillotome
Tonsillotomie tonsillotomy
Tonus tone, tonus
Topektomie topectomy
Tophus e. e.
tophusartig tophaceous
topisch topical
Topographie topography
topographisch topographical
Topologie topology
Tormentille tormentil
Torontoeinheit Toronto unit
torpid e. e.
Torpidität torpidity

Torricelli e.e.
Torsion e.e.
Torsiversion e.e.
Tortikollis torticollis
Torulose torulosis
tot dead
Totenbahre bier
totenblaß deadly pale
Totenkopf death's head
Totenschein certificate of death
Totenstarre cadaveric rigidity
totgeboren stillborn
Totgeburt stillbirth
–, verhaltene missed labor (a), missed labour (e)
Totische Operation Toti's operation
Totraum deadspace
Totschlag manslaughter
Toxämie toxaemia (e), toxemia (a)
toxämisch toxaemic (e), toxemic (a)
Toxikologe toxicologist
Toxikologie toxicology
Toxikologin toxicologist
toxikologisch toxicological
Toxikomanie toxicomania
Toxikose toxicosis
Toxin e.e.
toxisch toxic
Toxizität toxicity
Toxoid e.e.
toxophor toxophorous
Toxoplasma e.e.
Toxoplasmose toxoplasmosis
trabekulär trabecular
Tracer e.e.
Trachea e.e.
tracheal e.e.
Trachealkanüle tracheotomy tube
Trachealkatheter tracheal catheter
Trachealstenose tracheostenosis
Tracheitis e.e.
Trachelismus trachelism
trachelobregmatisch trachelo-bregmatic
Trachelopexie trachelopexy

Tracheloplastik tracheloplasty
Trachelotomie trachelotomy
Tracheobronchitis e.e.
tracheolaryngeal e.e.
Tracheomalazie tracheomalacia
tracheopharyngeal e.e.
Tracheoskopie tracheoscopy
tracheoskopisch tracheoscopic
Tracheostomie tracheostomy
Tracheotomie tracheotomy
tracheotomieren to tracheotomize
Trachom trachoma
trachomatös trachomatous
traditionell traditional
träge lazy
Träger conductor; vector
Träne tear
tränen to run with tears
Tränen lacrimation
Tränendrüse lacrimal gland
Tränendrüsenentzündung dacryadenitis
Tränengang lacrimal duct
Tränengangentzündung dacryo-canaliculitis
Tränensack tear sac
Tränensackentzündung dacryo-cystitis
träumen to dream
Tragant tragacanth
tragbar portable
Trage handbarrow
tragen to bear
Tragen bearing
trainieren to train
Training e.e.
Traktionsdivertikel traction diverticulum
Traktotomie tractotomy
Trank draft (a), draught (e), potion
Trank (veter.) drench
Tranquilizer e.e., minor tranquilizer (a)
Transaminase e.e.
transaurikulär transauricular
transbronchial e.e.

Transcriptase e.e.
transdiaphragmatisch transdiaphragmatic
Transferase e.e.
Transferrin e.e.
Transformation e.e.
Transformator transformer
transformieren to transform
Transformylase e.e.
transfundieren to transfuse
Transfusion e.e.
Transfusionszwischenfall transfusion incident
Transglutaminase e.e.
transhepatisch transhepatic
Transhydrase transhydrogenase
Transhydrogenase e.e.
Transhydroxymethylase e.
Transillumination e.e.
Transistor e.e.
transitorisch transitional
transjugulär transjugular
transkapillär transcapillary
Transkarbamylase transcarbamylase
Transketolase e.e.
transkranial transcranial
transkutan transcutaneous
Transmethylierung transmethylation
Transmissionscomputerton transmission computed
Transmitter e.e.
transmural e.e.
Transmutation e.e.
transorbital e.e.
transpalatal e.e.
transparent e.e.
Transpeptidase e.e.
transperitoneal e.e.
Transpiration e.e.
transpirieren to transpire
transplantabel transplant
Transplantat transplant,
Transplantation e.e.
transplantieren to transplant
transplazental transplace

Triangel triangle
Triarylboran trian
Trias triad
Triazetat triaceta
Triazetyloleandom oleandomycin
Tribadismus triba
Tribouletsche Pro test
Tribromäthylalkoh ethanol, tribrom
Tribromid tribrom
Tributyl e. e.
Trichiasis e.e.
Trichine trichina
Trichinella spiralis
trichinös trichino
Trichinose trichin
Trichlorid trichlor
Trichlorisobutylalk butanol
Trichlormethiazid zide
Trichlorphenol e.
Trichocephalus dis trichiura
Trichomona deninf trichomonas infe
Trichomona denmit monacide
Trichomonas vagin
Trichomykose tric
Trichophytia barba corporis trichop capitis / corporis
Trichophytie trich trichophytina
Trichophytin e.e.
Trichophyton acum
– gypseum Tricho asteroides
– tonsurans Triche crateriforme
– violaceum e.e.
Trichorrhexis nodos
Trichostrongylose strongylosis

Triphosphonukleosid triphosphonucleoside
Triplegie triplegia
triploid e. e.
Triplopie triplopia
Tripper gonorrhea (a), gonorrhoea (e)
Trishydroxymethylaminomethan trishydroxymethylaminomethane
Trismaleat trismaleate
Trismus e. e., lockjaw
trisomal e. e.
Trisulfid trisulfide (a), trisulphide (e)
Tritium e. e.
Trituration e. e.
triturieren to triturate
Trivialbezeichnung (eines Medikamentes) generic name
trochanterisch trochanteric
trochleär trochlear
trocken dry
Trockenschrank drying oven
trocknen to dry
Tröpfchen droplet
tröpfeln to trickle, to drop, to drip
Trokar trocar
Trommel drum
Trommelfell tympanic membrane
Trommelfellplastik tympanoplasty
Trommelschlägelfinger clubbed fingers
Trommersche Probe Trommer's test
Tropäolin tropeolin
Tropakokain tropacocaine
Tropein tropeine
Tropen tropics
Tropenkrankheit tropical disease
Tropenmedizin tropical medicine
Tropfen drop
tropfenweise by drops
Tropfer dropper
Tropfflasche dropping bottle
Tropfrohr drop tube

Trophik trophism
trophisch trophic
Trophoblast e. e.
Trophoneurose trophoneurosis
trophoneurotisch trophoneurotic
Trophonose trophonosis
Trophopathie trophopathy
Trophoplasma trophoplasm
trophotrop trophotropic
Tropin tropine
tropisch tropical
Trousseausches Zeichen Trousseau's sign
trüb muddy, turbid, cloudy, opaque
Trübung turbidity, opacity
Trugschluß false conclusion
Truncus brachiocephalicus innominate artery
Trunkenheit drunkenness
Trunksucht mania for drinking, dipsomania
trunksüchtige Person drunkard
Trypaflavin acriflavine hydrochloride
Trypanblau trypan blue
Trypanosoma brucei e. e.
– **cruzi** e. e.
– **equiperdum** e. e.
– **gambiense** e. e.
– **rhodesiense** e. e.
Trypanosomiasis e. e.
Trypanrot trypan red
Tryparsamid tryparsamide
Trypsin e. e.
Trypsinogen e. e.
Tryptamin tryptamine
Tryptase e. e.
tryptisch tryptic
Tryptophan e. e.
Tsetsefliege tsetse fly
Tsutsugamushifieber tsutsugamushi fever
tubar tubal
Tubargravidität tubal pregnancy
Tube (= Eileiter) fallopian tube

Tube (= Eustachische Röhre)
 eustachian tube
Tubektomie tubektomie
Tuberculum majus great tubercle
– **minus** lesser tubercle
Tuberkel tubercle
Tuberkelbazillus Mycobacterium
 tuberculosis
Tuberkelbildung tuberculation
tuberkulär tubercular
Tuberkulid tuberculide
Tuberkulin tuberculin
Tuberkulinanwendung tuberculinization
tuberkulös tuberculous
Tuberkulofibrose tuberculofibrosis
Tuberkulom tuberculoma
Tuberkulomanie tuberculomania
Tuberkulophobie tuberculophobia
Tuberkulose tuberculosis
Tuberkulose, fortschreitende
 progressive tuberculosis
–, **geschlossene** closed tuberculosis
–, **miliare** miliary tuberculosis
–, **offene** open tuberculosis
–, **zum Stillstand gekommene**
 arrested tuberculosis
tuberkulosekranke Person
 tuberculotic
Tuberkulosilikose tuberculosilicosis
tuberkulostatisch tuberculostatic
Tuberkulotoxin tuberculotoxin
tuberkulozid tuberculocide
tuberös tuberous
tuberoinfundibulär tuberoinfundibular
Tuberosität tuberosity
Tubocurarin tubocurarine
tubulär tubular
Tubuli contorti convoluted
 tubules
Tuchklemme towel forceps
Tüpfelung maculation, stippling
Türcksches Bündel Türck's
 bundle

Türkensattel pituitary fossa
Tularämie tularaemia (e),
 tularemia (a), rabbit fever
Tumenol e. e.
Tumor tumor (a), tumour (e)
tumorös tumorous
tupfen to dap, to touch lightly
Tupfen dot
Tupfer swab
Turbellaria e. e.
Turbidimeter e. e.
Turbidimetrie turbidimetry
turbidimetrisch turbidimetric
turbinal e. e.
Turbine e. e.
Turgor e. e.
Turmschädel steeple head,
 turricephaly
Turnbullblau Turnbull's blue
Turner-Syndrom Turner
 syndrome
Tutocain e. e.
Tylom tyloma
tympanal e. e.
Tympanektomie tympanectomy
Tympanie tympanites, tympany
– **des Pansens** hoven, bloat
tympanitisch tympanitic
tympanitischer Schall tympanitic
 sound
tympanomandibulär tympanomandibular
Tympanomastoiditis e. e.
Tympanoplastik tympanoplasty
Tympanotomie tympanotomy
Tyndall-Phänomen Tyndall
 phenomenon
Typ type
Typhlatonie typhlatony
Typhlitis e. e.
Typhlostomie typhlostomy
Typhlotomie typhlotomy
Typhloureterostomie typhloureterostomy
Typhobazillose typhobacillosis
typhös typhoid

Typhus abdominalis typhoid, typhoid fever
Typhusbazillus Eberthella typhosa
Typhusimpfstoff typhoid vaccine
Typhusimpfung typhoid vaccination
typisch typical
Typologie typology
typologisch typological
Tyramin tyramine
Tyrodelösung Tyrode's solution
Tyrosin tyrosine
Tyrosinase e. e.
Tyrosinose tyrosinosis
Tyrothricin e. e.
Tysonsche Drüse Tyson's gland

U

übel (= krank) ill, sick
Übel (= Krankheit) disease, illness, complaint
Übelbefinden indisposition
Übelkeit (= Brechreiz) nausea
übelriechend malodorous
Überalterung superannuation
überanstrengen to overexert
Überanstrengung overexertion
Überarbeitung overwork
Überbeanspruchung overexposure
Überbein exostosis, ganglion
Überbelichtung overexposure
Überbleibsel remains pl.
Überblick survey
Überdosierung overdosage
Überdruck overpressure, positive pressure
Übereinstimmung agreement
überempfindlich hypersensitive
Überempfindlichkeit hypersensitiveness
Überernährung overfeeding, hypernutrition
übererregbar hyperirritable
Übererregbarkeit hyperirritability
Übererregung overexcitation, surexcitation
überfärben to overstain
überfetten tu superfat
überflüssig abundant, redundant
überführen to transduce
überfüllen to glut
überfüttern to overfed
Überfütterung overfeeding
Überfunktion hyperfunction
Übergangsstadium transitional stage
Übergangszelle transition cell
übergeben, sich – to vomit
Übergewicht overweight
Übergreifen implication
Überhäutung cuticularization
Überholung (= Reparatur) overhaul
Über-Ich super-ego
Überkappung capping
Überkronung crownwork
überladen to overload
überlagern to superimpose
Überlagerung overlay
Überlappung overlapping
überlasten to overload
Überlastung overloading
Überlauf overflow
überleben to survive
Überlebende survivor
Überlebender survivor
Überlebensdauer duration of survival
Überlebensrate survival rate
Überleitung transconduction
Überleitungszeit transconduction time

übermangansauer permanganic
übermenschlich superhuman
übermüdet overtired
übernähen to oversew
übernormal supernormal, hypernormal
Überprüfung screening
überreif hypermature
übersättigen to oversaturate, to supersaturate
Übersättigung oversaturation, supersaturation
Übersäuerung superacidity
Überschallgeschwindigkeit supersonic speed
überschießend exuberant, overshooting
Überschuß excess
überschwellig supraliminal
übersegmentiert hypersegmented
übersinnlich transcendental
Überspanntheit exaltation
überstrecken to strain
Überstreckung strain
Überträger transmitter
übertragbar transmissible, communicable
Übertragbarkeit transmissibility
übertragen to transfer, to transmit
Übertragung transfer, transference; vection, transmission
übertrainieren to overtrain
übertreiben to exaggerate
Überwachung supervision
—, technische monitoring
Überwärmungsbad warming bath
überweich supersoft
überweisen to transfer
überweisen, einen Patienten to remit a patient
Überweisung eines Patienten remittance of a patient
überwinden to conquer, to overcome
Überwindung kosten to cost an effort
überzählig supernumerary

überzogen coated
Überzug coat, covering
üblich customary
Übung exercise, practice
Uffelmannsche Probe Uffelmann's test
Uhlenhuthsches Verfahren Uhlenhuth's test
Ulcus corneae corneal ulcer
— duodeni duodenal ulcer
— jejuni pepticum secondary jejunal ulcer
— ventriculi ulcer of stomach
Ulkus ulcer
Ulkusbildung ulceration
ulnar e. e.
ulnarwärts ulnad
ulnoradial e. e.
ultimobranchial e. e.
Ultrafilter e. e.
Ultrafiltration e. e.
Ultrahochvakuum ultra-high vacuum
Ultrakurzwelle ultrashort wave
Ultramikroskop ultramicroscope
ultramikroskopisch ultramicroscopical
Ultraschall ultra sound
Ultraschallbehandlung ultrasonic therapy
Ultraschallwelle ultrasonic wave
Ultrastruktur ultrastructure
ultrastrukturell ultrastructural
ultraviolett ultraviolet
— bestrahlen to uviolize
ultraviolettempfindlich uviosensitive
Ultraviolettlampe uviol
ultraviolettresistent uvioresistant
Ultravirus e. e.
ultravisibel ultravisible
Ultrazentrifuge ultracentrifuge
Ulzeration ulceration
ulzerativ ulcerative
ulzerieren to ulcerate
ulzerös ulcerous
umbilikal umbilical

Umdrehung revolution
Umdrehungen pro Minute revolutions per minute
Umfang circumference
umfangreich voluminous
umformen to transform
Umformung transformation
Umgebung peristasis, surroundings
umgehen to bypass
Umgehung bypass
Umkehrung reversal
Umleitung diversion, shunt
Umsatz turnover
Umschaltung changing
Umschlag (= Änderung) change
Umschlag (= Kataplasma) cataplasm
Umschneidung circumcision
Umstechung pursestring ligature
umstülpen to evert
Umstülpung eversion, subvolution
umwandeln to transform
Umwandlung transformation
Umwandlung, bösartige malignization
Umwelt environment
Umweltbedingungen environmental conditions
Umweltschutz environment protection
unabhängig independent
unauflösbar insoluble
unauflöslich indissoluble
unausbleiblich inevitable
unbeeinflußt unaltered
Unbehagen uneasiness
unbehaglich uneasy, uncomfortable
unbehandelt untreated
unberechenbar incalculable
unbeständig inconstant
Unbeständigkeit inconstancy
unbestimmt undetermined
unbeweglich immobile
Unbeweglichkeit immobility
unbewußt unconscious
unbrauchbar useless
Uncinariasis e. e.

undeutlich indistinct
Undichtigkeit leakage
Undichtigkeit, mikroskopische micro-leakage
Undulation e. e.
undulierend undulant
undulierendes Fieber undulant fever
undurchdringlich impenetrable
Undurchdringlichkeit impenetrability
undurchgängig impermeable
uneben uneven
unempfindlich insensible, insensitive
Unempfindlichkeit insensibility, insensitiveness
unenthaltsam incontinent
unerforscht unexplored
unergiebig unproductive, inefficient
unerkannt unrecognized
unerwartet unsuspected
unerziehbar ineducable
unfähig unable
Unfall accident
Unfallheilkunde traumatology
Unfallspezialist traumatologist
Unfallstation casualty department; ambulance station
unfreiwillig involuntary
unfruchtbar sterile, barren; unfruitful
Unfruchtbarkeit sterility, barrenness
ungebraucht unused
ungeeignet unable
ungeheilt uncured
ungeimpft unvaccinated
ungenau improper
ungenießbar not eatable
ungesättigt unsaturated
–, mehrfach polyunsaturated
ungesalzen unsalted
ungeschickt artless
Ungeziefer vermin
ungleichmäßig uneven
Unglücksfall misfortune, accident

ungual e. e.
Unguis incarnatus e. e.
ungünstig unfavorable (a), unfavourable (e)
unheilbar incurable
unhygienisch unsanitary, insanitary
unifokal unifocal
Unigravida e. e.
unilateral e. e.
unilokulär unilocular
Unipara e. e.
unipolar e. e.
unipotential e. e.
univalent e. e.
Univalenz univalence
Universität university
unkompliziert uncomplicated
unkontrollierbar uncontrollable
unlöslich insoluble
unmenschlich inhuman
Unmenschlichkeit inhumanity
unmerklich imperceptible
unmischbar immiscible
unmittelbar immediate
unnötig unnecessary
Unordnung disorder
unpäßlich unwell, indisposed
– sein to ail
Unpäßlichkeit ailment, indisposition, malaise
unpassend improper
unpathetisch apathetical
unphysiologisch unphysiological
unpigmentiert unpigmented
unpsychologisch unpsychological
unregelmäßig irregular
Unregelmäßigkeit irregularity
unreif immature
Unreife immaturity
unrein impure, unclean
Unreinheit uncleanness
unrichtig improper
unsauber impure
unschädlich innocuous
unsicher (= gefährlich) unsafe, insecure
unsicher (= ungeschickt) unsteady
– (= zweifelhaft) doubtful
Unsicherheit (= Gefahr) insecurity
– (= Ungeschicklichkeit) unsteadiness
– (= Zweifel) doubt
unsichtbar invisible
unsittlich immoral
unspezifisch nonspecific
unstet unsteady
unstillbar immitigable
unsympathisch unpleasant
Unterarm forearm
Unterart subspecies
Unterbauch lower abdomen
unterbewußt preconscious
Unterbewußtsein preconsciousness
unterbinden to ligate
Unterbindung ligation
unterbrechen to interrupt
Unterbrechung interruption
Unterdruck underpressure, negative pressure
unterdrückbar suppressible
unterdrücken to suppress
unterdrückend suppressant
unterdrückendes Mittel suppressant
Unterdrückung suppression
unterernährt undernourished, underfed
Unterernährung underfeeding, hypoalimentation, malnutrition
unterfärben to understain
Unterfütterungsmaterial reliner
Unterfunktion hypofunction
Untergewicht underweight
Untergruppe subgroup
Unterhaut subcutis
unterhöhlen to undermine
Unterkiefer lower jaw bone
unterlassen to omit
Unterlippe lower lip
Unterricht instruction
Unterricht am Krankenbett bedside teaching

Unterricht, programmierter programmed instruction
Unterschenkel lower leg
Unterschenkelgeschwür crural ulcer
unterschwellig subliminal
untersuchen to examine
untersuchen, einen Patienten gründlich – to check up a patient
Untersuchende examiner
Untersuchender examiner
Untersuchung examination
Untersuchungsbesteck diagnostic set
Untertauchen submersion
untertauchen to submerge
Unterwassergymnastik underwater gymnastics
ununterdrückbar nonsuppressible
unverändert unaltered
unverdächtig unsuspicious
unverdaulich indigestible
unverdauliche Nahrungsbestandteile roughage
Unverdaulichkeit indigestibility
unverdaut not digested
unverdünnt undiluted
unverestert unesterified
unverletzt uninjured, unhurt
unvermischt unmixed
unversehrt intact
unverträglich incompatible; intolerant
Unverträglichkeit incompatibility; intolerance
unverwundbar invulnerable
unvollständig incomplete
unvorhersehbar unpredictable
unweiblich unwomanly
unwiderruflich irrevocable
unwirksam ineffectual, ineffective, inefficient
Unwohlsein malaise
unzerbrechlich unbreakable
unzerstörbar indestructible
unzureichend insufficient

U.p.M. (= Umdrehungen pro Minute) rev./min. (= revolutions per minute)
urachal e. e.
Uracil e. e.
Uracil-Lost uracil-mustard
Urämie uraemia (e), uremia (a)
urämisch uraemic (e), uremic (a)
Uran uranium
Urat urate
uratisch uratic
Urea e. e.
Urease e. e.
Ureid ureide
Ureter e. e.
ureteral e. e.
Ureterektomie ureterectomy
Ureteritis e. e.
Ureterknickung ureteral angulation
Ureterographie ureterography
Ureterokolostomie ureterocolostomy
Ureterolithiasis e. e.
Ureterostomie ureterostomy
Ureterotomie ureterotomy
ureterotubal e. e.
Ureterozele ureterocele
Urethan urethane
Urethra e. e.
urethral e. e.
Urethritis e. e.
Urethrographie urethrography
Urethroskop urethroscope
Urethroskopie urethroscopy
urethroskopisch urethroscopic
Urethrostomie urethrostomy
Urethrotomie urethrotomy
Urethrozele urethrocele
Uridin e. e.
Uridinurie uridinuria
Urin urine
urinär urinary
Urinanalyse urine analysis, urinalysis
Urinflasche urinal
urinieren to urinate

Urinieren urination
urinös urinous
Urinsammelperiode urine collection period
Urinverhaltung retention of urine
Urinzucker urine sugar
Urne urn
Urning uranist
Urobilin e. e.
Urobilinämie urobilinaemia (e), urobilinemia (a)
Urobilinikterus urobilinicterus
Urobilinogen e. e.
Urobilinogenurie urobilinogenuria
Urobilinurie urobilinuria
Urochrom urochrome
Uroerythrin e. e.
urogenital e. e.
Urographie urography
urographisch urographic
Urokinase e. e.
Urolithiasis e. e.
Urologe urologist
Urologie urology
urologisch urological
Urometer urinometer
Uropepsin e. e.
Uropepsinogen e. e.
Uroporphyrin e. e.
Urosepsis e. e.
Ursache cause
ursächlich causative
Ursotherapie ursotherapy
Ursprung origin
Urticaria pigmentosa e. e.
Urtikaria urticaria
urtikariell urticarious

Urtyp archetype
Urzeugung spontaneous generation
uterin uterine
Uterinsegment segment of uterus
uteroabdominal e. e.
Uterographie uterography
uteroovariell uteroovarian
uteroplazentar uteroplacental
uterosakral uterosacral
uterovaginal e. e.
uterovesikal uterovesical
Uterus e. e.
Uterusblutung uterine haemorrhage (e), uterine hemorrhage (a)
Uterusfixation uterofixation
Uterustamponzange uterine dressing forceps
Uterusverlagerung displacement of uterus
Utilisation utilization
utilisieren to utilize
utrikulosakkulär utriculosaccular
Utrikulus utricle
Uvea e. e.
uveal e. e.
Uveaplastik e. e.
uveoparotisch uveoparotid
Uveoparotitis e. e.
Uvula e. e.
Uvulaödem stahyledema (a), staphyloedema (e)
Uvulitis e. e.
Uzara e. e.
Uzarin e. e.

V

väterlich paternal
Vagabund vagrant, vagabond

vagal e. e.
Vagina e. e.

vaginal e. e.
Vaginismus e. e.
Vaginitis e. e.
vaginolabial e. e.
vaginoperineal e. e.
Vagotomie vagotomy
Vagotonie vagotony, vagotonia
vagotonisch vagotonic
vagotrop vagotropic
Vagus e. e., pneumogastric nerve
vakuolär vacuolar
Vakuole vacuole
vakuolisieren to vacuolate
Vakuolisierung vacuolization
Vakuum vacuum
Vakuumextraktion vacuum extraction
Vakuumpumpe vacuum pump
vakzinal vaccinal
Vakzination vaccination
Vakzine vaccine
Vakzinebehandlung vaccinotherapy
Vakzinid vaccinide
vakziniform vacciniform
Valamin e. e.
valent e. e.
Valenz valence, valency
Valerianat valerianate
Valin valine
Valleixscher Punkt Valleix's point
vallekulär vallecular
Valsalvascher Versuch Valsalva's experiment
Valvotomie valvotomy
valvulär valvular
Valvulotom valvulotome
Valvulotomie valvulotomy
Valyl e. e.
Vanadium e. e.
Vancomycin e. e.
Vanillin e. e.
Vaquez-Oslersche Krankheit Vaquez's disease
variabel variable
Variation e. e.
varikös varicose

Varikose varicosis
Varikosität varicosity
Varikotomie varicotomy
Varikozele varicocele
Variola vera e. e.
variolär variolar
varioliform e. e.
variolös variolous
Variolois varioloid
Varizellen varicella, chickenpox
Varize varicose vein
Varizenbildung varication
Vas deferens e. e.
vasal e. e.
Vasektomie vasectomy
vasektomieren to vasectomize
Vaselin e. e.
–,**gelbes** petrolatum
–,**weißes** white petrolatum
Vaskularisation vascularization
vaskularisieren to vascularize
Vaskularisierung vascularization
Vasodilatation e. e.
vasodilativ vasodilative
Vasographie vasography
Vasokonstriktion vasoconstriction
vasokonstriktiv vasoconstrictive
vasomotorisch vasomotor
Vasoneurose vasoneurosis
vasoneurotisch vasoneurotic
Vasopressin e. e.
Vasopasmus vasospasm
vasospastisch vasospastic
Vasostomie vasostomy
Vasotomie vasotomy
Vater father
Vaterschaft fatherhood, paternity
Vatersche Papille Vater's papilla, duodenal papilla
Vegetarier vegetarian
Vegetarierin vegetarian
Vegetation e. e.
vegetativ vegetative
vegetative Dystonie autonomic nervous disorder
vegetatives Nervensystem autonomic nervous system

Vehikel vehicle
Veit-Smelliescher Handgriff Smellie's method, Veit-Smellie maneuver
Veitstanz Saint Vitus's dance
Vektor vector
vektoriell vectorial
Vektorkardiographie vectorcardiography
velamentös velamentous
Vena azygos azygos vein
– **basilica** basilic vein
– **cephalica** cephalic vein
– **epigastrica** epigastric vein
– **femoralis** femoral vein
– **pulmonalis** pulmonary vein
– **saphena** saphenous vein
– **thyreoidea** thyroid vein
– **umbilicalis** umbilical vein
Vene vein
Venektasie venectasia
Venenpunktion venipuncture
Venensektion phlebotomy
venerisch venereal
Venerologe venereologist
Venerologie venereology
venerologisch venereological
venoarteriell venoarterial
venös venous
Venographie venography
venographisch venographic
Venole venule
Ventilation e. e.
–, **maximale willkürliche** maximal voluntary ventilation
Ventilball valve bulb
ventilieren to ventilate
ventral e. e.
ventralwärts ventrad
Ventrikel ventricle
–, **dritter** third ventricle
–, **linker** left ventricle
–, **rechter** right ventricle
–, **vierter** fourth ventricle
Ventrikeldruck intraventricular pressure

Ventrikelseptumdefekt defect of interventricular septum, ventricular septal defect
ventrikulär ventricular
ventrikuloatrial ventriculoatrial
Ventrikulographie ventriculography
ventrikulographisch ventriculographic
Ventrikulostomie ventriculostomy
ventrodorsal e. e.
ventroinguinal e. e.
ventrolateral e. e.
ventromedial e. e.
Veränderung change
verästeln to ramify
Verästelung ramification
Verankerung anchorage
Veranlagung talent; disposition; constitution
Verapamil e. e.
Verarbeitung working through
veraschen to ash
Veraschung incineration, ashing
Veraschungsgerät asher
Veratmungspyelographie respiration pyelography
Veratrin veratrine
Veratrum album e. e.
– **viride** e. e.
verbal e. e.
Verband dressing, bandage
Verbandplatz infirmary
Verbandschere bandage scissors
Verbandstoff bandaging material, lint
Verbandstoffeimer waste-dressing pail
Verbandstofftrommel dressing drum
Verbascum thapsus e. e.
Verbenon verbenone
verbessern to ameliorate
Verbesserung amelioration
Verbigeration e. e.

verbilden to form wrongly
Verbildung malformation
verbinden to bandage, to dress, to bind
Verbindung connection, junction; linkage
Verbindungsstelle junction
verbluten to bleed to death
Verblutung exsanguination
Verbomanie verbomania
Verbrauch consumption
Verbrechen crime
Verbrecher criminal
Verbrecherin criminal
Verbreiterung enlargement
verbrennen to scorch, to burn
–, **Leichen** to cremate
Verbrennung burn, combustion
Verbrennungen (ersten/zweiten/dritten Grades) burns (of first/second/third degree)
Verbrennungshalle crematorium
Verbrennungsofen combustor
verbrühen to scald
Verbrühung scald
verchromt chrome plated
Verdacht suspicion
verdächtig suspicious
verdampfen to vaporize, to evaporate, to volatilize
Verdampfung vaporization, evaporation, volatilization
verdauen to digest
verdaulich digestible
Verdauung digestion
Verdauungsmittel digestive
Verdauungsstörung indigestion, digestive disorder
Verdauungstrakt digestive tract
verderben to deprave
verderblich perishable
Verdichtung condensation
verdicken to thicken, to inspissate
Verdoppelung duplication
Verdrängung displacement
verdünnen to attenuate; to dilute
Verdünnung attenuation; dilution

Verdünnungskurve dilution curve
Verdünnungsmittel diluent
Verdünnungsversuch, renaler renal dilution test
verdummen (trans.) to make stupid
– **(intrans.)** to become stupid
verdursten to die with thirst
vereinfachen to simplify
Vereinfachung simplification
vereinigen to unify, to pool
Vereinigung union, unification
vereinzelt sporadic
vereisen to glaciate
Vereisung glaciation
vereitern to suppurate
Vereiterung suppuration
verenden to perish
verengen to narrow
vererbbar hereditable
vererben to inherit
vererbt inherited
Vererbung inheritance
verestern to esterify, to esterize
Veresterung esterification
verfärben to discolor (a), to discolour (e)
Verfärbung discoloration (a), discolouration (e)
Verfahren procedure
verfallen to decay
Verfassung condition
verfaulen to rot
Verfettung pimelosis; fatty degeneration
verflüchtigen to volatilize
Verflüchtigung volatilization
verflüssigen to colliquate, to liquefy
Verflüssigung colliquation, liquefaction
Verfolgungswahn persecution mania, delusion of persecution
verfügbar available
Verfügbarkeit availability
–, **biologische** bioavailability
vergällen to denature, to embitter
vergehen to pass away

vergeßlich forgetful
Vergeßlichkeit forgetfulness
vergiften to poison
Vergiftung poisoning
Vergleich comparison
vergleichen to compare
Vergreisung dotage
vergrößern to magnify, to enlarge
Vergrößerung magnification, enlargement
Vergrößerungsglas magnifying glass, magnifying lens
Verhältnis ratio
Verhärtung hardening; concretion
verhalten to retain
Verhalten behaviour
verhalten, sich to behave
Verhaltung retention
verheben, sich – to injure oneself in lifting
verhindern to avert, to impede
verhornen to cornify, to keratinize
Verhornung cornification; callosity
verhüten to prevent
Verhütung prevention
verhungern to die of starvation
Verhungern starvation
verifizieren to verify
verjüngen to make young again
Verjüngung rejuvenescence
Verkäsung caseation, tyrosis
verkalken to calcify
Verkalkung calcification
verkapseln to encapsulate
Verkapselung encapsulation
Verkehr traffic
–,**geschlechtlicher** sexual intercourse
verkehren, geschlechtlich –
to have sexual intercourse
Verkehrsunfall road accident
Verkeilungsdruck wedge pressure
verkleben to paste
verklebend adhesive
verknöchern to ossify

Verknöcherung ossification, bone formation
verknorpeln to chondrify
Verknorpelung chondrification, cartilaginification
verkohlen to carbonize
verkrüppeln to cripple
verkühlen, sich to catch cold
verkümmern to become stunded
verkürzen to shorten
Verkürzung shortening
verlängern to lengthen
Verlängerung lengthening; prolongation
Verlagerung displacement
Verlagerungsoperation advancement
Verlauf issue; progress
Verlausung lousiness
verlegen (weiterleiten) to transfer
verlegen (= verstopfen) to obstruct
verlegen (= perplex) perplexed
Verlegung (Weiterleitung) transfer, transference
– **(= Obstruktion)** obstruction
verletzen to injure, to hurt
Verletzung lesion, injury
Verlust loss; deprival, deprivation
vermännlichen to masculinize, to virilize
Vermännlichung masculinization
vermehren to multiply; to increase
vermeiden to avoid
Vermeidung avoidance
vermengen to mix
vermindern to decrease, to diminish
Verminderung diminution
vermuten to suspect
vernähen to sew up
vernageln to nail
vernarben to cicatrize
Vernarbung cicatrization
vernebeln to nebulize
Vernebelung nebulization
Vernebler nebulizer
Verner-Morrison-Syndrom pancreatic cholera

vernichten to annihilate
Vernichtung annihilation
vernickelt nickel plated
verordnen to prescribe, to order
Verordnung prescription
Verpflanzung transplantation
Verpflegung catering
verpfuschen to bungle, to botch
verreiben to triturate
Verreibung trituration
verrenken to luxate
Verrenkung luxation, wrench, wrick
Verruca peruviana e. e.
verrückt crazy, mad
Verrücktheit madness
Versandgefäß mailing case
– **für bakteriologische Zwecke** mailing culture case
Verschattung opacity, shadow
Verschiebung shift
verschlacken to turn into dross
Verschlafenheit sleepiness
verschlechtern to make worse
Verschlechterung depravation; deterioration
verschleimen to obstruct with phlegm
Verschleppung (= **Verzögerung**) delay
verschließen to shut, to close up; to occlude
verschlimmern to make worse
–,**sich** – to become worse
Verschlimmerung change for the worse, depravation
verschlingen to devour
verschlucken to swallow
–,**sich** to swallow the wrong way
Verschluß fastening, closure
– (= **Okklusion**) occlusion
– (**photogr.**) shutter
– (= **Schloß**) lock
Verschlußikterus obstructive jaundice
Verschlußkrankheit, arterielle arterial occlusive disease

verschmähen to disdain
Verschmelzung fusion
verschmutzen to soil, to contaminate
Verschmutzung contamination
verschorfen to scab, to produce an eschar
verschreiben to prescribe
verschwinden to disappear
versehrt disabled
versehrte Person disabled
verseifen to saponify
Verseifung saponification
verseuchen to infect
Versorgung provision, supply, catering
–,**ärztliche** medical treatment
Versorgungsbehörde, militärische service for the care od veterans
Versorgungsgebiet supply area
Verspätung retardation
verspüren to feel
Verstädterung urbanization
Verstand intellect, understanding, intelligence
verstauchen to sprain
Verstauchung sprain
verstehen to understand
Verstehen understanding
versteifen to stiffen
Versteifung stiffening
versteinern to petrify
verstellbar adjustable
Verstimmung emotional deterioration
verstopfen to choke
verstopft (**obstipiert**) constipated
Verstopfung (**Obstipation**) constipation
verstümmeln to mutilate
Verstümmelung mutilation
Versuch experiment
Versuchsperson test person
–,**freiwillige gesunde** – healthy volunteer
Versuchstier experimental animal
vertebral e. e.

Vertebrata e. e.
vertebrosternal e. e.
Vertebrotomie vertebrotomy
Verteiler distributor
Verteilung distribution
Vertigo e. e.
vertikal vertical
verträglich tolerable, compatible
Verträglichkeit toleration, compatibility
Vertrauensarzt confidential medical officer
vertraulich confidential
verunglücken to meet with an accident
Verunreinigung soiling, contamination
verunstalten to disfigure
verursachen to cause
verursachend causative
Verursachung causation
Vervollständigung supplementation
verwachsen to grow together
Verwachsung concrescence, concretion
Verwaltung administration
Verwandlung metamorphosis
verweiblichen to feminize
Verweiblichung feminization, effemination
Verweilkatheter permanent catheter, indwelling catheter
verwenden to apply
verwerten to utilize
Verwertung utilization
verwesen to rot, to decompose, to putrefy
verwesend putrescent
Verwesung decomposition, putrefaction
Verwirrung confusion
verwundbar vulnerable
Verwundbarkeit vulnerability
verwunden to vulnerate
verwundet wounded
–,**schwer-** severely wounded
Verwundung wounding

Verwurmung vermination
Verzeichnung distortion
Verzerrung distortion
verzögern to delay
verzögert delayed, retarded
Verzögerung delay, retardation
Verzuckerung saccharification
verzweigen to ramify
verzweigt branched, ramified
Verzweigung ramification
vesikal vesical
vesikoabdominal vesicoabdominal
vesikoprostatisch vesicoprostatic
vesikopubisch vesicopubic
vesikorektal vesicorectal
vesikorenal vesicorenal
Vesikosigmoidostomie vesicosigmoidostomy
Vesikotomie vesicotomy
vesikoumbilikal vesicoumbilical
vesikoureteral vesicoureteral
vesikourethral vesicourethral
vesikouterin vesicouterine
vesikovaginal vesicovaginal
Vesikozele vesicocele
vesikulär vesicular
Vesikulektomie vesiculectomy
Vesikulitis vesiculitis
vesikulobronchial vesiculobronchial
Vesikulographie vesiculography
Vesikulotomie vesiculotomy
vestibulär vestibular
Vestibulotomie vestibulotomy
vestibulourethral e. e.
vestibulozerebellar vestibulocerebellar
Vestibulum e. e.
Veterinär veterinarian
Veterinärmedizin veterinary medicine
Vibration e. e.
Vibrio comma e. e.
Viburnum prunifolium e. e.
Vicq d'Azyrsches Bündel Vicq d'Azyr's bundle
Vieh cattle

Viehbremse gadfly
vierbeinig four-legged
viereckig quadrangular
Vierhügelplatte quadrigeminal plate
Vierling quadruplet
Vierte Krankheit rubeola scarlatinosa
vierwertig quadrivalent, tetravalent
vierzipfelig quadricuspid
vikariierend vicarious
villös villous
Vinblastin vinblastine
Vincaleukoblastin vincaleukoblastine
Vincristin vincristine
Vinyl e. e.
Viomycin e. e.
Viper e. e.
virginell virginal
viril virile
virilisieren to virilize
Virilismus virilism
Virologe virologist
Virologie virology
Virologin virologist
virologisch virological
virtuell virtual
virulent e. e.
Virulenz virulence
Virus e. e.
—,**Adeno-** adenovirus
—,**Coxsackie-** coxsackie virus
—,**ECHO-** ECHO virus
—,**Entero-** enterovirus
—,**Enzephalitis-** virus of encephalitis
—,**Gelbfieber-** virus of yellow fever
—,**Grippe-** virus of influenza
—,**Hepatitis-** virus of hepatitis
—,**Herpes-** herpes virus
—,**Influenza-** virus of influenza
—,**Katzenkratz-** cat-scratch virus
—,**Masern-** measles virus
—,**Oncorna-** oncorna virus
—,**Picorna-** picorna virus
Virus, Pocken- smallpox virus
—,**Poliomyelitis-** poliovirus
—,**Polyoma-** polyoma virus
—,**respiratorisches Synzytium-** respiratory syncytial virus
—,**Tollwut-** rabies virus
—,**Varizellen-** chickenpox virus
Virusforscher virologist
Virusforscherin virologist
Virushepatitis virus jaundice
Viruskrankheit virosis
Viruspneumonie virus pneumonia
Vision e. e.
viskoelastisch viscoelastic
viskös viscous
Viskosimetrie viscosimetry
Viskosität viscosity
visuell visual
viszeral visceral
viszeromotorisch visceromotor
viszeroparietal visceroparietal
viszeropleural visceropleural
Viszeroptose visceroptosis
viszerosensorisch viscerosensory
vital e. e.
Vitalfärbung vital staining
Vitalgranulation vital granulation
Vitalismus vitalism
vitalistisch vitalistic
Vitalkapazität vital capacity
Vitamin (A/B/C/D/E/K) vitamin (A/B/C/D/E/K)
Vitamin B-Komplex vitamin B complex
Vitamin B 12 e. e., cyanocobalamine
vitaminarme Kost low vitamin diet
Vitaminologie vitaminology
vitaminreiche Kost high vitamin diet
Vitaminträger vitamin carrier
Vitellin e. e.
vitiliginös vitiliginous
Vitiligo e. e.
Vitriol e. e.
Vivisektion vivisection
Vleminckxsche Lösung Vleminckx's solution

Vögtlin-Einheit Vögtlin unit
Völle repletion
Völlegefühl feeling of repletion
Vogel bird
vogelartig birdlike
Vogelmilbe bird mite
vokal vocal
volar e. e.
volatil volatile
Volhardsche Nierenfunktionsprüfung Volhard's test
Volkmannschiene Volkmann's splint
voll full
Vollbad full bath
vollblütig plethoric
Vollblütigkeit plethora, fullness of blood
vollbrüstig full-breasted
vollständig complete
Volt e. e.
Voltmeter e. e.
Volumen volume
Volumetrie volumetry
volumetrisch volumetric
voluminös voluminous
Volvulus e. e.
vomeronasal e. e.
vorangehend previous
vorangehender Eiteil presentation of fetus (a), presentation of foetus (e)
vorausgehend previous
Vorbehandlung pretreatment, previous treatment
Vorbereitung preparation
vorbeugen to prevent, to obviate
vorbeugend preventive
Vorbeugung prevention, prophylaxis
Vorbißstellung anterioocclusion
Vorderhaupt sinciput
Vorderhauptshaltung forehead position
Vorderwand anterior wall
voreheilich premarital
Vorfall accident

Vorfall (= Prolaps) prolapse
Vorhaut prepuce, foreskin
—,**überhängende** redundant prepuce
Vorherbestimmung predestination
vorherrschen to predominate
vorherrschend predominant, prepotent
vorhersagen to prognosticate
vorhersehbar predictable
Vorhof des Herzens, linker left auricle of the heart, left atrium of the heart
Vorhof des Herzens, rechter right auricle of the heart, right atrium of the heart
Vorhofdruck atrial pressure
Vorhofextrasystole atrial ectopic beat
Vorhofflattern auricular flutter
Vorhofflimmern auricular fibrillation
Vorhofseptumdefekt auricular septal defect, atrial septal defect
Vorkehrungen treffen to take precautions
vorklinisch preclinical
Vorkommen incidence
Vorläufer precursor
vorläufig provisional, preliminary
Vorlesung lecture
Vormilch colostrum
vorprogrammiert preprogrammed
Vorrichtung appliance
Vorschlag suggestion
vorschlagen to suggest
Vorschulalter preschool age
Vorsichtsmaßregel precaution, precautionary measure
Vorsteherdrüse prostate
Vorstellungsbild concept
Vorstufe precursor
vorübergehend transient, transitional
Vorverdauung predigestion
Vorwölbung hillock, eminence
Vorwort foreword, preface

vorzeitig premature, precocious
vulkanisieren to vulcanize
vulnerabel vulnerable
vulvär vulval
Vulvektomie vulvectomy

Vulvitis e. e.
vulvitisch vulvitic
vulvovaginal e. e.
Vulvovaginitis e. e.
Vuzin e. e.

W

Waage balance
wachen to be awake
— **bei jemandem** to sit up with one
Wacholder juniper
Wachs wax
Wachsabdruck wax model
Wachsbad wax bath
wachsen to grow
Wachsfließer wax molding spoon
Wachsmodell wax model
Wachstum growth
Wachstumshormon growth hormone
wachstumsregulierend growth-regulating
Wackelgelenk articular instability
Wade calf
Wadenbein perone
wächsern waxy
Wärme warmth
wärmebildend thermogenetic
Wärmebildung thermogenesis
Wärmegrad degree of heat
Wärmeleiter heat conductor
wärmen to warm
Wärmeregulation thermoregulation
Wärmflasche warming bottle
Wärter guard, attendant
Wäsche wash
wässerig aqueous
Wahlsches Zeichen Wahl's sign
Wahn delusion
wahnhaft delusional
Wahnsinn lunacy
wahnsinnig lunatic, mad

wahrnehmbar perceptible
wahrnehmen to perceive
Wahrnehmung perception, apperception
Wahrnehmungsvermögen perceptivity
Walchersche Hängelage Walcher's position
Waldeyerscher Rachenring Waldeyer's tonsillar ring
Wallach gelding
Wallenbergsches Syndrom Wallenberg's syndrome
Wallersche Degeneration wallerian degeneration
Wallung rush
Walroß walrus
Wand wall
wandern to migrate
wandernd migratory, wandering, vagrant
Wanderniere wandering kidney
Wanderpneumonie migratory pneumonia
Wanderung migration
Wanderzelle wandering cell
Wange cheek
Wangenhalter cheek retractor
Wangentasche cheek pouch
wanken to rock
Wanze bug
Wanzenstich bugbite
Warburgsches Atmungsferment Warburg's yellow enzyme
warm e. e.

warmblütig warm-blooded
Warteliste waiting list
Wartenbergsches Zeichen Wartenberg's sign
Wartezimmer waiting-room
Wartung maintenance
Warze wart, verruca
warzig warty, verrucous
waschbar washable
waschen to wash
Waschen wash
Waschflüssigkeit lotion
Waschung lavation, lavement, lavage, ablution
Wasser water
Wasserbad water bath
wasserdicht water-proof
wasserhaltig hydrous
Wasserklosett water-closet
Wasserkrebs noma
Wasserlassen micturition
wasserlöslich water-soluble
Wassermann-Reaktion Wassermann's reaction
Wasserstoff hydrogen
—,schwerer heavy hydrogen
Wasserstoffionenkonzentration hydrogen ion concentration
Wasserstoffsuperoxyd hydrogen peroxide
Wassersucht dropsy
wassersüchtig dropsical
Wasserverlust deprivation of water
Waterhouse-Friderichsen-Syndrom Waterhouse-Friderichsen syndrome
watscheln to waddle
watschelig waddling
Watt e. e.
Watte cotton
Watterolle cotton roll
Watteträger cotton carrier, cotton holder
Webe web
Weber e. e.
Weber-Ramstedtsche Operation Weber-Ramstedt's operation

Weberscher Versuch Weber's test
Webersches Syndrom Weber's syndrome
Wechselfieber intermittent fever
Wechselfußbad contrast foot bath
Wechselstrom alternating current
Wechselwirkung interaction
wegbrennen to burn away
Wegenersche Granulomatose Wegener's granulomatosis
wegführen to abduct
Wehe pain in labor (a), pain in labour (e)
weiblich female, feminine
Weichbrodtsche Reaktion Weichbrodt's reaction
weichmachend emollient
weichmachendes Mittel emollient
Weichmetall soft metal
Weichstrahltechnik soft ray method
Weichteile soft tissues
Weigertsche Färbemethode Weigert's method
Weil-Felixsche Reaktion Weil-Felix reaction
Weilsche Krankheit leptospiral jaundice
Weinstein tartar
Weisheitszahn wisdom tooth
weißen to blanch
Weiterbehandlung subsequent treatment
Weiterbildung, ärztliche medical postgraduate training
weitsichtig farsighted, longsighted
Weitsichtigkeit farsightedness
Weizenkeimöl wheat germ oil
welk flabby, withered
Welle wave
Welle, steile (EEG) sharp wave
Wellenlänge wave length
Wellensittich budgerigar
Wenckebachsche Periode Wenckebach's period
wenden to turn
Wendepunkt turning-point

Wendung turning, version
—, **äußere** abdominal version
— **auf den Kopf** cephalic version
—, **innere** internal version
— **nach Braxton Hicks** Braxton Hicks' version
Werdnig-Hoffmannscher Typ Werdnig-Hoffmann type
Werkzeug tool
Werlhofsche Purpura Werlhof's disease
Wermut wormwood
Wernersches Syndrom Werner's syndrome
Wert worth, value
Wertheimsche Operation Wertheim's operation
wertig (einwertig/zweiwertig/ dreiwertig/vierwertig/fünfwertig/sechswertig/siebenwertig/achtwertig) valent (monovalent/bivalent/trivalent/ tetravalent/pentavalent/hexavalent/septivalent/octavalent)
Wertigkeit valency
Wespe wasp
Westphalsches Zeichen Westphals' sign
Wettbewerb competition
wettbewerbsfähig competitive
wettbewerbsmäßig competitive
Whartonsche Sulze Wharton's jelly
Wheatstonesche Brücke Wheatstone's bridge
Whipplesche Krankheit Whipple's disease
Whisky e. e.
Wickel pack
—, **feuchter** wet-pack
wickeln to wrap, to pack
Widder ram
widerlich offensive, disgusting
Widerrist withers
Widerstand resistance
Widerstandsfähigkeit resistibility
widerstehen to resist

Widerwille aversion
Wiederaufleben revivescence
Wiederbelebung resuscitation, reanimation
Wiederbesiedelung repopulation
Wiedereinrichtung redressement
Wiedereintritt reentry
Wiedererweckung resuscitation
wiederherstellbar restorable
wiederherstellen to restore
Wiederherstellung restoration, restitution, recovery
Wiederholungsblutung re-bleeding
Wiederholungsimpfung boostershot
Wiederkäuen rumination
Wiederkäuer ruminant
Wiege cradle
Wiesel weasel
Wigandscher Handgriff Wigand's maneuver
Wilkinsonsche Salbe Wilkinson's ointment
Wille volition, will
willensmäßig volitional
willentlich volitional
Wilsonsche Krankheit Wilson's disease
Windel baby napkin (e), diaper (a)
Windpocken varicella
Windung winding
Winiwarter-Buergersche Krankheit Buerger's disease
Winkel angle
winkelig angular
Winkelstück anglepiece
Winterschlaf hibernation
—, **künstlicher** artificial hibernation
Wintrichscher Schallwechsel Wintrich's sign
Wirbel vertebra
Wirbelkörper vertebral body
Wirbelsäule vertebral column, spinal column, spine
Wirbelsäulensäge spine saw

Wirbelsäulenverbiegung deformity of spine
Wirbeltier vertebrate
Wirbeltuberkulose vertebral tuberculosis
wirken to have effect
wirksam efficient
Wirksamkeit effectiveness, potency, efficacy, efficiency, activity
Wirkstoff effective substance
Wirkung effect; response
–,**unerwünschte** untoward effect
Wirkungsdauer time of action
Wirkungsdosis effective dose
wirkungslos inefficient
Wirkungsverlust loss of effectiveness
Wirkungsweise mode of action
Wirt host
wischen to wipe
Wischer swab, wiper
Wismut bismuth
Wissenschaft science
wissenschaftlich scientific
Wittepepton Witte's peptone
Witzelfistel Witzel's fistula
Wochenbett childbed
Wochenbettfieber puerperal fever
Wöchnerin lying-in woman
Wohlbefinden wellbeing
Wohlfahrt welfare
Wohlgemuthsche Probe Wohlgemuth's test
Wolf e. e.
Wolff-Parkinson-White-Syndrom Wolff-Parkinson-White syndrome
Wolfram tungsten
wolhynisches Fieber Volhynia fever, trench fever, quintan fever
Wollfett wool fat
wollüstig voluptuous
Wollust volupty
Wortblindheit word blindness
Worttaubheit word deafness

Wucherung excrescence
Wuchs stature; growth
Wühlmaus vole
würgen to choke
Würze zest
Wulst ridge
wund sore
Wundausschneidung débridement, wound excision
Wunde wound
–,**Quetsch-** contused wound
–,**Riß-** incised wound
–,**Schnitt-** gunshot wound
–,**Schuß-** gunshot wound
–,**Stich-** punctured wound
Wundfieber wound fever
Wundhaken tissue retractor
Wundklammer wound clip
Wundklammerpinzette wound clip forceps
Wundmittel remedy for wounds
Wundrandpinzette approximation forceps
Wundsperrer self-retaining tissue retractor
Wurm worm
wurmartig vermicular
Wurmbefall verminosis, helminthiasis
wurmförmig vermiform
Wurmfortsatz appendix, vermiform process
wurmig wormy
wurmkrank suffering from worms
Wurmkur deworming
Wurmmittel vermifuge; vermicide
Wurmsamen wormseed
Wurmsamenöl oil of wormseed
wurmtötend vermicidal
wurmtötendes Mittel vermicide
wurmtreibend vermifugal
wurmtreibendes Mittel vermifuge
Wurstvergiftung sausagepoisoning
Wurzel root
Wurzelbehandlung root treatment
Wurzelhaut periodontal membrane, pericementum

Wurzelhautabszeß pericemental abscess
Wurzelheber root elevator
Wurzelkanal root canal
Wurzelkanalinstrument broach
Wurzelschraube root screw
Wurzelspitze root apex
Wurzelspitzenheber apical fragment ejector
Wurzelspitzenresektion apicoectomy
Wurzelsplitter root fragment
Wurzelsyndrom radicular syndrome
Wut rage, fury

X

Xanthelasma e. e.
Xanthen xanthene
Xanthin xanthine
Xanthinoxydase xanthinoxidase
Xanthinurie xanthinuria
xanthochrom xanthochromic
Xanthrochromie xanthochromia
Xanthom xanthoma
xanthomatös xanthomatous
Xanthomatose xanthomatosis
Xanthoprotein e. e.
Xanthopsie xanthopsia
Xanthosarkom xanthosarcoma
Xanthose xanthosis
Xanthosin xanthosine
X-Beine bandy legs
Xenon e. e.

Xeroderma e. e.
Xerographie xerography
xerographisch xerographical
Xerophthalmie xerophthalmia
Xeroradiographie xeroradiography
xeroradiographisch xeroradiographical
Xerose xerosis
Xerosebazillus Corynebacterium xerosis
Xylidin xylidine
Xylitol e. e.
Xylol xylene
Xylometazolin xylometazoline
Xylose e. e.
Xylulose e. e.

Y

Yamwurzel yam
Yoghurt yoghurt

Yohimbin yohimbine
Ytterbium e. e.
Yttrium e. e.

Z
(siehe auch:/look also for: C)

zackig pronged
Zähler counter
Zählkammer counting chamber
Zähnelung indenture
Zäpfchen (anat.) uvula
– (pharmacol.) suppository
Zäsium caesium (e), cesium (a)
Zahn tooth
–, eingeklemmter impacted tooth
–, verlagerter malposed tooth
Zahnärztin dentist
zahnärztlicher Stuhl dental chair
Zahnalveole tooth socket
Zahnarzt dentist
Zahnausfall loss of teeth, exfoliation of teeth
Zahnbogen dental arch
Zahnbohrer bur-drill
Zahnbrücke dental bridgework
Zahndurchbruch eruption of a tooth
Zahneinlage dental filling
Zahnextraktion extraction of a tooth
Zahnextraktionslehre exodontology
Zahnfäule dental caries
Zahnfistel dental fistula
Zahnfleisch gingiva, gum
Zahnfleischabszeß gingival abscess
Zahnfleischentzündung gingivitis, ulitis
Zahnfleischkappenstanze gum guillotine forceps
Zahnfleischmesser gum lancet
Zahnfleischrandwulst gum festoon
Zahnfleischsaum gingival margin
Zahnfleischschere gum scissors
Zahnfleischtasche gingival pocket
Zahnfokus dental focus
Zahnformel dental formula
Zahnfüllung dental filling
–, gegossene inlay

Zahnhals neck of tooth
Zahnhalteapparat paradentium
Zahnheilkunde dentistry, odontiatria
–, konservierende operative dentistry
–, prothetische prosthodontia
Zahnkrone dental crown
Zahnleiste tooth band
Zahnlockerung tooth-loosening
zahnlos edentulous
Zahnnerv dental nerve
Zahnpflegemittel dentifrice
Zahnpoliergerät dental burnisher
Zahnprothese denture
–, Oberkiefer- upper denture
–, provisorische temporary denture
–, Teil- partial denture
–, Unterkiefer- lower denture
–, Voll- complete denture
Zahnprothesenanpassung denture adaption
Zahnpulpa tooth pulp
Zahnpulver dentifrice
Zahnsäckchen dental sac
Zahnschmelz dental enamel
–, gesprenkelter mottled enamel
Zahnschmerz toothache, odontalgia
Zahnsequester dental sequestrum
Zahnstein dental tartar
Zahnsteinentferner scaler
Zahnsteinentfernung scaling
Zahnstellungsanomalie dental malalignment
Zahnstumpf tooth stump
Zahntechniker dental technician
Zahntrepanation odontotomy
Zahnung teething, dentition
Zahnwinkel tooth angle
Zahnwurzel dental root
Zahnwurzelkanal dental root canal

Zahnwurzelspitze dental root apex
Zahnzange extracting forceps
Zahnziehen tooth drawing
Zanderapparat Zander apparatus
Zange forceps
Zangemeisterscher Handgriff Zangenmeister's maneuver
Zangenentbindung forceps delivery
Zapfen (dent.) pivot
Zapfen und Stäbchen (der Retina) cones and rods (of the retina)
zart delicate
Zebra e. e.
Zebu e. e.
Zecke tick
Zeckenbefall ixodiasis, infestation with ticks
Zeckenfieber tick fever
Zeckenlähme tick paralysis
Zedernholzöl cedarwood oil
Zehe toe
Zehennagel toenail
Zehen, übereinanderstehende over-lapping toes
Zehenverwachsung webbed toes
Zeichen sign
Zeichnung, streifige striation
Zeigefinger index finger
Zeit time
zeitraubend time-consuming
Zeitschrift periodical
zeitsparend time saving
Zelle cell
zellenförmig celliform
zellfrei cell-free
Zellgewebe cellular tissue
Zellgewebeentzündung cellulitis
Zellhormon cytohormone
Zellmembran cytomembrane
Zellmetaplasie cytometaplasia
Zellmorphologie cytomorphology
Zellobiase cellobiase
Zellobiose cellobiose
Zellophan cellophane
Zellpathologie cytopathology
Zellphysiologie cytophysiology

Zellstoff wood pulp
Zellteilung cell division
zellulär cellular
Zellularchemie cytochemistry
Zellularpathologie cytopathology
Zellularphysiologie cytophysiology
Zellulartherapie cytotherapy
Zellulase cellulase
Zellulose cellulose
Zellwolle synthetic wool
Zelt tent
Zement cement
Zementbildung cementification
Zementoblast cementoblast
Zementoklasie cementoclasia
Zementoklast cementoclast
Zementom cementoma
Zementose cementosis
Zementozyt cementocyte
Zenkersches Divertikel Zenker's diverticulum
zentral central
zentrales Grau central gray
Zentralnervensystem central nervous system
zentralwärts centrad
zentrifugal centrifugal
Zentrifuge centrifuge
zentrifugieren to centrifuge
Zentrifugierung centrifugation
zentrilobulär centrilobular
Zentriole centriole
zentripetal centripetal
Zentrosom centrosome
Zentrum center (a), centre (e)
–, motorisches motor center
Zentrumsdialyse center dialysis (a), centre dialysis (e)
Zer cerium
zerbeißen to bite to pieces
Zerbröckelung comminution
zerebellar cerebellar
zerebellopontin cerebellopontile
zerebellorubrospinal cerebellorubrospinal
zerebral cerebral

Zerebralsklerose cerebral sclerosis, cerebrosclerosis
zerebromeningeal cerebromeningeal
Zerebrosid cerebroside
zerebrospinal cerebrospinal
Zerebrospinalflüssigkeit cerebrospinal fluid
Zerfahrenheit flightiness
Zerfall disintegration
zerfressen to corrode
Zerkarie cercaria
zermalmen to crush
zerreißen to lacerate
Zerreißung laceration; rupture
Zerrüttung disorganization
zerschneiden to cut to pieces
Zersetzung decomposition
Zerstäuber atomizer
zerstörbar destructible
zerstören to destruct
Zerstörung destruction
zerstreuen to distract
zerstreut absent-minded; distracted
Zerstreutheit absent-mindedness
Zerstreuung distraction
Zerumen cerumen
zeruminal ceruminal
zervikal cervical
zervikoaxial cervicoaxial
zervikobukkal cervicobuccal
zervikolingual cervicolingual
Zervix cervix
zerzupfen to tease
zeugen to procreate
Zeugnis certificate
Zeugung procreaction
zeugungsfähig procreative, capable of begetting
Zeugungskraft generative power
Zeugungsorgane genital organs
Ziege goat
Ziegelmehlsediment brick dust deposit
Ziegenmilch goat's milk

Ziegenpeter epidemic parotitis, mumps
Ziehen traction
Ziehl-Neelsen-Färbung Ziehl-Neelsen staining method
Ziel aim
Zielscheibe target
Zielscheibenzelle target cell
Zilie cilia
Zimmertemperatur room temperature
Zimt cinnamon
Zimtöl oil of cinnamon
Zink zinc
Zinkazetat zinc acetate
Zinkchlorid zinc chloride
Zinkoxyd zinc oxide
Zinkpaste zinc paste
Zinksalbe zinc ointment
Zinksulfat zinc sulfate (a), zinc sulphate (e)
Zinkvergiftung zincalism
Zinn tin
zinnhaltig stanniferous
– **(vierwertig)** stannic
– **(zweiwertig)** stannous
Zipfel cusp
Zirbeldrüse pineal gland
zirkadisch circadian
Zirkel circle
Zirbeldrüse pineal gland
Zirkel circle
Zirkonium zirconium
zirkulär circular
Zirkulation circulation
zirkulatorisch circulatory
zirkulieren to circulate
zirkumanal circumanal
zirkumartikulär circumarticular
Zirkumduktion circumduction
zirkumoral circumoral
zirkumorbital circumorbital
zirkumpulpal circumpulpal
zirkumskript circumscribed
zirkumvaskulär circumvascular
zirkumventrikulär circumventricular

Zirkumzision circumcision
zirzinär circinate
zischend sibilant
zisternal cisternal
Zisterne cistern
zitieren to cite
Zitrat citrate
Zitrin citrin
Zitrone lemon
Zitronenpresse lemon squeezer
Zitronensäure citric acid
Zitrullin citrulline
Zittern tremblement, trepidation
zittern to tremble
Zitze teat
Zögern hesitancy
zökal cecal (a), coecal (e)
Zökum cecum (a), coecum (e)
Zöliakie celiac disease (a), coeliac disease (e), idiopathic steatorrhea (a), idiopathic steatorrhoea (e)
Zollinger-Ellison-Syndrom Zollinger-Ellison syndrome
zonal e. e.
Zone e. e.
Zonierung zonation
Zonographie zonography
Zonula Zinni Zinn's zonule
Zonulolyse zonulolysis
Zoogonie zoogony
Zoologe zoologist
Zoologie zoology
Zoologin zoologist
zoologisch zoological
Zoonose zoonosis
Zopfbildung serpentine cording
Zoster e. e., zona, shingles
zosterartig zosteriform
Zoxazolamin zoxazoleamine
zubereiten to prepare
Zubereitung preparation; confection
Zucht (= Aufzucht) breeding
zucken to convulse
Zucker sugar

Zuckerkandlsches Organ Zuckerkandl's organ
zuckerkrank diabetic
Zuckerkranke diabetic
Zuckerkranker diabetic
zuckern to saccharate
Zuckertoleranz sugar tolerance
Zuckung convulsion, jerk
zufällig accidental
Zufall accident
zufriedenstellend satisfactory
zufügen to add
Zug traction
zugänglich accessible
Zugang access
Zugluft draught (e), draft (a)
zuheilen to heal up
Zukunftserwartung future expectation
Zulassung admission
Zunge tongue
—**,belegte** coated tongue, furred tongue
Zungenbrennen glossopyrosis
Zungendrücker tongue depressor
Zungenhalter tongue holder
Zungenlähmung glossoplegia
Zungenmandel lingual tonsil
Zungenplastik glossoplasty
Zungenspitze tip of the tongue
Zungenzange tongue forceps
zupfen to tease
Zurechnungsfähigkeit responsibility
zurückdrängen to stem
zurückgeblieben retarded
zurückhalten to retain
zurückspulen to rewind
zusätzlich additional
Zusammenballung conglobation
zusammendrücken to compress
Zusammendrücken compression
Zusammensetzung composition
zusammenwachsen to coalesce, to grow together
Zusammenwachsen coalescence
zusammenziehen to constrict

Zusammenziehung constriction
Zusatzdynamo booster
zwängen to force, to press
Zwang compulsion
Zwang (= Druck) pressure
Zwangbiß locked bite
zwanghaft compulsive
zwanghufig hoof-bound
Zwangsernährung forcible feeding
Zwangsjacke camisole
zwangsmäßig compulsory
Zwangsneurose compulsion neurosis
Zwangsvorstellung obsession
zwangsweise compulsory
Zwangszählen arithmomania
Zweck aim, purpose, intention
zweckbestimmt intentional
zwecklos aimless
zweckmäßig suitable
zweibasig dibasic
zweidimensional two-dimensional
zweieiig binovular
zweifach double
zweigeteilt bipartite
Zweigläserprobe two glass test
Zweiteilung bipartition
zweitgebärend biparous
Zweitgebärende bipara
Zweitimpfung revaccination
Zweiwegehahn two way stopcock
zweiwertig bivalent, diad
Zweiwertigkeit bivalence
Zwerchfell diaphragm, midriff
Zwerchfellkuppel dome of diaphragm
Zwerchfellrippenwinkel costophrenic angle
Zwerg dwarf
Zwergwuchs dwarfism, dwarfishness, nanism, nanosomia
zwergwüchsig nanous
Zwickzange pincers
Zwilling twin

Zwillinge, eineiige uniovular twins, enzygotic twins
Zwillinge, zweieiige binovular twins, dizygotic twins
Zwillingsbogen twin arch
Zwillingsspulenniere twin coil kidney
Zwischenfall incident
Zwischenergebnis intermediate result
Zwischenhirn betweenbrain
Zwischenmahlzeit between-meal
Zwischenphase interphase
Zwischenraum space
Zwischenstadium intergrade
Zwischenstufe intergrade
Zwischenumwandlung interconversion
Zwischenwirbelscheibe intervertebral disk
Zwitter hermaphrodite
Zwölffingerdarm duodenum
Zwölffingerdarmgeschwür ulcer of duodenum
Zyanamid cyanamide
Zyanid cyanide
Zyanidanol cyanidanol
Zyankali cyanide of potassium
Zyanoakrylat cyanoacrylate
Zyanokobalamin cyanocobalamine
Zyanose cyanosis
zyanotisch cyanosed
zygomatikofazial zygomaticofacial
zygomatikofrontal zygomaticofrontal
zygomatikoorbital zygomaticoorbital
zygomatisch malar
zygomaxillär zygomaxillary
zygot zygotic
zyklisch cyclic
Zyklitis cyclitis
Zyklopenthiazid cyclopenthiazide
Zyklopropan cyclopropane
Zykloserin cycloserine
zyklothym cyclothymic

zyklothyme Person cyclothymiac
Zyklothymie cyclothymia, cyclophrenia
Zyklotron cyclotron
Zyklus cycle
Zylinder cylinder
–,**Harn-** urinary cylinder, urinary cast
–,**granulierter** granular cast
–,**hyaliner** hyaline cast
–,**Koma-** Külz's cast, coma cast
–,**Wachs-** waxy cast
Zylinderepithel columnar epithelium
Zylindermeßglas graduated cylinder
zylindrisch cylindrical
Zylindrom cylindroma
Zylindrurie cylindruria
Zymarin cymarin
Zymase e. e.
Zymarose cymarose
Zymogen cymogen
Zymolyse zymolysis
Zystadenom cystadenoma
Zyste cyst
Zysteamin cysteamine
Zystein cysteine
Zystin cystine
Zystinose cystinosis
Zystinspeicherkrankheit cystine storage disease
Zystinurie cystinuria
zystisch cystic

Zystitis cystitis
zystitisch cystitic
Zystographie cystography
Zystopyelitis cystopyelitis
Zystoskop cystoscope
Zystoskopie cystoscopy
zystoskopisch cystoscopic
Zystourethroskop cystourethroscope
Zytidin cytidin
Zytoarchitektonik cytoarchitecture
zytoarchitektonisch cytoarchitectonic
Zytochemie cytochemistry
zytochemisch cytochemical
Zytochrom cytochrome
Zytogenese cytogenesis
Zytogenetik cytogenetics
zytogenetisch cytogenetic
Zytoglobin cytoglobin
Zytologie cytology
zytologisch cytologic
Zytolyse cytolysis
zytolytisch cytolytic
Zytomegalie cytomegaly
zytophil cytophilic
Zytoplasma cytoplasm
zytoplasmatisch cytoplasmic
Zytosin cytosine
Zytosom cytosome
Zytostase cytostasis
zytostatisch cytostatic
zytotoxisch cytotoxic

Anhang – Appendix

1. Temperaturskala – Scale of temperatures

° Celsius	° Reaumur	° Fahrenheit
– 40	– 32	– 40
0	0	+ 32
+ 20	+16	+ 68
+ 37	+29,6	+ 98,6
+ 40	+32	+ 104
+ 100	+80	+ 212

Formel: – *Equation:*

n° Celsius = 4/5 n° Reaumur = 9/5 n° + 32° Fahrenheit

2. Maße – Measures

1 inch = 2,54 cm
1 foot = 12 inches = 30,48 cm
1 yard = 3 feet = 91,44 cm
1 mile = 1760 yards = 1609,35 m

1 square inch = 6,45 cm^2
1 square foot = 144 square inches = 929,03 cm^2

1 cubic inch = 16,39 cm^3
1 cubic foot = 1728 cubic inches = 0,03 m^3

Die nichtmetrischen Maße sind allgemein gebräuchlich. Zum Teil wird jedoch auch das metrische System angewandt. – In Germany, Austria and Switzerland only the metric system is customary nowadays.

– – –

Apotheker-Flüssigkeitsmaß (vorwiegend in den USA gebräuchliches Flüssigkeitsmaß) – Apothecaries' fluid measure

1 minim (apoth.) = 0,00006161 Liter
1 fluidram (apoth.) = 60 minims (apoth.) = 0,0036966 Liter
1 fluidounce (apoth.) = 8 fluidrams (apoth.) = 480 minims (apoth.)
  = 0,0295729 Liter
1 pint (apoth.) = 16 fluidounces (apoth.) = 128 fluidrams (apoth.)
  = 7680 minims (apoth.) = 0,473179 Liter

1 quart (apoth.) = 2 pints (apoth.) = 32 fluidounces (apoth.)
 = 256 fluidrams (apoth.) = 15360 minims (apoth.) = 0,946358 Liter
1 gallon (apoth.) = 4 quarts (apoth.) = 8 pints (apoth.)
 = 128 fluidounces (apoth.) = 1024 fluidrams (apoth.)
 = 61 440 minims (apoth.) = 3,785434 Liter

„Imperial"-Flüssigkeitsmaß (in Großbritannien übliches Flüssigkeitsmaß) − Imperial fluid measure

1 minim (imperial) = 0,00005919 Liter
1 fluid drachm oder/or fluid dram (imper.) = 60 minims (imper.)
 = 0,0035515 Liter
1 fluidounce (imper.) = 8 fluid drams (imper.) = 480 minims (imper.)
 = 0,0284123 Liter
1 pint (imper.) = 20 fluidounces (imper.) = 160 fluid drams (imper.)
 = 9600 minims (imper.) = 0,5682454 Liter
1 quart (imper.) = 2 pints (imper.) = 40 fluidounces (imper.)
 = 320 fluid drams (imper.) = 19 200 minims (imper.)
 = 1,1364908 Liter
1 gallon (imper.) = 4 quarts (imper.) = 8 pints (imper.)
 = 160 fluidounces (imper.) = 1280 fluid drams (imper.)
 = 76 800 minims (imper.) = 4,5459631 Liter

3. Gewichte − Weights

In Großbritannien und in den USA ist das Gramm-Kilogramm-Gewichtssystem zwar bekannt; im allgemeinen wird aber mit dem „Avoirdupois"-Gewicht, das in Großbritannien auch „Imperial"-Gewicht heißt, gearbeitet. Zum Wiegen von Edelsteinen und Edelmetallen wird das „Troy"-Gewicht verwandt. Auf ärztlichen Rezepten benützt man zumeist das mit dem Troy-Gewicht identische „Apotheker"-Gewicht. − In Germany, Austria and Switzerland only the gram-kilogram-system is in use nowadays.

Avoirdupois- oder Imperial-Gewicht − Avoirdupois- or imperial weight

1 grain = 0,0647989 g
1 drachm oder/or dram (avoir) = 27,34 grains = 1,772 g
1 ounce (avoir) = 16 drams (avoir) = 437,5 grains = 28,35 g
1 pound (avoir) = 16 ounces (avoir) = 256 drams (avoir) = 7000 grains
 = 453,5924277 g
1 stone (e) = 14 pounds (avoir) = 6,35 kg
1 (short) quarter (a) = 25 pounds (avoir) = 11,34 kg
1 (long) quarter (e) = 28 pounds (avoir) = 12,70 kg

1 (short) hundredweight (a), Abkürzung/abbreviation: sh. cwt, = 4 short quarters = 100 pounds (avoir) = 45,36 kg
1 (long) hundredweight (e), Abkürzung/abbreviation: 1. cwt, = 4 long quarters = 112 pounds (avoir) = 50,80 kg

Apotheker- und Troy-Gewicht – Apothecaries' weight and Troy weight

1 grain = 0,0647989 g
1 scruple = 20 grains = 1,296 g
1 pennyweight (Troy) = 24 grains = 1,555 g
1 drachm oder/or dram (apoth.) = 3 scruples = 60 grains = 3,888 g
1 ounce (apoth., Troy) = 8 drams (apoth.) = 24 scruples = 480 grains = 31,103 g
1 pound (apoth., Troy) = 12 ounces (apoth., Troy) = 96 drams (apoth.) = 288 scruples = 5760 grains = 373,24177 g

4. Geschwindigkeit – Speed

16,09 km pro Stunde = 10 miles per hour (Abkürzung/abbreviation: m.p.h.)

5. Umrechnung Kalorie in Joule und umgekehrt – Conversion Calorie into Joule and vice versa

1 Joule = 0,239 Kalorien/calories
1 Kilojoule = 0,239 Kilokalorien/kilocalories
1 Kalorie/1 Calorie = 4,184 Joule
1 Kilokalorie/1 kilocalorie = 4,184 Kilojoule